CW01655827

MALT WHISKY YEARBOOK 2026

First published in Great Britain in 2025 by
MagDig Media Limited

ISBN 978-1-7394492-2-3

MagDig Media Limited
1 Brassey Road
Old Potts Way, Shrewsbury
Shropshire SY3 7FA
ENGLAND

E-mail: info@maltwhiskyyearbook.com
www.maltwhiskyyearbook.com

Contents

Introduction

Welcome to the 21st edition of the Malt Whisky Yearbook. The last couple of years have been challenging in so many ways; politically, environmentally and economically. For us as consumers and of course also for the producers. Let´s keep in mind though that we can learn from history. We´ve been there before and we found the way out. In the book you will find articles discussing everything from how peated whisky could be in danger and why the producers insist on launching ultra expensive bottlings to why China might become the new powerhouse of whisky, how sherry casks influence our favourite tipple and also a round of applause for those who dare build a whisky distillery in these times. And if you think the rise of Scotch in the late 1900s was due to Cognac being infected by phylloxera - think again.

And as usual there is the thoroughly revised and updated section on Scottish malt whisky distilleries; the chapter on distilleries from the rest of the world has been expanded; The Whisky Year That Was provides a summary of all the significant events during the year. You will also find a chapter about independent bottlers and suggestions on where to find more information about whisky in social media. Finally, the latest statistics answers your questions on production and consumption.

Thank you for buying Malt Whisky Yearbook 2026 - I wish you a pleasant read!

Acknowledgements

First of all I wish to thank the writers who have shared their great specialist knowledge on the subject in a brilliant and entertaining way – Justine Hazlehurst, Jonny McCormick, Nick Morgan, Gavin D Smith, Kristiane Westray and Ian Wisniewski. A special thanks to Ian who put in a lot of effort nosing, tasting and writing notes for this year´s independent bottlings. I am also deeply grateful to Stefan van Eycken and Philippe Jugé for their valuable input on Japanese and French distilleries.

The following persons have also made important photographic or editorial contributions and I am grateful to all of them:

Asa Abraham, Ryan Adair, Iain Allan, David Allen, Alasdair Anderson, Nuno Antunes, Sanjeev Banga, Stuart Baxter, Marilena Bidaine, Stewart Bowman, Ross Bremner, Keith Brian, Katie O´Brien, Jacqueline Broadfoot, Dave Broom, Andrew Brown, Angela Brown, Amy Brownlee, Gordon Bruce, Neil Bulloch, Robyn Bunting, Katie Burns, Gregor Butchert, Ruaridh Cameron, George Campbell, Rob Carpenter, Denny Chen, Jonathan Christie, David Clark, Suzanne Clark, Maria Coelho, Louisa Copping, Georgie Crawford, Mike Crutch, Ewa Czernecka, Steven Dalgarno, Alasdair Day, Paul Dempsey, Richard Devlin, Michael Elliot, Simon Erlanger, Graham Eunson, Carina Ewens, Katie Faulds, David Ferguson, Allan Findlay, Robert Fleming, Paddy Fletcher, John Fordyce, George Forsyth, Leah Forsyth, Callum Fraser, Kathrin Furst, Sophie Gall, Martin Gaughan, Graham Geddes, Gillian Gibson, Archie Gillies, Colin Gordon, Tomer Goren, Duncan Grant, Adam Hannett, Soichiro Harada, Jessica Haworth, Euan Henderson, Erik Hirschfeld, Peter Holroyd, David Hsieh, Robbie Hughes, Jonny Ingledew, Sandy Jamieson, Stephanie Jurado, Jenny Karlsson, Rebecca Kean, David Keir, Murray Kerr, Surrinder Kumar, Andrew Laing, Mark Lancaster, Miranda Lidgerwood, Ian Lochhead, Ian Logan, Polly Logan, Alistair Longwell, Daniel Lumsden, Iain McAlister, Brendan McCarron, Ali Macdonald, Alistair McDonald, Christy McFarlane, Sandy Macintyre, John McKee, Sarah McKeeman, Jaclyn McKie, Kirsty Mackinnon, Callum McLaughlin, Angus MacMillan, Jonny McMillan, Kevin MacPherson, Craig MacRitchie, Russell Main, Martin Markvardsen, Steve Marson, Roger Melander, Gary Mills, Andrew Millsopp, Scott Morrison, David Moule, Jamie Muir, David Ness, Katie O´Brien, Graham Omand, Colm O´Rourke, Jordan Paisley, Katie Palmer, Bruce Perry, Gemma Porter, Struan Grant Ralph, Malcolm Rennie, Ian Renwick, Charlotte Rietschel, Jay Robertson, Mairi Robertson, David Rogerson, Euan Ross, Joseph Sammons, Lauren Sendles White, Belen Silva, Jeff Simpson, Bruce Smith, Daniel Smith, Mackay Smith, Greig Stables, Tom Stacey, Piotr Stachura, Paul Stephenson, Fiona Stewart, Scott Stewart, Eddie Thom, Annabel Thomas, Laura Tolmie, Isabella Tricket, Kaitlyn Tsai, David Turner, Sandrine Tyrbas de Chamberet, Perry Unger, Gabriel Valentin, Mark van der Vijver, Stewart Walker, David Watt, Leon Webb, Sarah Webster, Iain Weir, Ronald Whiteford, Susan Williamson, Anthony Wills, Alan Winchester, Kristoffer Wittström, Rebecca Wood, Dave Worthington, Allison Young and Derek Younie.

Finally, to my wife Pernilla and our daughter Alice, thank you for your patience and your love!

Ingvar Ronde
Editor
Malt Whisky Yearbook

Faith in the Future

– the audacity to build in a downturn

by Gavin D Smith

It is no secret that the Scotch whisky industry is currently going through a tough phase caused by global economic turmoil, threats of tariffs and geopolitical instability. Yet there are still a vast number of distilleries being built in Scotland. What is the drive of these entrepreneurs?

Falling sales values, lack of consumer confidence, cost of living crises, Gen Z consumers who are averse to alcohol, crippling domestic duty levels, increasing construction and operating costs, voracious competition and an unpredictable US administration devoted to protectionism. Are you sure you want to build a new Scotch whisky distillery? Perhaps surprisingly, the answer in many cases remains 'yes.'

The past dozen years have seen around 50 new whisky distilleries come on stream in Scotland, with almost uninterrupted positivity in terms of global growth for the spirit, replicating trends seen during the latter decades of the 19th century and the 1960s and '70s, when distillery numbers grew and existing facilities were dramatically increased in capacity.

2022 saw exports exceed the £6bn mark for the first time, but two years later the figure had fallen to £5.4bn, and that apparent bellwether of the state of the industry – Diageo's share price – fell by an extraordinary 44% in just three years.

So, why would anyone build a new distillery in such apparently pessimistic times for Scotch whisky? Perhaps the most obvious answer is that a distillery does not go from plans in an architect's office to spirit flowing from stills in the blink of an eye. Many of the distilleries that recently came on stream or are approaching that stage will have been committed to during much rosier times.

However, Bari Reid, director of Organic Architects, the firm behind Ardnamurchan, Benbecula, Lindores Abbey, Moffat and Nc'Nean distilleries in Scotland, takes a slightly different view.

"I think you can talk about a long-term trend and short-term volatility," he declares. "There are ups

One of the stills going in at Kythe Distillery in Perthshire

and downs, but new distilleries are probably five years out from selling anything. If you can get funding, now is a great time! You're coming into the industry when it will be on the up!"

Reid also makes the point that "The headlines about a downturn have largely been generated by statements from the big players. Their first interest is shareholder profits, so you get knee-jerk downsizing. Cutting production and staff. But in a few years, they'll be increasing production and taking staff on again.

"A company like Diageo can be making something like 125m litres of malt spirit a year, while a small guy might make 100,000 litres. The people we are dealing with are level-headed and are working on 5-10-year projects. Mostly at Organic Architects they are of less than 1m litres at present. Some are building in future expansion rather than building big at the start."

The issue of Gen Z consumers drinking less clearly impacts whisky sales in many markets, but Bari Reid has a degree of optimism here, too, in terms of smaller, recent start-up distilling operations, noting that "Single malts are probably rather protected from the Gen Z drinkers' issue. Blends may be more vulnerable if they are being marketed as accessible to younger drinkers, and that will affect volume production for the big guys."

There is an old English proverb that states 'There's many a lip twixt cup and lip,' implying that events do not always turn out as anticipated, and Reid says that "There are dozens of distilleries in planning or with planning permission, but that doesn't mean they get built. They tend to be self-financing up to planning, then go out for funding. That's the biggest step. They are all competing for finance and sometimes you don't hear about these projects again for years. Creating a distillery takes big lumps of money, it's not cheap to do. Dozens have never got further than planning, and that's the same the world over."

It all starts with funding

Needless to say, distillery projects that do not require external funding for whatever reasons are more likely to get built than those that do in an economic climate where potential investors may be wary of commitment.

In the picturesque Argyllshire village of Inveraray, Stock Spirits Group (SSG) plans to build a whisky distillery close to Inveraray Castle, home to the chiefs of Clan Campbell.

The distillery is expected to produce up to 2m lpa, and if all goes well, spirit should be flowing in the latter half of 2027. The project involves investing some £25m, but SSG is not short of resources, boasting a portfolio of more than 70 brands available in 50 countries around the world. It employs in excess of 1,800 people and operates eight production plants – in Poland, the Czech Republic, Germany, Italy and France. The Group's stated ambition is to become the leading mainstream spirits company in Europe by 2027.

Part of that ambition includes building the Inveraray distillery to service the Clan Campbell blend, which Stock acquired from Pernod Ricard in 2023, and add a single malt to the portfolio in due course.

Leading the venture is Whisky Operations Director Graham Coull, formerly of Glen Elgin and Dingle distillery in Ireland, who explains the rationale behind the distillery's creation.

"With a blend, you don't need to build a distillery, but looking to the long term, you have to be a bit brave and confident. It will give us a guaranteed cost-effective spirit supply for the brand and for reciprocal trading, and it will give us more substance in the game. We are not going to private investors to get it off the ground – Stock is big, and the 10 years average growth for Scotch whisky is still pretty healthy."

Meanwhile, in Perthshire, the team behind Kythe distillery is hopeful of success due to a highly unusual series of factors that underlie its creation and operation. Heading up the Kythe venture are Angus MacRaild, who holds the title of Whisky Maker, Jonny McMillan, Distillery Manager, and Chairman Aaron Chang, all of whom are steeped in the world of whisky.

On the Kythe distillery website, the team declares that "Ours is an uncommonly ambitious project in pursuit of true and absolute quality - drawing on inspiration from the past to create a new Highland single malt that will stand as one of the most distinctive and charismatic in Scotland, and beyond. Our aim is to recreate an extinct style of Scottish single malt whisky - one not produced since the 1960s."

"Our ethos is to eschew outdated and tired obsessions about yield, efficiency, tourism and standardisation of character. Instead, we favour a ruthlessly ideological process founded in the best ingredients, the right equipment, exacting method and relentlessly holding ourselves to the standards demonstrated by the greatest bottled distillates from Scotland's past."

Kythe employs Maris Otter 'heritage' barley, fermentations using brewer's yeast lasting up to two weeks, and distillation in a wash still directly fired by sustainably-sourced air-dried logs.

The owners of Portintruan Distillery on Islay hope to start production in the early part of 2026

Jonny McMillan declares that "You need a very strong idea, a reason for creating a new distillery. Unless you have what I believe we have, you could be in trouble. Not all the whisky distilleries operational today will still be in business in 10 years' time. We are dyed-in-the-wool whisky guys who want to spend our lives doing it."

"Some new distilleries have been created because making whisky might have seemed an easy way to make money, because you're based near where a cruise ship regularly docks or a famous golf course, or you used to be a director with a whisky company. Very different to why we are doing it."

"We've had a boom period that's gone to snail's pace, but things were set in motion when all was looking good. You couldn't just stop. You're exposed if you don't have meaningful quality at its heart. The industry is contracting, and we live and die by quality. Some people are making half a million lpa per year. That's a lot of whisky! We expect to be selling around 15,000 x six-bottle cases per year."

Angus MacRaild adds that "I want to make money, but I'm not in this to make a fortune. We've done this through Brexit, Covid, and a Scottish independence referendum, and we didn't have land or money. Hopefully, in six years or so when we come to market, things may be more settled than they are now. Whisky doesn't just fly off the shelves anymore. You can no longer just sell over-priced, over-hyped stuff."

To gin or not to gin...

Many distilleries new to Scotch whisky have established reputations with white spirits such as gin and vodka, which means that they have an established business model, reliable, trained staff, practical knowledge of the complex legislation relating to producing and selling alcohol, supply chain infrastructure, routes to market, lucrative and known tourist offerings and sometimes a brand name already familiar to consumers.

They may have needed to expand or adapt their premises to accommodate whisky-making, and this, plus the additional distilling equipment will have come with a significant cost, but they already have experience of getting a viable drinks business up and running. Recent examples include Orkney, North Uist and Stirling.

Similarly, some of Scotland's start-up whisky-making ventures are based on existing agricultural businesses, with Daftmill in Fife being the first in

Witchburn Distillery located just north of Campbeltown, close to the airport

modern times to diversify in this way, followed by the likes of Arbikie, Ballindalloch, and Balmaud.

They have existing buildings that can be used, or land on which to build new structures, they are familiar with navigating through bureaucracy, capital can possibly be diverted from agricultural income or planned investment, and usually the presence of home-grown grain is part of the raison d'etre of creating a whisky distillery in the first place, reducing the cost of this raw material and giving the whisky produced 'grain to glass' cache.

Perhaps most importantly, agricultural-related income gives time to allow whisky to mature until the distillers feel it is genuinely ready for consumption, rather than three years and a day old, regardless of quality considerations. Daftmill did not release its first whisky until it was 12 years of age!

Not all 'new' whisky distilleries are 'new' in the purest sense, and Brora, Rosebank and Port Ellen have all been restored to active service after decades of silence. The motivation in these three cases was that the whiskies had become classics with connoisseurs, achieving iconic status, and producing 'more' of each seemed like a shrewd business move, especially with associated visitor revenue to add into the equation.

Now, however, there are plans to restore the museum distillery of Dallas Dhu and its Speyside sister of Coleburn to productivity. Whilst perfectly decent drams in their own right, Dallas Dhu and Coleburn were never exactly single malt classics. Rather they functioned to supply spirit for The Distillers Company Limited's plethora of blends.

Both fell silent during the 1980s Scotch whisky downturn and the reason for their intended resurrection relates principally to tourism. Dallas Dhu – preserved as it was when production ceased – has already proved a popular visitor attraction under the auspicies of Historic Environment Scotland, and now the distillery is to be brought back to life by Aceo Distillers Company Limited.

Aceo's Managing Director Edward Odim says that "The aim is to breathe life back into the distillery by first getting the original equipment working and traditional whisky distilling going once again. This revived, long-lost spirit will be matured in Dallas Dhu's well-preserved Victorian dunnage warehouses."

"Longer-term, the plan is for a state-of-the-art visitor centre with exhibition and museum space, and a café/restaurant, to be enjoyed by visitors and the local community. There will be a cooperage displaying the art of the cooper, a working malting floor and an interactive virtual reality whisky experience, that delves into the science behind Scotland's famous spirit. But, as well as show how whisky is made, we intend to tell the social and economic story – past and present – of whisky production in Speyside, Scotland's largest whisky producing region."

There are even more grandiose plans for Coleburn, owned by whisky sales and cask management specialists D&M Winchester Ltd, with a spokesperson noting that "Coleburn is now being prepared for a Destination Whisky Resort with associated 5-star hotel and lodging accommodation, spa and conference facilities including a working distillery and hospitality focal point."

"Ultimately, new distilleries, and revived ones like Coleburn, are being established not despite market challenges, but because of shifting consumer desires and a genuine interest in our heritage. Today's whisky enthusiasts want more than a dram, they want a story, a setting, and a sense of place and its people. That's exactly what we aim to deliver."

When location is key

While start-up whisky-making ventures can be found from Shetland to the Scottish Borders, two locations with long and honourable traditions of distilling are proving particularly popular for new distillery ventures, namely Islay and Campbeltown.

The 'whisky island' of Islay currently boasts 10 working distilleries, with another four in the pipeline, and one of the newcomers, is Portintruan, located close to Laphroaig and the work of independent bottlers Elixir Distillers, headed by Sukhinder and Rajbir Singh.

According to Sukhinder Singh, "We have been working on the Portintruan project for over a decade. It started firstly as a desire to have secure supply of new make spirit for a passion project. It was getting increasingly difficult to buy the whiskies we loved so we felt the best answer was to make them ourselves."

The choice of Islay as the location for Elixir's distillery was a relatively straightforward one, with Singh noting that "Demand for Islay whisky is still growing. The unique environment and community that surround the distilleries have been creating some of the world´s very best malt whisky for decades. Our hope is that Portintruan can be a place where young people from the Island can learn a trade and develop new ways of expressing their community. Though the whisky industry is clearly under pressure, there are still millions of people who have not discovered what this incredible place is creating and we feel very fortunate to be able to help give a platform for the island to continue shining."

Bari Reid of Organic Architects says that "Islay malts have a huge reputation, they've done very well. But I think you're now seeing expansion into the wider Hebrides, with the likes of Harris, Benbecula, Tiree and so on. Islay can't really support much more distilling in terms of infrastructure. With Port Ellen Maltings now only supplying Diageo distilleries, more malt has to be brought in, and in terms of ferries, roads and other aspects of infrastructure, can all the distilleries be serviced going forward?"

The second location finding favour with start-up distillers is the old whisky-making capital of Campbeltown, where three distilleries will soon become six. Organic Architects is working with the team behind the creation of Witchburn distillery, and Bari Reid points out that "You are talking different volumes in Campbeltown compared with Islay. Essentially, there are two-and-a-half distilleries working there. Campbeltown spirit is much harder to come by than that from Islay, and therefore more value is placed on it. Campbeltown has cache as a region for whisky-making, as have Speyside and Islay."

"If you get into distilling in either place, there's no room to distil terrible Islay or Campbeltown whisky because of the good reputation of their whiskies. There's a pressure. Witchburn is being developed by independent bottlers who are selling blends internationally. Polish and German guys. At present, they can't get enough peated malt to meet their requirements."

Witchburn is no boutique distillery, boasting an initial capacity of 2mlpa, with the potential to double to 4mlpa, starting with four Frilli stills. Reid emphasises that "Independent bottlers who can shift bulk are in a good position to create new distilleries. They have a route out to market for their spirit and will be able to generate cash flow quite quickly."

It seems that no matter what reasonable pessimism may lurk in the here and now or in the foreseeable future, there is no shortage of would-be distillers who hold a similar view to that of author William Faulkner, who wrote "Get it down. Take chances… it's the only way you can do anything really good."

Gavin D Smith is one of the world's leading whisky writers and Contributing Editor Scotland for Whisky Magazine. He regularly undertakes writing commissions for leading drinks companies and produces articles for a wide range of international publications. He is the author and co-author of some 30 books, and along with the late Dominic Roskrow, updated, revised and edited three editions of Michael Jackson's Malt Whisky Companion. Recent publications include Whisky Opus (with Jonny McCormick), The A9 Handbook and The Story of Whisky (with Charles MacLean). He is a Master of the Quaich and lives in the Scottish Borders.

Beyond the Bog

by Kristiane Westray

As the damage wreaked by commercial peat extraction becomes increasingly clear, the whisky industry faces a reckoning. Should peat be used as a flavouring agent at all, and what could the alternatives be?

Fly into Islay and on a clear day you'll get uninterrupted views of the island's peat bogs. One side of the airport's runway is flanked by the sweeping Strand beach. The other? An expanse of scrubby bog. Look closely and you'll spot shelves, lines etched through the land by centuries of peat extraction. The purpose? Once it was to heat homes. Today it's to impart that evocative smoky, earthy, medicinal quality into our whiskies.

Peat is present in whiskymaking far beyond Islay. It's used in the malting process as kiln fuel to create smoky drams. The heat 'kills off' barley as it germinates, essentially stunting growth at just the right moment so there are plentiful enzymes to help convert starch into sugar during mashing, the next stage of production. Maltsters making unpeated whiskies will typically use hot air as their weapon of choice. Looking for those smoky, earthy phenolics? Peat is your go-to.

Yet peat is a controversial topic. Sustainability has climbed up the social and political agenda. As climate breakdown intensifies, the understanding that we must all do our bit to minimise our carbon footprint has become starker. And peat has a profound role to play.

While peatland covers 3% of global land surface, it is what's known as a carbon sink, storing twice as much of the element as all the world's forest combined (source: UNEP). In the UK alone, peat bogs hold around 3 billion tonnes of carbon. This is released into the atmosphere if the land is damaged, for example, by peat extraction. You don't need to burn it – simply cutting it causes harm. Around 80% of the UK's remaining peat bogs are in a "degraded" condition. As a result, they contribute a whopping 4% of the country's greenhouse gas emissions.

Depending on who you ask, whisky accounts for between 3% and 6% of the UK's peat extraction. The vast majority is hoovered up by the horticultural and agricultural industries. Why is peated whisky so divisive if it isn't the main carbon culprit? Because peat-containing compost is due to be banned in the

Peat harvesting on Islay

UK in the coming months. Once that happens, whisky will become one of the biggest bog depleters.

"Peat will inevitably become political," reckons whisky broker Mark Littler. He thinks a ban on extraction for the whisky industry will come in the not too distant future. While he isn't calling for this legislation, he sees it as an "easy and highly visible" win for any government under pressure as the climate emergency intensifies.

He calculates that once agricultural peat use is banned, whisky will account for as much as 37% of UK peat extraction. Given that voluntary peat-use reductions within the industry haven't really worked, it paves the way for government action. He compares the situation to the introduction of the Ivory Act 2018, where almost all trade, even in antique pieces, was banned.

"Both involve the use of rare natural materials and both carry powerful environmental symbolism," Littler – who also deals in antiques – explains. "There used to be a legitimate market for antique ivory. Historical pieces, objects made 100 to 400 years ago, were not driving the modern poaching crisis." Illegal traders rightly drew global condemnation. Banning all ivory scored political points – but curtailing sales of 16th century chess pieces is useless if you're trying to protect today's living elephants.

In praise of peat

Many conservationists – and even some distillers – argue that whisky should be included in the peat ban. But there's something about peated expressions that just… grab us. They're evocative. They're steeped in deeply-held community traditions. Some of our oldest Scotch distilleries have been making malts using peat for centuries. It's hard to imagine the likes of Bowmore, Laphroaig, Lagavulin, Highland Park and Ardbeg without it.

The aromas and flavours are compelling. And there's a scientific reason you might have positive associations with it. "Our sensory [system] is intrinsically linked to our memories and our trigeminal nerve," explains Harmonie Bettenhausen, Ph.D. from the James B. Beam Institute for Kentucky Spirits. Depending on what you've been exposed to, you'll associate peat aromas with different things.

It's the same phenomenon that Nicola Brown, general manager at Aberdeen restaurant Amuse by Kevin Dalgleish, reports. When her customers try peated whisky, they light up. "It sparks this memory in their head. Something from their childhood, or a smell that they can relate to, whether that's a beach bonfire, the fire pit in the garden on a summer night, or something from their childhood. I think it's really cool."

What's going on with the flavour and aroma compounds to create something that's so captivating? Remarkably, peated profiles differ dramatically depending on where individual bogs are located and the centuries of plant composition that have contributed to it. There's no such thing as a generic 'phenol' compound. Instead, think of peat as a recipe of myriad phenols that give off different characteristics.

Guaiacol is associated with wood smoke, bacon and medicinal notes. "It's often the marker for smokiness in whisky," explains Bettenhausen. Then you've got methyl glycol, which contributes a clove-like spiciness. Hydroxy benzene brings antiseptic or tar notes to the party. A group of compounds called cresols can give elastoplast, sweeter barbecue sauce or even a barnyard funk. With such a vast flavour spectrum, it's no wonder that peated whiskies have such a loyal following.

And peat doesn't just resonate with established whisky drinkers. The style is reaching a whole new audience through cocktail culture. "There are more cocktails with peated whisky in them now," says Ahsoka Wallace, senior bartender at London's Leyton Calling. "The flavours are being used in more versatile ways." They put the increased interest down to the wider trend for savoury cocktails, and greater diversity in whisky. Broader demographics of people are enjoying malt now – and with that shift, attitudes like 'you can't mix malt' have lessened. "There are a lot more younger people drinking things like Penicillins."

That said, the main preservationists for peat are the old guard. Even the language used by the Scotch Whisky Association (SWA) points to this. The organisation stresses on its website that: "as a user of peat, we are determined to play a key role in preserving and restoring this habitat however we can." At the time of writing, an industry-specific framework for best practice is due for imminent publication.

Its most recent work in this area is 2023's 'The Commitment to Responsible Peat Use'. It states that the "harvesting and combustion of peat is an essential component in the production of unique Scotch whiskies". Even in the last few years, this positioning as 'essential' has become debated. The Scotch Whisky Technical File, often considered to be the bible of Scotch whisky-making, goes further. It claims that peat is "in plentiful supply across Scotland". In the era of significant bog degradation, this is surely outdated. Yet it is enshrined in law.

Peated whisky is at a crossroads. There's an environmental emergency, but also a strong demand for peated whisky from consumers and an industry deeply steeped in tradition. It's a complex tension that needs resolving.

Less is more

The drive to Loch Lomond Distillery is a discordant one. One moment you're immersed in the natural beauty of the national park, with its dense pine forests and glimmering loch. Then you're turning into an industrial estate where, on three sides, the distillery surrounds a ramshackle old shopping village that's slipped into disrepair.

What adds to the dissonance is that within this complex is housed one of Scotland's most forward-looking, bold makers. From the versatile still set-up that can create 11 different spirit styles to its chameleon-like approach to grain and peated whisky, Loch Lomond is a distillery like no other. "We talk about tradition and whisky, and I think tradition is sometimes misunderstood as keeping things the same," muses Michael Henry, master blender. We're chatting about the future of peat post-distillery tour. He quotes composer Gustav Mahler: "Tradition is the preservation of fire, not the worship of ashes."

It's a mantra that informs his work at Loch Lomond. Part of his remit is to nurture old stocks from the likes of ghost distillery Littlemill. But he's also

Michael Henry, master blender at Loch Lomond

Liam Hirt at Circumstance Distillery has decided they will never produce whisky using peat

laying down spirit and getting experimental with it. When it comes to peat, that means exploring ways to amp up perceived flavour by using less material.

Henry is running trials with chocolate malt, working out whether adding a small portion of the speciality grain can add emphasis to the phenol notes. This would require less peat in the kiln. "With chocolate malt we get coffee, roasted flavours – and I think it worked," he confirms. "There's a richness to the spirit that's not there with just peat." So far, he's trialled batches with just 5% chocolate malt, which will be upped to 10% next time.

He's fairly optimistic about the work the industry is doing to become more peat-efficient. Commercial maltsters are adapting, and small-scale traditional floor maltings don't use much anyway, he says. "Phenol recovery from peat has gone up. We're getting so much more flavour from what we're using now."

Island distillery Jura also has an interesting relationship with peat. Like many Hebridean makers, its signature profile is a balance of light-to-medium smoke notes backed by something fruitier. Jura achieves this by distilling peated malt for just one month a year, then cleaning everything down and reverting back to unpeated. Expressions are blended at a later date. But Jura distillery manager Graham Geddes says things are changing, especially as the brand focuses on lighter, fruitier output.

"We haven't done it since 2021 and don't plan to do it anytime soon," he tells me as we stand outside the stillhouse. While he's not certain if it's a permanent policy, there are still plenty of maturing casks filled with peated spirit. "It's more about giving a smoky kiss here or there," he describes the intended Jura character.

Geddes sees peated malt production as less efficient. "You'll lose with every changeover." Besides, even on Islay they're using less peat these days. Migrating birds have started nesting on some of the bogs which means distillers can't cut there anymore, he reports.

While peated whisky is most closely associated with Scotland, it's far from the only nation using it. The USA isn't known for its peat bogs, but some can be found in the Pacific Northwest. Spanning Washington, Oregon, and parts of Idaho, the region has become a hotbed for brewing and distilling excellence. One PNW maker exploring peat is Westland.

Based in Seattle, the distillery has been making whiskey inspired by its locale since 2011. And in 2023 the team released Solum. It's not made using conventional peat. In an effort to cut the environmental impact of extraction, it isn't cut. Instead, it is scooped up from the bottom of a Washington lake. Westland then developed its own process to form the peat into pellets and burn it in a custom-built kiln to max out the phenol impact. The expression is now on its third edition.

There are other ways to harness that peaty flavour, too. In July 2024, single malt Scotch distillery Kingsbarns released Coaltown, a smoky single malt that gets all its phenolic flavours from ex-Islay casks. Similarly, single grain Scotch brand Wee Smoky makes use of the island's casks to build its lightly peated character. The brand was developed with cocktails in mind. What's fascinating is that due to supply agreements neither the distillery producing the grain or the source of the casks can be named. The result? Wee Smoky customers are far more concerned by how tasty their drink is rather than provenance.

"As long as it looks good and it tastes good, that's all the customer really cares about," says Felix Bottomley, brand ambassador at Wee Smoky. "They don't really care about the process all that much."

As such, he is excited about alternative ways of getting phenolics into malt. He cites the Nordics, where everything from heather to broken-down casks are used in the kiln. "I think people are becoming more open to these sorts of whiskies. People are finally realising 'oh wait, actually these are very good'."

Celebrated bottlings include Finland's Kyrö Wood Smoke, which is made by smoking alder in a 100-year-old barn. Mackmyra's Svensk Rök, which translates as 'Swedish Smoke', is flavoured by burning juniper. Further afield, Namibia's Ondjaba Distillery uses elephant dung in the malting process for its smoky bottling. When you're not restricted by a technical file the possibilities are endless.

But some distilleries are choosing to eschew peat altogether. Based in Bristol, UK, Circumstance Distillery ruffled some feathers in March 2025 when it put out a statement loudly confirming that it would never produce a whisky using peat. "There were some people on Instagram saying 'you've lost a follower'," recalls Liam Hirt, director at Circumstance. "Some people took offence to it."

For the organic, B Corp-certified maker, not using peat makes perfect sense. "The whole idea of it doesn't really fit with our ethos," Hirt continues. "When you look at the impact of harvesting peat from peat bogs, it's relatively clear that it's undesirable." And with a commitment to source all ingredients from within 100 miles, it's illogical. "We don't have peat bogs in the centre of Bristol."

Peat futures

Few makers want to publicly discuss the future of peat. But trials are ongoing to explore alternatives. Off the record, I've gathered that one major Scotch whisky-maker is especially invested in this area. But all the while the core whisky categories, including single malt Scotch, are tightly defined in law, some seem to think it sacrilegious to even ask 'what if?'.

"Maybe it will go from being a purely raw material identity to a sensory category," muses Bettenhausen. "It'll be less about where the peat came from and more about the type of phenolic profile it expresses." Now that we can isolate different phenolic compounds, it's very possible to replicate them without cutting any more peat.

It's something Circumstance's Hirt has played around with. Smoked and roasted barley and wood smoke have all yielded positive results. "I can see with more experimentation there might be a way of doing it." The battle then could be normalising it with drinkers. But when I put the question to a bunch of whisky lovers, most said they'd eagerly explore 'alternatively smoked' whiskies if the end flavour was the same.

Another option to 'hack' peated flavour is yeast. "It's so easy to engineer, you can get it to do your job for you," Bettenhausen states. "From a biochemistry standpoint, it would not be unlikely if we saw some genetically modified or engineered yeast strains able to synthesise molecules during fermentation, or use some co-fermentations with microbes that naturally produce those phenolic off notes and recapture them." Yeast companies have worked out how to accentuate, replicate and even clean up groups of flavours in beer. Why not apply this to whisky? "The distilling industry is only starting to dip their toes into what yeast can do for us."

Whatever way you do it, it seems a future of alternative, peat-like whisky is possible. But, for now, there is hesitancy. "None of this is to diminish the economic and cultural importance of Scotch whisky," Littler sums up. "The issue is not whether peated whisky should exist, but whether its future can evolve in a way that balances heritage with environmental responsibility in a climate-conscious world." Can we continue to justify depleting crucial carbon stores just to flavour our whiskies? Surely not for much longer.

Kristiane Westray is a whisky writer, author, educator, consultant and judge. She writes about whisky culture, news and trends, and is fascinated by the evolution of global distilling. Her career has seen her head up the content team at multi-award-winning ecommerce site Master of Malt, and edit The Spirits Business magazine. Kristiane has chaired and judged at numerous tasting competitions, including the IWSC and the World Whiskies Awards. Her first book is *Savour: A guide to tasting and exploring whiskies of the world.* She was formerly writing under the name Kristiane Sherry.

China in your hand

by Jonny McCormick

Against a turbulent backdrop of tense China–U.S. trade relations and an increasingly challenging whisky market in the West, the investment and spirit of entrepreneurship in its homegrown whisky market is making China one of the most optimistic nations in world whisky in 2026.

China has ambitions to be the next whisky superpower. The country has rapidly urbanised, and now boasts the highest number of mega-cities and megalopolises on earth. Younger consumers are changing Chinese drinking culture, evolving traditional rituals of consuming alcohol with food shared with family and colleagues to embrace a more global perspective on premium drinks that encompasses whisky, cocktails, and collecting. With more than 30 operating distilleries in China, and plans for plenty more, China could overtake the number of operational distilleries in Ireland in the near future; a country that went through its own rapid expansion in distilling power not that long ago.

"China's whisky market is entering a golden phase of rapid growth," affirms Yvonne Chou, then Global Business Development Director for the Daiking Louis Distillery. The Chinese whisky industry is outperforming other Chinese spirits sectors, and it is set to quadruple by 2035, buoyed by double-digit growth forecasts for the next decade. China is on the cusp of becoming the second-largest whisky producing countries in Asia, after Japan, particularly for single malt, and it could become one of the world's top five whisky producing nations within the next decade.

"This growth is driven by improved consumer education, evolving lifestyles, and years of groundwork laid by international brands," explains Yvonne Chou. "Whisky is shifting from an imported luxury to a confident expression of local craftsmanship. By 2026, we expect more Chinese whisky brands to

Pernod Ricard´s Chuan Distillery

The spectacular setting of Daiking Distillery

expand both domestically and internationally, forming a distinct identity through flavour and cultural storytelling."

"It's a lot more promising than other markets for whisky, where there seems to be a downward trend in consumption," remarks Jay Robertson, CEO and founder of 9 Rivers Distillery. For years, Scotch marketing in China has leaned into establishing iconic brands, Lunar New Year special editions, and exclusive releases tactically produced in runs of 888 bottles. While Scotch is more heavily dependent on exports than domestic sales, the goal for Robertson is to develop and grow the market in China: self-sufficiency is key.

"We are crafting for local consumers, and we have no intention to export in the short-to-medium term," he says. "Local whisky will compete with, and eventually replace, imported whisky [*meaning Scotch*]. It really is that simple. There is bourbon in China, but it doesn't have the volumes to even be relevant in a conversation about 'whisky.' Japanese whisky isn't as popular in China as it has been in the west: culturally it can never be part of a conversation in a lot of China due to historical issues. Then there's an embargo on a lot of Japanese whisky because of Fukushima."

"Chinese consumers are highly adaptable, embracing global tastes, flavours, and cultures – with a particular curiosity for locally inspired offerings," says Jing-Yi Chiu, The Chuan International Brand Ambassador. As specialist whisky bars and cocktail culture flourish in the cities, which Chinese consumers are drawn to whisky?

"The core consumer base includes China's urban upper-middle class, fine dining venues, collectors, and premium buyers across Asia," Yvonne Chou reports. "Research shows the primary age group for whisky in China is between 25 and 45 years old, with a slight male preponderance. However, the number of female consumers and cocktail enthusiasts is growing rapidly."

Whisky consumption is often tied to social needs, including networking, casual gatherings in restaurants and bars, and gifting. "The distribution between on-trade and off-trade channels is relatively balanced, with modern trade such as chain liquor stores, supermarkets, E-commerce, and social-commerce platforms emerging as key purchase channels - especially for new brands," explains Jing-Yi Chiu.

Jay Robertson finds demographic stratification an oversimplification. "They are pretty much like whisky consumers all over the world," he states. "A plethora of ages, interests, backgrounds, careers, and of course, both men and women drink whisky. It is impossible to pigeonhole *anything* in China, not just whisky consumption, because the country is so varied from province to province, and even from city to city." Gifting culture is one striking difference between China and the West, and it is present in all aspects of life. Robertson notes, "Alcohol is one of the rarer types of gifts in modern times, as gifts are typically more modest and alcohol isn't cheap."

Made in China

Regular readers of the Yearbook will be more than aware that whisky can be made practically anywhere on planet earth. No matter if your country is too arid to grow barley, your yeast risks getting cooked in the fermentation tanks due to your climate's naturally high ambient temperature, you live on an island with no source of fresh running water, your country has no tradition of peat extraction for malting barley, or you live at a high latitude and elevation where cooperage-grade oaks can't grow: don't worry, you can still open a distillery and make whisky. We have the technical know-how and access to global trade routes to overcome all of these barriers.

The whisky industry in China is young and focused on the domestic market, so the West does not yet enjoy a wide selection of Chinese whiskies, nor is it at the front of the queue. While single malt is the dominant style produced, there are several distilleries in China equipped with column stills, and Chinese distillers are experimenting with a variety of grains, yeast, and cask types in order to add greater definition to the characteristics of Chinese whisky. Sustainability, climate change, and whisky tourism are also on the agenda of new distillery owners.

China has a long, colourful history of producing spirits, just not whisky, but the country has vast natural resources, an array of different climates, and the rapid growth in operational distilleries shows a determination to become a whisky powerhouse.

Chinese single malt closely follows Scotch from a production perspective, but can the provenance of local raw materials help distillers in China to establish their own signature styles and flavour characteristics reflective of its geographic origin? Jay Robertson is sceptical straight off the bat,

"Local barley – despite claims by some producers to be using it – is not suitable for beer, let alone whisky. The GN (*Glycosidic nitrile*) content is too high." The majority of malted barley for the brewing and distilling industries is imported from Europe or Australia, including peated malt. China has Qinke barley, a six-row huskless grain sometimes referred to as naked barley, which grows at altitude on the Qinghai-Tibet plateau. It has been used to make spirit using Baijiu methodology, applying solid-state fermentation akin to sorghum processing.

Chinese oak and Mongolian oak are terms in the parlance of some Chinese distillers, but what do whisky drinkers need to understand?

"Chinese oak? – there's no such thing available," says Jay Robertson, dismissing the notion. "China has a complete embargo on commercial logging, so any claims of cooperages creating 'Chinese oak casks' are questionable at best."

Robertson reports he has lab-tested samples from trading companies purportedly selling Chinese oak casks, and discovered they were actually made from American oak. The Chinese government banned commercial logging from designated forests and timber from illegal sources many years ago as part of a long-term silviculture recovery programme. This was stimulated by the devastating flooding of the Yangtze River in 1998 following heavy summer monsoons, where deforestation and soil erosion were contributing factors to the devastating loss of life and heavy economic impact.

The *Quercus mongolica* variety *crispula* is mizunara oak, which is familiar to Japanese whisky drinkers, whereas *Quercus mongolica* variety *mongolica* is Mongolian oak, which grows over a wider geographical area than China, though some Chinese whisky producers and cooperages may refer to this as Chinese oak. Researchers are also exploring the flavors from maturation in Liaodong oak casks, *Quercus mongolica* variety *liaotungensis*, another white oak species native to China.

Yeast, however, can be produced locally, and distilleries with their own maltings will be able to produce peated malt, as China has significant peatlands, especially in the northeast of the country, though most commercial harvesting is for horticultural use.

The Daiking Louis Distillery takes malt from the UK, Germany, and Australia, including both unpeated and peated supplies. All new make is matured at the distillery, which sits at an altitude of around 1,000m on Mount Daqin. This elevation provides stable cool temperatures and high humidity (often above 80%), accelerating flavour development while minimising the angels' share to around 6% per year.

The spirit is matured in American oak bourbon casks, Spanish sherry oak casks, and they use a small number of new French oak casks. Yvonne Chau adds, "We are also exploring locally-seasoned Mongolian oak, which imparts herbal, earthy, and resinous notes reflecting regional terroir." She recommends curious drinkers experience the Tea-Whisky Harmony: a pour of bourbon cask matured Daiking single malt delicately diluted with chilled high-mountain oolong tea.

"This pairing preserves the whisky's core character while infusing floral, mineral, and slightly tannic tea notes, creating a layered experience that resonates with both the refined balance of the Eastern tea tradition and the complexity of single malt whisky."

Pernod Ricard was the first international drinks company to open a distillery in China, unveiling The Chuan Distillery in Emeishan, Sichuan Province in 2021 as part of a £120 million investment over a ten-year period.

"The whisky production process at The Chuan distillery closely aligns with traditional Scotch methods, from milling, mashing, and fermentation, to double distillation, and maturation in oak casks," says Jing-Yi Chiu. "We utilize Chinese six-row malted barley and European two-row malted barley. The European malt primarily contributes sugars, while the Chinese malt, with its higher protein content, offers enhanced aromatic qualities."

The Chuan does not produce peated whisky or grain whisky at present. Master distiller Dr. Yang Tao matures the spirit in oak casks sourced from three continents: American oak bourbon barrels, European oak sherry casks, and *Quercus mongolica* variety *mongolica*, which imparts distinctive sandalwood and aged orange peel or chenpi notes. Sustainability is front and centre of this distillery, which runs on 100% renewable energy and offsets emissions to reduce its carbon footprint.

Since opening, they have offered an innovative private cask programme with bespoke cask finishing options, and launched The Chuan Pure Malt into the Chinese market just over 2 years after production started, a blended malt world whisky of their own young spirit and imported Scotch whiskies matured in bourbon, sherry, and Chinese oak casks i.e. *Quercus mongolica* variety *mongolica*. This is a porous wood that facilitates high evaporation but deep penetration into the wood.

As the international brand ambassador, Jing-Yi Chiu describes The Chuan's serving ritual alongside Chinese food, which pays homage to the three continents that shape the whisky's character.

"Just like the spirit itself, it embodies a uniquely Chinese touch, mirroring our tradition of ceremonial toasting during meals," he says. The ritual goes something like this: The first glass is poured for the guest on the left, honouring the influence of American oak bourbon barrels, then a second glass is offered to the guest on the right, celebrating the richness of European oak sherry casks. "The third glass," he reveals, "is reserved for the host, and symbolises reverence for the Chinese oak – a nod to both local craftsmanship and heritage."

The YunTuo Distillery opened late in 2024, Diageo's first malt whisky distillery in China, located in Eryuan in Yunnan Province in a high-altitude location 2,100m above sea level. Destined to be nicknamed the 1-2 distillery in Scot's vernacular, the distillery is being led by Jiao Changyi, supported by a handpicked team of Scotch whisky experts including former Johnnie Walker master blender Jim Beveridge, master blender Craig Wallace, and master distiller Andrew Millsopp.

Like The Chuan, sustainability is at the heart of the project, in line with Diageo's Society 2030: Spirit of Progress initiative. The distillery is carbon neutral, runs on renewable energy, and is a zero-waste site. Set in natural surroundings, production water comes from a natural spring that flows into the pristine Erhai Lake. One of the most eye-catching parts of the site is the 29m high tower of 1,000 used whisky casks from iconic distilleries around the world assembled for aesthetic purposes at the visitor centre.

For the foreseeable future, the number of Chinese whisky distilleries in the Asia section of the Yearbook is expected to rise, as more domestic and foreign companies – including cognac house Camus and Angus Dundee distillers – open their distilleries. But with rapid growth comes the need for regulation and standardisation to ensure this newborn industry is properly governed and able to compete in the international market.

The Chinese whisky guidelines

In February 2026, the China Alcoholic Drinks Association's new quality requirements for distilled spirits come into effect, which draw parallels with the 2009 Scotch Whisky Regulations. The guidelines state that Chinese whisky must be grain-based and produced as a result of mashing, fermentation, and double or triple distillation to below 95% ABV, and aged in oak casks of 700 litres or less for a minimum of three years. The only permitted additive to single malt whiskies is caramel colouring, and any age statement shown must indicate the youngest liquid in the bottle. Other styles of whisky are permissible within the grain whisky category; these are recognised as grain whisky unless they contain 51% or more of a single grain, such as rye, then they can be labelled as rye whiskey.

The most significant deviation from Scotch whisky guidelines refers to grain whisky maturation techniques, where oak chips can be added to increase flavour and colour beyond the oak staves, though this must be declared on the label, whether that whisky is bottled as a single grain whisky or used in a blend.

YuoTou in the Yunnan Province - Diageo´s first malt whisky distillery in China

There are additional rules on the production and regulations about the production of flavoured whiskies, though this is beyond the scope of this chapter.

As a member of China's Technical Standard Committee for Alcoholic Beverages, Pernod Ricard has been actively advocating for elevating the national whisky standards, such as extending the minimum aging requirement from two to three years. There could be more work to do. Jay Robertson is keen to see the industry block all forms of artificial colouring, whether through the addition of spirit caramel or other methods.

Daiking Louis Distillery believe the regulations are a major step forward, but can see further refinements worth striving for, such as requiring producers to declare the age of the youngest whisky in a blend on the label where an age statement appears and provide greater detail on permitted casks and other wood types.

They are also keen to allow greater flexibility on raw materials, opening the door to regionally meaningful grains such as sorghum or rice as ways to foster innovation in Chinese whisky styles. Like any new national whisky guidelines, producers in a competitive marketplace will disagree on the balance between standardisation and creative freedom as the industry matures.

What cannot be denied, however, is the ambition and scale of China's burgeoning whisky industry, fuelled by its agility in a fast-changing global economy and its potential to put Chinese whisky in the hands of new whisky drinkers both at home and abroad.

Jonny McCormick has been writing about whisky for 20 years and is Contributing Editor for Whisky Advocate magazine (M. Shanken Communications Inc.), the largest spirits title in the United States. He judges the Whisky Advocate Top 20 in New York each year and has reviewed more than 2,000 whiskies as a member of their tasting panel. He was made a Keeper of the Quaich in 2013, and co-wrote Whisky Opus (DK, 2024) with Gavin D. Smith. His work first appeared in the 2013 Edition of the Malt Whisky Yearbook.

The intricacies of Sherry Impact

by Ian Wisniewski

Ever wondered what various sherry styles can do to a whisky or what the impact of the seasoning period means? Or are you curious abot the difference between "seasoned to order" and ex-solera casks? Why don´t you follow Ian Wisniewski into the dark corners of sherry cask maturation?

Whisky Talk is far from being a language but it does include words that require sub-titles for anyone living in the World Beyond. 'Valinch' is a prime example, while 'Marriage' refers to casks not people, and a 'Sherry Bomb' does not possess a detonator.

"A great sherry bomb has elements such as dates and ginger at an intense peak, with layers of complexity and character in harmony with the distillery character. It's an elder statesman of whisky," says Dhavall Gandhi, Strategic Advisor in Luxury Whisky.

Various distilleries offer examples of full maturation in sherry casks, though ageing solely in sherry casks is rare. Glenfarclas is a classic example using only oloroso casks. Tamdhu has also used only oloroso casks since 2012 (following Ian Macleod's purchase of Tamdhu from Edrington). But this was a return to tradition as much as innovation, as the first ever cask filled at Tamdhu in 1898 was recorded as a sherry butt.

At that time sherry casks were acquired from 'local' wine merchants, who imported sherry into the UK in casks and bottled it themselves. That left plenty of empty casks, which malt whisky distillers needed, continuously. These sherry casks are thought to have been purpose-built for shipping, and 'seasoned' by sherry for as long as it took to reach Scotland.

This opportunity continued until 1986 when regulations required bodegas to bottle sherry in Jerez. Distillers then dealt directly with bodegas, initially purchasing casks withdrawn from solera systems. This traditional method of aging sherry comprises rows of casks stacked on top of each other. The first row (ie. ground level) is the solera containing the oldest sherry. The row above (the first criadera) contains sherry one stage younger. The row above that (the second criadera) contains sherry a stage younger than the first criadera, and so on, up to the youngest sherry in the top row of casks.

Sherry may be drawn from solera casks several times a year, up to a third of the contents, in order to be bottled. Solera casks are then replenished with equal amounts of sherry from the first criadera, which is replaced by sherry drawn from the second criadera, and so on. Casks in the final criadera are

The oak is toasted between 10 and 50 minutes Photo: J & M Martín S.L.

topped up with the youngest sherry.

The number of criaderas varies among bodegas, as does the number of criaderas for different styles of sherry. Oloroso for example, being an oxidative wine (ie. matures due to contact with air) typically has fewer criaderas than manzanilla and fino which mature beneath a layer of 'flor' (yeast).

Buying ex-bodega casks usually meant 'mixed bundles' comprising different criaderas, arriving without any identifying information. Casks which had contained sherry of different ages inevitably had varying influences on new make spirit.

As interest in malt whisky accelerated in the 1990s, distillers sought casks that provided greater consistency, and adopted a different approach: 'Seasoned To Order'. This 'a la carte' option enabled distillers to place orders with bodegas and cooperages in which every detail was stipulated: oak type, toasting level, cask size and seasoning regime.

Glenmorangie, for example, specifies American oak, a medium to heavy toast, and 18 months seasoning with oloroso and Pedro Ximenez. William Grant orders European oak, medium toast, mainly butts though also hogsheads and puncheons, seasoned for two years with oloroso.

William Grant, Glenmorangie and Tomatin are among distilleries that also supplement their 'Seasoned To Order' casks with some ex-bodega stock.

"Seasoned To Order casks are less romantic but more consistent than ex-bodega, which show more variety. This explains why we don't use ex-bodega casks in our core products," says Scott Adamson, Blender & Global Brand Ambassador, Tomatin.

Tannin levels

The majority of 'Seasoned To Order' casks are American oak (*quercus alba*), with the minority being European oak (*quercus robur*), including French and Spanish options. European oak is more assertive as tannin levels are up to several times greater than American oak. Tannins are praised for adding balance and structure, which are admittedly conceptual characteristics, whereas notes of brewed black leaf tea and dryness are more quantifiable. Dryness underlines flavours, while also enhancing mouthfeel, which (usually) also leads to a longer, richer finish.

"I generally prefer the softer character on the palate that American oak produces, together with a more luscious, creamy mouthfeel," says Dr Bill Lumsden, Head of Distilling & Whisky Creation, Glenmorangie.

Tannins are not entirely beneficial, however, and levels are deliberately reduced to prevent the risk of oak contributing bitterness. An initial step is air drying in the open, when tannins leach out and are 'rinsed' from the oak by rainfall.

"Our Spanish oak is air-dried for 2 years in the north of Spain, followed by two years air-drying in the south of Spain, prior to being coopered," says Sandy McIntyre, Distillery Manager, Tamdhu.

Air drying also enables micro-bacterial activity, which develops fruit and spice notes in the oak. Additional flavour compounds are created during the subsequent stage: toasting. The heat required is typically provided by burning off-cuts of oak within the 'carcass' of the cask (ie. body minus the heads) while avoiding physical contact between flames and staves.

Toasting levels

The scale of toasting is light, medium and heavy, but there are no definitions of the times and temperatures required, as each cooperage has its own approach. A light toast takes around 10-20 minutes, which affects the first mm of oak. A medium and heavy toast may take 20-30 minutes and 50 minutes respectively, while also attaining higher temperatures. This affects up to three mms of the stave (total thickness is about 32 mms in a hogshead and 35 mms in a butt). The heavier the toast the greater the level of vanilla, spice and nutty flavours created, though each type of oak has its own parameters.

"American oak requires at least a medium toast to unlock its aromatic potential. Toasting breaks down lignin and hemicellulose, producing pronounced vanilla (vanillin), caramel, coconut (thanks to high oak lactone levels), and sweet spice. While intense and expressive, American oak is generally less structurally complex than European oak," explains Alexandre Sakon, Founder, ASC Barrels.

Each toasting level provides a particular menu of flavours.

"Light toasting of French oak reveals buttery, brioche-like notes. Medium toasting brings roasted nuts, vanilla, coconut, and warm spices. A heavy toast shifts the profile toward leather, tobacco, and dark chocolate, with less vanilla than American oak," says Alexandre Sakon.

Such segmentation enables a highly individual approach. "We have a separate toasting regime for American and European oak, which is from northern Spain and southern France, in order to draw out the best of each cask type," says Alex Robertson, Head of Advocacy, The Macallan.

Air-dried oak waiting to be coopered into casks Photo: J & M Martín S.L.

Seasoning regimes

Another benefit of toasting is that heat 'opens up' the surface of the oak, and the greater the level of toasting, the more it opens up. This makes it easier for sherry to penetrate oak during the seasoning process, and the more 'opened up' the oak, the deeper the sherry penetrates. Sherry also finds it easier to penetrate the looser grain of European oak, than tighter grained American oak.

The favourite style of sherry is oloroso, which is available in two versions, together with the nuances of each bodega's house style.

"Oloroso casks provide a platform on which to build layers of flavour and create a great sherry cask whisky. Oloroso can be on the drier side, with more ginger and nutmeg coming through, and can also be on the sweeter side, with raisins and dried fruit," says Dhavall Gandhi.

The alcoholic strength of the 'seasoning sherry' can vary, 18% or 20% abv, for example, and the wine may be more youthful or more mature.

"While the extracted compounds are essentially the same, a higher alcohol content enhances the solubility of molecules (which are) less water-soluble, potentially resulting in subtle differences in the aromatic and sensory profile of the final spirit. A younger sherry does not extract a broader spectrum of compounds but rather a greater quantity in a shorter period," says Rocío Trillo, Master Distiller, González Byass.

The seasoning period is usually 18-24 months, though can reach 36 months, during which the key influence is sherry entering and exiting the staves. This movement peaks when the temperature rises, causing alcohol to expand and push into the staves. Flavour compounds within the sherry can remain in their original form, or interact with compounds in the staves to create new compounds.

"Ethanol could potentially combine with acids present in the oak to form new esters," says Kim Moller-Elshoj, Independent Whiskymaker.

When the temperature falls, liquid exits the staves taking flavour compounds from the oak into the bulk of the sherry.

"New oak has a lot of oomph and after 6 months you extract potent wood sugars and vanillin, with lactone formation only just beginning within the staves after adding the seasoning sherry, which acts as a kind of catalyst. After 24 months the oak has significantly less oomph, and the most desirable

Sherry casks maturing Photo: J & M Martín S.L.

aspect of this is a lower level of tannins," says Kim Moller-Elshoj.

From Spain to Scotland

Casks depart for Scotland with the addition of 'transport sherry,' perhaps 2.5 liters in a hogshead and 5 liters in a butt. This keeps casks fresh and moist during a journey lasting around 4-6 weeks. Without this precaution casks would become drier, decreasing the level of liquid within the staves, and reducing the influence on maturing whisky.

On arrival in Scotland 'transport sherry' must be emptied, though the staves are far from empty, retaining residual liquid from the seasoning process which can total up to 30 liters. Technically, this is not sherry but a residual wood extractive liquid, the sherry having been modified by interaction with oak.

An initial decision is the alcoholic strength at which new make spirit is filled into casks, 63.5% abv being standard.

"We have two filling strengths, 63.5% abv and 68.5% abv, with a greater level of alcohol-soluble flavours such as vanillin extracted at a higher strength. Ultimately it's the same range of compounds in both but slightly different ratios, which gives a broader range to work with," says Brian Kinsman, Master Blender, William Grant & Sons.

Similarly, Glenfarclas fills at 63.5% abv, except Glenfarclas 105 which is filled at receiver strength, 68% abv.

"A higher strength pulls out sherry flavours from the cask more quickly," says Callum Fraser, Production Manager, Glenfarclas.

Filling a cask instigates a series of complex reactions including 'indrink.' Occurring within 24-48 hours, this refers to staves absorbing new make spirit. Indrink can total 1-3% of the contents, depending on the freshness of the cask: the more saturated the staves, the lower the volume of indrink.

Simultaneously, residual wood extractive liquid seeps from the staves and integrates with the new make spirit. Residual liquid was traditionally considered the principal influence during ageing, though this was subsequently challenged by another school of thought which cited oak as the primary influence, and residual liquid secondary.

"When I first joined the industry I was seasoning casks myself, importing Sherry wine in bulk, and my conclusion was that while oak plays a part, about 75% of the influence is from the wine itself," says Dr Bill Lumsden.

Comparing the profile of residual wood extractive liquid in 'Seasoned To Order' and ex-bodega casks would be fascinating, but what really matters is how the 'sherry influence' interacts with the distillery character.

"We see a lot of oloroso sherry influence within the first 2-3 years. This adds Christmas cake notes which integrate with, and balance, the juicy green apple notes in the new make spirit," says Callum Fraser.

New make spirit develops most rapidly during the first three years, and then the rate slows down.

"After 3 years orchard fruits present in the new make spirit are still at the forefront, the sherry influence is in the background though it still accentuates the sweetness in the new make spirit, but the oak influence is not quite there, 3 years later you see the oak influence," says Scott Adamson.

Another opportunity to fine-tune the cask influence is with the 'fill,' as each time a cask is refilled the influence on the new make spirit modifies and decreases. The profile of residual liquid within the staves also evolves with each fill. The 'sherry character' is increasingly 'diluted' with new make spirit, and takes longer to become visible. This also enables the distillery character to show more clearly.

"Most Glenfarclas bottlings are a mix of different fills of oloroso casks, as it's all about balance and each fill provides a different ingredient in the recipe. I like a second fill cask, the distillery character is not masked by the sherry notes which are more toffee and caramel. A third fill has an apple note with caramel, and hint of vanilla, while a fourth fill has even more of the apple distillery character, like spicy apple crumble with cinnamon and a hint of vanilla, but it takes a bit longer to achieve this," says Callum Fraser.

Oloroso undoubtedly plays the lead role among sherry styles, but it also makes a great partner. A 30 year old Bladnoch bottling, for example, is a marriage of two oloroso hogsheads with one moscatel butt.

"This gives the whisky an overall nuttyness, with apricots and refreshing citrus notes of Seville oranges. I wanted the balance of softness and roundness from oloroso with the fresh fruitiness of moscatel," says Dr Nick Savage, Master Blender, Bladnoch Distillery.

Filling sherry casks with mature whisky to apply a finish (typically months), or secondary maturation (years), does of course give different results compared to ageing new make spirit. One reason for this is that mature malt whisky enters casks at a lower alcoholic strength than new make spirit, and so extracts a different range of characteristics.

"First fill oloroso casks add a lot of sultana, raisin and candied orange peel to the new make spirit. Finishing mature Glenmorangie in first fill oloroso produces a lot of lovely toffee, caramel, cinnamon and ginger. Finishing in a refill cask gives more walnut, hazelnut, and leather character," says Dr Bill Lumsden.

Finishing casks extend way beyond the favourite oloroso, and include a rarity such as palo cortado.

"In early 2020 we bought a batch of ex-bodega butts. These included casks that had held 30 year old palo cortado, used for a 3 year finish. After one year the palo cortado influence was discernible but not yet balanced, with burnt orange and maple syrup, with some toffee and bonfire notes. It was deeper and richer than I expected, with a well rounded, full mouthfeel which had a syrupy, treacle texture," says Scott Adamson.

As a finishing cask adds plenty of nuance, can 'twin finishes' add twice as much ? The Glenfiddich 18 year old Triple Sherry Cask is a marriage of oloroso-aged malt whisky with a moscatel finish and a fino finish.

"Each brings distinctive notes to the marriage: Fino adds yeasty, bakery notes, moscatel gives cinnamon, nutmeg and demerara sugar, with oloroso providing rich dried fruit," says Brian Kinsman.

Such innovation depends of course on cask availability, which is hardly a case of ordering on-line with overnight delivery.

"The key to sourcing rare casks is a good network of cooperages and bodegas. I tell them, if you get anything interesting just ring me," says Dr Nick Savage. Brian Kinsman adds, "I'm constantly on the look out for casks to try, and then see how it goes."

I would also like to see how it goes. Please let me know !

Ian Wisniewski is a freelance drinks writer focusing on spirits, particularly Scotch whisky. He contributes to various publications including Whisky Magazine France, and is the author of twelve books, the latest being 'A Passion For Whisky: How the tiny Scottish island of Islay creates malts that captivate the world,' published October, 2023. He regularly visits distilleries in Scotland to learn more and is a Master of the Quaich.

Picture of Ian Wisniewski by Alastair Duncan

Aged 52 Years
080 | 232
BOWMORE®
Est. 1779
ISLAY SINGLE MALT
SCOTCH WHISKY
1965
Matured over five
decades in the finest
Oloroso sherry cask
Carefully nurtured by generations
of distillers, this extremely rare
limited edition bottling unlocks the
exotic fruit tastes renowned in the
most collectible aged Bowmore.
WASHBACK
WOOD
SPECIAL EDITION CABINET
1 of 2

Premiumisation – a matter of perspective

by Justine Hazlehurst

The word premium triggers all sorts of emotions and arguments amongst whisky enthusiasts. But what defines a premium whisky, when was the expression coined and what lies in the future for this category?

Premium, it seems, is a matter of perspective. And when it comes to premium whisky, one person's *modus ponens* is another person's *modus tollens*. For some, if a whisky is labelled as premium, it stands to reason that it must be of exceptional quality. And once they've acknowledged that quality, they can feel confident making the purchase – irrespective of the price. For others – those who reside in the *that's more style over substance* camp – this logic is flipped. Unlike, however, the bottles they inevitably end up purchasing. But, more on that later.

That the word premium can trigger all sorts of conflicting emotions and arguments amongst whisky enthusiasts, only indicates that our perspective is undeniably shaped by our own individual experiences. Premium, it seems, is also entirely subjective.

But with so-called premium offerings now at unprecedented levels - and with announcements of the latest super- or ultra-premium whisky becoming more and more frequent – it raises the question: how did we get to this point? To answer this, we must travel back in time to post-war Britain.

The Second World War had a profound impact on Scotch whisky: the 1940s saw its production

Mortlach Become - one part of the Mortlach L´Evolution collaboration between Diageo and Phillipe Starck

severely curtailed as part of the war effort with duty, on the other hand, significantly increased. And so, whereas the appeal of Scotch whisky remained strong, limited availability together with its hefty price tag put it out of reach for most.

The industry's post-war years continued to play a key role in reshaping the perception of Scotch whisky. Despite the gradual lifting of restrictions on distilling, supply was still not able to keep up with demand. To all intents and purposes, Scotch whisky was well on the way to becoming a precious commodity.

At this time, however, there was no real single malt market – whisky drinkers were almost invariably steered towards one of the many blends placed on the shelves of shops and pubs. But during the industry's post-war boom years, moves to differentiate these 'standard' blends from more premium options were already underway.

As early as the 1960s, the Distillers Company Limited's subsidiary – The Distillers Agency – launched a series of advertisements for its flagship whisky, King George IV. These adverts not only emphasised the blend's 'majestic qualities' but also introduced the consumer to King George IV Supreme – a premium variant positioned as the perfect choice for either a 'special occasion' or a 'special treat'. Even at this stage, a layered strategy of premiumisation was beginning to take shape.

By the mid 1980s, the biggest issue the Scotch whisky industry faced was that of declining consumption. The so-called *whisky loch* of that decade forced many Scotch whisky producers to reassess their marketing and advertising strategies. Subsequently, in a race to the bottom, an increasing number of low-cost bottles appeared on the shelves, devaluing the product without necessarily yielding the desired increase in sales.

In 1986, shortly after Guinness plc launched what would become a successful takeover bid for the Distillers Company Ltd, its soon-to-be-disgraced chairman, Ernest Saunders, announced that the company was "undertaking a worldwide review of advertising and marketing."

"The future of Scotch whisky," Saunders declared, "depends on attracting consumers to premium brands. As the industry leader, we have a responsibility to show the way".

And show the way they did. Before the end of the decade, United Distillers – now newly formed and backed by a fresh executive team – launched the premium-priced Classic Malts range and, by the middle of the next decade, had released the inaugural Rare Malts Selection – both of which spearheaded single malts as a high-value category. And in between? The company, unwilling to neglect the blended Scotch whisky market it commanded, used aged single malts – conveniently aiding the necessary drainage of the *whisky loch* – to create what is now one of the best-known premium blends on the market: Johnnie Walker Blue Label.

As a result, not only did other Scotch whisky producers (such as Allied Distillers and Chivas) quickly follow suit, but firms which had been sitting quietly on the periphery of the industry also moved to capitalise on the opportunity. In response to what it perceived as a growing demand for specialty glass and packaging – aimed at premiumising Scotch whisky brands – Premier Glass Packaging was established in 1991, in the somewhat paradoxical setting of an industrial estate in Cumbernauld.

In *The Scotsman*, a PGP company spokesperson noted that "one way of making a whisky brand more distinctive is to repackage it in a decorated bottle" – a strategy which remains central today, not only for premium releases but increasingly for super- and ultra-premium whiskies.

Premiumisation accelerates

The recently released Mortlach L'Evolution brings together the distillery and French designer Philippe Starck, resulting in the *Begin, Become, and Beyond* collection. Each variant features the Beast of Dufftown's iconic square bottle encased in a 3D-printed cage, crafted from aluminium and copper for the £10,000 ultra-premium *Begin* and *Beyond* duo, or from cask wood chip and resin, with a "soft-to-touch finish", for a somewhat more modest £310 for the *Become* release. Naturally, the *modus ponens* crowd would argue that if it's both exclusive and expensive, then it must surely be worth the money. Those in Camp Modus Tollens, however, might perceive the only soft touch as being the person who paid a small fortune for it.

Heading into the new millenium, whisky marketers' premiumisation strategies continued apace. Pernod-Ricard – whose marketing director, Jean-Paul Richard, is often credited as the first within the company to coin such a phrase – witnessed signficant growth in revenue before his retirement in 2009 after thirty-five years with the company. In September 2007, Pernod-Ricard reported a 6.9% increase in year-on-year revenue and by May the following year, growth throughout the group had risen by 3.9% – with its Irish whiskey brand, Jameson, not only seeing a 14% rise in volume but also breaking into the Top 40 Global Premium Spirits chart for the first time. An illustration, according to then chairman Patrick Ricard, of the huge success of the company's premiumisation strategy, which had involved the introduction of more upmarket versions of its flagship brands.

Whisky's premium sector continued to grow and grow. In 2017, £4.36 billion of Scotch whisky had been exported - a new record at that time - and the demand for more luxury whisky products was on the up.

According to data published by the IWSR (International Wine and Spirits Record), the fastest growing sectors for Scotch whisky over the previous five years had been the prestige, super- and ultra-premium categories.

Indeed, in its annual report to the US Securities and Exchange Commission in 2018, a statement from Diageo's chairman, Javier Ferrán, explained that the company would "seize the opportunities presented by demographic change and rising incomes that allow people to choose premium brands" and expected "730 million new consumers will be able to afford international premium spirits over the next ten years, driving growth...".

Additionally, it was affirmed that "single malt whisky is increasingly seen as an investment of passion by high-net worth collectors, particularly in Asia" in an article entitled *Casks of Gold*, written by Andrew Shirley, for the 2019 Knight Frank Wealth Report.

Few, however, could have foreseen the profound global upheaval that began to unfold towards the end of that year. The impact of Covid-19 on the Scotch whisky industry – exacerbated by the 25% tariff imposed on imports of single malt Scotch whisky by the United States – was nothing short of extraordinary.

Exports of Scotch whisky fell sharply in 2020, dropping by 23% to £3.8 billion – the lowest level in a decade. As they recovered over the following two years – to £4.51 and £6.2 billion respectively – an interesting shift was taking place: the trend towards premiumisation appeared to be accelerating.

With no in-person tastings or festivals for whisky enthusiasts to attend, the industry's pivot to online events was both swift and effective. An increase in webinars, vlogs, and podcasts soon followed, creating an unprecedented wealth of information and education available to whisky enthusiasts right at their fingertips. Alongside this, it's perhaps therefore unsurprising that the move towards more premium offerings gathered pace, echoing the industry's growing marketing strategy of *drinking less, but better*.

For those whose incomes remained steady during this period – but whose usual opportunities for spending, such as travel and dining out, now precluded – that money was often redirected towards higher-end whiskies, allowing them to stretch their usual budgets and trade up to more premium bottles.

As whisky education became increasingly accessible, it's perhaps no surprise that the category – at least in the eyes of whisky drinkers – became

The Macallan and Bentley have been working together for the past few years

a victim of its own success. It had now become possible for anyone to recognise which releases were considered the most sought after – not only escalating the bun fights for bottles and driving up competition, but also framing these acquisitions as alternative investments.

Many of these alternative investments were short-term – very short-term, in fact – judging by the number of bottles flipped onto the secondary market. Of course, none of this was unique to Covid; prior to the pandemic, whisky had already been seen as a way to make a quick buck. At the end of the day, *flippers gonna flip*. But as the saying goes *money goes to money* and the pandemic certainly propelled the notion of whisky – and, particularly, of prestige bottlings – as an investment opportunity, into the mainstream.

Naturally, none of this came without consequences. As more people bought these bottles – in the hope that prices would rise even further on the secondary market – the value of premium whisky in general was artificially inflated.

The temptation for some producers – not just in Scotland but also elsewhere – to jump on the bandwagon proved too strong, with an increasing number of premium bottlings hitting the market. Take The Lakes Distillery just over the border, for example: since launching their Whiskymaker's Editions in 2020, no fewer than twenty-eight of these special edition bottlings have been released. In the eyes of drinkers and collectors alike, this influx runs the risk of not only diluting the prestige of the collection but also, as a consequence, the demand for individual bottles.

One way to resist the urge to flood the market with numerous releases is to focus on a single, ultra-premium bottling. In 2019, the London-based brand experience design studio Jordan Design was brought on board to strategically rebrand The Dalmore – to elevate it from a respected whisky into a luxury product. Later that year, The Dalmore released the first decanter (of three) of its 60 year-old-whisky to commemorate the 180th anniversary of the brand. Bottled at 41.7%, the angels certainly enjoyed their share over the course of those six decades. And, naturally, where there are angels, there are halos.

The entire range is elevated

The so-called halo effect is when the success or brilliance of one standout bottle filters down to make the entire range seem more desirable. In 2019, The

Dalmore's flagship 15-ye... single malt retailed for £70 in the UK. Thre... later and the price had increased to £90. ... it commands a price tag of £110 – a stag... 57% leap in just six years. For some, this is ... the halo shining brightly; for others, it's ... that the halo has simply slipped.

Although ... the ... ages of this premiumisation strategy ... obvious, any whisky producer that pursu... ing out genuine enthusiasts – the ... bottles to open and enjoy – potentially ... of its most loyal supporters.

One ... us neatly to The Macallan: the distil... become almost synonymous with this ... h.

... turn of the millenium, when Ken Grier ... e company's brands director, owners ... gton have positioned this Speyside single malt ... a force to be reckoned with in the luxury whisky market.

In an interview with The Spirits Business back in 2013, Grier explained that "What's happened at Macallan is that we very much appeal to über-collectors, to people who are real connoisseurs for whom price is no object. Once you've crossed that rubicon into the Macallan franchise, it's difficult to go back."

And accordingly, those über-collectors tend to have pockets that are über deep. As demand for ultra-premium offerings increases, so the dial on the premium-ometer is turned up. The Macallan's collaborations and associations with other luxury brands – most notably Lalique and Bentley – demonstrate how marketing a whisky alongside other luxury names serves to reinforce its image of exclusivity and quality, strengthening consumers' perception of it as a premium product.

But with the risk of alienating loyal customers, together with the forecast of an ever shrinking market – buffeted by global economic squalls – why do whisky producers continue to navigate the choppy waters of super- and ultra-premium releases?

Because they're sailing full speed ahead on the good ship Veblen, where those aboard have – and likely always will have – serious money to spend.

The Veblen Effect demonstrates how demand for certain products actually increases as their prices rise, as the high cost itself signals rarity, status, and exclusivity. In the world of ultra-premium whisky, über-collectors see the price tag not as a barrier but as part of the appeal. For them, these bottles – especially when paired with luxury collaborations and prestigious 'experiences' – serve to elevate not only their collection, but also their status.

For the rest of us who aren't among the super-rich, these economically turbulent times are likely to make us hold on to our wallets just that little bit tighter. Many of us will turn to the bottles already in our collection – perhaps built up during those two long years of lockdown – or seek out releases that offer real value for money, with independent bottlers at the forefront of our minds.

It's often said that in times like these, it's the middle market that gets squeezed as the whisky world splits into two extremes: affordable entry-level options at one end, and high-end luxury at the other, with little activity in between.

But Megan Brown, co-founder of independent bottler Woodrow's of Edinburgh, sees things differently.

"When premiumised whiskies retail at higher prices than our bottles, we're seen as better value by comparison, so retailers tend to take in more of our stock. Competing becomes less of a struggle when the alternatives are priced so much higher," she explains.

As for the super-premium releases? Megan does... see them as a direct threat. "They're really a diffe... rent category from what we offer," she says. "W... not competing head-to-head. There's very much ... market for both."

What constitutes premium whisky remains p... and subjective. It's a concept shaped by indiv... tastes, budgets, and expectations. And while ... ultra-premium market thrives on exclusivity ... status – appealing to those for whom price ... ject – there are plenty of whisky enthusiast... affordable and accessible bottles that offe... value for money.

Bottles, incidentally, that will be opene... contents enjoyed – usually with others. ... something to bear in mind as we face t... geopolitical turmoil together is the adv... person once offered me: *regardless o... you'll never know the true value of a... you've tasted it.*

Justine Hazlehurst is the founder of Kask Whisky - a tasting events and tour company - as well as the co-founder and co-director of the annual Fife Whisky Festival. Her passion and enthusiasm for whisky has led to her being selected as a judge for several whisky awards and her knowledge of Scotch whisky history has led her to work with a number of distilleries, organisations and publications delving into the heritage of brands. Justine recently published her first book - O... of Pattisons' Whisky.

ersonal
dual
the
and
s no ob-
s seeking
genuine
d and the
Perhaps
e current
ice a wise
the price tag,
whisky until
pening The Case: The Affairs

Sherry & Scotch – a complex relationship

by Nick Morgan

The prevailing view is that the the growth of Scotch in the late 19th century was a result of phylloxera and the subsequent decline of cognac and brandy. Instead it was the crash of sherry imports to the United Kingdom that propelled sales but also changed the style and character of Scotch.

It is widely held that the dizzying rise in the consumption of Scotch whisky in England in the final quarter of the nineteenth century was at the expense of brandy, following the devastation caused to the Charente vineyards by *phylloxera* from the mid 1870s. But it just doesn't add up. The vacuum created by the decline in imported brandy consumption between 1870 and 1900 was nowhere near as large as the increase in whisky consumption. So what really happened?

It was the decline in sherry drinking, which fell by 4 million gallons compared to brandy's 1.6 million gallons, not brandy, that first opened the doors of the English middle classes to Scotch whisky, and it was whisky that replaced sherry in the ubiquitous decanter, and *phylloxera* was only part of the story. 'The great volume of increase in the consumption has been in Scotch whisky, consumed in better class families, where wine has been, and still is, habitually used. But whisky has taken the place of a great deal of wine', wrote *Ridley's Monthly Wine And Spirit Trade Circular* (hereinafter *Ridley's*) in 1893

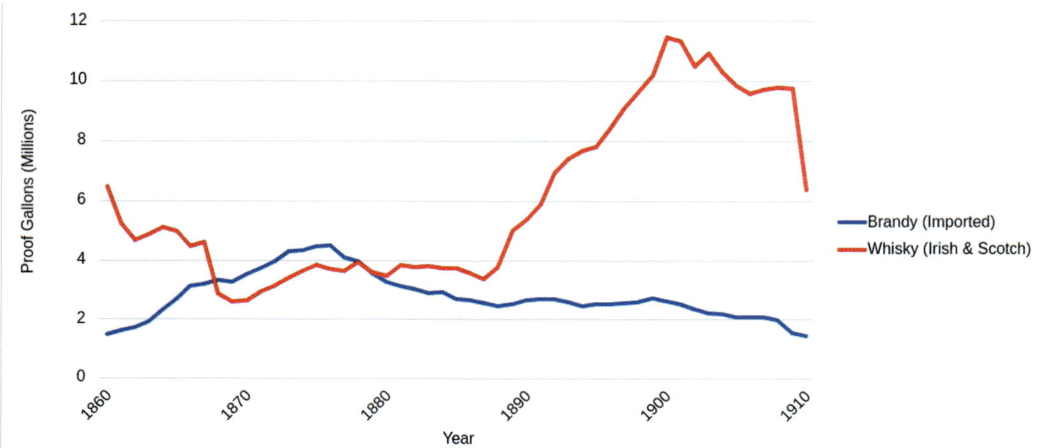

The consumption of imported brandy in Great Britain, and Irish and Scotch whisky in England, 1860-1910. Source: G B Wilson, Alcohol and the Nation (1940)]

Wine consumption increased dramatically after Gladstone's duty and licensing reforms in the early 1860s, which brought light table wines within reach of 'the ordinary sort of person': the age of 'the grocer's claret' was nigh. Nonetheless fortified wines, and particularly sherry, held a particular place in domestic and social discourse in the 1860s and 1870s – 'for three centuries sherry has been the favourite drink of Englishmen' claimed one authority. 'Sherry is a genteel drink; many well-to-do English people take some of this wine at their meals, some more afterwards, and some a great deal more than is good for them, between their meals'.

Sherry was also the darling of the medical profession. Charles Dickens was grateful that his doctor 'had great confidence in the virtue of juicy mutton and generous wine'. 'Two glasses of sherry at once and a nourishing dinner' was his prescription: 'Chicken broth and a glass of Amontillado sherry' the perfect restorative, the perfect cure-all. As sherry consumption reached a peak of over six million gallons in 1873 its position as the nation's favourite drink seemed assured. However, this was just the tip of a very problematic iceberg.

The traditional home of sherry was Jerez in Andalusia in southern Spain. Even under normal circumstances its vineyards could never produce the quantities of wine being consumed in Britian by the 1860s, which accounted for around 87% of its production. But after a series of poor harvests and periodic outbreaks of disease the need for producers and shippers to find wine from elsewhere to ship as sherry became imperative. So it was, traditional sherry wines were being blended with wines from elsewhere in Spain and Europe in order to meet the seemingly insatiable demand from England. These wines needed to be fortified with brandy to prevent a secondary fermentation occurring during transit, and the shippers, many of whom were of English origin, believed 'nothing but strong liquid would suit the English palate'. As a result, the wines were often 'highly brandied'. Moreover, some wine merchants would fortify the wine again before sale, sometimes using German spirit (it would later be alleged that this was used in Jerez too).

At a time when the adulteration of both food and drink was a bogeyman that loomed large in the imagination of the British public, and in attention grabbing headlines of newspapers, allegations of the malpractice in Spain began to gain traction. Sherry's reputation was also suffering from a host of cheap impersonators of variable quality, such as Cape sherry, Australian sherry and Hambourg sherry (not captured in the 'sherry' consumption figures in the graph below).

'Sherry has long been the favourite wine' wrote T G Shaw in *Wine, the Vine and the Cellar*, published in 1864, 'but the quantity of bad quality now shipped and sold under that name has already injured its reputation …'. The mode of consumption of these over-strengthened sherries was also a cause for concern: 'no discredit' said *The Saturday Review*, in 1871 'is now attached to visiting the luncheon bar for frequent drams, provided the liquor be sherry, and that it is consumed at a gulp standing, not sitting, and with a brief interval between each glass'. And the liquid? 'Many people who would be shocked at the idea of drinking spirits, and especially raw spirits, think nothing of a glass of sherry; yet in the majority of cases, the sherry is only cheap bad brandy in disguise'.

The dangers of this dramming of spiritous sherry-wine came to a head at the end of 1873, at the height of sherry consumption, when a man in Blackburn was found to have died of alcohol poisoning after drinking four gills of sherry. Reported in *The Times*, it provoked a correspondence there from wine merchants, analysts and self-styled experts which brought forward more allegations of malpractice and adulteration in Jerez, and resulted in a newsprint pile-on throughout the country that lasted for months, with sporadic outbreaks for a decade or more.

The decline of sherry

The public, wrote Henry Vizetelly in *Facts About Sherry* (1876) 'naturally grew alarmed, and for a time the subject formed a common topic of conversation at all diner-tables … middle aged gentlemen, too, perfectly hale and hearty on their daily pint of sherry, fancied that perhaps for them a day of reckoning may soon be near'. By the end of the decade sherry consumption had fallen by two and a half million gallons, and although the wine trade hit back with publications such as Vizetelly's, sales continued to plummet. 'Sherry seems to be the unfortunate scapegoat of all the branches of the Wine and Spirit Trade, on which the literary hack vents his yearning for criticism when more promising subjects fail' complained *Ridley's* in 1886.

Times were hard, and getting harder. Sherry's peak consumption year of 1873 also marked the start of a sustained period of over two decades of agricultural decline and commercial stagnation. Typically an item of discretionary spending, sales of alcohol were closely tied to economic conditions. 'The real cause of reduced consumption of wine' argued R C Cosens in *Sherryana*, 'is simply a question of means', although there would be no revival for sherry as economic conditions began to improve in the 1890s.

Brandy's decline, which began slightly later than sherry's was also hastened by this financial downturn. It was precipitated by shortages of liquid as the *phylloxera* beetle went to work on the vines of Charente and worsened as stocks of maturing Cognac dwindled. Like sherry, brandy's reputation suffered because of poor practice on the part of some producers. It was after 1876, explained *Ridley's*, 'that certain French firms turned their attention to shipping blended and imitation brandies … a large demand arose for Spirits shipped from Charente, no matter what they were made of, so long as they were cheap …'.

Poor imitations were also coming into the market from elsewhere on the continent, principally Germany. One London wholesaler, supplying public houses in the provinces, confessed to *Ridley's* that 'for every hogshead of real Brandy he sold, he got rid of ten hogsheads of the three and sixpenny'.

For over a decade the downward trajectory of sherry and brandy was almost identical. When brandy consumption stabilised in 1890 sherry continued to sink into the abyss. During this period there had been no sudden upsurge in the popularity of either Scotch or Irish whisky, despite the trade enthusiastically talking them up in order to try and recover millions of gallons of very profitable lost business. If these two categories were going to succeed they needed to win over the hearts and palettes of Londoners – from where trends and fashions spread throughout the country – and the world.

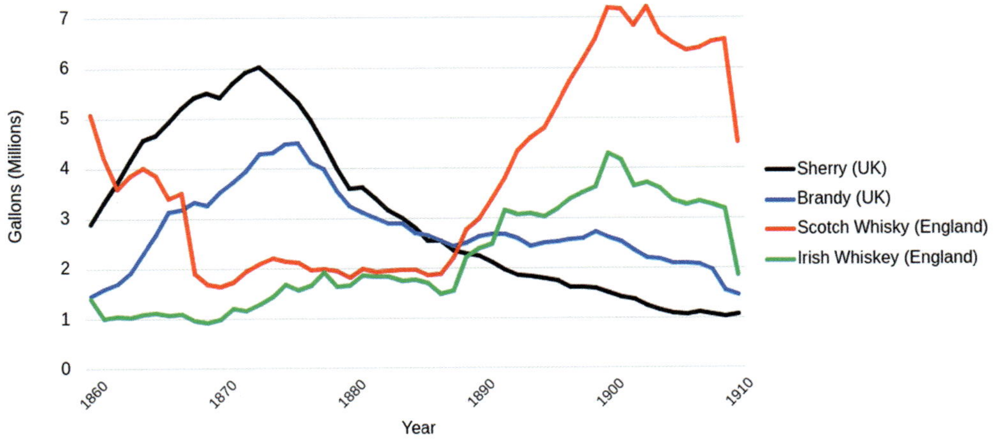

The consumption of sherry ('Spanish white wine') and imported brandy in Great Britain, and Irish and Scotch whisky in England, 1860-1910. Sherry in imperial gallons, spirits in proof gallons.
Sources: G B Wilson, Alcohol and the Nation (1940), Ridley's 12/3/1921

A sherry bodega in Jerez

Greenlees Brothers, with their Lorne Highland Whisky, 'unrivalled for toddy', opened a London branch in 1871. Alexander Walker followed in 1873. Years of losses followed, but in 1886 Walker could write to his son George, then managing the London office, 'I am glad that you say that the prospect of our London business is so bright. I never expected anything else since I first started there but no one but myself knows the hard work I had to make it …'.

This was just as consumption of Scotch and Irish whisky was turning a corner in England, as wages started to rise and prices fell. In the space of fifteen years, from 1888, consumption of Scotch whisky in England increased by an astonishing 200% to a peak of just over seven million gallons, taking up all the headroom left by the decline of sherry and brandy. Consumption of Scotch and Irish whiskies also increased in their home markets, but England now accounted for almost 70% of all the whisky drunk in the Kingdom.

A number of factors helped to make Scotch more palatable to these new English consumers: the shift from single malts to blended Scotch whisky; the consequent change from heavy and oily to lighter and delicate spirits; the fashion for whisky and soda rather than whisky toddy, relentless advertising and promotion of a scale and sophistication never witnessed before, and most important of all, the use of sherry casks to mature and 'soften' grain and malt spirit.

At the root of Scotch's success, observed Dublin whisky merchant Adam Findlater in 1898, was quality: 'getting the best pot still, and after that, patent still which made from the very finest and purest grain and stored in sherry casks for a long time'. 'We are not sure', said Scotland's *Victualling Trades Review*, 'that the taste for the Scotch article has not been largely due to the softness and roundness imparted by maturing the article in fresh sherry wood'.

Sherry and brandy had been deserted by important advocates in favour of whisky: 'the chief cause however of the recent popularity of whisky is, no doubt, the fact that the medical profession now very extensively recommend it … as being … one of the best of all alcoholic stimulants'. Discussing 'the falling off of the wine trade' *Ridley's* lamented that 'the consumer once having left the line, takes a great deal of persuading to return to it. Moreover 'the medical profession has had a large finger in the pie by recommending whisky.' It was wine (fortified and table wines) that suffered more than brandy.

Whisky, said *Ridley's* in 1893, 'has gone up in the world … in thousands of middle-class households, alcohol in the form of whisky has permanently ousted a considerable amount of alcohol in the form of wine'. It was the same in restaurants and fashionable resorts where, said *The Wine and Spirits Trade Record*, 'whisky has reaped the benefit, and men who formerly drank wine at lunch take whisky and

Apollinaris or soda instead'. 'It is passing strange to those who frequented fashionable restaurants years ago, to notice how the ubiquitous Whisky bottle has usurped the place of everything else upon many of the tables', said *Ridley's*. 'Sherry has come to be regarded merely as a flavouring for soups owing to the modern craze for whisky and soda' wrote a disgruntled correspondent to *The Daily Mail* in 1907.

The need for sherry wood

The decline of sherry (and to a lesser extent brandy) afforded Scotch whisky the opportunity to grow; the widespread adoption of sherry casks helped deliver the required quality to grow. Ironically, in tandem the declining availability of genuine sherry wood threatened the continued ability of Scotch distillers and blenders to maintain the tastes and flavours that were driving growth.

In the 1850s and 1860s unwanted shipping butts (around 110 gallons), worth around twelve shillings each, were routinely sent back to Cadiz. As production at Scottish distilleries began to increase from the early 1870s demand for them increased, as did the price. By the 1890s, if they could be got, shipping butts peaked in price at fifty shillings each - the cost paid indicating the premium blenders placed on the influence of sherry-wood. In 1870 around 50,000 shipping butts would have been emptied, in 1900 less than 1,500. Scotland's requirements for butts – assuming all spirit was being filled into sherry-wood (which was certainly not the case) would have been around 125,000 in 1870, 290,000 in 1900.

'For the past ten or fifteen years' said *The Wine and Spirits Trade* record in 1904, 'the difficulty of procuring really good sherry casks has been steadily becoming greater, and anyone accustomed to the fine sherry wood of, say, twenty years ago, can only think, with regret, of its almost total disappearance'. The trade believed that 'no better casks for maturing Whisky were ever got than the old-fashioned golden sherry casks when second fills'. In 1904 it was estimated 'that there is only enough freshly emptied sherry wood to receive about one-thirtieth part of the whisky produced'. Home coopered plain wood would have been the most common form of cask for maturation.

Blenders needed sherry wood whisky for top dressing to ensure 'fine and useful' blends. Cutbacks in wine production in Jerez in the late 1880s led to the availability of unwanted (larger) bodega butts; once exhausted, shippers started supplying wine-seasoned shipping butts and hogsheads of variable quality. In 1896 Ridleys complained that 'certain Houses in Jerez have of late sent over a quantity of new casks, both butts and hogsheads, the seasoning of which has been of a decidedly limited character, but for which, inasmuch as they come from Cadiz, have a ready sale. The casks, is said, were 'little, if any better, than "plain"'.

Particularly despised were the wine-seasoned hogsheads. One journal warned of danger to the reputation of Scotch due 'the "faking" that is going on by the shippers of so-called sherry wine casks … there is a big swindle going on, which is sure to have a detrimental effect one day'. Shippers, it was said, were making more out of their casks than they were their sherry. Blenders looked for wood from other sherry consuming markets often receiving 'casks said to be continental emptied or American-emptied which never saw either America or the continent' or, for that matter, any wine.

Coopers turned their attention to the possibility of wine seasoning casks at home, like Glasgow's William Lowrie's, who had registered a patent for steam seasoning plain casks in 1888, and promised to deliver from a adaptation of the patent a 'soft matured spirit, together with that fine sherry flavour and colour which is now so much appreciated.' They had 'already established a considerable trade in these casks, which are … equal in every respect to those procured from the finest sherry wood'.

Sherry and Scotch had a strange symbiotic relationship. When the decline of sherry consumption created the opportunity for Scotch to grow, the decline in the availability of genuine sherry wood forced producers to find alternatives, which meant that the use of inferior wine-treated or sherry seasoned casks changed the character of the blends the public had taken to their heart. 'The task of blenders is, year by year, becoming a more arduous one, and blends will persist in turning out thinner than they should'.

Blends were, wrote *Ridley's* in 1915, 'quite different to the taste of a quarter of a century ago'. By then blenders, and for that matter distillers, and the trade press, must also have been beginning to ask themselves, rather like today, what the term 'sherry cask' actually meant.

Nick Morgan's career as a historian and writer was rudely interrupted by a thirty-year, award-winning spell in the Scotch whisky business. His first role was as Archivist for United Distillers, after which he deftly side-stepped into marketing, becoming Diageo's Global Marketing Director for Single Malts, managing the largest portfolio of malts in the world. He has now returned to the relative sanity of the past, and is researching and writing about the whisky industry, the booze business and Scottish history more generally.

Picture of Nick Morgan by Amara Eno

Cabrach Distillery

Malt distilleries

Including the subsections:
Scottish distilleries | New distilleries
Distilleries around the globe

A brief explanation

There are five protected whisky regions or localities in Scotland today; Highlands, Lowlands, Speyside, Islay and Campbeltown. Where useful we mention a location within a region e.g. Orkney, Northern Highlands etc.

The year in which the distillery was founded is usually considered as when construction began and capacity is expressed in litres of pure alcohol (LPA). The historical chronology focuses on the official history of the distillery and (vc) under status means the distillery is open to visitors.

For all the Scottish distilleries we present tasting notes of what, in most cases, can be called the core expression (mainly their best selling 10 or 12 year old). The whiskies have been tasted either by Gavin D Smith (GS), Ian Wisniewski (IW) or by Ingvar Ronde (IR). All notes have been prepared especially for Malt Whisky Yearbook.

Distilleries that have not started production yet or are in a planning stage are all presented in the chapter The Year That Was, pages 272-275.

Closed distilleries

In earlier editions of the Malt Whisky Yearbook there was a chapter dedicated to closed distilleries. With closed distilleries we mean distilleries that stopped production after 1970. The reason for that cut-off point is that bottlings from all of them were possible to buy when the first Yearbook was published in 2005.

Today, stock from most of them have been depleted and only rarely will you be able to find them. At the same time a huge number of new distilleries have been founded. In order for the Yearbook not to grow out of proportion, we have decided to simply list the closed ones here.

For a deeper knowledge about them, we happily refer to the excellent book "Scotch Missed", written by Brian Townsend and published by Neil Wilson. Here is the list;

Banff • Ben Wyvis • Caperdonich • Coleburn • Convalmore Dallas Dhu • Glen Albyn • Glenesk • Glen Flagler Glenlochy • Glen Mhor • Glenugie • Glenury Royal • Imperial Inverleven • Killyloch • Kinclaith • Ladyburn • Littlemill Lochside • Millburn • North Port • Pittyvaich • St Magdalene

Aberfeldy

[ah•bur•fell•dee]

Owner:
John Dewar & Sons (Bacardi)

Region/district:
Southern Highlands

Founded:
1896

Status:
Active (vc)

Capacity:
3 400 000 litres

Address: Aberfeldy, Perthshire PH15 2EB

Website:
aberfeldy.com

Tel:
01887 822010 (vc)

Writing about Aberfeldy without mentioning Dewar's is of course impossible. Aberfeldy was the only distillery that the famous whisky family founded and it has been intrically linked with the brand ever since.

The family lost control in 1925 when DCL took over (and eventually in 1998 Bacardi became the custodians), but the single malt remains the backbone of Dewar's blended Scotch, White Label. It was introduced in 1899 and was registered as a brand in 1906. Since then it has been one of the Top 10 Scotch whiskies in the world and currently it occupies place 6 with 40 million bottles sold in 2024. For decades it was the most sold Scotch in USA but that position was overtaken by Johnnie Walker Black Label two years ago. In autumn 2024 the owners launched the "Here's to the Story" marketing campaign in USA to boost the brand. Apart from the big seller White Label there are 12, 15 and 18 year olds. In recent years the Double Double series with 21, 27 and 32 year olds has been introduced as well as the Cask Series where a range of 8 year olds have been finished in various casks such as rum and mezcal. The Aberfeldy single malt led a hidden existence for a long time but following a relaunch in 2014, sales have increased substantially to 1.6 million bottles in 2023.

The equipment consists of a 7.6 ton stainless steel, full lauter mash tun, eight washbacks made of larch, three made of stainless steel with an average fermentation time of 72 hours, and four stills. 15 mashes a week are planned for 2025 which equates to just over 2 million litres of alcohol.

The core range consists of **12, 16, 21** and **25** year **olds**. Recent limited expressions include an **18 year old** finished in red wine casks from Napa Valley, a **15 year old** Cadillac white wine finish, a **15 year old** from Tuscan red wine casks and an **18 year old** finished in Sangiovese red wine casks. For the duty free market there are three expressions; **12, 16** and **21 year olds,** allt of them finished in different types of Madeira casks.

12 years old

History:

- 1896 John and Tommy Dewar embark on the construction of the distillery, a stone's throw from the old Pitilie distillery which was active from 1825 to 1867. Their objective is to produce a single malt for their blended whisky - White Label.
- 1898 Production starts in November.
- 1917 The distillery closes.
- 1919 The distillery re-opens.
- 1925 Distillers Company Limited (DCL) takes over.
- 1972 Reconstruction takes place, the floor maltings is closed and the two stills are increased to four.
- 1991 The first official bottling is a 15 year old in the Flora & Fauna series.
- 1998 Bacardi buys John Dewar & Sons from Diageo at a price of £1,150 million.
- 2000 A visitor centre opens and a 25 year old is released.
- 2005 A 21 year old is launched in October, replacing the 25 year old.
- 2009 Two 18 year old single casks are released.
- 2010 A 19 year old single cask, exclusive to France, is released.
- 2011 A 14 year old single cask is released.
- 2014 The whole range is revamped and an 18 year old for duty free is released.
- 2015 A 16 year old is released.
- 2018 A 16 year old and a 21 year old madeira finish are released for duty free.
- 2020 A limited 15 year old finished in Pomerol casks is released.
- 2021 A limited 18 year old finished in Côte Rôtie casks is released.
- 2022 Limited 15 year and 18 old finished in red wine casks are released.
- 2023 A limited 18 year finished in red wine Napa Valley casks and a 15 year old Cadillac white wine cask finish are released.
- 2024 A 25 year old is added to the range.

Tasting notes Aberfeldy 12 years old:

GS – Sweet, with honeycombs, breakfast cereal and stewed fruits on the nose. Inviting and warming. Mouth-coating and full-bodied on the palate. Sweet, malty, balanced and elegant. The finish is long and complex, becoming progressively more spicy and drying.

Aberlour

[ah•bur•lower]

Owner: Chivas Brothers Ltd (Pernod Ricard)

Region/district: Speyside

Founded: 1879

Status: Active (vc)

Capacity: 3 800 000 litres

Address: Aberlour, Banffshire AB38 9PJ

Website: aberlour.com

Tel: 01340 881249

For quite some time now, Aberlour has been closed for distillery tours but tastings can still be booked. The reason for closure is a substantial expansion in progress, an idea that started growing a decade ago.

These plans were announced in 2017 but they were later withdrawn and a new application for expansion was submitted to the local council in 2020. The work started shortly thereafter and if everything goes according to plan the new distillery should be commissioned in August 2026 with a staggered plan to bring it into production during the autumn. The plans are impressive and include a doubling of the capacity to 7.6 million litres of alcohol. The number of stills will double to eight and there will be 14 washbacks. When it comes to mash tuns, Scottish distilleries usually buy them from Briggs, Newmill, Northern Fabricators or Forsyth. For Aberlour the owners contacted the German company GEA founded in 1920 for their new 13 ton mash tun. The plans for a new visitor centre have been pushed to the future.

At the time of writing, the distillery is equipped with a 12 ton semi-lauter mash tun, six stainless steel washbacks and two pairs of large and wide stills in a spacious still room. To achieve the desired fruity character of the new make, the operators run a very slow distillation. With a 7.5 hour spirit cycle, the middle cut (73-63%) takes two hours to complete.

The core range includes **12, 14, 16** and **18 year olds** – all matured in a combination of ex-bourbon and ex-sherry casks. Other core expressions include **Casg Annamh** (bourbon/oloroso matured) and **Aberlour a'bunadh** (bottled at cask strength). For select markets **12 year old** non chill-filtered and **White Oak** are available and for France the **10 year old Forest Reserve** and the **Triple Cask**. A selection of bottlings are available at the distillery only including a limited edition of **a'bunadh** which appeared in October 2025. Finally a new range for travel retail was launched in April 2025 – the NAS **Suthainn,** a **13yo** and **16 yo Double Charred Selection**.

12 years old

History:

1879 The local banker James Fleming founds the distillery.

1892 The distillery is sold to Robert Thorne & Sons Ltd who expands it.

1896 A fire rages and almost totally destroys the distillery. The architect Charles Doig is called in to design the new facilities.

1921 Robert Thorne & Sons Ltd sells Aberlour to a brewery, W. H. Holt & Sons.

1945 S. Campbell & Sons Ltd buys the distillery.

1962 Aberlour terminates floor malting.

1973 Number of stills are increased from two to four.

1974 Pernod Ricard buys Campbell Distilleries.

2000 Aberlour a´bunadh is launched.

2001 Pernod Ricard buys Chivas Brothers and merges Chivas Brothers and Campbell Distilleries under the brand Chivas Brothers.

2002 A new, modernized visitor centre is inaugurated in August.

2008 The 18 year old is also introduced outside France.

2013 Aberlour 2001 White Oak is released.

2014 White Oak Millenium 2004 is released.

2018 Casg Annamh is released.

2019 A´bunadh Alba is released.

2021 A 14 year old is released.

2025 A new range for travel retail and a limited edition of a´bunadh are released.

Tasting notes Aberlour 12 year old:

GS – The nose offers brown sugar, honey and sherry, with a hint of grapefruit citrus. The palate is sweet, with buttery caramel, maple syrup and eating apples. Liquorice, peppery oak and mild smoke in the finish.

Allt-a-Bhainne

[alt a•vain]

Owner:
Chivas Brothers Ltd
(Pernod Ricard)

Region/district:
Speyside

Founded:
1975

Status:
Active

Capacity:
4 200 000 litres

Address: Glenrinnes, Dufftown, Banffshire AB55 4DB

Website:
-

Tel:
01542 783200

In the 1960s blended Scotch whisky experienced a tremendous growth thanks to the demand in the USA - the demand for single malts was still low at the time but would surge later.

Around 30 malt distilleries were refurbished and severely expanded in the early 70s and from 1962 to 1975 no less than 16 new distilleries were built. These were often quite large as opposed to the recent two decades' (2005-2025) total of over 50 new distilleries where the majority are much smaller. One of the sixteen, and the last to open before the great slump in the early 1980s, was Allt-a-Bhainne near Glenlivet in Speyside.The initiator was the Canadian producer Seagrams who had opened Braeval a 15 minute drive to the south two years earlier.

The distillery was then mothballed for a few years in the early millennium but has since again produced malt, not least for the blend 100 Pipers which is very popular in Asian markets and especially so in India. Twenty years ago, and at the time widely available in European markets, it sold 42 million bottles per year while in 2024 the sales figures were down to 20 million bottles.

The equipment at Allt-a-Bhainne consists of a nine ton lauter mash tun, eight stainless steel washbacks with a fermentation time of 48-50 hours and two pairs of stills. In recent years, the distillery has been working seven days a week with 25 mashes resulting in 4 million litres of alcohol. Usually the peated production constitutes 30-50% of the total output and has a phenol specification in the barley between 10 and 20ppm. The distillery was re-opened two years ago after closure due to an upgrade with increased sustainability in mind. The upgrade resulted in saving 3,000 tons of carbon emissions yearly.

In 2018 Allt-a-Bhainne was for the first time released by the owners (unless you count the occasional single casks available at the company's visitor centres). With sales figures around 50,000 bottles the lightly peated **Allt-a-Bhainne** without age statement never seemed to attract the consumers and it has now been more or less discontinued.

History:

1975 The distillery is founded by Chivas Brothers, a subsidiary of Seagrams, in order to secure malt whisky for its blended whiskies. The total cost amounts to £2.7 million.

1989 Production has doubled.

2001 Pernod Ricard takes over Chivas Brothers from Seagrams.

2002 Mothballed in October.

2005 Production restarts in May.

2018 An official, lightly peated bottling is released.

Allt-a-Bhainne NAS

Tasting notes Allt-a-Bhainne NAS:

IR – Subtle smokiness is mixed with butterscotch, honey, apples and a touch of pepper. Sweet peat on the palate, oranges, ginger, melon, more pepper and vanilla.

Ardbeg

[ard•beg]

Owner: The Glenmorangie Co (Moët Hennessy)

Region/district: Islay

Founded: 1815

Status: Active (vc)

Capacity: 2 400 000 litres

Address: Port Ellen, Islay, Argyll PA42 7EA

Website: ardbeg.com

Tel: 01496 302244 (vc)

Quite a few distilleries in Scotland have been personified by great individuals. Almost always it is down to a blender or a distillery manager. A large part of Ardbeg's popularity though can be attributed to Jackie Thomson, in charge of the visitor centre.

Jackie has been with the distillery since 1997 when it was re-opened by Glenmorangie. For almost 30 years she has been welcoming thousands of visitors to the distillery, personifying the spirit of Ardbeg and Islay at the same time. In 2021 she became the chair person of the illustrious Ardbeg Committee and in 2024 she was inducted into the Whisky Magazine Hall of Fame. For many Ardbeg fans it came almost as a shock when she did her last Ardbeg Day end of May 2025. Her new adventure lies ahead in taking over the upcoming visitor experience at Portintruan distillery just a few miles south of Ardbeg. But the change of guards didn´t stop there. In July 2025 it was announced that Colin Gordon, who took over from Mickey Heads as distillery manager in 2000, was also leaving Ardbeg. Before his tenure at Ardbeg he was managing Lagavulin distillery.

Following a recent expansion the equipment today consists of a five ton stainless steel semi lauter mash tun and 12 Oregon pine washbacks holding 23,000 litres. The last four were installed in 2022 and the fermentation times at the moment consists of 6 short (60 hours) and 11 long (120 hours) runs. Furthermore, there are two pairs of stills, with the spirit stills fitted with purifiers to help create the special fruity character of the spirit. The phenol specification of the malted barley is 50-55ppm and with 10 minutes of foreshots, the cut points for the heart range from 72.5% down to 62.5% which means the heaviest compounds are avoided at the end of the distillation. The 2025 plan is to mash 17 times per week which will result in around 1.5 million litres of alcohol which to 90% is filled into American oak. There are two dunnage and three racked warehouses holding a total of 18,000 casks.

The core range consists of the **10 year old**, **Uigeadail,** a marriage of bourbon and sherry casks, **Corryvreckan**, a combination of bourbon casks and new French oak, **An Oa**, a vatting of whiskies that have been married together for a minimum of three months in three huge vats, the **5 year old Wee Beastie**, matured in a combination of bourbon and oloroso casks and a **25 year old**.

This year's Ardbeg Day release **Smokiverse**, aged in boubron casks, was the first Ardbeg release made with a hig-gravity mash. Other limited releases include the 6th batch of the **19 year old Traigh Bhan**, the 14 year old **The Unicorn´s Tale**, partly matured in maderira casks and the second release in the Anthology Collection and **Eureka**, matured in a combination of PX sherry and bourbon casks, celebrating the 25th anniversary of the Ardbeg Committee. The travel retail exclusive **Smoketrails Napa Valley** was complemented in autumn 2024 by the 21 year old **Seann Chreag** which had been aged in a combination of oloroso- and bourbon casks.

History:

1794 First record of a distillery at Ardbeg. It was founded by Alexander Stewart.

1798 The MacDougalls, later to become licensees of Ardbeg, are active on the site through Duncan MacDougall.

1815 The current distillery is founded by John MacDougall, son of Duncan MacDougall.

1853 Alexander MacDougall, John's son, dies and sisters Margaret and Flora MacDougall, assisted by Colin Hay, continue the running of the distillery. Colin Hay takes over the licence when the sisters die.

1888 Colin Elliot Hay and Alexander Wilson Gray Buchanan renew their license.

1900 Colin Hay's son takes over the license.

1959 Ardbeg Distillery Ltd is founded.

1973 Hiram Walker and Distillers Company Ltd jointly purchase the distillery.

1977 Hiram Walker assumes single control of the distillery. Ardbeg closes its maltings.

1979 Kildalton, a less peated malt, is produced over a number of years.

1981 The distillery closes in March.

1987 Allied Lyons takes over Hiram Walker.

1989 Production is restored. All malt is taken from Port Ellen.

1996 The distillery closes in July.

1997 Glenmorangie plc buys the distillery. Ardbeg 17 years old and Provenance are launched

2000 Ardbeg 10 years is introduced and the Ardbeg Committee is launched.

Jackie Thomson - an Ardbeg icon

History continued:

2001 Lord of the Isles 25 years and Ardbeg 1977 are launched.

2002 Ardbeg Committee Reserve and Ardbeg 1974 are launched.

2003 Uigeadail is launched.

2004 Very Young Ardbeg (6 years) and a limited edition of Ardbeg Kildalton are launched.

2005 Serendipity is launched.

2006 Ardbeg 1965 and Still Young are launched. Almost There (9 years old) and Airigh Nam Beist are released.

2007 Ardbeg Mor, a 10 year old in 4.5 litre bottles is released.

2008 The new 10 year old, Corryvreckan, Rennaissance, Blasda and Mor II are released.

2009 Supernova is released.

2010 Rollercoaster and Supernova 2010 are released.

2011 Ardbeg Alligator is released.

2012 Ardbeg Day and Galileo are released.

2013 Ardbog is released.

2014 Auriverdes and Kildalton are released.

2015 Perpetuum and Supernova 2015 are released.

2016 Dark Cove and a Twenty Something 21 year old are relased.

2017 An Oa, Kelpie and Twenty Something 23 year old are released.

2018 Grooves and Twenty Something 22 year old are released.

2019 Drum and Traigh Bhan are released.

2020 Blaaack, Wee Beastie and Traigh Bhan batch 2 are released.

2021 An 8 year old, a 25 year old, Arrrrrrrdbeg, Scorch and Traigh Bhan batch 3 are released.

2022 Fermutation, Ardcore, Smoketrails and Traigh Bhan batch 4 are launched.

2023 Bizzarebq, Heavy Vapours and the 13 year old Harpy´s Tale are launched.

2024 Anamorphic, Spectacular, Vintage Y2K and The Abyss are launched.

2025 Smokiverse, The Unicorn´s Tale, Eureka and Seann Chreag are released.

Tasting notes Ardbeg 10 year old:

GS – Quite sweet on the nose, with soft peat, carbolic soap and Arbroath smokies. Burning peats and dried fruit, followed by sweeter notes of malt and a touch of liquorice in the mouth. Extremely long and smoky in the finish, with a fine balance of cereal sweetness and dry peat notes.

Eureka

Smokiverse

The Unicorn´s Tale

An Oa

Wee Beastie

Smoketrails

10 years old

Uigeadail

Corryvreckan

Ardmore

[ard•moor]

Owner: Suntory Global Spirits

Region/district: Highland

Founded: 1898

Status: Active

Capacity: 4 900 000 litres

Address: Kennethmont, Aberdeenshire AB54 4NH

Website: ardmorewhisky.com

Tel: 01464 831213

The majority of the famous whisky families in the 1800s bought already established distilleries to produce malts for their blends. Only a handful actually built their own distilleries from scratch.

In this respect, Peter Mackie and Craigellachie, Dewars and Aberfeldy and James Buchanan and Glentauchers all come into mind. And then there is of course Adam Teacher, the son of William Teacher, who founded Ardmore in the last years of the 19th century. Adam passed away before the building was completed but the distillery has ever since been a cornerstone of their blend Teacher's Highland Cream.

It was launched in 1884 and was exported to America as early as in 1903. Ten years later it acquired fame when William Manera Bergius, nephew of Adam Teacher, introduced the replaceable cork which didn't require a corkscrew to open. It was sold under the slogan "Bury the corkscrew!" Today Teacher's blend is a far cry from its glory days. In just ten years the brand has lost 85% of its volumes with 3.4 million bottles sold in 2023. Ardmore single malt on the other hand is gaining more and more recognition. In just a decade sales have gone up by almost 300% to 730,000 bottles.

The distillery is equipped with a cast iron semi lauter mash tun (possibly to be replaced in 2026) with a copper lid. The mash charge is 12.5 tonnes. There are 16 Douglas fir washbacks – six of them with a capacity of 90,000 litres and ten with 45,000 litres each. Two of the former were added in April 2022 and the fermentation time is 70 hours regardless if it is about producing Ardmore or the un-peated Ardlair. Finally there are four pairs of stills in a large still house. In 2025 the distillery will be working a seven-day week with 23 mashes and the goal is to reach 4.9 million litres of alcohol. Around 50% of the production will be peated (12-14ppm in the barley) and the rest, to be used for blends, unpeated. Sometimes there is one week of heavily peated (45ppm) production as well.

The only core expression is **Legacy**, a mix of 80% peated and 20% unpeated malt. whereas the 12 year old Port Finish has been discontinued. **Traditional Peated** is exclusive to travel retail.

Legacy

History:

1898 Adam Teacher, son of William Teacher, starts the construction of Ardmore Distillery which eventually becomes William Teacher & Sons´ first distillery.

1955 Stills are increased from two to four.

1974 Another four stills are added, increasing the total to eight.

1976 Allied Breweries takes over William Teacher & Sons and thereby also Ardmore. The own maltings (Saladin box) is terminated.

1999 A 12 year old is released to commemorate the distillery's 100th anniversary. A 21 year old is launched in a limited edition.

2002 Ardmore is one of the last distilleries to abandon direct heating (by coal) of the stills in favour of indirect heating through steam.

2005 Jim Beam Brands becomes new owner when it takes over some 20 spirits and wine brands from Allied Domecq for five billion dollars.

2007 Ardmore Traditional Cask is launched.

2008 A 25 and a 30 year old are launched.

2014 Beam and Suntory merge. Legacy is released.

2015 Traditional is re-launched as Tradition and a Triple Wood and a 12 year old port finish are released.

2017 A 20 year old, double matured is released.

2018 A 30 year old is released.

Tasting notes Ardmore Legacy:

GS – Vanilla, caramel and sweet peat smoke on the nose, while on the palate vanilla and honey contrast with quite dry peat notes, plus ginger and dark berries. The finish is medium to long, spicy, with persistently drying smoke.

Exceptional Designs

The visitor centre at
Chuan Distillery in China

Auchentoshan

[ock•en•tosh•an]

Owner:
Suntory Global Spirits

Region/district:
Lowlands

Founded:
1823

Status:
Active (vc)

Capacity:
2 500 000 litres

Address: Dalmuir, Clydebank, Glasgow G81 4SJ

Website:
auchentoshan.com

Tel:
01389 878561

It probably hasn't escaped anyone that Scotch is made from barley, yeast and water. There has been a lot of focus recently at Auchentoshan on the latter ingredient, water.

In order to save water that is used for cooling the spirit vapours, a closed loop cooling system has been installed which has drastically reduced the required volume of water from 250 litres per litre of alcohol down to 25 litres. At the same time the new system guarantees an even temperature, even in the summer. In the new system there is also an independent trim chiller for the worts which gives a consistent output on the mashing side regardless of season.

The equipment consists of a semi-lauter mash tun with a 7.05 ton charge. There are four Oregon pine washbacks and five made of stainless steel – all of them with a 38,000 litre capacity and with a fermentation time of 70 hours (previously 52 hours). There are three stills; a wash still (17,500 litres), an intermediate still (8,200 litres) and a spirit still (11,500 litres). Due to triple distillation the spirit cut is narrow, between 82.5% and 80%. In 2025 the distillery has reduced the production to 13 mashes per week. That translates into around 1.2 million litres of alcohol in the year. Auchentoshan is one of two distilleries in Scotland practicing triple distillation for the entire production. The newly re-opened Rosebank is the other.

The core range consists of **American Oak**, without age statement, **12 years, Three Woods, 18 years** and **24 years**. The 21 year old was discontinued in 2023. There are also plans to replace the current 12 year old with a Double Oak 12 year old. The duty free range is made up of **Blood Oak**, matured in a combination of bourbon and red wine casks, **American Oak Reserve** matured in first fill bourbon and **Dark Oak** which is a vatting of whiskies matured in ex-bourbon, PX and oloroso casks.

12 years old

History:

1817 First mention of the distillery Duntocher, which may be identical to Auchentoshan.

1823 The distillery is founded by John Bulloch.

1823 The distillery is sold to Alexander Filshie.

1878 C.H. Curtis & Co. takes over.

1903 The distillery is purchased by John Maclachlan.

1941 The distillery is severely damaged by a German bomb raid.

1960 Maclachlans Ltd is purchased by the brewery J. & R. Tennent Brewers.

1969 Auchentoshan is bought by Eadie Cairns Ltd who starts major modernizations.

1984 Stanley P. Morrison, eventually becoming Morrison Bowmore, becomes new owner.

1994 Suntory buys Morrison Bowmore.

2002 Auchentoshan Three Wood is launched.

2004 More than a £1 million is spent on a new, refurbished visitor centre. The oldest Auchentoshan ever, 42 years, is released.

2006 Auchentoshan 18 year old is released.

2007 A 50 year old, the oldest ever Auchentoshan to be bottled, was released.

2008 New packaging as well as new expressions - Classic, 18 year old and 1988.

2010 Two vintages, 1977 and 1998, are released.

2011 Two vintages, 1975 and 1999, and Valinch are released.

2012 Six new expressions are launched for the Duty Free market.

2013 Virgin Oak is released.

2014 American Oak replaces Classic.

2015 Blood Oak and Noble Oak are released for duty free.

2017 Bartender´s Malt is launched.

2018 Bartender´s Malt 2 and 1988 PX Cask are released.

2019 American Oak Reserve and Dark Oak are released for the travel retail market.

2024 A 24 year old is released.

Tasting notes Auchentoshan 12 year old:

IR – Green and herbal on the nose with notes of pine needles, citrus and fresh oak. Quite dry on the palate with spicy notes coming through (nutmeg, clove and bay leaf) as well as vanilla and roasted nuts and sunflower seeds.

Auchroisk

[ar•thrusk]

Owner: Diageo

Region/district: Speyside

Founded: 1974

Status: Active

Capacity: 5 900 000 litres

Address: Mulben, Banffshire AB55 6XS

Website: malts.com

Tel: 01542 885000

In the early 1970s, International Distillers & Vintners, were looking for higher production capacity in order to fulfil the needs for single malt to support their blend J&B.

The company already owned three distilleries (Knockando, Glen Spey and Strathmill) but they were all rather small. Auchroisk on the other hand would be able to produce more than the three combined. At a cost corresponding to £55m in today's value, not only a distillery was built but also warehouses and blending facilities.

The Scottish whisky industry underwent a serious recession just a few years after the opening of Auchroisk as demand fell. In 1975 Allt-a-Bhainne was the last Scotch malt distillery to open for a period of 15 years until another was built. Between 1981 and 1986 no less than 23 distilleries were closed. The modern and efficient Auchroisk survived these hard times and, apart from producing whisky for blends, it even became a single malt brand on its own for a few years.

The equipment consists of a 12.75 ton stainless steel semi-lauter mash tun, eight stainless steel washbacks with a fermentation time of 42-46 hours and four pairs of stills. The washbacks are large, holding 50,000 litres each, and one washback can serve all four wash stills with a capacity of 12,700 litres each. The very short fermentation time and the cloudy wort make for a nutty/malty character of the newmake although Auchroisk has produced a variety of different styles over the years governed by Diageo's need for their blends. Normally, Auchroisk is doing 25 mashes per week, producing 6.1 million litres of alcohol per year.

Auchroisk single malt is an important part of the J&B blend. While still a prominent brand it has definitely seen better days. Twenty-five years ago it came in second just after Johnnie Walker Red with 72 million bottles. Today it sells less than half that, 29 million bottles, placing it as number 9 on the top list.

The only official bottling is the **10 year old Flora & Fauna**. The most recent limited bottling was a **47 year old** in the Prima & Ultima range in September 2021.

10 year old Flora & Fauna

History:

- 1972 Building of the distillery commences by Justerini & Brooks (which, together with W. A. Gilbey, make up the group IDV) in order to produce blending whisky. In February the same year IDV is purchased by the brewery Watney Mann which, in July, merges into Grand Metropolitan.
- 1974 The distillery is completed and production begins.
- 1978 The first bottling appears.
- 1986 From this year the malt is sold under the name Singleton.
- 1997 Grand Metropolitan and Guinness merge into the conglomerate Diageo. Simultaneously, the subsidiaries United Distillers (to Guinness) and International Distillers & Vintners (to Grand Metropolitan) form the new company United Distillers & Vintners (UDV).
- 2001 The name Singleton is abandoned and the whisky is now marketed under the name of Auchroisk in the Flora & Fauna series.
- 2003 A 28 year old from 1974, the distillery's first year, is launched in the Rare Malt series.
- 2010 A Manager´s Choice single cask and a limited 20 year old are released.
- 2012 A 30 year old from 1982 is released.
- 2016 A 25 year old from 1990 is released.
- 2021 A 47 year old Prima & Ultima from 1974 is launched.

Tasting notes Auchroisk 10 year old:

GS – Malt and spice on the light nose, with developing nuts and floral notes. Quite voluptuous on the palate, with fresh fruit and milk chocolate. Raisins in the finish.

Aultmore

[ault•moor]

Owner:
John Dewar & Sons (Bacardi)

Region/district:
Speyside

Founded:
1896

Status:
Active

Capacity:
6 000 000 litres

Address: Keith, Banffshire AB55 6QY

Website:
aultmore.com

Tel:
01542 881800

Production at Aultmore was disrupted last year as the distillery was in the final stages of a major expansion. Due to this Aultmore became the largest Scottish distilery of the five owned by Bacardi.

It was in 1998 that the world famous rum producer became a prominent player also in the Scotch whisky industry. That year they bought Dewar´s from Diageo - a deal which included four distilleries. Five years previously Macduff became the first distillery operated by the world´s largest family-owned spirits company, founded already in 1862 in Cuba. Today Bacardi is resposible for more than 7% of the global sale of Scotch.

This has mainly to do with owning two of the Top 10 blends - William Lawson´s and Dewar´s. Even though their five malts were relaunched a decade ago with completely new expressions and new packaging, it is only Aberfeldy that can be easily found on the shelves. Aultmore sold around 180,000 bottles in 2023.

Aultmore is easily spotted as "that white distillery" on the right hand side of the road when travelling the A96 from Keith towards Fochabers. While it doesn't normally cater to visitors the distillery has in the last couple of years been part of the "open distillery" theme during the Speyside Festival in May.

Since last year Aultmore is equipped with a 10.25 ton Steinecker full lauter mash tun. There are now 15 wooden washbacks with a fermentation time that has increased from 56 hours to 79 hours. Finally, there are three pairs of stills. Three wash stills, equipped with modern TVR (thermal vapour recompression) technology to save energy are situated in a new still house while the three spirit stills can be found in an older building. With slightly descending lyne arms, not allowing for very much reflux, and a generous middle cut between 73% and 61%, the new make carries a body and character which can make a lot of difference in a blend.

The core range includes **12, 18** and a **21 year old** as well as a **25 year old** exclusive to Asia. Included are also limited releases ranging from 12 to 25 years old for travel retail and select markets in the **Exceptional Cask Series**.

12 years old

History:

1896 Alexander Edward, owner of Benrinnes and co-founder of Craigellachie Distillery, builds Aultmore.

1897 Production starts.

1898 Production is doubled; the company Oban & Aultmore Glenlivet Distilleries Ltd manages Aultmore.

1923 Alexander Edward sells Aultmore for £20,000 to John Dewar & Sons.

1925 Dewar's becomes part of Distillers Company Limited (DCL).

1930 The administration is transferred to Scottish Malt Distillers (SMD).

1971 The stills are increased from two to four.

1991 United Distillers launches a 12-year old Aultmore in the Flora & Fauna series.

1996 A 21 year old cask strength is marketed as a Rare Malt.

1998 Diageo sells Dewar's and Bombay Gin to Bacardi for £1,150 million.

2004 A new official 12 year old bottling is launched

2014 Three new expressions are released – 12, 25 and 21 year old for duty free.

2015 An 18 year old is released.

2019 Three 22 year old single casks with different second maturations are released for duty free.

2021 A 21 year old is added to the core range.

2024 The capacity is expanded to 6 million litres.

Tasting notes Aultmore 12 years old:

GS – A nose of peaches and lemonade, freshly-mown grass, linseed and milky coffee. Very fruity on the palate, mildly herbal, with toffee and light spices. The finish is medium in length, with lingering spices, fudge, and finally more milky coffee.

Balblair

[bal•blair]

Owner:
Inver House Distillers
(International Beverage Holdings)

Region/district:
Northern Highlands

Founded:
1790

Status:
Active (vc)

Capacity:
1 800 000 litres

Address: Edderton, Tain, Ross-shire IV19 1LB

Website:
balblair.com

Tel:
01862 821273

Of the four single malts actively promoted by the owners, Inver House, Balblair is the least selling. In 2023 it was 130,000 bottles. It is possible that the figure might have been higher if it wasn't for a decision made in 2007.

That year the owners decided to sell the malt based on vintages rather than with an age statement. While vintage is a prerequisite in the wine business as the weather conditions in a certain year can severely impact the flavour, this is not so in the whisky industry. Vintages are not often seen and the whisky consumer tends to rely on the label's age statement. Come 2019 and Balblair abandoned the practice but so far sales haven't really picked up. The only other distillery that practised the vintage concept, Glenrothes, changed to age statements the year before and, to be honest, sales figures for that brand haven't really increased either.

It is a shame though that Balblair is not widely recognised as there is a lot speaking for the brand. Apart from producing a good spirit it belongs to an exclusive club of 9 working malt distilleries in Scotland that were all founded in the 1700s. Balblair is the 4th oldest even though it hasn't been in the same location the entire time. There is also a lovely visitor centre well worth the travel.

The distillery is equipped with a stainless steel, 4.5 tonnes semi lauter mash tun. There are six Oregon pine washbacks with a capacity of 19,000 litres and a fermentation time of 68 hours. Furthermore there is one wash still (19,000 litres) and one spirit still (11,700 litres) with a 10 minute foreshot and a spirit run between 74 and 64%.. In 2023 the stills were equipped with a TVR system (thermal vapour recovery) to save energy and water consumption. For the past few years they have been alternating between a five- and a seven-day week but for 2025 the plan is to run more or less at capacity with 18 mashes per week.

The core range consists of **12, 15, 18** and **25 year old**. In 2023 a **21 year old** with a 6 year long second maturation in first fill oloroso sherry butts was added. There is also a **17 year old** oloroso finish available in travel retail.

12 years old

History:

1790 The distillery is founded by James McKeddy.

1790 John Ross takes over

1836 John Ross dies and his son Andrew Ross takes over with the help of his sons.

1872 The distillery is moved to the present location.

1873 Andrew Ross dies and his son James takes over.

1894 Alexander Cowan takes over and rebuilds the distillery

1911 Cowan is forced to cease payments and the distillery closes.

1941 The distillery is put up for sale.

1948 Robert Cumming buys Balblair for £48,000.

1949 Production restarts.

1970 Cumming sells Balblair to Hiram Walker.

1988 Allied Distillers becomes the new owner through the merger between Hiram Walker and Allied Vintners.

1996 The distillery is sold to Inver House Distillers.

2000 Balblair Elements and the first version of Balblair 33 years are launched.

2001 Thai company Pacific Spirits (part of the Great Oriole Group) takes over Inver House.

2004 Balblair 38 years is launched.

2005 12 year old Peaty Cask, 1979 (26 years) and 1970 (35 years) are launched.

2006 International Beverage Holdings acquires Pacific Spirits UK.

2007 Three new vintages replace the former range.

2008 Vintage 1975 and 1965 are released.

2009 Vintage 1991 and 1990 are released.

2011 Vintage 1995 and 1993 are released.

2012 Vintage 1975, 2001 and 2002 are released. A visitor centre is opened.

2013 Vintage 1983, 1990 and 2003 are released.

2014 Vintage 1999 and 2004 are released for duty free.

2016 Vintage 2005 is released.

2019 A new range with age statements is launched.

2024 A 21 year old is released.

Tasting notes Balblair 12 year old:

IR – Sugary and malty on the nose with herbal and earthy notes coming through. Rich, creamy and sweet on the palate, grilled corn cobs, caramel, honey and some bitter, oaky notes.

Balmenach

[bal•<u>men</u>•ack]

Owner:
Inver House Distillers
(International Beverage Holdings)

Region/district:
Speyside

Founded:
1824

Status:
Active

Capacity:
2 900 000 litres

Address: Cromdale, Moray PH26 3PF

Website:
inverhouse.com

Tel:
01479 872569

Most people who come to visit Balmenach have no idea that whisky is produced on the site. Instead they are there for the premium gin Caorunn. The fact that the distillery was founded as a whisky distillery two centuries ago usually escapes them completely.

The tour at the distillery is thus promoted as a gin experience and the whisky side is not included in it. Balmenach was one of the first established distilleries also adding super-premium gin production to its mission. It started already in 2009 (with a visitor centre opening in 2016) and was followed later by the likes of Bruichladdich and Benromach. Already in 2018 Caorunn became Scotland's best selling super-premium gin overtaking Hendrick's and it is now one of the top sellers in the category in UK.

The Balmenach single malt is, unlike its four stable mates in Inver House, not promoted by the owners. The meaty and heavy style lends itself perfectly when it comes to adding character to a blend and in the case of Inver House that blend is Hankey Bannister which in 2023 sold 4.4 million bottles. Other blends in the company's range include Catto's and McArthur's.

Balmenach is equipped with a 7.6 ton stainless steel semi-lauter mash tun with a copper dome and a seven hour mash cycle and there are six washbacks made of Douglas fir. The fermentation time during a seven-day week is 54 hours. Finally, there are three wash stills and three spirit stills, all equipped with boil balls, descending lyne arms and connected to worm tubs. The distillation is fairly quick with little reflux and the spirit cut is unusually wide (72-58%), The production plan is for 20 mashes per week in 2025 which corresponds to 2.5 million litres of alcohol.

There are no official bottlings of Balmenach but there used to be a 12 year old from the previous owners (United Distillers) in the 1990s. The independent bottler Aberko though, has been working with the distillery for a long time and has released Balmenach under the name Deerstalker.

History:

1824 The distillery is licensed to James MacGregor who operated a small farm distillery by the name of Balminoch.

1897 Balmenach Glenlivet Distillery Company is founded.

1922 The MacGregor family sells to a consortium consisting of MacDonald Green, Peter Dawson and James Watson.

1925 The consortium becomes part of Distillers Company Limited (DCL).

1930 Production is transferred to Scottish Malt Distillers (SMD).

1962 The number of stills is increased to six.

1964 Floor maltings replaced with Saladin box.

1992 The first official bottling is a 12 year old.

1993 The distillery is mothballed in May.

1997 Inver House Distillers buys Balmenach from United Distillers.

1998 Production recommences.

2001 Thai company Pacific Spirits takes over Inver House at the price of £56 million. The new owner launches a 27 and a 28 year old.

2002 To commemorate the Queen's Golden Jubilee a 25-year old Balmenach is launched.

2006 International Beverage Holdings acquires Pacific Spirits UK.

2009 Gin production commences.

Deerstalker 12 years old

Tasting notes Deerstalker 12 years old:

IR – The nose is sweet and fruity, with green garden notes and sweet liquorice coming through. Sweet, fruity barley on the palate with notes of honey, custard, apricots, peaches and slightly bitter notes from the oak.

Balvenie

[bal•ven•ee]

Owner:
William Grant & Sons

Region/district:
Speyside

Founded:
1892

Status:
Active (vc)

Capacity:
7 000 000 litres

Address: Dufftown, Keith, Banffshire AB55 4DH

Website:
thebalvenie.com

Tel:
01340 820373

Balvenie is, together with Dalmore, the one brand on the Top 10 list of single malts that has increased its sales the most in the past ten years. In 2023 it was number 6 with a total sale of 5.3 million bottles!

The owners, William Grant & Sons, now have three of the best selling brands, including the number one, Glenfiddich, as well as the blended malt Monkey Shoulder. Balvenie is one of the single malts contributing to the latter´s character. For many years Balvenie has formed its flavour profile on the maturation in and blending of different types of casks. Sometimes this is called finishing, sometimes it is known as double maturation. This technique was explored more than three decades ago by the distillery´s master blender David Stewart who, in 2022, passed the torch to a new blender – Kelsy Mckechnie.

Balvenie is equipped with an 11.8 ton full lauter mash tun and nine wooden and five stainless steel washbacks with a fermentation time of 64-68 hours. In the original still house there are six spirit stills. An extension to the building harbours five wash stills more or less densely packed together. In recent years, the plan has been 30 mashes per week and 7 million litres of alcohol. The main part is unpeated but each year one week of production comes from peated barley (20-40 ppm).

An unusual feature for Balvenie is that they malt part of their barley in-house and there is also a cooperage on site which combined makes a tour around the distillery a highlight for any whisky aficionado.

The core range consists of **Doublewood 12, Caribbean Cask 14, French Oak 16** and **Portwood 21**. There is also the **Rare Marriage** series (**25, 30** and **40 years old**). In 2024 **A Collection of Curious Casks** was introduced and this was expanded in 2025 with **12 year old Montilla Cask, 13 year old Refill Port Puncheon** and a **20 year old Peated Sherry Cask Finish**. There is also a recent second edition of the **50 year old** single cask, first released in 2024. Exclusive to duty free are **The Creation of a Classic**, a **15 year old Madeira Cask**, an **18 year old PX Cask** and **The Week of Peat 19 years**.

Doublewood 12 years old

History:

1892 William Grant rebuilds Balvenie New House to Balvenie Distillery.

1893 The first distillation takes place in May.

1957 The two stills are increased by another two.

1965 Two new stills are installed.

1971 Another two stills are installed.

1973 The first official bottling appears.

1982 Founder's Reserve is launched.

1996 Port wood finish is launched.

2001 The Balvenie Islay Cask is released.

2002 A 50 year old is released.

2006 New Wood 17 years old, Roasted Malt 14 years old and Portwood 1993 are released.

2007 Vintage Cask 1974 and Sherry Oak 17 years old are released.

2008 Signature, Vintage 1976, Balvenie Rose and Rum Cask 17 year old are released.

2009 Vintage 1978, 17 year old Madeira finish, 14 year old rum finish and Golden Cask 14 years old are released.

2010 A 40 year old, Peated Cask and Carribean Cask are released.

2012 A 50 year old and Doublewood 17 years old are released.

2013 Triple Cask 12, 16 and 25 years are launched.

2014 Single Barrel 15 and 25 years, Tun 1509 and two new 50 year olds are launched.

2015 The Balvenie DCS Compendium is launched.

2017 The Balvenie Peat Week 2002 and Peated Triple Cask are released.

2019 The Balvenie Stories is launched.

2020 A 21 year old is released together with a fourth instalment in the Balvenie Stories series.

2021 The Second Red Rose, The Tale of the Dog and a 25 year old are released.

2022 French Oak 16 years and A Rare Discovery From Distant Shores are released. Kelsey Mckechnie replaces David Stewart as Malt Master.

2023 A Revelation of Cask and Character 19 years are released.

2024 A Collection of Curious Casks is introduced.

2025 The second edition of A Collection of Curious Casks is launched.

Tasting notes Balvenie Doublewood 12 years:

GS – Nuts and spicy malt on the nose, full-bodied, with soft fruit, vanilla, sherry and a hint of peat. Dry and spicy in a luxurious, lengthy finish.

Ben Nevis

[ben nev•iss]

Owner:
Ben Nevis Distillery Ltd
(Nikka, Asahi Breweries)

Region/district:
Western Highlands

Founded:
1825

Status:
Active (vc)

Capacity:
2 000 000 litres

Address: Lochy Bridge, Fort William PH33 6TJ

Website:
bennevisdistillery.com

Tel:
01397 700200

With the highest mountain in the UK majestically rising in the background, Ben Nevis distillery is celebrating its 200th anniversary in 2025. It has never been one the most talked-about distilleries but it has always had a devoted fanbase.

When the distillery was re-opened in 1990, with the well-known Japanese producer Nikka as the new owner, a visitor centre was inaugurated which is quite busy. Part of the reason is that it is situated in the popular holiday resort of Fort William. Nikka's main focus, however, has been on producing malt for their Japanese blends so promoting the brand as a single malt always came second and in 2023 only 19,000 bottles were sold.

But the range is also made up of the blended malt Glencoe, created in the 1960s and recently re-launched as a 10 year old. There is also the blended Scotch Dew of Ben Nevis which was introduced already in the 1800s. Today it is called Nevis Dew and exists in two versions – Red and Blue Label. These blended brands sold more than 300,000 bottles together last year. In 2024 an in-house bottling plant for single malts was set up which, hopefully, could entail larger volumes from Ben Nevis in the future.

The distillery is equipped with a nine ton full lauter mash tun made of stainless steel, six stainless steel and two made of Oregon pine washbacks with a 48 hour fermentation as well as two pairs of stills. Normally, mashing takes place 13 times per week and will produce a total of 2 million litres of alcohol. Around 50,000 litres of this will be heavily peated (40ppm in the barley).

The **10 year old** was relaunched with a new design in 2021. There is also the peated **MacDonald's Traditional Ben Nevis** as well as **Coire Leis** without age statement. Very old versions of Ben Nevis have turned up and three vintages from **1966, 1967** and **1968** were released in Taiwan a few years ago.

10 years old

History:

1825 The distillery is founded by 'Long' John McDonald.

1856 Long John dies and his son Donald P. McDonald takes over.

1878 Demand is so great that another distillery, Nevis Distillery, is built nearby.

1908 Both distilleries merge into one.

1941 D. P. McDonald & Sons sells the distillery to Ben Nevis Distillery Ltd headed by the Canadian millionaire Joseph W. Hobbs.

1955 Hobbs installs a Coffey still which makes it possible to produce both grain and malt whisky.

1964 Joseph Hobbs dies.

1978 Production is stopped.

1981 Joseph Hobbs Jr sells the distillery back to Long John Distillers and Whitbread.

1984 After restoration and reconstruction totalling £2 million, Ben Nevis opens up again.

1986 The distillery closes again.

1989 Whitbread sells the distillery to Nikka Whisky Distilling Company Ltd.

1990 The distillery opens up again.

1991 A visitor centre is inaugurated.

1996 Ben Nevis 10 years old is launched.

2006 A 13 year old port finish is released.

2010 A 25 year old is released.

2011 McDonald´s Traditional Ben Nevis is released.

2014 Forgotten Bottlings are introduced.

2015 A 40 year old "Blended at Birth" single blend is released.

2018 Ben Nevis 10 years old Batch No. 1 is released.

2021 The design of the 10 year bottle is revamped and Coire Leis is released.

Tasting notes Ben Nevis 10 years old:

GS – The nose is initially quite green, with developing nutty, orange notes. Coffee, brittle toffee and peat are present on the slightly oily palate, along with chewy oak, which persists to the finish, together with more coffee and a hint of dark chocolate.

Benriach

[ben•ree•ack]

Owner:
BenRiach Distillery Company (Brown Forman)

Region/district:
Speyside

Founded:
1897

Status:
Active (vc)

Capacity:
2 800 000 litres

Address: Longmorn, Elgin, Morayshire IV30 8SJ

Website:
benriachdistillery.com

Tel:
01343 862888

In 2016 the American producer Brown Forman took over the ownership of Benriach, Glendronach and Glenglassaugh at a price of £285m. The American producer was, and is, best known as the custodian of Jack Daniel's and Woodford Reserve.

Their interest in expanding into Scotch did not come as a surprise. In the 1990s they had a 10% share in Glenmorangie and when that distillery came up for sale in 2004 the Americans placed a bid for the entire company but were, surprisingly, beaten by Moet Hennessy. The opportunity that came twelve years later in 2016 was, however, not missed although the brands at that time were far less well-known to the public compared to Glenmorangie.

Brown Forman have put much effort into its distilleries and since the take-over Benriach alone has increased its sales (in terms of volumes) by 65% compared to a 25% increase for the general malt whisky category. They have also slowly opened up the distillery to visitors and there is more to come in the near future.

Benriach is equipped with a 5.8 ton traditional cast iron mash tun with a stainless steel shell, eight washbacks made of stainless steel with short (58 hours) and long (120 hours) fermentations. There are two 20,900 litre wash stills and two 12,700 litre spirit stills with slightly descending lyne arms. The 2025 plan is to produce 700,000 litres of pure alcohol. Usually there has been a part of peated production (at 25-30ppm) but not for this year. The floor maltings were re-commissioned in 2013 but haven't been used since 2022..

The core range consists of **The Original Ten, The Smoky Ten, The Twelve, The Smoky Twelve, The Sixteen, The Twenty One, The Twenty Five, The Thirty, The Forty** and, released in 2024 as the oldest ever from BenRiach, **The Fifty**. Exclusive to travel retail is **The Forty Octave Cask Matured**.

The Twelve

History:

1897 John Duff & Co founds the distillery.

1900 The distillery is closed.

1965 The distillery is reopened by the new owner, The Glenlivet Distillers Ltd.

1972 Production of peated Benriach starts.

1978 Seagram Distillers takes over.

1985 The number of stills is increased to four.

1998 The maltings is decommissioned.

2002 The distillery is mothballed in October.

2004 Intra Trading, buys Benriach together with the former Director at Burn Stewart, Billy Walker.

2004 Standard, Curiositas and 12, 16 and 20 year olds are released.

2005 Four different vintages are released.

2006 Sixteen new releases, i.a. a 25 year old, a 30 year old and 8 different vintages.

2007 A 40 year old and three new heavily peated expressions are released.

2008 Peated Madeira finish, a 15 year old Sauternes finish and nine single casks are released.

2009 Two wood finishes (Moscatel and Gaja Barolo) and nine single casks are released.

2010 Triple distilled Horizons and heavily peated Solstice are released.

2011 A 45 year old and 12 vintages are released.

2012 Septendecim 17 years is released.

2013 Vestige 46 years is released. The maltings are working again.

2015 Dunder, Albariza, Latada and a 10 year old are released.

2016 Brown Forman buys the company. BenRiach cask strength is released.

2017 10 year old Triple Distilled and Peated Cask Strength are released.

2018 A 12 and a 21 year old, Temporis 21 years and Authenticus 30 years are released.

2020 The entire core range is relaunched with seven new expressions.

2021 Malting Season First Edition is launched.

2022 The Sixteen is released.

2024 A 50 year old is launched.

Tasting notes BenRiach The Twelve:

IR – Fresh on the nose with notes of furniture polish, eucalyptus, tropical fruits, honey and brown sugar. A dry start on the palate is followed by raisins soaked in port, baked apples with vanilla, chocolate, cinnamon and almonds.

Benrinnes

[ben rin•ess]

Owner:
Diageo

Region/district:
Speyside

Founded:
1826

Status:
Active

Capacity:
3 500 000 litres

Address: Aberlour, Banffshire AB38 9NN

Website:
malts.com

Tel:
01340 872600

When you leave the town of Aberlour heading south on the A95 you will soon find two exit roads on your left. The first one takes you to Glenallachie and the second leads to Benrinnes.

While the first distillery was founded in 1967, the second will be celebrating its 200th anniversary next year. As you drive along the road with the majestic 840 metre Benrinnes rising in the background you almost get the feeling that very little has changed since those times. There are few houses along the road and sooner than you would expect you end up at Benrinnes distillery. It's existence has definitely not been uneventful, with one flooding and a fire forcing the owners to move the distillery to different sites twice.

And yet Benrinnes has been continuously producing through the years but it was never promoted as a single malt in its own right. Whisky aficionados love it, mostly having to rely on independent bottlings, but so do the blenders who have used it as a vital part in many blends over the years. From 1966 to 2008 an unusual practise of partial triple distillation was performed at the distillery in a similar way as Mortlach and Springbank still do.

The equipment consists of an 8.5 ton semi-lauter mash tun, eight washbacks made of Oregon pine with a fermentation time of 65 hours (when working seven days). There are also two wash stills and four spirit stills connected to worm tubs. The tubs were replaced during 2023 and after the temporary closure in connection with that work, the distillery moved to full capacity which means 21 mashes per week and 3.5 million litres. The fact that the spirit vapours are cooled using worm tubs contributes to the character of Benrinnes newmake, which is light sulphury. The wide spirit cut (73%-58%) also plays its part in creating a robust and meaty spirit.

The **Flora & Fauna 15 year old** is the only core, official bottling. In 2024 a **21 year old** Special Release appeared, matured for 8 years in refill casks and then double matured for thirteen years in wine-seasoned American oak, European oak and rejuvenated casks with charred ends.

15 years old

History:

1826 Lyne of Ruthrie distillery is built at Whitehouse Farm by Peter McKenzie.

1829 A flood destroys the distillery and a new distillery is constructed by John Innes a few kilometres from the first one.

1834 John Innes files for bankruptcy and William Smith & Co takes over.

1864 William Smith & Co goes bankrupt and David Edward becomes the new owner.

1896 Benrinnes is ravaged by fire which prompts major refurbishment. Alexander Edward takes over.

1922 John Dewar & Sons takes over ownership.

1925 John Dewar & Sons becomes part of Distillers Company Limited (DCL).

1956 The distillery is completely rebuilt.

1964 Floor maltings is replaced by a Saladin box.

1966 The number of stills doubles to six.

1984 The Saladin box is taken out of service and the malt is purchased centrally.

1991 The first official bottling from Benrinnes is a 15 year old in the Flora & Fauna series.

1996 United Distillers releases a 21 year old cask strength in their Rare Malts series.

2009 A 23 year old is launched as a part of this year´s Special Releases.

2010 A Manager´s Choice 1996 is released.

2014 A limited 21 year old is released.

2024 A 21 year old appears in Special Releases.

Tasting notes Benrinnes 15 years old:

GS – A brief flash of caramel shortcake on the initial nose, soon becoming more peppery and leathery, with some sherry. Ultimately savoury and burnt rubber notes. Big-bodied, viscous, with gravy, dark chocolate and more pepper. A medium-length finish features mild smoke and lively spices.

Benromach

[ben•ro•mack]

Owner: Gordon & MacPhail

Region/district: Speyside

Founded: 1898

Status: Active (vc)

Capacity: 700 000 litres

Address: Inverernе Road, Forres, Morayshire IV36 3EB

Website: benromach.com

Tel: 01309 675968

The well-established independent bottler Gordon & MacPhail surprisingly announced in July 2023 that they would cease purchasing stock from other producers for their independent bottlings.

Instead the Urquhart family, who owns Gordon & MacPhail, intend to focus on their own two distilleries – Benromach and the newly founded The Cairn. While it may has come as a shock to to Gordon & MacPhail fans, it soon became evident that the company still holds a huge stock in their warehouses for consumers to enjoy for decades to come.

The role of an independent bottler, even one with the reputation of Gordon & MacPhail, has been discussed vividly in recent years. With the rising demand for Scotch single malt it has been suggested that the producers would like to retain their stock for own bottlings. However, sometimes there are rapid changes in the whisky business and the past 18 months of diminishing sales of single malt Scotch may suggest a different future, if perhaps only short term, for independent bottlers.

Benromach is equipped with a 1.5 ton semi-lauter mash tun with a copper dome and 13 washbacks – nine made of European larch and four from Scottish larch and with fermentation times of between 67 and 115 hours. There is also one pair of stills with straight lyne arms and with exterior condensers. The 2025 plan entails 18 mashes per five-day week for 44 weeks and 500,000 litres of pure alcohol. Two of the weeks are served for heavily peated spirit and another two for organic production. There are six dunnage and one racked warehouse on site with space for 35,000 casks but over the next two years expansion for holding another 15,000 casks will take place.

The core range consists of **10, 15** and **21 year old** as well as **Cask Strength Vintage**. Since 2021 there are annual releases of a **40 year old** and in September 2024 a very limited **50 year old** was launched. There are also special editions in the Contrasts range; **Organic 2015** and **Peat Smoke 2014**. In 2024 these were complemented by **Virgin Oak 2013** and **Unpeated 2014**.

10 years old

History:

- 1898 Benromach Distillery Company starts the distillery.
- 1911 Harvey McNair & Co buys the distillery.
- 1919 John Joseph Calder buys Benromach and sells it to Benromach Distillery Ltd.
- 1931 The distillery is mothballed.
- 1937 The distillery reopens.
- 1938 Joseph Hobbs buys Benromach and sells it on to National Distillers of America (NDA).
- 1953 NDA sells Benromach to Distillers Company Ltd.
- 1968 Floor maltings is abolished.
- 1983 Benromach is mothballed.
- 1993 Gordon & McPhail buys Benromach.
- 1998 The distillery is once again in operation.
- 2004 The first bottle distilled by the new owner is 'Benromach Traditional'.
- 2005 A Port Wood finish, a Vintage 1968 and Classic 55 years ar released.
- 2006 Benromach Organic is released.
- 2007 Peat Smoke, the first heavily peated whisky from the distillery, is released.
- 2008 Benromach Origins Golden Promise is released.
- 2009 Benromach 10 years old is released.
- 2015 A 15 year old and two wood finishes (Hermitage and Sassicaia) are released.
- 2016 A 35 year old and 1974 single cask are released.
- 2017 A 1976 single cask and a 2009 Triple Distilled are released.
- 2018 A 20th Anniversary bottling and a Sassicaia 2010 are released.
- 2019 Peat Smoke Sherry Cask Matured and a 50 year old are released.
- 2020 A new core range is released.
- 2021 A 40 year old is released together with Peat Smoke Sherry Cask Matured 2012.
- 2022 Cara Gold and Triple Distilled are released.
- 2023 Air Dried Oak and Kiln Dried Oak are released.
- 2024 Virgin Oak 2013, Unpeated 2014 and a 50 year old are released.

Tasting notes Benromach 10 year old:

GS – A nose that is initially quite smoky, with wet grass, butter, ginger and brittle toffee. Mouth-coating, spicy, malty and nutty on the palate, with developing citrus fruits, raisins and soft wood smoke. The finish is warming, with lingering barbecue notes.

Bladnoch

[blad•nock]

Owner: David Prior

Region/district: Lowlands

Founded: 1817

Status: Active (vc)

Capacity: 2 000 000 litres

Address: Bladnoch, Wigtown, Wigtonshire DG8 9AB

Website: bladnoch.com

Tel: 01988 402605

Despite a great many distilleries having been established in the Scottish lowlands over the past decade, Bladnoch still holds the position of the southernmost whisky distillery in Scotland.

Founded as early as in 1817, the distillery is situated in Wigtown in southwest Scotland. The town was officially designated as Scotland's national book town in 1998 and is home to a wide range of litterature-related businesses. The distillery itself is the oldest Lowland distillery still producing. Historically, its future was insecure on a couple of occasions but the owner since 2015 seems determined to keep it alive and running. It was once owned by the mighty Diageo, while the current proprietor, David Prior, hails from Australia. Initially relying on old stock, the first bottlings from Prior's tenure as the custodian appeared in spring 2024.

The distillery is equipped with a 5.5 ton stainless steel semi-lauter mash tun and six Douglas fir washbacks. There used to be a combination of short and long fermentations but due to increased production it is now at 66 hours. There are also two pairs of stills with a 15 minute foreshot and cut points between 72% and 62%. The production for 2025 will be 16 mashes per week giving around 1.5 million litres of pure alcohol. Around 130,000 litres of that will be made from heavily peated barley (68-72ppm).

The core range is split into two collections; Bold Collection (no age statement) with **Vinaya**, **Samsara,** the peated **Alinta** and **Liora** and the new Galloway Collection with an **8 year old**, a **13 year old**, a **16 year old** and a **19 year old.** In 2023 the **Dragon Series** was launched with five no age statement expressions and it was followed by **The Samhla Collection** with three ultra rare vintages and the **Peated Collection**. In June 2024 the first installment in a new series called **The Wave** appeared. The idea is to showcase the five pillars of whisky making. Finally there is the **Loch Maberry** range with the first installment appearing in spring 2024 and with chapter 2 released in September 2025.

Vinaya

History:

1817 Founded by Thomas and John McClelland.

1878 John McClelland's son Charlie reconstructs and refurbishes the distillery.

1905 Production stops.

1911 Dunville & Co. buys T. & A. McClelland Ltd. Production is intermittent until 1936.

1937 Dunville & Co. is liquidated and Bladnoch is wound up. Ross & Coulter from Glasgow buys the distillery after the war. The equipment is dismantled and shipped to Sweden.

1956 A. B. Grant (Bladnoch Distillery Ltd.) takes over and restarts production with four new stills.

1964 McGown and Cameron becomes new owners.

1973 Inver House Distillers buys Bladnoch.

1983 Arthur Bell and Sons take over.

1985 Guiness Group buys Arthur Bell & Sons which, from 1989, are included in United Distillers.

1988 A visitor centre is built.

1993 United Distillers mothballs Bladnoch in June.

1994 Raymond Armstrong buys Bladnoch in October.

2000 Production commences in December.

2003 The first bottles from Armstrong are launched.

2008 First release of whisky produced after the take-over in 2000 - three 6 year olds.

2009 An 8 year old of own production and a 19 year old are released.

2014 The distillery is liquidated.

2015 The distillery is bought by David Prior.

2016 Samsara, Adela and Talia are released.

2017 Production starts again.

2018 A 10 year old is released.

2019 A visitor centre is opened.

2020 An 11 year old and the Waterfall Collection are launched.

2022 Alinta and Liora are released together with 5 single casks.

2023 The Dragon Series and the Samhla Collection are launched.

2024 Wave I: Time & Maturation is released.

2025 Loch Maberry Chapter 2 appears.

Tasting notes Vinaya:

IW – Oak laced with herbaceous and citrus notes, then grapefruit emerges accompanied by hay. Silky mouthfeel, sweetness rapidly escalates with lusciousness and a hint of dried herbs, before citrus and walnuts emerge, followed by green tea and honey.

Blair Athol

[blair ath•ull]

Owner: Diageo

Region/district: Southern Highlands

Founded: 1798

Status: Active (vc)

Capacity: 2 800 000 litres

Address: Perth Road, Pitlochry, Perthshire PH16 5LY

Website: malts.com

Tel: 01796 482003

Blair Athol is the spiritual home of Bell's blended whisky and, while Arthur Bell and his sons, Robert and Arthur, may have been the founders of the brand it was Raymond Miquel who made it the best selling whisky in England.

Miquel joined the company in 1956 and became managing director in 1968. He soon discovered that the company had a very traditional way of working or, as he himself would put it: "I thought I'd gone back to the Middle Ages." His improvements led to a sales increase in the home market from £20m in 1970 to £159m ten years later. This success attracted the interest from the Guinness Group and its manager, Ernest Saunders. A hostile take-over bid was launched and Bell's was absorbed into the giant brewing company. A disappointed Miquel soon went into other business opportunities and living at Gleneagles Hotel, which he himself bought in 1984 on behalf of Arthur Bell & Sons, Miquel passed away in 2021.

While Bell's is still one of the Top 20 blends in the world (16 million bottles in 2024), sales have actually dropped by 38% in the past couple of years. It is still however number three in the UK market after Famous Grouse and Whyte & Mackay.

The distillery is equipped with an 8.2 ton semi-lauter mash tun, six washbacks made of stainless steel with a fermentation time of 46 hours and two pairs of stills. A cloudy wort, together with the short fermentation time, gives Blair Athol newmake a nutty and malty character. The part of the spirit which blends into Bell's is matured mainly in bourbon casks, while the rest is matured in sherry casks. In 2025 twelve mashes per week on a five-day operation, will result in 2 million litres of alcohol.

The official bottling is the **12 year old Flora & Fauna**. In April 2025 a limited **20 year old** (available at the distillery and through malts.com) was released. It had been finished in four types of wood; rejuvenated casks, refill casks and wine-finished American and European oak.

20 years old

History:

1798 John Stewart and Robert Robertson found Aldour Distillery, the predecessor to Blair Athol. The name is taken from the adjacent river Allt Dour.

1825 The distillery is expanded by John Robertson and takes the name Blair Athol Distillery.

1826 The Duke of Atholl leases the distillery to Alexander Connacher & Co.

1860 Elizabeth Connacher runs the distillery.

1882 Peter Mackenzie & Company Distillers Ltd of Edinburgh (future founder of Dufftown Distillery) buys Blair Athol and expands it.

1932 The distillery is mothballed.

1933 Arthur Bell & Sons takes over by acquiring Peter Mackenzie & Company.

1949 Production restarts.

1973 Stills are expanded from two to four.

1985 Guinness Group buys Arthur Bell & Sons.

1987 A visitor centre is built.

2003 A 27 year old cask strength from 1975 is launched in Diageo's Rare Malts series.

2010 A distillery exclusive with no age statement and a single cask from 1995 are released.

2016 A distillery exclusive without age statement is released.

2017 A 23 year old is released as part of the Special Releases.

2025 A limited 20 year old is launched.

Tasting notes Blair Athol 12 years old:

GS – The nose is mellow and sherried, with brittle toffee. Sweet and fragrant. Relatively rich on the palate, with malt, raisins, sultanas and sherry. The finish is lengthy, elegant and slowly drying.

Bowmore

[bow•moor]

Owner: Suntory Global Spirits

Region/district: Islay

Founded: 1779

Status: Active (vc)

Capacity: 2 150 000 litres

Address: School Street, Bowmore, Islay, Argyll PA43 7GS

Website: bowmore.com

Tel: 01496 810441

Whisky enthusiasts travelling to Islay – and they are many – will if arriving by ferry land in either Port Askaig or Port Ellen. Their accommodation though is often in Bowmore village.

With only 750 people living in Bowmore, it is still the largest village on the island and has a good range of both accommodation and restaurants. On top of that, it is never more than a five minute walk to the oldest working distillery on Islay regardless of where you stay in Bowmore.

The distillery Bowmore was built by David Simpson only a decade after the village itself had been planned by Daniel Campell 'The younger'. The distillery has always been known for making a whisky which is less smoky than those from the three Kildalton cousins. This has probably been one of the reasons for the success amongst consumers who like smoke "but not too much of it".

Bowmore is one of three distilleries on the island with its own floor maltings (Laphroaig and Kilchoman being the other two). One malting on three floors produces 42 tonnes of malt which is kilned in three batches starting with 10 hours on peat and then 34 hours on dry air. Around 25% of the malt requirement is produced in-house. The remaining part is bought from Simpson's. Both parts have a phenol specification of 25-30 ppm and are always mixed in a ratio of 2 tons in-house malt and 6 tons of malt from Simpsons.

The distillery is equipped with an eight ton stainless steel semi-lauter mash tun. The are seven washbacks made of Oregon pine with a fermentation time of 72 hours. Finally, there are two wash stills (30,940 litres) and two spirit stills (14,750 litres) with a foreshot of 35 minutes in the spirit run and a cut between 74% and 61%. In 2025, the plan is to make 11 mashes in a five-day week which should correspond to 1.4 million litres of alcohol. Recently a closed loop cooling system (similar to the one installed at its sister distillery Auchentoshan) was installed in order to save water and keep the production consistent during the summer months.

The core range includes **12, 15, 18** and **25 years**. There are also recurrent but limited release of a **30 and 40 year old**. An additional **Sherry Oak Cask** range was added in October 2024 – **12, 15, 18** and **21 years old**. Recent limited bottlings include the Timeless Collection from spring 2021 with a **27 year old** and a **31 year old**. They were followed by a **29** and a **33 year old** in 2023. In 2022 there was also the **25 year old Distiller´s Anthology**. The **Feis Ile** bottling for 2025 was a 100% floor-malted single cask, matured for **8 years** in an oloroso sherry cask and bottled at 56%

The old duty free range (10, 15 and 18 years old) was replaced in October 2024 by the Appellations series with four finishes of different ages; **14 year old Bordeaux, 16 year old Ruby Port, 19 year old Pinot Noir** and **22 year old Sauternes**. The distillery has also entered into a collaboration with car maker **Aston Martin** including limited releases.

History:

1779 Bowmore Distillery is founded by David Simpson and becomes the oldest Islay distillery.

1837 The distillery is sold to James and William Mutter of Glasgow.

1892 After additional construction, the distillery is sold to Bowmore Distillery Company Ltd, a consortium of English businessmen.

1925 J. B. Sheriff and Company takes over.

1929 Distillers Company Limited (DCL) takes over.

1950 William Grigor & Son takes over.

1963 Stanley P. Morrison buys the distillery and forms Morrison Bowmore Distillers Ltd.

1989 Japanese Suntory buys a 35% stake in Morrison Bowmore.

1993 The legendary Black Bowmore is launched.

1994 Suntory now controls all of Morrison Bowmore.

1996 A Bowmore 1957 (38 years) is bottled at 40.1% but is not released until 2000.

1999 Bowmore Darkest with three years finish on Oloroso barrels is launched.

2000 Bowmore Dusk is launched.

2001 Bowmore Dawn with two years finish on Port pipes is launched.

2002 A 37 year old Bowmore from 1964 and matured in fino casks is launched.

2003 Another two expressions complete the wood trilogy which started with 1964 Fino - 1964 Bourbon and 1964 Oloroso.

2005 Bowmore 1989 Bourbon (16 years) and 1971 (34 years) are launched.

2006 Bowmore 1990 Oloroso (16 years) and 1968 (37 years) are launched.

2007 An 18 year old is introduced. 1991 (16yo) Port and Black Bowmore are released.

History continued:

2008 White Bowmore and a 1992 Vintage with Bourdeaux finish are launched.

2009 Gold Bowmore, Maltmen´s Selection, Laimrig and Bowmore Tempest are released.

2010 A 40 year old and Vintage 1981 are released.

2011 Vintage 1982 and new batches of Tempest and Laimrig are released.

2012 100 Degrees Proof, Springtide and Vintage 1983 are released for duty free.

2013 The Devil´s Cask and Vintage 1984 are released

2014 Black Rock, Gold Reef and White Sands are released for duty free.

2015 New editions of Devil´s Cask, Tempest and the 50 year old are released as well as Mizunara Cask Finish.

2016 Bowmore Vault Edit1on is released as well as the final batch of Black Bowmore.

2017 No. 1 is released together with three new expressions for travel retail.

2018 Vintner´s Trilogy is launched.

2019 Vault Edit1on Peat Smoke and the 36 year old Dragon Edition are released.

2020 Black Bowmore DBS is launched.

2021 Timeless 27 and 31 years old are released.

2022 The second batch of No Corners To Hide Collection is launched.

2023 Timeless 29 years old is released.

2024 Sherry Oak Cask range and a new range for travel retail are released.

Tasting notes Bowmore 12 year old:

GS – An enticing nose of lemon and gentle brine leads into a smoky, citric palate, with notes of cocoa and boiled sweets appearing in the lengthy, complex finish.

Timeless 31 year old | 1971 50 year old | Feis Ile 2025

12 year old Sherry Oak Cask | 12 year old | 15 year old

Braeval

[bre•vaal]

Owner:
Chivas Brothers (Pernod Ricard)

Region/district:
Speyside

Founded:
1973

Status:
Active

Capacity:
4 200 000 litres

Address: Chapeltown of Glenlivet, Ballindalloch, Banffshire AB37 9JS

Website:
secret-speyside.com

Tel:
01542 783042

When Chivas Brothers opened Braeval distillery in 1973, the blending company was owned by Seagram's – the famous Canadian spirits producer with roots going back to 1857.

Founded by English immigrants it was Sam Bronfman who grew the company in the late 1920s to become one of the biggest players in the industry. Born in what today is Moldovia, Bronfman was just a year old when his family arrived in America in 1889. Today he is considered one of the greatest characters in the spirits industry of the 1900s. Having gained control of Seagrams, Bronfman soon launched brands that are still very much in demand – Seagram's 7 Crown and Crown Royal. The company's first entry into the Scottish market was the purchase of the Glasgow whisky house Robert Brown Ltd. in 1936. The successful saga continued with further purchases of Chivas Brothers (1949), Strathisla (1950) and Glenlivet, Glen Grant and Longmorn (1977).

The good years came to an end and the fall of the once successful company, was instigated by Sam's grandson, Edgar Bronfman Jr. who decided to diversify the company into film and recording ventures as well. The debt grew larger and larger and the company was eventually acquired by the Vivendi Group, who in their turn sold the wine part of the operation to Diageo and the spirits part to Pernod Ricard in 2001.

The equipment at Braeval consists of a 9 ton stainless steel, full lauter mash tun, 13 stainless steel washbacks with a fermentation time of 70 hours and six stills. Two of them are wash stills with aftercoolers and four are spirit stills. The usual production is 26 mashes per week and 4.2 million litres. A few years ago, Braeval became Chivas Brothers' first zero carbon impact distillery by switching to a rapeseed residue-based bio-fuel.

The first official bottling appeared in 2017. In 2019, a new range called The Secret Speyside Collection from four different distilleries was launched. The initial three from Braeval were replaced in April 2024 by a **26 year old** matured in first fill American oak. Finally there is an **18 year old** Distillery Reserve Collection available at the visitor centres.

History:

1973 The distillery is founded by Chivas Brothers (Seagram´s) and production starts in October.

1975 Three stills are increased to five.

1978 Five stills are further expanded to six.

1994 The distillery changes name to Braeval.

2001 Pernod Ricard takes over Chivas Brothers.

2002 Braeval is mothballed in October.

2008 The distillery starts producing again in July.

2017 The first official bottling, a 16 year old single cask, is released.

2019 Three new official bottlings in a new range, The Secret Speyside Collection, are released.

2024 A 26 year old in The Secret Speyside Collection is released.

26 years old

Tasting notes Braeval 16 year old:

GS – Marzipan, milk chocolate-coated Turkish Delight and orange peel on the nose. The palate is sweet and fruity, with stewed apples, sugared almonds, nutmeg and ginger. Medium to long in the finish, consistently sugary and spicy.

Whisky in Social Media

There are a lot of blogs, websites and YouTube channels discussing whisky and other spirits. Some are excellent and others are not so great. Below are the ones I follow frequently and while these are all well worth visiting or tuning into, the ones marked with * are my personal favourites.

Aqvavitae (Youtube) *
ascotonscotch.com
bestshotwhiskyreviews.com *
blog.thewhiskyexchange.com *
canadianwhisky.org *
dramface.com *
dramfinecom.wordpress.com
First Phil Whisky (Youtube)
greatdrams.com
GWhisky (Youtube)
insidethecask.com *
islaywhisky.se
jeffwhisky.com
Liquorhound (Youtube)
longpouramour.com
maltandoak.com
maltfascination.com
malt-review.com *
masterofmalt.com/blog *
meleklerinpayi.com
nononsensewhisky.com*
notanotherwhiskypodcast.com*
ozwhiskyreview.com.au *
Ralfydotcom (Youtube)
scotchmaltwhisky.co.uk *
scotchnoob.com
Scotch Test Dummies (Youtube)
scotchwhisky.com *
scotch-whisky.org.uk
thedramble.com *
The Single Malt Review (YouTube)
thewhiskeyjug.com *
thewhiskeywash.com *
thewhiskyphiles.com *
The Whiskey Tribe (Youtube)
thewhiskyardvark.com
thewhiskyviking.com
thewhiskywire.com *
timeforwhisky.com
tjederswhisky.se
whiskyandwisdom.com *
whiskyboys.com
whiskycast.com *
whiskycritic.com
whisky-distillery.net *
whiskyfacile.com
whiskyfanblog.de
whiskyforeveryone.blogspot.com *
whiskyfun.com *
whiskyintelligence.com *
Whisky in the 6 (Youtube)
whiskyisrael.co.il *
Whisky Jason (Youtube)
whiskymylife.wordpress.com *
whisky-news.com *
whiskynotes.be *
whiskeyreviewer.com
whiskysaga.com *
whiskytalk.fireside.fm *
wordsofwhisky.com

Bruichladdich

[brook•lad•dee]

Owner: Rémy Cointreau

Region/district: Islay

Founded: 1881

Status: Active (vc)

Capacity: 2 000 000 litres

Address: Bruichladdich, Islay, Argyll PA49 7UN

Website: bruichladdich.com

Tel: 01496 850221

When Bruichladdich changed owners 25 years ago it went from being a rather neglected distillery selling just 70,000 bottles to a combination of a maverick and pioneer in the Scotch industry.

There was very little in the production that wasn't challenged over the years, not least in terms of "terroir" – how the flavour could be impacted by the barley variety and also where it had been grown. Even if the plethora of experiments have been toned down a bit in recent years, Bruichladdich is still at the forefront, especially when it comes to sustainable production. In 2023 the brand sold almost one million bottles.

The distillery is equipped with a 7 ton cast iron, open mash tun with rakes. There are six 60,000 litre washbacks made of Oregon pine with fermentation times varying between 72 and 110 hours. Furthermore, there are two wash stills and two spirit stills with a 35 minute foreshot and cut points for the spirit run going from 70% down to 63%. In 2025 the production will be ten mashes per week and around one million litres of alcohol. The breakdown of the three whisky varieties is 50% Bruichladdich, 40% Port Charlotte and 10% Octomore.

Bruichladdich has three product lines; unpeated Bruichladdich, heavily peated (40ppm) Port Charlotte and ultra-heavily peated (in the excess of 100ppm) Octomore. The core expressions include **The Classic Laddie**, the limited **Bruichladdich Eighteen** and **Thirty, Port Charlotte 10 year old** and the limited **Port Charlotte 18 year old.** Released more or less yearly are **Bruichladdich Bere Barley** and **Islay Barley.** As for Port Charlotte, **SYC:01** was released in autumn 2024. In September 2025, another batch of the heavily peated Octomore, was released; **16.1**, **16.2** and **16.3** and these were followed in November by **16.4**. Recent bottlings for Feis Ile 2025 were **Port Charlotte Rock'ndaal** as well as the 15 year old **Octomore Polyphonic**, the oldest version of Octomore to date. For travel retail there is the **Classic Laddie Sherry Cask Edition, The Bruichladdich Twenty One** and the **16 year old Bruichladdich Organic Barley**.

The Classic Laddie

History:

1881 Barnett Harvey builds the distillery with money left by his brother William III.

1886 Bruichladdich Distillery Company Ltd is founded and reconstruction commences.

1929 Temporary closure.

1936 The distillery reopens.

1938 Joseph Hobbs, Hatim Attari and Alexander Tolmie purchase the distillery through the company Train & McIntyre.

1952 The distillery is sold to Ross & Coulter.

1960 A. B. Grant buys Ross & Coulter.

1961 Own maltings ceases.

1968 Invergordon Distillers take over.

1975 The number of stills increases to four.

1983 Temporary closure.

1993 Whyte & Mackay buys Invergordon Distillers.

1995 The distillery is mothballed in January.

1998 In production again for a few months.

2000 Murray McDavid buys the distillery from JBB Greater Europe for £6.5 million.

2001 The first distillations of Port Charlotte and Bruichladdich starts in July.

2002 Octomore (80ppm) is distilled for the first time.

2006 The first official bottling of Port Charlotte; PC5.

2008 More than 20 new expressions including the first Octomore.

2009 New releases include Classic, Black Art and X4+3 - the first quadruple distilled single malt.

2011 The first 10 year old from own production is released as well as PC9 and Octomore 4_167.

2012 Rémy Cointreau buys the distillery.

2016 The Laddie Eight, Octomore 7.4 and Port Charlotte 2007 CC:01 are released.

2018 The Port Charlotte range is revamped and a 10 year old and Islay Barley 2011 are released.

2022 The Biodynamic Project and Bruichladdich 1988/30 are launched.

2023 The Regeneration Project made from rye is released.

2025 Octomore 16.1, 16.2, 16.3, 16.4 and Polyphonic are launched.

Tasting notes The Classic Laddie:

IR – Fresh on the nose with notes of pears, green apples, vanilla, citrus and paint. The palate starts with a sweet maltiness and lively pepper followed by vanilla and pears.

Bunnahabhain

[buh•nah•hav•enn]

Owner: CVH Spirits

Region/district: Islay

Founded: 1881

Status: Active (vc)

Capacity: 3 800 000 litres

Address: Port Askaig, Islay, Argyll PA46 7RP

Website: bunnahabhain.com

Tel: 01496 840646

Of the eleven whisky distilleries on Islay only two make unpeated whisky on a regular basis. One is Bruichladdich and the other is Bunnahabhain. Caol Ila is also known to do it but not annually.

In Bunnahabhain's case, it will be a 50/50 split during 2025 where 1.2 million litres are peated to a phenol specification of 35-45ppm. What many people don´t know though is that the distillery regularly produces a punchy, heavily peated newmake (200,000 litres in 2025) where the barley contains 70ppm of phenols.

In recent years much effort at the distillery has been directed towards sustainability issues. A biomass plant was commissioned in 2022, providing steam by burning both wood chips and draff from the production and there is also a high gravity mash which reduces the amount of water used and saves energy.

The distillery is equipped with a traditional stainless steel mash tun (with plans to exchange it for a semi lauter tun in the future) with a copper lid and with a charge between 7.6 and 8.4 tonnes. There are six, large washbacks made of Oregon pine with a volume of 100,000 litres but filled to 70%. The fermentation time is 58 hours. Finally, there are two wash stills (16,500 litres) and two spirit stills (8,500 litres) with slightly descending lyne arms. The cut points for the spirit run are 74-64% for unpeated and 72-61.5% for peated. The intention in 2025 is to mash 22 times per week and produce 2.8 million litres of pure alcohol.

The core range consists of **12, 18, 25, 30** and a **40 year old**. There is also the **12 year old cask strength**. The peated side is represented by **Toiteach a Dha** matured in both bourbon and sherry casks, **Stiùireadair**, matured in first and re-fill sherry casks and **Moine**. Releases for Feis Ile 2025 were **Turas Math No. 2** which had been finished in palo cortado casks and **Turas Math No. 3**, a 19 year old with an armagnac finish. Finally, there are three travel retail exclusives – the heavily peated **Cruach-Mhòna**, **Eirigh Na Greine**, matured in bourbon, sherry and red wine casks and the sherry-matured **An Cladach**.

12 years old

History:

- 1881 William Robertson founds the distillery together with the brothers William and James Greenless.
- 1883 Production starts in January.
- 1887 Islay Distillers Company Ltd merges with William Grant & Co. in order to form Highland Distilleries Company Limited.
- 1963 The two stills are augmented by two more.
- 1982 The distillery closes.
- 1984 The distillery reopens. A 21 year old is released to commemorate the 100th anniversary.
- 1999 Edrington takes over Highland Distillers and mothballs Bunnahabhain but allows for a few weeks of production a year.
- 2001 A 35 year old from 1965 is released.
- 2002 Auld Acquaintance 1968 is launched.
- 2003 Edrington sells Bunnahabhain and Black Bottle to Burn Stewart Distilleries for £10 million. A 40 year old from 1963 is launched.
- 2004 The first limited edition of the peated version is a 6 year old called Moine.
- 2005 Three limited editions are released - 34 years old,18 years old and 25 years old.
- 2006 14 year old Pedro Ximenez and 35 years old are launched.
- 2008 Darach Ur is released for travel retail and Toiteach is launched in few selected markets
- 2010 The peated Cruach-Mhòna and a limited 30 year old are released.
- 2013 A 40 year old is released.
- 2014 Eirigh Na Greine and Ceobanach are released.
- 2017 Moine Oloroso, Stiùireadair and An Cladach are released.
- 2018 Toiteach a Dha and a 20 year old Palo Cortado are released.
- 2019 A 2007 brandy finish and a 39 year old are released.
- 2020 A 2008 manzanilla, a 1997 PX finish and a 2005 burgundy finish are released.
- 2021 12 year old cask strength is launched.
- 2023 Three bottlings are released for Feis Ile.
- 2025 Turas Math No. 2 and No. 3 are released for Feis Ile.

Tasting notes Bunnahabhain 12 years old:

GS – The nose is fresh, with light peat and discreet smoke. More overt peat on the nutty and fruity palate, but still restrained for an Islay. The finish is full-bodied and lingering, with a hint of vanilla and some smoke.

Caol Ila

[cull eel•a]

Owner: Diageo

Region/district: Islay

Founded: 1846

Status: Active (vc)

Capacity: 6 800 000 litres

Address: Port Askaig, Islay, Argyll PA46 7RL

Website: malts.com

Tel: 01496 302760

It is a fact that Caol Ila single malt is only in seventh place in terms of sales of the ten active distilleries on Islay. At the same time it is by far the largest distillery on the island.

One of the reasons behind its modest ranking is that the owners, Diageo, for a long time saw Caol Ila as a producer for blends while its sister Lagavulin was the one to shine in terms of a malt brand. Still, this is very much the role of Caol Ila today but since 2002, in connection with that year's Islay festival, it has also been promoted on its own merits. In 2023 close to 800,000 bottles were sold, to be compared to Lagavulin's 2.5 million.

Caol Ila is equipped with a 12.5 ton full lauter mash tun. There are eight wooden washbacks and two made of stainless steel, all with a volume of 58,000 litres and a fermentation time of 55-60 hours. The last of the original washbacks from the 1974 refurbishment was replaced in 2025. Finally, there are three wash stills with descending lyne arms and three spirit stills with straight lyne arms. With 24-25 mashes per week during 2025 the total production is 6.4 million litres of pure alcohol. Caol Ila is best known for its peated whisky made from Port Ellen malt with a phenol specification of 42ppm (same as Lagavulin). Unpeated spirit is also sometimes produced but not at the moment.

In summer 2022 the distillery was in for a major revamp on the visitor side. The tiny shop was replaced by an impressive heritage centre including a shop/bar/restaurant providing a stunning view towards the Sound of Islay and Jura.

The core range consists of **Moch** without age statement, **12, 18** and **25 year old** and **Distiller's Edition** with a moscatel finish. The surprising release for Feis Ile 2025 was an **8 year old** which had been matured in a combination of refill casks and PX/Oloroso casks and then finished in new Colombian oak! In 2022 a **14 year old Four Corners of Scotland** distillery exclusive was launched and in 2024 an **11 year old** matured in refill and rejuvenated ex-wine American and European oak casks was released as part of the Special Releases.

12 years old

History:

1846 Hector Henderson founds Caol Ila.

1852 Henderson, Lamont & Co. is subjected to financial difficulties and Henderson is forced to sell Caol Ila to Norman Buchanan.

1863 Norman Buchanan sells to the blending company Bulloch, Lade & Co. from Glasgow.

1879 The distillery is rebuilt and expanded.

1920 Bulloch, Lade & Co. is liquidated and the distillery is taken over by Caol Ila Distillery.

1927 DCL becomes sole owners.

1972 All the buildings, except for the warehouses, are demolished and rebuilt.

1974 The renovation, which totals £1 million, is complete and six new stills are installed.

1999 Experiments with unpeated malt.

2002 The first official bottlings since Flora & Fauna/Rare Malt appear; 12 years, 18 years and Cask Strength (c. 10 years).

2003 A 25 year old cask strength is released.

2006 Unpeated 8 year old and 1993 Moscatel finish are released.

2007 Second edition of unpeated 8 year old.

2009 The fourth edition of the unpeated version (10 year old) is released.

2010 A 25 year old, a 1999 Feis Isle bottling and a 1997 Manager´s Choice are released.

2011 An unpeated 12 year old and the unaged Moch are released.

2012 An unpeated 14 year old is released.

2013 Unpeated Stitchell Reserve is released.

2014 A 15 year old unpeated and a 30 year old are released.

2016 A 15 year old unpeated is released.

2017 An 18 year old unpeated is released.

2018 Two bottlings in the Special Releases - a 15 year old and a 35 year old.

2020 A 35 year old is released as part of the new Prima & Ultima range.

2022 A 24 year old anniversary bottle and a 14 year old Four Corners of Scotland are released.

2024 An 11 year old is released as part of the Special Releases.

Tasting notes Caol Ila 12 year old:

GS – Iodine, fresh fish and smoked bacon feature on the nose, along with more delicate, floral notes. Smoke, malt, lemon and peat on the slightly oily palate. Peppery peat in the drying finish.

Cardhu

[car•doo]

Owner: Diageo

Region/district: Speyside

Founded: 1824

Status: Active (vc)

Capacity: 3 400 000 litres

Address: Knockando, Aberlour, Moray AB38 7RY

Website: malts.com

Tel: 01479 874635

Despite its moderate capacity, in this respect ranked 16 of the 31 Diageo malt distilleries, Cardhu has always enjoyed a very special position within the company. There are two reasons for this.

In 1893 Cardhu became the very first distillery that Alexander Walker II (grandson of John Walker) acquired for the family company. The year before he had investigated the potential of taking over Glen Albyn in Inverness and the year after the company leased Ananndale in the Lowlands. The purchase meant that Cardhu from that moment became an integral part of what would ultimately become the best-selling Scotch in the world.

The second reason for its prominence in the company is the fact that very early on Cardhu was promoted as a single malt. The Grant's had led the way in 1963 with Glenfiddich and DCL with its Cardhu was one of the first of the other companies to follow suit. A Cardhu 8 year old appeared in the early 1960s and in the following decades sales improved rapidly, not least in the Mediterranean markets. In the year 2000 it was actually number four after Glenfiddich, Glenlivet and Glen Grant. Things have changed since then though, and in 2023 it had dropped down to place 13 with 2.7 million bottles sold.

Cardhu is equipped with an eight ton stainless steel full lauter mash tun with a copper top, ten washbacks (eight of wood and two of stainless steel), all with a fermentation time of 75 hours, and three pairs of stills. For several years now, the distillery has been in production seven days a week with 21 mashes per week and a total of 3.4 million litres of alcohol. Cardhu is the third best selling single malt from Diageo after The Singleton and Talisker, but Lagavulin is gaining fast.

The core range from the distillery consists of **12, 15** and **18 year old** and two expressions without age statement – **Amber Rock** and **Gold Reserve**. To celebrate the distillery´s 200th anniversary, a limited **12 year old** was launched in 2024 and there is also a limited **16 year old Four Corners of Scotland** bottling, available only at the distillery.

History:

1824 John Cumming applies for and obtains a licence for Cardhu Distillery.

1846 John Cumming dies and his wife Helen and son Lewis takes over.

1872 Lewis dies and his wife Elizabeth takes over.

1884 A new distillery is built to replace the old.

1893 John Walker & Sons purchases Cardhu for £20,500.

1908 The name reverts to Cardow.

1960 Expansion of stills from four to six.

1981 The name changes to Cardhu.

1998 A visitor centre is constructed.

2002 Diageo changes Cardhu single malt to a vatted malt with contributions from other distilleries in it.

2003 The whisky industry protests sharply against Diageo's plans.

2004 Diageo withdraws Cardhu Pure Malt.

2005 The 12 year old Cardhu Single Malt is relaunched and a 22 year old is released.

2009 Cardhu 1997, a single cask in the new Manager´s Choice range is released.

2011 A 15 year old and an 18 year old are released.

2013 A 21 year old is released.

2014 Amber Rock and Gold Reserve are launched.

2016 A distillery exclusive is released.

2019 A 14 year old appears in the Special Releases and Cardhu is also part of the Game of Thrones series.

2020 An 11 year old Rare by Nature bottling is released.

2021 A 14 year old Rare by Nature and a 16 year old Four Corners of Scotland bottling are released.

2022 A 16 year old rum finish is released.

2024 A 200th anniversary bottling is released.

12 years old

Tasting notes Cardhu 12 years old:

GS – The nose is relatively light and floral, quite sweet, with pears, nuts and a whiff of distant peat. Medium-bodied, malty and sweet in the mouth. Medium-length in the finish, with sweet smoke, malt and a hint of peat.

Clynelish

[cline•leash]

Owner: Diageo

Region/district: Northern Highlands

Founded: 1967

Status: Active (vc)

Capacity: 4 800 000 litres

Address: Brora, Sutherland KW9 6LR

Website: malts.com

Tel: 01408 623003 (vc)

A current focus for Scottish distilleries is to minimise the water consumption and reduce the carbon footprint. These sustainability goals come from both the producers themselves as well as from governmental regulations.

In the case of Clynelish this means saving 20 million litres of water (a 20% reduction) in the past two years and reducing CO^2 emissions by 260 tonnes since 2024. Still though, the Clynelish boiler is fed by using gas. Brora however, their neighbouring distillery, uses a wood chip plant and there is an ongoing project to connect this to be used by Clynelish as well and thereby reducing the reliance on fossil fuels by yet another 40%.

In 2021 Clynelish became one of the "four corners of Scotland", which entailed a huge investment in the visitor experience (with Glenkinchie, Cardhu and Caol Ila making up the other three corners). This includes an amazing terrace bar overlooking the North Sea with an opportunity to enjoy not just whisky but also cocktails of all sorts.

Clynelish is known for its rare, waxy newmake – a style which is not often encountered. In the case of Clynelish it is achieved from residues being built up over time in the feints and foreshots receiver. The achieved flavour is much adored by single malt enthusiasts, yet at the same time Clynelish is an essential contribution to blended Scotch such as Johnnie Walker Gold Label

The distillery is equipped with a 12.2 ton full lauter mash tun, eight wooden washbacks and two made of stainless steel with a 58,000 litres capacity each and a fermentation time of 85 hours. The still room holds three pairs of stills. In 2025, Clynelish will be operating a seven-day week with 18 mashes weekly producing around 4.8 million litres of alcohol. On site there is also a plant which takes care of the copper residues that derive from the spent lees during the distillation process.

The only official core expressions are a **14 year old** and the **16 year old** distillery exclusive. In autumn 2025 the **Waxen Sun 18 year old** appeared in the Special Releases.

18 year old Waxen Sun

History:

1819 The 1st Duke of Sutherland founds a distillery called Clynelish Distillery.

1827 The first licensed distiller, James Harper, files for bankruptcy and John Matheson takes over.

1846 George Lawson & Sons become new licensees.

1896 James Ainslie & Heilbron takes over.

1912 James Ainslie & Co. narrowly escapes bankruptcy and Distillers Company Limited (DCL) takes over together with James Risk.

1916 John Walker & Sons buys a stake of James Risk's stocks.

1931 The distillery is mothballed.

1939 Production restarts.

1960 The distillery becomes electrified.

1967 A new distillery, also named Clynelish, is built adjacent to the first one.

1968 'Old' Clynelish is mothballed in August.

1969 'Old' Clynelish is reopened as Brora and starts using a very peaty malt.

1983 Brora is closed in March.

2002 A 14 year old is released.

2006 A Distiller´s Edition 1991 finished in Oloroso casks is released.

2009 A 12 year old is released for Friends of the Classic Malts.

2010 A 1997 Manager´s Choice single cask is released.

2014 Clynelish Select Reserve is released.

2015 Second version of Clynelish Select Reserve is released.

2017 The distillery produces again after a year long closure for refurbishing.

2019 Clynelish House Tyrell is released as part of the Game of Thrones series.

2020 A 26 year old Prima & Ultima is released.

2021 A 16 year old Four Corners of Scotland is launched.

2022 A 12 year old Special Release is launched.

2023 A 10 year old Special Release is launched together with a 26 year old Prima & Ultima matured in PX and oloroso sherry.

2025 The 18 year old Waxen Sun is released.

Tasting notes Clynelish 14 year old:

GS – A nose that is fragrant, spicy and complex, with candle wax, malt and a whiff of smoke. Notably smooth in the mouth, with honey and contrasting citric notes, plus spicy peat, before a brine and tropical fruit finish.

Cragganmore

[crag•an•moor]

Owner: Diageo

Region/district: Speyside

Founded: 1869

Status: Active (vc)

Capacity: 2 200 000 litres

Address: Ballindalloch, Moray AB37 9AB

Website: malts.com

Tel: 01479 874700

Cragganmore may be one of the smaller distilleries in the Diageo group and sales of its single malt does not amount to more than 200,000 bottles per year but there are definitely reasons why it is worth a visit.

The distillery is beautifully tucked away in the Spey valley, close to the A95 with Glenfarclas as its closest neighbour on the other side of the road. In fact, John Smith who already owned Glenfarclas at the time was the founder of it. Smith had a great interest in railroads and the distillery was founded the same year as the Strathspey Railway which meant that Cragganmore was one of the first distilleries in the Speyside area to make use of the railway as a means of transportation for its produce.

In 1988 Cragganmore became one of the original six Classic Malts. Sales in 2023 amounted to 206,000 bottles which rendered the brand a 12th place amongst Diageo malts. On site there is the beautiful Clubroom. With a library, an open fire and Chesterfield furniture, this used to be the distillery office from where John Smith ran the business in the 1870s.

The distillery is equipped with a 7 ton stainless steel full lauter mash tun clad with wood and with a copper canopy. There are six washbacks made of Oregon pine and since five-day weeks are worked there are six short (50 hours) and six long (100 hours) fermentations. Finally, there are two large wash stills with sharply descending lyne arms and two considerably smaller spirit stills with boil balls and long, slightly descending lyne arms. The stills are attached to stainless steel worm tubs on the outside for cooling the spirit vapours. Cragganmore has the capacity to produce 2.2 million litres of pure alcohol based on a seven-day production with 16 mashes but over the years there have also been five-day weeks with 1.5 million litres.

The official core range of Cragganmore is made up of a **12 year old** and a **Distiller's Edition** with a finish in port pipes. A **48 year old** appeared in the Prima & Ultima range 2022. The spirit was distilled just after the distillery went from coal-fired stills to using steam.

12 years old

History:

- 1869 John Smith, who already runs Glenfarclas distillery, founds Cragganmore.
- 1886 John Smith dies and his brother George takes over operations.
- 1893 John's son Gordon, at 21, is old enough to assume responsibility for operations.
- 1901 The distillery is refurbished and modernized with help of the famous architect Charles Doig.
- 1912 Gordon Smith dies and his widow Mary Jane supervises operations.
- 1917 The distillery closes.
- 1918 The distillery reopens and Mary Jane installs electric lighting.
- 1923 The distillery is sold to the newly formed Cragganmore-Glenlivet Distillery Co. where Mackie & Co. and Sir George Macpherson-Grant of Ballindalloch Estate share ownership.
- 1927 White Horse Distillers is bought by DCL which thus obtains 50% of Cragganmore.
- 1964 The number of stills is increased from two to four.
- 1965 DCL buys the remainder of Cragganmore.
- 1988 Cragganmore 12 years becomes one of six selected for United Distillers´ Classic Malts.
- 1998 Cragganmore Distillers Edition Double Matured (port) is launched for the first time.
- 2002 A visitor centre opens in May.
- 2006 A 17 year old from 1988 is released.
- 2010 Manager´s Choice single cask 1997 and a limited 21 year old are released.
- 2014 A 25 year old is released.
- 2016 A Special Releases vatting without age statement and a distillery exclusive are released.
- 2019 A 12 year bottled at cask strength appears in the Special Releases series.
- 2020 A 48 year old and a 20 year old are released.
- 2022 A 48 year old Prima & Ultima is released.

Tasting notes Cragganmore 12 years old:

GS – A nose of sherry, brittle toffee, nuts, mild wood smoke, angelica and mixed peel. Elegant on the malty palate, with herbal and fruit notes, notably orange. Medium in length, with a drying, slightly smoky finish.

Craigellachie

[craig•ell•ack•ee]

Owner: John Dewar & Sons (Bacardi)

Region/district: Speyside

Founded: 1891

Status: Active

Capacity: 4 300 000 litres

Address: Aberlour, Banffshire AB38 9ST

Website: craigellachie.com

Tel: 01340 872971

The word "dirty" in a tasting note may seem strange to many but for a group of seasoned whisky aficionados the term awakens fond memories of how whisky was made several decades ago.

What the term usually comprises is a whisky with oily, malty and robust flavours and Craigellachie usually falls into that camp. Other single malts that come to mind in this respect are Ledaig, Springbank, Glen Scotia, Mortlach and Benrinnes. All these bar Ledaig and Glen Scotia use wormtubs for cooling the spirit vapours which is one explanation for the character. Others have to do with whether or not you are looking for cloudy or a clear worts and the shape of the stills. As always many factors are in play.

Some would claim that the style is an acquired taste which might explain why Craigellachie is the one of the five Dewar's malts that sells the least – 170,000 bottles in 2023. As a matter of fact it hasn't been around as a widely available single malt for more than ten years. Before that the owners bottled a 14 year old which didn't get that much recognition. Independent bottlers though have always been keen on presenting it.

Craigellachie is equipped with a 10 ton full lauter mash tun, eight 47,000 litre washbacks made of larch with a fermentation time that currently combines shorts (57 hours) and longs (105 hours). There are also two pairs of stills attached to worm tubs. The production plan for 2025 involves 15 mashes in a five-day week and shy of 2.8 million litres of alcohol. The heavy character of Craigellachie relies on the worm tubs and massive stills with little reflux. This is balanced by a clear wort and a reasonably high cut (64%) on the spirit run to add fruitier elements as well.

The core range consists of **13, 17, 19, 23** and **33 year old**. The limited Cask Collection, was introduced in spring 2022 by way of a **13 year old** with a one year finish in Armagnac casks. Recent releases for travel retail also include a **27 year old** with a brandy finish and a **37 year old** finished in bourbon casks.

13 years old

History:

1890 The distillery is built by Craigellachie–Glenlivet Distillery Company which has Alexander Edward and Peter Mackie as part-owners.

1891 Production starts.

1916 Mackie & Company Distillers Ltd takes over.

1924 Peter Mackie dies and Mackie & Company changes name to White Horse Distillers.

1927 White Horse Distillers are bought by Distillers Company Limited (DCL).

1930 Administration is transferred to Scottish Malt Distillers (SMD), a subsidiary of DCL.

1964 Refurbishing takes place and two new stills are bought, increasing the number to four.

1998 United Distillers & Vintners (UDV) sells Craigellachie together with Aberfeldy, Brackla and Aultmore and the blending company John Dewar & Sons to Bacardi Martini.

2004 The first bottlings from the new owners are a new 14 year old which replaces UDV's Flora & Fauna and a 21 year old cask strength from 1982 produced for Craigellachie Hotel.

2014 Three new bottlings for domestic markets (13, 17 and 23 years) and one for duty free (19 years) are released.

2015 A 31 year old is released.

2016 A 33 year old and a 1994 Madeira single cask are released.

2018 A 24 year old and and a 17 year old palo cortado finish are released for duty free and the oldest official Craigellachie so far, 51 years old, is launched.

2019 A 19 and a 23 year old are released.

2020 A 39 year old is launched.

2021 A 33 year old is added to the core range.

2022 A 13 year old Armagnac finish is released.

Tasting notes Craigellachie 13 years old:

GS – Savoury on the early nose, with spent matches, green apples and mixed nuts. Malt join the nuts and apples on the palate, with sawdust and very faint smoke. Drying, with cranberries, spice and more subtle smoke.

Dailuaine

[dall•yoo•an]

Owner: Diageo

Region/district: Speyside

Founded: 1852

Status: Active

Capacity: 5 200 000 litres

Address: Carron, Banffshire AB38 7RE

Website: malts.com

Tel: 01340 872500

A minute or so of travel on the small road from the A95 towards Carron, you will encounter a number of warehouse roofs on your left side. They are so close it's almost as if you and your car will be landing on top of them if you stray off the road.

They belong to Dailuaine but haven't been used since 1989. This is a pity as they are some of the most beautiful dunnage warehouses in Speyside. Of other features at Dailuaine that have been closed, the floor maltings that were replaced by a Saladin box in 1960 (these days the malt comes from any of the commercial maltsters) can be mentioned, while the wonderful malting floors still are in pristine condition.

Dailuaine has cemented its place in whisky history thanks to a new innovation that was tested here for the first time in 1889. At that time the architect, Charles Cree Doig, constructed the first pagoda roof (as it was named later) to make it easier to ventilate the smoke coming from the kiln. Unfortunately, the roof collapsed in 1917 but the same design can still be seen today at many of the distilleries around Scotland albeit the vast majority of them these days just have an ornamental purpose rather than functional.

The distillery is equipped with a stainless steel, 11.25 ton full lauter mash tun. There are also eight washbacks made of Douglas fir plus two stainless steel ones placed outside – all with a charge of 52,000 litres. The charge has recently been reduced due to trials with high gravity mashing for water-saving purposes. Finally, there are three pairs of stills with foreshots running for 20 minutes and a spirit cut ranging from 77% way down to 58%. When they started working on waxy newmake in 2015, the fermentation times were very long (between 80 and 107 hours) but since 2022, in connection with aiming for a nutty style, Dailuane is back to just 46 hours. In later years the distillery has also switched between five-day (12 mashes) and seven-day weeks (22 mashes).

The only core bottling is the **16 year old Flora & Fauna.** In 2015, a **34 year old** from 1980 was launched as part of the Special Releases.

History:

1852 The distillery is founded by William Mackenzie.

1865 William Mackenzie dies and his widow leases the distillery to James Fleming, a banker from Aberlour.

1879 William Mackenzie's son forms Mackenzie and Company with Fleming.

1891 Dailuaine-Glenlivet Distillery Ltd is founded.

1898 Dailuaine-Glenlivet Distillery Ltd merges with Talisker Distillery Ltd and forms Dailuaine-Talisker Distilleries Ltd.

1915 Thomas Mackenzie dies without heirs.

1916 Dailuaine-Talisker Company Ltd is bought by the previous customers John Dewar & Sons, John Walker & Sons and James Buchanan & Co.

1917 A fire rages and the pagoda roof collapses.

1920 The distillery reopens.

1925 Distillers Company Limited (DCL) takes over.

1960 Refurbishing. The stills increase from four to six and a Saladin box replaces the floor maltings.

1965 Indirect still heating through steam is installed.

1983 On site maltings is closed down and malt is purchased centrally.

1991 The first official bottling, a 16 year old, is launched in the Flora & Fauna series.

1996 A 22 year old cask strength from 1973 is released as a Rare Malt.

1997 A cask strength version of the 16 year old is launched.

2000 A 17 year old Manager´s Dram matured in sherry casks is launched.

2010 A single cask from 1997 is released.

2012 The production capacity is increased by 25%.

2015 A 34 year old is launched as part of the Special Releases.

16 years old

Tasting notes Dailuaine 16 years old:

GS – Barley, sherry and nuts on the substantial nose, developing into maple syrup. Medium-bodied, rich and malty in the mouth, with more sherry and nuts, plus ripe oranges, fruitcake, spice and a little smoke. The finish is lengthy and slightly oily, with almonds, cedar and slightly smoky oak.

Dalmore

[dal•moor]

Owner:
Whyte & Mackay Ltd
(Emperador Inc)

Region/district:
Northern Highlands

Founded:
1839

Status:
Active (vc)

Capacity:
9 000 000 litres

Address: Alness, Ross-shire IV17 0UT

Website:
thedalmore.com

Tel:
01349 882362

In the midst of a temporary slowdown for Scotch whisky, Dalmore has carried on with their huge investments and changes both on the production side as well as for their visitors experience.

A completely new still house has been built where the – now demolished – Saladin maltings used to sit. The additional equipment will all be commissioned in August 2025 and the new capacity will be no less than 9 million litres making Dalmore the ninth largest malt distillery in Scotland. The £40m investment includes a stunning new visitor experience, incorporating parts of the old architecture with exciting, contemporary additions. Design was by 360 Architecture with Stefano Faeilla, previously involved with Port of Leith and The Cairn, as the lead architect. An unofficial opening for selected guests took place in September 2025 but the public opening is expected in the beginning of 2026.

A possible expansion has been discussed ever since Emperador took over Whyte & Mackay in 2014 and the timing couldn't be better. Dalmore is one of the fastest growing single malt Scotch and volumes have increased by almost 300% in the last decade, reaching 3.3 million bottles in 2023.

After the expansion, the distillery is equipped with two 10.4 ton stainless steel, semi-lauter mash tuns, 17 washbacks (48,500 litres) made of Oregon pine with a fermentation time of 50 hours and eight pairs of stills. All the wash stills have flat tops while the spirit stills are equipped with water jackets increasing the reflux. It is expected to produce 5.4 million litres of alcohol in 2025.

The core range consists of **12, 12 Sherry Cask Select, 15, 18, 21** and **25 year old, King Alexander III, Cigar Malt Reserve** and **Port Wood Reserve**. Recent limited bottlings include a **17 year old** as the third edition of the **Luminary Series** and the **Cask Curation Series** where the second iteration, influenced by Port wine, appeared in October 2024. For travel retail a new range was introduced in October 2024. The Portfolio Series consists of a **Bordeaux Wine Cask finish,** a **Châteauneuf-du-Pape Wine finish** and a **Bordeaux Cabernet Sauvignon finish**.

12 years old

History:

1839 Alexander Matheson founds the distillery.

1867 Three Mackenzie brothers run the distillery.

1891 Sir Kenneth Matheson sells the distillery for £14,500 to the Mackenzie brothers.

1917 The Royal Navy moves in to start manufacturing American mines.

1922 The distillery is in production again.

1956 Floor malting replaced by Saladin box.

1960 Mackenzie Brothers (Dalmore) Ltd merges with Whyte & Mackay.

1966 Number of stills is increased to eight.

1982 The Saladin box is abandoned.

1990 American Brands buys Whyte & Mackay.

1996 Whyte & Mackay changes name to JBB (Greater Europe).

2001 Through management buy-out, JBB (Greater Europe) is bought from Fortune Brands and changes name to Kyndal Spirits.

2002 Kyndal Spirits changes name to Whyte & Mackay.

2007 United Spirits buys Whyte & Mackay.

2008 1263 King Alexander III is released.

2009 New releases include an 18 year old, a 58 year old and a Vintage 1951.

2011 More expressions in the River Collection and 1995 Castle Leod are released.

2012 The visitor centre is upgraded and Constellaton Collection is launched.

2014 Emperador Inc buys Whyte & Mackay.

2016 Three new travel retail bottlings are released as well as a 35 year old and Quintessence.

2017 Vintage Port Collection is launched.

2018 The Port Wood Reserve is released.

2019 A new travel retail range is launched.

2020 A 51 year old is released.

2021 The Decades of Dalmore is released.

2022 A 21 year old is released.

2023 Cask Curation Series is launched.

2024 Cask Curation II and the Portfolio Series are released.

2025 The production capacity is doubled.

Tasting notes Dalmore 12 years old:

GS – The nose offers sweet malt, orange mar-malade, sherry and a hint of leather. Full-bodied, with a dry sherry taste though sweeter sherry develops in the mouth along with spice and citrus notes. Lengthy finish with more spices, ginger, Seville oranges and vanilla.

Dalwhinnie

[dal•whin•nay]

Owner:
Diageo

Region/district:
Speyside

Founded:
1897

Status:
Active (vc)

Capacity:
2 200 000 litres

Address: Dalwhinnie, Inverness-shire PH19 1AB

Website:
malts.com

Tel:
01540 672219 (vc)

Dalwhinnie was chosen as one of the six original Classic Malts, representing the Highlands, back in 1988. Today it is Diageo's 6th best selling single malt with 1.2 million bottles sold in 2023.

It is also a key malt in two major Scotch blends – Buchanan's and Black & White. Both brands were established in the 1890s by one of Scotch whisky's most prominent profiles – James Buchanan. Born in Canada by Scottish emigrants, he returned to Scotland and started as a whisky blender in 1884. While Black & White soon became the second best selling whisky in the UK, Buchanan's sales were less remarkable. In the second half of the 20th century, Black & White had lost most of its popularity and from the start of the new millennium it was Buchanan's that harvested success, not least in Latin America. Buchanan's is still doing well but in the last decade, Black & White has made one of the most extraordinary come-backs in the industry.

Sales have gone up by 200% to 40 million bottles and it is now the 7th best selling Scotch in the world! In 2023 though, sales in South America went gone down as it did for almost every foreign spirit in favour of local spirits such as tequila and cachaca. In 2024 however, the figures were on the positive side again.

Dalwhinnie is equipped with a 7.3 ton full lauter mash tun and six wooden, 34,000 litre washbacks (two of them to be replaced in 2026). There is one pair of stills attached to worm tubs. During 2023 and 2024 the distillery was working 24/7 but for 2025 they have gone back to the usual scheme of a five-day week which means 10 mashes per week with short (60 hours) and long (110 hours) fermentations and a total of 1.4 million litres of alcohol.

The core range is made up of a **15 year old**, **Distiller's Edition** with a finish in oloroso casks and **Dalwhinnie Winter's Gold**. A limited expression, a **30 year old**, appeared in 2020 as part of the Special Releases range.

15 years old

History:

1897 John Grant, George Sellar and Alexander Mackenzie commence building the facilities. The first name is Strathspey.

1898 The owner encounters financial troubles and John Somerville & Co and A P Blyth & Sons take over and change the name to Dalwhinnie.

1905 Cook & Bernheimer in New York, buys Dalwhinnie for £1,250 at an auction.

1919 Macdonald Greenlees & Willliams Ltd headed by Sir James Calder buys Dalwhinnie.

1926 Macdonald Greenlees & Williams Ltd is bought by Distillers Company Ltd (DCL) which licences Dalwhinnie to James Buchanan & Co.

1930 Operations are transferred to Scottish Malt Distilleries (SMD).

1934 The distillery is closed after a fire in February.

1938 The distillery opens again.

1968 The maltings is decommissioned.

1987 Dalwhinnie 15 years becomes one of the selected six in United Distillers´ Classic Malts.

1991 A visitor centre is constructed.

1992 The distillery closes and goes through a major refurbishment costing £3.2 million.

1995 The distillery opens in March.

2002 A 36 year old is released.

2006 A 20 year old is released.

2012 A 25 year old is released.

2014 A triple matured bottling without age statement is released for The Friends of the Classic Malts.

2015 Dalwhinnie Winter´s Gold and a 25 year old are released.

2016 A distillery exclusive without age statement is released.

2018 Lizzie´s Dram, a distillery exclusive bottling, is released.

2019 Dalwhinnie Winter´s Frost, part of the Game of Thrones series, is released as well as a 30 year old in the annual Special Releases.

2020 A 30 year old is released as part of the Rare by Nature series.

Tasting notes Dalwhinnie 15 years old:

GS – The nose is fresh, with pine needles, heather and vanilla. Sweet and balanced on the fruity palate, with honey, malt and a very subtle note of peat. The medium length finish dries elegantly.

Deanston

[deen•stun]

Owner: CVH Spirits

Region/district: Southern Highlands

Founded: 1965

Status: Active (vc)

Capacity: 3 000 000 litres

Address: Deanston, Perthshire FK16 6AG

Website: deanstonmalt.com

Tel: 01786 843010

It has taken a wee while for Deanston single malt to be discovered by the whisky aficionados but the recent progression speaks for itself. In the past four years sales have gone up by 100% to reach 770,000 bottles in 2023.

A first class visitor experience and the location, just a 15 minute drive north of Stirling, are all factors behind this significant boost. For die-hard Scotch whisky fans there is yet another reward to be found; Deanston is one of very few single malts that displays the waxy notes that are so rarely found. They originate from a deliberately overlooked cleaning of the low wines and feints receiver, much in the same way that Clynelish operates.

Deanston is equipped with an amazing, open top, stainless steel mash tun with rakes with an 8 ton charge. There are eight 64,000 litre stainless steel washbacks and since the distillery is now working seven days a week, the fermentation time is an even 85 hours. Finally there are two 16,000 litre wash stills and two 14,400 litre spirit stills with ascending lyne arms. To produce a fruity newmake the owners are looking for a clear wort (without too many solids) which can be difficult to create with a traditional mash tun. With 22 mashes per week, the aim in 2025 is to produce 2.9 million litres of alcohol of which 10,000 litres will be organic.

The core range is a **12** and an **18 year old** and the **Virgin Oak** matured in ex-bourbon and with a finish in virgin oak casks. Recent limited bottlings include a **15 year old Tequila Finish,** a **Virgin Oak Distillery Edition,** a **Virgin Oak Cask Strength,** a **2002 Organic PX Cask finish** and a **20 year old Organic** – distilled in 2002 and matured in American oak.

The only available duty-free exclusive is a **10 year old Bordeaux red wine finish**. Finally, there are three fairly recent distillery exclusives – a **2012 Red Wine Matured,** a **2012 Lepanto Matured** and a **2006 Oloroso Finish**.

History:

1965 A weavery from 1785 is transformed into Deanston Distillery by James Findlay & Co. and Brodie Hepburn Ltd.

1966 Production commences in October.

1971 The first single malt is named Old Bannockburn.

1972 Invergordon Distillers takes over.

1974 The first single malt bearing the name Deanston is produced.

1982 The distillery closes.

1990 Burn Stewart Distillers from Glasgow buys the distillery for £2.1 million.

1991 The distillery resumes production.

1999 C L Financial buys an 18% stake of Burn Stewart.

2002 C L Financial acquires the remaining stake.

2006 Deanston 30 years old is released.

2009 A new version of the 12 year old is released.

2010 Virgin Oak is released.

2012 A visitor centre is opened.

2013 Burn Stewart Distillers is bought by South African Distell Group for £160m

2014 An 18 year old cognac finish is released.

2015 An 18 year old is released.

2016 Organic Deanston is released.

2017 A 40 year old and Vintage 2008 are released.

2018 A 10 year old Bordeaux finish is released for duty free.

2019 1997 Palo Cortado finish, 2006 Cream Sherry finish and a 2012 Beer finish are launched.

2020 A 1991 Muscat finish, a 2002 Organix PX and a 2002 Pinot Noir finish are released.

2021 Kentucky Cask and Dragon´s Milk are released.

2023 CVH becomes new owner.

12 years old

Tasting notes Deanston 12 years old:

GS – A fresh, fruity nose with malt and honey. The palate displays cloves, ginger, honey and malt, while the finish is long, quite dry and pleasantly herbal.

Dufftown

[duff•town]

Owner: Diageo

Region/district: Speyside

Founded: 1896

Status: Active

Capacity: 6 000 000 litres

Address: Dufftown, Keith, Banffshire AB55 4BR

Website: malts.com thesingleton.com

Tel: 01340 822100

Even though Dufftown has been operating more or less constantly since its founding in 1895 and being a distillery of quite a substantial size, very few people had any knowledge of Dufftown and its single malt before 2006.

The distillery was owned by Arthur Bell & Sons for more than 30 years before it was taken over by Guinness in 1985 and later became a part of the Diageo stable of distilleries. Soon after the take-over it was launched as a 15 year old in the Flora & Fauna range of whiskies together with more than 20 other single malt brands. It gained just a little more recognition at that time, but it wasn't until 2006, when Dufftown became part of the trio of distilleries (Dufftown, Glendullan and Glen Ord) grouped under the Singleton umbrella, that things took off.

With water being one of the key prerequisites for making whisky, many distilleries like Dufftown are built next to a river. To be able to control the water intake, dams are often constructed but these can sometimes become a barrier for wild fish. A few years ago a fish ladder was built by the distillery to ensure that the brown trout population of the Dullan river are able to make it up the river beyond the distillery's dam wall.

Dufftown distillery is equipped with a 14 ton full lauter mash tun, 12 stainless steel washbacks and three pairs of stills. Furthermore, all stills have sub coolers. The style of the newmake is green and grassy which is achieved by a clear wort and long fermentations (75 hours minimum). The fore shots in the spirit still run for 15 minutes and the middle cut is collected between 73 and 58% abv. There are 23 mashes per week, if producing for seven days, which translates into six million litres per year.

The core range consists of **Malt Master's Selection** and **The Singleton of Dufftown 12, 15** and **18 year old**. A range for duty-free consists of **Trinité, Liberté** and **Artisan**. A number of older expressions have been released in later years including a **54 year old** which at the time was the oldest official bottling of a Diageo single malt ever.

Singleton of Dufftown 12 year

History:

1895 Peter Mackenzie, Richard Stackpole, John Symon and Charles MacPherson build the distillery Dufftown-Glenlivet in an old mill.

1896 Production starts in November.

1897 The distillery is owned by P. Mackenzie & Co., who also owns Blair Athol in Pitlochry.

1933 P. Mackenzie & Co. is bought by Arthur Bell & Sons for £56,000.

1968 The floor maltings is discontinued and malt is bought from outside suppliers. The number of stills is increased from two to four.

1974 The number of stills is increased from four to six.

1979 The stills are increased by a further two to eight.

1985 Guinness buys Arthur Bell & Sons.

1997 Guinness and Grand Metropolitan merge to form Diageo.

2006 The Singleton of Dufftown 12 year old is launched as a special duty free bottling.

2008 The Singleton of Dufftown is made available also in the UK.

2010 A Manager´s Choice 1997 is released.

2013 A 28 year old cask strength and two expressions for duty free - Unité and Trinité - are released.

2014 Tailfire, Sunray and Spey Cascade are released.

2016 Two limited releases are made - a 21 year old and a 25 year old.

2018 Malt Master´s Selection is released.

2020 A 30 year old Prima & Ultima and a 17 year old Rare by Nature are released.

2021 A 54 year old is released.

2023 A 37 year old bottled at 47,7% is launched as part of the Prima & Ultima range.

Tasting notes Dufftown 12 years old:

GS – The nose is sweet, almost violet-like, with underlying malt. Big and bold on the palate, this is an upfront yet very drinkable whisky. The finish is medium to long, warming, spicy, with slowly fading notes of sherry and fudge.

Edradour

[ed•ra•dow•er]

Owner:
Signatory Vintage
Scotch Whisky Co. Ltd

Region/district:
Southern Highland

Founded:
1825

Status:
Active

Capacity:
340 000 litres

Address: Pitlochry, Perthshire PH16 5JP

Website:
edradour.com

Tel:
01796 472095

After 15 years as an independent bottler, Andrew Symington finally got what he was looking for – a distillery of his own which could supplement the rest of his business.

After a series of attempts to buy distilleries like Scapa, Glenturret and Ardbeg, he was finally rewarded when Pernod Ricard sold him Edradour in 2002. Symington certainly had vision and foresight. Established producers are nowadays often reluctant to sell whisky to independent bottlers, but if you produce your own whisky, you can always swap casks.

At the same time Symington has managed to establish Edradour single malt as a brand of its own, in, admittedly, small quantities, but nevertheless with a devoted following. Its success has been so obvious that a second distillery with two new stills was added to the site in 2018. Edradour, located just a 5 minute drive off the A9 when you reach Pitlochry, used to be one the most visited distilleries in Scotland but has been closed to the public since the pandemic. In 2023 the brand sold 450,000 bottles.

Following the expansion the site is now made up of two distilleries. The combined equipment consists of two open, traditional cast iron mash tuns with a mash size of 1.1 tons producing a cloudy wort. There are two refrigerators to cool the wort and eight washbacks made of Oregon pine with both short (50 hours) and long (120 hours) fermentation. The two stills in each distillery are attached to worm tubs and the spirit cut is usually collected between 75% and 63%. In recent years the owners have run one shift at the old distillery and two at the new weekly. This has resulted in a total of 340,000 litres of alcohol. The amount of peated production (for the Ballechin brand) has diminished in the last couple of years due to the demand for the unpeated Edradour.

The core range consists of a **10 year old** and the **12 year old Caledonia Selection** and there is also the **10 year old peated Ballechin**. Regular but limited bottlings include **12, 21** and **25 year olds** – all sherrymatured and bottled at cask strength. There are also a number of expressions of both Edradour and Ballechin either fully matured or finished in wine casks.

History:

1825 Probably the year when a distillery called Glenforres is founded by farmers in Perthshire.

1837 The first year Edradour is mentioned.

1841 The farmers form a proprietary company, John MacGlashan & Co.

1886 John McIntosh & Co. acquires Edradour.

1933 William Whiteley & Co. buys the distillery.

1982 Campbell Distilleries (Pernod Ricard) buys Edradour and builds a visitor centre.

1986 The first single malt is released.

2002 Edradour is bought by Andrew Symington from Signatory for £5.4 million. The product range is expanded with a 10 year old and a 13 year old cask strength.

2003 A 30 year old and a 10 year old are released.

2004 A number of wood finishes are launched as cask strength.

2006 The first bottling of peated Ballechin is released.

2007 A Madeira matured Ballechin is released.

2008 A Ballechin matured in Port pipes and a 10 year old Edradour with a Sauternes finish are released.

2009 Fourth edition of Ballechin (Oloroso) is released.

2010 Ballechin #5 Marsala is released.

2011 Ballechin #6 Bourbon and a 26 year old PX sherry finish are relased.

2012 A 1993 Oloroso and a 1993 Sauternes finish as well as the 7th edition of Ballechin (Bordeaux) are released.

2013 Ballechin Sauternes is released.

2014 The first release of a 10 year old Ballechin.

2015 Fairy Flag is released.

2017 New releases include an 8 year old vatting of Edradour and Ballechin.

2018 The new distillery is commissioned.

10 years old

Tasting notes Edradour 10 years old:

GS – Cider apples, malt, almonds, vanilla and honey ar present on the nose, along with a hint of smoke and sherry. The palate is rich, creamy and malty, with a persistent nuttiness and quite a pronounced kick of slightly leathery sherry. Spices and sherry dominate the medium to long finish.

Fettercairn

[fett•er•cairn]

Owner:
Whyte & Mackay (Emperador)

Region/district:
Eastern Highlands

Founded:
1824

Status:
Active (vc)

Capacity:
2 200 000 litres

Address: Fettercairn, Laurencekirk, Kincardineshire AB30 1YB

Website:
fettercairnwhisky.com

Tel:
01561 340205

The well established producer Whyte & Mackay seems to be doing everything right at the moment. Three of the four single malts (Dalmore, Jura and Tamnavulin) belong to the fastest growing brands in the industry.

Forthermore, the classic blend Whyte & Mackay (established already in 1896) appears to have found a new lease of life, not least in the UK where it is now the second best selling blended Scotch after Famous Grouse. The final piece of the puzzle is to create more consumer awareness of the Fettercairn single malt. One part of the branding is the focus on sustainability: The Fettercairn 200 Club – a partnership together with Bairds Maltings and 200 local farms - make sure that all the barley required for production will be locally sourced. On top of that 13,000 saplings of oak (both Q. robur and Q. petrea) have been planted on the Fasque Estate where the distillery is situated, to be used to mature future spirit.

The distillery is equipped with a traditional, 5 ton cast iron mash tun but a new tun (still traditional) with a charge of 6 tons will be installed in 2025. There are eleven 39,000 litre washbacks with a fermentation time of 56 hours and also two pairs of stills. The spirit stills are quite unique in Scotland. They both have a cooling ring attached which sprays the head of the stills with water which is then collected at the base for circulation towards the top again. The whole idea is to increase the reflux during distillation. Both spirit stills were exchanged for identical new ones in 2024 but the coils and pans for heating were replaced by more energy efficient radiators. The goal for 2025 is 24 mashes per week and 2.2 million litres.

The core range consists of **12, 16, 22, 24** and **28 year olds**. In 2022 an **18 year old** was added to the range – the first from the distillery in the Sottish oak programme and released in yearly batches. Older versions in the range include **40, 46** and **50 year old**. For the duty free market there is a **14,** a **17** and a **25 year old**. To celebrate the 200th anniversary a limited set of six whiskies ranging from **60 years old** to **3 years old** was launched in 2024.

12 years old

History:

- 1824 Sir Alexander Ramsay founds the distillery.
- 1830 Sir John Gladstone buys the distillery.
- 1887 A fire erupts and the distillery closes for repair.
- 1890 Thomas Gladstone dies and his son John Robert takes over. The distillery reopens.
- 1912 John Gladstone buys out the other investors.
- 1926 The distillery is mothballed.
- 1939 The distillery is bought by Associated Scottish Distillers Ltd. Production restarts.
- 1960 The maltings discontinues.
- 1966 The stills are increased from two to four.
- 1971 The distillery is bought by Tomintoul-Glenlivet Distillery Co. Ltd.
- 1973 Tomintoul-Glenlivet Distillery Co. Ltd is bought by Whyte & Mackay Distillers Ltd.
- 1974 The mega group of companies Lonrho buys Whyte & Mackay.
- 1988 Lonrho sells to Brent Walker Group plc.
- 1989 A visitor centre opens.
- 1990 American Brands Inc. buys Whyte & Mackay for £160 million.
- 1996 Whyte & Mackay and Jim Beam Brands merge to become JBB Worldwide.
- 2001 Kyndal Spirits buys Whyte & Mackay from JBB Worldwide.
- 2002 The whisky changes name to Fettercairn 1824.
- 2003 Kyndal Spirits changes name to Whyte & Mackay.
- 2007 United Spirits buys Whyte & Mackay.
- 2009 24, 30 and 40 year olds are released.
- 2010 Fettercairn Fior is launched.
- 2012 Fettercairn Fasque is released.
- 2015 Emperador Inc buys Whyte & Mackay.
- 2018 12, 28, 40 and 50 year old are launched.
- 2019 A 12 year old PX finish is released for duty free.
- 2020 A 16 year old and a 22 year old are added.
- 2021 Two first batches of Warehouse 2 are released.
- 2022 An 18 year old is released.
- 2023 Warehouse 14 is released.
- 2024 The 200th Anniversary Collection is launched.

Tasting notes Fettercairn 12 years old:

IR – A delicious combination of pineapple, banana and mango together with coffee beans, cured ham and dried flowers. Still fruity on the palate but also becomes more spicy and malty and with a bit of mint at the end.

Glenallachie

[glen•alla•key]

Owner: The Glenallachie Distillers Co.
Region/district: Speyside
Founded: 1967
Status: Active (vc)
Capacity: 4 000 000 litres
Address: Aberlour, Banffshire AB38 9LR
Website: theglenallachie.com
Tel: 01236 422120

Since Pernod Ricard acquired Glenallachie in 1989, the distillery's main task was to produce malt whisky aimed as an integral part of the Clan Campbell blend. They made very few attempts to market it as a single malt.

When Billy Walker bought Glenallachie in 2017 the distillery went from being oblivious in the shadows to becoming a brand that caught an attention amongst whisky aficionados. Walker was well suited for the job. He joined the industry in 1972 and has over the years worked for HiramWalker & Sons and Burn Stewart. In 2004 he bought, together with partners, Benriach and subsequently also Glendronach and Glenglassaugh distilleries. His skills, not least as a blender, are undisputed.

Glenallachie is equipped with a 9.4 ton semi-lauter mash tun and eight stainless steel washbacks with a fermentation time of 160-164 hours, although longer fermentations have been trialled. There are also two pairs of stills. Production was stopped from March to July 2025 due to the instalment of MVR on the wash stills. MVR stands for Mechanical Vapour Recompression. It is a process which recycles waste heat to improve efficiency. It reduces both energy consumption as well as carbon dioxide emissions and quite a few distilleries around Scotland are currently employing this process. In 2025 the production will be 5 mashes per week and around 1 million litres of alcohol, of which 10% will be heavily peated.

The core range consists of **10, 12, 15, 18, 21** and **30 year old**. Three of them (10, 21 and 30) are bottled at batch strength. Recent limited releases include three **9 year olds** that have been finished in **fino sherry, amontillado sherry** and **oloroso sherry** respectively and **Sinteis #1**, a 2014 Vintage matured in a combination of PX sherry and **Chingquapin oak**. In 2023 a separate range of peated whiskies was launched under the name Meikle Tòir. It is made up of **The Original, The Sherry One, The Chingquapin One** and **The Turbo** – all of them aged for 5 years.

12 years old

History:

- 1967 The distillery is founded by Mackinlay, McPherson & Co., a subsidiary of Scottish & Newcastle Breweries Ltd. William Delmé Evans is architect.
- 1985 Scottish & Newcastle Breweries Ltd sells Charles Mackinlay Ltd to Invergordon Distillers which acquires both Glenallachie and Isle of Jura.
- 1987 The distillery is decommissioned.
- 1989 Campbell Distillers (Pernod Ricard) buys the distillery, increases the number of stills from two to four and takes up production again.
- 2005 The first official bottling for many years is a Cask Strength Edition from 1989.
- 2017 Glenallachie Distillery Edition is released and the distillery is sold to The Glenallachie Consortium.
- 2018 A series of single casks is released followed by a core range consisting of 12, 18 and 25 year old.
- 2019 A range of wood finishes is launched as well as a 15 year old core bottling. A visitor centre is opened.
- 2020 A 21 year old cask strength and three new wood finishes are launched; rye, port and moscatel.
- 2021 A 30 year old cask strength and the Wine Cask Finish series are launched.
- 2022 The 50th Anniversary Trilogy is launched together with 2012 Cuvée Cask Finish.
- 2023 The peated Meikle Tòir range is introduced.
- 2024 The core range is revamped.

Tasting notes Glenallachie 12 years old:

IR – Baked apples with almonds and custard, lemon zest and pine needles on the nose. Rich and lively on the palate, sweet spices, ginger, bananas, liquorice, raisins and hints of pepper.

Glenburgie

[glen•bur•gee]

Owner:
Chivas Brothers (Pernod Ricard)

Region/district:
Speyside

Founded: 1810

Status: Active

Capacity: 4 250 000 litres

Address: Glenburgie, Forres, Morayshire IV36 2QY

Website:
-

Tel:
01343 850258

Despite its size, with a production of over 4 million litres per year, Glenburgie is a distillery that doesn't get a lot of mention. You can clearly see the chimney from the A96 between Forres and Elgin.

However, if you decide to go there (which actually you shouldn´t because it´s not open to the public), you need to choose the correct junction exit. Coming from Forres, don't take the first right when you've spotted the chimney. It will take you to the distillery but the road is narrow and winding. Instead take the next right and you will end up right at a distillery. Albeit being founded so far ago as in the early 1800s it appears perfectly modern. The reason for this is that the whole distillery, with the exception of the customs house which is now used as a tasting area, was demolished in 2003 and a new distillery was built. Glenburgie single malt has been intimately linked to the Ballantine's blended Scotch since the late 1920s and for more than 50 years both the distillery and Ballantine's were under Hiram Walker's umbrella. Today they are both owned by Chivas Brothers (Pernod Ricard). Ballantine's has been the second most sold Scotch since 2007 when J&B Rare's figures were overtaken. In the troublesome year of 2024 it performed really well (up by 13%) selling 112 million bottles.

As for many other Chivas distilleries, Glenburgie is in for an upgrade to save energy. A planning application to install MVR (mechanical vapour recompression) on the wash stills was approved in October 2024.

Glenburgie is equipped with a 7.5 ton full lauter mash tun with a copper dome and 12 stainless steel washbacks with a fermentation time of 52 hours. There are also three pairs of large stills with straight lyne arms producing a fruity newmake. The majority of the production is filled into bourbon casks and a part thereof is matured on site in four dunnage, two racked and two palletised warehouses.

There are three official bottlings – **12, 15** and **18 year old**. A **17 year old cask strength** in the range The Distillery Reserve Collection is also available at Chivas's visitor centres.

15 years old

History:

1810 William Paul founds Kilnflat Distillery. Official production starts in 1829.

1870 Kilnflat distillery closes.

1878 The distillery reopens under the name Glenburgie-Glenlivet, Charles Hay is licensee.

1884 Alexander Fraser & Co. takes over.

1925 Alexander Fraser & Co. files for bankruptcy and the receiver Donald Mustad assumes control of operations.

1927 James & George Stodart Ltd (owned by James Barclay and R A McKinlay since 1922) buys the distillery which by this time is inactive.

1930 Hiram Walker buys 60% of James & George Stodart Ltd.

1936 Hiram Walker buys Glenburgie Distillery in October. Production restarts.

1958 Lomond stills are installed producing a single malt, Glencraig. Floor malting ceases.

1981 The Lomond stills are replaced by conventional stills.

1987 Allied Lyons buys Hiram Walker.

2002 A 15 year old is released.

2004 A £4.3 million refurbishment and reconstruction takes place.

2005 Chivas Brothers (Pernod Ricard) becomes the new owner through the acquisition of Allied Domecq.

2006 The number of stills are increased from four to six in May.

2017 A 15 year old is released.

2019 An 18 year old is released.

Tasting notes Glenburgie 15 years old:

IR – Very fruity on the nose with notes of pears, apple pie, honey, marzipan and roasted nuts. The palate reveals tropical fruits, white chocolate, marmalade, vanilla and caramel.

Glencadam

[glen•ka•dam]

Owner: Angus Dundee Distillers

Region/district: Eastern Highlands

Founded: 1825

Status: Active

Capacity: 1 300 000 litres

Address: Brechin, Angus DD9 7PA

Website: glencadamwhisky.com

Tel: 01356 622217

Glencadam is celebrating its 200th anniversary this year and what could be more fitting than opening a new visitor centre – a project which has been in the works for quite some time now.

One part of the tour shows the water wheel that was installed already in 2021. It is situated in the heart of the distillery and is there not just to offer a pleasant sight but also to supply the distillery with electricity. The 4.3 meter i diameter wheel replaces one which was installed when the distillery was founded and was working for almost a century.

Wooden or steel washbacks' impact on the spirit is often debated. The usual standpoint is that you don't change material when it's time to replace the vessels. Last year though, two stainless steel ones were replaced by those made from Oregon pine and in 2025 another two wooden washbacks were installed. The fact that the distillery now caters to visitors and that wooden washbacks look so much nicer may have influenced the decision.

The equipment consists of a traditional 5 ton stainless steel mash tun, two stainless steel washbacks and four made from wood with a fermentation time of 52 hours and one pair of stills. On site, two dunnage warehouses from 1825, three from the 1950s and one modern racked can be found. The distillery is currently working a seven-day week, which enables 16 mashes per week and 1.3 million litres of alcohol. The owners also produce a large number of blends and they are vatted together in 16 huge steel tanks next to the distillery.

The core range consists of **Origin 1825, Reserva Andalucia, American Oak, 10, 13, 15, 18, 21** and **25 year old**. A **27 year old Reserva de Jerez** (oloroso finish) was added in July 2024. A limited range of five NAS cask finishes including **PX sherry, white port, tawny port, merlot** and **pinot noir** casks appeared in 2023 and was followed in 2024/2025 by **madeira** and **amarone.**

10 years old

History:

1825 George Cooper founds the distillery.

1827 David Scott takes over.

1837 The distillery is sold by David Scott.

1852 Alexander Miln Thompson becomes the owner.

1857 Glencadam Distillery Company is formed.

1891 Gilmour, Thompson & Co Ltd takes over.

1954 Hiram Walker takes over.

1959 Refurbishing of the distillery.

1987 Allied Lyons buys Hiram Walker Gooderham & Worts.

1994 Allied Lyons changes name to Allied Domecq.

2000 The distillery is mothballed.

2003 Allied Domecq sells the distillery to Angus Dundee Distillers.

2005 The new owner releases a 15 year old.

2008 A re-designed 15 year old and a new 10 year old are introduced.

2009 A 25 and a 30 year old are released in limited numbers.

2010 A 12 year old port finish, a 14 year old sherry finish, a 21 year old and a 32 year old are released.

2012 A 30 year old is released.

2015 A 25 year old is launched.

2016 Origin 1825, 17 year old port finish, 19 year old oloroso finish, an 18 year old and a 25 year old are released.

2017 A 13 year old is released.

2019 The 15 year old is back in the range and batch two of the 25 year old is released.

2020 Reserva Andalucia is released.

2022 American Oak is released.

2023 The 18 year old re-appears and a limited 15 year old with an oloroso finish in released.

2024 A 27 year old Reserva de Jerez is launched.

2025 Two finishes (Madeira and Amarone) are released.

Tasting notes Glencadam 10 years old:

GS – A light and delicate, floral nose, with tinned pears and fondant cream. Medium-bodied, smooth, with citrus fruits and gently-spiced oak on the palate. The finish is quite long and fruity, with a hint of barley.

GlenDronach

[glen•dro•nack]

Owner: Benriach Distillery Co (Brown Forman)

Region/district: Highlands

Founded: 1826

Status: Active (vc)

Capacity: 2 000 000 litres

Address: Forgue, Aberdeenshire AB54 6DB

Website: glendronachdistillery.com

Tel: 01466 730202

In spite of the current downturn in whisky sales (and, to be honest, in all kinds of alcoholic drinks) there are still a number of major expansions going on in the Scotch whisky industry.

Admittedly most of the decisions behind them were made a few years ago when the economic climate was different and tariffs and geopolitical turmoil were not an issue. Yet, at the same time it exemplifies an industry which has to focus on a reality and a market that seems likely ten years from now. The expansion at Glendronach is a good example of this. The decision to double the capacity was made by Brown Forman at least five years ago and the completion destined for 2024 has now been shifted to summer 2026 which happens to coincide with the distillery's 200th anniversary.

Virtually everything at the distillery will be upgraded which, in terms of production means more washbacks and another pair of stills. On top of that there is a multitude of issues that need to be taken care of – the mill, malt intakes, the malt bins etc.

The current equipment consists of a 3.76 ton cast iron mash tun with rakes, nine washbacks made of larch with a fermentation time of 50 to 65 hours, two wash stills with sharply descending lyne arms while those on the spirit stills have a much less accentuated angle. In 2025, 28 mashes per week and a total output of 1.9 million litres is expected.

The newly revamped core range consists of **Aged 12 years** and **Aged 15 years** – both of them matured in a combination of ex-oloroso and ex-PX casks. Furthermore there is the **Aged 18 years** matured solely in oloroso casks and **Aged 21 years,** again a combination of oloroso and PX sherry. Recent limited releases include The Master´s Anthology series launched in late 2024 with **Ode to the Valley** matured in a combination of ex-sherry and ruby port casks, the peated **The Embers** from oloroso/PX casks and **Ode to the Dark** – matured solely in PX casks. Finally, the range for duty-free consists of the **Aged 10 years** (PX and oloroso) and the **Aged 16 years** (PX, oloroso and port).

12 years old

History:

1826 The distillery is founded by a consortium with James Allardes as one of the owners.

1837 Parts of the distillery is destroyed in a fire.

1852 Walter Scott (from Teaninich) takes over.

1887 Walter Scott dies and Glendronach is taken over by a consortium from Leith.

1920 Charles Grant buys Glendronach for £9,000.

1960 William Teacher & Sons buys the distillery.

1966 The number of stills is increased to four.

1976 Allied Breweries takes over William Teacher & Sons.

1996 The distillery is mothballed.

2002 Production is resumed on 14th May.

2005 The distillery closes to rebuild from coal to indirect firing by steam. Reopens in September. Chivas Brothers (Pernod Ricard) becomes new owner through the acquisition of Allied Domecq.

2008 Pernod Ricard sells the distillery to the owners of BenRiach distillery.

2009 Relaunch of the whole range including 12, 15 and 18 year old.

2010 A 31 year old, a 1996 single cask and a total of 11 vintages and four wood finishes are released. A visitor centre is opened.

2011 The 21 year old Parliament and 11 vintages are released.

2012 A number of vintages are released.

2013 Recherché 44 years and a number of new vintages are released.

2014 Nine different single casks are released.

2015 The Hielan, 8 years old, is released.

2016 Brown Forman buys the distillery. Peated GlenDronach and Octaves Classic are released.

2017 A range of new single casks is released.

2018 Two bottlings for duty free are released - 10 year old Forgue and 16 year old Boynsmill.

2019 Port Wood, Traditionally Peated and batch 18 of the Cask Bottlings are released.

2022 A 50 year old is released.

2023 Cask Strength batch 12 is released.

2024 The Master´s Anthology Series is launched.

Tasting notes GlenDronach 12 years old:

GS – A sweet nose of Christmas cake fresh from the oven. Smooth on the palate, with sherry, soft oak, fruit, almonds and spices. The finish is comparatively dry and nutty, ending with bitter chocolate.

Glendullan

[glen•dull•an]

Owner: Diageo

Region/district: Speyside

Founded: 1897

Status: Active

Capacity: 5 000 000 litres

Address: Dufftown, Keith, Banffshire AB55 4DJ

Website: thesingleton.com

Tel: 01340 822100

With just 1,500 inhabitants, Dufftown's reputation as the major whisky town is nothing short of extraordinary. Mortlach was the first distillery to open in 1823 and when Glendullan started in 1897 it became the seventh distillery.

The founder, a blender from Aberdeen by the name of William Williams, was well acquainted with the owners of Glenfiddich, the Grant family, and when Glenfiddich started producing in 1888, an agreement was made entailing that Williams would buy the entire volume produced at the distillery. This contract was dissolved in 1890, when the two parties had differing opinions about the terms and conditions. Two years later, when the Grants founded Balvenie, Williams approached them again, looking for a new agreement but was rejected. Finally he had no other alternative than to build his own distillery, Glendullan, on a site by the river Fiddich just one kilometre south of Glenfiddich. The working distillery we see today, however, is of a much later date built in 1972, and the two plants operated simultaneously until 1985 when the old distillery was closed. Since 2007 Glendullan has been one of three single malts marketed under the brand The Singleton by Diageo. The other two are Glen Ord and Dufftown and in 2023 the trio sold 8.5 million bottles.

Glendullan is equipped with a 12 ton full lauter stainless steel mash tun. There are ten very large washbacks holding 88,000 litres each – eight made from larch and two (placed outdoors) made of stainless steel. The fermentation time during a seven-day production is 75 hours. Finally there are three pairs of stills producing a green/grassy newmake. Usually the distillery is mashing 21 times per week, producing five million litres of alcohol.

The core range consists of **12, 15** and **18 year old**. The Singleton Reserve Collection with **Classic** (American oak), **Double Matured** (American and European oak) and **Master's Art** (Muscat finish) is exclusive to duty free. The most recent limited expression was a **14 year old**, part of the Special Releases 2023 series,.

12 years old

History:

- 1896 William Williams & Sons, a blending company with Three Stars and Strahdon among its brands, founds the distillery.
- 1902 Glendullan is delivered to the Royal Court and becomes the favourite whisky of Edward VII.
- 1919 Macdonald Greenlees buys a share of the company and Macdonald Greenlees & Williams Distillers is formed.
- 1926 Distillers Company Limited (DCL) buys Glendullan.
- 1930 Glendullan is transferred to Scottish Malt Distillers (SMD).
- 1962 Major refurbishing and reconstruction.
- 1972 A brand new distillery is constructed next to the old one and both operate simultaneously during a few years.
- 1985 The oldest of the two distilleries is mothballed.
- 1995 The first launch of Glendullan in the Rare Malts series is a 22 year old from 1972.
- 2005 A 26 year old from 1978 is launched in the Rare Malts series.
- 2007 Singleton of Glendullan is launched in the USA.
- 2013 Singleton of Glendullan Liberty and Trinity are released for duty free.
- 2014 A 38 year old is released.
- 2015 Classic, Double Matured and Master´s Art are released.
- 2018 The Forgotten Drops 40 years old is released.
- 2019 House of Tully, part of the Game of Thrones series, as well as a 41 year old are released.
- 2021 A 19 year old with a cognac finish and a 28 year old with a second maturation in madeira casks are released.
- 2023 A 14 year old Chardonnay finish is a part of the 2023 Special Releases.

Tasting notes Singleton of Glendullan 12 years:

GS – The nose is spicy, with brittle toffee, vanilla, new leather and hazelnuts. Spicy and sweet on the smooth palate, with citrus fruits, more vanilla and fresh oak. Drying and pleasingly peppery in the finish.

Glen Elgin

[glen el•gin]

Owner: Diageo

Region/district: Speyside

Founded: 1898

Status: Active

Capacity: 2 700 000 litres

Address: Longmorn, Morayshire IV30 8SL

Website: malts.com

Tel: 01343 862100

While Glen Elgin may not be one the more well-known single malts on the market, it has often been a favourite amongst both whisky enthusiasts and blenders alike.

Its fruity, yet complex, character is derived from a combination of clear worts, long fermentations, a slow distillation and the use of worm tubs for the condensing of the spirit vapours. This makes it perfect as a top note to any quality blend, historically not least White Horse. This famous Scotch, registered as a brand in 1891, has seen a tremendous turn-around in the last decade selling 25 million bottles in 2024.

For a brief period Glen Elgin appeared in the ongoing Flora & Fauna range but in 2002 the owners decided to create The Hidden Malts which consisted of Glen Elgin, Caol Ila, Clynelish and Glen Ord. That range lasted for a few years before it was abandoned and today the official bottling of Glen Elgin sells about 40,000 bottles.

The distillery has been closed for some years now, mainly due to a substantial refurbishing but most likely also because the owners, Diageo, sometimes do this to balance their future inventory of single malt. According to the owners the plan is to start production again some time in 2027. By then there will have been a replacement of two stills, several washbacks and the four worm tubs as well as new roofs on the warehouses and a new office building.

Glen Elgin is equipped with an 8.4 ton Steinecker full lauter mash tun, nine washbacks (39,400 litres) made of larch and six small stills. The stills are connected to six wooden worm tubs in which the spirit vapours are condensed. When the distillery starts to produce again it will initially be a five-day week with 12 mashes before probably ramping it up to seven-days production with 16 mashes.

The only official bottling of the single malt is a **12 year old**, but a limited **18 year old**, matured in ex-bodega European oak butts was one of the Special Releases in 2017.

History:

- 1898 The former manager of Glenfarclas, William Simpson and banker James Carle found Glen Elgin.
- 1900 Production starts in May but the distillery closes just five months later.
- 1901 The distillery is auctioned for £4,000 to the Glen Elgin-Glenlivet Distillery Co. and is mothballed.
- 1906 The wine producer J. J. Blanche & Co. buys the distillery for £7,000 and production resumes.
- 1929 J. J. Blanche dies and the distillery is put up for sale again.
- 1930 Scottish Malt Distillers (SMD) buys it and the license goes to White Horse Distillers.
- 1964 Expansion from two to six stills plus other refurbishing takes place.
- 1992 The distillery closes for refurbishing and installation of new stills.
- 1995 Production resumes in September.
- 2001 A 12 year old is launched in the Flora & Fauna series.
- 2002 The Flora & Fauna series malt is replaced by Hidden Malt 12 years.
- 2003 A 32 year old cask strength from 1971 is released.
- 2008 A 16 year old is launched as a Special Release.
- 2009 Glen Elgin 1998, a single cask in the new Manager´s Choice range is released.
- 2017 An 18 year old is launched as part of the Special Releases.

12 years old

Tasting notes Glen Elgin 12 years old:

GS – A nose of rich, fruity sherry, figs and fragrant spice. Full-bodied, soft, malty and honeyed in the mouth. The finish is lengthy, slightly perfumed, with spicy oak.

Glenfarclas

[glen•fark•lass]

Owner: J. & G. Grant

Region/district: Speyside

Founded: 1836

Status: Active (vc)

Capacity: 3 500 000 litres

Address: Ballindalloch, Banffshire AB37 9BD

Website: glenfarclas.com

Tel: 01807 500257

With the sixth generation working at the distillery, Glenfarclas is one of the oldest family-owned distilleries in Scotland. There was a time though when external owners were brought in and it could have ended with a disaster.

In 1896, the infamous Pattison brothers joined the company as partners. Two years later they were accused of fraud on a scale that would bring the entire Scotch whisky industry to its knees. Needless to say, this was not the time to "be in bed" with the Pattisons who went into liquidation. Fortunately the agreement between Glenfarclas and the brothers opened up for the Grant family to buy out their shares from the liquidator and the distillery was once again wholly owned by the Grant family.

Glenfarclas is known for its devotion to sherry casks, an expensive way to mature whisky nowadays as ex-sherry casks can be hard to come by. Glenfarclas way of solving this has been to build a very long relationship with the winemaker and cooperage José y Miguel Martin near Huelva in Andalucia which supplies all their casks. The company was founded in 1915 and is, just like Glenfarclas, family-owned.

Glenfarclas is a classic single malt with a large fan base. Their whiskies, especially the older releases, are also competitively priced which perhaps comes from the fact that it is family-owned lacking share holders interested in quick revenues. In 2023 the brand sold 2.3 million bottles which puts it ahead of such a well-known single malt as Bowmore.

The distillery is equipped with a 16.5 ton semi-lauter mash tun, the largest in Scotland, and twelve stainless steel washbacks with a minimum fermentation time of 60 hours (but currently with an average of 106 hours). There are three pairs of directly fired stills. These are extremely important for the character of Glenfarclas single malt and it is the only distillery left in Scotland employing direct fire to all of their stills. The 2025 goal is to mash 8-9 times per week with a total of 2.2 million litres of pure alcohol. On site are no less than 42 dunnage warehouses and another six are currently being built.

The Glenfarclas core range consists of **10, 12, 15, 21** and **25 year old**. The previous 8 year old and the Heritage will join the range in late 2025 as the new **Heritage 8 year old**. Finally there are the **105 Cask Strength**, a **16 year old** version of the same as well as a **17 year old** reserved for the USA, Japan and Sweden. Limited releases (although released regularly) include the Warehouse Series with a **30, 35** and a **40 year old** as well as a recent addition, a **70 year old** – the first for Glenfarclas. A few years ago Glenfarclas withdrew from the global travel retail market but end of 2025 they are making a re-entry by way of an **11 year old** and a **16 year old**. The owners also continue to release bottlings in their **Family Casks** series with vintages ranging from **1954** to **2010**.

History:

- 1836 Robert Hay founds the distillery on the original site since 1797.
- 1865 Robert Hay passes away and John Grant and his son George buy the distillery. They lease it to John Smith at The Glenlivet Distillery.
- 1870 John Smith resigns in order to start Cragganmore and J. & G. Grant Ltd takes over.
- 1889 John Grant dies and George Grant takes over.
- 1890 George Grant dies and his widow Elsie takes over the license while sons John and George control operations.
- 1895 John and George Grant take over and form The Glenfarclas-Glenlivet Distillery Co. Ltd with the infamous Pattison, Elder & Co.
- 1898 Pattison becomes bankrupt. Glenfarclas encounters financial problems after a major overhaul of the distillery but survives by mortgaging and selling stored whisky to R. I. Cameron, a whisky broker from Elgin.
- 1914 John Grant leaves due to ill health and George continues alone.
- 1948 The Grant family celebrates the distillery's 100th anniversary, a century of active licensing. It is 9 years late, as the actual anniversary coincided with WW2.
- 1949 George Grant senior dies and sons George Scott and John Peter inherit the distillery.
- 1960 Stills are increased from two to four.
- 1968 Glenfarclas is first to launch a cask-strength single malt. It is later named Glenfarclas 105.
- 1972 Floor maltings is abandoned and malt is purchased centrally.
- 1973 A visitor centre is opened.
- 1976 Enlargement from four stills to six.
- 2002 George S Grant dies and is succeeded as company chairman by his son John L S Grant.

History continued:

2005 A 50 year old is released to commemorate the bi-centenary of John Grant´s birth.

2007 Family Casks, a series of single cask bottlings from 43 consecutive years, is released.

2008 New releases in the Family Cask range. Glenfarclas 105 40 years old is released.

2010 A 40 year old is released.

2011 Chairman´s Reserve and 175th Anniversary are released.

2012 A 58 year old and a 43 year old are released.

2013 An 18 year old for duty free is released as well as a 25 year old quarter cask.

2014 A 60 year old and a 1966 single fino sherry cask are released.

2015 A 1956 Sherry Cask and Family Reserve are released.

2016 40 year old, 50 year old, 1981 Port and 1986 cask strength are released.

2018 A 22 year old version of the 105 Cask Strength is released.

2019 Glenfarclas Trilogy is released.

2020 Pagoda Ruby Reserve 62 and 63 years old are released.

2021 A 185th anniversary bottling is launched.

2022 A 50 year old is launched.

2024 A 16 year old version of the 105 Cask Strength is released.

2025 A 70 year old is launched together with two new entries to the travel retail market.

Tasting notes Glenfarclas 10 year old:

GS – Full and richly sherried on the nose, with nuts, fruit cake and a hint of citrus fruit. The palate is big, with ripe fruit, brittle toffee, some peat and oak. Medium length and gingery in the finish.

105 Cask Strength

16 years old

12 years old

18 years old

Family Cask 1959

21 years old

70 years old

Glenfiddich

[glen•fidd•ick]

Owner:
William Grant & Sons

Region/district:
Speyside

Founded:
1886

Status:
Active (vc)

Capacity:
21 000 000 litres

Address: Dufftown, Keith, Banffshire AB55 4DH

Website:
glenfiddich.com

Tel:
01340 820373 (vc)

The largest malt distillery in Scotland is about to expand again, only five years since the capacity was increased by almost 60%. There are several reasons for that but one is most probably an acquisition announced a year ago.

A press release presented the plans for W Grant to buy Famous Grouse from Edrington and in March 2025 the UK Competition and Markets Authority gave the green light for the deal to go through. With sales of 40 million bottles per year for the legendary blend, the take-over was, if not completely surprising, definitely one of the biggest news last year. On top of that it included the blended malt Naked Malt with a volume of 600,000 bottles.

Previously owning the number one single malt (Glenfiddich) and the number four blend (Grant's) there was obviously need for more malt production for the future. In spring 2024 a planning application was approved by the Moray council for eight more washbacks (with an option for another eight) as well as three wash stills, equipped with TVR (Thermal Vapour Recompression) for energy efficiency, and four spirit stills. While no figures have been communicated by the owners this could mean the total capacity some time next year could be 25 million litres!

Currently Glenfiddich is equipped with four, stainless steel full lauter mash tuns – all with a ten ton mash. There are 48 washbacks (40,000 litres) made of Douglas fir with a fermentation time of 74 hours. The total number of stills is 43; 16 wash stills (9,500 litres) and 27 spirit stills (5,900 litres). 15 of them, in the old still house number two, are directly fired using gas. An interesting new project, completed in 2022, was to install separate receivers on one wash still and two spirit stills. This will enable the owners to run experimental trials without interfering with the normal production. In recent years the production plan has entailed 105 mashes per week and 21 million litres of pure alcohol.

The latest expansion was signified by an attention to aesthetic beauty. The stairs of the granite stillhouse lead up to a magnificent glazed entrance. On entering, the stills are lined up on each side of an elegant dark grey shale floor. When reaching the back of the building, the room curves left where another 12 stills are placed.

The core range consists of **12, 15** and **18 year old.** Included are also a **19 year old** (USA). an **18 year old amontillado** (Taiwan), a **14 year old bourbon barrel reserve** (USA, Canada and France) and a **Triple Oak Twelve** (France). A separate range is the Grand Series with **21 year old Gran Reserva, 22 year old Grand Cortez** (for Asia), **23 year old Grand Cru, 26 year old Grand Couronne** and the **Grand Chateau 31 year old**. In the Time series we find **30, 40** and **50 year olds** and the Experimental Series include **Project XX, Fire & Cane** and **The Orchard Experiment**. In recent limited releases we find the **Archive Collection** of different single casks. For travel retail there is the **Perpetual Collection** with **Vat 01** and **Vat 02** without age statements, the **15 year old Vat 03** and the **18 year old Vat 04.**

History:

1886 The distillery is founded by William Grant.

1887 The first distilling takes place on Christmas Day.

1892 William Grant builds Balvenie.

1898 The blending company Pattisons, largest customer of Glenfiddich, files for bankruptcy and Grant decides to blend their own whisky. Standfast becomes one of their major brands.

1903 William Grant & Sons is formed.

1957 The famous, three-cornered bottle is introduced.

1958 The floor maltings is closed.

1963 Glennfiddich becomes the first whisky to be marketed as single malt in the UK and the rest of the world.

1964 A version of Standfast's three-cornered bottle is launched for Glenfiddich in green glass.

1969 Glenfiddich becomes the first distillery in Scotland to open a visitor centre.

1974 16 new stills are installed.

2001 1965 Vintage Reserve is launched in a limited edition of 480 bottles. Glenfiddich 1937 is bottled (61 bottles).

2002 Glenfiddich Gran Reserva 21 years old, Caoran Reserve 12 years and Glenfiddich Rare Collection 1937 (61 bottles) are launched.

2003 1973 Vintage Reserve (440 bottles) is launched.

2004 1991 Vintage Reserve (13 years) and 1972 Vintage Reserve (519 bottles) are launched.

2006 1973 Vintage Reserve, 33 years (861 bottles) and 12 year old Toasted Oak are released.

2007 1976 Vintage Reserve, 31 years is released.

2008 1977 Vintage Reserve is released.

2009 A 50 year old is released.

History continued:

2010 Rich Oak, 1978 Vintage Reserve, the 6th edition of 40 year old and Snow Phoenix are released.

2011 1974 Vintage Reserve and a 19 year old Madeira finish are released.

2012 Cask of Dreams and Millenium Vintage are released.

2013 A 19 year old red wine finish and 1987 Anniversary Vintage are released. Cask Collection is released for duty free.

2014 The 26 year old Glenfiddich Excellence, Rare Oak 25 years and Glenfiddich The Original are released.

2015 A 14 year old for the US market is released.

2016 Finest Solera is released for travel retail. Two expressions in the Experimental Series are launched; Project XX and IPA Experiment.

2017 Winter Storm is released.

2018 Fire & Cane is released.

2019 Grand Cru 23 year old and Rare Collection Cask No. 20050 are released.

2020 Gran Cortes 22 year old, Grande Couronne 26 year old and two 1975 Vintages are released. The distillery capacity is doubled.

2022 The cider finished Orchard Experiment and the Perpetual Collection are released.

2023 The 29 year old Grand Yozakura is launched.

2024 Grand Chateau 31 year old and Archive Collection are launched.

Tasting notes Glenfiddich 12 year old:

GS – Delicate, floral and slightly fruity on the nose. Well mannered in the mouth, malty, elegant and soft. Rich, fruit flavours dominate the palate, with a developing nuttiness and an elusive whiff of peat smoke in the fragrant finish.

Project XX

Orchard Experiment

Perpetual Vat 01

Our Original Twelve

Grand Chateau 31 years

Grand Yozakura 29 years

Our Solera Fifteen

Our Small Batch Eighteen

Glen Garioch

[glen gee•ree]

Owner: Suntory Global Spirits

Region/district: Eastern Highlands

Founded: 1797

Status: Active (vc)

Capacity: 1 350 000 litres

Address: Oldmeldrum, Inverurie, Aberdeenshire AB51 0ES

Website: glengarioch.com

Tel: 01651 873450

Quite often you hear whisky aficionados claim that the "big companies" are focused on efficiency and yield and by doing that they stand the risk of sacrificing flavour and character in their product.

While they praise those new and smaller distilleries in Scotland whose aim is to mimic how whisky was made in the 1950s by using heritage barley and old production techniques. There may be a bit of truth in this generalisation but several of the larger producers are also on the quest of improving flavour and one of the best examples is Suntory. This Japanese owner of five Scottish malt distilleries have made huge investments in the last five years where the pay-off isn't more spirit but an improved taste.

It all started at Glen Garioch four years ago when floor malting was re-installed and the wash still went back to being directly heated. These two measures will lower the yield but add to the flavour. Trials with brewer's yeast (commonplace in the industry forty years ago) have the same effect. More washbacks at the other distilleries were installed by Suntory - not to produce more alcohol but to increase fermentation time and by that adding more fruity flavours.

Glen Garioch is equipped with a four ton full lauter mash tun, nine stainless steel washbacks with an average fermentation time of 72 hours, one direct-fired wash still and one spirit still. Some 25% of their malt needs is produced in-house. In 2025 they will be trialing both medium and heavily peated malt The two stills have some of the sharpest descending lyne arms in the industry with very little reflux. Together with a very clear wort, the owners attempt to obtain a robust, yet fruity, newmake. In 2025, 15 mashes per week and a total of 650,000 litres of pure alcohol are planned.

The core range is the **1797 Founder's Reserve** and a **12 year old.** Previous limited expressions have included **Virgin Oak, The Renaissance** series, **The American Trilogy** and a number of vintage single casks. The latest, in May 2023, was a **1979 single cask** (44 years old) exclusively available at the distillery.

12 years old

History:

- 1797 John Manson founds the distillery.
- 1798 Thomas Simpson becomes licensee.
- 1825 Ingram, Lamb & Co. bcome new owners.
- 1837 The distillery is bought by John Manson & Co.
- 1884 The distillery is sold to J. G. Thomson & Co.
- 1908 William Sanderson buys the distillery.
- 1933 Sanderson & Son merges with the gin maker Booth's Distilleries Ltd.
- 1937 Booth´s Distilleries Ltd is acquired by Distillers Company Limited (DCL).
- 1968 Glen Garioch is decommissioned.
- 1970 It is sold to Stanley P. Morrison Ltd.
- 1973 Production starts again.
- 1978 Stills are increased from two to three.
- 1994 Suntory controls all of Morrison Bowmore Distillers Ltd.
- 1995 The distillery is mothballed in October.
- 1997 The distillery reopens in August and from now on, it is using unpeated malt.
- 2004 Glen Garioch 46 year old is released.
- 2005 15 year old Bordeaux Cask Finish is launched. A visitor centre opens in October.
- 2006 An 8 year old is released.
- 2009 Complete revamp of the range - 1979 Founders Reserve (unaged), 12 year old, Vintage 1978 and 1990 are released.
- 2010 1991 vintage is released.
- 2011 Vintage 1986 and 1994 are released.
- 2012 Vintage 1995 and 1997 are released.
- 2013 Virgin Oak, Vintage 1999 and 11 single casks are released.
- 2014 Glen Garioch Renaissance Collection 15 years is released.
- 2018 The fourth and final installment of the Rennaisance Collection is released.
- 2021 Floor malting is re-installed.
- 2023 A 44 year old single cask is released.

Tasting notes Glen Garioch 12 years old:

GS – Luscious and sweet on the nose, peaches and pineapple, vanilla, malt and a hint of sherry. Full-bodied and nicely textured, with more fresh fruit on the palate, along with spice, brittle toffee and finally dry oak notes.

Exceptional Designs

A wooden Coffey still
at Spirit of Hven Distillery in Sweden

Glenglassaugh

[glen•gla•ssa]

Owner: Glenglassaugh Distillery Co (BenRiach Distillery Co.)

Region/district: Highlands

Founded: 1875

Status: Active (vc)

Capacity: 1 100 000 litres

Address: Portsoy, Banffshire AB45 2SQ

Website: glenglassaugh.com

Tel: 01261 842367

It probably hasn't escaped anyone that the current economic and geopolitical climate has slowed down sales of Scotch, as with any other alcohol product for that matter, in the last year or two.

This has led to some producers balancing their future stock of spirit – or in short – to temporarily cut down on production. This has not been unusual in the past. However, when news appeared that Glenglassaugh and Benriach would share workforce during 2025 meaning that each distillery would be ”silent” for part of the year, it was in social media taken as either the end of Glenglassaugh or indeed Scotch as a category.

The truth is that since its resurrection in 2008, Glenglassaugh has never produced at full capacity. During a few years in the past decade there was actually no production at all. In 2024 the production was 620,000 litres of alcohol and this will be slightly lowered to 500,000 litres in 2025. While it is always tragic if one or two people are laid off, the news about Glenglassaugh are far less dramatic on a grander scale. Rachel Barrie, one of the most respected and talented master blenders in the industry, is responsible for the owners', Brown Forman, Scotch whiskies. The new range of Benriach in 2020 lifted the sales figures and her new core range for Glenglassaugh in 2023 will hopefully do the same for that brand.

The distillery equipment consists of a 5 ton cast iron mash tun with rakes, four wooden washbacks and two stainless steel ones, with a fermentation time between 54 and 80 hours. There is one pair of stills. Around 50,000 litres of the production in 2025 will be peated spirit (30ppm).

The core range is headed by a **12 year old** matured in bourbon, sherry and red wine casks. There are also two expressions with no age statement; **Sandend** matured in bourbon and manzanilla sherry and **Portsoy** in a combination of sherry, bourbon and port. In January 2024 three single casks were released in the **Serpentine Coastal Cask Collection**; a **48 year old** red wine barrique, a **49 year old** bourbon barrel and a **51 year old** oloroso puncheon.

12 year old

History:

1873 The distillery is founded by James Moir.

1887 Alexander Morrison embarks on renovation work.

1892 Morrison sells the distillery to Robertson & Baxter. They in turn sell it on to Highland Distilleries Company for £15,000.

1908 The distillery closes.

1931 The distillery reopens.

1936 The distillery closes.

1957 Reconstruction takes place.

1960 The distillery reopens.

1986 Glenglassaugh is mothballed.

2005 A 22 year old is released.

2006 Three limited editions are released - 19 years old, 38 years old and 44 years old.

2008 The distillery is bought by the Scaent Group for £5m. Three bottlings are released - 21, 30 and 40 year old.

2009 New make spirit and 6 months old are released.

2010 A 26 year old replaces the 21 year old.

2011 A 35 year old and the first bottling from the new owners production, a 3 year old, are released.

2012 A visitor centre is inaugurated and Glenglassaugh Revival is released.

2013 BenRiach Distillery Co buys the distillery and Glenglassaugh Evolution is released.

2014 The peated Torfa is released as well as eight different single casks and Massandra Connection (35 and 41 years old).

2015 The second batch of single casks is released.

2016 Brown Forman buys the distillery. Octaves Classic and Octaves Peated are released.

2017 Three wood finishes are released.

2018 Batch three in the Rare Cask series and the second release of Octaves are released

2020 Ten single casks in the series Coastal Casks are launched.

2021 A 50 year old is released.

2023 A new core range is introduced; 12 year old, Sandend and Portsoy.

2024 Serpentine Coastal Cask Collection is launched.

Tasting notes Glenglassaugh 12 years old:

IW – Fresh, ripe fruit drizzled with caramel sauce on the nose, becomes more luscious when butterscotch appears. Light texture on the palate from which butterscotch and caramel emerge. Then fudge joins in, poached fruit in syrup and cinnamon hints make it richer and luscious.

Glengoyne

[glen•goyn]

Owner:
Ian Macleod Distillers

Region/district:
Southern Highlands

Founded:
1833

Status:
Active (vc)

Capacity:
1 200 000 litres

Address: Dumgoyne by Killearn, Glasgow G63 9LB

Website:
glengoyne.com

Tel:
01360 550254 (vc)

The owners of Glengoyne, Ian Macleod Distillers, have been unusually busy in the last few years. Operating two distilleries (Tamdhu being the other one) alongside working as bottlers and blenders of a range of spirits simply didn't seem enough for them.

In 2023 they re-opened the legendary Rosebank distillery in Falkirk. Not just in terms of production, but they also built one of the most impressive visitor centres in the business. Meanwhile they had been working on plans to establish a malt distillery in India and in March 2024 they fired up the stills at the Una distillery in Himachal Pradesh in northern India. The Indian whisky market is thriving and several Scottish whisky companies have seen it as important of being present there also as producers. Finally, back in Scotland, near the airport on Islay, Ian Macleod Distillers have recently opened up Laggan Bay, the 11th whisky distillery on Islay with a one million litre capacity. Glengoyne, beautifully situated in the Trossachs, were the first to introduce biological treatment of the environmentally harmful by-products from distillation, especially the copper from the spent lees. In 2011 they created wetlands where 15,000 plants absorb the impure compounds.

The distillery is equipped with a 3.84 ton semi lauter mash tun. There are also six Oregon pine washbacks, as well as the rather unusual combination of one wash still and two spirit stills. Both short (56 hours) and long (110 hours) fermentations are practiced. The plan for 2025 is to vary between eight and ten mashes over the year and produce just over 600,000 litres of alcohol.

The core range consists of **10, 12, 15, 18** and **Cask Strength** (released in batches). Included are also **21, 25** and **30 year old** in the Sherry Oak range. The Oak Master´s Series include **White Oak, White Oak 24 year old** and (launched in August 2025) **Mizunara Oak**. For travel retail there is The Spirit of Time range which consists of the **12 year old First Fill**, predominantly from ex-bourbon and recently replacing a 10 year old, the **15 year old PX Cask Edition** and the **26 year old** oloroso matured.

12 years old

History:

1833 The distillery is licensed under the name Burnfoot Distilleries by the Edmonstone family.

1876 Lang Brothers buys the distillery and changes the name to Glenguin.

1905 The name changes to Glengoyne.

1965 Robertson & Baxter takes over Lang Brothers and the distillery is refurbished. The stills are increased from two to three.

2001 Glengoyne Scottish Oak Finish (16 years old) is launched.

2003 Ian MacLeod Distillers Ltd buys the distillery plus the brand Langs from the Edrington Group for £7.2 million.

2005 A 19 year old, a 32 year old and a 37 year old cask strength are launched.

2006 Nine "choices" from Stillmen, Mashmen and Manager are released.

2007 A new version of the 21 year old, two Warehousemen´s Choice, Vintage 1972 and two single casks are released.

2008 A 16 year old Shiraz cask finish, three single casks and Heritage Gold are released.

2009 A 40 year old, two single casks and a new 12 year old are launched.

2010 Two single casks, 1987 and 1997, released.

2011 A 24 year old single cask is released.

2012 A 15 and an 18 year old are released as well as a Cask Strength with no age statement.

2013 A limited 35 year old is launched.

2014 A 25 year old is released.

2018 A new range for duty free is released – Cuartillo, Balbaine, a 28 year old and Glengoyne PX.

2019 Glengoyne Legacy is launched.

2020 A 50 year old and Glengoyne Legacy Chapter Two are released.

2022 The Spirit of Time series is released for travel retail.

2024 White Oak 10 and 24 year old are released.

2025 Mizunara Oak is launched in the Oak Master´s Series.

Tasting notes Glengoyne 12 years old:

GS – Slightly earthy on the nose, with nutty malt, ripe apples, and a hint of honey. The palate is full and fruity, with milk chocolate, ginger and vanilla. The finish is medium in length, with milky coffee and soft spices.

Glen Grant

[glen grant]

Owner: Campari Group
Region/district: Speyside
Founded: 1840
Status: Active (vc)
Capacity: 6 200 000 litres
Address: Elgin Road, Rothes, Banffshire AB38 7BS
Website: glengrant.com
Tel: 01340 832118

Glen Grant has been closed to visitors for quite some time now and will remain so until spring 2026. The reason is a complete make-over of not only the visitor centre but also the magnificent garden.

The Major's Garden, as it is called, was founded in 1886 by then owner, Major James Grant. Covering 22 acres of the glen behind the distillery, the Victorian garden is filled with beautiful orchards, lawns and flowerbeds. The refurbishment includes a 27 metre long and 10 metre high glasshouse which will not only house exotic plants but will also have space for up to 25 seated visitors.

Major James Grant was the nephew of one of the founders. He took over the distillery in 1872 and ran it for almost 60 years until his death in 1931. James was an officer in the Rifle Volunteers, advanced to the rank of major and was always referred to, even after his retirement from the army, as The Major. He had a great interest in technology and in 1883 Glen Grant became the first distillery in Scotland to install electricity for the purpose of lighting. He also took active part in the building of the Strathspey railway which ran through Rothes. As a true Victorian gentleman, he was also a keen hunter and often went on expeditions to India and Africa.

Glen Grant is equipped with a 12.3 ton semi-lauter mash tun, ten Oregon pine washbacks with a minimum fermentation time of 48 hours and four pairs of stills. The wash stills are peculiar in that they have vertical sides at the base of the neck and all eight stills are fitted with purifiers. The plan for 2025 is to mash 20 times per week for 25 weeks which will result in 2.5 million litres of alcohol. An extremely efficient £5m bottling hall was inaugurated in 2013. It has a capacity of 12,000 bottles an hour and Glen Grant is unique among the large distillers in bottling its entire production on site.

The core range for Glen Grant is made up by **Arboralis** without age statement and matured in a combination of ex-bourbon and ex-sherry, a **10 year old,** a **12 year old** matured in both bourbon and sherry casks, a **15 year old batch strength** and an **18 year old** bourbon matured. Added in 2023, in what is known as the Glasshouse Collection, were a **21 year old** and a **25 year old** and these were recently complemented by a **30 year old**.

While the oldest official bottling of Glen Grant that has ever appeared was a 70 year old to celebrate Queen Elizabeth II and her 70 years on the throne, a number of old expressions can be expected in the new Splendour Collection. A **65 year old**, matured in an ex-sherry butt and bottled at the remarkable strength of 55.5%, was the first release in March 2025. Finally there is the Exploration series available in travel retail. The first release, **Exploration No. 1**, appeared in spring 2025 and had been finished in Carribean rum casks.

History:

1840 The brothers James and John Grant, managers of Dandelaith Distillery, found the distillery.

1861 The distillery becomes the first to install electric lighting.

1864 John Grant dies.

1872 James Grant passes away and the distillery is inherited by his son, James junior (Major James Grant).

1897 James Grant decides to build another distillery across the road; it is named Glen Grant No. 2.

1902 Glen Grant No. 2 is mothballed.

1931 Major Grant dies and is succeeded by his grandson Major Douglas Mackessack.

1953 J. & J. Grant merges with George & J. G. Smith who runs Glenlivet distillery, forming The Glenlivet & Glen Grant Distillers Ltd.

1961 Armando Giovinetti and Douglas Mackessak found a friendship that leads to Glen Grant becoming the most sold malt whisky in Italy.

1965 Glen Grant No. 2 is back in production, but renamed Caperdonich.

1972 The Glenlivet & Glen Grant Distillers merges with Hill Thompson & Co. and Longmorn-Glenlivet Ltd to form The Glenlivet Distillers.

1973 Stills are increased from four to six.

1977 The Chivas & Glenlivet Group (Seagrams) buys Glen Grant Distillery. Stills are increased from six to ten.

2001 Pernod Ricard and Diageo buy Seagrams Spirits & Wine, with Pernod acquiring Chivas Group.

2006 Campari buys Glen Grant for €115m.

2007 The entire range is re-launched.

Exploration No. 1 15 years old 30 years old

History continued:

2008 Two limited cask strengths - a 16 year old and a 27 year old - are released.

2009 Cellar Reserve 1992 is released.

2010 A 170th Anniversary bottling is released.

2011 A 25 year old is released.

2012 A 19 year old Distillery Edition is released.

2013 Five Decades is released and a bottling hall is built.

2014 A 50 year old and the Rothes Edition 10 years old is released.

2015 Glen Grant Fiodh is launched.

2016 A 12 year old and an 18 year old are launched and a 12 year old non chill-filtered is released for travel retail.

2018 A 15 year old is released for the duty free market.

2020 Arboralis with no age statement is released.

2021 A 60 year old Dennis Malcolm Anniversary bottling is released.

2023 A 21 and a 25 year old are added to the core range and a 70 year old is launched.

2025 A 65 year old and Exploration No. 1 are released.

Tasting notes Glen Grant 12 year old:

GS – A blast of fresh fruit – oranges, pears and lemons – on the initial nose, before vanilla and fudge notes develop. The fruit carries over on to the palate, with honey, caramel and sweet spices. Medium in length, with cinnamon and soft oak in the finish.

12 years old Arboralis

Glengyle

[glen•gajl]

Owner: Mitchell´s Glengyle Ltd

Region/district: Campbeltown

Founded: 2004

Status: Active

Capacity: 750 000 litres

Address: Glengyle Road, Campbeltown, Argyll PA28 6LR

Website: kilkerran.scot

Tel: 01586 551710

The most prosperous time for Campbeltown was in the Victorian days when shipbuilding, fishing and coal mining made most of the inhabitants quite wealthy.

This was also the time when at least 25 whisky distilleries were operating in this little town with, today, only 5,000 people. The downturn came during the first world war and by 1934, when Rieclachan closed, only two distilleries remained – Glen Scotia and Springbank. Seventy years later the number grew to three when Glengyle (closed in 1925) was re-opened by the owners of Springbank. In 2009 the Campbeltown Malts Festival was launched to celebrate the town's whisky heritage and it now runs yearly at the end of May. On top of that there are at least three distilleries either being built or planned in and around the town.

Glengyle, which lies more or less on the same ground as Springbank, is equipped with a 4.2 ton semi-lauter mash tun and four wooden washbacks with a fermentation time varying between 72 and 110 hours. There is also one wash still (18,000 litres) and one spirit still (15,000 litres). Malt is obtained both from the neighbouring Springbank and from external maltsters but there are also plans to install drum maltings at Glengyle. Operations between Glengyle and Springbank are managed by the same staff. The capacity is 750,000 litres, but considerably smaller amounts have been produced over the years. In 2025 the plan is to mash five times per week between October and December. This will amount to around 90,000 litres with 85% made up of 'regular' Kilkerran and the rest of heavily peated spirit. A large bottling hall which will serve both distilleries is currently being built next to Glengyle and will be ready in mid 2026.

The whiskies from Glengyle are sold under the name Kilkerran. The first core **12 year old** was launched in 2016. In 2017, an **8 year old cask strength** appeared. This is an annual release but released in batches. Finally in 2020 a **16 year old** was added to the range. The first batch of **Kilkerran Heavily Peated** (with a phenol specification of 80ppm in the barley) was released in spring 2019 and in summer 2024 a series of **single casks** were released to celebrate the distillery´s 20th anniversary.

12 years old

History:

- 1872 The original Glengyle Distillery is built by William Mitchell.
- 1919 The distillery is bought by West Highland Malt Distilleries Ltd.
- 1925 The distillery is closed.
- 1929 The warehouses (but no stock) are purchased by the Craig Brothers and rebuilt into a petrol station and garage.
- 1941 The distillery is acquired by the Bloch Brothers.
- 1957 Campbell Henderson applies for planning permission with the intention of reopening the distillery.
- 2000 Hedley Wright, owner of Springbank Distillery and related to founder William Mitchell, acquires the distillery.
- 2004 The first distillation after reconstruction takes place in March.
- 2007 The first limited release - a 3 year old.
- 2009 Kilkerran "Work in progress" is released.
- 2010 "Work in progress 2" is released.
- 2011 "Work in progress 3" is released.
- 2012 "Work in progress 4" is released.
- 2013 "Work in progress 5" is released and this time in two versions - bourbon and sherry.
- 2014 "Work in progress 6" is released in two versions - bourbon and sherry.
- 2015 "Work in progress 7" is released in two versions - bourbon and sherry.
- 2016 Kilkerran 12 years old is released.
- 2017 Kilkerran 8 year old cask strength is released.
- 2019 Kilkerran Heavily Peated is released.
- 2020 A 16 year old is released.
- 2021 Batch four of Heavily Peated and batch two of the 16 year old are released.
- 2022 Two new batches of the 8 year old cask strength are launched.
- 2023 New batches of the 8 year old and Heavily Peated are released.
- 2024 A series of single casks is released.

Tasting notes Kilkerran 12 year old:

GS – Initially, quite reticent on the nose, then peaty fruit notes develop. Oily and full on the palate, with peaches and more overt smoke, plus an earthy quality. Castor oil and liquorice sticks. Slick in the medium-length finish, with slightly drying oak and enduring liquorice.

Exceptional Designs

Egg-shaped, concrete washbacks
at Maison Lineti Distillery in France

Glen Keith

[glen keeth]

Owner:
Chivas Brothers (Pernod Ricard)

Region/district:
Speyside

Founded:
1957

Status:
Active

Capacity:
6 000 000 litres

Address: Station Road, Keith, Banffshire AB55 3BU

Website:
secret-speyside.com

Tel:
01542 783042

History:

1957 The Distillery is founded by Chivas Brothers (Seagrams).

1958 Production starts.

1970 The first gas-fuelled still in Scotland is installed, the number of stills increases from three to five.

1976 Own maltings (Saladin box) ceases.

1983 A sixth still is installed.

1994 The first official bottling, a 10 year old, is released as part of Seagram's Heritage Selection.

1999 The distillery is mothballed.

2001 Pernod Ricard takes over Chivas Brothers from Seagrams.

2012 The reconstruction and refurbishing of the distillery begins.

2013 Production starts again.

2017 A Distillery Edition is launched.

2019 Three bottlings in The Secret Speyside Collection are launched.

2024 A 31 year old is released in the Secret Speyside Collection.

Every time I came to Keith during the first years of the new millennium, I was dumbfounded by the fact that Glen Keith was not producing. Obviously being a fairly new and large distillery and owned by one of the big companies – it didn't make sense to me.

To understand the reason we need to look at the history. There were two recessions, 1980 to 1983 and 1990 to 1992, which impacted the economy as a whole especially in the UK and Europe and this was followed by another one in 1997-1998 in the rather young whisky market of Far East. Soon after, Chivas Brothers (including Glen Keith) was taken over by Pernod Ricard (in 2001). For five years in the early new millennium consumption of Scotch didn't increase but remained pretty stable comparing to the volumes from the mid 1990s. Glen Keith and Imperial had been mothballed in 1999 by Seagrams and Pernod Ricard, as the new owners, did the same with Allt-a-Bhainne and Braeval in 2002. Production volumes were simply too high compared to the consumption at the time. While Imperial remained closed, Allt-a-Bhainne and Braeval reopened in 2005 and 2008 and Glen Keith in 2013. The similarities with the current downturn are striking and reminds us of the intricacies of producing whisky when you have to predict future sales at least ten years in advance.

Glen Keith is equipped with a Briggs 8.4 ton full lauter mash tun. There are three tun rooms with three wooden washbacks in number one, another six wooden in number two and six made of stainless steel in the third together with the mash tun. Finally there are six stills with unusually long, slightly descending lyne arms. The production is usually between 38 and 41 mashes per week with the possibility to produce 6 million litres of pure alcohol.

The official expression from Glen Keith is **Distillery Edition**, exclusive to the UK. There is also The **Secret Speyside Collection** where Glen Keith is represented by a **31 year old** released in 2024. Finally, there is a **22 year old cask strength** bottling in the Distillery Reserve Collection, available at all Chivas visitor centres.

Distillery Edition

Tasting notes Glen Keith Distillery Edition:

IR – Sweet and fruity on the nose with notes of toffee and apples. Smooth on the palate, vanilla, tropical fruits, marzipan, sponge cake, honey, pears and a hint of dry oak in the finish.

Glenkinchie

[glen•kin•chee]

Owner:
Diageo

Region/district:
Lowlands

Founded:
1837

Status:
Active (vc)

Capacity:
2 500 000 litres

Address: Pencaitland, Tranent, East Lothian EH34 5ET

Website:
malts.com

Tel:
01875 342004

Glenkinchie is located in a part of the country known as East Lothian. It takes its name after Lot, the alleged ruler of southeast Scotland in ancient times and the brother-in-law of King Arthur. It is often referred to as Scotland's garden county.

With more hours of sunshine than anywhere else in Scotland, the farmland consisting of an abundance of meadows, groves and gardens is striking. Sometimes Diageo call Glenkinchie "the garden distillery" which has been emphasised in the new visitor centre that was opened up a few years ago as a part the Four Corners of Scotland. This was a huge investment in whisky tourism by Diageo, also including Cardhu, Clynelish and Caol Ila distilleries. Buildings were torn down to give way for a large landscaped garden leading up to the distillery. In 2020 they also partnered with a local honey manufacturer and put up bee hives in the garden. The proximity to Edinburgh makes it perfect for a day trip while visiting the city.

The character of the matured Glenkinchie single malt is elegant, floral and citrusy. The newmake, on the other hand, has a completely different character. Clear wort and long fermentations indicate fruitiness but the declining lyne arms and the worm tubs compensate for what estery notes came from the wash and the newmake ends up grainy and sulphury.

The distillery is equipped with a 9 ton full lauter mash tun and six wooden washbacks with a combination of short (66 hours) and long fermentations (110 hours). There are two stills, connected to a wormtub, with the wash still being the largest in Scotland. The production regime for several years now has been a five-day week with 10 mashes, producing just under 2 million litres of alcohol.

The core range consists of a **12 year old** and a **Distiller's Edition** with a finish in amontillado sherry casks. A limited **16 year old** available only at the distillery was released in 2020. In autumn 2023 a **27 year old**, matured in a combination of refill American barrels and European oak butts, appeared in the Special Releases range.

History:

1825 A distillery known as Milton is founded by John and George Rate.

1837 The Rate brothers are registered as licensees of a distillery named Glenkinchie.

1853 John Rate sells the distillery to a farmer by the name of Christie who converts it to a sawmill.

1881 The buildings are bought by a consortium from Edinburgh.

1890 Glenkinchie Distillery Company is founded. Reconstruction and refurbishment is on-going for the next few years.

1914 Glenkinchie forms Scottish Malt Distillers (SMD) with four other Lowland distilleries.

1939-1945 Glenkinchie is one of few distilleries allowed to maintain production during the war.

1968 Floor maltings is decommissioned.

1969 The maltings is converted into a museum.

1988 Glenkinchie 10 years becomes one of selected six in the Classic Malt series.

1998 A Distiller's Edition with Amontillado finish is launched.

2007 A 12 year old and a 20 year old cask strength are released.

2010 A cask strength exclusive for the visitor centre, a 1992 single cask and a 20 year old are released.

2016 A 24 year old and a distillery exclusive without age statement are released.

2019 A limited version is released in connection with The Royal Edinburgh Military Tattoo.

2020 A new visitor experience is opened and a 16 year old distillery exclusive is released.

2023 A 27 year old is released as part of this year´s Special Releases

Tasting notes Glenkinchie 12 years old:

GS – The nose is fresh and floral, with spices and citrus fruits, plus a hint of marshmallow. Notably elegant. Water releases cut grass and lemon notes. Medium-bodied, smooth, sweet and fruity, with malt, butter and cheesecake. The finish is comparatively long and drying, initially rather herbal.

12 years old

Glenlivet

[glen•<u>liv</u>•it]

Owner: Chivas Brothers (Pernod Ricard)

Region/district: Speyside

Founded: 1824

Status: Active (vc)

Capacity: 21 000 000 litres

Address: Ballindalloch, Banffshire AB37 9DB

Website: theglenlivet.com

Tel: 01340 821720 (vc)

At least since the mid 1960s, Glenfiddich had been the number one single malt in terms of sales. Then, in 2014 and 2015, Glenlivet managed to take over the leader and this happened again in 2021 and 2022.

In the troublesome year of 2023, however, Glenlivet slipped by more than 10% while Glenfiddich managed to hold its ground and even increased by 5% to almost 20 million bottles. There are no official figures for 2024 from the owners of Glenfiddich (W Grant) but since sales of Glenlivet slipped by another 7% in 2024 it seems safe to say that Glenfiddich is still in the lead. In USA however, Glenlivet is still number one.

Following the Spirits Act of 1823, founder George Smith was one of the first producers to take out a license to distil whisky – much to the dismay of all the remaining illicit distillers in the Livet valley who threatened to burn down his distillery. The buildings we see today, however, are of a later date. The first distillery was Upper Drumin a few kilometres to the north of the current distillery. A decade later George Smith took over another distillery at Delnabo Farm near Tomintoul and in 1859 the current distillery was erected at Minmore.

Since 2009 the distillery capacity has been expanded in two steps from 5.8 million litres to the current 21 million. The last step, completed in 2018, was a second distillery behind the warehouses. The current complete equipment at Glenlivet consists of two Briggs full lauter mash tuns, each with a 14 ton charge. Sixteen wooden washbacks are augmented by 16 made of stainless steel in the new distillery – all filled with 59,000 litres and with a fermentation time of 50-52 hours. Fourteen pairs of stills are divided with four pairs in the oldest still room, three in the beautiful room that was built in 2010 and another seven in the third and latest still room.

The core range is made up of **Founder's Reserve, Caribbean Reserve** finished in rum casks, **12 year old Double Cask, 15 year old French Oak Reserve**, and an **18 year old.** The Sample Room Collection is made up of a **21 year old** triple finished in casks that have held oloroso, cognac and vintage port, a **25 year old** has a finish in PX casks and cognac and the new **40 year old** was finished in PX and oloroso casks. There is also the **Fusion Cask**, exclusive to the US market, with a finish in dismantled rum and bourbon casks that had been reassembled together

Recent limited expressions include the first edition in the Eternal Collection - a **55 year old** and the oldest expression from the owners to date. There is also the third instalment in the Winchester Collection - a **50 year old** distilled in 1967. The travel retail range includes **Triple Cask White Oak Reserve, Caskmakers** and **The Journey Inward** which is the first chapter in the new Groundbreaker Collection. Finally, a number of expressions are available at the distillery visitor centre only including a **14 year old American oak,** a **15 year old first fill sherry** and a **16 year old Double oak.**

History:

1817 George Smith inherits the farm distillery Upper Drumin.

1840 George Smith buys Delnabo farm near Tomintoul and leases Cairngorm Distillery.

1845 George Smith leases three other farms, one of which is situated on the river Livet and is called Minmore.

1846 William Smith develops tuberculosis and his brother John Gordon moves back home to assist his father.

1858 George Smith buys Minmore farm and obtains permission to build a distillery.

1859 Upper Drummin and Cairngorm close and all equipment is brought to Minmore which is renamed The Glenlivet Distillery.

1871 George Smith dies and his son John Gordon takes over.

1880 John Gordon Smith applies for and is granted sole rights to the name The Glenlivet.

1890 A fire breaks out and some of the buildings are replaced.

1901 John Gordon Smith dies.

1904 John Gordon's nephew George Smith Grant takes over.

1921 Captain Bill Smith Grant, son of George Smith Grant, takes over.

1953 George & J. G. Smith Ltd merges with J. & J. Grant of Glen Grant Distillery and forms the company Glenlivet & Glen Grant Distillers.

1966 Floor maltings closes.

1970 Glenlivet & Glen Grant Distillers Ltd merges with Longmorn-Glenlivet Distilleries Ltd and Hill Thomson & Co. Ltd to form The Glenlivet Distillers Ltd.

1978 Seagrams buys The Glenlivet Distillers Ltd. A visitor centre opens.

2000 French Oak 12 years and American Oak 12 years are launched

Triple Cask White Oak Reserve

Groundbreaker Collection

Carribean Reserve

History continued:

2001 Pernod Ricard and Diageo buy Seagram Spirits & Wine. Pernod Ricard thereby gains control of the Chivas group.

2004 French Oak 15 years replaces 12 year old.

2005 The Glenlivet 12 year old First Fill and Nadurra are launched.

2007 Glenlivet XXV is released.

2009 Four more stills are installed and Nadurra Triumph 1991 is released.

2010 Another two stills are commissioned and Glenlivet Founder´s Reserve is released.

2011 Glenlivet Master Distiller´s Reserve is released for the duty free market.

2012 1980 Cellar Collection is released.

2014 Nadurra Oloroso, Nadurra First Fill Selection, The Glenlivet Guardian´s Chapter and a 50 year old are released.

2015 Founder´s Reserve is released as well as Solera Vatted and Small Batch.

2016 The Glenlivet Cipher and the second edition of the 50 year old are launched.

2018 Captain´s Reserve and Code are released. A new distillery is commissioned.

2019 Enigma and a 14 year old cognac finish are released.

2020 Spectra, Carribean Reserve and Illicit Still are released.

2021 The Licensed Dram is released.

2022 The Sample Room Collection is launched.

2024 A 12 year old 200th anniversary edition and a 55 year old are released.

2025 A 40 year old, The Journey Inward and Jamaica Edition are launched

Tasting notes Glenlivet 12 year old:

GS – A lovely, honeyed, floral, fragrant nose. Medium-bodied, smooth and malty on the palate, with vanilla sweetness. Not as sweet as the nose might suggest. The finish is pleasantly lengthy and sophisticated.

Founder´s Reserve

Caskmakers

40 years old

12 years old

18 years old

Glenlossie

[glen•loss•ee]

Owner:
Diageo

Region/district:
Speyside

Founded:
1876

Status:
Active

Capacity:
3 700 000 litres

Address: Birnie, Elgin, Morayshire IV30 8SS

Website:
malts.com

Tel:
01343 862000

There are two sibling distilleries situated just a mere 15 minute drive south from Elgin, Glenlossie and Mannochmore, but the difference in age is substantial. While Glenlossie was founded in 1876 it took almost a century until Mannochmore saw the light of day.

For quite a few years the two distilleries shared workforce working 6 months at a time at each distillery but at least since 2007 they have their own designated managers and teams. Both distilleries have continuously been producing malts for blends and, in the case of Glenlossie, it is not least Haig Gold Label. The difference between the newmake from the two sisters is striking; both distilleries run the same foreshots (20 minutes) and have roughly the same cut points for the spirit run but while Glenlossie is green and oily due to a 20 hour shorter fermentation time and larger stills, Mannochmore turns out sweet and fruity.

Glenlossie is equipped with an eight ton stainless steel full lauter mash tun, eight washbacks made of larch and two – placed outdoors – made of stainless steel. The fermentation time is 80 hours. There are three wash stills (15,800 litres) and three spirit stills (13,500 litres), all with horizontal lyne arms and equipped with purifiers and a fairly wide spirit cut going from 75% down to 62%. The distillery has been alternating in the last few years between five and seven-day production and from July 2025 runs for five days and makes 12 mashes per week. On site there used to be one biomass boiler and two fed by gas but since July 2025 all three are using sawdust as fuel.

As mentioned Glenlossie, together with Glenkinchie and Linkwood, is one of the major contributors to the Haig Gold Label blend. In terms of sales Haig is a far cry from the heydays of the 1970s but it still sells around 4 million bottles per year, mainly in India.

The only official bottling of Glenlossie single malt available today is a **10 year old Flora & Fauna**.

10 years old

History:

1876 John Duff, former manager at Glendronach Distillery, founds the distillery. Alexander Grigor Allan (to become part-owner of Talisker Distillery), the whisky trader George Thomson and Charles Shirres (both will co-found Longmorn Distillery some 20 years later with John Duff) and H. Mackay are also involved in the company.

1895 The company Glenlossie-Glenlivet Distillery Co. is formed. Alexander Grigor Allan passes away.

1896 John Duff becomes more involved in Longmorn and Mackay takes over management of Glenlossie.

1919 Distillers Company Limited (DCL) takes over the company.

1929 A fire breaks out and causes considerable damage.

1930 DCL transfers operations to Scottish Malt Distillers (SMD).

1962 Stills are increased from four to six.

1971 Another distillery, Mannochmore, is constructed by SMD on the premises. A dark grains plant is installed.

1990 A 10 year old is launched in the Flora & Fauna series.

2010 A Manager´s Choice single cask from 1999 is released.

Tasting notes Glenlossie 10 years old:

GS – Cereal, silage and vanilla notes on the relatively light nose, with a voluptuous, sweet palate, offering plums, ginger and barley sugar, plus a hint of oak. The finish is medium in length, with grist and slightly peppery oak.

Exceptional Designs

A cubistic exterior
at Puni Distillery in Italy

Glenmorangie

[glen•mor•run•jee]

Owner:
The Glenmorangie Co (Moët Hennessy)

Region/district:
Northern Highlands

Founded:
1843

Status:
Active (vc)

Capacity:
7 100 000 litres

Address: Tain, Ross-shire IV19 1PZ

Website:
glenmorangie.com

Tel:
01862 892477 (vc)

The year that the covid pandemic hit the world, in 2020, was disastrous for most single malt brands but not for Glenmorangie. While sales increased by just 3% the brand was still on the plus side.

Since then volumes have gone up by 38% to 9 million bottles in 2023 which means it's the fourth best selling single malt in the world. The only brand that is close to challenge that position is The Singleton. Few people have influenced the character of a distillery's whisky for such a long time as Bill Lumsden has done with Glenmorangie. He joined the company in 1995 as the distillery manager but soon he moved on to a position where he was responsible for the actual creation of the whiskies that were bottled. For a number of years his title has been Head of Distilling and Whisky Creation and it is applied not only for Glenmorangie but also for its sister distillery Ardbeg as well.

The distillery is equipped with a full lauter mash tun with a 10 ton charge (down from the previous 11.5 tonnes). There are also 12 stainless steel washbacks with a fermentation time of 52 hours. Finally there are six wash stills (12,000 litres) and six spirit stills (8,100 litres) with the longest necks in Scotland. These are quite often referred to as giraffe stills and were originally designed to make gin. The newmake is light, yet complex, with a 15 minute foreshots, cut points for the spirit distillation going from 74% down to 60% and using hard water for the production.

A couple of years ago a separate innovation distillery named The Lighthouse was constructed. Here, the team can try out new methods without disturbing the work in the original distillery. It is equipped with a one ton mash tun but there is also a mash conversion vessel that can handle more complex mash bills. Furthermore, there are two 5,000 litre wash backs and one pair of stills.

The pinnacle of the core range uised to be a 10 year old which in 2024 was replaced by a **12 year old**. Included is also an **18 year old** which was recently renamed **Infinita**. There are three wood finishes: **Quinta Ruban**, a 14 year old with an extra maturation in ruby port pipes. **Lasanta**, a 12 year old with a finish in oloroso and PX sherry casks which was relaunched as a 15 year old in spring 2025 and the 16 year old **Nectar D'Or** with time spent in Sauternes casks. A new addition to the core range in spring 2024 was **Triple Cask Reserve** where three types of casks are used for the maturation – bourbon, new charred oak and rye. The **Signet**, where part of the mashbill is chocolate malt, has been around for many years and in 2024 the **Signet Reserve** appeared which is Signet further matured in PX sherry casks. .

Recent limited releases include batch 4 of the **Cadboll Estate** and **A Tale of Ice Cream** where the casks had been toasted to create a high vanillin impact.Finally, for travel retail there are **12 year old The Accord, 14 year old The Elementa, 16 year old The Tribute** and a **19 year old.** In autumn 2024 the range was complemented by the **16 year old Vindima** finished in madeira casks and the **21 year old Aureum,** all matured in ex-bourbon.

History:

1843 William Mathesen applies for a license for a farm distillery called Morangie, which is rebuilt by them. Production took place here in 1738, and possibly since 1703.

1849 Production starts in November.

1887 The distillery is rebuilt and Glenmorangie Distillery Company Ltd is formed.

1918 40% of the distillery is sold to Macdonald & Muir Ltd and 60 % to the whisky dealer Durham. Macdonald & Muir takes over Durham's share by the late thirties.

1931 The distillery closes.

1936 Production restarts in November.

1980 Number of stills increases from two to four and own maltings ceases.

1990 The number of stills is doubled to eight.

1994 A visitor centre opens. Glenmorangie Port Wood Finish is released.

1995 Glenmorangie´s Tain l´Hermitage is launched.

1996 Two different wood finishes are launched, Madeira and Sherry. Glenmorangie plc is formed.

2001 Cask strength port wood finish, Cote de Beaune Wood Finish and Three Cask (ex-Bourbon, charred oak and ex-Rioja) are launched.

2002 A 20 year old Sauternes finish is launched.

2003 Burgundy Wood Finish and cask strength Madeira-matured are released.

2004 Glenmorangie buys the Scotch Malt Whisky Society. The Macdonald family decides to sell Glenmorangie plc (including the distilleries Glenmorangie, Glen Moray and Ardbeg) to Moët Hennessy at £300 million.

2005 A 30 year old is launched.

2007 The entire range gets a complete makeover.

History continued:

2008 Astar and Signet are launched.

2009 Sonnalta PX is released for duty free.

2010 Glenmorangie Finealta is released.

2011 28 year old Glenmorangie Pride is released.

2012 Glenmorangie Artein is released.

2013 Glenmorangie Ealanta is released.

2014 Companta, Taghta and Dornoch are released.

2015 Túsail and Duthac are released.

2016 Milsean, Tayne and Tarlogan are released.

2017 Bacalta, Astar and Pride 1974 are released.

2018 Spios, Cadboll and Grand Vintage Malt 1989 and 1993 are released.

2019 Allta, Cask 1784 and Grand Vintage Malt 1991 are launched.

2020 A new range of travel retail exclusives is released as well as the 26 year Truffle Oak, Grand Vintage Malt 1996 and A Tale of Cake.

2021 X by Glenmorangie, Grand Vintage Malt 1997, a 13 year old cognac finish, Signet Ristretto and Tale of Winter are launched.

2022 A Tale of Forest and Barrel Select Palo Cortado are released. An experimental distillery is commissioned.

2023 Barrel Select Amontillado is released.

2024 A 12 year old replaces the 10 year old and Triple Cask Reserve and Signet Reserve are released.

2025 Lasanta 15 year old and A Tale of Icecream are released.

Tasting notes Glenmorangie Original 12 year old:

IR – The nose is charming where notes of oranges and citrus sit together with heather, herbs and vanilla. Very creamy on the palate, honeyed sweetness, sweet garden fruits and a hint of coconut.

The Elementa

Signet Reserve

Barrel Select Calvados

12 years old

La Santa

Infinita 18 years

Glen Moray

[glen mur•ree]

Owner:
La Martiniquaise (COFEPP)

Region/district:
Speyside

Founded:
1897

Status:
Active (vc)

Capacity:
8 400 000 litres

Address: Bruceland Road, Elgin,
Morayshire IV30 1YE

Website:
glenmoray.com

Tel:
01343 542577

Until 2008, when under the umbrella of LVMH together with Glenmorangie and Ardbeg, Glen Moray was very much a neglected brand of single malt. It was mainly supplying malt for the blends that the owner held at that time.

When the current owner took over things changed rapidly. Not only was the distillery expanded to reach a position today where it is the 10th largest in Scotland. The brand itself also became known to a wider audience. In 2023 it sold 1.9 million bottles and it is especially popular in the UK where 40% of the volume was sold. The success for Glen Moray in recent years has to a certain extent been built on the whisky being very reasonably priced and, not least, on a wide range of expressions available. Usually I proclaim Glencadam or Tomintoul as the winners in this category but this year it must be Glen Moray with no less than 14 core expressions in the range.

The distillery is equipped with a 10 ton full lauter mash tun and a 6 ton semilauter tun with a high gravity (1075) in the worts to save energy. There are 21 stainless steel washbacks placed outside with a fermentation time of 58 hours. Finally there are ten stills – four wash stills equipped with TVR technology (thermal vapour recompression) for energy efficiency and six spirit stills. In 2025, the owners will be doing 26 mashes per week in each tun with a total outcome of 7,5 million litres of alcohol.

The extensive core range consists of **Classic, Classic Port Finish, Classic Chardonnay Finish, Classic Sherry Finish, Classic Shiraz Finish, Classic Cabernet Sauvignon Finish, Classic Peated**, **Phoenix Rising, Smoky 12 year old** and **Twisted Wine** as well as **12, 15, 18 year old** and **21 year old portwood finish**. Recent limited editions include a **tequila cask finish** and a **peated tequila cask finish** – both distilled in 2014. There is also the **Forbidden Fruit** – matured in calvados casks.

12 years old

History:

1897 Elgin West Brewery, dated 1830, is reconstructed as Glen Moray Distillery.

1910 The distillery closes.

1920 Financial troubles force the distillery to be put up for sale. Buyer is Macdonald & Muir.

1923 Production restarts.

1958 A reconstruction takes place and the floor maltings are replaced by a Saladin box.

1978 Own maltings are terminated.

1979 Number of stills is increased to four.

1996 Macdonald & Muir Ltd changes name to Glenmorangie plc.

1999 Three wood finishes are introduced.

2004 Louis Vuitton Moët Hennessy buys Glenmorangie plc and a 1986 cask strength, a 20 and a 30 year old are released.

2006 Two vintages, 1963 and 1964, and a new Manager's Choice are released.

2007 New edition of Mountain Oak is released.

2008 The distillery is sold to La Martiniquaise.

2009 A 14 year old Port finish and an 8 year old matured in red wines casks are released.

2011 Two cask finishes and a 10 year old Chardonnay maturation are released.

2012 A 2003 Chenin Blanc is released.

2013 A 25 year old port finish is released.

2014 Glen Moray Classic Port Finish is released.

2015 Glen Moray Classic Peated is released.

2016 Chardonnay Finish and Sherry Finish are released as well as a 15 and an 18 year old.

2017 Glen Moray Mastery is launched.

2018 10 year old Fired Oak is released.

2019 Glen Moray Rhum Agricole is released.

2020 A 13 year old Madeira Cask is released.

2021 A 30 year old sherry finish and a 14 year old matured in Sauternes casks are launched.

2022 Batch 2 of the Warehouse 1 Collection is released.

2023 Twisted Vine and batch 2 of the Warehouse 1 Collection are launched.

2025 Smoky 12 years and two tequila finishes are released.

Tasting notes Glen Moray 12 years old:

GS – Mellow on the nose, with vanilla, pear drops and some oak. Smooth in the mouth, with spicy malt, vanilla and summer fruits. The finish is relatively short, with spicy fruit.

Glen Ord

[glen ord]

Owner: Diageo

Region/district: Northern Highlands

Founded: 1838

Status: Active (vc)

Capacity: 11 900 000 litres

Address: Muir of Ord, Ross-shire IV6 7UJ

Website: malts.com

Tel: 01463 872004 (vc)

Glen Ord distillery, just a twenty minute drive west from Inverness and on the opposite side of the Beauly Firth, is currently the sixth largest malt distillery in Scotland.

A visit is highly recommended. Already in 1988 a visitor centre was added and upgrades have been made over the years. The current visitor experience, completely refurbished and expanded in 2022, is beautiful and includes a large shop and a bar. One of the available tours also includes a rare opportunity to see the adjacent drum maltings. In terms of sales Glen Ord is the most prominent of the three distilleries gathered under The Singleton brand umbrella with Dufftown and Glendullan being the other two.

Glen Ord is equipped with two stainless steel, full lauter mashtuns, each with a 13.5 ton mash. There are 22 wooden washbacks, allowing for a capacity of 59,000 litres and with a fermentation time of 75 hours. Fourteen of them were installed during the last decade of expansion – 12 in the old floor maltings and two in the old kiln. Three wash stills and three spirit stills can be found in still house No. 1 facing the road, while the eight latest stills to be installed are all in a new building on site. The condensers are run hot and, together with long fermentation and a clear wort, it results in a green/grassy newmake. Running at full capacity the distillery can mash 47 times per week and make close to 12 million litres of alcohol. On site there are also the Glen Ord drum maltings installed in 1968. With 18 drums and four kilns, the capacity is 45,000 tons per year.

The core range is the **Singleton of Glen Ord 12, 15** and **18 year old**. The duty free range consists of **Signature, Trinité, Liberté** and **Artisan**. There is also a **Celebratory** bottling available only at the distillery. Recent limited bottlings include three of substantial age (**38, 39** and **40 year old**). There is also the highly limited The Singleton Gourmand Collection released in spring 2025 and consisting of three **42 year olds** – all with a different maturation story. In autumn 2025 a **17 year old**, part finished in ex-mezcal casks, was released in the yearly Special Relesaes

12 years old

History:

1838 Thomas Mackenzie founds the distillery.

1855 Alexander MacLennan and Thomas McGregor buy the distillery.

1870 Alexander MacLennan dies and the distillery is taken over by his widow who marries the banker Alexander Mackenzie.

1877 Alexander Mackenzie leases the distillery.

1878 Alexander Mackenzie builds a new still house and barely manages to start production before a fire destroys it.

1896 Alexander Mackenzie dies and the distillery is sold to James Watson & Co. for £15,800.

1923 John Jabez Watson, James Watson's son, dies and the distillery is sold to John Dewar & Sons. The name changes from Glen Oran to Glen Ord.

1961 A Saladin box is installed.

1966 The two stills are increased to six.

1968 Drum maltings is built.

1983 Malting in the Saladin box ceases.

1988 A visitor centre is opened.

2002 A 12 year old is launched.

2005 A 30 year old is launched.

2006 A 12 year old Singleton of Glen Ord is launched.

2010 A Singleton of Glen Ord 15 year old is released in Taiwan.

2012 Singleton of Glen Ord cask strength is released.

2013 Singleton of Glen Ord Signature, Trinité, Liberté and Artisan are launched.

2015 The Master´s Casks 40 years old is released.

2017 A 41 year old reserved for Asia is released.

2018 A 14 year old triple-matured is launched as part of the Special Releases.

2019 A 43 year old is released as well as an 18 year old in the Special Releases.

2022 A 34 year old Prima & Ultima and a 15 year old Special Release are launched.

2023 A 40 year old with a 28 year secondary maturation in rum casks is released.

2024 A 14 year old appears in Special Releases.

2025 The Gourmand Collection and a 17 year old Special Release are launched.

Tasting notes Glen Ord 12 years old:

GS – Honeyed malt and milk chocolate on the nose, with a hint of orange. These characteristics carry over onto the sweet, easy-drinking palate, along with a biscuity note. Subtly drying, with a medium-length, spicy finish.

Glenrothes

[glen•roth•iss]

Owner: The Edrington Group

Region/district: Speyside

Founded: 1878

Status: Active

Capacity: 5 600 000 litres

Address: Rothes, Morayshire AB38 7AA

Website: theglenrothes.com

Tel: 01340 872300

The role of a distillery manager has changed considerably over the past few decades. Being compliant with health and safety regulations and, not least, reducing the impact on the environment has become increasingly important tasks.

The background of a manager is also very different today. Alasdair Anderson, who retired in spring 2025, spent his entire career working for Highland Distillers and, later, Edrington. It all started in 1980 at Tamdhu maltings when he shovelled 44 tonnes of green malt daily. Eventually he moved on to brewing and distilling learning the trade, and for the past 15 years he managed Glenrothes. "Old school" managers like Alasdair, working their way through the various steps of whisky production, is a dying breed. Today it is not uncommon that managers are recruited from the oil business or the chemical industry. While that may not be a bad thing it is certainly a sign of times changing.

The distillery is equipped with a 5.5 ton stainless steel full lauter mash tun. Twelve washbacks made of Oregon pine are in one room, whilst an adjacent modern tun room houses eight stainless steel washbacks – all of them with a 58 hour fermentation time. The magnificent, cathedral-like still house has five pairs of stills performing a very slow distillation. For 2025, the aim is 44 mashes per week, producing around 3.6 million litres of alcohol.

Two years ago the ten and twelve year old expressions as well as Whisky Maker's Cut were discontinued and were replaced in the core range by an **18 year old** (all matured in European oak sherry casks) and a **25 year old** (a combination of European and American oak sherry). In autumn 2024 the range was expanded with a **15 year old** matured predominantly in American oak sherry. There have also been limited releases aged 40 years and above, some of them designated for certain markets.

Alasdair Anderson

18 years old

History:

1878 James Stuart & Co. begins planning the new distillery with Robert Dick, William Grant and John Cruickshank as partners.

1879 Production starts in December.

1884 The distillery changes name to Glenrothes-Glenlivet.

1887 William Grant & Co. joins forces with Islay Distillery Co. and forms Highland Distillers Company.

1897 A fire ravages the distillery.

1903 An explosion causes substantial damage.

1963 Expansion from four to six stills.

1980 Expansion from six to eight stills.

1989 Expansion from eight to ten stills.

1999 Edrington and William Grant & Sons buy Highland Distillers.

2002 Four single casks from 1966/1967 are launched.

2005 A 30 year old is launched together with Select Reserve and Vintage 1985.

2008 1978 Vintage and Robur Reserve are launched.

2009 The Glenrothes John Ramsay, Alba Reserve and Three Decades are released.

2010 Berry Brothers takes over the brand.

2011 Editor´s Casks are released.

2013 2001 Vintage and the Manse Brae range are released.

2014 Sherry Cask Reserve and 1969 Extraordinary Cask are released.

2015 Glenrothes Vintage Single Malt is released.

2016 Peated Cask Reserve and Ancestor´s Reserve are released.

2017 The brand returns to Edrington and The Glenrothes Wine Merchant´s Collection is introduced.

2018 The entire range is revamped and four new bottlings with age statements are introduced.

2019 A 40 year old and a 50 year old are released.

2023 A 42 year old is launched.

2024 A 15 year old is released.

Tasting notes Glenrothes 18 year old:

IR – Ripe pear and sweet vanilla pods, invigorating almond notes and a hint of dried ginger. A rich and deep flavour with sweet ginger, pear and rose water, aromatic fruit and light oak with an undercurrent of creamy vanilla.

Exceptional Designs

An ingenious way of malting the barley
at Stauning Distillery in Denmark

Glen Scotia

[glen sko•sha]

Owner: Loch Lomond Group (Hillhouse Capital Management)

Region/district: Campbeltown

Founded: 1832

Status: Active (vc)

Capacity: 800 000 litres

Address: High Street, Campbeltown, Argyll PA28 6DS

Website: glenscotia.com

Tel: 01586 552288

Why Glen Scotia was the only Campbeltown distillery apart from Springbank to survive into the new millennium is a mystery. The author Angus Martin, in one of his books, calls it "survival of the unfittest".

The distillery changed hands on a number of occasions and was quite frequently closed or mothballed. Martin is convinced that if it hadn't been for Sir Maurice Bloch, blender and broker from Glasgow, taking over Glen Scotia in 1933, the distillery wouldn't have survived. Sir Maurice's involvement lasted until 1954 but a nephew of his headed the distillery until 1970. Five decades with various owners followed and in 2019 a Hong Kong based private equity company stepped in. Since then the distillery and the portfolio of malts have undergone a huge shift for the better.

An expansion of the distillery to increase capacity was announced in 2023 but part of it was later postponed. At the moment Glen Scotia is equipped with a traditional 3 ton stainless steel mash tun which replaced a similar tun made of cast iron in October 2024. There are ten (the latest installed in 2024) stainless steel washbacks – six interior and four exterior – holding 25,000 litres but filled to 15,000 litres. The fermentation time is an unusual mix ranging from 70 hours to 120 hours. There is one wash still and one spirit still with normal cut points ranging from 72% to 63% but for peated whisky, goes down to 61%. In 2025 it is planned to do 13 mashes per week resulting in 750,000 litres including six weeks of both lightly (20ppm) and heavily (54ppm) peated production.

The core range consists of **Double Cask, Double Cask Rum Finish, 10, 15, 18** and **25 year old**. There are also **Victoriana** and **Glen Scotia Harbour**, both gently peated. Two core additions in 2025 were the **Double Cask Bordeaux** finish and a **12 year old**. The duty free range consists of **Glen Scotia Campbeltown 1832, Crosshill Cask Strength**, a **22 year old** port finish and a **32 year old**, Recent limited releases include the second installment in the Icons of Campbeltown series, the 14 year old **The Dragon** with a red wine finish. In spring 2025, the oldest ever bottling, a **50 year old**, was released.

Double Cask

History:

- 1832 The families of Stewart and Galbraith start Scotia Distillery.
- 1891 The distillery is sold to Duncan McCallum.
- 1919 Sold to West Highland Malt Distillers.
- 1924 West Highland Malt Distillers goes bankrupt and Duncan MacCallum buys back the distillery.
- 1930 The distillery closes
- 1933 Bloch Brothers Ltd take over and production restarts.
- 1954 Hiram Walker takes over.
- 1955 A. Gillies & Co. becomes new owner.
- 1970 A. Gillies & Co. becomes part of Amalgamated Distilled Products.
- 1979 Reconstruction takes place.
- 1984 The distillery closes.
- 1986 Amalgamated Distilled Products is taken over by Gibson International.
- 1989 Production starts again.
- 1994 Glen Catrine Bonded Warehouse Ltd takes over and the distillery is mothballed.
- 1999 The distillery re-starts using staff from Springbank.
- 2000 Loch Lomond Distillers runs operations with its own staff from May onwards.
- 2005 A 12 year old is released.
- 2006 A peated version is released.
- 2012 A new range is launched.
- 2014 A 10 year old and one without age statement are released - both heavily peated.
- 2015 A new range is released; Double Cask, 15 year old and Victoriana.
- 2017 A 25 year old and an 18 year old as well as two bottlings for duty-free are released.
- 2019 The distillery is sold to Hillhouse Capital Management.
- 2021 A 46 year old is released.
- 2022 Double Cask Rum Finish is launched.
- 2023 The Mermaid and a 48 year old are released.
- 2024 The Dragon is released.
- 2025 A 50 year old, a 12 year old and Double Cask Bordeaux Finish are released.

Tasting notes Glen Scotia Double Cask:

GS – The nose is sweet, with bramble and redcurrant aromas, plus caramel and vanilla. Smooth mouth-feel, with ginger, sherry and more vanilla. The finish is quite long, with spicy sherry and a final hint of brine.

Glen Spey

Photo: © Raymond MacDonald

[glen spey]

Owner:
Diageo

Region/district:
Speyside

Founded:
1878

Status:
Active

Capacity:
1 500 000 litres

Address: Rothes, Morayshire AB38 7AU

Website:
malts.com

Tel:
01340 831215

Glen Spey is the fourth smallest of Diageo's malt distilleries and it is probably the least known to the average malt whisky consumer. It was taken over by the gin producer W. & A. Gilbey in 1887 – the first time an English company bought a Scottish distillery.

Given the history of that ownership over the next 80 years, it is interesting to see that Glen Spey has actually been producing gin rather than whisky for the past five years. While it may seem surprising, one has to remember that Diageo is the owner of two famous gin brands – Gordon's and Tanqueray. Since at least 1989 the GNS (grain neutral spirit) for these has been produced at Cameronbridge distillery in Fife but there has always been a backup amongst some of their malt distilleries (including also Auchroisk, Pittyvaich and Strathmill) to step in if need be.

A recent increase in capacity at Cameronbridge made Glen Spey superfluous in terms of gin production and Diageo ceased to distill at Glen Spey in November 2024. The official plan is to bring the distillery back to whisky production but while not yet confirmed by the owners, this could probably take a couple of years.

While producing whisky, the distillery has been equipped with a 4.4 ton semi-lauter mash tun, eight stainless steel washbacks with both short (46 hours) and long (100 hours) fermentations and two pairs of stills. The two spirit stills are equipped with purifiers which add reflux and also help eliminate the heavier esters. Due to a cloudy wort, the Glen Spey new make is usually nutty and slightly oily.

Virtually all of the produce has gone into blends and especially that of J&B. From time to time independent bottlers take an interest in Glen Spey and the Scotch Malt Whisky Society have released more than 50 single casks over the years. The only official single malt is the **12 year old Flora & Fauna** bottling. In 2010, two limited releases were made – a **1996 single cask** from new American oak and a **21 year old** with maturation in ex-sherry American oak..

History:

1878 James Stuart & Co. founds the distillery which becomes known by the name Mill of Rothes.

1886 James Stuart buys Macallan.

1887 W. & A. Gilbey buys the distillery for £11,000.

1920 A fire breaks out and the main part of the distillery is re-built.

1962 W. & A. Gilbey combines forces with United Wine Traders and forms International Distillers & Vintners (IDV).

1970 The stills are increased from two to four.

1972 IDV is bought by Watney Mann which is then acquired by Grand Metropolitan.

1997 Guiness and Grand Metropolitan merge to form Diageo.

2001 A 12 year old is launched in the Flora & Fauna series.

2010 A 21 year old is released as part of the Special Releases and a 1996 Manager´s Choice single cask is launched.

12 years old

Tasting notes Glen Spey 12 years old:

GS – Tropical fruits and malt on the comparatively delicate nose. Medium-bodied with fresh fruits and vanilla toffee on the palate, becoming steadily nuttier and drier in a gently oaky, mildly smoky finish.

Glentauchers

[glen•tock•ers]

Owner: Chivas Brothers (Pernod Ricard)

Region/district: Speyside

Founded: 1897

Status: Active

Capacity: 4 200 000 litres

Address: Mulben, Keith, Banffshire AB55 6YL

Website: -

Tel: 01542 860272

There are some striking historic similarities between Glentauchers and Imperial. Both were founded in the last shivering years of the 19th century and both suffered badly, like most of the industry, almost immediately due to the Pattison crash.

The two distilleries came under DCL ownership around 1925 and remained under that umbrella for sixty years until they were mothballed. At least they weren't closed, a destiny affecting many distilleries in the mid eighties. In 1989, United Distillers (the successor of DCL) sold the two distilleries to Allied Distillers who decided to reopen them in 1991/1992. After this date their destinies took different turns: While Imperial was mothballed again in 1998, Glentauchers continued to produce. Pernod Ricard became new owners in 2005 and later demolished Imperial to build Dalmunach on the same grounds. Glentauchers on the other hand is still thriving doing the same thing it has always done, namely producing malt whisky for blends. It is one of the cornerstones in the mega brand Ballantines and has until recently been almost completely unknown to malt whisky drinkers.

Glentauchers was the first of Chivas Brothers' twelve malt distilleries to become carbon neutral. This was accomplished in 2022 and the next in line was Allt-a-Bhainne, followed by Dalmunach. The fundamental change at all three distilleries was installing MVR technology (mechanical vapour recompression) on the stills. The energy reduction during distillation amount to 90% and the site energy demand has been reduced by half.

The distillery is equipped with a 12.2 ton stainless steel full lauter mash tun with a copper dome. There are six washbacks made of Oregon pine with a fermentation time of 56 hours and three pairs of stills. Depending on whether or not the distillery is on a five-day or a seven-day week, the number of mashes are 12 or 18.

There is an official **23 year old** in the Ballantine's Single Malt Series as well as a **21 year old** cask strength bottling in the Distillery Reserve Collection.

History:

- 1897 James Buchanan and W. P. Lowrie, a whisky merchant from Glasgow, found the distillery.
- 1898 Production starts.
- 1906 James Buchanan & Co. takes over the whole distillery and acquires an 80% share in W. P. Lowrie & Co.
- 1915 James Buchanan & Co. merges with Dewars.
- 1923 Mashing house and maltings are rebuilt.
- 1925 Buchanan-Dewars joins Distillers Company Limited (DCL).
- 1930 Glentauchers is transferred to Scottish Malt Distillers (SMD).
- 1965 The number of stills is increased from two to six.
- 1969 Floor maltings is decommissioned.
- 1985 DCL mothballs the distillery.
- 1989 United Distillers (formerly DCL) sells the distillery to Caledonian Malt Whisky Distillers, a subsidiary of Allied Distillers.
- 1992 Production recommences in August.
- 2000 A 15 year old Glentauchers is released.
- 2005 Chivas Brothers (Pernod Ricard) become the new owner through the acquisition of Allied Domecq.
- 2017 A 15 year old is released in the Ballantine´s Single Malt Series.
- 2021 A 23 year old is launched.

15 years old

Tasting notes Glentauchers 15 years old:

IR – Delicious on the nose, both floral and fruity, vanilla, pastry, heather and honey. Still fruity on the palate with additional notes of roasted nuts, toffee and milk chocolate..

Glenturret

[glen•turr•et]

Owner: Lalique Group/Hansjörg Wyss

Region/district: Southern Highlands

Founded: 1763

Status: Active (vc)

Capacity: 500 000 litres

Address: The Hosh, Crieff, Perthshire PH7 4HA

Website: theglenturret.com

Tel: 01764 656565

From 2002 until 2019, when Edrington sold the distillery, Glenturret was the spiritual home of Famous Grouse blended Scotch. Visitors came in thousands every year to see The Famous Grouse Experience.

When joining such a tour one would hear the narrative about the importance of Glenturret single malt for the character of Famous Grouse. If one takes into account that the popular blend sells around 20 million bottles every year and that if every drop of Glenturret whisky was used it would still just make up only 3% of the "recipe". Furthermore, for many years only 50% of the capacity at Glenturret was used and some of the spirit was bottled as single malt. So the stories from the tour guides were perhaps stretching it a bit.

The new owners since 2019, Lalique Group, have not only changed focus to strengthening Glenurret as a brand of its own but have also turned the site itself into an exciting destination. Part of that includes a two star Michelin restaurant! The distillery can also boast that it is the oldest producing distillery in Scotland, dating as far back as to 1763.

Glenturret is equipped with a semilauter mash tun where the charge was recently lowered from 1.9 tons to 1.8 in order to increase the esters in the spirit. The old mash tun (replaced in May 2022) had an open top and was uniquely hand-stirred. There are eight 8,000 litre Douglas fir washbacks with a fermentation time of 100-120 hours and one pair of stills. The production target for 2025 is 13 mashes per week and 440,000 litres which is an increase from last year by almost 25%.

The core range consists of eight expressions, all with different abv; **Triple Wood, 7 year old Peat Smoked, 10 year old Peat Smoked, 14 year old Peat Smoked** (new in 2024), **12, 15, 25** and **30 year old**. Recent limited bottlings include **Distiller´s Dram Edition 1** in November 2024 which was followed in late 2025 by **Edition 2.** In spring 2024 the distillery also released their first gin – Aberturret.

12 years old

History:

1763 A distillery by the name of Thurot is operating on the site of todays Glenturret.

1818 John Drummond is licensee until 1837.

1826 A distillery in the vicinity is named Glenturret, but is decommissioned before 1852.

1852 John McCallum is licensee until 1874.

1875 Hosh Distillery takes over the name Glenturret Distillery and is managed by Thomas Stewart.

1903 Mitchell Bros Ltd takes over.

1921 Production ceases and the buildings are used for whisky storage only.

1929 Mitchell Bros Ltd is liquidated, the distillery dismantled and the facilities are used as storage for agricultural needs.

1957 James Fairlie buys the distillery and re-equips it.

1959 Production restarts.

1981 Remy-Cointreau buys the distillery and invests in a visitor centre.

1990 Highland Distillers takes over.

1999 Edrington and William Grant & Sons buy Highland Distillers for £601 million. The purchasing company, 1887 Company, is a joint venture between Edrington (70%) and William Grant (30%).

2002 The Famous Grouse Experience, a visitor centre costing £2.5 million, is inaugurated.

2003 A 10 year old Glenturret replaces the 12 year old as the distillery´s standard release.

2007 Three new single casks are released.

2013 An 18 year old bottled at cask strength is released as a distillery exclusive.

2014 A 1986 single cask is released.

2015 Sherry, Triple Wood and Peated are released.

2016 Fly´s 16 Masters is released.

2017 Cameron´s Cut, Jamieson´s Jigger Edition and Peated Drummond Edition are launched.

2019 Lalique Group and Hansjörg Wyss buy the distillery.

2020 A completely new core range is launched.

2021 Glenturret Jaguar E-Type is released.

2024 14 year old Peat Smoked is launched.

2025 Distiller´s Dram Edition 2 is released.

Tasting notes Glenturret 12 years old:

GS – Initial hints of Christmas cake and old leather, warm spices, dried fruits and old oak. Sweet and rich on the palate with tangy orange notes, cinnamon, dates, walnuts, caramel and lingering ginger.

Highland Park

[hi•land park]

Owner:
The Edrington Group

Region/district:
Highlands (Orkney)

Founded:
1798

Status:
Active (vc)

Capacity:
2 500 000 litres

Address: Holm Road, Kirkwall, Orkney KW15 1SU

Website:
highlandparkwhisky.com

Tel:
01856 874619

Following a closure, both in terms of production and for visitors, lasting a year, Highland Park finally opened up again in March 2025. The substantial refurbishment was implemented not least to secure high sustainability standards.

The £13m project included a more efficient mash tun and new, stainless steel washbacks equipped with cooling jackets. The old washbacks were all made of wood. A new heat recovery system will capture heat generated during distillation and will be used to dry the malt which was previously dried by coke. All these modifications are a step on the way to fulfil their target of reducing carbon dioxide by 50% by 2030. The new visitor experience now offers no less than five different tours ranging in price from £30 to £1,600. While the distillery is located on the outskirts of Kirkwall, there is also a flagship store right in the middle of the town.

In June 2025 it was announced that the master whisky maker since 2009, Gordon Motion was to retire. He has been with Edrington since 1998 and took over from John Ramsay in 2009. His final creation for the brand was Sherry Skies released in 2025. His successor as the blender for Highland Park is Marc Watson who left Holyrood in 2023 to become the blender for Famous Grouse and Naked Malt. Both brands were, however, sold to William Grant in 2025.

Highland Park is currently equipped with a 12 ton semi-lauter mash tun although with a 6.5 ton mash. There are twelve new 29,200 litre washbacks made of stainless steel with a fermentation time of 60 hours. There are two 14,600 litre wash stills and two 9,000 litre spirit stills – all with horizontal lyne arms and condensers outside. Foreshots are 30 minutes and the cut points for the spirit run are 74-64%. In the last couple of years there have been 22 mashes per week which means a total of 2.5 million litres of alcohol. Highland Park is malting roughly 25% of its malt on-site and there are three malting floors with a capacity of almost 36 tons of barley. The malted barley is dried using peat for the first eight hours and hot air for the final 19. This gives a phenol specification of 30-40ppm whereas the malt sourced from Simpsons is unpeated.

The current core range of Highland Park consists of **12, 15, 18, 21, 25, 30** and **40 year olds**. Included in the core range is also **Cask Strength** which is released in batches. A new range for the travel retail market was introduced in October 2024 but basically it is the same spirit in the bottles as before but without any nods to viking legends. Instead the names relate to the nature that make up the Orkneys; **14 year old Land of Orkney, 16 year old Sea of Orkney** and **18 year old Sky of Orkney**. Recent limited expressions include the oldest release ever from the distillery – a **54 year old** which was launched in spring 2023. Since spring 2025 there are also the **16 year old Swallows Return** and the **19 year old Sherry Skies**.

History:

1798 David Robertson founds the distillery. The local smuggler and businessman Magnus Eunson previously operated an illicit whisky production on the site.

1816 John Robertson, an Excise Officer who arrested Magnus Eunson, takes over production.

1826 Highland Park obtains a license and the distillery is taken over by Robert Borwick.

1840 Robert´s son George Borwick takes over but the distillery deteriorates.

1869 The younger brother James Borwick inherits Highland Park and attempts to sell it as he does not consider the distillation of spirits as compatible with his priesthood.

1895 James Grant (of Glenlivet Distillery) buys Highland Park.

1898 The distillery is expanded from two to four stills.

1937 Highland Distilleries buys Highland Park.

1979 Highland Distilleries invests considerably in marketing Highland Park as single malt which increases sales markedly.

1986 A visitor centre, considered one of Scotland's finest, is opened.

1997 Two new Highland Park are launched, an 18 year old and a 25 year old.

1999 Highland Distillers are acquired by Edrington Group and William Grant & Sons.

2005 Highland Park 30 years old is released. A 16 year old for the Duty Free market and Ambassador´s Cask 1984 are released.

2006 The second edition of Ambassador´s Cask, a 10 year old from 1996, is released.

2008 A 40 year old and the third and fourth editions of Ambassador´s Cask are released.

History continued:

2009 Two vintages and Earl Magnus 15 year are released.

2010 A 50 year old, Saint Magnus 12 year old, Orcadian Vintage 1970 and four duty free vintages are released.

2011 Vintage 1978, Leif Eriksson and 18 year old Earl Haakon are released.

2012 Thor and a 21 year old are released.

2013 Loki and a new range for duty free, The Warriors, are released.

2014 Freya and Dark Origins are released.

2015 Odin is released.

2016 Hobbister, Ice Edition, Ingvar and King Christian I are released.

2017 Valkyrie, Dragon Legend, Voyage of the Raven, Shiel, Full Volume, The Dark and The Light are released.

2018 New duty free bottlings include Spirit of the Bear, Loyalty of the Wolf and Wings of the Eagle. The limited Valknut is also released.

2019 Twisted Tattoo, Valfather, Triskelion and a 21 year old are released.

2020 A cask strength is added to the core range.

2021 A 15 year old and a 50 year old are released.

2023 A 54 year old, the oldest expression from Highland Park so far, is launched.

2025 The range is revamped and Swallows Return and Sherry Skies are released.

Tasting notes Highland Park 12 year old:

GS – The nose is fragrant and floral, with hints of heather and some spice. Smooth and honeyed on the palate, with citric fruits, malt and distinctive tones of wood smoke in the warm, lengthy, slightly peaty finish.

Gordon Motion

Swallows Return

54 year old

Sherry Skies

12 years old

14 year old
Land of Orkney

18 years old

Inchgower

[inch•gow•er]

Owner: Diageo
Region/district: Speyside
Founded: 1871
Status: Active
Capacity: 3 200 000 litres
Address: Buckie, Banffshire AB56 5AB
Website: malts.com
Tel: 01542 836700

When Arthur Bell & Sons bought Inchgower from Buckie Town Council it must have been considered a win-win situation for both parties. The town had taken over the distillery for £1,000 by the end of 1936 when the original owners went bankrupt.

Just a few months later the town sold it to Bell's for £6,000. Bell's, of course, were happy with the price and so was the town council. They made a profit of £5,000 but, more importantly, they still held the water rights that were part of the original deal. Just four years earlier, Bell's had paid £56,000 for Blair Athol and Dufftown distilleries. One of Bell's less successful ventures on the distillery front was building Pittyvaich on the outskirts of Dufftown. The distillery was inaugurated in 1974 and less than 30 years thereafter, it was closed for good but, by then, Bell's had been long since acquired by Diageo.

Inchgower single malt remains an important part of Bell's blended Scotch. It used to be the second best selling Scotch in the UK but was recently surpassed by Whyte & Mackay. Worldwide it comes in as number 17 with 16 million bottles sold in 2024.

The distillery is equipped with an 8.4 ton stainless steel semilauter mash tun, where the cloudy wort adds to the spirit character, and six 50,000 litre washbacks made from Oregon pine divided into two separate rooms. When the distillery is operating a seven-day week with 19 mashes the fermentation time is 50-52 hours. During a five-day week there are both short (42 hours) and long (90 hours) fermentations. Two wash stills (13,640 litres) and two spirit stills (8,155 litres) are all onion-shaped and with sharply descending lyne arms. A quick distillation and a middle cut which goes down to an unusually low 55% enhances the nutty and robust style of the newmake.

Besides the official **Flora & Fauna 14 year old**, there have also been a few limited bottlings of Inchgower single malt. The most recent was a **27 year old** in autumn 2018 which was part of the yearly Special Releases.

14 years old

History:

1871 Alexander Wilson & Co. founds the distillery.

1936 Alexander Wilson & Co. becomes bankrupt and Buckie Town Council buys the distillery and the family's home for £1,600.

1938 The distillery is sold on to Arthur Bell & Sons for £3,000.

1966 Capacity doubles to four stills.

1985 Guinness acquires Arthur Bell & Sons.

1987 United Distillers is formed by a merger between Arthur Bell & Sons and DCL.

1997 Inchgower 1974 (22 years) is released as a Rare Malt.

2004 Inchgower 1976 (27 years) is released as a Rare Malt.

2010 A single cask from 1993 is released.

2018 A 27 year old is launched as part of the Special Releases.

Tasting notes Inchgower 14 years old:

GS – Ripe pears and a hint of brine on the light nose. Grassy and gingery in the mouth, with some acidity. The finish is spicy, dry and relatively short.

Jura

[joo•rah]

Owner:
Whyte & Mackay
(Emperador Inc)

Region/district:
Highlands (Jura)

Founded:
1810

Status:
Active (vc)

Capacity:
2 500 000 litres

Address: Craighouse, Isle of Jura PA60 7XT

Website:
jurawhisky.com

Tel:
01496 820240

Truth be told, for a number of years Jura single malt did not enjoy the best reputation amongst enthusiasts. The reason for that can be found in the casks that they were using for maturation.

From the re-start in 1963 until 1994 the spirit was often filled into wood of a lower quality. In 1998 a gargantuan project of re-racking 30,000 casks of maturing spirit into high quality oak was launched. It took more than a decade before it was completed but the whisky was dramatically improved. Around the same time the owners decided that the main part of Jura newmake would begin its maturation in first fill bourbon casks. The scheme paid off. Sales figures in 1998 were around 350,000 bottles and 25 years later the brand sold almost 3 million and is on the verge to become of the Top Ten malts. In 2023 warehouse No. 2 was knocked down to give space to a new biomass plant fed by wood chips. This is one step towards becoming carbon-neutral by 2030. It took the construction of a temporary slip to transport the equipment including the 40 ton boiler to the distillery. The boiler was commissioned in April 2025.

The distillery has a five ton semi-lauter mash tun, six stainless steel washbacks with a fermentation time of 60 hours and two pairs of stills. The plan for 2025 is 26 mashes per week and 2.3 million litres of alcohol.

The core range (recently revamped) consists of **Bourbon Cask, 12 year old, 14 year old Rye cask, Seven Wood, 12** and **15 year old Sherry Cask, 18 year old, French Oak** and the **21 year old Tide**. There is also a series called **Cask Editions** where the latest include **Pale Ale Cask, Red Wine Cask, Winter Edition** and **Rum Cask**. For duty-free a new range was introduced in October 2025 including **White Oak Cask**, a **13 year old**, a **16 year old** and a **19 year old**. There is also the **Islander´s Expression** collection where **No. 3**, finished in red wine casks, was recently released. A new series, **Perspective**, was introduced in 2024 with a **16 year old oloroso finish** as the first edition. Finally, the 2025 bottling for Feis Ile was a **27 year old** matured in a sherry cask.

12 years old

History:

- 1810 Archibald Campbell founds a distillery named Small Isles Distillery.
- 1853 Richard Campbell leases the distillery to Norman Buchanan from Glasgow.
- 1867 Buchanan files for bankruptcy and J. & K. Orr takes over the distillery.
- 1876 Licence transferred to James Ferguson & Sons.
- 1901 Ferguson dismantles the distillery.
- 1960 Charles Mackinlay & Co. extends the distillery. Newly formed Scottish & Newcastle Breweries acquires Charles Mackinlay & Co.
- 1963 The first distilling takes place.
- 1985 Invergordon Distilleries acquires Charles Mackinlay & Co. from Scottish & Newcastle.
- 1993 Whyte & Mackay (Fortune Brands) buys Invergordon Distillers.
- 1996 Whyte & Mackay changes name to JBB (Greater Europe).
- 2001 The management buys out the company and changes the name to Kyndal.
- 2002 Isle of Jura Superstition is launched.
- 2003 Kyndal reverts back to its old name, Whyte & Mackay. Isle of Jura 1984 is launched.
- 2006 The 40 year old Jura is released.
- 2007 United Spirits buys Whyte & Mackay.
- 2009 Prophecy and Paps of Jura are released.
- 2012 The 12 year old Jura Elixir is released.
- 2013 Camas an Staca, 1977 Juar and Turas-Mara are released.
- 2014 Whyte & Mackay is sold to Emperador Inc.
- 2016 The 22 year old "One For The Road" is released.
- 2017 The limited One and All is released.
- 2018 A new core range is released; 10, 12 and 18 year old as well as Journey and Seven Wood.
- 2020 Red Wine Cask and Winter Edition are released.
- 2021 Cask Editions are launched.
- 2022 The 14 year old Rye Cask is released.
- 2023 Bourbon Cask replaces Journey.
- 2024 The Perspective series is introduced.
- 2025 A new range for duty-free is released.

Tasting notes Jura 10 years old:

GS – Resin, oil and pine notes on the delicate nose. Light-bodied in the mouth, with malt and drying saltiness. The finish is malty, nutty, with more salt, plus just a wisp of smoke.

Kilchoman

[kil•ho•man]

Owner: Kilchoman Distillery Co.

Region/district: Islay

Founded: 2005

Status: Active (vc)

Capacity: 650 000 litres

Address: Rockside farm, Bruichladdich, Islay PA49 7UT

Website: kilchomandistillery.com

Tel: 01496 850011

The first edition of the Malt Whisky Yearbook was published almost at the same time (the second half of 2005) as Kilchoman fired up its stills on Islay. This was in many ways the start of an incredible expansion of new distilleries in Scotland.

Since Kilchoman opened up, another 60 whisky distilleries have been founded and I have a feeling that if an audacious Englishman could start the first distillery on Islay for 124 years, a lot of would-be distillers were encouraged to embark on their own adventures. Anthony Wills' idea from the very start was to build a farm distillery where the barley for the whisky was grown in the surroundings. The take-over of Rockside farm from its owner in 2015 is in line with this. A decision was also taken early on to malt as much of their own barley by themselves. The barley is dried for 15-20 hours using peat (to 15-20ppm) and then for another 30 hours on hot air. Currently around 15% of their needs are floor malted on site and they are looking to increase that, possibly by adding yet another type of malting – Saladin box or drums.

The current equipment consists of two 1.2 ton stainless steel semi-lauter mash tuns providing a clear wort, 14 stainless steel, 6,000 litre washbacks with an average fermentation time of 85 hours and two pairs of stills with foreshots running for just 5 minutes and spirit collected between 75% and 65%. In 2025, the distillery is looking to produce 640,000 litres of pure alcohol. Some 60% of the spirit is filled into ex-bourbon casks, 30% into ex-sherry and the final 10% divided between various types of wood.

The core range consists of **Machir Bay, Sanaig** and **Batch Strength**. Limited but regular releases are **Loch Gorm** matured in oloroso casks and **100% Islay** purely made from barley grown and malted on the island. Recent limited releases include a **13 year old** matured in a combination of ex-bourbon, octaves and calvados casks and the **Feis Ile 2025** bottling – a madeira matured version of the 100% Islay. For travel retail **Coull Point** and **Saligo Bay** are available.

Machir Bay

History:

- 2002 Plans are formed for a new distillery at Rockside Farm on western Islay.
- 2005 Production starts in June.
- 2006 A fire breaks out in the kiln causing a few weeks´ production stop but malting has to cease for the rest of the year.
- 2007 The distillery is expanded with two new washbacks.
- 2009 The first single malt, a 3 year old, is released on 9th September followed by a second release.
- 2010 Three new releases and an introduction to the US market. John Maclellan from Bunnahabhain joins the team as General Manager.
- 2011 Kilchoman 100% Islay is released as well as a 4 year old and a 5 year old.
- 2012 Machir Bay, the first core expression, is released together with Kilchoman Sherry Cask Release and the second edition of 100% Islay.
- 2013 Loch Gorm and Vintage 2007 are released.
- 2014 A 3 year old port cask matured and the first duty free exclusive, Coull Point, are released.
- 2015 A Madeira cask maturation is released and the distillery celebrates its 10th anniversary.
- 2016 Sanaig and a Sauternes cask maturation are released.
- 2017 A Portugese red wine maturation and Vintage 2009 are released.
- 2018 Original Cask Strength and 2009 Vintage are released.
- 2019 Capacity is doubled with two more stills. A limited STR Cask Matured is released.
- 2020 Am Burach and a fino sherry cask are released.
- 2021 Two bottlings matured in PX sherry cask and madeira cask respectively are launched.
- 2022 Casado and a Madeira cask matured are released.
- 2023 Expressions matured in casks that had held cognac, fino sherry and PX sherry are released.
- 2024 Batch Strength and Sanaig Cask Strength are launched.

Tasting notes Kilchoman Machir Bay:

GS – A nose of sweet peat and vanilla, undercut by brine, kelp and black pepper. Filled ashtrays in time. A smooth mouth-feel, with lots of nicely-balanced citrus fruit, peat smoke and Germolene on the palate. The finish is relatively long and sweet, with building spice, chili and a final nuttiness.

Kininvie

[kin•in•vee]

Owner: William Grant & Sons
Region/district: Speyside
Founded: 1990
Status: Active
Capacity: 4 500 000 litres
Address: Dufftown, Keith, Banffshire AB55 4DH
Website: kininvie.com
Tel: 01340 820373

It is probably safe to declare Kininvie as one of Scotland's most unknown malt distilleries. Its equipment is split between two sites, visitors are not allowed and bottlings are almost impossible to find.

In 1990 it was the first Scotch malt distillery to open in 15 years. Even if the general interest in single malt was still in its cradle at the time, the founder, W Grant & Sons, had for years experienced regularly growing sales of both Glenfiddich and Balvenie. At the same time these malts were also used for the megablend Grant's. More malt was needed and Kininvie was tailored to produce exclusively for blends.

In 2003 the blended malt Monkey Shoulder was launched and Kininvie became an important part of that as well. Some 20 years later that brand has grown to become the fourth best selling Scottish malt with almost ten million bottles sold in 2023. As a brand in its own right Kininvie had by then since a decade, starting in 2013, been bottled by the owners – both with age statements and as experimental releases – but this seems now to have ceased.

Kininvie distillery consists of one separate still house with three wash stills and six spirit stills. There is a 9.8 ton stainless steel full lauter mash tun which is placed in the nearby Balvenie distillery. Ten Douglas fir washbacks with a fermentation time between 60 and 70 hours can also be found at Balvenie. The volumes vary depending on what style is in the making. For "floral" (normally 25% of the production) there will typically be 20 mashes per week with a fermentation time of at least 70 hours. The other style, "cereal", takes 60 hours to ferment and there can be 25 mashes. Towards the end of the year there is also one week (10 mashes) of rye whisky production.

The first official bottling appeared in 2013 and since then a few experimental whiskies have been launched; the **KVSM001** was a 5 year old triple distilled single malt while the **KVSG002** was made from malted rye and barley, matured in virgin American oak. Finally, there is **KVSB003** which was a blend of double distilled malt and the aforementioned rye/barley whisky.

Kininvie KVSB003

History:

- 1990 Kininvie distillery is inaugurated and the first distillation takes place on 25th June.
- 1994 Another three stills are installed.
- 2006 The first expression of a Kininvie single malt is released as a 15 year old under the name Hazelwood.
- 2008 In February a 17 year old Hazelwood Reserve is launched at Heathrow´s Terminal 5.
- 2013 A 23 year old Kininvie is launched in Taiwan.
- 2014 A 17 year old and batch 2 of the 23 year old are released.
- 2015 Batch 3 of the 23 year old is released and later in the year, the batches are replaced by a 23 year old signature bottling. Three 25 year old single casks are launched.
- 2019 Three expressions in the Kininvie Works series are released.

Tasting notes Kininvie 17 years old:

GS – The nose offers tropical fruits, coconut and vanilla custard, with a hint of milk chocolate. Pineapple and mango on the palate, accompanied by linseed oil, ginger, and developing nuttiness. The finish dries slowly, with more linseed, plenty of spice, and soft oak.

Knockando

[nock•an•doo]

Owner: Diageo.

Region/district: Speyside

Founded: 1898

Status: Active

Capacity: 1 400 000 litres

Address: Knockando, Morayshire AB38 7RT

Website: malts.com

Tel: 01340 882000

John Thompson founded Knockando in 1898 but was already forced to close it two years later, in the aftermath of the disastrous Pattison crash.

When the famous English gin producer W&A Gilbey bought the distillery in 1903 it was at a real bargain price of £3,500 (which is the equivalent of £370,000 in today's value). This was their third acquisition of a whisky distillery in Scotland. The first was Glen Spey in 1887 (at £11,000) which was followed by Strathmill in 1895 (£9,500). All three distilleries were of approximately the same size, with just the one pair of stills at the time.

Knockando single malt soon became a vital part of Gilbey's blended Scotch Spey Royal and, after Gilbey's and Justerini & Brooks joined forces in 1962, it became one of the signature malts of J&B. It was also one of the first to be bottled as a single malt in the 1970s and, by the early 1990s, it was one of the top ten single malt brands of the world. It was, and to a certain degree still is, particularly popular in France and Spain. In 2023 the brand sold almost 700,000 bottles.

The distillery was closed in 2017 and re-opened again in autumn 2023. It is equipped with a small (4.4 ton), semi-lauter mash tun, eight Douglas fir washbacks and two pairs of stills. Historically, Knockando has always worked a five-day week with 16 mashes – eight short fermentations (50 hours) and eight long (100 hours). The nutty character of the newmake, a result of the cloudy worts coming from the mash tun, has given it its fame. However, in order to balance the taste, the distillers use boiling balls on the spirit stills to increase reflux and thereby creating the typical Speyside floral notes.

The core range of Knockando single malt used to consist of four expressions but has recently been diminished to just one – the **12 year old**. The 15 year old Richly Matured, 18 year old Slow Matured and 21 year old Master Reserve have all been discontinued.

History:

1898 John Thompson founds the distillery. The architect is Charles Doig.

1899 Production starts in May.

1900 The distillery closes in March and J. Thompson & Co. takes over administration.

1903 W. & A. Gilbey purchases the distillery for £3,500 and production restarts in October.

1962 W. & A. Gilbey merges with United Wine Traders (including Justerini & Brooks) and forms International Distillers & Vintners (IDV).

1968 Floor maltings is decommissioned.

1969 The number of stills is increased to four.

1972 IDV is acquired by Watney Mann who, in its turn, is taken over by Grand Metropolitan.

1978 Justerini & Brooks launches a 12 year old Knockando.

1997 Grand Metropolitan and Guinness merge and form Diageo; simultaneously IDV and United Distillers merge to United Distillers & Vintners.

2010 A Manager´s Choice 1996 is released.

2011 A 25 year old is released.

2017 The distillery closes for refurbishing.

2023 Production is resumed.

12 years old

Tasting notes Knockando 12 years old:

GS – Delicate and fragrant on the nose, with hints of malt, worn leather, and hay. Quite full in the mouth, smooth and honeyed, with gingery malt and a suggestion of white rum. Medium length in the finish, with cereal and more ginger.

Knockdhu

[nock•doo]

Owner:
Inver House Distillers
(International Beverage Holdings)

Region/district:
Speyside

Founded:
1893

Status:
Active (vc)

Capacity:
2 000 000 litres

Address: Knock, By Huntly, Aberdeenshire AB54 7LJ

Website:
ancnoc.com

Tel:
01466 771223

John Morrison is sometimes mentioned as the founder of Knockdhu. It is true that he bought the land in 1892 and discovered a high quality water source which he sent for analysis with distilling purposes in mind.

That is, however, as far as he became involved. Instead he sold the land to DCL which built the distillery. DCL was the largest player in the industry and their influence would strengthen over the years. The founders of the company, back in 1877, were seven grain distilleries in the Lowlands. Their expansion strategy was focussed on acquiring operational distilleries but Knockdhu was the first and one of few which they built by themselves.

The distillery is equipped with a 5 ton stainless steel lauter mash tun with a copper dome, eight washbacks made of Oregon pine (two of them used as intermediate vats) with a fermentation time of 65 hours and one pair of stills. The cooling is a combination of shell and tube condensers (including TVR heat recovery) and a wormtub which reduces the energy consumption. The production for 2025 runs a seven-day week and 19 mashes but due to an extended summer shutdown with the wormtub and the pot on the spirit still being replaced, the actual output will be slightly lower than last year. Towards the end of the year 500 tonnes of heavily peated malt (45 ppm) will be used.

The first official of anCnoc (as the single malt is called) was released in 1993 and today the brand sells around 250,000 bottles yearly which makes it the third biggest in the InverHouse stable after Old Pulteney and Speyburn.

The core range was revamped in early 2025 and now consists of **12 year old,** the new **16 year old,** the **Peated Sherry Cask Finish** and another novelty - the **10 year old Peated**. This means that the **18** and **24 years old** as well as the smoky **Peatheart** have all been discontinued. The only expression for the travel retail market, **Black Hill Reserve**, is also gone but there may still be stock available in the market.

12 years old

History:

1893 Distillers Company Limited (DCL) starts construction of the distillery.

1894 Production starts in October.

1930 Scottish Malt Distillers (SMD) takes over production.

1983 The distillery closes in March.

1988 Inver House buys the distillery from United Distillers.

1989 Production restarts on 6th February.

1990 First official bottling of Knockdhu.

1993 First official bottling of anCnoc.

2001 Pacific Spirits purchases Inver House Distillers at a price of $85 million.

2003 Reintroduction of anCnoc 12 years.

2004 A 14 year old from 1990 is launched.

2005 A 30 year old from 1975 and a 14 year old from 1991 are launched.

2006 International Beverage Holdings acquires Pacific Spirits UK.

2007 anCnoc 1993 is released.

2008 anCnoc 16 year old is released.

2011 A Vintage 1996 is released.

2012 A 35 year old is launched.

2013 A 22 year old and Vintage 1999 are released.

2014 A peated range with Rutter, Flaughter, Tushkar and Cutter is introduced.

2015 A 24 year old, Vintage 1975 and Peatlands are released as well as Black Hill Reserve and Barrow for duty free.

2016 Vintage 2001, Blas and Rùdhan are released.

2017 Vintage 2002 and Peatheart are released.

2019 A 16 year old cask strength is released.

2021 Vintage 2009 is released.

2023 Peatheart batch 3 is launched.

2025 A 16 year old is released.

Tasting notes anCnoc 12 years old:

GS – A pretty, sweet, floral nose, with barley notes. Medium bodied, with a whiff of delicate smoke, spices and boiled sweets on the palate. Drier in the mouth than the nose suggests. The finish is quite short and drying.

Lagavulin

[lah•gah•voo•lin]

Owner: Diageo

Region/district: Islay

Founded: 1816

Status: Active (vc)

Capacity: 3 200 000 litres

Address: Port Ellen, Islay, Argyll PA42 7DZ

Website: malts.com

Tel: 01496 302749 (vc)

For various reasons, including consumers' less purchasing power due to inflation and the overall geopolitical uncertainty, sales of Scotch whisky and spirits in general as well as beer and wine has taken a downturn in the last two years.

The reaction to this from a majority of Scotch malt producers is to, temporarily, slow down production. This can be achieved by implementing a five-day week with fewer mashes instead of running 24/7 or, in some cases, simply stopping production for a few months. Lagavulin on the other hand will be running at full capacity during 2025 which means 30 mashes per week and a total of 3 million litres of pure alcohol. The same goes for its sister distillery on Islay, Caol Ila. In the case of Lagavulin the brand has actually had a good progress in the past decade increasing sales by 55% to 2.5 million bottles in 2023 which makes it the second best selling Islay malt after Laphroaig and just ahead of Ardbeg.

The sudden interest in smoky Islay whiskies that started in the early 1990s, can to a large extent be attributed to Lagavulin and the fact that it was marketed as one of the Classic Malts from 1988 onwards. For many years it was the most sold Islay single malt but was surpassed by Laphroaig, in 2001.

On a peninsula next to the distillery stands the ruins of Dunyvaig Castle. In the 14th and 15th centuries it was used by the clan Macdonald (or Lord of the Isles) to protect the island from attacks from the sea. While Dunyvaig was used as a naval base, then actual settlement was located more inland on the north part of the island. The last person bearing the title Lord of the Isles, John Macdonald, had to give up his empire in 1493 and two centuries of fights between the Macdonalds and the Campbells followed. The main parts of Dunyvaig Castle were demolished in 1677.

The distillery is equipped with a 5.4 ton stainless steel full lauter mash tun and ten washbacks made of larch with a volume of 21,000 litres and a 55 hour fermentation cycle. Six of the washbacks have been replaced over the past few years. There are also two pairs of stills with three of them replaced in 2021. Foreshots are 30 minutes and the spirit cut starts at 72% and goes down to 59%. The usual phenol specification for the malt is 36ppm but three weeks per year heavily peated malt (50-70ppm) is also run. The newmake is, almost without exception, filled into ex-bourbon hogsheads. There are only around 7,000 casks maturing at the distillery and all of the new production is now shipped to the mainland for maturation.

The core range of Lagavulin consists of an **8 year old**, a **16 year old** and the **Distiller's Edition**, a PX sherry finish. There is also a **12 year old cask strength** which actually forms part of the yearly Special Releases. In 2025 this version had been matured in a combination of refill casks and PX and oloroso casks. In spring 2025 a **15 year old** with a two year finish in moscatel casks was released for the Feis Ile.

History:

- 1816 John Johnston founds the distillery.
- 1825 John Johnston takes over the adjacent distillery Ardmore.
- 1836 John Johnston dies and the two distilleries are merged and operated under the name Lagavulin. Alexander Graham, a wine and spirits dealer from Glasgow, buys the distillery.
- 1861 James Logan Mackie becomes a partner.
- 1867 The distillery is acquired by James Logan Mackie & Co. and refurbishment starts.
- 1878 Peter Mackie is employed.
- 1890 J. L. Mackie & Co. changes name to Mackie & Co. Peter Mackie launches White Horse with Lagavulin included in the blend.
- 1895 James Logan Mackie retires and Peter Mackie takes over the distillery.
- 1908 Peter Mackie uses the old distillery buildings to build a new distillery, Malt Mill, on the site.
- 1924 Peter Mackie passes away and Mackie & Co. changes name to White Horse Distillers.
- 1927 White Horse Distillers becomes part of Distillers Company Limited (DCL).
- 1930 The distillery is administered under Scottish Malt Distillers (SMD).
- 1952 An explosive fire breaks out and causes considerable damage.
- 1962 Malt Mills distillery closes and today it houses Lagavulin's visitor centre.
- 1974 Floor maltings are decommisioned and malt is bought from Port Ellen instead.
- 1988 Lagavulin 16 years becomes one of six Classic Malts.
- 1998 A Pedro Ximenez sherry finish is launched as a Distillers Edition.
- 2002 Two cask strengths (12 years and 25 years) are launched.

History continued:

2006 A 30 year old is released.

2010 A new edition of the 12 year old and a Manager´s Choice single cask are released.

2011 The 10th edition of the 12 year old cask strength is released.

2012 The 11th edition of the 12 year old cask strength and a 21 year old are released.

2013 A 37 year old and the 12th edition of the 12 year old cask strength are released.

2014 A triple matured for Friends of the Classic Malts is released.

2016 An 8 year old and a 25 year old are launched.

2017 A new edition of the 12 year old cask strength is released.

2018 An 18 year old is released for Feis Ile.

2019 A 19 year old is released for Feis Ile, a 9 year old House Lannister in the Game of Thrones series and a 10 year old for duty free.

2020 The 11 year old Offerman Edition and a 20 year old for Feis Ile are released.

2021 A second Offerman Edition, a 13 year old for Feis Ile and a 26 year old are launched.

2022 A third Offerman and a 28 year old Prima & Ultima are released.

2023 A 14 year old Feis Ile bottling and 25 year old 1997 Prima & Ultima are launched.

2024 The 29 year old Shies of Feis Ile, with an amoroso finish, is released.

2025 A 12 year old Special Releases and a 15 year old Feis Ile are launched.

Tasting notes Lagavulin 16 year old:

GS – Peat, iodine, sherry and vanilla merge on the rich nose. The peat and iodine continue on to the expansive, spicy, sherried palate, with brine, prunes and raisins. Peat embers feature in the lengthy, spicy finish.

Offerman Edition
11 years old

12 year old
Special Release 2025

15 year old
Feis Ile 2025

16 years old

8 years old

Distiller´s Edition

Laphroaig

[lah•froyg]

Owner: Suntory Global Spirits

Region/district: Islay

Founded: 1815

Status: Active (vc)

Capacity: 3 300 000 litres

Address: Port Ellen, Islay, Argyll PA42 7DU

Website: laphroaig.com

Tel: 01496 302418

Since 2001 Laphroaig has been the best selling of all the Islay malts. That was the year they passed Lagavulin on the list and today they are firmly cemented at the top with no contenders.

In 2023 Laphroaig sold just over 4 million bottles and with the continued increase in demand comes a need to also increase the production capacity. This has been discussed for a good many years and in April 2024 a request for a planning permission to expand the distillery was sent in to the Argyll & Bute council. It was approved a year later. The expansion project includes taking down the current visitor centre, which will be re-located on-site, and restore the original ground floor of the malting building. As it looks, the number of washbacks will increase by another twelve but it has not yet been communicated exactly how many stills there will be in a new still house. The plan is to increase the capacity from 3.3 million litres to 4.8.

Laphroaig is currently equipped with a 5.5 ton stainless steel full lauter mash tun and eight stainless steel washbacks. Two of them were added in March 2023, not to add to the capacity but to increase fermentation time from 53 hours to 72 hours. This will generate a more complex and fruitier flavour profile. The distillery uses an unusual combination of three wash stills (4,700 litres), one large spirit still (9,400 litres) and three smaller spirit stills (4,700 litres). All stills are fitted with ascending lyne arms and foreshots are unusually long – 45 minutes. The middle cut starts at 72% and goes down to 60%. The plan for 2025 is to produce 2.9 million litres of alcohol.

Laphroaig malts 20% of its own requirement on six malting floors to a specification of 45-50ppm with 10-12 hours on peat and 15-18 hours on hot air. For the past couple of years Laphroaig hasn't been able to buy peated malt from Port Ellen on the island. Instead they have relied on Simpsons on the mainland and have also shipped some of their Islay peat to them. In 2025 a closed loop cooling system to reduce the amount of water being used was installed similar to the ones already in place at sister distilleries Auchentoshan and Bowmore.

The core range consists of **Oak Select**, **10 year old, 10 year old cask strength**, **10 year old Sherry Oak Finish**, **Quarter Cask, Lore** and a **25 year old cask strength**. In June 2024 the popular **18 year old** was also re-introduced. The travel retail range consists of **Four Oak,** the **Cask Legacy, Port Wood** and **PX Cask**.

Recent limited releases include a **33 year old** in the new series **Strong Characters** from autumn 2024. There is also the second installment in the **Archive Collection** - a **38 year old** oloroso finish released in June 2025. This year´s edition in the Elements Series was **Elements No. 3** displaying unusual, toasty flavours due to an accidental kiln fire. There is also the **39 year old Rope** in the Wall Collection, released in August 2025. Finally, this year´s Feis Ile bottling was **Càirdeas Lore Cask Strength** - a marriage of five different cask types.

History:

1815 Brothers Alexander and Donald Johnston found Laphroaig.

1836 Donald buys out Alexander and takes over.

1837 James and Andrew Gairdner found Ardenistiel a stone's throw from Laphroaig.

1847 Donald Johnston is killed in an accident in the distillery. The Manager of neigh-bouring Lagavulin, Walter Graham, takes over.

1857 Operation is back in the hands of the Johnston family when Donald's son Dougald takes over.

1877 Dougald, being without heirs, passes away and his sister Isabella, married to their cousin Alexander takes over.

1907 Alexander Johnston dies and the distillery is inherited by his two sisters Catherine Johnston and Mrs. William Hunter (Isabella Johnston).

1908 Ian Hunter arrives in Islay to assist his mother and aunt with the distillery.

1924 The two stills are increased to four.

1927 Catherine Johnston dies, Ian Hunter takes over.

1928 Isabella Johnston dies and Ian Hunter becomes sole owner.

1950 Ian Hunter forms D. Johnston & Company

1954 Ian Hunter passes away and management of the distillery is taken over by Elisabeth "Bessie" Williamson.

1967 Seager Evans & Company buys the distillery through Long John Distillery, having already acquired part of Laphroaig in 1962. The number of stills is increased from four to five.

1972 Bessie Williamson retires. Another two stills are installed bringing the total to seven.

1975 Whitbread & Co. buys Seager Evans (now renamed Long John International) from Schenley International.

1989 The spirits division of Whitbread is sold to Allied Distillers.

1995 A 10 year old cask strength is launched.

2001 A 40 year old is released.

Oak Select | Quarter Cask | Lore

History continued:

2004 Quarter Cask is launched.
2005 Fortune Brands becomes new owner.
2007 A vintage 1980 and a 25 year old are released.
2008 Cairdeas and Triple Wood are released.
2009 An 18 year old is released.
2010 Cairdeas Master Edition is launched.
2011 Laphroaig PX and Cairdeas - The Ileach Edition are released.
2012 Brodir and Cairdeas Origin are launched.
2013 QA Cask, An Cuan Mor and Cairdeas Port Wood Edition are released.
2014 Laphroaig Select is released.
2015 A 21 year old and a 32 year old sherry cask are released and the 15 year old is re-launched.
2016 Lore, Cairdeas 2016 and a 30 year old are released.
2017 Four Oak and The 1815 Edition are released.
2018 A 28 year old and Cairdeas Fino are released.
2019 A 30 year old is the first release in a new series named The Ian Hunter Story.
2020 The Ian Hunter Story chapter 2 and a 16 year old are released.
2021 A 10 year old sherry oak finish and The Ian Hunter Story chapter 3 are released.
2022 Chapter 4 in the Ian Hunter Story is released.
2023 Chapter 5 in the Ian Hunter Story and Cairdeas White Port & Madeira are released.
2024 A 10 year old Cairdeas and Elements 2.0 are released.
2025 A 38 year old Archive Collection, Elements No. 3 and Cairdeas Lore Cask Strength are launched.

Tasting notes Laphroaig 10 year old:

GS – Old-fashioned sticking plaster, peat smoke and seaweed leap off the nose, followed by something a little sweeter and fruitier. Massive on the palate, with fish oil, salt and plankton, though the finish is quite tight and increasingly drying.

10 year old sherry finish | 18 year old

10 years old | 33 years old Strong Characters | Cairdeas Feis Ile 2025

Linkwood

[link•wood]

Owner: Diageo

Region/district: Speyside

Founded: 1821

Status: Active

Capacity: 5 600 000 litres

Address: Elgin, Morayshire IV30 8RD

Website: malts.com

Tel: 01343 862000

If one would poll with die-hard malt whisky aficionados which Diageo-owned single malts they would like to see more of on the shelves, there are a couple that would most probably occupy the top two spots – Clynelish and Linkwood.

Both have a complexity and depth that the consumers adore. Ironically, these characters are also what makes them scarce on the single malt market. They are simply too valuable for the owner to be used to enhance the character of any of their blends, not least Johnnie Walker. Both are represented by just a 14 and a 12 year old respectively and in the foreseeable future this doesn't seem to change.

Linkwood incorporates the best from two worlds by combining fresh, fruity, green/grassy flavours with a powerful mouth feel. To achieve the desired character, the wort is made as clear as possible, the fermentations are long and the stills are only filled just above the man door to enhance the copper contact. Furthermore, the spirit stills are allowed to rest for a minimum of one hour between runs to allow for the regeneration of the copper.

Linkwood is equipped with a 12.5 ton full lauter mash tun and 11 wooden washbacks holding 52,000 litres in one room. The fermentation time is either 80 hours in a seven-day week or varying between 65 hours and 105 hours on a five-day week. In two other rooms there are three 12,800 litre wash stills and three 14,200 spirit stills. The plan for 2025 is to reduce to five days production from July. In April 2024 a planning application was submitted to replace the existing gas boiler with one fuelled by wood pellets and this transition was completed by the end of 2025.

The only official bottling is the **12 year old Flora & Fauna**. In 2021, a 39 year old matured in American oak/PX and oloroso sherry was launched as part of the Prima & Ultima range.

History:

1821 Peter Brown founds the distillery.

1868 Peter Brown passes away and his son William inherits the distillery.

1872 William demolishes the distillery and builds a new one.

1897 Linkwood Glenlivet Distillery Company Ltd takes over operations.

1902 Innes Cameron, a whisky trader from Elgin, joins the Board and eventually becomes the major shareholder and Director.

1932 Innes Cameron dies and Scottish Malt Distillers takes over in 1933.

1962 Major refurbishment takes place.

1971 The two stills are increased by four. Technically, the four new stills belong to a new distillery referred to as Linkwood B.

1985 Linkwood A (the two original stills) closes.

1990 Linkwood A is in production again for a few months each year until 1996.

2002 A 26 year old from 1975 is launched as a Rare Malt.

2005 A 30 year old from 1974 is launched as a Rare Malt.

2008 Three different wood finishes (all 26 year old) are released.

2009 A Manager´s Choice 1996 is released.

2013 Expansion of the distillery including two more stills.

2016 A 37 year old is released.

2021 A 39 year old in the Prima & Ultima range is released.

12 years old

Tasting notes Linkwood 12 years old:

GS – Floral, grassy and fragrant on the nutty nose, while the slightly oily palate becomes increasingly sweet, ending up at marzipan and almonds. The relatively lengthy finish is quite dry and citric.

Loch Lomond

[lock low•mund]

Owner:
Loch Lomond Group
(Hillhouse Capital et al)

Region/district:
Western Highlands

Founded:
1965

Status:
Active

Capacity:
5 000 000 litres

Address: Lomond Estate, Alexandria G83 0TL

Website:
lochlomondwhiskies.com

Tel:
01389 752781

Situated in an old dye factory, Loch Lomond has never been suited to accomodate visitors. This has been mourned by many whisky enthusiasts as the brand has a colourful and interesting story to tell.

Recently the owners have come up with a solution which will not give access to the distillery itself but will create a brand home for the whisky including tastings, a bar and a shop in which to purchase the different products. This will all take place in Luss by the bank of Loch Lomond just a 15 minute drive to the north of the distillery in Alexandria. Planning permission was secured in early 2025 to repurpose an old smokehouse. The main purpose for the building will be a new distillery for the owners' award-winning Ben Lomond gin which until now has been produced at another location.

Loch Lomond has an unusual equipment setup with a 9.5 ton full lauter mash tun and 21 stainless steel washbacks (10 x 25,000 litres and 11 x 50,000 litres) with a fermentation time of 92 to 160 hours. It is on the still side however where things stand out. There is one pair of traditional pot stills and six pot stills with straight necks equipped with internal plates. Finally, a continuous still is there for distillation of malted barley. There are also two column stills with a capacity of 20 million litres for the production of grain whisky. In the last few years the distillery has been working at full capacity with 28 mashes per week. One important feature at Loch Lomond is the cooperage operated by nine full-time coopers. Together they repair and rejuvenate 40-60,000 casks per year.

The core range consists of **Loch Lomond Classic, Original, 10, 12** and **18 year old**. Furthermore there is **Loch Lomond Inchmurrin 12 year old** and **Loch Lomond Inchmoan 12 year old**. Recent limited releases include a new series named Waypoint with the cognac finished **16 year old Falls of Falloch** and the **31 year old Inversnaid to Inverarnan** finished in tawny port as the first editions. The duty-free range consists of **Origins, Alchemy** finished in Colombian oak, **Ingenuity** with a Swedish oak finish and **Copper** with a full bourbon maturation.

Loch Lomond 12 year old

History:

1965 The distillery is built by Littlemill Distillery Company Ltd owned by Duncan Thomas and American Barton Brands.

1966 Production commences.

1971 Duncan Thomas is bought out.

1984 The distillery closes.

1985 Glen Catrine Bonded Warehouse Ltd buys Loch Lomond Distillery.

1987 The distillery resumes production.

1993 Grain spirits are also distilled.

1997 A fire destroys 300,000 litres of maturing whisky.

1999 Two more stills are installed.

2005 Inchmoan and Craiglodge as well as Inchmurrin 12 years are launched.

2006 Inchmurrin 4 years, Croftengea 1996 (9 years), Glen Douglas 2001 (4 years) and Inchfad 2002 (5 years) are launched.

2010 A peated Loch Lomond with no age statement is released as well as a Vintage 1966.

2012 New range for Inchmurrin released – 12, 15, 18 and 21 years.

2014 The distillery is sold to Exponent Private Equity. Organic versions of 12 year old single malt and single blend are released.

2015 Loch Lomond Original Single Malt is released together with a single grain and two blends, Reserve and Signature.

2016 A 12 year old and an 18 year old are launched.

2017 This year´s releases include Inchmoan 12 year old and Inchmurrin 12 and 18 year old.

2018 A 50 year old Loch Lomond is released.

2019 The distillery is sold to Hillhouse Capital Management and a 50 year old is released.

2020 The core range is revamped and expanded.

2021 The 45 year old oloroso finish Remarkable Stills is released.

2022 A range of four grain expressions is launched.

2023 Steam and Fire and a 50 year old are released.

2024 The travel retail range is revamped and the Waypoint series is launched.

Tasting notes Loch Lomond 12 years old:

IR – Starts out malty on the nose followed by pears, apple pie with custard and digestive. Herbal at first on the palate with cinnamon and thyme, roasted root vegetables and nuts, caramel, vanilla and a hint of peat.

Lochranza

[lock•ran•sa]

Owner: Isle of Arran Distillers

Region/district: Highlands (Arran)

Founded: 1993

Status: Active (vc)

Capacity: 1 200 000 litres

Address: Lochranza, Isle of Arran KA27 8HJ

Website: arranwhisky.com

Tel: 01770 830264

To simplify things one could say that there are two approaches to adding more equipment and expanding a distillery's capacity – either you just make it cost-effective or you see the opportunity to enhance the aesthetics of the distillery.

Arran Distillers definitely took the second path when they added four more washbacks in November 2023. They could have just teared down a wall of the existing tun room to make some more space. Instead they built a new extension with an elegantly curved glass wall which created an excellent view, not least towards the nearby mountain, and let more light into the distillery. It was obviously more expensive but this attention to detail improved the looks of an already beautiful distillery.

Lochranza is equipped with a 2.5 ton semi-lauter mash tun with a copper top. There are ten 13,000 litre Oregon pine washbacks with the last four installed in November 2023. The extra washbacks were not intended to increase production but were installed to be able to run long fermentations (85 hours) throughout a seven day production. Finally there are two wash stills (6,500 litres) and two spirit stills (4,500 litres). 18 mashes per week with a total target of 750,000 litres of pure alcohol are expected in 2025.

The core range consists of **10, 18** and **25 year old, Quarter Cask The Bothy, Sherry Cask The Bodega, Barrel Reserve** and **Robert Burns**. The much appreciated **14 year old** will also return to the range The peated side of Arran is represented by **Machrie Moor Cask Strength** without age statement as well as a **10 year old** version. Limited (yet annual) expressions include three wood finishes – **Amarone, Port** and **Sauternes**. In spring 2025 the **10 year old - Arran Barley Edition** using locally grown barley appeared and a couple of months later the third edition of Arran Signature Series was released – the 12 year old **Duero Discovery** having spent the final six years in Spanish red wine casks. Expected in autumn 2025 are **Arran Rare Batch** and **Arran 30 year old First Release**.

10 years old

History:

1993 Harold Currie founds the distillery.

1995 Production starts in full on 17th August.

1998 The first release is a 3 year old.

1999 The Arran 4 years old is released.

2002 Single Cask 1995 is launched.

2003 Single Cask 1997, non-chill filtered and Calvados finish is launched.

2004 Cognac finish, Marsala finish, Port finish and Arran First Distillation 1995 are launched.

2006 Arran 10 years old is released.

2007 Four new wood finishes and Gordon´s Dram are released.

2008 The first 12 year old is released.

2009 Peated single casks, two wood finishes and 1996 Vintage are released.

2010 A 14 year old, Rowan Tree, three cask finishes and Machrie Moor (peated) are released.

2011 The Westie, Sleeping Warrior and a 12 year old cask strength are released.

2012 The Eagle and The Devil´s Punch Bowl are released.

2013 A 16 year old is released.

2014 A 17 year old and Machrie Moor cask strength are released.

2015 A 18 year old and The Illicit Stills are released.

2017 The Exciseman is released.

2018 A 21 year old and Brodick Bay are released.

2019 The core range is revamped and the limited Lochranza Castle is released.

2020 A 25 year old and the 21 year old Kildonan & Pladda are released.

2021 Drumadoon Point and two 15 year olds are released.

2022 Ten year old Machrie Moor and Rare Batch are released.

2023 A 17 year old and Remnant Renegade are launched.

2024 The 15 year old Peated Sherry Butts and Barrel Bonfire are released.

2025 Arran Barley Edition, Arran Rare Batch and Arran 30 year old are launched.

Tasting notes Arran 14 year old:

GS – Very fragrant and perfumed on the nose, with peaches, brandy and ginger snaps. Smooth and creamy on the palate, with spicy summer fruits, apricots and nuts. The lingering finish is nutty and slowly drying.

Longmorn

[long•morn]

Owner:
Chivas Brothers
(Pernod Ricard)

Region/district:
Speyside

Founded:
1894

Status:
Active

Capacity:
4 500 000 litres

Address: Longmorn, Morayshire IV30 8SJ

Website:
secret-speyside.com

Tel:
01343 554139

Having celebrated its 130th anniversary last year, Longmorn has entered into a more quite 2025. It was shut down in March to allow for the installation of MVR on the wash stills.

MVR (mechanical vapour recompression) is basically a heat pump attached to the wash still whereby energy is recovered and reintroduced back into the distillation process. This method of saving energy and thus reducing the emissions of CO^2 has already been implemented on a few of the Chivas distilleries since 2022 and the rest are to follow.

Longmorn has always been a blender's malt which means it can do wonders to the character of a blend – in Longmorn's case Chivas Regal and, not least, Royal Salute. The drawback of this is that whisky enthusiasts have a hard time finding official bottlings of the single malt. The owners have made a few attempts to establish Longmorn as a brand in its own right but without immediate success. Sales in 2023 amounted to just 52,000 bottles. Luckily there are independent bottlers who offer this very distinct and full-bodied single malt to the market.

The distillery is equipped with an 8.5 ton Briggs full lauter mash tun and ten stainless steel washbacks. There are eight, large onion-shaped stills with declining lyne arms producing a rich new make combining both depth and fruitiness. In the last few years, production has been running for five days per week with 18 mashes which means roughly three million litres of alcohol.

The previous core range, introduced in 2015/2016, consisting of The Distiller's Choice, a 16 year old and a 23 year old was replaced in February 2024 by an **18 year old** and a **22 year old**, both expressions being single batches and bottled at cask strength. They were recently complemented by a **30 year old**. There are also a **22 year old** and a **24 year old** in the Distillery Reserve Collection.

18 years old

History:

1893 John Duff & Company, which founded Glenlossie already in 1876, starts construction. John Duff, George Thomson and Charles Shirres are involved in the company. The total cost amounts to £20,000.

1894 First production in December.

1897 John Duff buys out the other partners.

1898 John Duff builds another distillery next to Longmorn which is called Benriach (at times aka Longmorn no. 2). Duff declares bankruptcy and the shares are sold by the bank to James R. Grant.

1970 The distillery company is merged with The Glenlivet & Glen Grant Distilleries and Hill Thomson & Co. Ltd. Own floor maltings ceases.

1972 The number of stills is increased from four to six. Spirit stills are converted to steam firing.

1974 Another two stills are added.

1978 Seagrams takes over through The Chivas & Glenlivet Group.

1994 Wash stills are converted to steam firing.

2001 Pernod Ricard buys Seagram Spirits & Wine together with Diageo and Pernod Ricard takes over the Chivas group.

2004 A 17 year old cask strength is released.

2007 A 16 year old is released replacing the 15 year old.

2012 Production capacity is expanded.

2015 The Distiller´s Choice is released.

2016 A 16 year old and a 23 year old are released.

2019 Three expressions in the new The Secret Speyside Collection are released.

2024 A new core range is introduced – an 18 year old and a 22 year old.

2025 A 30 year old is added to the range.

Tasting notes Longmorn 18 year old:

IW – Rich fudge, cappuccino dusted with cocoa powder and Creme de Cassis on the nose. Silky mouthfeel, elegant and balanced notes of fudge, espresso, Creme de Cassis and chocolate truffles, with a base line of maltyness and dryness.

Macallan

[mack•al•un]

Owner:
Edrington Group

Region/district:
Speyside

Founded:
1824

Status:
Active (vc)

Capacity:
15 000 000 litres

Address: Easter Elchies, Craigellachie, Morayshire AB38 9RX

Website:
themacallan.com

Tel:
01340 871471

In 2023 the club of single malt brands selling more than one million cases per year (i. e. 12 million bottles) was expanded from two to three. Since 2014 it had only been Glenfiddich and Glenlivet but recently they were joined by Macallan.

The distillery has undergone a tremendous development in recent years. In 2017 the old distillery was closed and a new, state of the art, distillery was commissioned. The first years following the opening the owners declared that the old distillery was just mothballed in case Edrington would need the additional capacity going forward. In 2024 however, when Macallan celebrated its bi-centennial anniversary, the company submitted plans to the local council to tear down the old distillery in order to revamp the industrial site into a home for nature.

The redevelopment of the old site has been named named "Project Marley" by the owners and demolition of some of the buildings started in spring 2025. Parts of the old structures will be kept as industrial artefacts while at the same time the creation of wetlands and a naturalised garden landscape will take place. Meanwhile, Macallan has been working with EDF Renewables to install solar panels which will take care of 25% of the distillery's electricity requirements.

Macallan is equipped with a full lauter mash tun with a 17 ton mash and 21 washbacks made of stainless steel with a fermentation time of 60 hours. There are also 12 wash stills and 24 spirit stills – quite small and with steeply descending lyne arms. They are not attached to any spirit safe and the spirits flow into a buffer tank and from there to the spirits filling store. Since the opening of the new distillery in 2017, the production has continuously been ramped up and in 2025 production will be fairly close to capacity which is 15 million litres of pure alcohol. There are 16 dunnage and 35 racked warehouses on site.

The core range of Macallan consists of **Sherry Oak 12, 18, 25** and **30 years old** and **Double Oak 12, 15, 18** and **30 years old.** Macallan Estate and Triple Cask (which used to be named Fine Oak) have been discontinued. The number of limited expressions is huge; **The Red Collection** with old and ultra-rare bottlings and a **78 year old** as the latest, the M Collection with **M Decanter, M Black** and **M Copper,** the **Harmony Collection** with two expressions inspired by tea as the latest, **Edition, Distil Your World, A Night on Earth, Tales of Macallan** and the **Fine & Rare** with single casks from 1926 to 1995. In 2024 a collaboration with Bentley Motors resulted in **The Macallan Horizon** and the same year, to celebrate the 200th anniversary, **Time:Space** and **Time:Space Mastery** were launched. The Macallan Quest Collection reserved for duty-free was in 2023 replaced by **The Colour Collection** with **12, 15, 18, 21** and **30 year olds**. Also available in duty-free is **Rare Cask Black**. Finally in 2025 six limited expressions were released to celebrate the **James Bond 60th Anniversary**.

History:

1824 The distillery is licensed to Alexander Reid under the name Elchies Distillery.

1847 Alexander Reid passes away and James Shearer Priest and James Davidson take over.

1868 James Stuart takes over the licence. He founds Glen Spey distillery a decade later.

1886 James Stuart buys the distillery.

1892 Stuart sells the distillery to Roderick Kemp from Elgin. Kemp expands the distillery and names it Macallan-Glenlivet.

1909 Roderick Kemp passes away and the Roderick Kemp Trust is established to secure the family's future ownership.

1965 The number of stills is increased from six to twelve.

1966 The trust is reformed as a private limited company.

1968 The company is introduced on the London Stock Exchange.

1974 The number of stills is increased to 18.

1975 Another three stills are added, now making the total 21.

1984 The first official 18 year old single malt is launched.

1986 Japanese Suntory buys 25% of Macallan-Glenlivet plc stocks.

1996 Highland Distilleries buys the remaining stocks. 1874 Replica is launched.

1999 Edrington and William Grant & Sons buys Highland Distilleries for £601 million through The 1887 Company with 70% held by Edrington and 30% by William Grant & Sons. Suntory still holds 25% in Macallan.

2000 The first single cask from Macallan (1981) is named Exceptional 1.

2002 Elegancia, 1841 Replica, Exceptional II and Exceptional III are launched.

Double Cask 30 years | Double Cask 18 years | Sherry Oak 12 years

History continued:

2003 1876 Replica and Exceptional IV, single cask from 1990 are released.

2004 Exceptional V, single cask from 1989 is released as well as Exceptional VI, single cask from 1990. The Fine Oak series is launched.

2005 New expressions are Macallan Woodland Estate, Winter Edition and the 50 year old.

2007 1851 Inspiration and Whisky Maker´s Selection are released as a part of the Travel Retail range.

2008 Estate Oak and 55 year old Lalique are released.

2009 The mothballed No. 2 stillhouse is re-opened. The Macallan 1824 Collection and a 57 year old Lalique bottling is released.

2010 Oscuro is released for Duty Free.

2011 Macallan MMXI is released for duty free.

2012 Macallan Gold, the first in the new 1824 series, is launched.

2013 Amber, Sienna and Ruby are released.

2014 1824 Masters Series (with Rare Cask, Reflexion and No. 6) is released.

2015 Rare Cask Black is released.

2016 Edition No. 1 and 12 year old Double Cask are released.

2017 Folio 2 is released. The new distillery is commissioned.

2018 The Quest Collection is released for duty free and Macallan M Black and Genesis are launched. Concept No. 1 and a 72 and a 52 year old are released.

2019 Macallan Estate, Edition No. 5 and Concept No. 2 are released.

2020 Double Cask 15 and 18 year old are released as well as the Red Collection.

2021 The third and final bottling in the Concept range is launched as well as Tales of The Macallan Volume I.

2022 The Harmony Collection, a 30 year old Double Cask and the 81 year old The Reach are released.

2023 The Colour Collection is launched.

2024 The Macallan Horizon is released.

2025 The James Bond 60th Anniversary collection is launched.

Tasting notes Macallan 12 year old Sherry oak:

GS – The nose is luscious, with buttery sherry and Christmas cake characteristics. Rich and firm on the palate, with sherry, elegant oak and Jaffa oranges. The finish is long and malty, with slightly smoky spice.

Double Cask 12 years

Harmony Green Meadow

73 years old

Colour Coll. 12 years old

M Copper

Rare Cask Black

Rare Cask Batch 3

Macduff

[mack•duff]

Owner: John Dewar & Sons Ltd (Bacardi)

Region/district: Highlands

Founded: 1960

Status: Active

Capacity: 4 100 000 litres

Address: Banff, Aberdeenshire AB45 3JT

Website: lastgreatmalts.com

Tel: 01261 812612

When you cross the river Deveron going from the Banff side to the Macduff side, you find the distillery on your right. The location is stunning and you would think that this distillery has been perfectly situated there for ages. Well, it hasn't.

In fact it was built in the early 1960s, surfing on the wave of Scotch whisky's popularity at the time. The distillery was in the forefront of modern whisky production: They were pioneers when it came to heating the stills using internal steam coils and instead of using a worm tub to cool the spirit vapours they introduced shell and tube coolers. Built by Scots it soon came under Italian ownership when Martini & Rossi bought it in the early 1970s.

Almost a decade before Martini & Rossi took over Macduff they had acquired the William Lawson's Scotch blend brand and it didn't take long until the single malt from Macduff became an integral part of that blend. It remains so to this day. Even though William Lawson's was the biggest loser of the Top 10 blends in 2024 (-9%) it is still number six on the Top Ten list of Scotch whiskies and sold 38 million bottles in 2024.

In 2022 a new Steinecker full lauter mash tun with a 8.7 ton mash (an increase from last years 7.8 ton) was installed. Included in the rest of the equipment are nine stainless steel washbacks (of 34,000 litres each). The fermentation time in a seven-day week used to be 55 hours but since the distillery has moved to a five-day week in 2025 there are both short (52 hours) and long fermentations (104 hours). Finally there are two wash stills with vertical condensers and three spirit stills with horizontal condensers and sub coolers. Foreshots run for 20 minutes and the cut points for the spirit run are between 74% and 64%. During 2025 the production will be based on 18 mashes per week resulting in 2.8 million litres.

The core range from the distillery is known under the name The Deveron and consists of a **10 year old** and a **12 year old**. For duty free there is a range, first launched in 2013, named Glen Deveron The Royal Burgh encompassing **16, 20** and **25 year olds**.

10 years old

History:

1960 The distillery is founded by Marty Dyke, George Crawford, James Stirrat and Brodie Hepburn (who is also involved in Tullibardine and Deanston). Macduff Distillers Ltd is the name of the company.

1964 The number of stills is increased from two to three.

1967 Stills now total four.

1968 The first bottling from the distillery is launched - the 5 year old Macduff Pure Highland Malt Scotch Whisky.

1972 William Lawson Distillers, part of General Beverage Corporation which is owned by Martini & Rossi, buys the distillery from Glendeveron Distilleries.

1990 A fifth still is installed.

1993 Bacardi buys Martini Rossi (including William Lawson) and eventually transfered Macduff to the subsidiary John Dewar & Sons.

2013 The Royal Burgh Collection (16, 20 and 30 years old) is launched for duty free.

2015 A new range is launched - 10, 12 and 18 years old.

Tasting notes The Deveron 12 years old:

GS – Soft, sweet and fruity on the nose, with vanilla, ginger, and apple blossom. Medium-bodied, gently spicy, with butterscotch and Brazil nuts. Caramel contrasts with quite dry spicy oak in the finish.

Mannochmore

[man•och•moor]

Owner: Diageo

Region/district: Speyside

Founded: 1971

Status: Active

Capacity: 6 000 000 litres

Address: Elgin, Morayshire IV30 8SS

Website: malts.com

Tel: 01343 862000

Mannochmore was founded almost a century after Glenlossie with which it shares the site south of Elgin. For many years they lived very much in symbiosis with the same workforce alternating between the two distilleries.

For almost twenty years though the two have been producing more or less at full capacity. The huge number of warehouses are still shared and are also used to mature whisky from many other Diageo distilleries. Until recently there were two boilers fed by gas but in the name of sustainability these were exchanged for three new boilers (shared with Glenlossie) in July 2025, all fuelled by wood pellets.

Mannochmore is one of the signature malts for the blended Scotch Haig which was first introduced in the late 1880s. The Haig family belonged to the top of Scottish whisky aristocracy and had been involved in distilling since the middle of the 17th century. Today the brand sells around 4 million bottles per year.

The distillery is equipped with a 12 ton Briggs full lauter mash tun. Capacity used to be 11 tonnes but since last year the distillery is practising high gravity mashing which requires less water and also increases the yield per tonne barley. There are eight wooden washbacks and another eight external washbacks made of stainless steel (all 52,000 litres each) as well as four pairs of stills. Clear wort and long fermentations (up to 100 hours) create a new-make spirit with a fruity character. Unlike Glenlossie (which will resume to a temporary five-day production from July 2025) Mannochmore will continue to run a seven-day production with 5.8 million litres.

The only current official bottling is a **12 year old Flora & Fauna**. A limited release in the Prima & Ultima range appeared in 2022 – a **31 year old** having spent almost thirty years in virgin European oak.

History:

- 1971 Distillers Company Limited (DCL) founds the distillery on the site of their sister distillery Glenlossie. It is managed by John Haig & Co. Ltd.
- 1985 The distillery is mothballed.
- 1989 In production again.
- 1992 A Flora & Fauna series 12 years old becomes the first official bottling.
- 2009 An 18 year old is released.
- 2010 A Manager´s Choice 1998 is released.
- 2013 The number of stills is increased to eight.
- 2016 A 25 year old cask strength is released.
- 2022 A 31 year old Prima & Ultima is released.

12 years old

Tasting notes Mannochmore 12 years old:

GS – Perfumed and fresh on the light, citric nose, with a sweet, floral, fragrant palate, featuring vanilla, ginger and even a hint of mint. Medium length in the finish, with a note of lingering almonds.

Miltonduff

[mill•ton•duff]

Owner:
Chivas Brothers (Pernod Ricard)

Region/district:
Speyside

Founded:
1824

Status:
Active

Capacity:
5 800 000 litres

Address: Miltonduff, Elgin, Morayshire IV30 8TQ

Website:
-

Tel:
01343 547433

For almost ninety years the whisky from Miltonduff has been linked to the world famous blend Ballantine's. At that time (in the 1930s) the distillery as well as the Scotch brand, were taken over by the Canadian company Hiram Walker.

While owners as well as the set-up of the distillery have changed over the years it compares to nothing with the huge overhaul of the distillery that is now taking place and is a major expansion of Miltonduff. A number of warehouses northwest of the existing distillery are being demolished to make space for a new distillery. The expansion is in two phases where the first one brings the capacity up to ten million litres and the second up to 16 million litres. This will eventually make Miltonduff one of the three largest malt distilleries in Scotland.

The distillery is situated seven kilometres south-west of Elgin, in the peaceful rural surroundings of Pluscarden. Once called the Garden of Scotland, this is excellent land for growing barley. That was one of the reasons for an abbey to be founded here by Alexander II in 1230. The influence of the abbey grew and a big part of the surroundings soon belonged to the monks of Pluscarden, including the site where Miltonduff now lies.

Miltonduff is currently equipped with an 8 ton full lauter mash tun with a copper dome, 16 stainless steel washbacks with a fermentation time of 56 hours and six, large stills. The lyne arms are all sharply descending which allows for very little reflux. This makes for a rather robust and oily new make in contrast to the lighter and more floral Glenburgie which is another huge influence in the Ballantine blend.

Official bottlings of Miltonduff first appeared in 2017 in the Ballantine's Single Malt Series. From 2024 however Miltonduff is no longer part of that range. Instead the only official bottlings are a **24 year old** in the Secret Speyside Collection (released in April 2024).

History:

1824 Andrew Peary and Robert Bain obtain a licence for Miltonduff Distillery. It has previously operated as an illicit farm distillery called Milton Distillery but changes name when the Duff family buys the site it is operating on.

1866 William Stuart buys the distillery.

1895 Thomas Yool & Co. becomes new part-owner.

1936 Thomas Yool & Co. sells the distillery to Hiram Walker Gooderham & Worts. The latter transfers administration to the newly acquired subsidiary George Ballantine & Son.

1964 A pair of Lomond stills is installed to produce the rare Mosstowie.

1974 Major reconstruction of the distillery.

1981 The Lomond stills are decommissioned and replaced by two ordinary pot stills, the number of stills now totalling six.

1986 Allied Lyons buys 51% of Hiram Walker.

1987 Allied Lyons acquires the rest of Hiram Walker.

1991 Allied Distillers follow United Distillers´ example of Classic Malts and introduce Caledonian Malts in which Tormore, Glendronach and Laphroaig are included in addition to Miltonduff. Tormore is later replaced by Scapa.

2005 Chivas Brothers (Pernod Ricard) becomes the new owner through the acquisition of Allied Domecq.

2017 A 15 year old is released.

2020 A 19 year old exclusive to Asia is released.

2024 A 24 year old in the Secret Speyside Collection is launched.

24 years old

Tasting notes Miltonduff 15 years old:

IR – Fresh citrus and honey on the nose together with heather, ginger and peaches. More spicy on the palate with cinnamon and clove, vanilla, honey, red berries and liquorice.

Mortlach

[mort•lack]

Owner: Diageo

Region/district: Speyside

Founded: 1823

Status: Active

Capacity: 3 800 000 litres

Address: Dufftown, Keith, Banffshire AB55 4AQ

Website: mortlach.com, malts.com

Tel: 01340 822100

Diageo, the owners of Mortlach, have always known what a rare gem of a distillery they were sitting on. A very unusual production regime results in a powerful whisky with plenty of character.

This is the kind of spirit that can make all sorts of wonders in a blend and over the years Johnnie Walker Black Label, not least, has benefitted from having Mortlach in the "recipe". Meanwhile the malt itself, with a 16 year old sherry bomb, was a part of the Flora & Fauna range until 2014 when a completely new range was launched. This range never took off and why is difficult to say but a new attempt was made four years later. This time it was a success and by 2023 almost one million bottles were sold.

The distillery is equipped with a 12 ton full lauter mash tun and six washbacks made of Douglas fir. For many years there have been both short and long fermentations but since mid 2023, it has been working at full capacity seven days a week with 16 mashes which means all fermentations are 55-59 hours. There are three wash stills and three spirit stills – all of them attached to worm tubs for cooling the spirit vapours. The distilling regime is probably one of the oddest in the Scotch whisky industry and with all the various distillations taken into account, it could be said that Mortlach is distilled 2.81 times.

The core range consists of **12 year old Wee Witchie**, **16 year old Distiller's Dram**, **20 year old Cowie's Blue Seal** and, for duty-free, the **14 year old Alexander's Way**. In 2024 a bottling that had been finished in Ramandolo white wine and Sangiovese red wine casks appeared as part of the **Special Releases**. The world-famous industrial designer Philippe Starck and Mortlach have initiated a collaboration with a trio of spirits, L´Evolution Collection, appearing in autumn 2024. It was made up of the new-make **Begin,** the **Beyond** which is a mariage of casks from five decades and finally **Become** – aged in virgin oak, red wine and refill casks.

12 years old

History:

1823 The distillery is founded by James Findlater.

1824 Donald Macintosh and Alexander Gordon become part-owners.

1831 The distillery is sold to John Robertson for £270.

1832 A. & T. Gregory buys Mortlach.

1837 James and John Grant of Aberlour become part-owners. No production takes place.

1842 The distillery is now owned by John Alexander Gordon and the Grant brothers.

1851 Mortlach is producing again after having been used as a church and a brewery for some years.

1853 George Cowie joins and becomes part-owner.

1867 John Alexander Gordon dies and Cowie becomes sole owner.

1896 Alexander Cowie joins the company.

1897 The number of stills is increased to six.

1923 Alexander Cowie sells the distillery to John Walker & Sons.

1925 John Walker becomes part of Distillers Company Limited (DCL).

1964 Major refurbishment.

1968 Floor maltings ceases.

1996 Mortlach 1972 is released as a Rare Malt.

1998 Mortlach 1978 is released as a Rare Malt.

2004 Mortlach 1971, a 32 year old is released.

2014 Rare Old, Special Strength, 18 year old and 25 year old are released.

2018 A new range is presented; 12 year old Wee Witchie, 16 year old Distiller´s Dram and 20 year old Cowie´s Blue Seal.

2019 The oldest official Mortlach bottling ever, 47 years, is released and a 26 year old appears in the Special Releases.

2020 A 25 year old Prima & Ultima is released followed by a 21 year old Rare by Nature.

2021 A 13 year old, partly matured in virgin oak, is released.

2022 The 30 year old Midnight Malt is launched.

2023 A NAS Special release bottling appears, partly matured in ex-Japanese casks.

2024 The first appearance of the Mortlach x Starck collaboration.

Tasting notes Mortlach 12 years old:

IR – Fresh and intense on the nose with notes of sherry, apple cider, dark plums, tobacco and toffee. The palate is robust with orange marmalade, dark chocolate, espresso and chili pepper.

Oban

[oa•bun]

Owner: Diageo

Region/district: Western Highlands

Founded: 1794

Status: Active (vc)

Capacity: 925 000 litres

Address: Stafford Street, Oban, Argyll PA34 5NH

Website: malts.com

Tel: 01631 572004 (vc)

Not only did the two Stevenson brothers, John and Hugh, build the distillery. They played a vital part in transforming Oban from a tiny fishing hamlet in the late 1700s into a modern and thriving town.

The two brothers had arrived in Oban around 1780 and they soon started a business that would be the foundation of their future wealth. They bought the small island of Belnahua, south-west of Oban, and opened a slate quarry. Together with another three islands (Easdale, Luing and Seil), Belnahua formed what was known as Slate Islands. For 200 years, starting already back in 1630, these four islands dominated the slate industry in Scotland with up to 8 million slates produced per year. Many of these slates went into building the houses when Oban was growing, but they were also exported to markets as far away as Australia. But the Stevenson brothers were industrial in many ways. They were involved in construction work, ship building and also started a tannery and a brewery before founding Oban distillery in 1793.

The equipment consists of a 7 ton stainless steel mash tun with rakes. The four wooden washbacks are made from Oregon pine and there is one wash still (16,880 litres) and one spirit still (8,296 litres) attached to a stainless steel worm tub to condensate the spirit vapours. For many years there have been five long fermentations (110 hours) and one short (65 hours) but with the new wash charger all fermentations are 119 hours. In contrast to the use of worm tubs, which often results in a heavy spirit, Oban newmake is fruity not least thanks to the long fermentations. In recent years the production plan has consisted of seven mashes per week. The distillery also boasts one of the best visitor centres in the business with 50,000 visitors every year.

The core range consists of **Little Bay**, a **14 year old**, an **18 year old** exclusive to the US market and a **Distiller's Edition** with a montilla fino sherry finish. Recent limited editions include **Old Teddy, Young Teddy** and, in October 2024, the final release in the MacLean series – **Grandson Derek**. Finally there is a **12 year old** matured in bourbon casks which was released in autumn 2025 in the Special Releases series.

Grandson Derek

History:

1793 John and Hugh Stevenson found the distillery.

1820 Hugh Stevenson dies.

1821 Hugh Stevenson's son Thomas takes over.

1829 Bad investments force Thomas Stevenson into bankruptcy. His eldest son John takes over.

1830 John buys the distillery from his father's creditors for £1,500.

1866 Peter Cumstie buys the distillery.

1883 Cumstie sells Oban to James Walter Higgins who refurbishes and modernizes it.

1898 The Oban & Aultmore-Glenlivet Co. takes over with Alexander Edwards at the helm.

1923 The Oban Distillery Co. owned by Buchanan-Dewar takes over.

1925 Buchanan-Dewar becomes part of Distillers Company Limited (DCL).

1931 Production ceases.

1937 In production again.

1968 Floor maltings ceases and the distillery closes for reconstruction.

1972 Reopening of the distillery.

1979 Oban 12 years is on sale.

1988 United Distillers launches Classic Malts and Oban 14 year old is included.

1998 A Distillers' Edition is launched.

2002 The oldest Oban (32 years) so far is launched.

2013 A limited 21 year old is released.

2015 Oban Little Bay is released.

2016 A distillery exclusive is released.

2018 A 21 year old is launched as a part of the Special Releases.

2019 Night´s Watch - Oban Bay Reserve and Old Teddy are released.

2021 A 12 year old Rare by Nature is released.

2022 A 10 year old Special Release with an amontillado finish is launched.

2023 Young Teddy and an 11 year old Special Release rum finish are released.

2024 A 10 year old Special Release is launched.

2025 A 10 year old Special Release and Grandson Derek are released.

Tasting notes Oban 14 years old:

GS – Lightly smoky on the honeyed, floral nose. Toffee, cereal and a hint of peat. The palate offers initial cooked fruits, becoming spicier. Complex, bittersweet and oak a. The finish is quite lengthy, with spicy oak, toffee and new leather.

Pulteney

[poolt•ni]

Owner: Inver House Distillers (International Beverage Holdings)

Region/district: Northern Highlands

Founded: 1826

Status: Active (vc)

Capacity: 1 700 000 litres

Address: Huddart St, Wick, Caithness KW1 5BA

Website: oldpulteney.com

Tel: 01955 602371

During the time when Pulteney was owned by Allied, the single malt produced was mainly destined for a part of the Ballantines blend. It wasn't until the current owners, Inver House, took over in 1995 that the brand was promoted on its own merits.

The company has worked hard making Old Pulteney available in markets all over the world and in 2023 it sold 730,000 bottles. This makes it the best selling malt in the Inver House group of distilleries. In older days the single malt was known as "the manzanilla of the north" in order to describe the dry, briny and slightly salty character of the spirit. Lately, the owners are instead using "The maritime malt" in their marketing which makes sense with fewer people today knowing what a manzanilla sherry is or tastes like. Pulteney is located in Wick and not only was the distillery closed between 1930 and 1951, but the entire town was dry. A law gave communities in Scotland the right to implement prohibition similar to the one that was enforced in the USA, provided a majority voted for it. The ban came into place in 1922 and it took 25 years until pubs were allowed to serve alcohol again.

The distillery is equipped with a stainless steel semi-lauter mash tun and seven stainless steel washbacks. Fermentation time is a mix of short (50 hours) and long cycles (110 hours). The wash still, equipped with a huge boil ball, is quaintly chopped off at the top. Both stills use stainless steel worm tubs for condensing the spirit. For the past few years, the distillery has been working a five-day week producing around 1.3 million litres of alcohol.

The core range is made up of **Harbour** and the smoky **Huddart,** both without age statements, as well as **12, 15, 18** and **25 years old**. For the travel retail market there is a **10 year old** matured in bourbon barrels, a **13 year old** finished in Spanish oak casks and a **16 year old** with a finish in oloroso casks. Limited releases include two in the Coastal Series – **Pineau des Charentes** and **Port**. There is also a new distillery exclusive, **French Oak**, bottled at 53%.

12 years old

History:

1826 James Henderson founds the distillery.

1920 The distillery is bought by James Watson.

1923 Buchanan-Dewar takes over.

1930 Production ceases.

1951 In production again after being acquired by the solicitor Robert Cumming.

1955 Cumming sells to James & George Stodart, a subsidiary to Hiram Walker & Sons.

1958 The distillery is rebuilt.

1959 The floor maltings close.

1961 Allied Breweries buys James & George Stodart.

1981 Allied Breweries changes name to Allied Lyons.

1995 Allied Domecq sells Pulteney to Inver House Distillers.

1997 Old Pulteney 12 years is launched.

2001 Pacific Spirits (Great Oriole Group) buys Inver House at a price of $85 million.

2004 A 17 year old is launched.

2005 A 21 year old is launched.

2006 International Beverage Holdings acquires Pacific Spirits UK.

2010 WK499 Isabella Fortuna is released.

2012 A 40 year old and WK217 Spectrum are released.

2013 Old Pulteney Navigator, The Lighthouse range (3 expressions) and Vintage 1990 are released.

2014 A 35 year old is released.

2015 Dunnet Head and Vintage 1989 are released.

2017 Three vintages (1983, 1990 and 2006) are released together with a 25 year old.

2018 A completely new core range is launched.

2020 A limited 34 year old is released.

2022 A limited 38 year old is released.

2023 The Coastal Series is introduced and a 13 year old is launched for duty free.

Tasting notes Old Pulteney 12 years old:

GS – The nose presents pleasingly fresh malt and floral notes, with a touch of pine. The palate is comparatively sweet, with malt, spices, fresh fruit and a suggestion of salt. The finish is medium in length, drying and decidedly nutty.

Royal Brackla

[royal brack•lah]

Owner: John Dewar & Sons (Bacardi)

Region/district: Highlands

Founded: 1812

Status: Active

Capacity: 4 300 000 litres

Address: Cawdor, Nairn, Nairnshire IV12 5QY

Website: lastgreatmalts.com

Tel: 01667 402002

Whether a washback (where the fermentation takes place) should be made from traditional wood or more modern stainless steel has always been up for debate.

A quick survey of the 1 300 or so washbacks in operation in the Scotch malt whisky industry shows that just about a majority (51%) are still made from wood. While these may be harder to clean compared to stainless steel ones, they also tend to contain small volumes of bacteria that could be essential for that particular distillery's character. That is also why the owners almost always exchange like for like when it's replacement time. An additional reason for that, essential to those distilleries accepting visitors, is that the wooden ones look much more interesting for the tour takers.

This is also what Royal Brackla did in 2025. The six wooden washbacks had reached the age of 40 plus years and six new ones made from Oregon pine were installed. The supplier was Joseph Brown Vats in Dufftown, established in 1921 and today owned buy the still manufacturer Forsyths. They have supplied washbacks to a huge number of distilleries over the years.

Royal Brackla is equipped with a 12.9 ton full lauter mash tun with a six hour mash cycle. There are six wooden washbacks and another two made of stainless steel – all with a fermentation time of 68 hours. Finally, there are also two pairs of large stills with tall necks and slightly ascending lyne arms. In 2025, due to a prolonged silent season to install the new washbacks and the fact that they have gone from a seven-day week to a five-day week, production has been reduced to 2.3 million litres instead of last year's 4.3 million.

The core range consists of a **12 year old** oloroso finish, an **18 year old** palo cortado finish**,** a **20 year old** finished in a combination of PX, oloroso and palo cortado and a rather new **25 year old** PX finish. There are also recurrent, limited releases for the travel retail market in the Exceptional Cask Series, a **25 year old oloroso finish** being one of the latest.

History:

- 1812 The distillery is founded by Captain William Fraser.
- 1833 Brackla becomes the first of three distilleries allowed to use 'Royal' in the name.
- 1852 Robert Fraser & Co. takes over the distillery.
- 1897 The distillery is rebuilt and Royal Brackla Distillery Company Limited is founded.
- 1919 John Mitchell and James Leict from Aberdeen purchase Royal Brackla.
- 1926 John Bisset & Company Ltd takes over.
- 1943 Scottish Malt Distillers (SMD) buys John Bisset & Company Ltd and thereby acquires Royal Brackla.
- 1964 -1966 The distillery closes for a big refurbishment and the number of stills is increased to four. The maltings closes.
- 1970 Two stills are increased to four.
- 1985 The distillery is mothballed.
- 1991 Production resumes.
- 1993 A 10 year old Royal Brackla is launched in United Distillers´ Flora & Fauna series.
- 1997 UDV spends more than £2 million on improvements and refurbishing.
- 1998 Bacardi–Martini buys Dewar´s from Diageo.
- 2004 A new 10 year old is launched.
- 2014 A 35 year old is released for Changi airport in Singapore.
- 2015 A new range is released; 12, 16 and 21 year old.
- 2019 A new range for travel retail, including 12, 18 and 20 year olds, is launched.
- 2021 The 18 year old palo cortado finish and the 20 year old sherry finish (three different types of sherry) become part of the core range.

12 years old

Tasting notes Royal Brackla 12 years old:

GS – Warm spices, malt and peaches in cream on the nose. The palate is robust, with spice and mildly smoky soft fruit. Quite lengthy in the finsh, with citrus fruit, mild spice and cocoa powder.

Royal Lochnagar

[royal loch•nah•gar]

Owner:
Diageo

Region/district:
Eastern Highlands

Founded:
1845

Status:
Active (vc)

Capacity:
500 000 litres

Address: Crathie, Ballater, Aberdeenshire AB35 5TB

Website:
malts.com

Tel:
01339 742700

The distillery lies beautifully in the lush greenery of the Royal Deeside – a wonderful area which stretches from the village of Banchory in the east to Braemar in the west.

This is a spectacular part of Scotland. My favourite route to the distillery is coming from the north on the old military road (A939), turning right at Gairnshiel Lodge onto the B976, enjoying the scenery as I continue south, driving a few hundred metres on the A93, then back on the B976 which crosses the river Dee right where the Balmoral car park is and then leading me to the distillery.

Royal Lochnagar is one of very few whisky brands holding a royal warrant. The background is the unlikely story of the owner at the time, John Begg, inviting his "neighbours", Queen Victoria and Prince Albert, in 1848 to come and visit the distillery. Prince Albert had recently acquired Balmoral Castle, just a kilometre away, and the royals apparently took a liking to the whisky and awarded Begg a royal warrant. Currently there are seven brands or companies in the Scotch whisky business that have earned the same recognition; Royal Lochnagar, Laphroaig, Dewar's, Johnnie Walker, Matthew Gloag & Sons, Berry Brothers and Justerini & Brooks. The latest time Royal Lochnagar's warrant was renewed was by Queen Elizabeth II in 2021 and again by King Charles III in 2024.

The distillery is equipped with a 5.4 ton open, traditional stainless steel mash tun. There are two wooden washbacks with short fermentations of 70 hours and long ones of 110 hours. The two stills are small with a charge in the wash still of 6,100 litres and 4,000 litres in the spirit still and the spirit vapours are condensed in cast iron worm tubs. The whole production (usually four mashes per week) is filled on site with 1,000 casks being stored in its only warehouse.

The official core range of single malts consists of the **12 year old** and **Selected Reserve**. The latter is a vatting of casks, usually around 18-20 years of age. A limited release in the Prima & Ultima range appeared in 2022 – a **40 year old** matured in refill hogsheads, bottled at 52.5%.

12 years old

History:

1823 James Robertson founds a distillery in Glen Feardan on the north bank of River Dee.

1826 The distillery is burnt down by competitors but Robertson decides to establish a new distillery near the mountain Lochnagar.

1841 This distillery is also burnt down.

1845 A new distillery is built by John Begg, this time on the south bank of River Dee. It is named New Lochnagar.

1848 Lochnagar obtains a Royal Warrant.

1882 John Begg passes away and his son Henry Farquharson Begg inherits the distillery.

1896 Henry Farquharson Begg dies.

1906 The children of Henry Begg rebuild the distillery.

1916 The distillery is sold to John Dewar & Sons.

1925 John Dewar & Sons becomes part of Distillers Company Limited (DCL).

1963 A major reconstruction takes place.

2004 A 30 year old cask strength from 1974 is launched in the Rare Malts series (6,000 bottles).

2008 A Distiller´s Edition with a Moscatel finish is released.

2010 A Manager´s Choice 1994 is released.

2013 A triple matured expression for Friends of the Classic Malts is released.

2016 A distillery exclusive without age statement is released.

2019 House Baratheon is released as part of the Game of Thrones series.

2021 A 16 year old Rare by Nature is released.

2022 A 40 year old Prima & Ultima is released.

Tasting notes Royal Lochnagar 12 years old:

GS – Light toffee on the nose, along with some green notes of freshly-sawn timber. The palate offers a pleasing and quite complex blend of caramel, dry sherry and spice, followed by a hint of liquorice before the slightly scented finish develops.

Scapa

[ska•pa]

Owner: Chivas Brothers (Pernod Ricard)

Region/district: Highlands (Orkney)

Founded: 1885

Status: Active

Capacity: 1 300 000 litres

Address: Scapa, St Ola, Kirkwall, Orkney KW15 1SE

Website: scapawhisky.com

Tel: 01856 876585

In the 1980s and 90s Scapa single malt had a solid, while not large, fanbase. Apart from the quality of the spirit there was something fascinating about this remote, underdog distillery overshadowed by the much larger Highland Park.

Scapa was taken over by Chivas in 2005 and the core 12 year old was replaced by a 14 year old and later by a 16 year old. At that time yearly sales figures were around 100,000 bottles. In 2015/2016 Skiren and Glansa appeared and sales more than doubled for a few years but soon dropped back again. The two expressions were exchanged for three with age statements (10, 16 and 21 year old) in late 2024. Hopefully this change will propel the interest in Scapa which celebrates its 140th anniversary in 2025.

The location is not just about whisky. After Germany's surrender in the First World War in 1918, the allied forces ordered the German navy to sail to Scapa Flow and lay anchor. In June 1919 the German admiral Ludwig von Reuter and his crew were successful in sinking 52 of the 74 vessels to prevent them from being used by any of the allied forces. During the following 15 years most were recovered and sold for scrap. The wrecks that remain under water have become popular to explore for scuba divers.

The equipment at Scapa consists of a 2.9 ton semi-lauter mash tun from Forsyth with a copper dome. Since 2019 there are four washbacks made of wood and eight made of stainless steel. The fermentation time is unusually long – 160 hours. Finally there are two stills. The wash still is a Lomond still sourced from Glenburgie distillery although with the adjustable plates removed. There is also a visitor centre with a lovely tasting room with a view to Scapa Bay.

The official core range is represented by a **10, 16** and **21 year old**. All three have been matured predominantly in first fill American oak. There is also a huge number of limited releases including vintages going back to 1977 as well as three expressions available only at the distillery - the NAS **Island Games,** an **11 year old** and a **14 year old**.

History:

- 1885 Macfarlane & Townsend founds the distillery with John Townsend at the helm.
- 1919 Scapa Distillery Company Ltd takes over.
- 1934 Scapa Distillery Company goes into voluntary liquidation and production ceases.
- 1936 Production resumes.
- 1936 Bloch Brothers Ltd (John and Sir Maurice) takes over.
- 1954 Hiram Walker & Sons takes over.
- 1959 A Lomond still is installed.
- 1978 The distillery is modernized.
- 1994 The distillery is mothballed.
- 1997 Production takes place a few months each year using staff from Highland Park.
- 2004 Extensive refurbishing takes place at a cost of £2.1 million. Scapa 14 years is launched.
- 2005 Production ceases in April and phase two of the refurbishment programme starts. Chivas Brothers becomes the new owner.
- 2006 Scapa 1992 (14 years) is launched.
- 2008 Scapa 16 years is launched.
- 2015 The distillery opens for visitors and Scapa Skiren is launched.
- 2016 The peated Glansa is released.
- 2020 Three vintages are released - 1977, 1979 and 1990.
- 2024 A new core range (10, 16 and 21 year old) is introduced.

10 years old

Tasting notes Scapa 10 year old:

IW – Intense vanilla and gingerbread on the nose followed by lemon tart, orange marmalade and apple crumble. Soft mouthfeel with immediate richness which turns to sweetness and creamy vanilla lusciousness, orange marmalade and tarte tatin, then gingerbread.

Speyburn

[spey•burn]

Owner:
Inver House Distillers
(International Beverage Holdings)

Region/district:
Speyside

Founded:
1897

Status:
Active (vc)

Capacity:
4 600 000 litres

Address: Rothes, Aberlour, Morayshire AB38 7AG

Website:
speyburn.com

Tel:
01340 831213

The start of the 20th century was harsh for the Scotch whisky industry and many of the smaller distillers trying desperately to survive were swallowed up by a few big companies.

The largest of these players was Distillers Company Limited (DCL) but along them there were "The Big Three" operating (John Walker & Sons, John Dewar & Sons and James Buchanan & Co). All four companies joined forces in 1925 in what has then been called "the big amalgamation". But before that DCL managed to pick up casualties along the way and one of the first was Speyburn in 1916. This distillery had been founded by John Hopkins & Co some twenty years earlier and they were also owners at the time of Tobermory. The price for the company and the two distilleries was £85,000. Speyburn was also the first distillery in Scotland to make use of drum maltings (already from the start in 1897) and although they were shut down in 1968 they are still there for visitors to be experienced as an unusual and exciting addition to the tour.

The distillery is equipped with a 6.25 ton stainless steel, semilauter mash tun. There are four wooden, 27,000 litre washbacks in a separate room and 15 made of stainless steel in an old dunnage warehouse. Fermentation time in a seven-day week is 72 hours. Finally there is unusual combination of one 27,000 litre wash still connected to a shell and tube condenser and two 12,500 litre spirit still attached to a worm tub. With a 20 minute foreshots and a wide spirit cut ranging from 74% down to 61%, the owners are aiming for a fruity character yet still retaining some body. Usually the production is 40 mashes per week and 4.6 million litres.

The core range is made up of **Bourbon Cask. 10, 15** and **18 year old** as well as the **Rum Cask Finish**. Hopkins Reserve and a 16 year old were recently discontinued in the travel retail range and were replaced by **Jerez** - finished in three types of sherry casks, **Kentucky** - matured in first fill bourbon and **Bordeaux** with a finish in cabernet sauvignon and merlot casks.

10 years old

History:

1897 Brothers John and Edward Hopkins and their cousin Edward Broughton found the distillery through John Hopkins & Co. They already own Tobermory. The architect is Charles Doig. Building the distillery costs £17,000 and the distillery is transferred to Speyburn-Glenlivet Distillery Company.

1916 Distillers Company Limited (DCL) acquires John Hopkins & Co. and the distillery.

1930 Production stops.

1934 Productions restarts.

1962 Speyburn is transferred to Scottish Malt Distillers (SMD).

1968 Drum maltings closes.

1991 Inver House Distillers buys Speyburn.

1992 A 10 year old is launched as a replacement for the 12 year old in the Flora & Fauna series.

2001 Pacific Spirits (Great Oriole Group) buys Inver House for $85 million.

2005 A 25 year old Solera is released.

2006 Inver House changes owner when International Beverage Holdings acquires Pacific Spirits UK.

2009 The un-aged Bradan Orach is introduced for the American market.

2012 Clan Speyburn is formed.

2014 The distillery is expanded.

2015 Arranta Casks is released.

2017 A 15 year old and Companion Casks are launched.

2018 Two expressions for duty free are released - a 10 year old and Hopkins Reserve. A core 18 year old is launched.

2023 The distillery opens to the public.

2024 Bourbon Cask and Rum Cask Finish are launched.

2025 A new range for travel retail is launched.

Tasting notes Speyburn 10 years old:

GS – Soft and elegant on the spicy, nutty nose. Smooth in the mouth, with vanilla, spice and more nuts. The finish is medium, spicy and drying.

Speyside

[spey•side]

Owner: Speyside Distillers Co.
Region/district: Speyside
Founded: 1990
Status: Temp. closed
Capacity: 850 000 litres
Address: Glen Tromie, Kingussie, Inverness-shire PH21 1NS
Website: speysidedistillery.co.uk
Tel: 01540 661060

Since 2012, Harvey's of Edinburgh have been leasing the piece of land south of Kingussie where Speyside distillery is situated. The lease expired in 2025 and the company is now moving the distillery to a new site near Strathmashie.

The new location is 15 kilometres to the west and close to the source of river Spey. Planning permission was secured already in 2023 and in early 2025 mash tun, washbacks and stills were sent to Forsyths for maintenance and storage until the new distillery is ready to start production. Meanwhile Glasgow Whisky, who took over the lease and the existing buildings, will build a new distillery named Glentromie. The construction is supervised by Graham Geddes who recently managed Jura distillery. The new distillery (with a capacity of 1.4 million litres) is expected to be up and running in the first half of 2026.

Before the closure in early 2025, Speyside distillery was equipped with a 4.2 ton semi-lauter mash tun, six stainless steel washbacks with a 120-180 hour fermentation time, one 10,000 litre wash still and one 7,000 litre spirit still. For the last years a six-day week has been in force with a total production of 600,000 litres of alcohol. Peated spirit has been produced for about two weeks a year. The plan is to increase capacity at the new site to 1.2 million litres of pure alcohol.

Spey single malt has been particularly popular in the Far East and not least in Taiwan. The owners are now looking to strengthen the brand's presence in the UK and other European markets.

The core range of Spey single malt used to consist of Tenné (port finish), Trutina (bourbon matured) and Fumare, similar to Trutina but smoky. All these were discontinued in late 2024 and replaced by **12, 15, 18, 26** and a **30 year old**. The only expression remaining from the old range is the **Chairman´s Choice PX** as well as the "black whisky" **Beinn Dubh** finished in ruby port casks. A version with age statement of the latter is expected in late 2025.

12 year old

History:

- 1956 George Christie buys a piece of land at Drumguish near Kingussie.
- 1957 He starts a grain distillery near Alloa.
- 1962 Christie commissions the drystone dyker Alex Fairlie to build a distillery in Drumguish.
- 1986 Scowis assumes ownership.
- 1987 The distillery is completed.
- 1990 The distillery is on stream in December.
- 1993 The first single malt, Drumguish, is launched.
- 1999 Speyside 8 years is launched.
- 2000 Speyside Distilleries is sold to a group of private investors including Ricky Christie, Ian Jerman and Sir James Ackroyd.
- 2001 Speyside 10 years is launched.
- 2012 Speyside Distillers is sold to Harvey´s of Edinburgh.
- 2014 A new range, Spey from Speyside Distillery, is launched (NAS, 12 and 18 year old).
- 2015 The range is revamped again. New expressions include Tenné, 12 years old and 18 years old.
- 2016 "Byron´s Choice - The Marriage" and Spey Cask 27 are released.
- 2017 Trutina and Fumare are released.
- 2019 Cask strength versions of Tenné, Trutina and Fumare are released.
- 2020 A 10 year old bourbon/port, a peated 12 year old and a 12 year old port cask are released.
- 2024 A PX version of Chairman´s Choice is released.
- 2025 A new core range is introduced and all the equipment is dismantled to be moved to a new location.

Tasting notes Spey 12 year old:

IW – Integrated fruityness on the nose then baked apples emerge, followed by honey, camomile tea, fresh apples, nutmeg and caramel. Indulgent mouthfeel, dry oak underlines crisp green apples and juicy pears, with creamy maltyness and linseed hints following.

Springbank

[spring•bank]

Owner: Springbank Distillers (J & A Mitchell)
Region/district: Campbeltown

Founded: 1828
Status: Active (vc)
Capacity: 500 000 litres

Address: Well Close, Campbeltown, Argyll PA28 6ET

Website: springbank.scot
Tel: 01586 551710

Many whisky lovers believe that Springbank has always been the one distillery which walks its own path, always relying on sales of their single malts for their success.

But this was not always the case. In the 1960s and 1970s, part of the whisky produced was sold to blenders and that is also why Springbank, like many others, were hit by the crash in the 1980s. They were forced to close the distillery from 1979 to 1987 and when they reopened, Hedley Wright, the owner and the great-great-grandson of one of the founders, made a decision. Never again should they sell their whisky to third parties but instead build their fortune on single malts. Springbank has also been famous for being the only Scottish distillery malting all their barley themselves but from 1960 to 1992, the maltings were closed.

The distillery is equipped with a 3.5 ton open cast iron mash tun and six wooden washbacks with fermentations between 72 and 110 hours. There is also one wash still and two spirit stills. The wash still is unique in Scotland, as it is fired by both an open oil-fire and internal steam coils. Ordinary condensers are used to cool the spirit vapours, except in the first of the two spirit stills, where a worm tub is used.

Springbank produces three distinctive single malts: Springbank is distilled two and a half times (12-15ppm), Longrow is distilled twice (40-45 ppm) and the unpeated Hazelburn is distilled three times. All the barley is malted on site. Lately the yearly production has been 210,000 litres of Springbank and 25,000 litres each of Longrow and Hazelburn.

The core range, **Springbank 10, 15** and **18 year old** and a **12 year old cask strength**, will be joined by **100° Proof**. There are also recurrent releases of **21, 25** and **30 year olds**. Recent limited releases include **Springbank Local Barley** and the **Countdown Collection** – this time a **30 year old**. The core **Longrow** is without age statement and is complented by **100° Proof**. For Hazelburn, the core expression is a **10 year old** complemented by limited annual releases.

Springbank 10 years old

History:

1828 The Reid family founds the distillery.
1837 The Reid family encounters financial difficulties and John and William Mitchell buy the distillery.
1897 J. & A. Mitchell Co Ltd is founded.
1926 The depression forces the distillery to close.
1933 The distillery is back in production.
1960 Own maltings ceases.
1979 The distillery closes.
1985 A 10 year old Longrow is launched.
1987 Limited production restarts.
1989 Production restarts.
1992 Springbank takes up its maltings again.
1997 First distillation of Hazelburn.
1998 Springbank 12 years is launched.
2000 A 10 year old is launched.
2001 Springbank 1965 'Local barley' is launched.
2002 Number one in the series Wood Expressions is a 12 year old with five years in rum casks.
2004 Springbank 10 years 100 proof is launched.
2005 Springbank 21 years and the first version of Hazelburn (8 years) are launched.
2008 The distillery closes temporarily. Three new releases of Longrow - CV, 18 year old and 7 year old Gaja Barolo.
2010 Springbank 12 year old cask strength is released.
2012 Springbank 21 year old and Longrow Red are released.
2014 Hazelburn 10 year old is launched.
2016 Springbank Local Barley is released.
2019 Springbank 25, Hazelburn 14 and a 21 year old Longrow are released.
2022 Longrow Red 15 year old pinot noir, a 21 year old Hazelburn and a 30 year old Springbank are released.
2023 Longrow Red 11 year old tawny and Local Barley 11 year old are released. Hedley G. Wright dies.
2024 Longrow Red 7 year old and a 26 year old are released.
2025 A 30 year old and Springbank 100° Proof are launched.

Tasting notes Springbank 10 years old:

GS – Fresh and briny on the nose, with citrus fruit, oak and barley, plus a note of damp earth. Sweet on the palate, with developing brine, nuttiness and vanilla toffee. Coconut oil and drying peat.

Strathisla

[strath•eye•la]

Owner: Chivas Bros (Pernod Ricard)

Region/district: Speyside

Founded: 1786

Status: Active (vc)

Capacity: 2 450 000 litres

Address: Seafield Avenue, Keith, Banffshire AB55 5BS

Website: chivas.com

Tel: 01542 783044

Sales of officially bottled Strathisla is virtually non-existent and the same goes for any independent expressions. The malt is made simply to become a part of the blend Chivas Regal.

The famous brand was established in 1909 and was for a long time owned by the Canadian company Seagrams. Since 2001 however it is in the hands of Pernod Ricard. It was one of a few brands who's sales were not affected in 2020 when the pandemic hit the world and in the two consecutive years volumes went up by a staggering 60%. It slowed down in 2023 (as it did for almost every brand) but the following year it was on the plus side again. A total of 58 million bottles were sold which rendered it a third place behind Johnnie Walker and Ballantine's in 2024. In 2024 the owners of Chivas Regal struck a promotion deal with Arsenal football club and this has been followed up by a collaboration with Ferrari and not least their top Formula 1 driver Charles Leclerc who has become the brand´s global brand ambassador.

Strathisla is the oldest working distillery in Speyside and third oldest in Scotland after Glenturret and Bowmore. Its picturesque appearance is adored by whisky tourists and every year around 15,000 visitors come here.

Strathisla is equipped with a 5.12 ton traditional mash tun with a raised copper canopy, seven washbacks made of Oregon pine and three of larch – all with a 54 hour fermentation cycle. There are two pairs of stills. The wash stills are of lantern type with descending lyne arms and the spirit stills have boiling balls with the lyne arms slightly ascending. The spirit produced at Strathisla is piped to nearby Glen Keith distillery just a couple of hundred metres down the road for filling or to be transported away. A small amount is stored on site in two racked and one dunnage warehouse.

For a long time there has been a 12 year old core bottling but this has now been discontinued. Official expressions though are still available in the way of seven bottlings (**8-29 years old**) in the limited **Distillery Reserve Collection** and there are also four bottlings (**11-21 years old**) exclusive to distillery visitors.

12 years old

History:

1786 Alexander Milne and George Taylor found the distillery under the name Milltown, but soon change it to Milton.

1823 MacDonald Ingram & Co. purchases the distillery.

1830 William Longmore acquires the distillery.

1870 The distillery name changes to Strathisla.

1880 William Longmore retires and hands operations to his son-in-law John Geddes-Brown. William Longmore & Co. is formed.

1890 The distillery changes name to Milton.

1942 Jay Pomeroy acquires a majority of the shares in William Longmore & Co. Pomeroy is jailed as a result of dubious business transactions and the distillery goes bankrupt in 1949.

1950 Chivas Brothers buys the run-down distillery at a compulsory auction for £71,000 and starts restoration.

1951 The name reverts to Strathisla.

1965 The number of stills is increased from two to four.

1970 A heavily peated whisky, Craigduff, is produced but production stops later.

2001 The Chivas Group is acquired by Pernod Ricard.

2019 Chivas Distillery Collection Strathisla 12 year old is released.

Tasting notes Strathisla 12 years old:

GS – Rich on the nose, with sherry, stewed fruits, spices and lots of malt. Full-bodied and almost syrupy on the palate. Toffee, honey, nuts, a whiff of peat and a suggestion of oak. The finish is medium in length, slightly smoky and with a final flash of ginger.

Strathmill

[strath•mill]

Owner: Diageo
Region/district: Speyside
Founded: 1891
Status: Active
Capacity: 2 600 000 litres
Address: Keith, Banffshire AB55 5DQ
Website: malts.com
Tel: 01542 883000

Morayshire in northeast Scotland is definitely the epicentre of Scotch and a must-visit destination for any whisky tourist. The towns of Dufftown and Rothes have ten distilleries altogether but in the eastern parts there is also the sometimes forgotten Keith.

This is where you will find Strathmill, Strathisla and Glen Keith distilleries and it is also one of the terminal stops of the heritage Keith and Dufftown Railway, also known as the Whisky Line. A lesser known fact is that Keith is one of the towns in Scotland where you will have a good chance of hearing doric being spoken. This is an ancient Scottish dialect which used to be common in Aberdeenshire and Morayshire and if you are generally having difficulties understanding Scots, doric will definitely be a challenge.

Whereas Strathisla is one of the main attractions along the Whisky Trail, Strathmill is hidden away on a side road right by the river Isla and with no visitor facilities. For many years, Strathmill single malt has been a key ingredient in the J&B Scotch blend. Until 2007, this was the second best selling blend in the world but since then sales have dropped considerably and it now resides in place number ten with around 29 million bottles sold in 2024.

The equipment consists of a 9.1 ton stainless steel semi-lauter mash tun and six stainless steel washbacks. There are two pairs of stills and Strathmill is one of few distilleries still using purifiers on the spirit stills. This device is mounted between the lyne arm and the condenser and acts as a mini-condenser, allowing the lighter alcohols to travel towards the condenser and forcing the heavier alcohols to flow back into the still for another distillation. The result of this is a lighter spirit. For quite a few years, Strathmill has been producing gin but when on whisky, it generally operates on a five-day week with 10 mashes per week and 2 million litres of alcohol in the year.

The only official bottling is the **12 year old Flora & Fauna**, but a limited **25 year old** was launched in 2014 as part of the Special Releases.

12 years old

History:

- 1891 The distillery is founded in an old mill from 1823 and is named Glenisla-Glenlivet Distillery.
- 1892 The inauguration takes place in June.
- 1895 The gin company W. & A. Gilbey buys the distillery for £9,500 and names it Strathmill.
- 1962 W. & A. Gilbey merges with United Wine Traders (including Justerini & Brooks) and forms International Distillers & Vintners (IDV).
- 1968 The number of stills is increased from two to four and purifiers are added.
- 1972 IDV is bought by Watney Mann which later the same year is acquired by Grand Metropolitan.
- 1993 Strathmill becomes available as a single malt for the first time since 1909 as a result of a bottling (1980) from Oddbins.
- 1997 Guinness and Grand Metropolitan merge and form Diageo.
- 2001 The first official bottling is a 12 year old in the Flora & Fauna series.
- 2010 A Manager´s Choice single cask from 1996 is released.
- 2014 A 25 year old is released.

Tasting notes Strathmill 12 years old:

GS – Quite reticent on the nose, with nuts, grass and a hint of ginger. Spicy vanilla and nuts dominate the palate. The finish is drying, with peppery oak.

Talisker

[tal•iss•kur]

Owner: Diageo

Region/district: Highlands (Skye)

Founded: 1830

Status: Active (vc)

Capacity: 3 500 000 litres

Address: Carbost, Isle of Skye, Inverness-shire IV47 8SR

Website: malts.com

Tel: 01478 614308 (vc)

In the year 2000 Talisker single malt sold around 500,000 bottles which by no means was bad at a time when single malts had just started to take off. It was ranked as 17th place in the sales list.

Around that time the owners, Diageo, were putting a lot more attention to their malts. Admittedly they had launched the Classic Malts concept (of which Talisker was part) already in 1988 and this had a tremendous impact on the interest in malt whisky and not just for Diageo. Their ambitions for Talisker however were greater and they took a decision to invest in the brand hoping that it would make it into the Top 10 in the near future. Their plans paid off. In 2023 Talisker sold 4,5 million bottles and is the seventh best selling Scotch single malt in the world.

At the same time it is not a large distillery (just 3.5 million litres) so plans were hatched to increase capacity. In October 2024 a planning application was submitted to the local council. The plans entail a demolition of the current distillery but not until a completely new one has been built. The re-development is a huge undertaking and in view of the recent downturn in the spirits business it remains to be seen when it will all start to happen.

The distillery is equipped with a stainless steel lauter mash tun with a capacity of 8.75 tonnes and eight washbacks made of Oregon pine. Before mashing, the malted barley is mixed to a ratio of 25% unpeated and 75% peated which has a phenol specification of 20-25ppm. There are five stills – two wash stills and three spirit stills. The wash stills are equipped with a special type of "purifiers" or, more specifically, return pipes, which use the colder outside air, and there is also a u-bend in the lyne arms. The return pipes and the peculiar bend of the lyne arms allow for more copper contact and increases the reflux during distillation. All of the stills are connected to wormtubs. The fermentation time is around 60 hours and the middle cut from the spirit still is collected between 76% and 65% which, together with the phenol specification, gives a medium peated spirit. With 20 mashes per week and a high-gravity mash the result in 3.5 million litres of alcohol in a year.

Talisker's core range consists of **Skye** and **Storm**, both without age statement, **10, 18, 25** and **30 year old, Distiller's Edition** with an Amoroso sherry finish and **Port Ruighe**, finished in ruby port casks. There is also **Dark Storm** which is exclusive to duty free together with **Surge**. In spring 2023 **Wilder Seas**, finished in cognac casks, became the second installment in a range aimed at preserving sea forests around the planet and it was followed in November by the **45 year old Glacial Edge**. In spring 2025 **The Wild Blue** without age statement was launched. Finished in red wine casks from South Africa, a £3 donation per sold bottle goes to the Blue Marine Foundation. In autumn 2025 a **14 year old** that had been finished in toasted American oak appeared as part of this years **Special Releases**.

History:

1830 Hugh and Kenneth MacAskill found the distillery.

1848 The brothers transfer the lease to North of Scotland Bank and Jack Westland from the bank runs the operations.

1854 Kenneth MacAskill dies.

1857 North of Scotland Bank sells the distillery to Donald MacLennan for £500.

1863 MacLennan experiences difficulties in making operations viable and puts the distillery up for sale.

1865 MacLennan, still working at the distillery, nominates John Anderson as agent in Glasgow.

1867 Anderson & Co. from Glasgow takes over.

1879 John Anderson is imprisoned after having sold non-existing casks of whisky.

1880 New owners are now Alexander Grigor Allan and Roderick Kemp.

1892 Kemp sells his share and buys Macallan Distillery instead.

1894 The Talisker Distillery Ltd is founded.

1895 Allan dies and Thomas Mackenzie, who has been his partner, takes over.

1898 Talisker Distillery merges with Dailuaine-Glenlivet Distillers and Imperial Distillers to form Dailuaine-Talisker Distillers Company.

1916 Thomas Mackenzie dies and the distillery is taken over by a consortium consisting of, among others, John Walker, John Dewar, W. P. Lowrie and Distillers Company Limited (DCL).

1928 The distillery abandons triple distillation.

1960 On 22nd November the distillery catches fire and substantial damage occurs.

1962 The distillery reopens after the fire.

1972 Own malting ceases.

1988 Classic Malts are introduced, Talisker 10 years included. A visitor centre is opened.

1998 A Distillers Edition with an amoroso sherry finish is released.

History continued:

2004 An 18 year old and a 25 year old are launched.

2005 Talisker 175th Anniversary is released.

2006 A 30 year old and the fourth edition of the 25 year old are released.

2008 Talisker 57° North is launched.

2009 New editions of 25 and 30 year old are released.

2010 A 1994 Manager´s Choice single cask and a new edition of the 30 year old are released.

2013 Four new expressions are released – Storm, Dark Storm, Port Ruighe and a 27 year old.

2014 A bottling for the Friends of the Classic Malts is released.

2015 Skye and Neist Point are released.

2018 A 40 year old, the new Bodega Series and an 8 year old Special Release are launched.

2019 A 41 year old Bodega Series and House Greyjoy in the Game of Thrones series are released.

2020 A 31 year old Prima & Ultima and an 8 year old rum finish Rare by Nature are released.

2021 A 43 year old and an 8 year old Special Releases are released.

2022 The 27 year old Talisker Elements, the 44 year old Forests of the Deep and Talisker Surge are launched.

2023 Wilder Seas and the 45 year old Glacial Edge are launched.

2024 An 8 year old Special Release and a 30 year old are released.

2025 The Wild Blue and a 14 year old Special Releases are launched.

Tasting notes Talisker 10 years old:

GS – Quite dense and smoky on the nose, with smoked fish, bladderwrack, sweet fruit and peat. Full-bodied and peaty in the mouthy; complex, with ginger, ozone, dark chocolate, black pepper and a kick of chilli in the long, smoky tail.

Port Ruighe

Storm

30 year old

10 years old

18 years old

Surge

The Wild Blue

Special Release 2025

Tamdhu

[tam•doo]

Owner:
Ian Macleod Distillers

Region/district:
Speyside

Founded:
1897

Status:
Active

Capacity:
4 000 000 litres

Address: Knockando, Aberlour, Morayshire AB38 7RP

Website:
tamdhu.com

Tel:
01340 872200

Tamdhu has now been in the capable hands of Ian Macleod Distillers for fourteen years. Once a workhorse for blends in the Edrington stable of distilleries, it has been completely renewed and rebranded in recent years.

The new owners carried on with Edrington's dedication to sherry casks for maturation. That approach came as no surprise as this is exactly what made Glengoyne, another distillery owned by Ian Macleod, successful. First and second fill oloroso casks made from both European and American Oak is the key to Tamdhu's flavour profile. The concept seems successful as sales have gone from virtually nothing to 250,000 bottles in just a few years.

On a narrow sideway of the B9102 leading down to Spey, Tamdhu is beautifully situated just by the river. Unfortunately the distillery is only open to the public during the Speyside Whisky Festival. However there are daily opportunities to take part in a 90 minute tasting of Tamdhu at the sister distillery Rosebank in Falkirk – booking is required.

Tamdhu is equipped with an 11.85 ton semilauter mash tun and nine Oregon pine washbacks with a fermentation time of 59 hours. There are three 22,500 litre wash stills with sustainable TVR (thermal vapour recompression) installed in 2023 and three 18,300 litre spirit stills. An on-site cooperage for repairing and testing casks became operational in 2019. The production for 2025 is set on 18 mashes per week and 3 million litres of pure alcohol. On site there are also no less than 28 warehouses - dunnage, racked and palletised.

The core range consists of a **12 year old**, a **15 year old,** an **18 year old** and a **21 year old** which was added to the range in May 2025. The non-chill filtered **Batch Strength** is released yearly. Recent limited releases include the fourth edition of **Cigar Malt** in autumn 2024, a **43 year old** and a **46 year old** in the Dedication Collection and **Tamdhu Distinction IV** being released in 2025. Finally, for the travel retail market there are **Ámbar Vintage, Gran Reserva** and **Cuatro Reserva**.

12 years old

History:

1896 The distillery is founded by Tamdhu Distillery Company, a consortium of whisky blenders with William Grant as the main promoter. Charles Doig is the architect.

1897 The first casks are filled in July.

1898 Highland Distillers Company, which has several of the 1896 consortium members in managerial positions, buys Tamdhu Distillery Company.

1911 The distillery closes.

1913 The distillery reopens.

1928 The distillery is mothballed.

1948 The distillery is in full production again in July.

1950 The floor maltings is replaced by Saladin boxes when the distillery is rebuilt.

1972 The number of stills is increased from two to four.

1975 Two stills augment the previous four.

1976 Tamdhu 8 years is launched as single malt.

2005 An 18 year old and a 25 year old are released.

2009 The distillery is mothballed.

2011 The Edrington Group sells the distillery to Ian Macleod Distillers.

2012 Production is resumed.

2013 The first official release from the new owners – a 10 year old.

2015 Tamdhu Batch Strength is released.

2017 A 50 year old is released.

2018 A 12 year old, a 15 year old and the Dalbeallie Dram are released.

2019 Two expressions for duty-free - Ámbar and Gran Reserva First Edition.

2020 Iain Whitecross Single Cask and Cigar Malt are launched.

2021 Quercus Alba Distinction is released.

2022 Tamdhu Club Single Cask, Tamdhu Distinction II and an 18 year old are launched.

2023 Tamdhu Distinction III is launched.

2024 The 43 year old Dedication Collection is released.

2025 A 21 year old and Distinction IV are released.

Tasting notes Tamdhu 12 years old:

IR – Distinct sherry notes on the nose with raisins and prunes as well as menthol and green leaves. The taste is wellbalanced with dried fruit, crème brûlée, roasted nuts, bananas and cinnamon.

Tamnavulin

[tam•na•voo•lin]

Owner: Whyte & Mackay (Emperador)

Region/district: Speyside

Founded: 1966

Status: Active

Capacity: 4 500 000 litres

Address: Tomnavoulin, Ballindalloch, Banffshire AB3 9JA

Website: tamnavulinwhisky.com

Tel: 01807 590285

The progress of Tamnavulin single malt in terms of sales during the past five years is extraordinary. The closest contestants are stablemates Dalmore and Jura, all three owned and operated by Whyte & Mackay.

In 2023 Tamnavulin sold 2.6 million bottles which makes it the 14th best selling Scotch single malt in the world (and number five in the UK), ahead of such prominent brands as Lagavulin, Highland Park and Ardbeg. While being a very well-made malt whisky, part of its success can probably be attributed to the fact that it is positioned in the lower bracket in terms of price – not least important in times of economic uncertainty.

There are now solid plans to follow up on the brand's popularity by adding a brand home to welcome visitors. It probably won't be ready until 2026/27 but the intention is to use the same building from the 1830s which used to house a visitor centre yet at the same time expanding with new buildings.

Tamnavulin distillery is equipped with a full lauter mash tun with an 11 ton charge, nine 48,500 litre washbacks made of stainless steel with a fermentation time of 57-60 hours and three pairs of stills. The wash stills, with horizontal lyne arms, are all equipped with sub-coolers while the spirit stills with their descending lyne arms have purifiers, although currently not in use. The foreshots are running for 25 minutes and the heart is collected from 75% down to 60% resulting in a slightly grassy new make. In 2025 the distillery will be mashing 22 times per week for 46 weeks, aiming for 4.5 million litres of alcohol. There are two racked warehouses on site holding 40,000 casks.

The core expression is **Double Cask** with a sherry finish. In 2019 a **Sherry Cask Edition** with a finish in three types of oloroso casks was launched and in 2020 three wine cask finishes were added – **Cabernet Sauvignon, Grenache** and **Pinot Noir**. These were recently followed by a **Sauvignon Blanc** finish and, in 2024, a **Port Cask Edition**. There are also a **Tempranillo finish**, an **Oloroso finish** and a **Sauvignon Blanc finish** for duty free.

History:

- 1966 Tamnavulin-Glenlivet Distillery Company, a subsidiary of Invergordon Distillers Ltd, founds Tamnavulin.
- 1993 Whyte & Mackay buys Invergordon Distillers.
- 1995 The distillery closes in May.
- 1996 Whyte & Mackay changes name to JBB (Greater Europe).
- 2000 Distillation takes place for six weeks.
- 2001 Company management buy out operations for £208 million and rename the company Kyndal.
- 2003 Kyndal changes name to Whyte & Mackay.
- 2007 United Spirits buys Whyte & Mackay. Tamnavulin is opened again in July after having been mothballed for 12 years.
- 2014 Whyte & Mackay is sold to Emperador Inc.
- 2016 Tamnavulin Double Cask is released.
- 2019 Sherry Cask Edition and Tempranillo Finish are released.
- 2020 Three wine cask finishes are released; cabernet sauvignon, grenache and pinot noir.
- 2022 A sauvignon blanc finish is released.
- 2024 A port cask finish is launched.

Double Cask

Tasting notes Tamnavulin Double Cask:

GS – The nose offers malt, soft toffee, almonds and tangerines. Finally, background earthiness. Smooth on the palate, with ginger nut biscuits, vanilla and orchard fruits, plus walnuts. The finish is medium in length, with lingering fruity spice.

Teaninich

[tee•ni•nick]

Owner: Diageo

Region/district: Northern Highlands

Founded: 1817

Status: Active

Capacity: 10 200 000 litres

Address: Alness, Ross-shire IV17 0XB

Website: malts.com

Tel: 01349 885001

For 25 years Teaninich has been an anomaly in the Scotch whisky industry due to the fact that a hammer mill is used to grind the malted barley and a mash filter used to convert the starch into sugar.

In recent years a few distilleries have taken up on that very unusual scheme – most notably Inchdairnie. The investment is substantial compared to common practise but the advantage is that any type of mashbill can be handled with a decent yield. In the case of Teaninich it means that they have been capable of distilling whisky made from rye, even if it that hasn´t been done on a yearly basis.

Teaninich is the second oldest of the distilleries north of Inverness that survived into the new millennium. Balblair, the oldest, was founded 27 years earlier. At one time, back in the 1970s, it was one of the largest distilleries in Scotland with its capacity of 6 million litres. Situated in what is today an industrial area of Alness, one would have thought that a distillery with such a heritage would have had spells of glory over the years but it very much continued making whisky for blends in the shadows.

The equipment consists of a Meura hammer mill, a Meura mash filter (two times 7 ton mash) with 76 plates, 18 wooden and two stainless steel washbacks with a fermentation time of 78 hours, and six wash stills (18,000 litres) and six spirit stills (15,500 litres). A typical production year at Teaninich entails running full production from October to June, having a quiet run in July and slowly ramping up (due to water supply) from July and onwards.

In spite of its considerable size, Teaninich is definitely one of the most anonymous Scotch malt distilleries. The only official core bottling is a **10 year old** in the Flora & Fauna series. In autumn 2025 however, a limited **8 year old** in the yearly Special Releases series was released. What made this bottling so special was that is was made from rye and hence was labeled single grain whisky to comply with the SWA regulations.

8 years old
Special Releases 2025

History:

1817 Captain Hugh Munro, owner of the estate Teaninich, founds the distillery.

1831 Captain Munro sells the estate to his younger brother John.

1850 John Munro, who spends most of his time in India, leases Teaninich to the infamous Robert Pattison from Leith.

1869 John McGilchrist Ross takes over the licence.

1895 Munro & Cameron takes over the licence.

1898 Munro & Cameron buys the distillery.

1904 Robert Innes Cameron becomes sole owner of Teaninich.

1932 Robert Innes Cameron dies.

1933 The estate of Robert Innes Cameron sells the distillery to Distillers Company Limited.

1970 A new distillation unit with six stills is commissioned and becomes known as the A side.

1975 A dark grains plant is built.

1984 The B side of the distillery is mothballed.

1985 The A side is also mothballed.

1991 The A side is in production again.

1992 United Distillers launches a 10 year old Teaninich in the Flora & Fauna series.

1999 The B side is decommissioned.

2000 A mash filter is installed.

2009 Teaninich 1996, a single cask in the new Manager´s Choice range is released.

2015 The distillery is expanded with six new stills and the capacity is doubled.

2017 A 17 year old is launched as part of the Special Releases.

2025 An 8 year old single grain (containing rye in the mash bill) is launched as part of the Special Releases.

Tasting notes Teaninich 10 years old:

GS – The nose is initially fresh and grassy, quite light, with vanilla and hints of tinned pineapple. Mediumbodied, smooth, slightly oily, with cereal and spice in the mouth. Nutty and slowly drying in the finish, with pepper and a suggestion of cocoa powder notes.

Tobermory

[tow•bur•mo•ray]

Owner: CVH Spirits

Region/district: Highland (Mull)

Founded: 1798

Status: Active (vc)

Capacity: 1 250 000 litres

Address: Tobermory, Isle of Mull, Argyllsh. PA75 6NR

Website: tobermorydistillery.com

Tel: 01688 302647

Tobermory is a delight to visit. It is not just the distillery itself but also the village and the island of Mull with its unique natural beauty are worth seeing. Mull can be conveniently reached from Oban by a 55 minute ferry trip.

The whisky on the other hand is not as easily accessible. Tobermory single malt sells just 78,000 bottles per year (one third of these are sold in the UK) while the peated Ledaig from the same distillery reached 162,000 bottles in 2023. In comparison, the number one seller of the three single malts owned by CVH is Bunnahabhain with close to one million bottles. Usually a distillery production scheme stays more or less unchanged over the years to allow for a consistent spirit. There are small tweaks however that can improve things. In the case of Tobermory the fermentation times have recently been increased to 62 hours for the short ones (improving the yield) and 110-126 hours for the long ones (to add more fruity flavours). Two styles of whisky are produced at Tobermory – the unpeated Tobermory 30%) and the heavily peated Ledaig (70%). Foreshots are always 20 minutes but when producing Tobermory the cut during the spirit run are between 74% and 63% and when Ledaig is produced it is 71% down to 59% .

The equipment consists of a 7.5 ton, stainless steel semi lauter mash tun and four washbacks made of Oregon pine. Finally there are four stills, two of which were replaced in 2014 and the other two in 2019. Eight mashes per week aiming for 980,000 litres of pure alcohol are planned for 2025.

The core range consists of the **12** and **21 year old Tobermory** and the **10** and **18 year old Ledaig** as well as the NAS **Ledaig Sinclair rioja finish**. In 2021 a new limited series for Tobermory named The Hebridean was introduced. The final addition in March 2025 was a **27 year old** with an extra 12 years in oloroso casks. Limited Ledaig releases include **Triple Wood**, and (in May 2025) **Hebridean Moon** - the first ever **10 year old Ledaig** bottled at cask strength (58.8%). Finally there are more than 15 different distillery exclusives to choose from.

Ledaig 10 years old

History:

1798 John Sinclair founds the distillery.

1837 The distillery closes.

1878 The distillery reopens.

1890 John Hopkins & Company buys the distillery.

1916 Distillers Company Limited (DCL) takes over.

1930 The distillery closes.

1972 A shipping company and the sherrymaker Domecq refurbish the buildings and form Ledaig Distillery Ltd.

1975 Ledaig Distillery Ltd files for bankruptcy and the distillery closes again.

1979 The estate agent Kirkleavington Property buys the distillery, forms a new company, Tobermory Distillers Ltd and starts production.

1982 No production. Some of the buildings are rented to a dairy company for cheese storage.

1989 Production resumes.

1993 Burn Stewart Distillers buys Tobermory.

2002 CL Financial buys Burn Stewart Distillers.

2007 A Ledaig 10 year old is released.

2008 A Tobermory 15 year old is released.

2013 Burn Stewart Distillers is sold to Distell Group Ltd. A 40 year old Ledaig is released.

2015 Ledaig 18 years and 42 years are released together with Tobermory 42 years.

2019 A 12 year old Tobermory is released.

2020 A 23 year old Tobermory oloroso finish and Ledaig Sinclair rioja finish are released.

2021 The Hebridean series is launched.

2023 CVH becomes new owner and a 21 year old Tobermory is released.

2024 A 26 year old Tobermory and Ledaig Triple wood are launched.

2025 The 10 year old Ledaig Hebridean Moon, and a 27 year old Tobermory are released.

Tasting notes Tobermory 12 years old:

IR – Butterscotch and heather honey on the nose with peaches and a hint of orange peel. Mouthcoating, rich and malty with notes of fudge, Danish pastry, citrus, pineapple and a hint of pepper. The finish is slightly salty.

Tasting notes Ledaig 10 years old:

GS – The nose is profoundly peaty, sweet and full, with notes of butter and smoked fish. Bold, yet sweet on the palate, with iodine, soft peat and heather. The finish is medium to long, with pepper, ginger, liquorice and peat.

Tomatin

[to•mat•in]

Owner:
Tomatin Distillery Co
(Takara Shuzo Co., Kokubu & Co., Marubeni Corp.)

Region/district:
Highland

Founded:
1897

Status:
Active (vc)

Capacity:
5 000 000 litres

Address: Tomatin, Inverness-shire IV13 7YT

Website:
tomatin.com

Tel:
01463 248144 (vc)

A crucial part of the team left Tomatin in May 2025 when Graham Eunson, Master Distiller and Distillery Operations Director, was retired after 34 years in the Scotch whisky industry.

An Orcadian by birth, Graham found himself halfway through his career as the manager of one of the most respected distilleries in Scotland – Glenmorangie. In 2008 he accepted the challenge to resurrect the mothballed Glenglassaugh distillery which he embarked on until 2011 when be became the manager of Tomatin. For the past fourteen years he has been instrumental in establishing Tomatin as one of the distilleries undergoing the change from being a supplier of malt for blends into a single malt brand to be reckoned with. To recognise his amazing work, a Tomatin Legacy Makers – Graham Eunson edition, was released containing whisky from 1990 (the year that Graham started in the business) and from 2011 (when he moved to Tomatin).

The distillery is equipped with a 9.6 ton stainless steel, full lauter mash tun and 12 stainless steel washbacks with a fermentation time over 140 hours. Furthermore there are six wash stills and four spirit stills producing a fruity, sweet newmake. When producing unpeated Tomatin the cut point for the spirit run are 71% to 65% but when producing the peated Cù Bòcan the spirit is collected at 61%. The production plan for 2025 is to mash 14 times per week aiming for 1.8 million litres. For the Cù Bòcan range they will also be using 600 tonnes of barley with a phenol specification of 45ppm.

The core range consists of **Legacy, Double Cask, 10, 12, 18, 30** and **36 year old** as well as **Cask Strength, a 12 year old Sherry Cask** and **14 year old port finish**. Recent limited releases include three expressions in the **Sherry Collection** where whiskies aged from 10 to 17 years have been matured in different types of sherry casks. The duty free range consists of **8, 12, 16, 21** and **45 year old**. The smoky side of Tomatin is represented by **Cù Bòcan** with **Signature**, a **12 year old** rum maturation and a **15 year old** sherry maturation. There is also the limited **Creation #7** (matured in a combination of virgin oak and Pineau des Charentes casks).

Graham Eunson

12 years old

History:

1897 The distillery is founded by Tomatin Spey Distillery Company.

1906 Production ceases.

1909 Production resumes through Tomatin Distillers.

1956 Stills are increased from two to four.

1958 Another two stills are added.

1961 The six stills are increased to ten.

1974 The stills now total 23 and the maltings closes.

1985 The distillery company goes into liquidation.

1986 Takara Shuzo Co. and Okara & Co., buy Tomatin through Tomatin Distillery Co.

1998 Okara & Co is liquidated and Marubeni buys out part of their shareholding.

2004 Tomatin 12 years is launched.

2005 A 25 year old and a 1973 Vintage are released.

2008 A 30 and a 40 year old are released.

2009 A 15 year old and a 21 year old are released.

2010 The first peated release - a 4 year old exclusive for Japan.

2011 A 30 year old and Tomatin Decades are released.

2013 Cù Bòcan, the first peated Tomatin, is released.

2014 14 year old port finish, 36 year old, Tomatin Cuatro and Cù Bòcan Sherry Cask are released.

2015 Cask Strength and Cù Bòcan Virgin Oak are released.

2017 New releases include Wood, Fire and Earth as well as a 2006 Cù Bòcan.

2018 A 30 and a 50 year old are released.

2019 The entire range of Cù Bòcan is relaunched with three new expressions.

2020 A Vintage 1975 is released.

2021 The French Collection is released.

2022 Cù Bócan Creation #3 and #4 are released together with the Portuguese Collection.

2023 Cù Bócan 15 year old and Creation #5 are released together with Tomatin Italian Collection.

2024 A 12 year old Sherry Cask and The Sherry Collection are launched.

2025 The Graham Eunson Legacy Makers and Cù Bócan Creation #7 are released.

Tasting notes Tomatin 12 years old:

GS – Barley, spice, buttery oak and a floral note on the nose. Sweet and medium-bodied, with toffee apples, spice and herbs in the mouth. Medium-length in the finish, with sweet fruitiness.

Tomintoul

[tom•in•towel]

Owner:
Angus Dundee Distillers

Region/district:
Speyside

Founded:
1965

Status:
Active

Capacity:
3 300 000 litres

Address: Ballindalloch, Banffshire AB37 9AQ

Website:
tomintouldistillery.co.uk

Tel:
01807 590274

Without a doubt, Angus Dundee Distillers is the most prolific bottler in the Scotch industry when it comes to offering official expressions from their two distilleries – Glencadam and Tomintoul.

Currently there are 13 expressions in the Tomintoul core range. Add to that a range of wood finishes and you have another 13. Finally the three bottlings exclusive to travel retail makes a total of 29 different expressions. But it doesn't stop there. Heavily peated whisky is offered in a separate range named Old Ballantruan, so it is safe to say there is something for everyone in this distillery. Like most whisky companies in the past couple of years, Angus Dundee have seen the effects of geopolitical uncertainty, rising inflation and consumer cost-of-living challenges. The latest financial report (June 2024) saw sales dropping by 24%. What speaks in the company's favour despite this is that their business model relies more on value for money rather than prestige bottlings.

Tomintoul is equipped with a 12.2 ton semi lauter mash tun, six stainless steel washbacks with a fermentation time of 54-60 hours and two pairs of stills. There are currently 15 mashes per week, which means that capacity is used to its maximum, and the 19 warehouses (14 racked and 5 palletised) have a storage capacity of 130,000 casks. The malt used for mashing is unpeated, but every year since 2001, heavily peated (55ppm) spirit has also been produced. In 2025 that part will be 450,000 litres split between June and December to coincide with the following silent seasons.

The core range consists of **Tlàth** and **Seiridh**, both without age statement, **10, 14, 16, 18, 21, 25 year old** and **Cigar Malt.** The peaty side of Tomintoul is represented by **Peated** without age statement and **Peaty Tang 15 year old**. As a stand-alone range, there is also the heavily peated **Old Ballantruan** without age statement as well as a **10** and **15 year old**. Recent limited releases include a **40 year old,** the **50 year old Robert Fleming Anniversary Edition** as well as a wide range of wood finishes including **amarone, madeira** and **tawny port**. Finally, the travel retail range is represented by **Tor, Tundra** and **Tarn.**

10 years old

History:

- 1965 The distillery is founded by Tomintoul Distillery Ltd, which is owned by Hay & MacLeod & Co. and W. & S. Strong & Co.
- 1973 Scottish & Universal Investment Trust, owned by the Fraser family, buys both the distillery and Whyte & Mackay.
- 1974 The two stills are increased to four and Tomintoul 12 years is launched.
- 1978 Lonhro buys Scottish & Universal Investment Trust.
- 1989 Lonhro sells Whyte & Mackay to Brent Walker.
- 1990 American Brands buys Whyte & Mackay.
- 1996 Whyte & Mackay changes name to JBB (Greater Europe).
- 2000 Angus Dundee plc buys Tomintoul.
- 2002 Tomintoul 10 year is launched.
- 2003 Tomintoul 16 years is launched.
- 2004 Tomintoul 27 years is launched.
- 2005 The peated Old Ballantruan is launched.
- 2008 1976 Vintage and Peaty Tang are released.
- 2009 A 14 year old and a 33 year old are released.
- 2010 A 12 year old Port wood finish is released.
- 2011 A 21 year old, a 10 year old Ballantruan and Vintage 1966 are released.
- 2012 Old Ballantruan 10 years old is released.
- 2013 A 31 year old single cask is released.
- 2015 Five Decades and a 40 year old are released.
- 2016 A 40 year old and Tlàth without age statement are launched.
- 2017 15 year old Peaty Tang and 15 year old Old Ballantruan are launched.
- 2018 Tomintoul 1965 The Ultimate Cask is released.
- 2020 Seiridh and a number of bottlings celebrating Robert Fleming´s 30th anniversary are released.
- 2021 A 16 year old Sauternes finish is released.
- 2023 Tor, Tundra and Tarn are released for travel retail.

Tasting notes Tomintoul 10 years old:

GS – A light, fresh and fruity nose, with ripe peaches and pineapple cheesecake, delicate spice and background malt. Medium-bodied, fruity and fudgy on the palate. The finish offers wine gums, mild, gently spiced oak, malt and a suggestion of smoke.

Tormore

[tor•more]

Owner:
Elixir Distillers

Region/district:
Speyside

Founded:
1958

Status:
Active

Capacity:
4 800 000 litres

Address: Tormore, Advie, Grantown-on-Spey, Morayshire PH26 3LR

Website:
elixirdistillers.com

Tel:
01807 510244

More than three years have passed since brothers Sukhinder and Rajbir Singh took over Tormore distillery from Pernod Ricard. As expected things have moved forward pretty swiftly.

In terms of equipment the distillery was adjusted to their needs and a vast stock of maturing whisky was assessed. The latter part of the work has meant an intensive programme of re-racking the whisky into casks that blend in with the new profile of Tormore single malt. At the same time the distillery continues to produce single malt for Chivas' blends. The biggest news for 2025 is that the master blender Oliver Chilton and distillery manager Polly Logan have come up with no less than six different bottlings in anticipation of the first core expression, expected in early 2026. The owners are also gearing up for a visitor centre in the near future.

The distillery is equipped with a 10.4 ton stainless steel full lauter mash tun and eleven stainless steel washbacks divided into three rooms with fermentation times ranging from 54 hours up to 115-120 hours. In a very spacious still house, there are four 18,500 litre wash stills equipped with TVR (thermal vapour recompression) and sub coolers and four 13,900 litre spirit stills. A clear wort, long foreshots (25-30 minutes) and slow distillation gives a light and fruity character to the newmake. Currently the distillery is working a 5-day week with 17-18 mashes and 3.2 million litres of alcohol. In 2023 the new owners started filling casks again on-site – the first time since 2006.

In June 2025 the **Blueprint Series** was launched with three **10 year olds** matured in bourbon barrels, cream sherry casks and toasted barrels respectively. Just one month later the **Legacy Series** appeared with three vintages. Each vintage features a collection of single casks with the **2003 Vintage** and the **2009 Vintage** having matured in first fill bourbon while the **2012 Vintage** had been matured in a combination of first and second fill bourbon – a total of sixteen casks for the series.

Legacy 2012

History:

1958 Schenley International, owners of Long John, founds the distillery.

1960 The distillery is ready for production.

1972 The number of stills is increased from four to eight.

1975 Schenley sells Long John and its distilleries (including Tormore) to Whitbread.

1989 Allied Lyons (to become Allied Domecq) buys the spirits division of Whitbread.

1991 Allied Distillers introduce Caledonian Malts where Miltonduff, Glendronach and Laphroaig are represented besides Tormore. Tormore is later replaced by Scapa.

2004 Tormore 12 year old is launched as an official bottling.

2005 Chivas Brothers (Pernod Ricard) becomes new owners through the acquisition of Allied Domecq.

2012 Production capacity is increased by 20%.

2014 The 12 year old is replaced by two new expressions - 14 and 16 year old.

2022 The distillery is sold to Elixir Distillers.

2025 First bottlings since Elixir took over are launched; the Blueprint Series containing three 10 year olds with different maturations and the Legacy Series with three vintages.

Tasting notes Tormore Legacy 2012:

IW – Rich chocolate truffles on the nose, cappuccino with cocoa powder and an edge of piped icing. Soft mouthfeel, creme caramel and chocolate truffles, with oak and maltyness providing counterpoint, creaminess extends to chocolate eclairs and mille feuille.

Tullibardine

[tully•bar•din]

Owner:
Terroirs Distillers
(Picard Vins & Spiritueux)

Region/district:
Highlands

Founded:
1949

Status:
Active (vc)

Capacity:
3 000 000 litres

Address: Blackford, Perthshire PH4 1QG

Website:
tullibardine.com

Tel:
01764 682252

After a ten year closure, Tullibardine was bought in 2003 by former directors of DCL and United Spirits, Michael Beamish and Doug Ross. They made an excellent job resurrecting the distillery.

Their business plan was to combine the distillery with a large commercial outlet next door. In the following years however, most of the shops were closed, not least due to economical difficulties and the property crash which followed the financial crisis in 2008. Even though the owners managed to show positive figures in the balance sheet already in 2007, they confirmed in 2008 that they were considering offers from other companies to buy the distillery.

It would take another six years before the perfect buyer turned up, namely Picard Vins & Spiritueux. Tullibardine had always struggled with a blurry range of whiskies but the new owners created a core range which attracted the consumers' attention. The remains of the closed outlet have been turned into an excellent visitor centre, a bottling line, a vatting hall, more warehouses and a small cooperage and the distillery also serves as the spiritual home of the owners' blended Scotch – Highland Queen.

The distillery equipment consists of a 6.2 ton stainless steel semi-lauter mash tun and ten stainless steel washbacks. All the washbacks are sealed which will help the owners capturing 2,400 tonnes of CO^2. The fermentation time is 55-60 hours. There are also two pairs of stills with cut points between 75 and 64% on the spirit run. The plan in 2025 is to do 27 mashes per week which will result in 3 million litres of alcohol.

The core range consists of **Sovereign**, **225 Sauternes finish, 228 Burgundy finish, 500 Sherry finish** and a **15 year old**. An **18 year old** was added in late 2023. A vast number of expressions have so far been released in the Marquess Collection with the latest being **2008 Châteauneuf-du-Pape cask finish**. In 2024, to celebrate the 75th anniversary, a **Vintage 1993** was released which had spent the first years in bourbon casks and then finally eight years in virgin oak. Expressions available only at the distillery include a **2006 Madeira single cask**.

Sovereign

History:

- 1949 The architect William Delmé-Evans founds the distillery.
- 1953 The distillery is sold to Brodie Hepburn.
- 1971 Invergordon Distillers buys Brodie Hepburn Ltd.
- 1973 The number of stills increases to four.
- 1993 Whyte & Mackay buys Invergordon Distillers.
- 1994 Tullibardine is mothballed.
- 1996 Whyte & Mackay changes name to JBB (Greater Europe).
- 2001 JBB (Greater Europe) is bought out from Fortune Brands by management and changes name to Kyndal (Whyte & Mackay from 2003).
- 2003 A consortium buys Tullibardine for £1.1 million. The distillery is in production again.
- 2005 Three wood finishes from 1993, Port, Moscatel and Marsala, are launched together with a 1986 John Black selection.
- 2006 Vintage 1966, Sherry Wood 1993 and a new John Black selection are launched.
- 2007 Five different wood finishes and a couple of single cask vintages are released.
- 2008 A Vintage 1968 40 year old is released.
- 2009 Aged Oak is released.
- 2011 Three vintages and a wood finish are released. Picard buys the distillery.
- 2013 A completely new range is launched – Sovereign, 225 Sauternes, 228 Burgundy, 500 Sherry, 20 year old and 25 year old.
- 2015 A 60 year old Custodian Collection is released.
- 2016 A Vintage 1970 and The Murray from 2004 are released.
- 2017 Vintage 1962 and The Murray Chateauneuf-du-Pape are released.
- 2018 The Murray Marsala Finish is released.
- 2019 A Vintage 1964 is released.
- 2020 A 15 year old is released.
- 2021 The Murray Double Wood Finish is released.
- 2023 An 18 year old and The Murray Triple Port are released.
- 2024 A 2008 Châteauneuf-du-Pape cask finish is released.

Tasting notes Tullibardine Sovereign:

GS – Floral on the nose, with new-mown hay, vanilla and fudge. Fruity on the palate, with milk chocolate, brazil nuts, marzipan, malt, and a hint of cinnamon. Cocoa, vanilla, a squeeze of lemon and more spice in the finish.

Angus MacMillan, proud founder and owner of Benbecula Distillery

New distilleries

Until Kilchoman was founded in 2005, only three malt distilleries had been opened in Scotland during the preceeding 15 years. In the past twenty years, no less than 61 new distilleries have been built! Even though many of them have released whisky, and a few of them of a considerable age, we still call them New Distilleries in this section. Some of them, with a capacity of less than 30,000 litres, are presented on pages 182-183. Many more are yet to come – you can read about them in the chapter The Year That Was, pages 272-275.

8 Doors

[eyt doars]

Owner:
Kerry and Derek Campbell

Region/district:
Highlands

Founded:
2022

Status:
Active (vc)

Capacity:
150 000 litres

Address: John O´Groats, Wick KW1 4YR

Website:
8doorsdistillery.com

Tel:
01955 482000

For many years, Pulteney was Scotland's most northerly situated mainland whisky distillery. Then Wolfburn in Thurso came in 2013 but their claim to the title only lasted nine years.

In September 2022 the 8 Doors Distillery started production in John O´Groats which is about as far north you can get on the mainland. The founders, Kerry and Derek Campbell, managed to hire John Ramsay as a consultant to define their spirit. With a 40 year long career as master blender for the Edrington Group (Macallan, Highland Park, Glenrothes etc.), Ramsay is a legend in the whisky industry. The day to day whisky production at the distillery is looked after by Ryan Sutherland and Andrew Adamson.

While there is no mill on site, the grist is bought from an external supplier. The equipment at 8 Doors is interesting as the owners have decided on both a mash conversion vessel and a 0.4 ton semi lauter mash tun to process the grains. The MCV can be used to process grains other than malted barley but for now it's used as the first step of of the barley mash conversion. They are also looking for a clear wort with a slightly higher gravity. With five stainless steel wash backs (2,000 litres each) the distillery is currently working a 5-day week with two short (70 hours) and three long (120 hours) fermentations.There is also one 1,700 litre wash still and one 1,300 litre spirit still, both from Speyside Copperworks and with slightly descending lyne arms. The foreshots last 10 minutes and they they cut the spirit between 74% and 64% aiming for a fruity new make spirit.

In waiting of their own spirits to mature the owners have launched a range of sourced Scotch blends and single malts under the name Seven Sons. There is also the 874 Club, named after the distance by road between Land's End and John O´Groats (the whole length of Great Britain), where fans initially could buy there own cask from the distillery.

Aberargie

[aber•arg•gee]

Owner:
Morrison Scotch Whisky Distillers Ltd.

Region/district:
Lowlands

Founded:
2017

Status:
Active

Capacity:
750 000 litres

Address: Aberargie, Perthshire PH2 9LX

Website:
morrisondistillers.com

Tel:
01738 787044

The Morrison family boasts a five-generation legacy of whisky-making, and Aberargie Distillery marks their return to distilling since the 1960s.

Stanley P. Morrison acquired Morrison Bowmore in 1963, establishing the foundation for his distilling, blending, and brokering business before selling his final share to Suntory in 1994. In 2014, the Morrison family announced plans to build a new distillery on their Aberargie farm, which previously supplied barley to maltsters. Approval was granted for both the distillery and a separate blending and bottling hall located adjacent to the distillery. With the family´s majority stake in the venture, construction for both projects commenced promptly.

Groundbreaking took place in June 2016 with the first cask filled in November 2017. Aberargie Distillery is equipped with a 2-ton semi-lauter mash tun, nine stainless steel washbacks, a 15,000-litre wash still, and a 10,000-litre spirit still. The stills, featuring steeply descending lyne arms, were crafted by Forsyths and are heated with panels instead of coils or pans.

Primarily, Aberargie operates a grain-to-glass process, with Morrison Scotch Whisky Distillers responsible for managing operations and bottling when the whisky is ready. Every step except malting occurs on-site to ensure complete quality control.

The independent bottling division has grown successfully, offering three distinct whisky ranges: Càrn Mòr, showcasing expressions from various Scottish malt distilleries; Mac-Talla, reflecting Morrison's connection with Islay and peated malts; and Old Perth, highlighting sherry-matured blended malts. Additionally, the distillery has announcced the release of its inaugural whisky in early 2026.

Ailsa Bay

[ail•sah bey]

Owner: William Grant & Sons
Region/district: Lowlands
Founded: 2007
Status: Active
Capacity: 12 000 000 litres
Address: Girvan, Ayrshire KA26 9PT
Website: ailsabay.com
Tel: 01465 713091

William Grant & Sons have always been known to do the walk rather than the talk – at least when it comes to establishing new distilleries.

When Girvan grain distillery came on stream in 1963 it came out of the blue and the distillery was accomplished in record time. The same when Kininvie malt distillery was founded in 1990 and the new Tullamore distillery in Ireland saw the light of day in 2014. Ailsa Bay distillery (on the same site as Girvan) came about due to a need for malt whisky for the company's blends. Glenfiddich and Balvenie were established as single malt brands, Kininvie was producing not least for the highly successful Monkey Shoulder while at the same time Grant's blended Scotch was consistently on the way up. In 2023 it was number four on the top ten list of Scotch selling almost 50 million bottles.

Ailsa Bay is equipped with two 12.1 tonne full lauter mash tuns, 24 washbacks made of stainless steel and 16 stills. Each washback holds 50,000 litres and fermentation time is 60 hours for the heavier styles and 72 hours for the lighter style. Maturation for the tiny part that is bottled as single malt starts in small ex-bourbon barrels and after 6-9 months the spirit is transferred to regular sized barrels as well as into new oak. The plan is to perform around 50 mashes per week, producing 10-12 million litres of alcohol.

Five different types of spirit are produced. The most common is a light, sweet spirit. Then there is a heavy, sulphury style and three peated with the peatiest having a malt specification of 50ppm. In 2016, a peated single malt Ailsa Bay was released. This was followed up in 2018 by Ailsa Bay Sweet Smoke and the same year Aerstone Land Cask was launched which is a 10 year old Ailsa Bay single malt matured inland. Shortly after, Aerstone Sea Cask was launched.

Annandale

[ann•an•dail]

Owner: Annandale Distillery Co.
Region/district: Lowlands
Founded: 2014
Status: Active (vc)
Capacity: 500 000 litres
Address: Northfield, Annan, Dumfriesshire DG12 5LL
Website: annandaledistillery.com
Tel: 01461 207817

In the new millenium Annandale, which had produced whisky from 1836, and was owned by Johnnie Walker from 1895 until it closed in 1918, was restored as a working distillery.

Professor David Thomson and his wife Teresa Church bought the site, which was in a poor condition, and with the aid of the late Dr. Jim Swan they meticulously refurbished it into a working distillery. The first cask was filled in November 2014 and the distillery is equipped with a 2.5 ton semi-lauter mash tun with a copper dome. There are three wooden washbacks (with a fermentation time of 72-96 hours), one wash still (12,000 litres) and two spirit stills (4,000 litres). In 2023 a £3.6m project was announced which will use a new thermal energy storage technology enabling Annandale to produce a carbon-neutral whisky.

Both unpeated and peated (45ppm) whisky is distilled. In 2018, the first two single malts were released, both matured in ex-Buffalo Trace barrels. Annandale's bottling regime is based on single casks bottled at cask strength. The back bone is made up of the unpeated Man O'Words, in honour of Robert Burns who was an exciseman in Annandale, and the peated Man O' Sword to commemorate King Robert the Bruce who was the 7th Lord of Annandale. Limited bottlings include Storyman in collaboration with actor James Cosmo. In spring 2025 the first official bottlings carrying an age statement (10 years) were released. Since the very start Annandale have been diligent and innovative when it comes to using different casks for the maturation.

Annandale lies a bit off the beaten track when it comes to whisky tourism. Situated in the very south, a 30 minute drive from Dumfries, it still gets its fair share of visitors. The distillery offers a variety of tours and there is even a virtual reality tour for those who experience limited mobility.

Arbikie

[ar•bi•ki]

Owner: The Stirling family
Region/district: Eastern Highlands
Founded: 2015
Status: Active
Capacity: 200 000 litres
Address: Inverkeilor, Arbroath, Angus DD11 4UZ
Website: arbikie.com
Tel: 01241 830770

The Stirling family has been farming since the 17th century and the 2000-acre Arbikie Highland Estate in Angus has now been in their possession for four generations.

The three brothers (John, Iain and David) started their careers within other fields but then returned to the family lands to open up a single-estate distillery. The definition of a single-estate distillery is that the whole chain of production takes place on site, and all the ingredients are grown on the farm. It doesn't stop there for the Stirlings: Their goal is to become the world's first hydrogen-powered distillery by installing a wind turbine, electrolyser, hydrogen storage and a hydrogen boiler system.

The barley is thus grown in fields on the premises and the distillery is equipped with a stainless steel, semi-lauter mash tun with a 0.75 ton charge and four washbacks (two 4,400 litre and two 9,000 litre) with a fermentation time of 96-120 hours. There is also one 4,000 litre wash still and one 2,400 litre spirit still. For the final stages of vodka and gin production, there is a 40 plate rectification column.

Arbikie were the first to take a serious interest in producing rye whisky in Scotland, something that hadn't been done for 200 years. Historically Scotch whisky was made from a variety of different mash bills. The current expressions from Arbikie are typically made from 60% winter rye, 25% malted barley and 15% winter wheat. To comply with the SWA rules the 1794 Highland Rye must be labelled as a single grain Scotch whisky. The current core range of 1794 Highland Rye consists of The Original, The Peated and The PX. There is also the recent limited Distiller´s Edition One – a 5 year old. The Stirlings intend to launch their first single malt whisky made from barley first in 2029/2030.

Ardgowan

[ard•gau•one]

Owner: Roland Grain et al
Region/district: Lowlands
Founded: 2025
Status: Active (vc)
Capacity: 900 000 litres
Address: Bankfoot Farm, Inverkip PA16 0DT
Website: ardgowandistillery.com
Tel: -

With a handful of exceptions, whenever one hears of a new distillery being built, it usually takes a much longer period of time to see it in production than what has been communicated.

This is certainly the case with Ardgowan. The idea was hatched in the mid 2010s and planning permission was granted in 2017. The entire project then stalled due to the aftermath of Brexit and the covid pandemic but the persistence of the initiators was admirable. Due to the magnitude of the project it couldn't rely on crowd funding or selling future casks. A proper investor was needed and in stepped Distil Ventures but not least Roland Grain, an Austrian investor and the current CEO and major shareholder.

A number of luminaries from the Scotch whisky industry got involved; Ian Macmillan (ex Burn Stewart), Max Macfarlane (ex Highland Park), Mike Keillor (ex Morrison Bowmore) and Stuart Macpherson and Willie Phillips (both ex Macallan) were among the people landing the project. Lately, Paul Currie, co-founder of Arran and Lakes distillery, joined the team as the chairman.

The distillery lies on the Ardgowan Estate near Inverkip in Inverclyde, less than an hour's drive from Glasgow. The first distillation was in April 2025 and the distillery is equipped with a 5 ton full lauter mash tun and six stainless steel, 32,000 litre, washbacks with a fermentation time of 96 hours. There is one 12,500 litre wash still equipped with the latest TVR (thermal vapour recompression) for heat recovery and one 9,000 litre spirit still. Both unpeated and peated (80ppm) malt is produced. The spirit will be matured predominantly in sherry cask matured European oak.

The distillery was formally opened in June 2025 with visitors being welcomed from August. From early on Blackwoods gin and vodka has been produced by the owners.

Ardnahoe

[ard•na•hoe]

Owner: Hunter Laing & Company
Region/district: Islay
Founded: 2017
Status: Active (vc)
Capacity: 1 000 000 litres
Address: Isle of Islay, Port Askaig PA46 7RU
Website: ardnahoedistillery.com
Tel: 01496 840711

Regular visitors to Islay know that the road to Ardnahoe distillery used to be a challenge for most drivers. Narrow, poorly maintained and always with the risk of a meeting with a lorry.

Well, things have changed recently. The owners of Ardnahoe, Hunter Laing, have spent money on refurbishing the track when you leave the A846 and head to the distillery and CVH Spirits have done the same for the remainder of the road leading to Bunnahabhain. The trip is recommended as both distilleries have excellent visitor centres.

In late 2018 Ardnahoe became the ninth distillery on Islay to start production in modern times and almost six years later the two first bottlings appeared. The first was the limited Inaugural followed by Infinite Loch – both a combination of ex-bourbon and ex-sherry. The next to appear was Bholsa predominantly matured in oloroso casks.

Ardnahoe is equipped with a 2.75 ton semi lauter mash tun with a copper lid. The lauter gear is used as little as possible in order to obtain a clear wort. There are four 25,000 litre washbacks made from Oregon pine with an average fermentation time of 72 hours, one wash still (12,500 litres) and one spirit still (8,000 litres) with a slow distillation, both with the longest lyne arms in Scotland (7.5 metres). The spirit is collected between 74% and 63% and the character of the newmake is fruity. The distillery is also equipped with wooden worm tubs – the only ones on Islay. Around 90% of the production is peated (using malt typically peated to 40ppm) while the rest is unpeated. The plan for 2025 is to produce around 550,000 litres of pure alcohol. So far the spirit has been filled into casks on the mainland and some of them have been transported back to mature on the island. In 2025 however an on-site filling store was completed making the handling more efficient and sustainable.

Ardnamurchan

[ard•ne•mur•ken]

Owner: Adelphi Selection
Region/district: Western Highlands
Founded: 2014
Status: Active (vc)
Capacity: 500 000 litres
Address: Glenbeg, Ardnamurchan, Argyll PH36 4JG
Website: adelphidistillery.com
Tel: 01972 500 285

Reaching Ardnamurchan Distillery requires more than a quick jaunt. The drive from Fort William takes approximately an hour and a half, winding out to the remote peninsula north of Mull, but it is more than worth the journey.

The distillery is fitted with a two-tonne semi-lauter stainless steel mash tun capped with copper, and seven washbacks – four Douglas Fir, three stainless steel. Fermentation runs between 72 and 96 hours. The stillhouse holds one 10,000-litre wash still and one 6,000-litre spirit still, both now paired with recently installed stainless steel sub-coolers. Three distinct spirit styles flow from the stills: unpeated, peated (30ppm), and heavily peated (80ppm). For 2025, the production target is 12 mashes per week, yielding around 370,000 litres of alcohol – half of it peated.

Throughout the production process, the goal is to create a spirit that befits its remote location on the West Coast of Scotland: rich with salinity and tempered smoke, but still with enough nuance to encourage fruity and floral tones to shine as well. Sustainability is a foundational tenet of the distillery. All power and heat are drawn from local renewable sources. Cooling water from the nearby river and streams off the hills behind the site drive a hydroelectric generator; a biomass boiler burns renewably harvested woodchip from surrounding forests; and 138 solar panels contribute additional energy such that Ardnamurchan Distillery puts more into the local grid than it takes.

Ardnamurchan's inaugural single malt, AD/09.20:01, was released in October 2020. This was followed in 2022 by the AD/ Cask Strength Release. More recent bottlings include AD/ The Midgie – matured in a mix of ex-port and bourbon casks with a single sherry butt – in May 2025 and the AD/ Sauternes Release, Peated in autumn 2025.

Ardross

[ard•ross]

Owner: Greenwood Distillers
Region/district: N Highland
Founded: 2019
Status: Active
Capacity: 1 000 000 litres
Address: Ardross Mains, Ardross, Alness
Website: theardross.com
Tel: -

While most of the new distilleries in Scotland are focused on more or less traditional production of malt whisky, Ardross is definitely staking out its own path.

The reason for this is Theodore House, an innovation distillery opened on the site in 2023. The main Ardross distillery has consistently been producing malt whisky since 2019 but the owners wanted the opportunity to experiment with other styles as well as other spirits while at the same time not interfering with the daily production.

Theodore House is equipped with a 0.65 ton mash tun, three wooden washbacks (5,000 litres each), one wash still, one cooker for grains, one small distillation column and three spirit stills of different shapes. Both copper and stainless steel condensers are in place and the multitude of equipment offers the possibility of producing a wide range of spirits including ones made from maize, wheat and rye. Around 30,000 litres will be produced in 2025.

The main Ardross distillery is equipped with a 4.4 ton semi-lauter mash tun, ten wooden washbacks of 20,000 litres each and with a fermentation time of 100-130 hours, one 16,800 litre wash still and one 12,000 litre spirit still, both fitted with purifiers although these are currently not used. The capacity is one million litres of pure alcohol and in 2025 the plan is to achieve 800,000 litres with 10 mashes per week. The signature style is unpeated but peated new-make (65ppm in the malted barley) will amount to 200,000 litres. There is also a designated gin still.

The owners, Greenwood Distillers, are involved in other companies in the industry: a mezcal producer in Mexico, an armagnac distillery in France, a bourbon distillery in Kentucky and a cooperage in Japan. With a 50 year long career in the Scotch whisky business Andrew Rankin is now the chairman and master blender at Greenwood Distillers.

Ballindalloch

[bal•lin•da•lock]

Owner: The Macpherson-Grant family
Region/district: Speyside
Founded: 2014
Status: Active (vc)
Capacity: 100 000 litres
Address: Ballindalloch, Banffshire AB37 9AA
Website: ballindallochdistillery.com
Tel: 01807 500 331

The concept of opening small farm distilleries where the grain grown on site is used for their whisky has spread around the world lately.

Depending on where in the world you are it can be called barley-to-bottle, grain-to-glass, paddock-to-bottle or single estate distillery. The general idea is to use your own grain, sometimes even malting it yourself, and then proceeding through distillation and maturation until you, preferably, bottle it yourself. While it is more and more common in the USA and Australia, there are still just a handful of these distilleries in Scotland. First in line was of course Francis Cuthbert and Daftmill in Fife in 2005. They were later followed by Arbikie, Lochlea and Ballindalloch.

The latter was built on the Ballindalloch Estate in Speyside, owned by the Macpherson-Grant family. The family already possessed a legacy in the whisky business as part-owners of nearby Cragganmore distillery from 1923 to 1965. Travelling north on the A95 you can't miss Ballindalloch on the right hand side just before the road to Ballindalloch Castle and within a stone's throw from River Spey.

The distillery is equipped with a 1 ton semi lauter mash tun with a copper dome. There are four washbacks made of Oregon pine with four long fermentations (140 hours) and one short (92 hours). Finally there is a 5,000 litre lantern-shaped wash still and a 3,600 litre spirit still with a reflux ball. Both stills are connected to two wooden worm tubs for cooling the spirit vapours. The distillery is currently working five days a week, making 75,000 litres of alcohol.

The first two expressions were released at the distillery in August 2023 and have been followed by a wide variety of limited bottlings. Some of the latest include The Castle matured in a combination of bourbon casks and ex-peated casks. In June 2025 there were also a single PX sherry butt and a single virgin oak hogshead.

Balmaud

[bal•mah]

Owner:
Balmaud Distillery Co. Ltd

Region/district:
Highlands

Founded:
2024

Status:
Active

Capacity:
1 000 000 litres

Address: Yonderton Farm, Turriff AB53 5PT

Website:
-

Tel:
-

With a family legacy in farming, the Strachans decided to expand their business by building a whisky distillery in the picturesque and fertile landscapes of Turriff in Aberdeenshire.

The farm-to-glass distillery lies ten kilometres south of Banff and with Macduff as its closest distillery neighbour. It is an old farm owned by the family but the buildings were just not suited for a modern distillery and so they were knocked down and replaced with new. A planning application was submitted to the local council in September 2021 followed by revised plans in July 2022 which were finally approved in April 2023. With every piece of equipment installed, the owners started production in late January 2025. The first released products from the distillery will be gin, vodka and rum with whisky (for obvious reasons) coming later.

Sustainability is not just a buzz word for the Strachans. The barley comes from the surrounding fields owned by the family and the distillery is powered by wind turbines. A heat recovery and storage system will also optimize energy efficiency of the distillery. The distillery manager is Allan Findlay with over two decades in the whisky industry, most recently at Speyside Distillery.

The distillery is equipped with a 3 ton semi lauter mash tun and eight stainless steel washbacks with a capacity of 26,000 litres but filled with 15,000 litres. The fermentation time is 80-140 hours. There is one 15,000 litre wash still fitted with TVR heat recovery and one 10,000 litre spirit still. There is also one smaller still (500 litres) for production of rum, gin and vodka. The distillery is capable of producing 1 million litres annually and there are two warehouses on site with space for 10,000 casks. The owners also have plans for their own maltings in the future.

Benbecula

[ben•be•cuelah]

Owner:
MacMillan Spirits

Region/district:
Highlands (Islands)

Founded:
2024

Status:
Active (vc)

Capacity:
150 000 litres

Address: Gramsdale, Benbecula HS7 5QP

Website:
benbeculadistillery.com

Tel:
-

Between North and South Uist in the Outer Hebrides lies the small island of Benbecula with 1,200 inhabitants. The very idea of building a whisky distillery there may seem ludicrous.

Not to Angus MacMillan though. He grew up on the island and later left for the mainland as many young islanders did. In his early 30s he came back and founded an organic salmon farm which eventually grew to incorporate eleven locations. Twenty-eight years later he sold it and in 2006 he was part of a legendary community buyout of South Uist, Eriskay and Benbecula from absentee landlords.

After selling the salmon farm MacMillan nurtured the idea of building a whisky distillery. Something that came to his mind was to use the ancient bere barley that is grown on the island. While the distillery doesn't malt the barley themselves, they send it off to a maltster in Montrose on the mainland together with local peat and also heather. The heather is used for small parts of the production.

To get help setting up the distillery MacMillan called upon Brendan McCarron with many years of experience from various companies in the industry. In 2024 Mary Margaret Connarty, raised on the island and with a long career at North British distillery, was hired as a distillery manager.

The first distillation took place in June 2024 and the distillery is equipped with a one ton semi lauter mash tun, nine 5,000 litre stainless steel washbacks and two stills made by Speyside Copper Works. Most fermentations are around 75 hours but longer ones occur. Currently they are doing 7-9 mashes per week and 150,000 litres.

In anticipation of their first whisky a range of sourced spirits (whisky and rum) is available under the name MacMillan Spirits as well as gin produced on site.

Bonnington

[bon•ing•tun]

Owner: Halewood Artisinal Spririts

Region/district: Lowlands

Founded: 2020

Status: Active

Capacity: 720 000 litres

Address: 21 Graham Street, Edinburgh EH6 5QN

Website: crabbiewhisky.com

Tel: 0151 480 8800

The second malt whisky distillery to open up in Edinburgh in recent times is owned by a company that was started in 1978 by John Halewood.

Run as a family company for many years it became transformed in 2015, with new investors on board, into one of the largest spirits distillers and distributors in the UK. In 2020 the name of the company changed to Halewood Artisanal Spirits and it currently operates two whisky distilleries (Bonnington and Aber Falls in Wales) as well as one rum and two gin distilleries. Their portfolio of brands include John Crabbie's Scotch whisky, The Pogues Irish whiskey, J.J. Whitley gin, Dead Man's Fingers rum and Aber Falls Welsh whisky.

The first distillation took place in March 2020 and the distillery is equipped with a 2 ton semi lauter mash tun, 15 stainless steel washbacks with a fermentation time of 75-138 hours, a 10,500 litre wash still and an 8,000 litre spirit still. Nine of the washbacks were installed in spring 2023 as part of a major expansion which eventually could give the distillery a capacity of one million litres. Currently the distillery is mashing 21 times per week and around 5% of that will be using peated malt (50ppm).

The inaugural, limited, release appeared in January 2024 and was influenced by the use of a ruby port cask for the maturation. It was followed up in May by four casks of PX-matured whisky being vatted together. The first consistently available expression was named John Crabbie Bonnington Single Malt and had been matured in virgin American oak. The most recent limited releases (in April 2025) were two versions, one peated and one unpeated, matured in muscat casks and bottled at 47 and 51% respectively.

The Borders

[boar•ders]

Owner: Borders Distillery Co. Ltd.

Region/district: Lowlands (Sc. Borders)

Founded: 2017

Status: Active (vc)

Capacity: 1 600 000 litres

Address: Commercial Road, Hawick TD9 7AQ

Website: thebordersdistillery.com

Tel: 01450 374330

While the southern parts of Scotland were historically known for its distilleries, there had been no new distillery opened in the region named The Borders since 1837.

That is until four gentlemen decided to do just that in the town of Hawick in 2017. All four had previously worked for William Grant & Sons and they decided to renovate some beautiful landmark buildings dating from the late 1880s and previously used by local businesses. The river Teviot runs just behind the distillery and similarly to the textile companies that the town is renowned for were using the water for dyeing and power, the distillery now uses it for cooling the spirit vapours.

The distillery is equipped with a 5 ton mash tun, eight stainless steel washbacks with a fermentation time of 80 hours, two wash stills (12,500 litres) and two spirit stills (7,500 litres) with all equipment provided by Forsyths. The whisky produced is unpeated and floral. Other spirits are also produced, for instance vodka and gin. In spring 2022, the distillery established a partnership with Simpsons Malt and 12 farms, all located within a 30 mile radius of the distillery. The aim is to support sustainable farming and improve the traceability of the supply chain.

The first bottling was released in 2018 when William Kerr's Borders Gin was launched and it was later followed by Puffing Billy Steam Vodka. The company then released a blended Scotch from sourced whisky called Clan Fraser and a new series of Scotch whiskies named Workshop Series appeared in autumn 2022 with the blend Borders Malt & Rye. This was followed by The Long and Short of It where spirit with short fermentation (55 hours) was blended with long fermentation (150 hours) produce as well as single grain. The third instalment, in June 2025, was Right as Rain.

Brora

[bro•rah]

Owner: Diageo

Region/district: Northern Highlands

Founded: 2021 (1819)

Status: Active (vc)

Capacity: 1 000 000 litres

Address: Clynelish Rd, Brora, Sutherland KW9 6LR

Website: malts.com

Tel: -

With Clynelish operating on the same site it is interesting (although not a surprise) that the re-opened Brora has a similar card up their sleeve when it comes to production.

Clynelish has always been famous and adored for its waxy character which derives from not cleaning the low wines and feints receiver where a residue builds up over time. Brora across the road does exactly the same. Another similarity is the clear wort producing a fruity newmake. However, Brora uses worm tubs for the cooling and also produces both unpeated and peated spirit so there is certainly a difference in the character between the two.

The distillery is equipped with a new 6 ton traditional mash tun with rakes made of stainless steel (just like the one from the closed didtillery). There are six new Oregon pine washbacks filled with 27,000 litres. The wash still (14,400 litres) and the spirit still (13,200 litres) are the same, yet refurbished, stills that were in place when the distillery closed in 1983. Foreshots are 15-20 minutes and cut points for the spirit run go from 74% down to 63-64%. The stills are attached to wooden worm tubs and usually the distillery works seven days per week with nine mashes.

The distillery is open for visitors but by appointment only. The tours start at £225 rising to £900 for an even more exclusive alternative. This 5 hour tour includes a three course lunch as well as tasting of several old Brora expressions.

Remaining stock from Brora is scarce and limited bottlings have included a set of three 50 cl bottles named Brora Triptych, the 50 year old Iris (the oldest Brora ever bottled) and sold for charity at Sotheby's for £400,000 and the 44 year old distillery exclusive Untold Depths in July 2024. There is also the possibility for visitors to try the newmake as well as a 3 year old Brora from the new production.

Burnobennie

[burn•o•benni]

Owner: Ardent Spirits

Region/district: Eastern Highlands

Founded: 2020

Status: Active

Capacity: 680 000 litres

Address: Burn Ó Bennie Road, Banchory, Aberdeenshire AB31 5NN

Website: burnobennie.com

Tel: 01330 202172

In 2017, Mike Bain opened up a small experimental craft distillery in Banchory and named it Deeside Distillery. It only operated for 18 months though before it closed.

It was a part of Deeside Brewery in Lochton of Leys, also owned by Bain, but the intention from the beginning was more or less that this would serve as a pilot distillery where the team could put some of their ideas into practice. Only 100 casks were filled at Deeside of which 88 were sold to help finance the new distillery.

In 2019 Mike Bain teamed up with Liam Pennycook and moved the operation to larger premises in a business park in nearby Hill of Banchory. The distillery started production in 2020 and was recently expanded. It is now equipped with a 1.6 ton mash tun which is designed specifically to accommodate wash for whisky distillation in addition to beer and rye wash. Furthermore, there are 13 stainless steel wash-backs with a fermentation time of 168 hours, one 5,000 litre wash still and one 3,600 litre spirit still. Foreshots are one hour and a slow distillation is practiced.

The distillery is definitely at the cutting edge when it comes to searching for new flavours involving experimenting with yeast, fermentation, fractional distillation and sour beer washes. It produces both peated and unpeated single malt as well as small batches of rye and corn whisky. One feature which stands out is the owners' interest in various speciality malts that are typically used in the brewing business but not so much by distilleries. These include for instance crystal and chocolate malt but also the use of the heritage bere barley.

In 2024 Mike Bain sent in a planning application for yet another distillery, this time in Aberdeen on the site of the old Bon-Accord drinks plant.

Cabrach

[ca•brach]

Owner: The Cabrach Trust

Region/district: Speyside

Founded: 2024

Status: Active

Capacity: 100 000 litres

Address: Inverharroch Farm, Lower Cabrach, Historic Banffshire AB54 4EU

Website: thecabrach.com

Tel: 01466 702103

Recently we have seen an increasing number of distilleries being opened up where one of their objectives has been to play an important role for the community where they are located.

Raasay and Glen Wyvis are perfect examples of this and, if we go back in time, Springbank has for many years functioned as an important employer in Campbeltown. The latest in the line is The Cabrach Distillery which, in the hands of The Cabrach Trust, is a cornerstone project of a regeneration masterplan for this remote area in north-east Scotland.

The Trust was established in 2013 and the distillery is registered as a Community Interest Company. The last distillery in the area, which has a long history of whisky-making, closed over 170 years ago but in autumn 2024 Cabrach stills were fired up again. The Cabrach Distillery (which is already welcoming visitors via appointment) will create important employment, with future profits used to progress the Trust's long-term regeneration vision.

The distillery is equipped with 0.5 ton semilauter mash tun, six wooden washbacks, a 2,500 litre wash still and an 1,800 litre spirit still – both attached to worm tubs. They are also commissioning a third, 1,250 litre pot still. Locally grown barley at Inverharroch, complimented by a very local barley growers group, forms an important part of the distillery's production philosophy, alongside weeklong fermentations, and slow, patient distillations.

The first own-produced whisky will not be launched within the next few years but a blended malt under the name The Feering, is already on the market. The inaugural edition, Early Harvest, is a blend of casks donated by four local Speyside distilleries. The whisky has been curated by the legendary Alan Winchester who spent decades overseeing all distilleries in the Chivas Group.

The Cairn

[cairn]

Owner: Gordon & MacPhail

Region/district: Speyside

Founded: 2022

Status: Active (vc)

Capacity: 1 000 000 litres

Address: Craggan, Grantown-on-Spey PH26 3NT

Website: thecairndistillery.com

Tel: 01479 816543

In 2023, when the independent bottler Gordon & MacPhail announced that purchasing stock from other distilleries would cease in 2024, it became obvious that the plans for The Cairn had been in the pipeline for quite some time.

That did not come as a surprise. The legendary family-owned company had always had a reputation for long-time planning. In 1993 they bought their first distillery (Benromach) and they spent five years meticulously refurbishing it. Already at that time they realised that relying solely on spirit from others would not be sustainable. The Cairn thus became the result of that insight. Unlike Benromach, on the outskirts of Forres, the location for The Cairn was quite different. Situated on the edge of the beautiful Cairngorms, it is the first distillery you approach when you follow the A95 into the heartland of Speyside.

The Cairn is open to visitors and boasts a magnificent tasting room with a view towards the Spey river and the Cairngorms as well as a shop with various bottlings from the Gordon & MacPhail range. It is equipped with a 5.8 ton full lauter mash tun. There are six 26,300 litre stainless steel washbacks with cooling jackets and both short (67 hours) and long (110 hours) fermentations. Finally, there are two traditional wash stills and four spirit stills. The production plan for 2025 entails 9 mashes per week which will result in one million litres of pure alcohol – the actual, current capacity. With an additional six washbacks in the future, the capacity would rise to 2 million litres.

They produce an unpeated single malt, definitely lighter in style compared to Benromach, and the newmake is fruity with sweet, malty notes. The first whisky from the distillery is not expected to be released until in the mid 2030s.

The Clydeside

[klajdsajd]

Owner: Morrison Glasgow Distillers

Region/district: Lowlands

Founded: 2017

Status: Active (vc)

Capacity: 620 000 litres

Address: 100 Stobcross Road, Glasgow G3 8QQ

Website: theclydeside.com

Tel: 0141 2121401

The location of Clydeside distillery in the Queens Docks is absolutely oozing of Glaswegian industry/whisky history and there is also an amazing connection to the current owners.

The founder Tim Morrison represents the fourth generation of one of Scotland's best known whisky families and his great grandfather designed the pumphouse where the distillery is now situated. This was designed to power the hydraulic gates allowing ships going in and out of the docks. Originally known as Stobcross Dock it was opened in 1877 and eventually closed in 1969 due to a decline in river traffic. Part of the distillery tour includes unique photos of this important part of Scottish history. In a short time the distillery has become a main attraction on the tourist tracks of Glasgow and in June 2025 an amazing bar with a marvellous view of the Clyde was added to the experience.

The equipment consists of a 1.5 ton semi lauter mash tun made of stainless steel, 8 stainless steel washbacks with a fermentation time of 72 hours, a 7,500 litre wash still and a 5,000 litre spirit still. The foreshots are 15 minutes with a slow distillation and the cutpoints for the spirit run are 76-71%. In 2025 it is planned is to make 18 mashes per week and a total of 500,000 litres of pure alcohol.

It would take until autumn 2021 before the inaugural release of a Clydeside single malt was released. It was named Stobcross after the cross that once marked the route to Dumbarton Rock, which was later demolished to make way for the Queen's Dock. The latest bottling of Stobcross is over 6 years old and a cask strength version has also been released. In June 2024 the 6 year old Napier with two years in oloroso sherry butts was added to the range. In May 2025 a limited rum finish appeared and it is hoped that the release of the first peated expression (54ppm), named Fortnight, will take place later in the year.

Daftmill

[daf•mil]

Owner: Francis Cuthbert

Region/district: Lowlands

Founded: 2005

Status: Active

Capacity: c 65 000 litres

Address: By Cupar, Fife KY15 5RF

Website: daftmill.com

Tel: 01337 830303

I can't think of any other whisky operation in Scotland that more clearly resembles the classic view of a 19th century farm distillery where production of whisky was but one part of the general operation.

For the two brothers Francis and Ian it is also very much about growing the fields of barley and the herd of cattle. The distillery in Fife is not easily found (I've been there three times and every time I took the wrong turn) and it doesn't have any kind of visitor centre. Francis, who came up with the idea of making whisky in 2008, is now responsible for the production. Yet at the same time he is a farmer and whisky production only happens for a few months – in June-July and November-February.

Daftmill's first distillation was in 2005 and the barley is grown on the farm while also supplying other distilleries.

The equipment consists of a one tonne semi-lauter mash tun with a copper dome, two stainless steel washbacks with fermentation time between 96 and 120 hours and one pair of stills. The stills, with a slow distillation, are designed to give a lot of copper contact and a lot of reflux. The wash still has a capacity of 3,000 litres and the spirit still 2,000 litres. The aim is to do a light, Lowland-style whisky. In order to achieve this they have very short foreshots (seven minutes) and the spirit run starts at 78% to capture all of the fruity esters and already comes off at 73%. Taking care of the farm obviously prohibits Francis from producing whisky full time and the plan for 2024 is 2-3 mashes per week and 20,000 litres of alcohol.

The first whisky was launched in 2018 by Berry Brothers and since then a number of Summer and Winter releases, including various single casks, have appeared including one distilled in 2011 and bottled in 2025.

Dalmunach

[dal•moo•nack]

Owner: Chivas Brothers
Region/district: Speyside
Founded: 2015
Status: Active
Capacity: 10 000 000 litres
Address: Carron, Banffshire AB38 7QP
Website: -
Tel: -

The last decade has seen an impressive expansion of malt whisky production capacity in Scotland adding some 70 million litres of pure alcohol.

The lions share of this comes from three large companies; Diageo expanded Glen Ord, Clynelish and Glenlossie/Mannochmore while W Grant completed a doubling of Glenfiddich´s capacity in 2020. The third producer, Pernod Ricard, are in the midst of an impressive expansion of both Aberlour and Miltonduff. All this meant and means adding capacity to already existing distilleries. The latest megadistillery being built from scratch, and also belonging to Pernod Ricard, was Dalmunach in 2015.

The chosen location in Carron was the site of the demolished Imperial distillery. Founded in 1897 it was producing intermittently until 1998 when it was mothballed. Chivas Brothers took over the distillery in 2005 but never re-started production. Instead the company demolished it in 2013 leaving only the dunnage warehouses. This was at a time when optimism in the Scotch whisky industry was high. The owner´s expansion of Glenlivet distillery was ongoing but more malt whisky was needed. Dalmunach was not only huge (10 million litres) but the architecture was definitely something that stood out

Dalmunach is equipped with a 13 ton Briggs full lauter mash tun and 16 stainless steel washbacks charged with 56,000 litres and with a fermentation time of 56-62 hours. There are four pairs of stills of a considerable size – wash stills 28,000 litres and spirits stills 18,000. In similar with Glentauchers and Allt-a-Bhainne, MVR technology (mechanical vapour recompression) was installed on the stills during 2024 to save energy. In 2019, the first official release of Dalmunach single malt appeared – a 4 year old bottled at cask strength – and more releases have followed.

Dornoch

[dor•nock]

Owner: Thompson Bros Distillers
Region/district: Northern Highlands
Founded: 2016
Status: Active
Capacity: 12 000 litres
Address: Castle Street, Dornoch, Sutherland, IV25 3 SD
Website: thompsonbrosdistillers.com
Tel: 01862 810 216

The Thompson bothers (Phil and Simon) were amongst the first to take an interest in producing what could best be described as ”old-school Scotch whisky”.

What this entailed was emphasis on the raw materials and the production process for determining flavour rather than allowing the casks and the maturation decide this. In 2016 they set up a very small distillery in an old fire station next to the family-owned hotel in Dornoch. Since then whisky, gin and other spirits have been produced on a small scale while at the same time, the two brothers have acted as independent bottlers.

Time has now come to expand the business and a planning application for a much larger distillery (of more than 200,000 litres) was approved in February 2024. The £7m distillery, named Struie, will be located on Shore Road within Blailiath Industrial Estate. It will be equipped with no less than 12 washbacks and one pair of stills and and a visitor centre is also in planning. Crowdfunding for the new distillery was launched in spring 2024 and when it closed a year later it had raised £2.4m – 129% over the original goal! In April 2025 three whisky luminaires were appointed to the board of the new distillery - Ryan Chetiyawardana, Rebecca Jago and Nick Ravenhall.

The current distillery is equipped with a 300 kg stainless steel, semi-lauter mash tun, six washbacks made of oak with a minimum fermentation time of seven days, a 1,000 litre wash still and a 600 litre spirit still. The stills are directly fired using gas but they are also equipped with steam coils. There is also a 2,000 litre still with a column for the production of gin and other spirits. The first single malt release appeared in 2020 and more releases have followed since.

Dunphail

[done•<u>fail</u>]

Owner: Dunphail Distillery Ltd.
Region/district: Highlands
Founded: 2023
Status: Active (vc)
Capacity: 200 000 litres
Address: Wester Greens, Dunphail, Forres IV36 2QR
Website: dunphaildistillery.com
Tel: 01309 611309

The owners of Bimber distillery, which opened in London in 2015, had always had their mind set on another distillery in Scotland as well.

The idea was to implement the same basic ideas as at Bimber; floor malted barley and long fermentation times were essential parts of the the process. The location of Dunphail, near Forres was chosen due to the proximity to a supply of Sassy grain from the Altyre Estate and mineral-rich water from a borehole on site. The important distinction from the London site was that here they would do all the malting in-house. The first distillation took place in October 2023.

The distillery is equipped with a one ton semi-lauter mash tun and 12 open-top washbacks made from Douglas fir, each holding 5,000 litres. Fermentations are long, usually around seven days. There are two 2,250 litre wash stills and one spirit still of the same size. Since spring 2024 the wash stills have been direct-fired. On top of that there is a 5 ton floor malting which makes it the second distillery in Scotland (after Springbank) malting all their barley on site.

The owners produce both unpeated and peated whisky where the eight week peat session usually takes place in spring. The phenol specification in the barley is 45ppm and the cut-off on the spirit run tends to be slightly lower when distilling peated spirit. For both styles a fruity newmake is desired. The cask policy will favour refill wood over first fill. Initially Dunphail will produce 100,000 litres of pure alcohol while the maximum capacity is 200,000 and the first release of their single malt is expected in late 2028. All in all, Dunphail is one of the best representatives of new distilleries featuring time-honoured processes to achieve and preserve as much as possible of the character from the production (malting, fermentation and distillation) rather than relying on the influence of the casks.

Eden Mill

[eden mill]

Owner: Inverleith LLP
Region/district: Lowlands
Founded: 2012
Status: Active (vc)
Capacity: 100 000 litres
Address: 96 Market St, St Andrews, Fife, KY16 0UU
Website: edenmill.com
Tel: 01334 834038

In 2012, Eden Mill was founded in Guardbridge just west of St. Andrews. What started as a brewery was extended in 2014 with a distillery.

Equipped with three 1,000 litre alambic stills made by Hoga in Portugal he first gin and new make was distilled that same year, with the very first whisky casks laid down. The distillery was situated on the site of an old paper mill next to the Eden estuary, and brought distilling back to St Andrews for the first time in over 150 years. The Haig family owned Seggie Distillery was operational on the same site between 1810 and 1860.

Eden Mill's first single malt appeared in 2018, matured in a combination of French virgin oak, American virgin oak, and Pedro Ximenez casks. Since then, the brand has gone on to launch a blended Scotch, a pair of signature single malts and an annual small-batch release called the 'Art of St Andrews' which sees the brand collaborate with local artists to create bespoke labels and packaging, inspired by the 'home of golf'.

In 2018, whisky production was paused to allow for the construction of a brand new distillery as the brand looked to expand its production and meet international demand. Private equity firm Inverleith LLP bought a majority stake in the company in 2022 bringing a wealth of industry expertise and expediting the distillery construction process. Planning permission from the local council for the new distillery at the mouth of the River Eden was received in March 2022.

The equipment consists of six 15,000 litre washbacks, one 15,000 litre wash still and one 11,500 litre spirit still. The gin still will be powered by the University of St Andrews solar plant and other renewable sources. The distillery produced its first spirit in April 2025 and by the end of August the new Eden Mill opened for visitors.

Falkirk

[fall•kirk]

Owner: Stewart family
Region/district: Lowlands
Founded: 2020
Status: Active (vc)
Capacity: 1 200 000 litres
Address: Grandsable Rd, Polmont, Falkirk FK2 0WA
Website: falkirkdistillery.com
Tel: 01324 281086

Just ten minutes apart there are now two whisky distilleries in the town of Falkirk west of Edinburgh; the classic and recently resurrected Rosebank and the newly established Falkirk.

The latter is the result of the tireless and persistent work of Fiona Stewart and her father George. Planning permission was granted as early as in 2010 but the founders' plans were interrupted by the discovery of the remnants of the Roman Antonine Wall built in the 2nd century and situated very close to the distillery. The Stewarts were not discouraged though and, adjusting their plans, the first distillation took place in September 2020.

The distillery is equipped with a 4.6 ton ex-Caperdonich traditional mash tun with rakes made of stainless steel and with a copper top producing a clear wort. There are six 34,000 litre stainless steel washbacks with a fermentation time of 72 hours, one 15,000 litre wash still and a 10,000 litre spirit still – both also from Caperdonich. Foreshots are 10 minutes and the spirit cut is made between 76% and 65%. The plan is to produce a light, traditional Lowland malt. At the moment the production is two mashes per week but this is expected to eventually scale up.

On site there are two dunnage warehouses, one of them with two floors. The main part of the produce is filled into ex-bourbon barrels but there are also ex-sherry casks in the warehouse. The first, limited expression from the distillery appeared in 2024 celebrating George Stewart's 79th birthday and were followed by more general releases including a sherried one with the latest appearing in October 2025. Tours are available by appointment but preparations have already been made for a visitor centre and benefitting from Falkirk's three existing visitor attractions (Callendar House, The Falkirk Wheel and The Kelpies) the owners hope to attract over 80,000 visitors every year.

Glasgow

[glas•go]

Owner: Liam Hughes, Ian McDougall
Region/district: Lowlands
Founded: 2015
Status: Active (vc)
Capacity: 365 000 litres
Address: Deanside Rd, Hillington, Glasgow G52 4XB
Website: glasgowdistillery.com
Tel: 0141 4047191

When Glasgow Distillery was opened in Hillington Business Park, it became the first purpose-built malt whisky distillery in Glasgow in more than a hundred years.

The distillery started production in February 2015 and the first distillation of whisky was unpeated. Since then peated spirit (50ppm) has become part of the production and since 2017, triple distillation is also practised one month per year. The distillery is equipped with a one ton mash tun, 8 stainless steel washbacks with a minimum fermentation of 72 hours, two 2,500 litre wash still, two 1,400 litre spirit stills and one 450 litre gin still .

The first product to be bottled was the Makar gin which now exists in several versions. In the beginning, the owners also bottled old, sourced single malts under the name Prometheus. The first single malt from their own production appeared in June 2018. Aged in ex-bourbon barrels and finished in virgin oak, the whisky was called 1770 Glasgow Single Malt, named after Glasgow's first distillery which was founded at Dundashill in 1770.

From that a signature range of three whiskies has evolved; The Original, Peated and Triple Distilled. They are released in batches with the type of wood changing slightly for every batch. Since autumn 2023 The Original and Peated are also available at cask strength. A new range, Small Batch Series, was introduced in 2022. This is where the owners can excel in bottlings that have been either finished or fully matured in a variety of casks. Some of the latest (in 2025) include two finishes - a 6 year old ruby port and a peated cognac cask finish. There is also a very limited 10 year old, the oldest release from the distillery so far. In July 2025 the distillery opened up to tours limited to 8 people including coopering demonstrations and sampling straight from the cask.

GlenWyvis

[glen•wivis]

Owner: GlenWyvis Distillery Ltd.

Region/district: Highlands

Founded: 2017

Status: Active

Capacity: 120 000 litres

Address: Upper Docharty, Dingwall IV15 9UF

Website: glenwyvis.com

Tel: 01349 862005

While most of the new distilleries in Scotland have one or a handful of owners, Glen Wyvis has more than 4,000! Most of them are based in Dingwall, where the distillery is situated, but 10% come from abroad.

This was the idea from the very beginning and while the every day operation is run by highly skilled professionals (the current manager Craig MacRitchie has been there since the start) some decisions are left to the owners who have one vote each. The business idea also includes part of the profits going back to the local community. The distillery, alas not open to visitors, is beautifully situated on elevated ground north of Dingwall which lies a 20 minute drive northwest of Inverness. The last time a whisky distillery was operating in Dingwall was in 1926.

The distillery is equipped with a 0.5 ton semi lauter mash tun, six washbacks (4,800 litres each) made of stainless steel with a fermentation time of 96-144 hours, one 2,500 litre wash still and one 1,700 litre spirit still with slightly declining lyne arms and performing a slow distillation. The water source is a bore hole delivering hard water due to limestone and the distillery is supported by a biomass boiler fed by wood chips.

The malt comes from Baird's in Inverness and for eleven months of the year unpeated spirit is produced and the final month it is peated (50 ppm). The newmake is semi-sweet with malty and fruity notes. The production plan for 2025 is to do 5 mashes per week and 42,000 litres of pure alcohol.

The newmake was first released for sale in 2019. A first, limited whisky release appeared in 2020 while the inaugural public release was in late 2021. A new series named The Highland Legacy appeared in 2025 with The Drover as the first instalment.

Harris

[har•ris]

Owner: Isle of Harris Distillers Ltd.

Region/district: Highlands (Isle of Harris)

Founded: 2015

Status: Active (vc)

Capacity: 399 000 litres

Address: Tarbert, Isle of Harris, Na h-Eileanan an Iar HS3 3DJ

Website: harrisdistillery.com

Tel: 01859 502212

The distillery, located in Tarbert on Harris, was the second distillery after Abhainn Dearg on Lewis to be founded in the Outer Hebrides in modern times.

For almost ten years these two were the only whisky producers in this remote part of Scotland but recently two distilleries have opened up on North Uist and Benbecula and another one is planned for Barra.

One of the founders, Simon Erlanger started his career in the business already in 1985 working with Johnnie Walker, just before Guinness took over the company. He joined Glenmorangie in 1993 eventually becoming commercial director. After a few years as a consultant he became part of the team that founded Isle of Harris distillery.

The first whisky at Harris was distilled in December 2015 and after years of successfully selling gin they launched their first single malt, The Hearach, in September 2023. One year later a second expression, this time matured exclusively in first fill oloroso butts, appeared. A limited bottling, fully matured in casks from the producer of sweet wines, Chateau Biac in France, was launched in spring 2025 and in September a 10th anniversary bottlings was released.

The equipment consists of a 1.2 tonne semi lauter mash tun made of stainless steel but clad with American oak and 8 washbacks made of Oregon pine with a fermentation time of 72-96 hours. There are also one 7,000 litre wash still and a 5,000 litre spirit still – both with descending lyne arms and made in Italy. For 2025 the goal is to do 10 mashes and 200,000 litres or more of pure alcohol. The style of the whisky is medium peated with a phenol specification in the barley of 12-14ppm although there are also a few batches of heavily peated malt (30ppm) made with local peat.

Holyrood

[holly•rude]

Owner: The Holyrood Distillery Ltd.
Region/district: Lowlands
Founded: 2019
Status: Active (vc)
Capacity: 250 000 litres
Address: 19 St Leonard´s Lane, Edinburgh EH8 9SH
Website: holyrooddistillery.co.uk
Tel: 0131 2858977

Whisky enthusiasts had been waiting for the first whisky distillery in modern days to open up in Edinburgh and, later on, for the first single malt distilled in Edinburgh to be launched.

It so happened that the honour was shared between two producers. Holyrood, founded in 2019, was the first "proper" distillery but the first single malt was actually launched in early 2022. The Chain Pier Single Malt had been distilled in the pilot distillery (where just 39 casks were filled) in the first months of 2019 of what later became the Bonnington distillery in Leith.

In October 2023 though, Holyrood released their first single malt at a charity auction and the next day it went on general sale. Named Arrival it had been matured in a combination of oloroso, PX sherry, bourbon and rum barrels. It was later followed by Pitch (exploring the impact of red wine yeast), Ambir (made from four different speciality malts) and Embra (based on seven different types of yeast). Located in the centre of Edinburgh, the distillery also houses a visitor centre.

It is currently equipped with a one ton semi-lauter mash tun and six 5,000 litre washbacks made of stainless steel. The fermentation time is typically between 48 and 120 hours but experiments with more than 300 hours of fermentation have also been conducted. There is one 5,000 litre wash still and one 3,750 litre spirit still – both very tall and fitted with descending lyne arms and boil balls. Attached to the spirit still is a water-cooled purifier. The newmake is filled into a variety of casks, including ex-bourbon, sherry, rum and virgin oak. The distillery uses a variety of different types of yeast as well as different mash bills based on traditionally malted barley, including heritage strains such as Chevalier and Golden Promise, but also including speciality varieties such as crystal and chocolate malt.

InchDairnie

[inch•dairnie]

Owner: InchDairnie Distillery Ltd
Region/district: Lowlands
Founded: 2015
Status: Active
Capacity: 4 000 000 litres
Address: Whitecraigs Rd, Glenrothes, Fife KY6 2RX
Website: inchdairniedistillery.com
Tel: 01595 510010

Inchdairnie, one of the most innovative of all the new Scottish distilleries in the past 20 years, experienced a change of guard in 2024.

The initiator and co-founder Ian Palmer resigned as managing director to continue as chairman of the board. Starting in the industry in 1978, Palmer has held a number of senior roles over the years, not least at Invergordon Distillers, Whyte & Mackay and La Martiniquaise. Since the start, the Danish spirits company MacDuff International has had an interest in the distillery. In May 2025 it was announced that the two companies would merge under the name InchDairnie Whisky Limited.

Inchdairnie is equipped with a hammer mill and a Meura mash filter. There are seven washbacks with a fermentation time of 50 hours and two pairs of traditional pot stills with double condensers and after-coolers increasing the copper to spirit ratio. The pot stills are complemented by a Lomond still with six plates to provide the opportunity for triple and experimental distillation.

At least five different types of whisky are produced. First of all Inchdairnie Single Malt which will form the core range together with RyeLaw made from malted rye and malted barley and KinGlassie which is a peated expression. Furthermore there is Strathenry which constitutes 80% of the distillery's production and will be used for blended whisky. The final expression is The PrinLaws Collection which will be a range of spirits from different yeasts, cereals and oaks. On top of that there are trials with single pot still and sour mash whisky. The first core expression appeared in May 2023 with RyeLaw. It was followed in May 2025 by two single malt expressions named KinGlassie. Both were heavily peated and 8 years old but while Raw had been fully matured in bourbon casks, the Double Matured had received a 3 year finish in amontillado casks.

Isle of Raasay

[ajl ov rassay]

Owner:
R&B Distillers

Region/district:
Highlands (Raasay)

Founded:
2017

Status:
Active (vc)

Capacity:
220 000 litres

Address: Borodale House, Raasay, By Kyle IV40 8PB

Website:
raasaydistillery.com

Tel:
01478 470177

Raasay distillery is an excellent example of a whisky distillery established in a remote area (in this case an island east of Skye), creating job opportunities for the locals.

An old Georgian house was turned into both a distillery and a six bedroom hotel with another 5 rooms, Na Bothain, added and opened in October 2025. The visitor centre was upgraded in 2022 with a new tasting room and a new bar. The distillery is equipped with a 1 ton mash tun and six stainless steel (5,000 litre) washbacks with cooling jackets currently with four short fermentations (67 hours) and six long (118 hours) adding up to 220,000 litres of alcohol in 2025. The 5,000 litre wash still has a cooling jacket around the lyne arm and there's also a 3,600 litre spirit still with a copper column attached should it be used for special runs. The production is a 50/50 combination of peated (48-52 ppm) and unpeated spirit. Some of the barley is grown on Raasay while the production in 2025 also will include organic barley from Orkney, bere barley from Berwickshire and barley from Campbeltown. All Raasay single malt is distilled, matured and bottled on the island.

The first release of a signature malt (R01), matured in a combination of virgin chinkapin oak, Bordeaux red wine barriques and first fill rye casks, appeared in 2021. New releases in 2025 include The Draam (the signature single malt), a cask strength bottling of the same and Dun Cana matured in ex rye casks finished in a mix of oloroso and PX quarter casks. Na Sia are single cask, cask strength bottlings comprising of unpeated spirit matured in ex rye casks, chinkapin oak and ex Bordeaux red wine as well as peated spirit matured in the same type of casks. Na Sia will be released every two years until 2030 when it will be 11 years old.

Jackton

[jack•ton]

Owner:
Raer Scotch Whisky Ltd.

Region/district:
Lowlands

Founded:
2020

Status:
Active

Capacity:
300 000 litres

Address: Hayhill Road, Jackton G74 5AN

Website:
raer.co.uk

Tel:
01355 202 590

The first few years of Jackton distillery in South Lannarkshire were, if not humble, then at least kept very much under the radar.

The Kean family, already involved in the local business, converted the O'Cathain Farm near East Kilbride in South Lannarkshire into a distillery without much fuss and the first distillation was in February 2020. Eventually a small shop was opened on site where their own gin and sourced whisky was offered under the name Raer, but there were no tours.

Since summer 2024 things have changed dramatically. Not only are you able to tour the distillery but the owners also offer accommodation with 12 double rooms fully equipped with a kitchenette and there is also a lovely tasting bar for the guests.

The distillery is equipped with a one ton stainless steel, semi-lauter mash tun and six 7,000 litre stainless steel washbacks (with room for another six in the future) with a fermentation time of 90 hours. There are two stills from Kothe – a 5,000 litre wash still and a 2,000 litre spirit still. The major development in the last year was installing their own maltings. The steeping takes place in separate tanks and the germination and kilning happens in two large, 5 ton drums. The system will be available to serve the own distillery's needs as well as supplying other producers with malted barley. Currently the distillery is mashing 4-5 times per week. There are three warehouses (both dunnage and racked) on site and the owners use a variety of casks for the maturation; bourbon, sherry, rum, port and different wine casks.

The current offering of Raer whisky, before their own production has matured, consists of three blended Scotch.

Kingsbarns

[kings•barns]

Owner: Wemyss family

Region/district: Lowlands

Founded: 2014

Status: Active (vc)

Capacity: 600 000 litres

Address: East Newhall Farm, Kingsbarns, St Andrews KY16 8QE

Website: kingsbarnsdistillery.com

Tel: 01333 451300

Kingsbarns distillery is currently undergoing a multi-million pound expansion focusing on both sustainability as well as securing more warehousing for their growing brand.

It started with a fifth washback in spring 2024 and was followed by the instalment of a new heat exchange system. This recovers heat from the pot ale and spent lees which is then used to preheat the wash for the following distillation. The procedure saves more than 100 tonnes of carbon emissions yearly. Finally, in 2025, four bonded warehouses with a total capacity of 57,000 casks, were erected in Glenrothes in Fife. The owners will also have the possibility of marrying casks, filling and re-racking.

Apart from owning Kingsbarns, the Wemyss family are also known for their brand of independent bottlings, Wemyss Malts, and their Scottish gin, Darnley's Gin.

The distillery is equipped with a 1.5 ton stainless steel mash tun and five stainless steel washbacks – four of them holding 7,500 litres and a fifth double that size. The fermentation time is 72-120 hours. Finally there is one 7,500 litre wash still and one 4,500 litre spirit still. A slow distillation and an early cut are important to achieve the fruity character. Mainly first fill bourbon barrels are used for maturation together with STR casks (wine barriques that have been shaved, toasted and re-charred). The production goal for 2025 will be 10 mashes per week and 300,000 litres of pure alcohol.

The first widely available release, Dream to Dram, appeared in 2019. In 2023 this was succeeded by Doocot. Before that they added an ex-oloroso matured single malt, Balcomie, to the range. In 2024 a third addition to the core range appeared by the way of Coaltown matured in ex-peated casks and this was followed in 2025 by a 10 year old – the first from the distillery with an age statement.

Kythe

[kyeth]

Owner: Kythe Distillery Co.

Region/district: Lowlands

Founded: 2025

Status: Active

Capacity: 60 000 litres

Address: Hills of Bendochy Farm, Blairgowrie PH13 9HN

Website: kythedistillery.com

Tel: -

Angus MacRaild and Jonny McMillan have been advocates of old-style whisky for more than a decade. It seemed inevitible that some day they would become distillers themselves.

In 2023 plans were revealed to build a distillery on Hills of Bendochy Farm in Perthshire just north of Coupar Angus and the two were joined by Aaron Chan who shared the same ethos for whisky as they did. As they themselves declare the goal is to be at the forefront of a new movement to revive ´old style´ Scottish single malt, specifically looking to the 1960s and beyond. What that entails is searching for flavour and character rather than efficiency and yield. Specifically, they are looking for tropical fruits, waxiness and a heavier texture.

This becomes obvious when you scrutinize their choices of raw material and production setup. At least for the first two years they will be using the classic (and low-yielding) Golden Promise barley, part of it being grown on the farm and floor-malted. Going forward there will also be a space for other heirloom barley varieties.

The one ton mash tun will be handstirred and they are planning for four mashes per week. A 14 day fermentation in the eight Douglas fir washbacks will be standard and yeast from local brewer´s will be used instead of distillers yeast which is predominant in the industry. The 6,000 litre wash still is directly fired, fitted with a rummager and the fire is fed by hand with logs. This is complemented by a 4,000 litre spirit still. The spirit vapours from both stills are condensed using worm tubs. In terms of maturation the idea is to let the newmake shine and the main part will be filled into refill wood but there will also be a place for sherry casks in the scheme. The plan is to have the distillery commissioned in autumn 2025.

Lagg

[laag]

Owner:
Isle of Arran Distillers Ltd.

Region/district:
Lowlands (s. Arran)

Founded:
2019

Status:
Active (vc)

Capacity:
750 000 litres

Address: Kilmory, Isle of Arran KA27 8PG

Website:
laggwhisky.com

Tel:
01770 870565

For six years now the Isle of Arran has been blessed with two whisky distilleries, both owned by Isle of Arran Distillers. The first to open, in 1995, is the one in Lochranza on the northern tip of the island.

It was followed by Lagg in the south which started distilling in 2019. Actually there used to be a Lagg distillery before but that closed its doors almost two centuries ago. The location of the new distillery is stunning, with a view to the Firth of Clyde, and the visitor experience is one of the best in Scotland. On the other side of the road from the distillery, 3,000 apple trees are growing to be used for small, yearly batches of cider and with a view to produce apple brandy in the future.

Lagg is all about peated whisky with a 50ppm phenol specification of the barley and the distillery has a four ton semilauter mash tun with a copper top. There are four Oregon pine washbacks holding 20,000 litres and with a fermentation time of either 54 or 72 hours. Finally there is one wash still (10,000 litres) and one spirit still (7,000 litres). Foreshots are 30 minutes long and the spirit run goes from 73% down to 63%. The cloudy wort, slightly descending lyne arms and a quick distillation gives a green/grassy newmake and the plan for 2025 is to do 5 mashes per week resulting in 300,000 litres of alcohol. If need be, there is space already for an additional four washbacks and one more pair of stills.

In 2022 the first limited single malts from the distillery appeared. These were followed in 2023 by the first core bottlings – Kilmory (46%, bourbon matured) and Corriecravie (55%, bourbon matured and with a sherry finish). New bottlings in 2025 include the globally available Small Batch Palo Cortado Finish bottled at 56.2% and, exclusive to the distillery, a Tequila Cask Finish bottled at 59,1%.

Laggan Bay

[laggan bei]

Owner:
Ian Macleod Distillers

Region/district:
Islay

Founded:
2025

Status:
Active

Capacity:
1 000 000 litres

Address: Glenegedale PA42 7AS

Website:
-

Tel:
-

Islay is the world's most legendary whisky island – famous for its smoky style and adored by enthusiasts globally. Probably early 2026 it will be blessed with its 11th distillery.

Mackay Smith and Donald MacKenzie, known as the Islay Boys, recently moved their Islay Ales Brewery to Glenegedale east of Islay airport. For years they also planned for an adjacent whisky distillery on the same site. One important reason for that was that over time their beer brewery had expanded into an independent whisky bottling business with brands such as Flatnöse and Bårelegs.

The planning for Laggan Bay Distillery was approved by the local council in June 2022 but between application and approval the idea for a smaller distillery had grown into one with a million litre capacity. More funding was required and Mack and Donald approached one of Scotland's largest spirits companies, Ian Macleod Distillers, to see if they were interested, which they were. Building started in September 2023 and the distillery will soon come on stream. Today the distillery is fully owned by Ian Macleod but with the Islay Boys having secured part of the production for their whisky business.

Laggan Bay is situated on an old RAF site and is equipped with a four ton semilauter mash tun and six 20,000 litre washbacks made from stainless steel. Fermentation time will initially be 66-90 hours. There is one 20,000 litre wash still with TVR and one 14,400 litre spirit still. Water and electricity is scarce on the island so while the process water will come from the nearby river, the cooling water is derived from a closed loop system. Until 2029 when they can be attached to the expanded island grid, the electricity is supplied by generators. The spent lees from the distillation will be cleaned by a four-cell wetland in similar with the one in place at Ian MacLeod's Glengoyne distillery.

Lerwick

[le•rick]

Owner: Lerwick Distillery Ltd.

Region/district: Highlands (Shetland)

Founded: 2024

Status: Active (vc)

Capacity: 250 000 litres

Address: 32 Market St, Lerwick ZE1 0JP

Website: shetlandwhisky.com

Tel: 01806 249226

For at least twenty years anticipation for the first Shetland whisky distillery has been high. The Blackwood project in the early millenium backfired and investors lost their money.

The plans, before the company was folded up, was to build the distillery at the former RAF site at Saxa Vord on Unst. Eventually, in 2013, a distillery was built on the site, this time initiated by the highly experienced Stuart Nickerson but so far it has been producing Shetland Reel gin.

In November 2022 however a planning application for a whisky distillery right in the middle of Lerwick was granted. Behind the distillery are the two born-and-bred Shetlanders Martin Watt and Calum Miller and they were joined by Carline MacIntyre who will be in charge of sales. They also managed to bring in the whisky icon Ian Millar, with lots of experience from many Scottish distilleries, as master distiller.

The distillery is equipped with a 0.55-0.75 ton semi lauter mash tun and there are six stainless steel washbacks holding 4,000 litres each with a fermentation time of plus 70 hours. Finally there are two 4,000 litre pot stills. Most of the equipment has been made in China. The long term plan is to grow and malt the barley on the island. The whisky will be matured at Scalloway but the owners are in no hurry to release their first expression. The plan is to wait at least eight years. Sourced whisky, curated by Ian Millar, is sold since November 2024 under the name Nørn and in 2025 the Smoorikin was added to the range.

The first distillation was planned for late 2024 but by August 2025 they were still waiting to commission. The distillery however is open for visitors.

Lindores Abbey

[linn•doors aebi]

Owner: The Lindores Distilling Co.

Region/district: Lowlands

Founded: 2017

Status: Active (vc)

Capacity: 225 000 litres

Address: Lindores Abbey House, Abbey Road, Newburgh, Fife KY14 6HH

Website: lindoresabbeydistillery.com

Tel: 01337 842547

Building a distillery at the old monastery of Lindores was a stroke of genius from the owners, Drew and Helen McKenzie.

In a letter from King James IV to Friar John Cor in 1494 he instructed the monk to make "aqua vitae from VIII bolls of malt". The archaeological and historical evidence for Lindores being the birthplace of Scotch whisky are by no way inconclusive but further excavations of the site may reveal some evidence.

Be that as it may, the location is stunning and with all the production equipment on one level you have a spectacular view of the surroundings. If you look down from the second floor you see the remnants of the old monastery and if you look further away you see Dundee.

The equipment consists of a 2 ton semi lauter mash tun with a copper lid, four Douglas fir washbacks with five 90 hour fermentations per week, one 10,000 litre wash still and two 3,500 litre spirit stills. The foreshots are 15-20 minutes and the spirit cut starts at 75% and goes down to 67% with the obvious aim of catching the fruity esters in the beginning and avoiding the pungent congeners at the end. The plan for 2025 is to produce 190,000 litres of pure alcohol. All the barley used in the distillery has been grown in the surrounding fields

In spring 2021, the first 1494 bottles of their inaugural release, available only to members of The 1494 Preservation Society, appeared and this was followed in July by the first widely available expression – the Lindores MCDXCIV. September 2024 saw the launch of Thiron, the first in an annual series bottled at 49.4%. Another series is the Friar John Cor Cask Strength Congregation where Chapter III was released in May 2025. Starting in ex-bourbon the whisky gets its character from both amontillado and PX sherry casks.

Lochlea

[lock•lee]

Owner: Lochlea Distilling Co.

Region/district: Lowlands

Founded: 2018

Status: Active

Capacity: 200 000 litres

Address: Lochlea Farm, South Ayrshire KA1 5NN

Website: lochleadistillery.com

Tel: 07585 661 605

Surrounded by 220 acres of their own barley fields, Lochlea is beautifully located on the site of a farm from the 1700s in rural Ayrshire just south of Kilmarnock.

Ten years ago the owner, Neil McGeoch, divided his time between the farm where he had cattle and the family business in Glasgow, which included property and renewable energy. He decided to change the focus of the farm into agriculture and the idea of starting a distillery was born. In 2022 John Campbell, with 27 years at Laphroaig, was hired as the production director and master blender but left in autumn 2024 to join Sespe Creek distillery in California. Lochlea's new master blender is Jill Boyd with a long experience from W Grant's and Compass Box.

The distillery is equipped with a 2 ton semi-lauter mash tun, six Douglas fir washbacks with both short (66 hours) and long (116) fermentations and two tall stills (10,000 and 6,250 litres respectively). Producing a semi-cloudy wort, conducting long fermentations and a distillation with a 25 minute long foreshot and a spirit cut of 75-67%, the aim is to produce a fruity newmake with a significant amount of cereal body. All the barley comes from own fields and 15-20% of that is floor malted on site while the rest is sent to Baird's to be malted. The 2025 production plan is five mashes in a five-day week and 195,000 litres of pure alcohol. So far, peated whisky has not been produced although it is in the pipeline.

The inaugural whisky appeared in 2022 and since then Our Barley has been launched as the core product. This was followed by the Seasonal Releases. In September 2025 that range was discontinued and Our Barley was joined by Orchard & Oak, Dark Briar and Smoke Without Fire. In May 2025 the limited batch 3 of the cask strength appeared.

Nc´nean

[nook•knee•anne]

Owner: Nc´nean Distillery Ltd.

Region/district: Western Highlands

Founded: 2017

Status: Active (vc)

Capacity: 100 000 litres

Address: Drimnin, By Lochaline PA80 5XZ

Website: ncnean.com

Tel: 01967 421698

Sustainability has been at the heart of the founder Annabel Thomas and her team from the moment the first plans for Nc´nean distillery were drawn up.

In 2021 Nc´nean became a certified net zero emissions whisky distillery – the first in the UK to achieve this and 20 years ahead of the Scotch industry target. In 2022 the distillery was one of two distilleries in Scotland to become a certified B Corporation for its social and environmetal standards. The distillery is powered with 100% renewable energy from a biomass boiler fired by woodchips from a nearby forest and all the trees are replanted.

The distillery is equipped with a one ton semi lauter mash tun and four stainless steel washbacks with a fermentation time between 65 and 115 hours. Furthermore there is a 5,000 litre wash still and a 3,500 litre spirit still, both with slightly descending lyne arms and sub coolers although the latter are currently not being used. The owner is working on two basic recipes of fruity whisky – "new style" to be enjoyed young and "old style", with lower cut points and destined for a longer maturation.

A botanical spirit was launched in 2018. The first single malt, Ainnir, was released in 2020 and this was followed by a core expression which is now bottled in batches. Quiet Rebels is a series of whiskies chosen by individuals working at Nc´Nean with Simon being the latest in October 2025, a stout cask matured whisky. Huntress is a series focusing on the distillery´s experiments not least with yeast, with the latest being Huntress Lemon Meadow, launched in April 2025. Lemon Meadow has been matured in a combination of STR casks and ex-bourbon. Finally, there are a number of single cask bottlings under the name Aon, which means 'one' in Gaelic. The distillery is situated on the Morvern peninsula with a stunning view towards Mull.

North Uist

[north uised]

Owner: North Uist Distillery Ltd.
Region/district: Islands (Benbecula)
Founded: 2024
Status: Active (vc)
Capacity: 50 000 litres
Address: Nunton Steadings, Benbecula HS7 5LU
Website: northuistdistillery.com
Tel: 01870 603 792

Establishing a new whisky distillery is a strenuous task by any means. If you decide to do it on an island you have set yourself up for an even greater challenge.

Logistics and finding staff are but a few of the challenges and yet in the last decade no less than ten distilleries have opened up in the Western Isles – four of them in the Outer Hebrides. The latest to come on stream was North Uist distillery. Already in 2019, Jonny Ingledew and Kate MacDonald (both with family ties to the island) started distilling gin on North Uist.

A year later they bought Nunton Steadings on Benbecula (south of North Uist) and transformed the 18th century farm into their new distillery, adding whisky to the menu.

The first whisky distillation took place in November 2024 and the distillery is equipped with a 0.5 ton mash tun and five Douglas fir washbacks holding 2,500 litres each. Both stills are from Forsyth's – wash still (2,500 litres) and spirit still (2,000 litres) and both are attached to shell and tube condensers. There are dunnage warehouses on site as well as additional storage off site. With five mashes per week the capacity is 50,000 litres of pure alcohol.

Bere barley is grown locally but other varieties (both heritage and modern) are also used. At the moment all barley is malted off the island but there are plans to build own floor maltings using local peat. Both unpeated and peated spirit is produced and for maturation first and refill bourbon casks are in place along with a small number of ex-sherry casks.

On site there is a fully functional visitor centre with a shop, bar and tasting room and there are daily tours in the summertime.

Port Ellen

[port ell•en]

Owner: Diageo
Region/district: Islay
Founded: 1825 (2024)
Status: Active (vc)
Capacity: 1 700 000 litres
Address: Port Ellen, Isle of Islay, Argyll PA42 7AJ
Website: malts.com
Tel: -

The decision to re-open both Brora and Port Ellen was made in autumn 2017. While it took four years to start up Brora, it lasted another three years until Port Ellen was running.

The formal opening was on 19 March 2024 when it became the 10th operational malt distillery on Islay. Its previous closure in 1983, seemingly for good, was at a time when the Scotch whisky industry encountered decreasing demand for its products and another twenty distilleries were also shut down. Unlike Brora, there were just a few of the existing buildings at Port Ellen that could be used and all the equipment was gone. Instead Diageo used the old drawings and embarked on recreating the original equipment. On site there is now a full lauter mash tun with mash charges ranging from 5.5 to 7.5 tonnes. The barley, coming from the adjacent maltings, has a phenol specification of 35ppm. There are six wooden 36,000 litre washbacks with a fermentation time between 90 and 120 hours and one pair of stills based one the ones which ran during 1967-1983. These are named Phoenix stills as a nod to the mythic bird that rose from the ashes. On the opposite side of the stillroom there is also one set of experimental stills (one third in size of the main pair). Foreshots are 30 minutes and cut points go from 74% down to 60%. A large courtyard separates the distillery from an elegant and well designed visitor centre. Diageo has decided to offer few but high-end tours of the distillery in similar with how they operate at Brora. Two options are available starting at £250. There is also a day each month open to the public which is complimentary but still has to be booked in advance.

In 2024 Gemini, a twin set of malts distilled in 1978, aged for 44 years and matured in different types of casks, were released. They were followed in 2025 by Prism and a 200th anniversary bottling.

Port of Leith

[port of leeth]

Owner: Muckle Brig
Region/district: Lowlands
Founded: 2023
Status: Active (vc)
Capacity: 400 000 litres
Address: 11 Whisky Quay, Edinburgh EH6 6FH
Website: leithdistillery.com
Tel: 0131 6000 144

When it comes to the architecture and the design, the Port of Leith distillery in Edinburgh is definitely one of the most unusual in Scotland, perhaps even in the world.

To start with, it's the world's tallest at 42 metres high with no fewer than 10 floors, solar panels on the roof and what must surely be the smallest service yard in the industry. The top five floors hold the hospitality area with bars, private dining rooms, tasting areas and shop. The lower floors contain the production zone with a CTS mill and hopper on the top floor, followed by a 1.5 ton semi-lauter mash tun and seven insulated, 7,500 litre washbacks with a 72 hour fermentation. Further down are one wash still and one spirit still, both with slightly descending lyne arms. The water for the production comes from a 132 metre deep bore hole on the site.

The two founders, Paddy Fletcher and Ian Stirling, chose the location with great care. The distillery can be found in Edinburgh's historic Port in Leith, just 50 metres from the Royal Yacht Britannia. From the early 1800s until the 1990s, Leith was an important area for the warehousing, blending and bottling of Scotch whisky.

The view from all floors towards the North Sea is also stunning. The distillery opened in October 2023 and the core spirit is unpeated with various strains of yeast and barley varieties being an important part. The newmake is filled into first fill bourbons, refills, and different types of sherry in both American and European oak along with various wine casks. Prior to opening, the owners had undertaken whisky trials with experimental yeasts in association with Heriot Watt University, research that will continue. In May 2022, they opened The Lind & Lime Distillery, a gin distillery also in Leith.

Rosebank

[rows•bank]

Owner: Ian Macleod Distillers
Region/district: Lowlands
Founded: 2022
Status: Active (vc)
Capacity: 1 000 000 litres
Address: Camelon Road, Falkirk FK1 5JR
Website: rosebank.com
Tel: 01324 374 100

The newborn Rosebank has now been distilling for a little more than two years and malt whisky enthusiasts couldn't be happier.

The distillery has always been close to the hearts of many aficionados thinking of Rosebank as the ultimate Lowland malt and the closure in 1993 was indeed a sad day. Ian Macleod, the new owners and already operating Glengoyne and Tamdhu, meticulously recreated the old distillery although all the equipment bar the Boby mill was gone.

The distillery is equipped with 3.2 ton semi lauter mash tun with a copper dome. There are eight 15,000 litre Douglas fir washbacks with fermentation times in a five-day production range from 72 hours up to 132 hours. Rosebank is triple distilled in a 15,000 litre wash still, an 8,000 litre intermediate still and a 5,200 litre spirit still. The swan neck on the wash still is chopped off and capped and the lyne arm stuck to the side of the neck. The spirit is cooled in individual worm tubs on the outside. Foreshots are 17 minutes and for a triple distilled whisky the spirit cut (around 4 hours) is quite wide starting at 81% and coming off spirit in the low 70's%. In 2025 twelve mashes per week is planned resulting in around 530,000 litres of pure alcohol. The newmake is an enigma, being both dry, floral, malty and peppery. The explanation lies in the combination of triple distillation, clear wort and using worm tubs.

The Rosebank visitor experience is excellent with all the equipment assembled on one floor and includes a stunning shop as well as various tasting rooms. When Ian Macleod took over the distillery the old stock of maturing whisky was included. Over the past few years the Legacy Series has been released, starting with a 30 year old distilled in 1990 and ending with a 32 year old. On top of that there are two 1990 vintages for global travel retail and two single casks (433 and 625) distilled in 1993.

Roseisle

[rose•eyel]

Owner:
Diageo

Region/district:
Speyside

Founded:
2009

Status:
Active

Capacity:
12 500 000 litres

Address: Roseisle, Morayshire IV30 5YP

Website:
-

Tel:
01343 832100

In the first decade of the new millennium the Scotch whisky industry was filled with optimism and the memories of distillery closures in the mid eighties had started to fade away.

Consumer interest was on the way up and I remember writing in the Malt Whisky Yearbook 2009 "Scotch whisky continues breaking records." Diageo, the largest company in the business, had for quite some time realised they needed to scale up their production. They owned 28 malt distilleries at the time but many of them were small. Simultaneously the interest in bottled single malt was growing stronger and stronger. What they needed was a large plant which could produce malt for their blends.

The huge Roseisle (12 million litres) was built close to Burghead maltings on the Moray coast a few miles west of Elgin. At the same time Diageo announced that they had plans to construct another two "Roseisle", possibly where Clynelish and Inchgower lies. These plans, however, were never fulfilled. Roseisle is equipped with two stainless steel, full lauter mash tuns with a 12.5 tonne charge each. There are 14 huge (112,000 litres) stainless steel washbacks and 14 stills. The wash stills are heated by external heat exchangers while the spirit stills are heated using steam coils. The spirit vapours are cooled through copper condensers but on three spirit stills and three wash stills there are also stainless steel condensers attached. They can be used for acquiring a more sulphury spirit. The fermentation time for a Speyside style of whisky is 90-100 hours and for a heavier style it is 50-60 hours.

In 2017, Roseisle single malt was part of the blended malt Collectivum XXVIII and in the 2023 Special Releases it was for the first time released as a single malt – a 12 year old. This was followed up by yet another 12 year old in autumn 2024, this time bottled at 55.6%.

Strathearn

[strath•earn]

Owner:
Douglas Laing

Region/district:
Southern Highlands

Founded:
2013

Status:
Active

Capacity:
60 000 litres

Address: Bachilton Farm Steading, Methven PH1 3QX

Website:
strathearndistillery.com

Tel:
-

When Strathearn distillery was founded in 2013, just ten kilometres west of Perth, it was one of Scotland's first craft distilleries.

Craft, in this case, referred not only to its small scale but also to its innovative and progressive approach to Whisky production. Founder Tony Reeman-Clark was determined to push boundaries set by the Scotch Whisky Association, experimenting with maturation in non-oak woods such as chestnut, mulberry, and cherry, as well as trialling older barley varieties, including Maris Otter, where flavour took precedence over yield.

In 2019, the Distillery was acquired by independent bottler Douglas Laing. While alternative woods were set aside, the focus on heirloom and speciality malts continued. Today, Strathearn operates with a copper-clad 0.4-tonne stainless steel mash tun, eight stainless steel washbacks, two 1,000-litre wash stills, and a 1,000-litre spirit still. Fermentations are notably long, averaging 144 hours, with planned production reaching around 60,000 litres of pure alcohol in 2025. Whereas the previous owners also produced peated whisky, the distillery is now dedicated entirely to un-peated spirit. Following a career in brewing, Angela Brown has served as lead distiller since 2020.

The first single malt Scotch from the distillery was released in 2016 and the first from the new owners appeared three years later. In July 2022, a single malt spirit named "The Heart", bottled at 63.5%, was launched. In April 2024, the inaugural Strathearn Single Malt was unveiled, marrying whisky distilled by Douglas Laing with spirit from the original owners, aged six to eight years. It was followed by Batch 2 - a global limited release. Comprising a vatting of 31 casks (mostly ex-bourbon but also sherry and virgin oak casks), it reflects both inherited stock and whisky distilled under Douglas Laing's stewardship

Torabhaig

[tor•a•vaig]

Owner: Mossburn Distillers
Region/district: Highlands (Skye)
Founded: 2016
Status: Active (vc)
Capacity: 500 000 litres
Address: Teangue, Sleat, Isle of Skye IV44 8RE
Website: torabhaig.com
Tel: 01471 833447

Torabhaig is owned by a fairly young company, Mossburn Distillers which was founded in 2012. But one of the initiators has a much longer background in the spirits business.

Neil Mathiesons interest in spirits started with cognac, armagnac and wine in the early 1990s. He founded Eaux de Vie which in large parts functioned as an importer and independent bottler. He later joined hands with Swiss-based Marussia Beverages and eventually Mossburn Distillers was founded. Apart from Torabhaig, the company owns and operates the small Reivers distillery in the Scottish Borders where rye whisky and other spirits are produced. They also have an interest in Kaikyo distillery in Japan and within a few years the plans are to have a quite large distillery near Jedburgh for production of both malt and grain whisky.

Torabhaig is equipped with a 1.5 ton stainless steel semi lauter mash tun with a copper top. There are eight washbacks made of Douglas fir (10,000 litres) with a fermentation time between 80 and 120 hours, one 8,000 litre wash still and one 5,000 litre spirit still. The production plan entails 18 mashes per week in the winter and 12 in the summer aiming for 500,000 litres of heavily peated spirit.

The first single malt from the distillery, "2017. The Legacy Series", was released in 2021 and had been made from heavily peated barley (55-60ppm). It was followed by Allt Gleann matured in a combination of first fill bourbon barrels and re-fill casks. The second edition of Allt Gleann appeared in 2022 and was followed by a cask strength version in 2023. In 2024 there was the Cnoc na Mòine and new releases in 2025 include Sound of Sleat and a batch strength version of the same. Their first 10 year old is only a matter of a few years away now.

Wolfburn

[wolf•burn]

Owner: Aurora Brewing Ltd.
Region/district: Northern Highlands
Founded: 2013
Status: Active (vc)
Capacity: 135 000 litres
Address: Henderson Park, Thurso, Caithness KW14 7XW
Website: wolfburn.com
Tel: 01847 891051

Traditionally the release of a 12 year old single malt has been the mark of a distillery entering into adulthood. Today the consumers are less fixated by age but it still remains a milestone.

As far north as one can travel on the Scottish mainland lies Caithness. Next comes the Pentland Firth and then Orkney. This beautiful and rugged part of the country was never famous for its distilleries but for a short period in the 1820s there was one known as Wolfburn. Almost two centuries later a "new" Wolfburn (close to the old one) was founded in Thurso. In just twelve years this has made a name for itself and a completely new core range from the owners, including a 12 year old, celebrates just that.

While situated in an industrial park it may not resemble the traditional, romantic distillery setting and yet visitors come from near and afar. It is equipped with a 1.1 ton semi-lauter stainless steel mash tun with a copper canopy, four stainless steel washbacks with a fermentation time of 70-92 hours, holding 5,500 litres each, one wash still (5,500 litres) and one spirit still (3,600 litres). The main part of the malt is unpeated but a lightly peated spirit is also produced. Yearly production is around 125,000 litres

The inaugural bottling in 2016 had a smoky profile from being partly matured in quarter casks from Islay. This was followed over the years by more widely available expressions including Northland, Aurora, Morven and Langskip. In 2025 these were all exchanged for a new core range consisting of two 8 year olds – one matured in quarter and the other lightly peated. There is also the 10 year old (first released in 2023) from oloroso sherry casks and, introduced in May 2025, a 12 year old with influences from both bourbon and sherry casks. On top of that there is the limited Perthrö, the 14th edition in the Kylver series, matured in two oloroso casks as well a Cognac cask finish

Active distilleries per owner

Diageo
Auchroisk
Benrinnes
Blair Athol
Brora
Caol Ila
Cardhu
Clynelish
Cragganmore
Dailuaine
Dalwhinnie
Dufftown
Glendullan
Glen Elgin
Glenkinchie
Glenlossie
Glen Ord
Glen Spey
Inchgower
Knockando
Lagavulin
Linkwood
Mannochmore
Mortlach
Oban
Port Ellen
Roseisle
Royal Lochnagar
Strathmill
Talisker
Teaninich

Chivas Brothers (Pernod Ricard)
Aberlour
Allt-a-Bhainne
Braeval
Dalmunach
Glenburgie
Glen Keith
Glenlivet
Glentauchers
Longmorn
Miltonduff
Scapa
Strathisla

Edrington Group
Glenrothes
Highland Park
Macallan

InterBev
Balblair
Balmenach
Knockdhu
Pulteney
Speyburn

John Dewar & Sons (Bacardi)
Aberfeldy
Aultmore
Craigellachie
Macduff
Royal Brackla

William Grant & Sons
Ailsa Bay
Balvenie
Glenfiddich
Kininvie

Whyte & Mackay (Emperador)
Dalmore
Fettercairn
Jura
Tamnavulin

Suntory Global Spirits
Ardmore
Auchentoshan
Bowmore
Glen Garioch
Laphroaig

Ian Macleod Distillers
Glengoyne
Rosebank
Tamdhu
Laggan Bay

CVH Spirits
Bunnahabhain
Deanston
Tobermory

Benriach Dist. Co. (Brown Forman)
Benriach
Glendronach
Glenglassaugh

Loch Lomond Group
Glen Scotia
Loch Lomond

J & A Mitchell
Glengyle
Springbank

Glenmorangie Co. (LVMH)
Ardbeg
Glenmorangie

Angus Dundee Distillers
Glencadam
Tomintoul

Campari Group
Glen Grant

Isle of Arran Distillers
Lagg
Lochranza

Signatory
Edradour

Tomatin Distillery Co.
Tomatin

J & G Grant
Glenfarclas

Rémy Cointreau
Bruichladdich

David Prior
Bladnoch

Gordon & MacPhail
Benromach
The Cairn

La Martiniquaise
Glen Moray

Ben Nevis Distillery Ltd (Nikka)
Ben Nevis

Picard Vins & Spiritueux
Tullibardine

Harvey´s of Edinburgh
Speyside

Kilchoman Distillery Co.
Kilchoman

Cuthbert family
Daftmill

Mark Tayburn
Abhainn Dearg

Aurora Brewing Ltd
Wolfburn

Douglas Laing
Strathearn

Annandale Distillery Co.
Annandale

Adelphi Distillery Co.
Ardnamurchan

Wemyss
Kingsbarns

Mcpherson-Grant family
Ballindalloch

Inverleith LLP
Eden Mill

Isle of Harris Distillers
Harris

The Glasgow Distillery Company
Glasgow

InchDairnie Distillery Ltd.
Inchdairnie

Stirling family
Arbikie

Thompson Bros.
Dornoch

Mossburn Distillers
Torabhaig

R & B Distillers
Isle of Raasay

The Lindores Distilling Company
Lindores Abbey

Morrison Glasgow Distillers
Clydeside

Nc´nean Distillery Ltd.
Nc´nean

Borders Distillery Company Ltd.
The Borders

The Glenallachie Distillers Co.
Glenallachie

Morrison Scotch Whisky Distillers
Aberargie

GlenWyvis Distillery Ltd.
GlenWyvis

Hunter Laing
Ardnahoe

The Holyrood Distillery Ltd.
Holyrood

Greenwood Distillers
Ardross

Lalique Group/Hansjörg Wyss
Glenturret

John Crabbie & Co.
Bonnington

Lochlea Distilling Co.
Lochlea

Stewart family
Falkirk

Ardent Spirits
Burnobennie

Raer Scotch Whisky Ltd.
Jackton

Elixir Distillers
Tormore

Kerry and Derek Campbell
8 Doors

Dunphail Distillery Ltd.
Dunphail

Dark Sky Spirits
Moffat

Muckle Brig
Port of Leith

Jon and Victoria Erasmus
Uile-bheist

June & Cameron McCann
Stirling

Tiree Whisky Co. Ltd.
Isle of Tiree

Orkney Distilling Ltd.
Orkney

Deerness Distillery Ltd.
Deerness

North Coast Distillers Ltd.
North Point

Lerwick Distillery Ltd.
Lerwick

The Cabrach Trust
Cabrach

Balmaud Distillery Co Ltd.
Balmaud

Roland Grain et al
Ardgowan

MacMillan Spirits
Benbecula

Kythe Distillery Co.
Kythe

North Uist Distillery Ltd.
North Uist

Simpson family
Ben Cumhaill

O´Rourke family
Blackness Bay

Graham Taylor
Crafty

Nelson family
Toulvaddie

Scottish micro distilleries

Abhainn Dearg

Founded:	Capacity:	Website:	
2008	20 000 l	abhainndeargdistillery.co.uk	
Owner:	**Address:**		**Region:**
Mark Tayburn	Carnish, Isle of Lewis HS2 9EX		Islands

Using mainly barley grown on Lewis, this was the first distillery on the island since 1840. The first release appeared in 2010 and this has been followed by many more, for instance a 10 year old in 2018. Production has been very intermittent for quite a few years now.

Crafty

Founded:	Capacity:	Website:	
2017	25 000 l	craftydistillery.com	
Owner:	**Address:**		**Region:**
Graham Taylor	Newton Stewart DG8 6AS		Lowlands

Originally set up as a gin distillery the owners have been producing small volumes of malt whisky since 2022. They use only Scottish barley and fermentations are up to 168 hours. In late 2024 an application to build a larger distillery was approved. Open to visitors.

Ben Cumhaill

Founded:	Capacity:	Website:	
2025	7 000 l	bencumhaill.co.uk	
Owner:	**Address:**		**Region:**
Simpson family	Dumfries DG2 0RZ		Lowlands

In a building dating back to 1750, Jeff and Jessica Simpson have opened a distillery equipped with two stills and with very long fermentations (up to 168 hours). The first bottling is probably not due until 2033. First distillation was in September 2025 and soon visitors will be welcomed.

Deerness

Founded:	Capacity:	Website:	Region:
2016	10 000 l	deernessdistillery.com	Islands
Owner:		**Address:**	
Deerness Distillery Ltd.		Deerness, Orkney, KW17 2QJ	

Having produced gin for several years, distillation of whisky started in spring 2025 in copper stills (2,400 and 1,200 litres respectively) made in Portugal. The plan is to malt the barley on site. A sourced blend is sold under the name Deer Sound. Open to the public.

Blackness Bay

Founded:	Capacity:	Website:	
2024	2 000 l	blacknessbaydistillery.co.uk	
Owner:	**Address:**		**Region:**
O´Rourke fam.	Blackness, Linlithgow EH49 7NL		Lowlands

With rum being the main produce, malt whisky is also distilled under the name Mary Queen of Scotch. Equipped with a 75 kilo mash tun, three stainless steel washbacks and two copper pot stills the wash is allowed to ferment for 4-6 days. Visitors are welcome by appointment.

Moffat

Founded:	Capacity:	Website:	Region:
2023	12 000 l	moffatdistillery.com	Lowlands
Owner:		**Address:**	
Dark Sky Spirits		Moffat, DG10 9FE	

Nick Bullard, founder of the blending company Dark Sky Spirits together with his wife Erin, decided to also become a distiller in summer 2023. Some 90% of the barley is grown and malted on a single estate and the wash still is directly fired. The distillery is open for tours.

Scottish micro distilleries

North Point

Founded:	Capacity:	Website:	Region:
2023	18 000 l	northpointdistillery.com	Highlands

Owner:	Address:
North Coast Distillers Ltd.	Thurso, KW14 7UZ

With rum as the primary venture it didn´t take long until malt whisky was produced. A two ton mash tun and six washbacks indicate plans to increase capacity. The first whisky expression is planned for 2028 and currently sourced whisky named Dalclagie is sold. Open for tours.

Isle of Tiree

Founded:	Capacity:	Website:	Region:
2018	5 000 l	tireegin.com	Islands

Owner:	Address:
Tiree Whisky Co. Ltd	Isle of Tiree, PA77 6UF

In the Inner Hebrides this distillery founded by Alain Campbell and Ian Smith has been quietly producing gin since 2018 with malt and rye whisky added in 2020. The three stills are direct-fired and fitted to wormtubs and the first single malt was released January 2025.

Orkney Distillery

Founded:	Capacity:	Website:	Region:
2018	30 000 l	orkneydistilling.com	Islands

Owner:	Address:
Orkney Distilling Ltd.	Kirkwall, Orkney, KW15 1QX

Beautifully situated on Kirkwall´s harbour front, the distillery produced Kirkjuvagr gin for the initial six years with the first whisky being distilled in March 2024. Later that year new Hoga stills from Portugal were installed increasing the capacity. The distillery is open for tours.

Toulvaddie

Founded:	Capacity:	Website:	Region:
2022	17 000 l	toulvaddiedistillery.com	N Highland

Owner:	Address:
Heather & Bobby Nelson	Fearn, Tain IV20 1XW

In the abandoned Fearn Airfield southeast of Tain the Nelson´s have built a distillery which, with the tiny bar, adds beautifully to the local community. First distillation was in April 2024 and including a hand stirred mash tun the character of the newmake is extremely complex.

Stirling

Founded:	Capacity:	Website:	Region:
2015	12 000 l	stirlingdistillery.com	Lowlands

Owner:	Address:
June & Cameron McCann	Stirling FK8 1EN

June and Cameron McCann started producing gin in this small distillery in the shadow of Stirling Castle in 2015. In autumn 2023 malt whisky was also added to the range with the aim for a first release in 2027. This is the first time whisky has been distilled in Stirling since 1852.

Uile-bheist

Founded:	Capacity:	Website:	Region:
2023	20 000 l	uilebheist.com	Highlands

Owner:	Address:
Jon & Victoria Ersamus	Ness Bank, Inverness IV2 4SG

The first new distillery (and currently the only one) in Inverness to open in 130 years. The first distillation was in April 2023 and the distillery is powered both by water from river Ness as well as rooftop solar installations. Combined with a brewery, Uile-bheist is open to visitors.

Distilleries
around the globe

Including the subsections:
Europe
North America | Australia & New Zealand
Asia | Africa | South America

The term ”world whisky” has always been used a bit carelessly but I think most people get the meaning behind it. These are countries outside the Big Five (Scotland, Ireland, USA, Canada and Japan) that produce whisky. To make the Malt Whisky Yearbook as easy to navigate as possible, this chapter however deals with all distilleries that are not Scottish.

The rapid rise of world whisky distilleries in the last two decades is absolutely amazing. Twenty years ago, in the first edition of the book, I reported on 33 distilleries. This year they are more than 750 and four countries have been added to the list; Chile, Lebanon, Romania and Uruguay. While Scotch may still be dominating on the malt side, what we are seeing around the world is a curiosity when it comes to using new techniques and methods in order to create new flavours.

Of course there are producers that try their hardest to make their whisky taste as Scottish as possible, adhearing more or less strictly to the rules and regulations set up by the Scotch Whisky Association. But the vast majority try to create something that is influenced by where the whisky was made – the raw material, the climate, cultural traditions...

As discussed in other parts of this book, the alcohol industry is currently on a bumpy road with customers having less to spend due to economic factors and at the same time worrying about geopolitical instability. The question is how this may affect distilleries that started up quite recently, many times burdened by loans and especially in countries that were never famous for whisky?

Actually this could be a really good time to enter the market. Younger consumer groups are looking for authenticity. Brands that don´t just tell a well polished marketing story but the ones that they can relate to. There are also signs that consumers in times of trouble try to buy locally from companies nearby. Their purchase decisions become emotional and, perhaps, less rational.

I know that most readers of this book were probably introduced to whisky when they tried their first Scotch and many of you still rely on that category or style when you make your next purchase. Still, world distilleries have strengthend and broadened the entire whisky scene and there is so much more to discover today than there was twenty years ago. In the end, I feel that the ”old” and the ”new” together will benefit the growth of the world´s most popular spirit – whisky.

Opposite page; Về Để Đi - the first whisky producer in Vietnam

Europe

Austria

Destillerie Haider

Roggenreith, founded in 1995

waldviertlerwhisky.at

The owners released the first Austrian whisky in 1998. In 2005, they opened up a Whisky Experience World with tours and tastings. The distillery is equipped with two Christian Carl copper stills. The main part of the production is made from either 100% malted rye or a combination of rye and malted barley while the rest is from malted barley. Five expressions make up the core range and apart from them there are peated versions as well as limited releases. One of the latest was a 10 year old 30th anniversary edition in June 2025.

Broger Privatbrennerei

Klaus, founded in 1976 (whisky since 2008)

broger.info

The production of whisky is supplementing the distillation and production of eau de vie from apples and pears. The distillery is equipped with a 150 litre Christian Carl still. The current range of whiskies consists of Triple Cask, Medium Smoked, Burn Out and the limited Distiller´s Edition. Whiskies made from alternative grains are sold under a separate brand name - Hoamat.

Other distilleries in Austria

Arno Pauli, Brennerei

Absam, founded in 1930 (whisky since 2005)

arnopauli.at

Whisky is produced in this combination of a guesthouse, brewery and distillery. Besides a 6 year old single malt from barley, they have also released whiskies made from maize, dinkel and wheat.

Dachstein Destillerie (Mandlberggut)

Radstadt, founded in 2007

mandlberggut.com

Apart from production of various spirits from berries, malt whisky is also produced. Their two core expression are Rocky and the peated Smokey.

Egilse Destillerie

Würmla, founded in 2001

egilse-whisky.at

Focusing mainly on whisky the distillery has three product ranges; Classic made from malted barley, Dark which entails the use of different mash bills and Peat made from smoked malted barley.

Farthofer, Destillerie

Öhling, founded in 1867 (whisky since 2014)

destillerie-farthofer.at

Producing schnapps and liqueurs for more than a century, whisky production started in recent years and apart from the blend AWA, the owners have released both single rye and single malt whiskies. The production is organic and they also have their own maltings.

Franz Kostenzer, Edelbrennerei

Maurach/Achensee, founded in 1998, whisky since 2006

schnaps-achensee.at

A huge range of different spirits as well as whisky is produced. Several expressions under the name Whisky Alpin have been released including a 14 year old single malt sherry cask finish, an 11 year old amarone finish and a 6 year old heavily peated.

Hermann Pfanner, Destillerie

Lauterach, founded in 1854 (whisky since 2005)

pfanner-destillate.com

Two core expressions are produced, Pfanner Single Malt Classic and Single Malt Red Wood with a maturation in red wine casks. There are also several limited releases including smoky versions as well as various finishes.

Keckeis Destillerie

Rankweil, founded in 2003 (whisky since 2008)

destillerie-keckeis.at

The core expression is Keckeis Single Malt but in 2021 the limited Stillman´s Finest was launched. Part of the barley has been smoked with beech and maturation is in small ex-sherry casks.

Kuenz Naturbrennerei

Dölsach, founded in 1643 (whisky since 2014)

kuenz-schnaps.at

The distillery recently added whisky to their range. The first single malt, named Rauchkofel, was released in 2017 and since then several different batches have appeared including a smoked one.

Old Raven

Neustift, founded in 2004

oldraven.at

A brewery supplies the wash for the whisky. The core expression is the triple distilled Old Raven and special versions include the 5 year old Smoky Devil, the 10 year old Lockdown and Black Edition.

Puchas, Destillerie (former Lagler, Spezialitätenbrennerei)

Kukmirn, founded in 2009

destillerie-puchas.at

One of few distilleries that are using vacuum distillation. Two single malts are available under the name Kukmirn.

Reisetbauer & Son

Kirchberg-Thening, founded in 1994 (whisky since 1995)

reisetbauer.at

Specialising in brandies and fruit schnapps, a range of malt whiskies is also produced. The current range of whiskies have all been matured in casks that have previously contained Chardonnay and Trockenbeerenauslese and include 7, 12, 15 and 21 year old.

Rogner, Destillerie

Rappottenstein, founded in 1997

destillerie-rogner.at

The whisky range consists of Rogner Waldviertel Whisky 3/3 and single malt Whisky No. 2. Later releases include the 20 year old Red Road and the sherry finished Phönix. In early 2025 the 17/26 appeared.- a rye whisky combined of spirits that had matured for 17 and 26 years respectively.

See-Destillerie

St. Wolfgang im Salzkammergut, founded in 2018

see-destillerie.at

Originally a liqueur distillery the first expression of Wolfgangsee Whisky 1528 was launched in 2021 and there are now seven different varieties including two peated.

Weutz, Destillerie

St. Nikolai im Sausal, founded in 2002

weutz.at

The distillery added whisky to the range in 2004. Some of the whiskies are produced in the traditional Scottish style while others are more unorthodox, for example based on elderflower.

Wieser Destillerie

Wösendorf in der Wachau, founded in 1996

wieserwachau.com

Traditionally producing schnaps and liqueur, they have also launched the quadruple distilled Uuahouua whisky; American oak, French oak, Sherrywood, Pinot Noir and Smoke on the Water.

Belgium

Belgian Owl Distillery

Grâce Hollogne, founded in 1997

belgianwhisky.com

The first Belgian whisky distillery, equipped with two stills that were retrieved from the closed Caperdonich distillery, has certainly come a long way since they released their first expression in 2008. They are now exporting to Eastern Europe, Asia and the USA and the range of special expressions aged up to 11 years is growing. Two of the latest had been finished in casks that had held chocolate spirit and coffee spirit respectively. The core expressions used to be 3 years old and bottled at 46% or cask strength. In September 2024 however, the range was revamped and now includes a 5 year old and a 10 year old.

De Molenberg Distillery

Blaasveld, founded in 1471 (whisky since 2003)

stokerijdemolenberg.be

In 2010, the brewer Charles Leclef started a distillery at the family estate Molenberg. The wash still has a capacity of 3,000 litres and the spirit still 2,000 litres. The first bottles under the name Gouden Carolus Single Malt 3 years old appeared in 2008 and today there are also three varieties matured in sherry, madeira and port casks respectively as well as the smoky Blaasveld Broek and the Black Canvas series. Yearly anniversary bottlings also appear with the 5 year old Pedro, in autumn 2024, being one of the latest.

Other distilleries in Belgium

Braeckman Distillery

Oudenaarde, founded in 1918 (whisky since 2007)

braeckman.eu

A genever distillery also producing whisky. Their first release was a 9 year old single grain and currently there are four single grains available, the oldest a 13 year old. There are also the Double Cask single malt and single malt single casks (3 and 4 years old).

Filliers

Bachte-Maria-Leerne, founded in 1880 (malt whisky since 2008)

filliersdistillery.com

In 2007 a whisky was launched under the name Goldlys. Today the sherrymatured single malt is sold under the name Filliers and the oldest whisky available is currently a 10 year old matured in sherry casks. Single rye is also produced.

Pirlot, Brouwerij

Zandhoven, founded in 1998 (whisky since 2011)

brouwerijpirlot.be

Originally a brewery, the distillery is equipped with a continuous still and the spirit is matured in a combination of ex-bourbon and quarter casks from Laphroaig. The first of Kempisch Vuur single malt was released in 2016 and several releases have followed.

Radermacher, Distillerie

Raeren, founded in 1836

distillerie.biz

In a wide range of products from this classic distillery, there is also whisky to be found. The brand name is Lambertus and the range consists of both single grain and single malt, aged up to 10 years.

Sas Distillery

Stekene, founded in 2014

sasdistilleries.com

In a 200 litre column still, Sas is producing gin, rum, absinthe and whisky according to old recipes. In 2019 the Ignis Templi single malt was released with the latest batch appearing in autumn 2024.

Wilderen, Brouwerij & Distilleederij

Wilderen-St. Truiden, founded in 2011

brouwerijwilderen.be

A combination of a beer brewery with a history going back to 1642 and a distillery. The current core bottling of a single malt is Wild Weasel bottled at either 46% or 60%.

Cyprus

Aristides Distilling

Tseri, founded in 2020

aristidesdistilling.eu

After a number of years producing whisky in the American Ozark Mountains, Aris and Marianna Aristidou returned to Cyprus and opened up a distillery in Tseri, 10 kilometres south of Nicosia. Gin is produced but first and foremost whisky under the name Kythrea. Their single malt is made from the local, 6-row barley Kythrea and there are also two single grains made from malted barley and corn and malted barley and wheat respectively.

Czech Republic

Svachovka Distillery

České Budějovice, founded in 2016

svachovkadomu.cz

Owned by Vaclav Cvach, this is a combination of a brewery, distillery, hotel, restaurant and spa. Equipped with stainless steel washbacks and copper stills the distillery produces fruit brandy as well as Svach´s Old Well and Gold Well single malt whisky. The first 3 year old single malt was launched in autumn 2019 and a wide variety of expressions have been released since.

Gold Cock Distillery

Vizovice, founded in 1877

rjelinek.cz

The main product is slivovitz but whisky is produced in three versions – a 3 year old blended whisky, a 12 year old single malt and different versions of Small Batch single malt. Production was stopped for a while but after the brand and distillery were acquired by R. Jelinek a.s. the whisky began life anew.

Denmark

Stauning Whisky

Stauning, founded in 2006

stauningwhisky.com

The first Danish purpose-built malt whisky distillery entered a more adolescent phase in 2009, after having experimented with two small pilot stills bought from Spain. More stills were installed in 2012. The preconditions, however, were completely changed in 2015 when Diageo´s incubator fund project, Distil Ventures, invested £10m to increase the capacity. In 2018 a new distillery with no less than 24 copper stills, all directly fired, was opened. The floor malting were increased to 1,000 m^2 on four floors and the total production capacity is now 900,000 litres of pure alcohol. The core range consists of Rye (also available as cask strength), the smoky Kaos Triple Malt (both rye and barley), Smoke Single Malt and Høst Double malt (rye and barley). Recent limited expressions in autumn 2024 include the Smoke Tawny Port Cask single malt, a UK exclusive Madeira single cask rye and a single malt finished in a balsamic vinegar cask (!) from Acetaia Giusti.

Braunstein

Köge, founded in 2005 (whisky since 2007)

braunstein.dk

Denmark's first micro-distillery in Køge, just south of Copenhagen. The wash comes from the own brewery and a Holstein type of still is used for distillation. A substantial part of the required barley is ecologically grown in Denmark. The first release from the distillery and the first release of a malt whisky produced in Denmark was in 2010. Recent releases include the peated Library Collection 24:2, matured in oloroso sherry casks and the unpeated Cask Edition No: 16 matured in fino sherry casks. There is also Danica reserved for the duty-free market.

Thy Whisky

Fjerritslev, founded in 2009 (whisky since 2011)

thy-whisky.dk

A family-owned farm distillery where the ecological barley used for the production is grown in fields surrounding the distillery. The owners also use innovative smoking material for their whiskies. The first Thy single malt was released in 2014 and the current core range consists of Thy, Bøg, Spelt-Rye and the sherried Caramel malt. Meanwhile a series of limited releases came to and end in 2024 with edition 24 but the distillery continues to make special editions for various markets including releases for the Scotch Malt Whisky Society.

Copenhagen Distillery

Copenhagen, founded in 2014

copenhagendistillery.com

A wide range of gin, vodka and liqueurs were produced as an initial "bread and butter" but this is first and foremost a whisky distillery. The grain is milled using a plate mill and then mashed in a 0.6 ton mash tun. Following a 7-10 day fermentation on the grain, the liquid is distilled one time in a copper hybrid still attached with a column. The spirit is mainly matured in toasted casks made of Hungarian oak but more unusual casks are used as well. There are three ranges; Refined which is a more traditional whisky, Raw where all the flavours are "dialled up" and the experimental Rare bottlings where sometimes alternative grains are used. The First Edition was released in 2020 and has been followed by a number of limited bottlings.

Other distilleries in Denmark

Als, Destilleriet

Sydals, founded in 2018

destillerietals.dk

Built as a combined gin- and whisky distillerie, the whisky is distilled in a 350 litre column still. One of the latest release, a 4 year old PX maturation, appeared in September 2023.

Jakob Stjernholm - one of the founders and owners of Thy Whisky

Branderiet

Brande, founded in 2020 (whisky since 2021)

branderiet.dk

A producer of gin and schnapps which released their first two whiskies in 2024.

Brinkholm Øl og Whisky

Herlslev, founded in 2019

brinkholmale.dk

A brewery/distillery making small volumes of organic whisky. The first was launched in 2022 with more releases planned for 2025.

Dyrehøj Vingård

Kalundborg, founded in 2007 (whisky since 2018)

dyrehoj-vingaard.dk

The largest vineyard in Denmark has in later years installed a distillery where gin, bitters and a whisky named Rös are produced.

Falster Destilleri & Bryghus

Væggerløse, founded in 2019

falsterdestilleri.dk

A combined brewery and distillery producing different types of spirits including malt whisky. The first whisky, matured in a combination of bourbon, oloroso and PX sherry was released in February 2023 and was then followed by a peated version in June.

Fary Lochan Destilleri

Give, founded in 2009

farylochan.dk

Most of the malted barley is imported from the UK but they also malt some themselves. The first whisky was released in 2013 and a number of bottlings have been released since then. The most recent releases include a 9 year old matured in a combination of bourbon, PX sherry and moscatel as well as the first installment of Saison 1.

Limfjorden, Braenderiet

Roslev, founded in 2013

braenderiet.dk

Apart from peated and unpeated single malt and rye, the distillery also produces gin and rum. The first single malt was released in 2016 while the latest, in October 2024, was the second edition of a 10 year old PX cask.

Nordisk Brænderi

Fjerritslev, founded in 2009

nordiskbraenderi.dk

For the first years the distillery produced whisky under the Thy whisky label with a first release in 2013. Since then the owners continued to produce different spirits as well as single malt under the name Hødal. The latest, Masters Choice, appeared in late 2024.

Nyborg Destilleri

Nyborg, founded in 1997 (whisky since 2009)

fioniawhisky.com

Opened as an extension to an existing brewery, the distillery moved in 2017 to new premises. The distillery is equipped with two copper pot stills with attached columns. The first release of Isle of Fionia single malt was in 2012. The core range is made up of Little Isle, Danish Oak, Peated, Peated Black and Danish Oak Black. Recent limited releases in October 2024 include Skipper´s Glow and a 15 year old matured in borbon casks.

Radius Distillery

Præstø, founded in 2019

radiusdistillery.com

A farmhouse distillery focused on gin and apple brandy but also producing malt whisky from their own barley. Unusually, the whisky is distilled on the grain with an anticipated release in 2025.

Sall Whisky Distillery

Sall, founded in 2018

sallwhisky.com

Gin, but above all, malt whisky made from ecologically grown barley is produced. New make was launched in 2019 and the inaugural single malt appeared in 2023. With the latest series in August 2024 (followed by further editions) a series of three expressed three different styles of their whisky; Muld from ex-bourbon casks, the peated Tørv and Glød with an impact from ex-sherry casks.

Søgaards Bryghus

Aalborg, founded in 2010 (whisky since 2018)

soegaardsbryghus.dk

Originally a brewery, the owners embarked on an exciting distillery adventure in 2018 where barley grown on four different islands were used to produce four malt whiskies. These were later matured on the respective islands and released in 2023 under the name Vindblæst (Windswept).

Søhøjlandets Destilleri

Silkeborg founded in 2020

sohojlandetsdestilleri.dk

Earning a reputation for their gin, their first single malt was produced in December 2022. The inaugural release is expected in 2025/2026.

Thornaes Destilleri

Helsinge, founded in 2018

thornaes.com

A distillery specialising in whisky but also producing gin. The first single malt was released in 2023 and the final releases in The Uncharted Series, in anticipation of a core range and reflecting various distilling techniques and maturation, were Saga and the smoky Sonoma Peat in early 2025.

Tranum Mølle Destilleri

Brovst, founded in 2018

tranummølle.dk

Starting with production of gin, the owners expanded into whisky named Koldmose two years later. So far it hasn´t been released.

Trolden Distillery

Kolding, founded in 2011

trolden.com

The distillery is a part of a brewery and the first single malt release was in 2014 and in 2020 the distillery moved to new premises. The whisky is sold under the name Nimbus and two of the latest (in March 2025) were Nimbus Cumulus XI and Nimbus Stratus Peated.

Ærø Whisky

Ærøskøbing, founded in 2013

ærøwhisky.dk

Situated on the island of Ærø the distillation started in stills from Portugal and in 2016, larger stills were installed. The first bottling was in 2017 and today the core expression is matured in a combination of casks made from new American, Spanish and Hungarian oak. Limited editions are released on a regular basis.

England

English Distillery, The

Roudham, Norfolk, founded in 2006

englishwhisky.co.uk

Started by father and son, James and Andrew Nelstrop, it became the first English malt whisky distillery for over a hundred years. In 2009, it was time for the release of the first whisky called Chapter 5. This was then followed by several more chapters but the sometimes uncomprehensible range was exhanged for a range with four core expressions; The English Original, The English Smokey Sherry Cask and an 11 year old.There are also regular, limited releases in the Small Batch series with Gently Smoked Double Cask, Oloroso Casks, the heavily smoked Cask Fusion and Virgin Oak as some of the latest. Recent releases in the Single Cask Series include Smokey Triple and a 17 year old Portuguese Cabernet Sauvignon. Another range is The Norfolk including innovative expressions made from different grains. The latest in that range was Popcorn made from a mash bill of maize, rye and barley. Finally there is the Founder´s Private Cellar range where a 13 year old matured in a brandy cask appeared in early 2025.

Cotswolds Distillery

Stourton, founded in 2014

cotswoldsdistillery.com

The distillery was originally equipped with one wash still, one spirit still and two Holstein stills. The distillery was substantially expanded in autumn 2022 when a completely new distillery was built to house both some of the old equipment as well as a new 2 ton mash tun and two much larger stills. All the barley is grown locally and is floor malted at Warminster Maltings. In 2023 a funding round, including an investment by Berry Brothers & Rudd, was completed. The first single malt, the 3 year old Odyssey, was launched in 2017. In 2018, the distillery started experimenting with rye whisky and later that year the owners made their first trials producing rum. Today, the two core expressions in the Classics Collection are Signature and Reserve, both matured in a combination of ex-bourbon and STR casks. The Cask Expressions Collection include Founder´s Choice (STR matured), Peated Cask (matured in ex peated quarter casks), Sherry Cask and Bourbon Cask. The third installment in the Harvest Series Collection was Amber Meadow matured in a combination of moscatel and bourbon casks and there is also the Hearts & Craft Collection with Pineau Des Charentes Cask as one of the latest releases. Single casks occur from time to time with a recent Banyuls cask in 2025.

Lakes Distillery

Bassenthwaite Lake, founded in 2014

lakesdistillery.com

The distillery is equipped with two stills for the whisky production, each with both copper and stainless steel condensers, and a third still for the distillation of gin. A £4.25m investment made it possible to install another eight washbacks in 2020 thereby increasing the production capacity to 375,000 litres of alcohol per year. The inaugural bottling, The Lakes Malt Genesis, was released in 2018. In 2019, the distillery launched its first widely available expression in the sherry-led Whiskymaker´s Reserve series with the seventh and last expression being released in September 2023. There is also the Whiskymaker´s Editions, with Galáxia, Equinox, Nostalgia and Kairos as the latest additions. In June 2024 the English sparkling wine producer Nyetimber acquired the distillery for £71m.

Spirit of Yorkshire Distillery

Hunmanby, founded in 2016

spiritofyorkshire.com

The farm distillery, founded by Tom Mellor and David Thompson, is actually situated over two separate locations. The mash tun and washbacks stand at Tom's farm, where they grow 100% of barley for their whisky regeneratively and houses sister company Wold Top Brewery, established in 2003. The wash still and the spirit still are 2,5 miles down the road in Hunmanby with a four plate rectifying column, designed to run in tandem with the spirit still. Part of the production is distilled using this column to achieve a lighter character of the new make, with all the barley used coming from their family farm. The distillery has also produced small volumes made from rye. There are plans to increase capacity of the distillery in the future and they also have a visitor centre open year-round, hosting daily tours for visitors. Their core bottling, first released in 2019, is the bourbon-matured Filey Bay Flagship. More recent limited expressions include Filey Bay Porter Cask in April 2024, where porter casks from World Top Brewery were part of the maturation, Filey Bay Orange Wine Barrique and Yorkshire Day 2025 bottled annually for the distillery open weekend in July.

Bimber Distillery

London, founded in 2015

bimberdistillery.co.uk

An innovative distillery equipped with open top wooden washbacks, direct-fired alembic stills and using floor malted barley. Distillation began in May 2016 and the first release from the distillery was a vodka. Today, however, only whisky is produced. In 2019, it was time for the distillery´s inaugural single malt bottling and a number of releases have followed since. Some of the latest include the Shoulders of Giants series of eleven single casks in 2024/2025 and in December 2024 the 8 year old The Harmony of Eight (bourbon and PX maturation) appeared. In September 2023 the owners opened up a second distillery (Dunphail) near Forres in Scotland.

Other distilleries in England

Abingdon Distillery

Abingdon, founded in 2022

abingdondistillery.com

Starting with rum and gin, malt whisky is now also produced. The first bottles, matured in Bulleit ex-rye casks, are expected in 2026.

Ad Gefrin Distillery

Wooler, founded in 2022

adgefrin.co.uk

Equipped with two pot stills, the first casks were filled in December 2022. In anticipation of a whisky from their own production a range of blended whiskies sourced from Scotland, Ireland, England and Scandinavia is offered under the name Tácnbora. The distillery also includes an Anglo-Saxon museum!

Adnams Copper House Distillery

Southwold, founded in 2010

adnams.co.uk

Adnams Brewery in Suffolk added distillation of spirits to their production in 2010 and, apart from whisky – gin, vodka and absinthe are produced. The first whisky was released in 2013 and the range now consists of Single Malt, Rye Malt and Triple Malt. The Distiller´s Choice range include a 12 year old expression.

Bankhall Distillery

Blackpool, founded in 2019

bankhallwhisky.com

Owned by Halewood Artisinal Spirits, the distillery has a broad perspective on whisky. Sweet mash whisky, expressions made from rye and wheat are produced and the first releases of single malts appeared in 2023.

BB Distillery

Wallingford, founded in 2016

bbdistillery.co.uk

Initially known as Black Bottle distillery, the main products are gin, rum and Randolph single malt whisky.

Canterbury Brewers and Distillers

Canterbury, founded in 2018

thefoundrycanterbury.co.uk

A combination of craft brewery, distillery, restaurant and bar. Equipped with a 500 litre still, gin and rum has been for sale for quite a while. The first whisky was distilled in 2019 and in 2023 Foundry Streetlight single malt was launched. This was followed in summer 2025 by Foundry Capstan finished in stout casks.

Circumstance Distillery

Bristol, founded in 2018

circumstancedistillery.com

The idea is to make whisky and rum in a flexible distillery equipped with a pot still with attached columns. The first bottling in 2019 was Circumstantial Barley 1:1:1:1:6, a spirit made from 100% malted barley. A number of different expressions from a variety of mashbills have occured since and in 2025 a whisky made from Maris Otter malt and matured in new European oak appeared..

Cooper King Distillery

Sutton-on-the-Forest, founded in 2018

cooperkingdistillery.co.uk

Equipped with a Tasmanian copper pot still and practising a combination of vacuum distillation and traditional distillation. The barley is floor malted at Warminster Maltings and the mash is stirred by hand. Whisky production started in 2019 and the first malt whisky, "First Edition: Fruit + Spice", was released in 2023. This has been followed by more expressions in the Cask Series.

Copper Rivet Distillery

Chatham, founded in 2016

copperrivetdistillery.com

The distillery is equipped with a copper pot still with a column attached as well as a special gin still. In 2017, Son of a Gun, an 8 week old grain spirit was released. The first Masthouse Single Malt was released in 2020 and the range now consists of Signature, Reserve and Grain Whisky.

Dartmoor Distillery

Bovey Tracey, founded in 2016

dartmoorwhiskydistillery.co.uk

The distillery is equipped with an old alembic still from Cognac, The first single malt was launched in 2020 and the current core range includes ex-bourbon, ex-oloroso and ex-Bordeaux wine casks. The latest limited release, in February 2025, had been matured in port casks.

Durham Whisky

Durham, founded in 2014 (whisky since 2018)

durhamwhisky.co.uk

The distillery has released gin and vodka and in 2018 whisky was added to the range. In 2021, the distillery moved to larger premises. The distillery is equipped with a 1,200 litre wash still and a 1,000 litre spirit still. No single malt has yet been released.

Ad Gefrin - one of the newer distilleries in England founded in 2022 Photo: Sally Ann Norman

East London Liquor Company

London, founded 2014

eastlondonliquorcompany.com

This combined distillery, bar and restaurant was the first distiller to open up in more than 100 years in East London. A variety of spirits are produced where their gin has become the most popular. On the whisky side there is both rye and single malt made from barley.

Ellers Farm Distillery

Stamford Bridge, whisky since 2022

ellersfarmdistillery.com

Having produced various spirits for some years, Ellers Farm commenced distilling malt whisky in 2022 with an aim to present its first release in late 2025. The distillery is equipped with a 20-plate column still as well as a traditional pot still.

Elsham Wold Distillery

Elsham Wolds, founded in 2019

elshamwolddistillery.co.uk

With the aim to produce vodka from their own potatoes, single malt whisky soon became a part of the business. The inaugural release in 2023 was Flarepath PX Sherry finish followed by a rum cask finish.

Forest Distillery, The

Macclesfield, founded in 2014

theforestdistillery.com

Established in an old stone barn in the Peak District National Park, the pot still was later moved to the legendary Cat & Fiddle Inn. A number of blends of their own single malt and sourced whiskies have been released and in December 2023 the 26th edition, using Cheshire malt and wild yeast, became their first core expression.

Hawkridge Distillery

Hampstead Norreys, founded in 2018

hawkridgedistillers.com

A larger distillery was opened in autumn 2024 in a converted 17th century barn. The main focus is on gin but in February 2025 Hawkridge Single Malt was also launched.

Henstone Distillery

Trewern, Shropshire, founded in 2017

henstonedistillery.com

First releases were gin, vodka, apple brandy and a corn "whisky". The first malt whisky was launched in 2021 and the range is now made up of single malts matured in bourbon, oloroso, PX, red wine and peated casks respectively. In 2024 the distillery moved to a new location at Dingle Farm.

Isle of Wight Distillery

Newport, founded in 2015

isleofwightdistillery.com

The distillery is currently focused on vodka and their Mermaid Gin. For the whisky, the fermented wash is bought from a local brewery and distilled in hybrid copper stills. The first whisky was distilled in December 2015 but has not yet been released.

Lancaster Spirits Company

Lancaster, founded in 2024

lancasterspirits.co.uk

Taking advantage of sister company Lancaster Brewery, a beer wash is fermented and distilled in the "whisky room" which was established in July 2024. The inaugural release is expected in 2027.

Ludlow Distillery

Ludlow, founded in 2014

ludlowdistillery.co.uk

Equipped with a 200 litre still, this tiny distillery released its first single malt, Young Prince, in November 2018. One of the latest releases, in December 2024, was a cask strength bottling finished in a ruby port cask.

Pendle Witch Distillery

Waddington, founded in 2020

pendlewitchdistillery.uk

Founded and run by the Moore family the distillery is specialising on whisky - mainly single malt (smoky and un-smoky) but also an American style version made from 50% corn. So far moonshine and gin have been released.

Pocketful of Stones

Penzance, founded in 2019

pocketfulofstones.com

This combination of a distillery, bar and restaurant produces a wide range of different spirits and one the latest Hell´s Stone Whisky was triple distilled and matured in a bourbon cask.

Retribution Distilling Co.

Frome founded in 2021

retributiondistilling.co.uk

With gin and rum already on the shelves, the owners produce small volumes of Somerset´s first malt whisky. The first release, a 3 year old matured in an ex-bourbon quarter cask and bottled at 63,3%, appeared in January 2025.

Spirit of Birmingham Distillery

Birmingham, founded in 2021

spiritofbirmingham.co.uk

Makers of both beer and vodka, the owners have also laid down whisky in barrels made from a five grain mash bill including both malted rye and malted barley including heritage Maris Otter. The first bottling was released in summer 2025.

Spirit of Manchester Distillery, The

Manchester, founded in 2016 (whisky since 2022)

spiritofmanchester.co.uk, onepointsixwhisky.com

Situated underneath the former railway arches on Watson Street in Manchester, the distillery started producing gin but since 2022 a malt whisky is also distilled, due to be released in 2025 under the name One Point Six.

Ten Hides Distillery

Melksham, founded in 2021

tenhides.com

Following a long career in the army, Andrew Wilson opened this distillery in 2021. Focus so far has been on gin and spiced rum but with Jack Mayo (ex Glasgow and Holyrood distilleries) it comes as no surprise that whisky is also in the works. The first release however is a few years away.

Weetwood Brewery & Distillery

Kelsall, founded in 1992 (whisky since 2019)

weetwoodales.co.uk

Established as a brewery, the owners added a distillery to the set-up in 2019. Gin, vodka, rum and brandy were first released and the inaugural Cheshire Single Malt appeared in September 2022. Recent limited releases include an IPA Cask Special Edition.

West Midlands Distillery, The

Rowley Regis, founded in 2017 (whisky since 2021)

westmidlandsdistillery.co.uk

Gin, vodka and rum have been on the market for quite a while and in 2021 the owners started distilling malt whisky with a first release in 2025. Heritage grain from Warminster Maltings and different strains of yeast are a vital part of the production.

Wharf Distillery

Towcester, founded in 2015

wharfdistillery.co.uk

What probably used to be the smallest whisky distillery in England was expanded with yet another still in 2022. The first malt whisky release appeared in 2019 followed by Solstice and Equinox (port matured). There is also a range of grain whiskies named Fyr Drenc.

White Peak Distillery

Ambergate, Derbyshire, founded in 2017

whitepeakdistillery.co.uk

The distillery started distillation in April 2018. Gin, rum, and a 30 months old malt spirit were released first followed by the inaugural, Wire Works Single Malt in 2022. Recent expressions include Madira, Moscatel, Virgin Oak and the lightly peated Caduro.

Whittaker´s Distillery

Harrogate, founded in 2015 (whisky since 2019)

whittakersgin.com

The owners have already had success with Whittaker Gin but whisky was in their thoughts from the beginning. In summer 2019, two new, larger stills were installed and whisky production started in the autumn. On 1st August 2024 their inaugural malt whisky was released.

Winchester Distillery

Winchester, founded in 2014

winchesterdistillery.co.uk

Paul Bowler started producing spirits in his own kitchen but soon moved to larger premises. The main seller so far is Twisted Nose gin but other spirits are also distilled including malt whisky.

Witchmark Distillery

Salisbury, founded in 2024

witchmark.co.uk

Vodka and gin were the first products for sale and in August 2024 the first cask with single malt new make was filled and a visitor centre was opened soon after.

Yarm Distillery

Eaglescliffe, founded in 2018

yarmdistillery.com

During the first two years, focus was on gin (both sloe and London dry) and in 2020 the first single malt whisky, made from wash from a local brewery, was distilled in their two alembic copper stills. The inaugural release appeared in August 2023.

Yorkshire Dales Distillery

Catterick Garrison, founded in 2017

yorkshiredalesdistillery.com

Equipped with three stills the distillery produces vodka, gin, rum and, quite recently, malt whisky under the name Ramskull Founders Reserve which could possibly be released in 2027

Faroe Islands

Einar´s Distillery

Klaksvik, founded in 2016

einarsdistillery.com

The first legal distillery in the Faroe Islands was built adjacent to the Föroya Bjór brewery and the wash obviously comes from the brewery´s 2 ton mash tun and is then fermented in three stainless steel washbacks and distilled in a pot still from Arnold Holstein. The first single malt was released in 2020. The most recent release, in July 2025, was Tróndur í Götu – a 6 year old matured in a combination of bourbon and sherry casks.

Faer Isles Distillery

Vestmanna, founded in 2023

faer.io

This is the second distillery in the Faroe Islands with a capacity of 600,000 litres of alcohol. Vodka, akvavit and gin have already been released. The whisky is matured in "open" warehouses (*opnahjallur*) similar to the ones that have been used for centuries to dry lamb and fish. The owners expect a substantial impact from the humid, windy and salty weather. The first launch of their whisky is expected in 2026.

Finland

Teerenpeli

Lahti, founded in 2002

teerenpeli.com

The original distillery, located in a restaurant in Lahti, is equipped with one pair of stills. A completely new distillery, with one 3,000 litre wash still, two 900 litre spirit stills and an annual capacity of 160,000 litres, was opened in 2015 in the same house as the brewery. The core range consists of a 10 year old, Kaski which is a 100% sherry maturation, Portti which is finished in port casks, the peated Savu, the 7 year old Kulo, matured in PX and oloroso casks, the peated Palo matured in sherry casks and Länki which is only available at the Teerenpeli resturants and Helsinki airport. To date, the oldest expression from the distillery is a 15 year old. Recent limited bottlings include the 11 year old Akte which is the third in a trilogy that had been finished in amarone red wine casks.

Other distilleries in Finland

Helsinki Distilling Company

Helsinki, founded in 2014

hdco.fi

Equipped with one mash tun, three washbacks and two stills. A gin was released in 2014 and on the whisky side, the focus is on malted rye but also single malt made from barley and whisky made from corn. The latest single malt from barley was a 7 year old matured in ex-applejack casks in November 2023.

Nagu Distillery

Lillandet, founded in 2018

nagudistillery.com

Located in an old boat factory in the southwestern Finnish archipelago the owners have released a number of gins and vodkas. Malt whisky is still maturing in the warehouses. The owners are currently moving to another location and building a new distillery.

Ägräs Distillery

Fiskars, founded in 2017

agrasdistillery.com

Located in the south of Finland in a small factory village dating back to the 17th scentury. Ägräs Distillery produces various spirits such as aqvavit, gin and also malt whisky. The first whisky is expected in 2025/26.

France

Distillerie Warenghem

Lannion, Bretagne, founded in1900 (whisky since 1993)

distillerie-warenghem.com

Leon Warenghem founded the distillery and in 1967, his grandson Paul-Henri Warenghem, together with his associate, Yves Leizour, took over the reins. They moved the distillery to its current location on the outskirts of Lannion in Brittany. Gilles Leizour, Yves' son, took over at the end of the 1970's and it was he who added whisky to the Warenghem range. WB, a blend from malted barley and wheat, saw the light in 1987 and Armorik – the first ever French single malt – was released in 1998. The distillery is equipped with a 6,000 litre semi-lauter mashtun, six stainless steel washbacks and two, traditional copper pot stills (a 6,000 litre wash still and a 3,500 litre spirit still). Around 180,000 litres of pure alcohol (including 20% grain whisky) are produced yearly. The single malt core range (certified organic) consists of Édition Originale and Sherry Finish. Both are 4 years old, matured in ex-bourbon casks and with a finish in sherry butts. There are also Classic, a mix of 4 to 8 year old whiskies and the 7 year old Double Maturation which has spent time in both new oak and sherry wood. These two are earmarked for export as well as the Sherry Cask and a 10 year old. Warenghem has also distilled rye whisky with the 10 year old Roof Rye being released in 2021. In 2022 a 15 year old was added to the core range. Peated expressions are released under the name Yeun Elez. In 2023 the distillery opened a cooperage in the centre of the city.

Grallet-Dupic

Rozelieures, Grand Est, founded in 1860 (whisky since 2003)

whiskyrozelieures.com

The Glen Rozelieures brand was launched in 2007. Following an expansion in summer 2024, the distillery is now one of the largest in France with a capacity of 400,000 litres. Five versions are currently available: Original Collection aged in ex-fino casks, the lightly peated Rare Collection matured in ex-sauternes, Fumé Collection (20ppm) matured in ex-fino, Tourbé Collection and the un-peated Subtil Collection. In 2018 they also opened a malting plant on site. Since 2023 all their whiskies are certified organic.

Distillerie des Menhirs

Plomelin, Bretagne, founded in 1986 (whisky since 1998)

distillerie.bzh

Originally a portable column still distillery, the owners settled down in 1986 with the idea of producing a 100% buckwheat whisky. Eddu Silver was launched in 2002, followed by Eddu Gold (to be replaced by Eddu 10 year old in 2026), Eddu Silver Brocéliande and Eddu Diamant. In 2019, Les Menhirs released a vintage 2004 which was the first whisky distilled from malted buckwheat. In June 2025 the second edition of Graal 21 years old appeared – the oldest French whisky to date.

Domaine des Hautes-Glaces

Saint Jean d´Hérans, Auvergne-Rhône Alpes, founded in 2009 (whisky since 2014)

hautesglaces.com

The distillery grows and malt their own organic barley. Principium, the first whisky made at the distillery has been available since 2014. The distillery was bought by Rémy Cointreau in 2015 and a second distillery started operating in 2020. The core range includes Les Moissons Malt and Les Moissons Rye and in 2021, XO^{0}, the first 10 year old was released. Indigene was recently launched together with experimental bottlings in the Épistéme range.

Teerenpeli is the distillery that put Finland on the whisky map

Miclo

Lapoutroie, Grand Est, founded in 1970 (whisky since 2012)

distillerie-miclo.com

Originally a producer of fruit spirits, the owners have since 2012 used wort from a local brewery to make whisky in four Holstein waterbath pot stills. In September 2021 the range was revamped and now consists of Welche Classique ex-Sauternes, Welche Fumé, Welche Tourbé and Welche Classique ex-Bourgogne.

Bercloux

Bercloux, Nouvelle Aquitaine, founded in 2000 (whisky since 2014)

distillerie-bercloux.fr

Opened as a brewery, a Stupfler pot still was installed in 2014 to produce whisky. This has later been complemented by a cognac still and a column still. The first bottlings of Bercloux Single Malt Whisky were released in 2018. In 2019, the distillery was bought by the company Les Bienheureux. Their intention was to secure stock and production for their own brand – Bellevoye triple malt whisky which now has a range of seven expressions. The original Bercloux brand changed name to Lefort to be sold mainly in supermarkets. Bellevoye and Lefort are now amongst the top five of the best selling French whiskies.

Celtic Whisky Distillerie (former Glann ar Mor)

Pleubian, Bretagne, founded in 1999

glannarmor.com

Jean Donnay, started his first trials in 1999 while regular production commenced in 2005. Two small stills were directly fired and worm tubs were used for condensation. The fermentation in wooden washbacks was long and the distillation slow. In 2020 Jean Donnay sold the distillery to Maison Villevert who changed the name in 2023 to Celtic Whisky Distillerie. In 2025 the distillery closed and has been dismantled. The idea is to build a new distillery, more adapted to new regulations, on the same site.

Hepp, Distillerie

Uberach, Grand Est, founded in 1972 (whisky since 2005)

distillerie-hepp.com

The distillery produces two core expressions without age statement; Tharcis Hepp (bourbon/sherry) and Johnny Hepp (bourbon/white wine). In 2018 new bottlings were released; Ouisky, Tharcis Hepp Tourbé and French Flanker. Hepp is also behind the brands Charmeval, Nelcius, Villa 16, 102 Lions and Maison Lacroix. End of 2024 Hepp took over the oldest French independent bottler - AWA.

Castan, Distillerie

Villeneuve Sur Vère, Occitanie, founded in 1946 (whisky since 2010)

distillerie-castan.com

In 2016 Sébastien Castan added a brewery to supply the beer for his distillery. The range consists of five bottlings: Vilanova Berbie (ex-white wine casks), Gost (new cask), Terrocita (peated), Roja (ex-red wine casks) and Segala (rye). Recent limited releases include Vilanova Gilbert Signature and Shed.

Rouget de Lisle

Bletterans, Bourgogne-Franche Comté, founded in 1994 (whisky since 2006)

brasserie-rouget-lisle.com

The brewery Rouget de Lisle commissioned the Brûlerie du Revermont in 2006 to distil whisky for them. The first Rouget De Lisle single malt whisky was released in 2009 and in 2012 the owners bought their own still. The core range consists of two NAS aged in ex-vin de paille and ex-Macvin casks. Recently a range of five whiskies aged from 5 up to 21(!) years were launched. In 2025 the owners bought two stills from Celtic Whisky distillery including the one that had been used by Jean Donnay since 1999 to produce the legendary Taol Esa whisky.

LN Mattei (former Mavela)

Corsica, founded in 1991 (whisky since 2001)

distilleriemattei.com/en/

Distilled in a Holstein still and aged in ex-Corsican muscat casks, the P&M single malt was sold for the first time in 2004. End of 2017, the distillery released its first 12 year old and in 2018 the owners unveiled a completely new range: P&M Signature, P&M Red Oak (aged in ex-red-wine casks) and P&M Tourbé (peated). In 2023, a corn whisky made from local corn was launched.

Naguelann, Distillerie

Languenan, Bretagne, founded in 2014

naguelann.bzh

Lenaïck Lemaitre launched Naguelann as an independent bottler. While working as a bottler, Lenaïck started to build his own distillery fitted with two small stills. Dieil Tantad released in 2020 was the first bottling. In 2021, a brewery and two more stills were installed and in 2024 the 10th anniversary series Dek was launched

Other distilleries in France

Auguste

Fontenay, Normandie, founded in 2020

whisky-augustericouard.fr

When Paul Ricouard took over the family farm he was convinced on adding a whisky distillery and equipped with a Portuguese Hoga still. Auguste, named after his grandfather, is aged in new oak barrels, lightly charred before being transferred into ex-white port cask.

Boinaud, Maison

Angeac Champagne, Nouvelle Aquitaine, founded in 1971 (whisky since 2018)

boinaud.com

Equipped with 41 pot stills, Maison Boinaud has become one of the most important cognac distilleries in recent years. Since 2018 they are also producing malt whisky two months per year. The first single malt, Hériose Le Classique, was launched in June 2022.

BOWS

Laure Minervois, Occitanie, founded in 2017

bowsdistillerie.com

Started by Benoit Garcia who alsodesigned and built the distillery. The first whiskies, Benleioc Original and Benleioc Tourbe Intense, both made from a stout beer, appeared in 2021. In 2022 the distillery moved to a new location and new equipment was installed to expand the production. In 2024 they released the first whisky where koji fungus had been a part of the malting process.

Brana, Domaine

Ossès, Nouvelle Aquitaine, founded in 1974 (whisky since 2018)

brana.fr

With a history of four generations working in the wine industry, the family started distilling spirits from pears in 1974. A new distillery equipped with three copper pot stills was opened in 2018 and in 2022 Laminak, matured in Irouléguy red wine casks, was launched. The three latest expressions appeared end of 2024.

Breuil, Château du

Le Breuil en Auge, Normandie, founded in 1952 (whisky since 2015)

chateau-breuil.biz

The company is a well-known maker of Calvados and, fitted with two Charentais stills, the distillery also produces malt whisky. The first expressions, including a smoky version after maturation in Laphroaig casks, appeared in 2021 under the name Le Breuil. Experiencing financial difficulties the distillery has decided to keep on going focusing on whiskies made from classic malt varieties such as Golden Promise, Chevalier and Maris Otter.

Brûlerie du Revermont

Nevy sur Seille, Bourgogne-Franche Comté, founded in 1991 (whisky since 2003)

marielouisetissot-levin.com

Relying upon a unique distillation set-up, a Blavier still with three pots, the Tissot family have been producing single malt whisky since 2003. In 2011 they launched their brand Prohibition with whiskies aged in "feuillettes" which is 114 litre half-casks.

Bughes, Distillerie des

Solignac, Auvergne, founded in 2017

homedistillers.fr

Starting with three, directly heated stills, a fourth and larger still was installed in 2021. Montagnac, aged in sherry casks, was released in 2020 followed by Mandrant matured in ex-red wine casks. In 2025 a peated single cask matured in STR casks was launched.

Busnel

Cormeilles, Normandie, founded in 1820 (whisky since 2019)

distillerie-busnel.fr

A well-known producer of calvados entering into whisky as well. The first two bottlings appeared in 2023 - Cormeil and Busnel followed by Cormeil Peated in late 2023. In 2025 the range was revamped with Whisky de France, Peated and a Calvados finish.

Camut, Domaine

La Lande Saint-Léger, Normandie, founded in 1981 (whisky since 2018)

A 6th generation producer of calvados making their whisky debut in 2018. Two bottlings, matured in barrels that held "balsamic" apple vinegar, have been released in 2022/2023.

Castor, Distillerie du

Troisfontaines, Grand Est, founded in 1985 (whisky since 2011)

distillerie-du-castor.com

Equipped with two small stills the distillery produces whisky as well as fruit and pomace brandies. The distillate is aged in ex-white wine casks and then finished in ex-sherry casks. The whisky (be tween 4 and 10 years old) is sold under the name St Patrick.

Charlier & Fils

Warcq, Grand Est, founded in 2015

facebook.com/laquinarde

The ambition from start was to create their whisky from indigeneous yeast and practising long fermentations. The first Charlier whisky was released in 2020. The production will increase in the coming years as the owner recently bought another still.

Claeyssens de Wambrechies, Distillerie

Wambrechies, Hauts de France, founded in 1817 (whisky since 2000)

wambrechies.com

The distillery´s first 3 year old whisky was released in 2003. In 2019 the distillery was bought by Saint-Germain brewery/distillery and was mothballed. In 2023 a new still was installed and distillation resumed. The range consists of Wambrechies 5 year old, Sherry and the peated Tourbé.

Didier Barbe Entreprise

Lusigny Sur Barse, Grand Est, founded in 2012

didierbarbeentreprise.com

Focusing on brandies, the first whisky was produced in 2017 using wash from local breweries. The first whisky, R, aged in ratafia barrels, was launched in 2020 and was followed by M in 2023.

Dreumont

Neuville-en-Avesnois, Hauts de France, founded in 2005

brasserie-distillerie-dreum.fr

In 2011 Jérôme Dreumont built his own 300 litre still and has since then been filling only one cask per year. His first whisky, was launched in 2015 and has been followed by more releases.

Fontagard Distillery is equipped with twelve stills

Ergaster, Distillerie

Passel, Hauts de Frances, founded in 2015

distillerie-ergaster.com

Peated and unpeated spirit is aging in Cognac, Pineau des Charentes, Vin Jaune and Banyuls casks. The organic Ergaster Nature was launched in 2018 and the latest was Fût D´Exception in 2022.

d´Escagnan, Domaine

Eauze, Occitanie, founded in 2019

moonshine-francais.fr

The distillery is equipped with its own brewery and a 2,500 litre Maresté Cognac still. After two eaux-de-vie the first whisky, Cavalcade, was released at the beginning of 2024. This was followed in 2025 by Cavalcade Peated and Sarra in 2025.

Fabrique à Alcools, La

Pecqueuse, Ile de France, founded in 2016

lafabriqueaalcools.com

Founded as Parisis Brewery in 2003, whisky production started in 2017. In 2021 a single cask named Le Premier de la Fabrique was launched followed by Alliage, Chevreuse and Fromenteau.

Faronville, Domaine de

Eauze, Occitanie, founded in 2019

lagomorphe.com

A farm distillery equipped with a Stupfler still, which is operated in one single run, as well as a brewery. The first three whiskes were launched in 2023 under the name Lagomorphe.

Fontagard

Neuillac, Nouvelle Aquitaine, founded in 1990 (whisky since 2018)

fontagard.com

Equipped with no less than 12 stills, the owners have been producing whisky for the last six years. The first three expressions appeared in late 2021 and the whisky production is now being increased. A number of new bottlings have appeared in 2024 and 2025.

Franc Tireur

Franqueville-Saint-Pierre, Normandie, founded in 2020

distillerie-franc-tireur.com

Inspired by a trip to Martinique, Julien Sevestre opened a distillery in Normandie built to a large extent from recycled equipment. First whiskies under the name Le Conquérant appeared in 2024.

Hagmeyer

Balbronn, Alsace, founded in 2016

distillerie-hagmeyer.com

The owners started whisky production based on beer from Perle brewery. WAH! was launched in 2019. From time to time, WAH! single cask and WAH! cask strength have been released since 2022.

Hautefeuille, Distillerie

Beaucourt En Santerre, Hauts de France, founded in 2015

distilleriedhautefeuille.com

The distillery is fitted with an 800 litre Stupfler still. The first whisky, Loup Hardi distilled at another distillery, was launched in 2018. The first release from their own production appeared in 2020 and end of 2022, Parcelle Hangard was launched followed by two expressions in 2023 - one peated and one un-peated.

Kentan

Tonquedec, Britanny, founded in 2017

kentan.fr

Equipped with a Charentais-style still, the distillery started production in 2018. The first releases, Season One and Season Two, have both been matured in ex-cognac casks. A three bottle series from 2023 was released as "regular", peated and rye respectively.

Lachanenche

Méolans Revel, Provence-Alpes-Côte d´ Azur, founded in 2008 (whisky since 2018)

lachanenche.com

Supplied with wash from a local brewery, the owners went from distilling spirits from raspberries to also making whisky. Laverq, matured in white wine and white port casks, appeared in late 2022 and since 2025 their whisky released is 5 years old.

La Seine

Le Havre, Normandie, founded in 2021

distillerie-seine.fr

Founded in a former slaughterhouse, the distillery is equipped with a hybrid Muller still and the wash comes from local breweries. The latest releases include the 777 La Source and a single cask bottled at 49.29% - the latitude of Le Havre.

La Tour

Pons, Nouvelle Aquitaine, founded in 1989

distillerie-de-la-tour.com

This fairly large producer of various spirits is in part supported by the major spirits company La Martiniquaise. Whisky is rather new in the range and the first expression, Alcée, appeared recently.

Laurens, Domaine

Clairvaux d'Aveyron, Occitanie, founded in 1983 (whisky since 2014)

domaine-laurens.com

This wine estate started production with the help of a brewery. The first versions. Red Léon, aged in white dry aveyron wine ex-casks, and Blue Léon, red ratafia ex-casks, were launched in 2017.

Lehmann, Distillerie

Obernai, Grand Est, founded in 1850 (whisky since 2001)

distillerielehmann.com

The first bottlings from this family-owned distillery appeared in 2008. The range includes Elsass Origine and Elsass Gold matured in white wine casks, and Elsass Premium matured in Sauternes casks. In 2020 a new range of three bottlings, Birdy, was launched.

Leisen

Malling, Grand Est, founded in 1898 (whisky since 2012)

distillerie-leisen-petite-hettange.fr

Since 1898, the Leisen family has distilled fruit spirits but also spirits made from rye and barley. The distillery is equipped with two Carl stills. In 2018 the first bottles appeared under the JML brand and today there are two 5 year old expressions available.

Les Pyrénées

Vieille Toulouse, Occitanie, founded in 2021

bear-brothers.com

Situated on the southern outskirts of Toulouse, the distillery is equipped with two 800 litre Stupfler stills. The first whisky appeared in 2024 - the 2B Double Malt, a blend of malts distilled in Brittany and Occitanie.

Mabillot, Domaine

Sainte-Lizaigne, Centre-Val de Loire, founded in 1992 (whisky since 2021)

domaine-mabillot.fr

The whisky is produced in a 250 litre Holstein still. In 2021 Mabillot Artry and Les Dordans were released followed by the peated Mabillot Bellevue and, in 2025, by Raffaut and Les Taboux.

Maison Victors

Vacquiers, Occitanie, founded in 2017

maison-victors.com

Equipped with two stills, the distillery produces organic whisky from barley and rye. The first whisky (a single PX sherry cask) appeared in 2022 and in 2024 the first core expressions were released. The owners are currently building a new distillery, ready in 2026.

Merlet & Fils

Saint-Sauvant, Nouvelle Aquitaine, founded in 1850 (whisky since 2015)

distillerie-merlet.com

Renowned for their liqueurs and cognacs, the Merlet family are also into whisky. The first, in 2020, was released under the name Coperies and it was followed by Coperies Les Ocres in 2023.

Meyer, Distillerie

Hohwarth, Grand Est, founded in 1958 (whisky since 2004)

distilleriemeyer.fr

The first bottlings from the distillery were launched in 2007 and currently there are two malt whiskies for sale, Meyer's Pur Malt and Meyer Pur Malt Le Fumé. In 2023 Lionel Meyer left the company.

Michard, Brasserie

Limoges, Nouvelle Aquitaine, founded in 1987 (whisky since 2008)

bieres-michard.com

The first whisky from this craft brewery was released in 2011 followed by a second batch in 2013. End of 2021 a 15 year old was launched followed by a 17 year old in December 2023.

Mine d´Or, La

Ploërmel, Bretagne, founded in 2017

laminedor.bzh

Originally fitted with an 800 litre still, a new distillery, with an additional 2,500 litre Charentais still, was opened in 2022. The whisky is sold under the name Galaad and three new editions were released in 2023. In 2025 the Beltaine 7 year old was launched.

Moon Harbour

Bordeaux, Nouvelle Aquitaine, founded in 2017

moonharbour.fr

The distillery is equipped with two 1,000 litre Stupfler stills. The first whisky was released in 2020 under the name Dock. In 2021 Dock 2, made from malted corn, and Dock 3 where malted barley smoked with seaweed was used, appeared.

Moutard

Buxeuil, Grand Est, founded in 1892 (whisky since 2017)

famillemoutard.com

Fitted with five pot stills, the distillery buys the wash from 5 local breweries in order to make whisky. Matured in Champagne ratafia barrels, the first whisky was released in 2020. A number of bottlings, all with a reference to the breweries have since been released.

Nalin, Distillerie

La Chana, Auvergne-Rhône Alpes, founded in 1919 (whisky since 2015)

distillerie-nalin.fr

For generations the Nalin family has distilled pear eaux-de-vie for other companies. In 2015, they started whisky production and the first bottling has been sold under the name of NP since 2018.

Ninkasi

Tarare, Auvergne-Rhône Alpes, founded in 2015

ninkasi.fr

The whisky was at first distilled in a Prulho Chalvignac still but a second still was installed in 2019 and in 2023 a completely new distillery with two stills operating under vacuum was commissioned. The first whiskies were released in 2018 and in 2023 the Ninkasi Lab range appeared. The range was completely revamped in 2025 to contain New Code, Manifesto, The Flow and Inspiration.

Northmaen, Distillerie de

La Chapelle Saint-Ouen, Normandie, founded in 1997 (whisky since 2002)

northmaen.com

Originally a craft brewery but later equipped with a portable still. Over the years Thor Boyo, Sleipnir, the peated Fafnir and Kenning have been released and in 2022 Cuvée 1110 Batch 1 appeared. The still is not portable anymore but now works in a real distillery.

O´Spirit

Chaingy, Centre-Val de Loire, founded in 2021

o-spirit.com

The distillery is equipped with one single hybrid still and fermentations last 3-4 days. The first whiskies were released in 2023 and the latest, in September 2025, was a 4 year old Margaux finish.

Ouche Nanon

Ourouer Les Bourdelins, Centre-Val de Loire, founded in 2015

ouche-nanon.fr

Equipped with a wood-fired still, they launched La Petite Bertha from Sauternes casks in 2018 followed by the peated Frog´s Peat and single casks or small batch (The Lost Barrel and Cardonaccum). Since late 2024 the range consists of Berry, Salamandre, Chardon and Peaty Frog – all whiskies being certified organic.

Paris, Distillerie de

Paris, Île de France, founded in 2016

distilleriedeparis.com

Equipped with a small Holstein still the distillery launched the first Parisian whisky in 2019 and it was followed in 2021 by whiskies made from corn and rice and a cask strength finished in chestnut wood

Persyn

Houlle, Hauts de France, founded in 1812 (whisky since 2021)

genievredehoulle.com

Traditionally a genever distillery, the whisky distillation is on the grains, a mix of rye, malted barley and oats and is conducted in four succesive runs without cutting heads and tails. First whisky, matured in cognac barrels was released in 2024.

Piautre, La

Ménitré Sur Loire, Pays de Loire, founded in 2004 (whisky since 2014)

lapiautre.fr

La Piautre is equipped with two direct-fired stills and malting their own barley. They released their first whiskies in 2018; Malt, Tourbé and Seigle. In 2025 two core expressions were launched – Empreintes (white wine casks) and Seson (French oak).

Quintessence, La

Herrberg, Grand Est, founded in 2008 (whisky since 2013)

distillerie-quintessence.com

Nicolas Schott produces fruit spirits and also liqueurs. End of 2016, he surprised everyone with the release of his first single malt whisky, Schott's, bottled at 42%.

Roche Aux Fées, La

Sainte-Colombe, Bretagne, founded in 1996 (whisky since 2010)

distillerie-larocheauxfees.com

A micro-brewery was in 2010 turned into a portable automatic batch still. The still is wood-heated and equipped with a worm tub. The first bottling, distilled from three malted cereals was released in 2016. In 2020, the brewery moved to a larger site. In 2025 the brand was renamed Skilt with two expressions – the non-peated Roc´Elf and the peated L´Omn Fort.

Saint-Palais

Saint-Palais de Negrignac, Nouvelle Aquitaine, founded in 2016

alfredgiraud.com

A distillery equipped with ten stills was built in 1963 with the capacity doubled in 1990. In 1995, Philippe Giraud joined the company to form the Alfred Giraud French Malt Whisky. In 2021 the distillery´s first own single malt, Pointe Blanche, was launched and in 2023 Alfred Giraud Horizon, the first whisky made entirely at Saint-Palais appeared. End of 2024, two permanent expressions were launched – Organic and Peated.

Soligny

Soligny Les Étangs, Grand Est, founded in 2020

solignywhisky.fr

Founded by Véronique and Vincent Godier, winegrowers and agricultural engineers by training. The distillery is equipped with two 2,000 litre Istill stills and four fermenters. Brewing, fermentation and distillation are carried out continuously in the same production device. The first whisky was launched in 2023. and in June 2024 the core expression Air de Plaine was released.

Sonneur

Le Mans, Pays de Loire, founded in 2020

distillerie-dusonneur.com

Originally a fruit-to-brandy distillery that has now entered into whisky. The first Le Mans whisky was released in June 2024, after aging in ex-Jasnières barrels, a white wine from Pays de Loire.

Tessendier

Cognac, Nouvelle Aquitaine, founded in 1880 (whisky since 2019)

cognac-tessendier.com

The famous producer of cognac has a distillery fitted with seven stills. The first bottlings appeared in 2022; Arlette and the peated Tourbé. They were later followed by two single malts finished in rum and pineau des Charentes cask respectively. Early 2025 another brand, Les Fratés, with two expressions was launched

T. O. S. Distillery

Aix-Noulette, Hauts de France, founded in 2017

tosdistillery.fr

Saint-Germain has been one of the greatest successes in the revival of French beer production and in 2017 the owners also took up whisky. Artesia single malt was released in 2020 followed by Artesia Rye, Artesia Sherry, Artesia Char#3 and Artesia Peated. In 2025, Artesia Double Maturation (bourbon and moscatel) completed the range.

Twelve, Distillerie

Laguiole, Occitanie, founded in 2017

whiskytwelve.fr

The distillery was built in the former presbytery of Laguiole. The first whisky, Basalte, was released in 2020 and was later followed by Basalte cask strength, Almandin (ex-rum), Aventurine (ex-cognac), the peated Azurite and Topaze (ex-sauternes). The more affordable Twelve 42 is also in the range.

Vercors, Distillerie

Saint-Jean En Vercors, Auvergne-Rhône Alpes, founded in 2015 (whisky since 2019)

distillerie-vercors.com

The distillery is equipped with a Charentais copper still and a steel boiler which works under vacuum. Two malt spirits, were launched in 2018 and in 2020 the first "proper" whisky was launched followed by a peated version in 2021. In 2023 the range was revamped and now consists of Sequoia and Tourbé Réserve and these were followed by the limited Zinc and Black Cat.

Vinet Delpech

Brie Sous Archiac, Nouvelle Aquitaine, founded in 1972 (whisky since 2019)

vinet-delpech.com

With a history of producing cognac and brandy the distillery, equipped with ten pot stills started whisky production in 2019. Palisson, matured in Limousin French oak, was released in September 2022 followed by a version from ex-rum barrels in 2023 and later one from ex-bourbon casks.

Volcans d´Auvergne

Brassac Les Mines, Auvergne-Rhône Alpes, founded in 2021

distillerie-volcans-auvergne.com

Already an established brewer, the business was expanded with whisky in 2021. They fill no less than 600 barrels per year and in 2024 the first whisky, Korma, was launched.

Germany

Whisky-Destillerie Blaue Maus

Eggolsheim-Neuses, 1980

fleischmann-whisky.de

The oldest malt whisky distillery in Germany distilling their first whisky in 1983. It took, however, 15 years before the first whisky, Glen Mouse 1986, appeared. A completely new distillery became operational in 2013. All whisky from Blaue Maus are single cask and there are around ten single malts in the range. Some of them are released at cask strength while others are reduced to 40%.

Slyrs Destillerie

Schliersee, founded in 1928 (whisky since 1999)

slyrs.de

The malt, smoked with beech, comes from locally grown grain and the spirit is distilled in 1,500 litre stills. The non chill-filtered whisky is called Slyrs after the original name of the surrounding area, Schliers. The core expressions are a the Classic, the 51 which has matured in casks that previously held sherry, port or sauternes and a 12 year old. There are also a peated version as well as a rye. Limited editions include a number of wood finishes and the Mountain Edition, with a new batch released yearly around 1st of May. In summer 2025 a completely new distillery was opened.

Hercynian Distilling Co (formerly known as Hammerschmiede)

Zorge, founded in 1984 (whisky since 2002)

hercynian-distilling.de

The distillery´s main products used to be spirits from fruit, berries and herbs but whisky distilling was embarked on in 2002. The first bottles were released in 2006. The core range goes under the name Elsburn and one subrange is called Alrik, represented by experimental and smoky whiskies while the Willowburn range consists of whiskies finished in different types of casks and Emperor´s Way is all about peated whisky. Several new releases appear every year in small batches and often sell out quickly.

Bayerwald-Bärwurzerei und Spezialitäten-Brennerei Liebl

Kötzting, founded in 1970 (whisky since 2006)

coillmor.com

In 2009 the first bottles bearing the name Coillmór were released. There is a wide range aged between 4 and 12 years currently available. Recent limited editions include Bayerische Weihnacht 2023 matured in a combination of oloroso and Ramandolo sweet wine casks.

St Kilian Distillers

Rüdenau, founded in 2015

stkiliandistillers.com

St Kilian is one of few German distilleries designed to make only whisky. Equipped with copper pot stills from Forsyths and wooden washbacks from Joseph Brown in Dufftown, the capacity is now 600,000 litres of pure alcohol. Recently they moved all the maturing casks to new warehouses up in the mountains. The first, limited single malt, Signature Edition One, was released in 2019 and has been folowed with another 14 versions. In 2023 two core expressions emerged; Classic and Peated.

Finch Whiskydestillerie

Heroldstatt, founded in 2001

finch-whisky.de

One of Germany´s biggest distilleries with a yearly production of 250,000 litres. A new distillery was commissioned in 2023. The range of whiskies is large and they are made from a variety of different grains. The age is between 5 and 12 years and include peated expressions as well as rye.

Eifel Whisky

Koblenz, founded in 2009

eifelwhisky.de

This is not a distillery per se. Instead the owner of the company, Stephan Mohr, decides on the mash bills and the malted barley and other grains are then sent to Feinbrennerei Sasse to be processed and distilled to Mohr´s specification. The newmake is then sent back to Eifel Whisky´s warehouses in Koblenz for maturation and blending. There are currently three ranges; Signatur, around 4 years old, Reserve, 6-8 years old and 746.9 Series, 10-12 years old.

Other distilleries in Germany

Altstadthof, Hausbrauerei

Nürnberg, founded in 1984

hausbrauerei-altstadthof.de

The current range of Ayrer´s organic single malts consists of Red, PX, Bourbon and Ayla (peated). Limited expressions include the 5 year old Mastercut, the 5 year old Alligator and three wood finishes.

Am Hartmannsberg, Schaubrennerei

Freital, founded in 2011

hartmannsberger.de

Working on a range of various spirits, the owner also produces small volumes of whisky. The first whisky was released in 2015 and the latest was a 7 year old single malt, matured in ex-sherry casks.

Bellerhof Brennerei

Owen, founded in 1925 (whisky since 1990)

dannes.de

The production of whisky made from barley, wheat and rye started in 1990 and today there is a range of various whiskies under the name Danne´s.

The new Slyrs Distillery

Bergwelt Brennerei

Pfaffenhausen-Salgen, founded in 2017

bergwelt-brennerei.de

Apart from a variety of spirits made from herbs, the distillery also produces gin and a single malt whisky under the brand name White Mountain. The mash bill is made up of five different malt varities.

Birgitta Rust Piekfeine Brände

Bremen, founded in 2011

br-piekfeinebraende.de

A producer of gin and other spirits but also single malt whisky. One of the latest releases is the Van Loon 6 year old single malt with a Tokajer finish.

Birkenhof-Brennerei

Nistertal, founded in 1848 (whisky since 2002)

birkenhof-brennerei.de

The first release from the distillery in 2008 was the 5 year old rye Fading Hill followed by a single malt. The current range consist of single malt, both peated and unpeated, and a rye.

Bosch Edelbrand

Lenningen, founded in 1948 (whisky since 1997)

bosch-edelbrand.de

Family run by the third generation, the distillery produces gin, edelbrände and single malt whisky. The range consists of whiskies (both grain and malt) up to the 12 year old single cask Sandhannes.

Brauhaus am Lohberg

Wismar, whisky since 2010

brauhaus-wismar.de, hinricusnoyte.de

The first release of Baltach single malt, a 3 year old sherry finish, was in 2013. Today there is also a peated version, finished in PX sherry casks.

Burger Hofbrennerei

Burg, founded in 2007 (whisky since 2012)

sagengeister.de

Apart from distillates from fruits and berries, the distillery also produces whisky made from malted barley. The first release of Der Kolonist single malt was in spring 2015.

Dolleruper Destille

Dollerup, founded in 1990 (whisky since 2014)

dolleruper-destille.de

A huge variety of spirits from fruits, berries and nuts are produced but also single malt whisky. A variety of different bottlings under the name Noord Molt, including peated, have been released.

Drexler, Destillerie

Arrach, whisky since 2007

drexlers-baerwurz.de

Malt whisky has been produced since 2009. The first release of Bayerwald Single Malt was in 2011 and in the past few years a number of 10 year olds have appeared.

Druffel, Brennerei

Oelde-Stromberg, founded in 1792 (whisky since 2010)

brennerei-druffel.de

A variety of spirits are produced including malt whisky. Two of the latest releases of Druffel single malt was a 13 year old in 2023 and a 6 year old in 2024 which had been matured in an Islay cask.

Dürr Edelbranntweine

Neubulach, founded in 2002

blackforest-whiskey.com

The first release from the distillery, the 4 year old Doinich Daal, reached the market in 2012. One of the latest expressions, Batch 07 in December 2024, had been finished in apple aperitif casks.

Edelbrände Senft

Salem-Rickenbach, founded in 1988 (whisky since 2009)

senft-destillerie.de

The first Senft Bodensee Whisky was released in 2012 and then followed by a cask strength version. One of the latest releases was a 10 year old.

Evermann-Whisky (Bimmerle KG)

Sasbach, founded in 1966 (whisky since 2015)

evermann-whisky.de

This family owned company is focused on fruit brandies but recently malt whisky has become a part of the range. Currently the range consists of Wilhelm single malt and Theo blended whisky.

Faber, Brennerei

Ferschweiler, founded in 1949

faber-eifelbrand.de

A producer of eau-de vie from fruits and berries, whisky has also been included in the production. The only whisky so far is a single malt that has matured for 6 years in American white oak.

FARO

Schretstaken, founded in 2019

faro-whisky.de

Founded by Fabian Rohrwasser and his wife Martina the distillery focuses entirely on whisky and they even have their own maltings. In 2023 the first whisky was launched under the name Feingeist.

Farny

Kisslegg, founded in 1833 (whisky since 2015)

farny.de

Originating as a brewery in the 1800s, a whisky distillery was added in 2015. Currently there are two single malts in the range under the name Falken – 5 and 10 years old respectively.

Feller, Brennerei

Dietenheim-Regglisweiler, founded in 1820
(whisky since 2008)

brennerei-feller.de

In 2012 the 3 year old single malt Valerie matured in bourbon casks, was released. It has since been followed by more expressions including 6 to 10 year old grain whiskies under the name Augustus.

Fessler Mühle

Sersheim, founded in 2013

fessler-muehle.de

For 625 years there has been a mill in Sersheim. On the same site a distillery was founded in 2013. Their Mettermalt whisky, matured in a variety of casks, is bottled in small batches.

Fitzke, Kleinbrennerei

Herbolzheim-Broggingen, founded in 1874 (whisky since 2004)

kleinbrennerei-fitzke.de

The first release of Derrina single malt was in 2007 and new batches have been launched ever since. The different varieties are made from malted grains (barley, rye, wheat, oats) or unmalted (barley, oats, buckwheat, rice, triticale, sorghum or maize).

Glina Whiskydestillerie

Werder a.d. Havel, founded in 2004

glina-whisky.de

The first Glina Single Malt was released in 2008. Most of the whiskies, malts and ryes, are between 3 and 8 years old. The oldest whiskies in the range have now reached the age of 12 years.

Grumsiner Distillery

Angermünde, founded in 2015

grumsiner.de

The first whiskies were released in 2019 and the latest release of Mammoth single malt was the 8 year old Edition 2023 finished for 3 years in PX casks. Single rye and single grain are also available.

Gutsbrennerei Joh. B. Geuting

Bocholt Spork, founded in 1837 (whisky since 2010)

muensterland-whisky.de

The first releases, two single malts and two single grain, appeared in 2013. Currently there are seven expressions of the J.B.G. Münsterländer whisky, the oldest 11 years.

Henrich, Brennerei

Kriftel, founded in 1983 (whisky since 2008)

brennerei-henrich.de, www.gilors.de

The first release was the 3 year old single malt Gilors in 2012. In 2023 the Gilors No. 1 was released to celebrate the company´s 50th anniversary. Different casks from 2008-2010 had been married together for two years in bourbon casks and bottled at 55,1%.

Heinrich Habbel

Sprockhövel, founded in 1878 (whisky since 1977)

habbel.com

A family distillery in its fourth generation. In 1977 they produced Uralter whisky, the first German whisky. In 2013 they built a designated whisky distillery where Hillock Park is now produced. The range is extensive with a 12 year old as the pinnacle.

Hinrichsen´s

Dunsum auf Föhr, founded in 2019

hinrichsens-whisky.de

Inspired by a trip to Hillrock Distillery in USA, the owners opened a distillery on a farm with rots going back to 1630 on the island of Föhr. The barley is grown on the estate and floor-malted on site. The first malt whisky, sold under the name Hinrichsen´s Frisian Whisky, appeared in 2023.

Höhler, Brennerei

Aarbergen, founded in 1895 (whisky since 2001)

brennerei-hoehler.de

The first whisky was released in 2004 as a 3 year old. One of the more recent releases of their Whesskey is a 6 year old matured in chestnut casks.

Kammer-Kirsch, Destillerie

Karlsruhe, founded in1961 (whisky since 2006)

kammer-kirsch.de

Working with a brewery the distillery is making their own Black Forest Rothaus whisky as well as a single malt under the name Black Forêt.

Kinzigbrennerei

Biberach, founded in 1937 (whisky since 2004)

biberacher-whisky.de

The first single malt release was the 4 year old Biberacher in 2010. Later releases include Schwarzwälder Rye, Kinzigtäler and Geroldsecker. The oldest whisky so far is the 15 year old Annorum XV bottled at both 40% and cask strength (54%).

Kymsee Whisky

Grabenstätt, founded in 1994 (whisky since 2012)

kymsee-whisky.de

In 2015 the first triple-distilled Kymsee single malt was released. Later editions include Triple Oak and two finishes - quarter cask and sherry cask.

Landgasthof Gemmer

Rettert, founded in 1908 (whisky since 2008)

landgasthof-gemmer.de

The only single malt released is the 3 year old Georg IV which has matured for two years in toasted Spessart oak casks and finished for one year in casks that have contained Banyuls wine.

Lübbehusen Malt Distillery

Emstek, founded in 2014

theluebbehusen.com

With one of the largest pot stills in the country, the distillery currently has three single malts in the range; Unpeated small batch 5 years old, Peated small batch 7 years old and a Vintage 2014.

Marder Edelbrände

Albbruck-Unteralpfen, founded in 1953 (whisky since 2009)

marder-edelbraende.de

The first release was the 3 year old Marder Single Malt. The oldest expression so far is a 12 year old matured in a combination of bourbon, new oak and port casks.

Märkische Spezialitäten Brennerei

Hagen, whisky since 2010

msb-hagen.de

The spirit is distilled four times and matured in a cave. The first DeCavo whisky was released in 2013 and the latest, in June 2023, was a 6 year old made from Chevalier heritage barley.

Mösslein, Destillerie

Zeilitzheim, founded in 1984 (whisky since 1996)

weingeister.de

Originally a winery, the first whisky was released in 2003 and the current range consists of single malt and a grain whisky including the 5 year old Bergwerk-Whisky.

Nordik Edelbrennerei

Horneburg, founded in 2012

nordik-edelbrennerei.de

A variety of spirits including whisky are produced. One of the latest, in 2023, was the 8 year old, peated Elbe Valley. The distillery moved to a new location in 2022.

Nordpfälzer Edelobst & Whiskydestille Höning

Winnweiler, founded in 2008

nordpfalz-brennerei.de

The first release was in 2011, a 3 year old single malt by the name Taranis with a full maturation in a Sauternes cask. Every year in September, a new version is released.

Number Nine Spirituosen-Manufaktur

Leinefelde-Worbis, founded in 1999 (whisky since 2013)

number-nine.eu

Production was expanded in 2013 to include rum, gin and whisky. The first single malt under the label The Nine Springs was launched in 2016. One of the latest releases was a 7 year old with an acacia finish.

Old Sandhill Whisky

Bad Belzig, founded in 2012

sandhill-whisky.com

The first whisky was released in 2015. The current range of six expressions include Oloroso, Bordeaux, German oak, American oak, Port and the 5 year old Bio Whisky.

Preussische Whiskydestillerie

Mark Landin, founded in 2009

preussischerwhisky.de

The spirit is distilled five to six times in a 550 litre copper still with a rectification column. Since 2013 only organic barley is used. The first whisky was launched as a 3 year old in 2012. Since 2015, all the whiskies have been at least 5 years old.

Ralf Hauer, Destillerie

Bad Dürkheim, founded in 1989 (whisky since 2012)

sailltmor.de

The first release, in 2015 was the 3 year old Saillt Mor single malt. The current range are all 5-6 years old; PX Sherry, Double Wood, Port Cask, Jamaika Rum, Madeira Finish and Pfälzer Eiche.

Rieger & Hofmeister

Fellbach, founded in 1994 (whisky since 2006)

rieger-hofmeister.de

First release was in 2009 and current expressions include a single malt made from barley and one made from wheat.

Sauerländer Edelbrennerei

Kallenhardt, founded in 2000 (whisky since 2004)

sauerlaender-edelbrennerei.de

The first release of the 3 year old Thousand Mountains McRaven appeared in 2007. One of the latest bottlings was the 6 year old Stefen 1624 matured in red wine casks.

Scheibel Mühle

Kappelrodeck, founded in 2015

scheibel-muehle.de

Originally distillers of Kirschwasser, the owners are now also producing whisky. The Emill range of single malts consists of Feinwerk, Stockwerk, Kraftwerk, Fasswerk and Spielwerk.

Schlitzer Destillerie

Schlitz, founded in 2006

schlitzer-destillerie.de

Apart from a range of different spirits, whisky is also produced. There are currently three Schlitzer single malt - Classic, Peaty and and Woody, the last one matured in virgin oak.

Schloss Neuenburg, Edelbrennerei

Freyburg, founded in 2012

schlossbrennerei.eu

The first whisky appeared in August 2016 and one of the most recent expression is is Schlosswhisky No. 8 matured in a tokaji cask.

Schwarzwaldbrennerei Walter Seeger

Calw-Holzbronn, founded in 1952 (whisky since 1990)

krabba-nescht.de

The first single malt was launched in 2009. Currently there are two expressions in the range; the 4 year old Black-Wood single malt matured in amontillado casks and an 8 year old wheat whisky.

Scriptor

Karlsruhe, founded in 2015

scriptor-brennerei.de

A number of small batch whiskies, both peated and unpeated, have been released including Brigant which has experienced a finish in amontillado sherry casks.

Seitz, Gasthof

Gräfenberg, founded in 2007 (whisky since 2013)

gasthof-seitz.de, elch-whisky.de

A combination of a brewery and a distillery. The latest releases include the 7 year old Fass No. 83 matured for the full time in a port wine cask.

Simon´s Feinbrennerei

Alzenau-Michelbach, founded in 1879 (whisky since 1998)

simon-brennt.de

A single pot still whisky has been produced since 2013 and the range also includes a blend, a whisky made from emmer and a single malt made from malted barley.

Singold Whisky

Wehringen, founded in 2017

singold-whisky.de

Although founded in 2017, the brand was produced at another distillery already in 2012. The core range consists of Singold Malt Whisky including a cask strength version and the recent port cask maturation.

Steinhauser Destillerie

Kressbronn, founded in 1828 (whisky since 2008)

weinkellerei-steinhauser.de

The main products are spirits derived from fruits, but whisky also has its niche. The first release was the single malt Brigantia which appeared in 2011 and a 12 year old has followed since.

Steinwälder Hausbrennerei

Erbendorf, founded in 1818 (whisky since 1920)

brennerei-schraml.de, stonewood-whisky.de

A kind of whisky was made here already in the early 1900s but was sold as "Kornbrand". When the current owner took over, the spirit was relaunched as a 10 year old single grain by the name Stonewood 1818. Latest releases include a 9 year old finished in vermouth casks.

Stork Club Whiskey-Destillerie

Schlepzig, founded in 2004

stork-club-whisky.com

The distillery had a history of producing a wide range of spirits but new owners decided to focus mainly on rye whisky. The range is called Stork Club and also includes a single malt made from barley

Störtebeker Brennerei

Mönchgut/Rügen, founded in 2009

stoertebeker-whisky.com

The first whisky was released in 2014 and the current core

expression is Klassik. Recent limited editions include a 5 year old Jubiläums Edition. The distillery was expanded in 2023.

Tecker Whisky-Destillerie

Owen, founded in 1979 (whisky since 1989)

tecker.eu

Apart from a variety of other spirits, whisky is also produced. The core expression is the 10 year old Tecker Single Malt matured for five years in ex-bourbon barrels, followed by five years in oloroso casks. Recently an 20 year old PX cask matured has been released.

Thomas Sippel, Destillerie

Weisenheim am Berg, founded in 1992 (whisky since 2011)

destillerie-sippel.de

Wines as well as distillates of all kinds are on the menu with whisky being introduced in 2011. The first release of the Palatinatus Single Malt came in 2014 and several expressions matured in different casks have since been released.

Vielanker Distillery

Vielank, whisky since 2008

vielanker.de

A combination of a restaurant, hotel, beer brewery and, most recently, a distillery. The brand name of their single malt is Aur Ox and the two oldest expressions so far are a 10 and a 12 year old.

Volker Theurer, Brennerei

Tübingen, founded in 1991

schwaebischer-whisky.de

The first whisky was released in 2003 as a 7 year old. Since then they have released the 8 year old Sankt Johann and the 10 year old Tammer (both single malts) as well as the blend Original Ammertal.

Wild Brennerei

Gengenbach, founded in 1855 (whisky since 2002)

wild-brennerei.de

Three 5 year old whiskies have been released so far – Wild Whisky Single Malt matured for 3 years in American white oak and another 2 in either sherry or port casks, Blackforest Wild Whisky Sherry Cask and Blackforest Wild Whisky Peated.

Zeitzer Whisky Manufaktur

Zeitz, founded in 2014

whisky-zeitz.de

The distillery is equipped with a Lomond still as well as a still built in Germany in 1935. Latest releases include a number of whiskies matured or finished in casks such as tequila, moscatel, gin, madeira and marsala.

Ziegler, Brennerei

Freudenberg, founded in 1865

brennerei-ziegler.de

Maturation takes place not only in oak casks, but also made from chestnut. Their single malt brand, Aureum 1865, was recently replaced by Freud Whisky matured in bourbon and chestnut casks and finished in their Obstbrand barrels.

Hungary

Gemenc Distillery

Pörböly, founded in 2014

gemencdistillery.hu

Unlike so many other distilleries in Hungary producing pálinka, Gemenc is completely focused on whisky. The owner´s, Lajos Szöke, interest lies mainly in whiskies made from various mash bills which are matured in casks made from Hungarian oak or acacia. Since 2017, Szöke has also filled casks with both peated and unpeated single malt made from barley.

Agárdi Distillery

Gárdony, founded in 2002

agardi.hu

A pálinka producer who also distills small amounts of Agárdi single malt and rye whisky. The current malt whisky has been matured in a combination of virgin oak and ex-tokaji barrels.

Seven Hills

Bodrogkisfalud, founded in 2020

sevenhillsdistillery.com

A new distillery focusing initially on vodka and gin but also with whisky on the agenda. In autumn 2024 their smoky single malt matured in a tokaji cask was released.

Iceland

Eimverk Distillery

Garðabær, founded in 2012

flokiwhisky.is

The country´s first whisky distillery where only organic barley grown in Iceland is used for the production and everything is malted on site. Both peat and sometimes sheep dung is used to dry the malted barley. The distillery has a capacity of 100,000 litres (including gin and aquavite) and the first, limited release of a 3 year old whisky was in 2017 and more bottlings have followed since then including one finished in beer casks and one with a partial maturation in birch casks. They are also making Eth made from rye.

Republic of Ireland

Midleton Distillery

Midleton, Co. Cork, founded in 1975

irishdistillers.ie

Midleton is by far the biggest distillery in Ireland and the home of Jameson´s Irish Whiskey. The production at Midleton comprises of two sections – grain whiskey and single pot still whiskey. The grain whiskey is needed for the blends, where Jameson´s is the biggest seller. Single pot still whiskey, on the other hand, is unique to Ireland. This part of the production is also used for the blends but is being bottled more and more on its own.

Instead of mash tuns, Midleton is equipped with three mash filters and following several major upgrades of the distillery in the last decade, the distillery is now equipped with 48 washbacks, 6 column stills and 10 pot stills. The total capacity of the distillery is 70 million litres of pure alcohol. In 2015 a micro distillery was opened to be used mainly for experiments and innovation. The owners announced in June 2022 that they would invest €50 million over the next four years to make the distillery carbon neutral by the end of 2026. A couple of months later, in September, Irish Distillers declared that they were going to build another distillery across the Dungourney river, just across the existing distillery. The investment is €250 million and the distillery was supposed to be operational by 2025. In March 2025 however, the owners announced that they would temporarily pause production for a few months and that decision also entails a delay in the completion of the new distillery.

Of all the brands produced at Midleton, Jameson´s blended Irish whiskey is by far the biggest. In 2024 the brand sold 130 million bottles. Apart from the core expression with no age statement, there are Crested, Black Barrel and Black Barrel Proof. Recent limited releases include 18 year old, 18 year old Bow Street and a Single Pot Still which had been matured in a combination of five different casks. There is also the Triple Triple series with three whiskies that had first been matured in a combination of bourbon and sherry and then received a finish in a third cask. The three versions are Malaga, Chestnut and Marsala. Finally there is the Caskmates series with two finishes, Stout and IPA.

Other blended whiskey brands include Powers with a 100% rye version launched in 2023, and the exclusive, yearly releases of Midleton Very Rare. The latter is also the name of a series of exceptionally old whiskies – Midleton Very Rare Silent Distillery. They have all been distilled at the old Midleton Distillery which closed in 1975. The sixth and final installment, in April 2025, was a 50 year old blend of grain and pot still.

In recent years, Midleton has invested increasingly in their second category of whiskies – single pot still. The main brand is Redbreast with a range of 12, 12 cask strength, 15, the new 18 year old, 21, Lustau Edition, PX Editionand a 27 year old. Recent limited releases include the Iberian Series with Tawny Port released in 2023 and with Cuatro Barriles, the fourth installment, appearing in March 2024. Finally the last edition of Redbreast Dream Cask, this time the 38 year old Zenith, was launched in 2024. Other single pot stills whiskies can be found in the Spot range; Green Spot without age statement and with three more varieties - the 12 year old Leoville Barton bordeaux finish, the Chateau Montelena finish and Quails´ Gate. Furthermore there are Yellow Spot 12 year old, Red Spot 15 year old, Blue Spot 7 year old and Gold Spot 13 year old which also comes in The Generations Edition. Powers John´s Lane and Powers Three Swallow are other examples of their single pot still whiskies and so is the Dair Ghaelach range of single casks, finished in virgin Irish oak and aged between 13 and 26 years. The innovative side of production at Midleton was displayed in 2017 when a first range of experimental whiskeys was introduced under the name Method and Madness. This range includes Japanese Trilogy, Oats and Malt and Malt and Rye.

Tullamore Dew Distillery

Clonminch, Co. Offaly, founded in 2014

tullamoredew.com

Until 1954, Tullamore D.E.W. was distilled at Daly´s Distillery in Tullamore. When it closed, production was temporarily moved to Power´s Distillery in Dublin, and was later moved to Midleton Distillery and Bushmill´s Distillery. William Grant & Sons acquired Tullamore D.E.W. in 2010 and in 2013, they started to build a new distillery at Clonminch, situated on the outskirts of Tullamore. The four stills produce both malt whiskey and single pot still whiskey and the capacity is 3.6 million litres of pure alcohol. In 2017, a bottling hall and a grain distillery with a capacity of doing 8 million litres of grain spirit was opened and in September 2023 another 12 acres of neighbouring land was acquired to increase warehousing. All whiskies at Tullamore are triple distilled. Tullamore D.E.W. is the second biggest selling Irish whiskey in the world after Jameson with around 20 million bottles. The core range consists of Original, 12 year old Special Reserve and 14 and 18 year old Single Malts. Exclusive to duty free and select markets there are also the Cider Cask Finish and Carribean Rum Cask Finish. Finally there is Tullamore D.E.W. Honey made from single malt, single pot still and grain whiskey and infused with Bohemian honey.

Cooley Distillery

Cooley, Co. Louth, founded in 1987

thetyrconnellwhiskey.com, connemarawhiskey.com

John Teeling has played a huge part in the resurrection of Irish whiskey which during the second half of the 20th century continuosly lost ground amongst the consumers. By the late 1980s there were only two distilleries left in the country. In 1987 he bought the disused Ceimici Teo distillery and renamed it Cooley distillery. Two years later he installed two pot stills and in 1992 he released the first single malt from the distillery, called Locke´s Single Malt. A number of brands were launched over the years. In 2011 Beam Inc. acquired the distillery and today Cooley is owned by Suntory Global Spirits The range of whiskies is made up of several brands. Connemara single malts, which are all more or less peated, consist of a no age Original, a 12 year old and a cask

Tullamore DEW Distillery

strength. Another brand is Tyrconnell with a core expression bottled without age statement. Other Tyrconnell varieties include three 10 year old wood finishes and Tyrconnell 16 year old with a finish in both oloroso and moscatel casks.

Teeling Distillery

Dublin, founded in 2015

teelingwhiskey.com

This was the first new distillery in Dublin in 125 years, founded by Jack and Stephen Teeling. In 2017, Bacardi acquired a minority stake in Teeling Whiskey and later upped its stake in the company on a couple of occasions to the present 79%. The distillery is equipped with two wooden washbacks, four made of stainless steel and three stills made in Italy; wash still (15,000 litres), intermediate still (10,000 litres) and spirit still (9,000 litres). Both pot still and malt whisky is produced. The core range from the distillery consists of the blend Small Batch which has been finished in rum casks, Single Grain which is fully matured in Californian red wine barrels, Single Malt - a vatting of five different whiskies that have been finished in five different types of wine casks, Single Pot Still (50% malted and 50% unmalted barley) and Blackpitts Peated Single Malt, triple distilled and matured in ex-bourbon and ex-Sauternes. Later a limited cask strength version of the same was launched. Recent limited bottlings include Wonders of Wood where the third edition had been fully matured in virgin Swedish oak. There is also Rising Reserve with three 21 year olds each with a different second maturation – white port, marsala and ruby port. Finally there is the Vintage Reserve Collection with a 40 year old as the pinnacle. The last two series are made from whiskies distilled at Cooley.

Dingle Whiskey Distillery, The

Milltown, Dingle, Co. Kerry, founded in 2012

dingledistillery.ie

The distillery is equipped with an unusual wooden mash tun and wooden washbacks with a minimum fermentation time of 72 hours. There are also three pot stills and a combined gin/vodka still. The first production of whiskey was in 2012 and the first general release of a single malt whiskey was in autumn 2016. Since then a range of different "small batches" of single malt and single pot still have been released. A limited series named The Celtic Wheel (reflecting the Celtic solar calendar) has also been launched with the ninth and final edition, the single pot still Lá an Dreoilín, released in November 2024.

Roayl Oak Distillery (fomerly known as Walsh Whiskey Distillery)

Carlow, Co. Carlow, founded in 2016

royaloakdistillery.com, thebusker.com

With succesful brands such as The Irishman and Writer´s Tears, Bernard Walsh opened his own distillery at Royal Oak, Carlow. With a back-up from the major Italian drinks company, Illva Saronno, the distillery was commissioned in 2016. The capacity is 2.5 million litres of alcohol and all types of whiskey is produced including grain- malt- and pot still whiskey. In 2019 Illva Saronno took full control of the distillery while Bernard Walsh continued with the brands Writer´s Tears and The Irishman. Walsh Whiskey was later acquired by Latvian, Luxemburg based Amber Beverage Group who are now looking to build their own distillery. The owners of Roayl Oak introduced their own brand, Busker, in November 2020 and the range now consists of Single Grain, Single Malt, Single Pot Still and Triple Cask.

Great Northern Distillery

Dundalk, Co. Louth, founded in 2015

gndireland.com

In 2013, the Irish Whiskey Company (IWC), with John Teeling as the majority owner, took over the Great Northern Brewery in Dundalk and turned it into a distillery. When it became operational in August 2015, it was the second biggest distillery in Ireland (and still is), with the capacity to produce 3.6 million litres of pot still whiskey and 8 million litres of grain spirit. A recent expansion, including another six pot stills and an additional eight washbacks has brought the capacity to 16 million litres. The idea behind the distillery is to sell new make or whiskey (single malt, single potstill and grain) to other companies. Around 60% of the volume sold is new make but the share of mature whiskey (including blends) is growing.

Roe & Co. Distillery

Dublin, founded in 2019

roeandcowhiskey.com

The opening of Roe & Co Distillery marked Diageo´s return to the Irish whiskey scene which they left in 2014 when they sold Bushmills. A blend named Roe & Co made from sourced whiskies was launched already in 2017 and at the same time plans to build a distillery in Dublin were revealed. The distillery is situated in The Liberties district in the former Guinness Power Station. Three stills and wooden washbacks make up part of the equipment for producing double- and tripledistilled whiskey. In 2020 the first whiskies, sourced from another distillery, appeared. The current range consists of Roe & Co blended whiskey and the 14 year old single grain Flor - both made from sourced whiskies. Finally, in February 2024, Solera single malt appeared, the first product distilled on site.

West Cork Distillers

Skibbereen, Co. Cork, founded in 2004

westcorkdistillers.com

The distillery, equipped with eight pot stills, two column stills and with a yearly capacity of no less than 4,5 million litres of pure alcohol, produces both malt whiskey and grain whiskey and some of the malting is done on site. The whiskey range is quite substantial with well over 15 expressions and include single malts, single pot stills, cask finished whiskies with a second maturation in cask that have held for example port, stout, IPA and sherry and finally, the Glengarriff series with peated expressions. In 2019 the founders bought out the majority stake in the business held by Halewood Group and in 2020 the company moved to a new and expanded distillery in Marsh Road in Skibbereen. An approved planning application (in 2023) to build six warehouses at Tullig near Reenascreena was refused in early 2025 after an appeal to An Bord Pleanála.

Blackwater Distillery

Ballyduff Upper, Co. Waterford, founded in 2014

blackwaterdistillery.ie

Originally located in Cappoquin, Co. Waterford, the distillery moved in 2018 to Ballyduff. At that time the company was already famous for their gin. In their new distillery, equipped with two former grappa stills from Frilli in Italy, whiskey is now also produced. Director and co-founder Peter Mulryan, with a background as TV-producer and whisky writer, is passionate about single pot still. The current legislation says it must be produced from malted and unmalted barley and that only 5% of other grains can be a part of the mash bill. According to legislators this is the traditional way. Going through hundreds of recipes from the 19th and 20th century Irish distilleries, Mulryan has shown that a substantially higher percentage of other grains were involved. A revised version of the technical file for production of single pot still is now imminent. Apart from distilling single malt, Mulryan is making single pot still from a huge variety of these ancient recipes. The first releases, named Dirtgrain Irish Whisky, were released in November 2022. Four different mashbills (including wheat, oats and rye) matured in four different types of casks were presented. In 2024 The Full Irish, a blend of single malt, single pot still and grain whiskey finished in stout casks, was released.

Other distilleries in Ireland

Achill Island Distillery

Achill Island, Co. Mayo, founded in 2019

irishamericanwhiskeys.com

Irelands first island-based whiskey distillery, owned by IrishAmerican Trading Company. The first products for sale were sourced whiskies but their inaugural release from own production appeared in 2022 and was followed by more. The latest, in November 2024, was a special edition matured in a combination of port and bourbon casks.

Ahascragh Distillery

Ahascragh, Co. Galway, founded in 2023

ahascraghdistillery.com

An old mill has been converted into a whiskey and gin distillery. Powered by renewable energy, the distillery opened to the public in July 2023 and started production a few months later. The distillery is equipped with a 47 plate mash filter and sourced whiskies have already been released under the names Clan Colla and Uais.

Ardara Distillery (a.k.a Sliabh Liag Distillers)

Ardara, Co. Donegal, founded in 2021

sliabhliagdistillers.com, ardaradistillery.com

In early 2022 the first whiskey (the main part being peated) was produced from three stills made by Forsyths. The Japanese drinks giant Asahi Group have invested €3m in the distillery and the current capacity is around 500,000 litres. The owners have with great success been selling a blended whiskey named Silkie and their first single malt, the smoky The Kilcar Release, appeared in 2023 with a moscatel finish being one of the latest in late 2024.

Ballykeefe Distillery

Ballykeefe, Co. Kilkenny, founded in 2017

ballykeefedistillery.ie

A farm distillery growing their own barley. The distillery is equipped with three copper pot stills and the first triple distillation was in 2018. Gin, vodka and poitin were released early on while the first Ballykeefe single pot still appeared in March 2021 followed by a single malt in November.

Baoilleach Distillery

Carrickart, Co. Donegal, founded in 2018

baoilleachdistillery.ie

Michael O´Boyle started off distilling gin, rum and poitín and later ventured into whiskey made from malted and unmalted barley. A new, direct-fired still was installed in March 2022. The Mountain Dew series of malt spirits - The Son, The Father and The Holy Smoke (not old enough to be called whiskey) have been launched.

Blacks Brewery & Distillery

Kinsale, Co. Cork, founded in 2013 (whiskey since 2020)

blacksbrewery.com

Starting off as a brewery, the owners later went on with distillation of gin and rum. In 2020, they purchased two copper pot stills from Frilli in Italy. Both single malt whiskey and single pot still are produced and sourced whiskey was offered early on. In December 2024 their first malt whiskey and single pot still whiskey from own production, both 4 years old, were released.

Boann Distillery

Drogheda, Co. Meath, founded in 2016

boanndistillery.ie

The distillery is equipped with three Italian-made copper pot stills and a gin still. Releases of sourced whiskey under the name The Whistler appeared early on. In 2022 the first whiskey from their own production, the PX-matured The Solstice, was released. The latest, in July 2024, was a trio of single pot still whiskeys matured in madeira, PX sherry and marsala respectively. In December 2023 it was announced that the company had secured €5 million to fund an expansion which dould double the capacity.

Diageo´s Roe & Co Distillery opened in Dublin in 2019

Burren Distillery

Ballyvaughan, Co. Clare, founded in 2019

burrendistillers.com

The owners are using locally grown barley which is floor malted at the distillery and for some of the maturation, casks made of Irish oak are used. Both single pot still and single malt whiskey is produced and the first release appeared in November 2023.

Church of Oak Distillery

Ballykelly Mills, Monasterevin, Co. Kildare, founded in 2021

churchofoak.com

A large distillery owned by Jewelfield Ltd with Bono as a shareholder was recently opened. The stills were delivered from Forsyths in August 2021 and the first spirit was distilled in May 2022. The whiskey is either double or triple distilled (and occasionally 2,5 times).

Clonakilty Distillery

Clonakilty, Co. Cork, founded in 2019

clonakiltydistillery.ie

For nine generations the Scully family have farmed the lands near Clonakilty in West Cork. The main product is a triple distilled pot still whiskey and sourced, at least partially, whiskey was launched early on. The first whiskey from their own production, a single pot still, appeared in July 2024.

Connacht Whiskey Company

Ballina, Co. Mayo, founded in 2016

connachtwhiskey.com

Equipped with three pot stills the first distillation of whiskey was made in 2016 and in 2017, triple distillation started as well. In 2021 a limited release from the first cask as well as a general release of Single Malt Batch 1 appeared and in 2023 the 5 year old single malt Spirit of the Atlantic was released. Distillery exclusives also occur. One of the latest, in 2024, had matured in a tequila cask. In September 2024 Terroirs Distillers (owners of Tullibardine distillery in Scotland) bought the distillery.

Crolly (Croithli) Distillery

Crolly, Co. Donegal, founded in 2020

thecrollydistillery.com

The former Crolly Doll factory from 1902 has been converted into a distillery with two cognac stills and in summer 2023 a larger mash tun was installed. The first distillation was in November 2020 and sourced whiskey is currently sold.

Dublin Liberties Distillery, The

Dublin founded in 2018

thedld.com

After eight years of preparations, the distillery finally started the production in early 2019. It is owned by Quintessential Brands (75%) and East European drinks company Stock Spirits (25%). The three coper pot stills produce both double and triple distilled whiskey as well as peated expressions and the total capacity is 700,000 litres of pure alcohol per year. The whiskeys currently available have all been produced at either Bushmills or Cooleys. Due to the current headwinds in the industry the distillery temporarily closed in May 2025.

Fore Distillery

Moortown, Co. Westmeath, founded in 2021

foredistillery.ie

A family owned distillery producing golden rum, white rum and poitín which have all been released. Resting in the warehouse with a possible release in 2026 is single pot still whiskey.

Glendalough Distillery

Newtown, Co. Wicklow, founded in 2013

glendaloughdistillery.com

Originally equipped with a 500 litre Holstein still the distillery has over the years released a combination of sourced and own whiskies also including gin and poitín. In 2016 Mark Anthony Brands invested in Glendalough and eventually took over the company.

Kilbeggan Distillery

Kilbeggan, Co. Westmeath, founded in 1757

kilbegganwhiskey.com

Brought back to life in 2007, Kilbeggan is the oldest producing whiskey distillery in the world, equipped with a wooden mash tun, four Oregon pine washbacks and two stills. The first single malt from the new production came in 2010 and the current range consists of a blended whiskey, a single pot still, a small batch rye and triple cask (whish used to be called single grain).

Killarney Brewing Distilling

Fossa, Co. Kerry, founded in 2023

killarneybrewingdistilling.com

Killarney Brewing Company started beer production in 2013 on a site in the centre of Killarney but a new brewery/distillery, of quite some size, was then built by Lough Leane on the western outskirts of the town. The brewing part became operational in summer 2022 and the distillery was commissioned in 2024. The distillery is equipped with three Italian 2,000 litre copper pot stills and while waiting for their first own whiskey to be launched in 2028, sourced whiskey has been released.

Lough Gill Distillery

Hazelwood House, Co. Sligo, founded in 2019

loughgilldistillery.com, athru.com

A group of investors led by David Raethorne came up with the idea in 2014 to build a distillery adjacent to the 18th century Hazelwood House. Equipped with three pot stills from Frilli, the distillery has a capacity of 1 million litres. Sourced whiskey can be found under the brand name Athrú. In summer 2022 The Sazerac Company (Buffalo Trace and Southern Comfort) acquired the distillery and at the same time Bushmill´s former master blender Helen Mulholland joined the team. In 2023 Sazerac bought the classic whiskey brand Paddy and now have plans to expand Lough Gill Distillery to create a brand home for their Irish whiskeys.

Lough Mask Distillery

Tourmakeady, Co. Mayo, founded in 2016

loughmaskdistillery.com

Equipped with two alambic stills, the distillery started production in early 2018 producing gin and vodka. After a few years whiskey was added to the range. The Loch Measc malt is double distilled and both peated and unpeated spirit is produced. The first whiskey is due for release in 2025. There is also a visitor centre on site.

Lough Ree Distillery

Lanesborough, Co. Longford, founded in 2018

lrd.ie

A family owned distillery west of Dublin, famous for its Slingshot Gin. Production of whiskey didn´t start until 2022 but sourced whiskey from Great Northern Distillery and other distilleries are sold under the name Bart´s and The Bridge.

Micil Distillery

Salthill, Co. Galway, founded in 2016

micildistillery.com

The first steps into distillation were producing gin and poitin.

In 2021, the operation was expanded into whiskey making, not least using local peat to dry the barley. According to the owners the family represents Irelands longest unbroken family distilling tradition. In July 2024 their first whiskey was released – a peated single malt matured in three different types of sherry casks.

Pearse Lyons Distillery

Dublin, founded in 2017

pearselyonsdistillery.com

Dr Pearse Lyons was a native of Ireland and used to work for Irish Distillers in the 1970s. In 2008, he opened a whiskey distillery in Lexington, Kentucky. Four years later he started a distillery in Carlow, Ireland. After a few years, the stills were moved to Dublin where Dr Lyons restored the old St James´ church and converted it to a distillery. The first distillation was in 2017 but early on the owners presented a range of aged malt whiskies made from whisky produced at Carlow and other distilleries. The range until recently consisted of two blended whiskies and two single malts. In June 2023 they launched the Limited Edition Pearse Genesis Release matured in ex-bourbon and virgin oak which had been produced entirely at the distillery in Dublin. Since then tey have released the Pearse Legacy blended malt with whiskies from both the Dublin distillery and the one in Kentucky.

Powerscourt Distillery

Enniskerry, Co. Wicklow, founded in 2017

powerscourtdistillery.com

The distillery is situated at the Powerscourt Estate south of Dublin. Equipped with three pot stills, distillation started in 2018 and a visitor centre was opened in 2019. A range of sourced whiskies are released under the name Fercullen and in September 2022 Fercullen Falls (a 50/50 blend of single malt and grain) was the first to use whiskey distilled on site. This was followed in summer 2024 by a single malt, bottled at cask strength and produced entirely on site. The company has recently run into financial difficulties and a receiver was appointed in June 2025.

Shed Distillery, The

Drumshanbo, Co. Leitrim, founded in 2014

thesheddistillery.com

Founded by entrepreneur P J Rigney, the distillery is equipped with five pot stills, three column stills and six washbacks. The focus is triple distilled single pot still whiskey but Drumshanbo gin has been on the market for years. The first whiskey distillation was in late 2014 and in 2019 the 5 year old Drumshanbo Single Pot Still was released. One of the latest versions, in early 2025, was a 7 year old matured in tawny port casks.

Slane Distillery

Slane, Co. Meath, founded in 2017

slaneirishwhiskey.com

The Conyngham family established a whiskey brand which became popular in the USA. The whiskey was produced at Cooleys but the family decided to start their own distillery. After an unsuccesful partnership with Camus, Brown-Forman stepped in and took over the entire project in 2015. Equipped with three copper pot stills and six column stills the distillery started production in 2018 and three types of whiskey are produced; single malt, single pot still and grain whiskey. The current range is Triple Casked Blend, Batch Strength, Special Edition and Extra Sherry Wood - the first release in the Wood Series.

Tipperary Boutique Distillery

Clonmel, Co. Tipperary, founded in 2020

tipperarydistillery.ie

Jennifer Nickerson and her husband Liam Ahearn chose the Ahearn family farm, Ballindoney, as the spot for their distillery. Sourced whiskey was released from early on and in November 2020, the first whiskey made from their own barley and distilled at another Irish distillery was released. Simultaneously, the owners made their first distillation at their own distillery which is equipped with four stills from Hoga in Portugal. More expressions distilled at other distilleries have followed.

Isle of Man

Fynoderee

Ramsey, Isle of Man, founded in 2017

fynoderee.com

Founded by local couple Paul and Tiffany Kerruish the distillery has so far focused on gin and rum. While trials making malt whisky started already in 2018, the first expression is not due until 2026.

Manx Whisky Company

Baldrine, Isle of Man, founded in 2020

manxwhisky.com

Magnus Grinneback moved from Sweden to the Isle of Man in 2018. With a background in beermaking, he started a micro distillery two years later.The small distillery is old school with floor malting, direct fired stills and wormtubs. The first whisky (a PX single cask) was released in December 2023 and was followed by a second in September 2024 and a third in May 2025.

Italy

Puni Destillerie

Glurns, South Tyrol, founded in 2012

puni.com

Located in South Tyrol this was the first designated whisky distillery in Italy. Apart from a spectacular distillery design, the combination of three malted cereals in the recipe – barley, rye and wheat – is unusual. The distillery is equipped with five washbacks and one pair of stills. The first single malt was released in 2015 and the core range consists of Sole (two years in ex-bourbon and two years in PX casks), Gold (5 years in ex-bourbon) and Vina (5 years in marsala casks). Recent limited releases include the fifth version of Arte, a 6 year old matured in ex-Islay casks and the fourth edition of Aura, a 7 year old matured in ex-Pinot Grigio casks.

Other distilleries in Italy

Exmu Brewery & Distillery

Sassari, founded in 2019

birrificioexmu.it

A Sardinian brewery expanding into whisky as well as gin. Growing their own barley and using long fermentation times, they recently launched the 3 year old Sassari single malt.

Poli Distillery

Schiavon, founded in 1898

poligrappa.com

A family-owned distillery with a large visitor centre mainly focusing on grappa. Recently two 5 year old single malt whiskies have been added to the range; the lightly peated Conclave and Segretario di Stato finished in Amarone casks.

Psenner Destillerie

Tramin, founded in 1947 (whisky since 2013)

psenner.com

Originally a producer of fruit spirits and grappa. Their first release of the single malt eRètico appeared in 2016 and currently there are two 7 year olds as well as a Distillery Cut available at the distillery.

St Urban Distillery

Girlan, founded in 2008

st-urban.it

Main products are spirits made from their own fruits. The first single malt from this distillery in South Tyrol appeared in 2019, matured in Gewürztraminer casks.

Silvio Carta

Zeddiani, founded in 1952 (distilled spirits since 2013)

silviocarta.it

Starting as wine producers the family later added a distillery to their Sardinian estate. The 4 year old malt whisky has been matured in casks made from chestnut.

Strada Ferrata Distillery

Seregno, founded in 2020

stradaferrata.xyz

The founders, all with a long experience of making beer, made their first distillation early 2021. The process involves long fermentations and unconventional malts and yeasts. Their first single malt was released in October 2024.

Villa de Varda

Mezzolombardo, founded in early 19th century

villadevarda.com

The Dolzan family has been distilling spirits for 6 generations in the Dolomites. In recent years three inQuota single malts have been added to the range, one of them finished in casks made from spruce.

The Netherlands

Zuidam Distillers

Baarle Nassau, founded in 1974 (whisky since 1996)

zuidam.eu

Started as a traditional, family distillery producing liqueurs, genever, gin and vodka the company is today managed by Patrick van Zuidam. It has also become the distillery that has defined Dutch whisky at its best in the world. The first release of the Millstone single malt was bottled in 2007 as a 5 year old. The current, substantial range includes a 5 year old which comes in both peated and unpeated versions, Peated American Oak, American Oak 10 years, French Oak 10 years, Sherry Oak 12 years and PX Cask 1999. Apart from single malts there is also the Millstone 100 Rye which is bottled at 50%, its younger sibling 92 Rye and the limited 10 year old Founder´s Reserve. Recent limited expressions include a 5 year old, heavily peated whisky matured in palo cortado sherry casks which was launched in June 2024. The oldest release so far, in December 2023, was a 27 year old matured in American oak. Two more stills from Forsyths were commissioned in 2020 and the distillery has also started to grow their own barley and rye at a nearby farm.

Other distilleries in The Netherlands

Bus Whisky

Loosbroek, founded in 2015

buswhisky.com

An estate distillery using barley from their own fields. The whisky starts the maturation in ex-bourbon and may then receive a finish in other types of casks. The first whisky appeared in 2019 and the latest release, matured in a moscatel quarter cask, appeared in 2025.

Cley Distillery

Rotterdam, founded in 2015

cleywhisky.com

The triple distilled Cley whisky is matured in ex-bourbon

Patrick van Zuidam, owner of the best know whisky distillery in The Netherlands, Zuidam Distillers

and finished in virgin American oak. Both single malts and combinations of malt and rye are bottled. One of the latest was a 4 year old finished in Islay casks.

Den Hool Distillery

Holsloot, founded in 2015

denhoolwhisky.nl

Originally a farm, the owners started brewing beer in the late 1990s. For the first few years the wash was sent to Zuidam Distillers for distillation into whisky. The first release of Veenhar single malt was in 2016 and the first to have been produced entirely at the distillery appeared in 2023. It was a 7 year old matured in a combination of new and first refill American oak and PX sherry.

Drumlin Distillery

Havelte, founded in 2018

drumlindistillery.com

The first release from this new distillery was a gin but both malt whisky and rye are also produced. In January 2023, the first bottling of Cromlech single malt (a 3 year old distilled in 2019) appeared and this has been followed by more releases.

Hemel Brewery and Distillery, De

Nijmegen, founded in 1983

brouwerijdehemel.nl

Situated in a 12th century monastery, a brewery has now been complemented by a distillery. The two releases of Anima whisky are technically "Bierbrands", i. e. distilled from a hopped beer.

Horstman Distillery

Losser, founded in 2000

distilleerderijhorstman.nl

Producers of genever and whisky, the distillery released their first bottling in 2016. The current single malt range includes a 5 year old matured in port casks and Whisky Blau – a 9 year old matured in sherry casks.

Ijsvogel Distillery, De

Arcen, founded in 2012

ijsvogel.com

A huge variety of different spirits are distilled including malt whisky. The first whisky was bottled in 2015 and the latest, released in March 2025, was a 4 year old matured in oloroso casks.

Kalkwijck Distillers

Vroomshoop, founded in 2009

kalkwijckdistillers.nl

The distillery is equipped with a 300 litre pot still with a column attached. In 2015, the first Eastmoor single malt was released as a 3 year old and in 2023 batch 9 appeared. Another range is named Higgledy Piggledy - made up of grain, rye and corn whiskies.

Lepelaar Distillery

Texel, founded in 2009 (whisky since 2014)

delepelaartexel.nl

This distillery, producing single malt as well as grain whisky and genever, is a part of a larger crafts centre. A first launch of Texelse Whisky was made for the crowd funders in 2018 and was later followed a number of general releases.

Stokerij Sculte

Ootmarsum, founded in 2004 (whisky since 2011)

stokerijsculte.nl

The distillery is equipped with a 500 litre stainless steel mashtun, 4 stainless steel washbacks and two stills. The first Sculte Twentse Whisky was released in 2014 and has been followed by a number of different releases. The 11th bottling appeared in December 2025.

Us Heit Distillery

Bolsward, founded in 2002

usheit.com

Frysk Hynder was the first Dutch whisky and made its debut in 2005 at 3 years of age. The barley is grown in the surrounding area and malted at the distillery. The whisky (3 to 5 years old) is matured in a variety of casks and there is also a cask strength version.

Northern Ireland

Bushmill´s Distillery

Bushmills, Co. Antrim, founded in 1784

bushmills.com

This, the third biggest of the Irish distilleries after Midleton and Great Northern, was sold by Pernod Ricard to Diageo in 2005 who, in turn, sold it to Proximo (producer of the José Cuervo tequila) in 2014. The new owners applied for a planning permission to expand the capacity and also to build another 29 warehouses over the next two decades on adjacent farmland. The local council gave the green light in 2019 and in spring 2023 a second distillery on the site, named Causeway Distillery, was opened. Equipped with one mash tun, eight washbacks and ten stills, it means that Bushmills has doubled their capacity to 9 million litres. Bushmills is the third most sold Irish whiskey after Jameson and Tullamore D.E.W. and in 2024 it sold just over 13 million bottles.

At Bushmill´s, triple distilled single malt whiskey is produced. For their range of blended whiskies, the grain part is brought in from Midleton Distillery. The blended range consists of Bushmill´s Original, Black Bush and Red Bush. In April 2021 two Bushmills Original Cask Finish were released. The single malt part of the two whiskies had been finished in American oak and rum respectively.

The core range of Bushmill´s single malts consists of a 10 year old, a 16 year old Triple Wood with a finish in Port pipes and a 21 year old finished in Madeira casks for two years. In April 2024 a 14 year old finished in Malaga wine casks was added. Two limited small batch expressions appeared in April 2023; a 25 year old with 21 years in ruby port pipes and a 30 year old with a 16 year long second maturation in PX sherry butts. In 2020 the limited The Causeway Collection appeared where, over the years, a number of single malts that have been finished in different casks are bottled at cask strength. The recent Private Reserve series saw a second wave in early 2025 when four expressions received a third maturation in different casks including Amarone, Moscatel, Bordeaux and Tequila. Recent limited expressions also include the 36 year old Hill Street Edition, the oldest expression of Bushmills at the time. This record was broken though in March 2025 when the 46 year old Secrets of the River Bush was released. Not only was it the oldest bottling of Bushmill´s but also the world´s oldest Irish single malt! Finally there is a recent new expression for travel retail - the 18 year old Three Wood aged in a combination of bourbon, sherry and Colheita port casks..

Other distilleries in Northern Ireland

Copeland Distillery

Donaghadee, Co. Down, founded in 2016

copelanddistillery.com

In early 2019, the distillery moved from Saintfield 20 kilometres south of Belfast to Donaghadee by the coast. Already established as a gin producer, the owners filled their first cask of malt whiskey in November 2019 and in December 2024 the double distilled The Founder´s Release, matured in a bourbon cask, was launched.

Echlinville Distillery

Kircubbin, Co. Down, founded in 2013

echlinville.com

Founded by Shane Braniff the distillery, having its own floor maltings, has been expanded over the years and a visitor centre has also been opened. In order to increase the maltings to an industrial scale, the former Ards Maltings in Newtownards was recently bought to be restored. Apart from single pot still and single malt whiskey, vodka and gin is also produced. Using sourced whiskey Braniff has revived the old Dunville´s brand of blended whiskey and included also single malt. The Matt D´Arcy brand has also been added to their range. The first whiskeys from their own distillation (The Beginning), a single malt and a single pot still both 7 years old, were released in autumn 2024.

Glenwinny Distillery

Lisbellow, Co. Fermanagh, founded in 2023

glenwinny.com

A family run micro distillery located in their own country inn The Dog and the Duck near Enniskillen and Lough Erne. In 2023 poitín was released vnd the first malt whiskey is expected in 2026.

Hinch Distillery

Ballynahinch, Co. Down, founded in 2020

hinchdistillery.com

The owner of Chateau de La Ligne in Bordeaux, Terry Cross, is the founder of this distillery within the grounds of Killaney Lodge just south of Belfast. A wide range of sourced whiskies were launched early on. The covid pandemic delayed the opening of the distillery but in November 2020, the first distillation was made. The distillery, practising triple distillation, is equipped with three pot stills (10,000 l, 5,500 l and 2,500 l).

Killowen Distillery

Newry, Co. Down, founded in 2017

killowendistillery.com

The distillery started producing gin in 2017 and in 2019 the first pot still whiskey was distilled. The spirit is double distilled and peated and fermentation takes place in open top wash backs for a week or longer. The two stills (one attached with a column) are direct heated and worm tub condensers are used. In 2019 the first in a range of sourced whiskeys appeared and in 2022 it was time for their first whiskey release from their own distillation. Under the name Barántúil, two single cask single pot still whiskeys were launched and in December 2024 a 5 year old Barántúil finished in a palo cortado cask was released. There is also a 5 year old single malt finished in rum casks and sherry butts in the range.

McConnell´s Distillery

Belfast, Co. Antrim, founded in 2023

mcconnellsirishwhisky.com

More than a decade ago it was announced that a distillery would be built in the old Crumlin Road Gaol jail. That never materialised and a group of American investors took over the £25m project. Three stills were installed in 2023 and the first cask was filled in July 2024. The distillery has a capacity of 500,000 litres of pure alcohol and in anticipation of the first whiskey from their own production, a sourced whiskey is sold under the name McConnell's – a historic whiskey brand from Belfast.

Mourne Dew Distillery

Warrenpoint, Co. Down, founded in 2018

mournedew.com

The distillery is unusually equipped with two vacuum stills as well as a conventional 500 litre hybrid still. The first products to be launched were poitin, gin and vodka but recently their triple distilled whiskey has been launched both in way of a blend as well as a single malt.

Rademon Estate Distillery

Downpatrick, Co. Down, founded in 2012

shortcrosswhiskey.com

Shortcross gin became a success for Rademon very quickly and in 2015 the production was expanded into whiskey, both single malt and single pot still. The capacity of the distillery was increased in 2018 with a new gin still as well as a new still for the whiskey production. The first release of a Shortcross single malt was a 5 year old in December 2021 which had been matured in Bordeaux red wines casks and finished in chinquapin oak. It has since been followed by rye & malt, peated single malt and single pot still.

Titanic Distillers

Belfast, Co. Antrim, founded in 2022

titanicdistillers.com

In 1911 The Titanic was moved from the ship builder Harland & Wolff to the newly constructed Thompson Dry Dock for the final fitting. More than hundred years later a distillery has been constructed in the old pump-house. Equipped with three copper pot stills from Forsyth, the distillery was opened to visitors in March 2023 and started distilling in early August. Whisky and vodka under the brand Titanic has been on the market for some time, distilled at the Great Northern Distillery. In February 2025 the distillery secured a £5m equity investment from Whiterock Finance.

Wild Atlantic Distillery

Aghyaran, Co. Tyrone, founded in 2019

wildatlanticdistillery.ie

Founded by brothers-in-law Brian Ash and Jim Nash the distillery made their first trials at whiskey in 2018 and then moved on to producing gin and vodka. Whisky was always in the plans though and late 2020 a pot still was installed. With no sourced whiskeys released underway their inaugural bottling, the limited Islandmen, appeared in December 2024.

Norway

Det Norske Brenneri

Grimstad, founded in 1952 (whisky since 2009)

eiktyrnewhisky.com

Founded in 1952 the company mainly produced wine from apples and other fruits. Whisky production started in 2009 and in 2012, Audny, the first single malt produced in Norway was launched. Under the name Eiktyrne a total of 17 expressions have been released so far.

Myken Distillery

Myken, founded in 2014

mykendestilleri.no

Situated on Myken, a group of islands in the Atlantic ocean, 32 kilometres from mainland Norway. Both peated and unpeated whisky is produced. The first launch of their single malt was in 2018. One of the latest releases, in November 2024, was the 4 year old Autumn Gale matured in a combination of sherry and bourbon.

Other distilleries in Norway

Anora (former Arcus)

Gjelleråsen, founded in 1996 (whisky since 2009)

arcus.no

Anora is the biggest supplier and producer of wine and spirits in Norway. The first whisky produced by the distillery was launched in 2013. Under the name Gjoleid, three whiskies made from malted barley and malted wheat have been released. One of the latest expressions was the 10 year old Mesterens Triple Cask.

Aurora Spirit

Tromsö, founded in 2016

bivrost.com

At 69.39^{O}N, Aurora is the northernmost distillery in the world. In the beginning the mash was bought from a brewery but since 2021 they do the mashing inhouse. Apart from single malt whisky, the owners also produce gin, vodka and aquavit. All their products are sold under the name Bivrost and a number of limited expressions occured until late 2024 when Yggdrasil, matured in oloroso casks, appeared as the first core expression.

Berentsen Distillery

Egersund, founded in 1895 (whisky since 2018)

berentsens.no

A producer of mineral water for more than 100 years, the company has started producing beer and spirits in recent years. By way of a £5m investment and using stills from Arnold Holstein in Germany the owners hope to become one of the biggest whisky producers in Norway. In March 2023 the inaugural 3 year old Vardberg Born single malt bottled at cask strength was released. It was later followed by a version bottled at 48% as well as an oloroso single cask.

Feddie Ocean Distillery

Island of Fedje, founded in 2019

feddiedistillery.no

On Fedje, the most westerly, populated island in Norway, an already existing brewery was complemented by a distillery in 2019 and production of organic whisky started. Founded by Anne Koppang, the distillery is owned by more than 100 investors. The bigger goal for the company is to contribute to the island by way of investments and inspiration. The first bottling of their whisky, a 4 year old matured in a combination of bourbon and oloroso casks, appeared in November 2024.

Klostergården Distillery

Tautra, founded in 2017

klostergardentautra.no

Equipped with two copper stills from Hoga in Portugal (1,000 and 600 litres repectively), this distillery is situated on the island of Tautra in the Trondheim fiord. There is also a brewery, hotel, restaurant and shop. No official bottling has yet been released.

Oss Craft Distillery

Flesland, founded in 2016

osscraft.no

Specialising in gin and other spirits made from herbs and botanicals, the distillery has already launched a range of spirits under the name Bareksten. In autumn 2024 the first single malt was released - the 7 year old One Ocean Expedition.

Poland

Piasecki Distillery

Stawiguda, founded in 1964 (whisky since 2014)

mazurskiemiody.pl/destylarnia/

A wide range of spirits are produced and recently also malt whisky. The 3 year old Langlander was released in 2017 and there is also Bee Keeper blended whisky.

Karczma Wrzos

Ustrón, whisky since 2019

karczma-wrzos.pl

A combination of a restaurant, brewery and distillery producing a variety of spirits including whisky. The 3 year old Glen Vistula, matured in virgin oak, was released in December 2022 and it was followed by a 5 year old smoky expression in August 2025.

Legacy Distillery

Oborniki, founded in 2021

legacydestillery.com.pl

Founded by Piotr Dubisz the distillery has been producing whisky at a temporary location since 2023 but have plans to move to a new site in 2025. Sourced whiskey from Ireland that have been further matured and finished in Poland are already in the range.

Millside Distillery

Debrzno, founded in 2023

millside.pl

What started in 2013 as a whisky shop (and later an independent bottler) has recently been complemented with a distillery. It is equipped with a 1,000 litre wash still, a 500 litre spirit still and a column still for making vodka. Golden Promise and peated Laureate barley are used for the whisky and the distillery started production in January 2025.

Silesia Distillery

Bieruń, founded in 2021

silesiadistillery.com

Founded by three people who had previously released independent bottlings. Equipped with 350 litre pot still with a column the owners plan to release their first malt whisky, finished in a marsala cask, in December 2025.

Portugal

Venakki Distillery

Alpiarça, founded in 2012

portuguesewhisky.com

Founded by Jay Venakki the distillery produces a wide range of spirits including malt whisky. They are using Spanish grain for the whisky and every step of the production is carried out on site. Their Woodwork single malts whiskies start their maturation in ex-bourbon barrels and are then finished in a variety of different Portuguese wine casks. A range of blended whisky named The Portuguese has also been added.

Romania

Carpathian Distillery

Ilfov, founded in 2017

carpathian-singlemalt.com

Part of the Alexandrion Group, the largest wine producer in the country, the malt whisky is produced in two traditional pot stills and often matured in casks from their own winery. The master distiller is Allan Anderson with a long career in the Scottish and Irish whisky industry. The first whisky was released in 2022 and the range is now quite substantial.

Slovakia

Nestville Distillery

Hniezdne, founded in 2008

nestville.sk

The distillery is owned by BGV and focuses mainly on production of ethanol and grain alcohol for industrial use. Whisky production started in 2008 and in 2012 the first Nestville whisky, a blend, was released as a three year old. The first single malt was released in 2018 and was followed my more including single casks.

Slovenia

Broken Bones Distillery

Ljubljana, founded in 2016

brokenbones.si

A family owned craft distillery producing gin and whisky. All of their whiskies are matured in casks made of American or Slovenian oak and released in small batches without chill filtration or artificial colouring. The range consists of the unpeated This Whisky, the lightly peated Kika and a number of cask strength versions.

Spain

Distilerio Molino del Arco

Segovia, founded in 1959

dyc.es

Equipped with six copper pot stills, the distillery has the capacity for producing eight million litres of grain whisky and two million litres of malt whisky per year. The big seller when it comes to whiskies is a blend simply called DYC which is around 4 years old. It is supplemented by an 8 year old blend and also by DYC Pure Malt, a blend of malt from the distillery and from Scottish distilleries. A new range called Colección Maestros Destiladores was launched in 2018 with a 12 year old blend as the first release. This was followed by a 20 year old single barrel in 2022.

Other distilleries in Spain

Acha, Destilerias

Àlava, founded in 1831 (whisky since 2006)

destileriasacha.com

One of the oldest distilleries in Spain, the production of vermouth and pacharán has been augmented by whisky production in recent years. The Ibar 3 and 8 year old malt whiskies have been made with 25% malted barley and 75% unmalted barley. All barley is local and smoked using heather roots.

Basque Moonshiners

Álava, founded in 2014

basquemoonshiners.es

Producing a variety of spirits, including vodka made from potatoes, there is also malt whisky on the agenda. Their main seller, Agot Single Malt, appeared in 2020 and there is also the blended malt Bikkun (including malts from Scotland) in the range.

Liber, Destilerias

Padul, Granada, founded in 2001

destileriasliber.com

Apart from whisky, the distillery produces rum, marc, gin and vodka. Maturation takes place in PX sherry casks that have been used in a solera system for 20-30 years. Whiskies include the 5 year old single malt Embrujo de Granada and the 13 year old Liber. Single casks aged 12-16 years have been released in small numbers.

Picos de Cabariezo

Cabezón de Liébana, founded in 2000

vinosylicorespicos.es

A young winery and distillery in Cantabria with liqueurs, gin, orujo (the Spanish form of grappa) and, more recently, malt whisky on their agenda. Their single malt, matured in sherry casks, is sold under the name AS de Picos.

Sweden

High Coast Distillery (former BOX Distillery)

Bjärtrå, founded in 2010

highcoastwhisky.se

Set in buildings from the 19th century, the distillery started production in November 2010 and in 2018 it was expanded. The equipment now consists of a semilauter mash tun with a capacity of 1,5 tonnes, seven stainless steel washbacks, two wash stills (3,800 litres) and two spirit stills (2,500 litres). The distillery makes two types of whisky – fruity/unpeated and peated. With a slow distillation, the flavour of the spirit is also impacted by the effective condensation using 2-6°C water from a nearby river. A fermentation time of 72-96 hours also affects the character. The first whisky was released in 2014 and three years later the first core expression, Dàlvve, was launched. This was replaced in 2019 by the current core range; Timmer, Hav, Älv and Berg. Recent ranges include the Mountains where the local history and geography plays a major part. There is also a small batch range (currently with batch 37 released) with bottlings for select markets as well as limited bottlings for their yearly festival on site.

Mackmyra Svensk Whisky

Valbo, founded in 1999

mackmyra.com

Mackmyra´s first distillery was built in 1999 and in 2012 a new distillery was built a few miles from the first one. The construction is quite extraordinary and with its 37 metre structure, it is one of the tallest distilleries in the world. The first release was in 2006 and the distillery now has three core expressions; Svensk Ek, the peated Svensk Rök and Mack. A range of limited editions called Moment was introduced in 2010 by the Master Blender, Angela D`Orazio who left the company in 2021. In autumn 2024 the company filed for bankruptcy but was later bought out by one of the previous owners (who died in July 2025) and an external company. Currently under reconstruction, the distillery launched Fusion, with a maturation in five different types of casks, in April 2025.

Spirit of Hven

Hven, founded in 2007

hven.com

The distillery, situated on the island of Hven right between Sweden and Denmark, was founded by Henric Molin, a trained chemist. It is equipped with a 0,5 ton mash tun, six washbacks made of stainless steel, one wash still, one spirit still and a designated gin still. Apart from that, a unique wooden Coffey still has been installed to be used mainly for distillation of rye and corn. Besides whisky, other products include rum made from sugar beet, vodka, gin and aquavit. For a couple of years there have been rumours that the distillery intend to move the production to the mainland while still using barley and other grains grown on the island. So far though nothing has happened. Their first whisky was the lightly peated Urania, released in 2012 and the first core expression, Tycho´s Star, was launched in 2015. New and innovative bottlings include Sweden´s first rye whisky, Hvenus Rye, and Mercurious, the first whisky in Sweden made predominantly (88%) from corn. The first Swedish blended whisky appeared in spring 2022.

Smögen Whisky

Hunnebostrand, founded in 2010

smogenwhisky.se

Founded by Pär Caldenby, the distillery is equipped with three washbacks, a 900 litre wash still and a 600 litre spirit still. An interesting addition to the equipment setup was made in 2018 when worm tubs were installed. Heavily peated malt is imported from Scotland and the aim is to produce an Islay-type of whisky. The first release from the distillery was the 3 year old Primör in 2014. This has over the years been followed by many limited releases, mostly single casks. In 2020 a wider release of a 6 year old "100 proof" from sherry seasoned quarter casks appeared. Recent, limited releases to celebrate the distillery´s 15th anniversary include two 10 year olds, both matured in small casks made from Swedish oak but with different toasting levels.

Agitator Whiskymakare

Arboga, founded in 2017

agitatorwhisky.se

The owners have chosen some rather unusual techniques in the production. Water is added during the milling and the fermented wash is split in half and distributed to the two pairs of stills. The stills operate under vacuum which is extremely rare in pot still whisky making. The distillery is experimenting with different kinds of grain apart from barley. The capacity is 500,000 litres of pure alcohol and the first distillation was made in 2018. The inaugural bottling appeared in 2021 and the current core range consists of The Swedish Malt, The Swedish Blend, Chestnut Cask, Rye Rye, Single Malt Rök and Blind Seal Straight Rye. A special, limited series (Argument) highlights the experimental side of the distillery where whiskies will have matured in unusual cask types such as maple syrup or mezcal. Finally, the Evidens range are whiskies filled into casks at 55% rather than the typical 63,5%.

Other distilleries in Sweden

Gammelstilla Whisky

Torsåker, founded in 2005

gammelstillawhisky.se

Built by the owners, the annual capacity is 20,000 litres per year. The first, limited release for shareholders was in 2017 with a general release in 2018 of the 4 year old Jern. The most recent release in May 2025 was "2025" followed by Jubilar, a 10 year old matured in a burgundy cask.

Gotland Whisky

Romakloster, founded in 2011

gotlandwhisky.se, isleoflime.com

The distillery is equipped with a 1,600 litre wash still and a 900 litre spirit still. Local barley is ecologically grown and part of it is malted on site. Unpeated and peated whisky is produced and the first launch of Isle of Lime single malt was in 2017. Apart from a core expression (Isle of Lime Gotland) recent releases in 2024 include the 7 year old Stainkalm with a maturation in bourbon casks and new oak and the 10 year old Bläse matured in bourbon casks.

Lihnell´s Distillery (former Bergslagens Destilleri)

Örebro, founded in 2014 (whisky since 2019)

lihnells.se

A family-owned distillery equipped with one Holstein still and four washbacks producing a number of different spirits including

Every year 20,000 visitors come to High Coast Distillery

malt whisky. In 2016 the company bought the whisky stock from the closed Grythyttans distillery and have since then released a vast number of expressions. The first bottling from their own production has not yet appeared. In 2024 the distillery changed its name and moved to a new location nearby.

Nordmarkens Destilleri

Årjäng, founded in 2014 (whisky since 2018)

nordmarkensdestilleri.se

In 2015 the owners produced newmake spirit at another Swedish distillery and following maturation at Nordmarken, Traukiol was released in 2021 and was followed by more releases. The first whisky distillation on their own premises, where gin and aqvavit are also produced, was in summer 2018 and both peated and unpeated malt spirit is distilled.

Norrtelje Brenneri

Norrtälje, founded in 2002 (whisky since 2009)

norrteljebrenneri.se

The production consists mainly of spirits from fruits and berries. Since 2009, a single malt whisky from ecologically grown barley is also produced. The first bottling was released in summer 2015 and the latest was a PX sherry matured in 2022.

Tevsjö Destilleri

Järvsö, founded in 2012 (whisky since 2014)

tevsjodestilleri.se

The owners are primarily focused on distillation of aquavit and other white spirits but whisky production is also included. In December 2019 the first malt whisky and "bourbon" were released. The distillery has recently expanded their capacity.

Vattudalen Whisky

Äspnäs, founded in 2016

vattudalenwhisky.com

A small distillery producing both gin and vodka apart from whisky. The first whisky release was a rye and in February 2024 it was time for the first single malt made from barley. Aged for five years in ex-bourbon casks and with a two year finish in ex-sauternes casks it was followed in autumn 2024 and May 2025 by two peated expressions.

Switzerland

Luchs & Hase (formerly known as Käsers Schloss)

Elfingen, Aargau, founded in 2001

luchsundhase.ch

The first whisky reached the market in 2004. under the name Castle Hill. Since then the range has been expanded. In 2023 the distillery changed its name to Luchs & Hase and the entire range was revamped. Today there are ´180 Grad´, an 8 year old with a 2 year madeira finish, the smoky ´Rauchzeichen´, ´Fassgeschichten´ with a maturation in multiple casks and ´Best of Vintage´ where the latest was a 12 year old from new, toasted French oak.

Brauerei Locher

Appenzell, founded in 1886 (whisky since 1999)

saentismalt.com

The distillery uses old beer casks for the maturation, sometimes with a finish in other types of casks. The core range consists of three expressions; Himmelberg, Kamor and Sigel. There is also a wide range of limited bottlings with the Jubiläums Edition - 10 Jahre Whiskytrek in July 2025 being one of the latest.

Langatun Distillery

Langenthal, Bern, founded in 2007

langatun.ch

The distillery was built under the same roof as a brewery and the single malts include Old Deer, Old Bear and the smoky Old Crow and Old Wolf. Other bottlings are Old Eagle rye, Old Mustang "bourbon" and the organic Old Woodpecker. Recent limited releases include a 6 year old Langatun in November 2024, matured in chardonnay casks and finished in a nerello mascalese red wine cask.

Other distilleries in Switzerland

Etter Distillerie

Zug, founded in 1870 (whisky since 2007)

etter-distillerie.ch

The main produce from this distillery is eau de vie from various fruits and berries but whisky production commenced in 2007. The first release of Johnett Single Malt was made in 2010 and in June 2022 a smoky 10 year old appeared.

The foundation of Penderyn distillery in 2000 eventually resulted in an entire new whisky category - Welsh Whisky

Humbel Brennerei

Stetten, Aargau, founded in 2004

humbel.ch

With a history going back to 1918, the distillery uses a wash from the brewery Unser Bier in Basel to produce their ValeReuss Whisky.

Lüthy, Bauernhofbrennerei

Muhen, Aargau, founded in 1997 (whisky since 2005)

brennerei-luethy.ch

The distillery is equipped with its own malting floor and the first single malt was Insel-Whisky in 2008. Several releases have since followed. Starting in 2010, the yearly bottling was given the name Herr Lüthy and the 14th release, matured in a combination ex-bourbon and a Blauburgunder barrique, was released in 2023.

Macardo Distillery

Amlikon-Bissegg, Thurgau, founded in 2007

macardo.ch

Built on a former cheese factory, the distillery moved to new premises in 2020. The core single malt, without age statement but typically 10 years old, is bottled at 42%. One of the latest, limited releases was The Life Cycle of a Cask Chapter Two, a cask strength expression maured in port wine casks.

Malt Age Distillery

Genève, founded in 2016

maltage.ch

Founded by five friends in the spirits/beer industry, this represents the first Genève malt whisky. Made from local barley and distilled in a small copper still, the first releases appeared in 2022 and were followed by more.

Rugen Distillery

Interlaken, Bern, founded in 2010

rugenbraeu.ch

An old brewery which was later expanded with a distillery. The brand name is Swiss Mountain and the core range consists of Classic, Double Barrel and the 7 year old Rock Label. A yearly expression is Ice Label where the latest edition in 2025 received a second maturation of 8 years at an altitude of 3,454 m.

Sempione Distillery

Brig-Glis, Valais, founded in 1976 (whisky since 2011)

sempione-distillery.ch

A family-owned distillery of fruits and berries but now focusing on whisky. Current single malts made from barley are Wallisky, Swiss Stone Eagle and the limited 10 year old Swiss Golden Eagle.

Z´Graggen Distillerie

Lauerz, Schwyz, founded in 1948

zgraggen.ch

Focusing on spirits distilled from fruits and berries, the owners also produce gin, vodka and whisky. The distillery is quite large, with a combined production of 400,000 litres per year. There are two single malts in the range – the 10 year old, smoky Bergsturz and Z´Graggen without age statement.

Zürcher, Spezialitätenbrennerei

Port, Bern, founded in 1954 (whisky from 2000)

lakeland-whisky.ch

The main focus of the distillery is specialising in various distillates of fruit, absinth and liqueur but a Lakeland single malt is also in the range. Since March 2024 there are two expressions, a 7 year old and a 13 year old, both matured in oloroso sherry casks.

Wales

Penderyn Distillery

Penderyn, founded in 2000

penderyn.wales

When Penderyn began producing in 2000, it was the first Welsh distillery in more than a hundred years. A new type of still, developed by David Faraday for Penderyn, differs from the Scottish and Irish procedures in that the whole process from wash to new make takes place in one single still producing a spirit at 92% abv. In 2013, a second still (almost a replica of the first still) was commissioned and in 2014, two traditional pot stills, as well as their own mashing equipment was installed.

In May 2021, the owners opened yet another distillery in Llandudno in north Wales. This is also equipped with the trademark Faraday still but production at the new distillery will be focused on production of peated single malt. The distillery has a visitor centre which the owners hope will attract 60,000 people yearly. In summer 2023, Copperworks Distillery, the third in the Penderyn group, opened in Swansea. This is the largest of the three bringing the combined capacity to 900,000 litres of alcohol. It is equipped with two Faraday stills and one pair of traditional pot stills. Penderyn has been influential advocating for a GI status (Geographical Indication) for Welsh whisky and this became fruitious in summer 2023. The first single malt was launched in 2004. The core range today is divided into two groups. Dragon consists of the Madeira finished Legend, Myth which is fully bourbon matured and Celt with a peated finish. The other range is Gold with Madeira, Peated, Portwood, Sherrywood and Rich Oak. The smoky notes from the distillery´s peated expressions comes from maturation in ex-Islay casks. A limited range is Icons of Wales where the 12th edition, Copperopolis, was released in 2025. The name refers to the huge importance Swansea had from the 1720s going forward for the copper smelting in the UK and indeed in the world.

Other distilleries in Wales

Aber Falls Distillery

Abergwyngregyn, founded in 2017

aberfallsdistillery.com

While Aber Falls started producing and selling gin, malt whisky is also produced and in spring 2019, they distilled rye for the first time. Their inaugural, limited single malt was released in May 2021 followed by a core expression in August. In December 2024 the limited Distiller´s Cut matured in a manzanilla cask appeared..

Coles Distillery

Llanddarog, founded in 1999 (whisky since 2014)

coles.wales

A combination of an inn, brewery and distillery. Two single malts (both aged for more than five years) have so far been released.

Dà Mhile Distillery

Llandyssul, founded in 2013

damhile.co.uk

Focusing on gin and grain whisky, malt whisky is also produced in a wood fired still. In 2019, their first organic single malt was released – The Tarian Edition. Recent releases in 2024 include two single malts aged in madeira casks and tokaji casks repectively.

In The Welsh Wind

Tan-y-groes, founded in 2021

inthewelshwind.co.uk

The distillery started by launching several expressions of gin. Whisky made from local barley has been maturing in the warehouses for quite some time and in autumn 2024 the first and second release appeared and the third in August 2025

North America

USA

Westland Distillery

Seattle, Washington, founded in 2011

westlanddistillery.com

Until 2012, Westland was a medium sized craft distillery but the year after the owners moved to another location equipped with a 6,000 litre brewhouse, five 10,000 litre fermenters and two Vendome stills. The distillery capacity is now 260,000 litres per year. In 2017, global spirits giant Remy Cointreau bought Westland distillery. Sine the start the distillery has been focusing on local barley varieties and also local peat. In February 2024 Westland became a Certified B Corporation which indicates a company that meets very high standards for social and environmental impact. The core expression, aptly named Flagship Single Malt (introduced in 2013) is based on a 6-malt grain bill and has matured for a minimum of 40 months in a combination of five different types of casks. There is also the Cask Exploration range currently with a 5 year old red wine finish and a beer finish as some of the latest. A limited range called Outpost has been introduced in order to highlight the owners´ interest in exploring new frontiers of whiskey making. Currently there are three expressions; Garryana edition 9 where the native garry oak has been used for part of the maturation, Colere edition 4 which has been made using local two-row spring barley from Skagit Valley Malting and Solum edition 3 which gets its character from local peat.

Balcones Distillery

Waco, Texas, founded in 2008

balconesdistilling.com

Founded by Chip Tate who left the company in 2014. The same year, another four, small stills were installed. The big step though, was a completely new distillery which was built 5 blocks from the old site and distillation started in February 2016. The new distillery is equipped with two pairs of stills and five fermenters. In 2022 Diageo bought the company for an undisclosed sum. All of Balcones´ whisky is mashed, fermented and distilled on site and they were the first to use Hopi blue corn for distillation. The core range currently consists of five expressions; Texas 1 Single Malt, Lineage Single Malt, Baby Blue (made from blue corn), Texas Rye 100 Proof and the smoky Brimstone. Two recent, limited additions to the range are Mirador Eclipse Single Malt and Cataleja Single Malt. The latter had been made from Golden Promise barley and matured in a variety of casks including different sherry casks.

Stranahans Whiskey Distillery

Denver, Colorado, founded in 2003

stranahans.com

Founded by Jess Graber and George Stranahan, the distillery was bought by Proximo Spirits in 2010. The Classic expression was in 2021 replaced by Original made up of older whiskies. Before that, in 2020, the four year old Blue Peak, matured using a solera system, was launched together with the 10 year old Mountain Angel fully matured in new American oak. From the old range there is still Diamond Peak, a vatting of casks that are 6-9 years old, a Single Barrel and Sherry Cask. As usual there was a limited Snowflake edition (#27 Redcloud Peak) in December 2024 with influences of a range of casks including port and madeira.

Hood River Distillers

Hood River, Oregon, 1934

hrdspirits.com

Since the foundation, the company acts as importer, distiller, producer and bottler of all kinds of spirits. Some of the products are distilled in-house while others are sourced. The role in the single malt segment came through buying Clear Creek Distillery in 2014. Founded by Steve McCarthy in Portland in 1985, Clear Creek Distillery was the first to produce single malt whiskey in the USA. In December 2017, Clear Creek closed their distillery in Portland and moved to Hood River. The only single malt whiskey produced by the company is the peated McCarthy´s Oregon Single Malt available both as a 3 year old and as a 6 year old. There are also 6 year olds finished in PX casks and Oloroso casks respectively.

Jared Himstedt, Head Distiller at Balcones, checking out the inventory

Copper Fox Distillery

Sperryville and Williamsburg, Virginia, founded in 2000

copperfoxdistillery.com

The distillery moved to another site in 2006 and in November 2016, they opened up a second distillery in Williamsburg. They do their own floor malting of barley which is dried using smoke from selected fruitwood (apple and cherry). After mashing, fermentation and distillation, the spirit is filled into oak barrels, together with hand chipped and toasted chips of apple wood and oak wood. In 2019 the entire range was rebranded and the core single malt expressions consist of Original Single Malt, Peachwood Single Malt, Apple Brandy Barrel Finish and Port Style Barrel Finish.

St. George Distillery

Alameda, California, founded in 1982

stgeorgespirits.com

Founded by Jörg Rupf, who was in 1996 joined by Lance Winters as a distiller and co-owner. In 2005, the two were joined by Dave Smith who now has the sole responsibility for the whisky production. The main produce is based on eau-de-vie and a vodka named Hangar One. Whiskey production was picked up in 1996 and the first single malt appeared on the market in 1999. St. George Single Malt used to be sold as a three year old but nowadays comes to the market as a blend of whiskeys aged from 5 to 22 years! The latest release is Lot 25 in autumn 2025. In 2022 a 40th anniversary bottle was released. Introduced a few years ago there is also the single malt Baller, intended to be used in a highball, which has been finished in umeshu casks.

Westward Whiskey (House Spirits Distillery)

Portland, Oregon, founded in 2004

westwardwhiskey.com

In the early days, the main products for House Spirits used to be Aviation Gin and Krogstad Aquavit but with new equipment installed in 2015 they drastically increased whiskey capacity. In 2018, Diageo´s "spirits accelerator" Distill Ventures acquired a minority stake in the brand which helped expand the capacity even further. In April 2025 the company filed for Chapter 11 bankruptcy protection to restructure the business. The first three whiskies were released in 2009 and in 2012 it was time for the first, widely available single malt under the name of Westward American Single Malt. In autumn 2020 the brand was revamped and the core range now consists of Westward Original, a cask strength version of the same, Stout Cask, Pinot Noir Cask and Rum Cask. On top of that a huge number of limited releases occur from time to time. One of the latest (in February 2025) had been finished in stout casks from Fort George Brewery.

Corsair Distillery

Nashville, Tennessee, founded in 2008

corsairdistillery.com

The first distillery was opened up in Bowling Green, Kentucky followed two years later by one in Nashville, Tennessee. The Bowling Green operation was closed in 2019 but a much larger distillery was opened in Nashville in 2023. Corsair Distillery has always had a wide range of experimental whiskies. This changed in 2020 when the owners settled for both a new design of the bottles and a more comprehensive range. This now consists of Triple Smoke, a single malt smoked using cherry wood, beech wood and peat, Dark Rye made from malted rye and chocolate rye, Tennessee Single Malt and two gins - barreled and unbarreled.

Virginia Distillery

Lovingston, Virginia, 2008 (production started 2015)

vadistillery.com

The idea for the distillery was conceived in 2007. The copper pot stills arrived from Turkey in 2008 but following several changes in ownership, the first distillation didn´t take place until 2015. Their first single malt appeared in 2019 and the current core range (Courage & Conviction) consists of Signature Malt, Double Cask Reserve, Bourbon Cask, Cuvée Cask, Sherry Cask, Bourbon Single Cask, Cuvée Single Cask, Fino Sherry Single Cask, Oloroso Sherry Single Cask and PX Sherry Single Cask. There is also a range of different wood finishes as well as a limited range where one of the latest (February 2025) was a collaboration with Foothills Brewing.

Long Island Spirits

Baiting Hollow, New York, founded in 2007

lispirits.com

Long Island Spirits, founded by Rich Stabile, is the first distillery on the island since the 1800s. The starting point for The Pine Barrens Whisky, the first single malt from the distillery, is a finished ale with hops and all. The whisky was first released in 2012 and has later been followed by a cherrywood smoked version.

Great Wagon Road Distilling Co.

Charlotte, North Carolina, founded in 2014

gwrdistilling.com

The distillery started with a 15 litre still but moved to a new location in 2020 and is now equipped with a 3,000 litres Kothe still and in 2021 a second still was installed. The mash comes from a neighbouring brewery and the fermentation is made in-house. The first batch of the Rua Single Malt was launched in 2015 and was later complemented by Rua Gold.

Hamilton Distillers

Tucson, Arizona, founded in 2011

whiskeydelbac.com

Stephen Paul came up with the idea of drying barley over mesquite, instead of peat. The first bottlings of Del Bac single malt appeared in 2013 and they now have three core expressions – aged Mesquite smoked (Dorado), aged unsmoked (Classic) and Sentinel Straight Rye. Three limited but annual expressions are Frontera (PX finish), Normandie (calvados finished) and Ode to Islay (heavily mesquited and the latest edition finished in Sauternes casks). On top of that there is the Distiller´s Cut range available only in Arizona.

Deerhammer Distilling Company

Buena Vista, Colorado, founded in 2010

deerhammer.com

The location of the distillery at an altitude of 2,500 metres with drastic temperature fluctuations and virtually no humidity, has a huge impact on the maturation of the spirit. The owners released their first single malt in 2012. The current, and more matured range, is made up of American Single Malt, Port Cask Finished Single Malt, Pot Still Rye and Four Grain Straight Bourbon. In 2019, the first edition of a new series, Progeny, was released. The fourth release, in 2023, was the 5 year old Vino Verso with a two year second maturation in three types of casks from Carboy Winery.

Hillrock Estate Distillery

Ancram, New York, founded in 2011

hillrockdistillery.com

The distillery was expanded in 2019 with a new pot still, a lauter mash tun and more fermentation tanks. The owners also floor malt their own barley. The first release from the distillery in 2012 was the Solera Aged Bourbon. Since then the range has been expanded with a Single Malt and a Double Cask Rye. Current single malts include an oloroso and PX finish, the 9 year old Founders 1806 Collection #2 and Owner´s Special Reserve Triple Finish.

Santa Fe Spirits

Santa Fe, New Mexico, founded in 2010

santafespirits.com

Founded by Colin Keegan, one of the pioneers of American malt whisky, the distillery was sold in April 2024 to Stockwell Reserve, a cooperative of craft distilleries. The first release of an aged single malt whiskey, Colkegan, appeared in 2013 and was followed by more. In late 2024 the range was completely revamped and six different single malts are now sold under the name Santa Fe rather than Colkegan; Original Mesquite, Bottled-in-Bond, Cask Strength, Apple Brandy Cask Finished, PX and Unsmoked.

Copperworks Distilling Company

Seattle, Washington, founded in 2013

copperworksdistilling.com

The distillery is currently equipped with two, large copper pot stills for the whiskey production, one smaller pot still for the gin and one column still. A cornerstone of their production is the Five Malt recipe, blending pale malt with four caramelized malts. The first distillation was in 2014 and the first batch of the single malt was launched in 2016. A new core range was launched in summer 2024 consisting of Maltsmith (made from a 5-malt mashbill), Farmsmith (made from Washington barley) and Peatsmith (made with Washington peat). In December 2024 two limited releases appeared; the 4 year old Color Cask fully matured in a very unusual sherry cask and the 6 year old Whidbey´s Port Cask.

Rogue Ales & Spirits

Newport, Oregon, founded in 2009

rogue.com

The company consists of one brewery, two combined brewery/pubs and two distillery pubs scattered over Oregon, Washington and California. The main business is producing Rogue Ales but apart from whiskey - rum and gin are also distilled. The first malt whiskey, Dead Guy Whiskey, was launched in 2009 and is still in the core range. Later additions are two expressions that have been finished in stout casks and wine casks respectively. Another, limited, release is the very ligthly smoked Morimoto single malt.

High West Distillery

Park City, Utah, founded in 2007

highwest.com

Starting as a blender of sourced rye whiskies the company opened a distillery at Blue Sky Ranch in Wanship, Utah in 2015 and in 2016 Constellation Brands became new owners. The 2018 versions of Rendezvous Rye and Double Rye, were the first including whiskey from their own production. In 2019, the first single malt made entirely by themselves and named High Country, was released.

Sons of Liberty Spirits Co.

South Kingstown, Rhode Island, founded in 2010

drinksol.com

The distillery is equipped with a stainless steel mash tun, open top fermenters and a combined pot and column still. The two core expressions are Uprising American Whiskey made from a stout beer and Battle Cry made from a Belgian style ale. Both versions are also released as 5 to 6 year old single barrels and an oloroso matured grain and malt whiskey was the latest limited release.

Talnua Distillery

Arvada, Colorado, founded in 2017

talnua.com

The distillery is focusing on single pot still whiskey. That means, in their case, using a mashbill of 50% unmalted and 50% malted barley as well as practising triple distillation. The range is made up of Peated Cask, Continuum, Bourbon Cask & Stave and Virgin White Oak. There is also Heritage Selection which is a blend of single pot still and grain. Limited releases include Olde Saint´s Keep, Black Dog Batch and the Aries Series where the first expression had been matured in casks that had been smoked using Irish peat before filling them with newmake. In October 2024 a 6 year old bottled-in-bond single barrel was released.

Oak & Grist Distilling Co.

Black Mountain, North Carolina, founded in 2015

oakandgrist.com

The owners are focusing on whiskey made from locally grown and malted barley. The core single malt was later complemented by Descendent, a single malt matured in a combination of new American oak and used bourbon barrels, the 3 year old Origins from bourbon barrels and the limited Rum Cask Finish. Two of the founders are father and son Ed and Russell Dodson. Ed, with a 40 year plus track record in the Scotch whisky industry, was the distillery manager of Glen Moray until 2005.

Other distilleries in USA

10th Street Distillery

San José, California, founded in 2017

10thstreetdistillery.com

Inspired by a trip to Islay, Virag Saksena and Vishal Gauri went on to build their own distillery. So far they have released Peated Single Malt, STR Single Malt, Distiller´s Cut and a Port Cask and a recent limited release is the Triple Cask STR Single malt.

117 West Spirits

Vista, California, founded in 2018

117westspirits.com

Apart from gin, rum, bourbon, malted rye and a malt/wheat whiskey there are two single malts in the range - the 117° West California Single Malt made from pale, Munich and caramel malt and the the 117° West Coast Whiskey including crystal, chocolate and roasted barley.

1911 Established

La Fayette, New York, founded in 2009 (whisky since 2017)

1911established.com

What started five generations ago and became one of the most famous apple orchards in the USA, eventually grew into producing apple cider in 1979, vodka and gin in 2010 and whisky since 2017. Their 1911 American Single Malt is also available in an applewood smoked version.

Acre Distilling

Fort Worth, Texas, founded in 2015

acredistilling.com

The distillery produces gin, vodka, bourbon, rye and different versions of single malt. The core expression, Texas Single Malt, is complemented by Smoked Single Malt and a recent 5 year old finished in a Scotch Ale barrel.

Alley 6 Craft Distillery

Healdsburg, California, founded in 2014

alley6.com

A small craft distillery with rye whiskey as the main product. The first bottles were released in 2015 followed by a single malt in 2016. The owners are using direct fired stills and are experimenting with a range of different barley varieties.

Amalga Distillery

Juneau, Alaska, founded in 2017

amalgadistillery.com

The distillery uses a 250 gallon pot still from Vendome and they are also floor malting their own barley, some of it grown in Alaska. The first core single malt was released in 2020 and one of the latest, (batch 20) was finished in a cognac cask.

Andalusia Whiskey

Blanco, Texas, founded in 2016

andalusiawhiskey.com

Focusing on whiskey production the first single malts were released in 2016. Core expressions are the mesquite-smoked Stryker, the lightly peated Revenant Oak and Triple-Distilled. Later releases include Bottled-in-Bond and American Soldier.

Arizona Distilling Company

Mesa, Arizona, founded in 2012

azdistilling.com

The first release from the distillery was Copper City bourbon followed by Desert Durum made from wheat, Humphrey's, a single malt first released in 2014 and Copper City Straight Rye. The distillery moved to Mesa in late 2023.

ASW Distillery

Atlanta, Georgia, founded in 2016

aswdistillery.com

Equipped with two traditional Scottish copper pot stills the distillery also has three tasting rooms in Atlanta. Focus is on bourbon but a variety of single malts have also been released over the years.

Atelier Vie Distillery

New Orleans, Louisiana, founded in 2012

ateliervie.com

The first product was Riz - a whiskey made from Louisiana rice. Owner Jedd Haas then went on to distil also malt whiskey from barley and Louisiana Single Malt was first released in 2019.

Axe and the Oak Distillery

Colorado Springs, Colorado, founded in 2013

axeandtheoak.com

A combination of a distillery, bar and restaurant, Axe and the Oak have so far released both bourbon (including a recent 10 year old) and rye whiskey but there is also single malt maturing.

Bellemara Distillery

Hillsborough, New Jersey, 2021

bellemaradistillery.com

The distillery is focused on single malt whisky and the inaugural bottlings (including a single cask barrel strength) were released in June 2023 with more batches (including one peated) following.

Bendt Distilling Co. (former Witherspoon Distillery)

Lewisville, Texas, founded in 2011

bendtdistillingco.com

Originally named Wiherspoon, the distillery recently introduced a new core range with Straight Malt, Straight Bourbon and Straight Wheat. There is also the blended whiskey Bendt No. 5.

Black Heron

West Richland, Washington, founded in 2013

drinkblackheron.com

A combined winery and distillery with two single malt whiskies made from local grain (and some Scottish for the peated version) in the range as well as bourbon and other spirits.

Black Sheep Distillery

Prattsburg, New York, founded in 2021

blacksheepdistilleryny.com

With gin already released, Kim and Dean Massaro also have a bourbon, a rye and a single malt in the pipeline.

Bogue Sound Distillery

Bogue, North Carolina, founded in 2018

boguesounddistillery.com

The distillery is equipped with a 500-gallon still and produces gin, vodka, rye and bourbon. A single malt, to be released under the John A.P. Conoley brand, is currently maturing.

Breckenridge Distillery

Breckenridge, Colorado, founded in 2008

breckenridgedistillery.com

Situated at a an altitude of 2,900 metres and claiming to be the world´s highest distillery, Breckenridge produces mainly bourbon and not least many cask finished versions. There is also the limited Dark Arts single malt, aged up to 10 years.

Breuckelen Distilling

Brooklyn, New York, founded in 2010

brkdistilling.com

The company focused first on gin and whiskies made from rye, corn and wheat. When locally malted barley became available the range was expanded and the first single malt, the 6 year old Brownstone Malt Whiskey, was released in 2020.

Brickway Brewery & Distillery (former Borgata)

Omaha, Nebraska, founded in 2013

drinkbrickway.com

The owners are focused on single malt whiskey but they also produce smaller amounts of bourbon and rye as well as gin and rum. Their first whisky appeared in 2014 and one of the most recent was batch 3 of their bottled-in-bond single malt.

Brother Justus

Minneapolis, Minnesota, founded in 2014

brotherjustus.com

Phil Steger is using local peat from Minnesota. The unusual approach is that for some of their bottlings they let the whisky rest in barrels with peat instead of burning it to dry the barley. The first whiskies, including Cold-Peated Whiskey, appeared in late 2020 and in late 2024 the Single Barrel Select range was introduced.

Bulleit Distilling Company

Shelbyville, Kentucky, founded in 1987 (distillery in 2017)

bulleit.com

The whiskey brand Bulleit was re-created in 1987 by Tom Bulleit. A decade later Seagrams took over and a few years into the new millenium Diageo became the owner of the brand. Bourbon, and later rye, was the foundation of the brand which in 2023 sold 25 million bottles worldwide. In 2017 the company opened a new distillery in Shelbyville and in 2024 a single malt was introduced.

Bull Run Distillery

Portland, Oregon, founded in 2009

bullrundistillery.com

The distillery is focused on 100% Oregon single malt whiskey although aged bourbons as well as brandy and gin are also in the range. The first release of a single malt was a 4 year old in 2016. Since then a huge number of different expressions have become available. Not least single barrels up to 16 years old in the Whiskey Reserve Flight range.

Burning Barrel Spirits

Placerville, California, founded in 2023

burningbarrelspirits.com

In 2023 Burning Barrel Brewing Co. expanded their operation

with a distillery in Placerville east of Sacramento. Casks have been filled with malt whiskey still maturing in their warehouse.

Caiseal Beer & Spirits Company

Hampton, Virginia, founded in 2017

caiseal.com

A combined brewery and distillery where the brewery produces the mash for various distilled products. The first spirits included vodka, gin and bourbon and was followed in 2019 by a single malt. Since then a peated version has also been added to the range.

Cedar Ridge Distillery

Swisher, Iowa, founded in 2003

cedarridgewhiskey.com

The first single malt was launched in 2013 and the core expression is The Quintessential. This has over the years been released in a large number of different versions including peated ones.

Charbay Winery & Distillery

St. Helena, California, founded in 1983

charbay.com

With a wide range of products such as wine, vodka, grappa, pastis, rum and port, the owners decided in 1999 to also enter in to whiskey making. They were pioneers distilling whiskey from hopped beer and over the years several releases have been made The latest, in early 2024, were Lot #3 of Doubled & Twisted and tha last lot of Charbay R5.

Chattanooga Whiskey

Chattanooga, Tennessee, founded in 2015

chattanoogawhiskey.com

The distillery, which moved to larger premises in 2017, is mainly focused on bourbon but quite a few whiskies made from malted barley have appeared. One of the latest, the 5 year old Triple Islay Cask Finished, had been made from three different peated malts and finished in three different Islay Scotch casks.

Chemist Spirits

Asheville, North Carolina, founded in 2018

chemistspirits.com

Founded by Debbie Word and her daugther Danielle the distillery earned fame for their gin made with wheat spirit and American botanicals. Soon single malt whisky became an important part of their production and Biltmore (finished in Sangiovese barrels) and Greenman Single Malt (made from Golden Promise malt) are two of the latest releases.

Coppersea Distilling

New Paltz, New York, founded in 2011

coppersea.com

A distillery with malting on site, open-top wooden washbacks and direct-fired alembic stills. One thing that makes Coppersea stand out is that they don´t dry the malted barley but instead produce a mash from green, unkilned barley. Big Angus is made from 100% green barley and in the range there is also bourbon and rye.

Cotherman Distilling

Dunedin, Florida, founded in 2015

cothermandistilling.com

All the whiskies are made from 100% malted barley. First launched in July 2016 and one of the latest releases, in November 2024, was a Stout Mash Single Malt.

Crater Lake Spirits (Bend Distillery)

Bend, Oregon, founded in 1996

craterlakespirits.com

While focusing on vodka and to a certain extent rye whiskey, the producers also recently launched the 10th release of Black Butte single malt aged for more than 5 years.

Tim Piersant and Grant McCracken - founders of Chattanooga

Current Spirits

Elmsford, New York, founded in 2019

currentspirits.com

The distillery focuses on gin and vodka. In 2020 the first cask strength single malt was released and in 2023, two versions of Perpetual single malt were released - Premier Blend and Sherry Cask Aged - followed by Empire Blend in 2024.

Cut Spike Distillery (formerly Solas Distillery)

La Vista, Nebraska, founded in 2009

cutspike.com

The first bottles of single malt were launched in 2013. A large number of new releases occur every year not least in the Small Batch range. Peated production commenced in 2020. Vodka, rye and other spirits are also produced.

Dampfwerk Distillery, The

St. Louis Park, Minnesota, founded in 2016

thedampfwerk.com

The distillery offers fruit brandies and herbal liqueurs as well as gin and whiskey. The first single malt (4 years old), made from pale ale and chocolate malt and finished in red wine barrels, was launched in 2021 and more batches have followed.

Dark Island Spirits

Alexandria Bay, New York, founded in 2015

darkislandspirits.com

By way of a device inside the casks, the owners are maturing their spirits with the help of soundwaves created by different genres of music. A variety of different spirits have been released including single malt under the name Eleanor Glen. The latest versions are Phantom Piper, Highlander and the peated 1000 Islays.

Dirty Water Distillery

Plymouth, Massachusetts, founded in 2013

dirtywaterdistillery.com

Starting with vodka, gin and rum, the distillery expanded into malt whiskey in 2015. The first release of Bachelor Single Malt, came in 2016 and one of the more recent releases was Night Shift Santilli IPA made from a beer wash.

Distillery 291

Colorado Springs, Colorado, founded in 2011

distillery291.com

The core range consists of several ryes, bourbons and American whiskies. In an experimental range there have also been two single malts made from 100% barley. In February 2021, the distillery moved to a new facility and doubled their capacity.

Dogfish Head Distillery

Milton, Delawere, founded in 2002

dogfish.com

Opened up as a brewery, the company later expanded into being a distillery as well. Two copper stills and a copper column are used to make rum, gin and vodka. On the malt whiskey side there are Let´s Get Lost, Hull & Helm and a number of different finishes.

Door County Distillery

Carlsville, Wisconsin, founded in 2011

doorcountydistillery.com

Originally a winery which was later complemented by a distillery. Gin, vodka and brandy are the main products but they also make single malt whiskey. The first Door County Single Malt was released in 2013 and there are also bourbon and rye in the range.

DownSlope Distilling

Centennial, Colorado, founded in 2008

downslopedistilling.com

Double-Diamond Whiskey was first released in 2010 and it is still the core expression. It was followed by a number of varieties of bourbon, malted rye, malted wheat and in February 2025 their latest single malt (peated) appeared.

Dry Diggings Distillery

El Dorado Hills, California, founded in 2012

drydiggings.com

In 2015, Dry Diggings bought Amador Distillery and has since produced spirits under both brand names. Together with gin, vodka, rye and bourbon, single malts have also been released - Bodie 5 Dog and Twin Bridges although the latter was distilled at Westland.

Dry Fly Distilling

Spokane, Washington, founded in 2007

dryflydistilling.com

Several styles of whisky are produced and the O´Danaghers single malt is the rarest. The distillery moved to a new location in 2021.

Eastern Kille Distillery (former Gray Skies Distillery)

Rockford, Michigan, founded in 2014

easternkille.com

Bourbon and rye are produced and the first bottle of Michigan Single Malt appeared in 2016 with more batches following. The distillery moved to a new location in Rockford in autumn 2023.

Edgefield Distillery

Troutdale, Oregon, founded in1998

mcmenamins.com

Part of the McMenamin chain of pubs and hotels in Oregon and Washington. Some of the pubs have adjoining microbreweries and the chain's first distillery opened in 1998 with Hogshead Whiskey being bottled in 2002. Limited releases occur every year on St Patrick´s Day under the name The Devil´s Bit. A second distillery was opened in 2011 at Cornelius Pass Roadhouse in Hillsboro.

Eleven Wells Distillery

St. Paul, Minnesota, founded in 2013

11wells.com

Equipped with open-top fermenters and two stills, whiskey is the main product and the first two releases, aged bourbon and rye, were released in 2014 followed by wheat whiskey, corn whiskey and a subtly smoky single malt made from malted barley.

Elgin Distillery (Arizona Craft Beverage)

Elgin, Arizona, founded in 2015

elginwd.com

What started out as a winery founded in 1982 by Bill Letarte, was later expanded to also a brewery and a distillery. Gin, rum, bourbon, rye and a 9 year old malt whiskey from 100% barley are produced.

Elk Fence Distillery

Santa Rosa, California founded in 2020

elkfencedistillery.com

A craft distillery founded by Scott Woodson and Gail Coppinger. Equipped with two copper Trident stills from Maine, the distillery produces vodka, gin, rum and a single malt whisky named The Briny Deep.

Fainting Goat Spirits

Greensboro, North Carolina, founded in 2015

faintinggoatspirits.com

First spirits on the shelves were gin and vodka. In 2017 C. B. Fisher´s single malt whiskey was launched as a 2 year old and there is also a yearly, limited Christmas Whiskey version. Rye and bourbon are also in the range.

FEW Spirits

Evanston, Illinois, founded in 2010

fewspirits.com

Equipped with three stills; a Vendome column still and two Kothe hybrid stills, the distillery released its inaugural single malt smoked with cherry wood (preceeded by both bourbon and rye) in 2015.

Finger Lakes Distilling

Burdett, New York, founded in 2008

fingerlakesdistilling.com

Focusing on bourbon, rye and single pot still they have also released the 10 year old McKenzie American Straight Malt and, in early 2025, Flower Power Malt Whisky distilled from a beer.

Glacier Distilling

Coram, Montana, founded in 2010

glacierdistilling.com

The distillery produces a wide range of spirits. On the malt whiskey side there is Bearproof flavoured with huckleberry juice, Two Med made from an ale and, released in July 2024, Logan Pass matured in ex-rye barrels.

Grand Teton Distillery

Driggs, Idaho, founded in 2012

tetondistillery.com

The biggest product from the distillery is vodka made from potatoes. Various whiskies are also produced, including bourbon, wheat and a 4 year old single malt. There is also the Private Stock single malt which has been aged for a minimum of 7 years.

Headframe

Butte, Montana, founded in 2010

headframespirits.com

John and Courtney McKee are not just running a micro-distillery but thye are also designing and manufacturing continuous stills (similar to the ones they are using) for other distilleries. The couple produce a variety of spirits including Kelley single malt matured in bourbon barrels and finished in oloroso sherry casks.

Herman Marshall Whiskey

Wylie, Texas, founded in 2008

hmwhiskey.com

The first products in the Herman Marshall range were launched in 2013 and were at that time produced at Dallas Distilleries in Garland. Late 2021 the brand was sold to Dry County Distilleries who moved the production in 2022 to Wylie. Bourbon, rye and single malt are in the range.

Hewn Spirits

Pipersville, Pennsylvania, founded in 2013

hewnspirits.com

Apart from rum, gin and vodka the distillery produces bourbon, rye and the Reclamation American Single Malt Whiskey, bottled at 55%. Recently the whiskey has been aged in American white oak, then used boubron barrels and finally chestnut casks.

High Peak Distilling

Lake George, New York, founded in 2016

highpeakdistilling.com

High Peaks obtains all of their fermented wash from the Adirondack Brewery which is then distilled and matured on site. The first release in 2018 was the peated Cloudsplitter Single Malt which in later releases has reached the age of 5 years.

Highside Distilling

Bainbridge Island, Washington, founded in 2018

highsidedistilling.com

Several expressions of gin and amaro had been released when production of single malt whiskey started in 2019. The first version, 3 years old, appeared in January 2023 and the 7th edition, slightly peated and made from four malts, was released in September 2024.

Hinterhaus Distilling

Arnold, California, founded in 2020

hinterhausdistilling.com

This Sierra Nevada distillery started with gin, vodka and sourced bourbon and rye. The first single malt (made from six different malts and named Discovery) appeared in April 2023. Batch 4 was released in January 2025.

Hogback Distillery

Boulder, Colorado, founded in 2017

hogbackdistillery.com

The founder is the Scotsman Graeme Wallace and the focus is to do a Scottish style single malt, sometimes peated. The first single malt was released in 2020 and this has been followed by a number of limited releases in the Wallace Collection. The plan is to relocate the distillery to Estes Park up in the Colorado Rocky Mountains.

Hollerhorn Distilling

Naples, New York, founded in 2018

hollerhorn.com

Focusing on spirits made from maple syrup the owners eventually expanded into whiskey. Singe malt as well as whiskey infused with habanero has been released and in 2022 a Malt in Motion Heavily Peated Single Malt was launched. The distillery more or less burned to the ground in 2022 but was rebuilt and opened again in 2023.

Idlewild Spirits

Winter Park, Colorado, founded in 2015

idlewildspirits.com

Production of the first batch of malt whiskey was in June 2016. Fermentation and distillation being on the grain add to the over-all character. Their Colorado Single Malt was first released in 2018.

Ironton Distillery

Denver, Colorado, founded in 2018

irontondistillery.com

The distillery produces a variety of spirits. The first whiskies were all released in 2019. The single malt is made from malted barley smoked with beech and a straight version was released in 2022. In 2026 the distillery will be moving to Louisville, Colorado.

Jersey Spirits Distilling Co

Fairfield, New Jersey, founded in 2015

jerseyspirits.com

Apart from gin and vodka, the owners have two bourbon varieties. The first single malt distillation was in 2018 and in 2020, Wild Woods Apple Wood Smoked and Cherry Wood Smoked single malts were released.

Jettywave

Half Moon Bay, California, founded in 2022

jettywave.com

Mishelle and David Westendorf practise a traditional style of distilling with open top fermenters made of redwood, fermenting on the grain. The range consists of gin, bourbon and Maritime Single Malt whisky.

John Emerald Distilling Company

Opelika, Alabama, founded in 2014

johnemeralddistilling.com

With the wash being fermented on the grain, the main product is John´s Alabama Single Malt which gets its character from barley smoked with a blend of southern pecan and peach wood. The first release was made in 2015 and the latest was aged in honey casks.

Journeyman Distillery

Three Oaks, Michigan and Valparaiso, Indiana, founded in 2010

journeymandistillery.com

The range of whiskies include bourbon, rye, wheat and single malt. The first release of Three Oaks Single Malt Whiskey was in 2013 and it had been aged in a combination of bourbon, rye and rum casks. In October 2023, the distillery opened up in a second location (of quite a substantial size) in Valparaiso, Indiana.

Judson & Moore

Chicago, Illinois, founded in 2020

judsonandmoore.com

Located in a former leather tannery in Chicago, the distillery focuses on whiskey; bourbon, rye and a single malt made from 65% smoked malted barley and 35% unsmoked. First releases were in spring 2022.

Kings County Distillery

Brooklyn, New York, founded in 2010

kingscountydistillery.com

The oldest distillery in Brooklyn where the wash is fermented in open-top, wooden fermenters and practising double distillation in copper pot stills. The distillery is primarily focused on bourbon and rye but a single malt (60% unpeated and 40% peated) was released already in 2016. In 2022 a 2 year old Irish style, triple distilled whiskey was released.

Krobar Craft Distillery

San Luis Obispo, California, founded in 2012

krobardistillery.com

Two wine businesses were turned into a distillery and today they are producing gin, vodka and whiskey. The current single malt range consists of a core expression made from Maris Otter barley and a port finish. In August 2023 they moved to a new location.

Liberty Call Spirits

San Diego, California, founded in 2014

libertycall.com

The distillery uses a range of barley varieties including caramel malts and the rare Maris Otter. Apart from bourbon, gin and rum there is also a single malt named Old Ironsides. In spring 2020, they opened up a second restaurant/distillery in San Diego.

Liquid Brands Distillery (Browne Family Vineyards)

Spokane, Washington, founded in 2018

warriorliquor.com

Rich and Mary Clemson started to produce a variety of spirits including the Warrior single malt made from malted barley. When they retired, the project was taken over by well known Browne Family Vineyards and the experienced distiller Aaron Kleinhelter.

Liquid Riot (now known as Pennant Brewing & Distilling)

Portland, Maine, founded in 2013

camppennant.com

At the waterfront in the Old Port, Maine´s first brewery/distillery/resto-bar, produces an extensive range of beers and spirits which include bourbon, rye, oat, rum, vodka, agave spirit and the cherry wood smoked Old Port Single Malt. In summer 2024 it was sold and is now working under the name Pennant.

Los Angeles Distillery

Culver City, California, founded in 2013

ladistillery.com

The distillery is very much focusing on whiskey. Different versions of bourbon and rye are produced as well as a number of varieties of malt whiskey from barley. Current expressions include three 7 year old versions of Glen L.A. single malt; matured in Tokaji casks, in a combination of Tokaji casks and new oak and in a combination of Tokaji casks, new oak and Bordeaux wine casks.

Lost Wood Whiskey

Minneapolis, Minnesota, founded in 2018

lostwoodswhiskey.com

Three single malts can be found in the range; 88 Proof, 110 Proof and, the latest release, 80 Proof. The founder and owner, Tom Schaeppi, gives back 1% of all sales to organisations supporting the environment.

Mad River Distillers

Warren, Vermont, founded in 2011

madriverdistillers.com

The distillery was built on a 150 year old farm in the Green Mountains. Focus is on rum, brandy and whiskey. Current single malts are the 8th edition of Hopscotch (first released in 2016) and (launched in November 2024) the limited Summit.

Maine Craft Distilling

Portland, Maine, founded in 2013

mainecraftdistilling.com

The distillery offers vodka, gin, rum as well as the Fifty Stone single malt in limited batches. The barley is floor malted on site and both peat moss and seaweed is used to dry the barley.

Maplewood Brewery and Distillery

Chicago, Illinois, founded in 2014

maplewoodbrew.com

This brewery/distillery currently has five malts in the range; Fat Pug made from five different malts, Oaty Otter with Maris Otter barley and oats, Fest inspired by festbier, Heritage and Peat Smoke Whiskey (the smoke coming from both peat and cherry wood).

Minden Mill Distillery

Minden, Nevada, founded in 2023

mindenmill.com

In 2016 Christopher Bentley opened a whiskey distillery in an old mill in Minden. Six years later he bought a huge estate in Scotland and at the same time the distillery in Nevada was put up for sale. A year later the distillery, part of the surrounding farm land and the stock of maturing whiskey was bought by Bill Foley. Apart from being the owner of Las Vegas Golden Knights hockey team Foley also runs Foley Family Wines since 1996 with renowned vineyards in Sonoma Valley, Oregon, Washington and New Zealand. The current single malt, made from barley malted in-house, has aged for 5 years in ex-oloroso, ex-bourbon and American oak.

Minturn

Minturn, Colorado founded in 2021

minturnwhisky.com

Following an inspirational trip to Scotland, Spence Neubauer and his wife Stefanie founded a distillery which focuses completely on malt whisky. In early days the whisky was named Eagle River Whisky but today the Minturn range consists of a single malt, a peated single malt and a blended malt.

Montgomery Distillery

Missoula, Montana, founded in 2012

montgomerydistillery.com

The owners use a hammer mill and the wash is fermented on the grain. The first whiskey was a rye in 2015, followed up by the 3 year old Montgomery Single Malt in 2016. The latest release, in November 2024, was an 8 year old.

Motor City Gas

Royal Oak, Michigan, founded in 2014

motorcitygas.com

The owners have an experimental approach using rare grains, different yeasts and unusual woods. The range includes rye, bourbon and single malt. Recent expressions include the 4 year old Shifter 7th Gear, the 5 year old Pile Driver and the 7 year old Guzzler. In 2021 the company bought a farm in Ann Arbour where they grow their own organic heirloom grain.

New Holland Brewing Co.

Holland, Michigan, founded in 1996 (whiskey since 2005)

newhollandbrew.com

The first bottlings were released in 2008 and among them were Zeppelin Bend, a 3 year old straight malt whiskey which is still very much in the range together with the 10 year old Walleye Run single malt. Included in the range is also a wide range of bourbon and rye.

Noco Distillery

Fort Collins, Colorado, founded in 2016

nocodistillery.com

With a fermentation of up to three weeks, slow distillation and up to nine different types of woods for maturation, the distillery produces gin, rum, vodka, bourbon, rye whiskey as well as single malt. The latter was first released in 2019. New hybrid stills were installed in early 2022.

Old Home Distillers

Lebanon, New York, founded in 2014

oldhomedistillers.com

The distillery produces bourbon, corn whiskey and New York Single Malt Whiskey. The mash is fermented on the grain for 4-5 days and the distillation takes place in a hybrid column still. The current malt whiskey expression is Empire.

Old Line Spirits

Baltimore, Maryland, founded in 2014

oldlinespirits.com

A peated version was launched in 2017 with a sherry cask finish appearing in 2018 and a cask strength a year later. From 2023 there is a core range with Flagship 95, Navy Strength 114, Bottled in Bond and Single Barrel. There is also the Double Oak Series of wood finishes and, in January 2025, the Sherry Cask Finish.

Old Trestle Distillery

Truckee, California, founded in 2012

oldtrestle.com

Using their own underground aquifer as the water source, the distillery is focused on whiskey production but the first spirit releases were vodka and gin. In summer 2020, their 3 year old Sierra Bourbon was launched and their first single malt was released in spring 2023.

Orange County Distillery

Goshen, New York, founded in 2013

orangecountydistillery.com

Malting their own barley and using their own peat, since 2014 they have launched a wide range of whiskies, including corn, bourbon, rye and single malt. The first single malt was launched in 2015 and more releases (peated as well as unpeated) have followed since.

Orcas Island Distillery

Orcas, Washington, founded in 2014

orcasislanddistillery.com

Apple brandy is the main produce but the 3 year old West Island single malt as well as the 4 year old Cask Strength are also in the range.

Painted Stave Distilling

Smyrna, Delaware, founded in 2013

paintedstave.com

Most of the production is centered on bourbon and rye but there is also Diamond State Pot Still Whiskey made from malted barley and rye and Double TroubleD made from a hopped beer.

Peach Street Distillers

Palisade, Colorado, founded in 2005

peachstreetdistillers.com

An extensive range of various spirits is complemented by a bourbon, a smoky rye, a hop flavoured whiskey, a peated single malt, an 8 year old version of the same and finally, in December 2024, a 10 year old peated single malt.

Pilot House Distilling

Astoria, Oregon, founded in 2013

pilothousedistilling.com

Starting off with vodka and gin, the owners eventually broadened the range to include whisky. The main product is the A-O American Whiskey made from corn and malted barley but small amounts of single malt are also produced and the first 2 year old was released in 2021 with batch 15 being released in December 2024.

PostModern Distilling

Knowville, Tennessee, founded in 2017

postmodernspirits.com

Focusing on gin, vodka and liqueur, a single barrel single malt whiskey was released in 2018. The current core expression is the Straight Malt Whiskey partly smoked using cherry wood.

Prichard´s Distillery

Kelso and Nashville, Tennessee, founded in 1999

prichardsdistillery.com

The main track of the production is rum. The first single malt was launched in 2010 and later releases usually have been vattings from barrels of different age (some up to 10 years old).

Quincy Street Distillery

Riverside, Illinois, founded in 2011

quincystreetdistillery.com

The distillery produces a range of spirits including gin, vodka, absinth, bourbon, corn whiskey and rye. The Golden Prairie single malt was first launched in 2015 and the latest, limited release was in autumn 2024.

Ranger Creek Brewing & Distilling

San Antonio, Texas, founded in 2010

drinkrangercreek.com

Focusing on beer brewing and whiskey production, the first whiskey release was Ranger Creek .36 Texas Bourbon in 2011. The first single malt, Rimfire, was launched in 2013. These days the mesquite, lightly smoked Texas Landmark, first released in September 2024, is the core single malt.

Red River Brewery & Distillery

Red River, New Mexico, founded in 2018

redriverbrewing.com

Founded by Michael and Sharon Calhoun this combined brewery/distillery produces beer, gin, vodka, rum and bourbon but also a single barrel single malt named Calhoun Family Reserve.

Redwood Empire Whiskey

Graton, California, founded in 2015

redwoodempirewhiskey.com

Located in the heart of the Russian River Valley, the distillery produces bourbon, rye and single malt whiskey in a continuous micro-column still. The Foggy Burl single malt is aged for a minimum of four years.

Rennaisance Artisan Distillers

Akron, Ohio, founded in 2013

renartisan.com

Apart from whiskey, the distillery produces gin, brandy, grappa and limoncello. The first whiskey release, The King´s Cut single malt, was made from a grain bill including toasted and caramel malts. In 2021 Kilted Peat Malt Whiskey was released.

Restless Spirits

Kansas City, Missouri, founded in 2016

restlessspiritsdistilling.com

The distillery produces gin, vodka and whiskey. Some of the whiskies (Sons of Erin) were inspired by Irish whiskey making while Gullytown is an American single malt whiskey

Rock Town Distillery

Little Rock, Arkansas, founded in 2010

rocktowndistillery.com

A grain-to-glass distillery where the backbone of the production is made up of several bourbons, rye, wheat whiskey and vodka but there is also a 4 year old single malt finished in ex-cognac casks.

Rock Valley Spirits

Long Eddy, New York, founded in 2018

rockvalleyspirits.com

A small, family-owned farm distillery located in the Catskill Mountains. First spririts that were launched were gin and vodka and they were followed in 2021 by a single malt whisky.

Routt Distillery

Steamboat Springs, Colorado, founded in 2022

routtdistillery.com

Founded by Brad Christensen, the distillery/tasting room started by releasing gin and vodka and now has American single malt maturing in the warehouse.

San Diego Distillery

Spring Valley, California, founded in 2015

sddistillery.com

A distillery focused almost entirely on whiskey. In 2016 the first six whiskies were released including an Islay peated single malt. Since then several limited single malts have appeared.

SanTan Spirits

Chandler and Phoenix, Arizona, founded in 2007 (2015)

santanbrewing.com

With two locations in Arizona, this brewery/restaurant added distilling to its concept in 2015. There are currently two single malts in the range; the Sacred Stave finished in red wine barrels (also available at cask strength) and the 4 year old J.W. Powell.

Seven Caves Spirits

San Diego, California, founded in 2016

the7caves.com

Apart from gin, rum and bourbon, Geoff Longenecker also makes whiskey from malted barley. One of the latest (in August 2022) was a peated 4 year old matured in a rum barrel.

Shadow Ridge Spirits

Oceanside, California, founded in 2017

srdistilled.com

While rum and gin may be a part of the range, the distillery is focused on whiskey; bourbon, rye and single malt. The latter has been made from a combination of different malts and also comes in a special, smoked version where peat and cherry wood were used.

Shelter Distilling

Mammoth Lakes, California, founded in 2018

shelterdistilling.com

Apart from gin, vodka, rum and liqueurs the distillery produces bourbon, rye and single malt. The core single malt expression has been matured in a combination of Hungarian and American oak and there is also the limited Dark Sky, released yearly in December.

Silver Brothers

Old Chatham, New York, founded in 2023

silverbrothers.com

A terroir-driven distillery in Hudson River Valley where they grow their own organic rye and barley. Two types of whiskey are produced; rye and American single malt. A typical fermentation is seven days and the first distillation was in February 2023 with a possible first release in 2025.

Sinister Distlling

Albany, Oregon, founded in 2015

sinisterdeluxe.com

Part of a brewstillery with DeLuxe Brewing as the other half. A variety of spirits are produced including Howard Jacob single malt. Batch 6 had been aged for 7 years in a French oak wine barrel.

Snitching Lady Distillery

Fairplay, Colorado, founded in 2018

snitchingladydistillery.net

The distillery, which moved to new premises in August 2019, has so far released peach brandy, bourbon, rye and blue corn spirit. Single malt made from barley was distilled for the first time in 2019 and released in September 2022.

Solar Spirits

Richland, Washington, founded in 2018

solarspirits.com

A "farm-to-bottle" distillery using 100% renewable energy thanks to onsite solar panels. The range currently consists of gin, vodka, brandy and a single malt whiskey.

South Mountain Distilling

Connelly Springs, North Carolina, founded in 2015

southmountaindistillery.com

Focus is very much on moonshine but there are also matured whiskies in the range including Dignified Single Malt and a corn whiskey named Sinister.

Spirit Hound Distillers

Lyons, Colorado, founded in 2012

spirithounds.com

The signature spirits are gin and malt whiskey. The first expression appeared in 2015 and apart from that there are now also a cask strength version, a bottled in bond and three finishes (sherry, stout and honey) available.

Spirit Lab Distilling

Charlottesville, Virginia, founded in 2015

spiritlabdistilling.com

Founded by Ivar Aass, the distillery is making gin, brandy and American malt whiskey. Using a solera system, batches of the cask strength Aass Single Malt are released regularly. The latest batch (#16) has 9 year old whiskey as its oldest component.

Spirits of St Louis Distillery (formerly known as Square One)

St. Louis, Missouri, founded in 2006

squareonebrewery.com

A combined brewery and restaurant. Apart from rum, gin, vodka and absinthe, the owners also produce J.J. Neukomm Whiskey, a malt whiskey made from 25% cherry wood smoked malt.

Stark Spirits

Pasadena, California, founded in 2013

starkspirits.com

The first single malt whiskey was distilled in 2015 and the first official distillery release of single malt (both peated and un-peated) came in February 2017. They have two stills with one reserved for all the peated production.

Storm King Distilling Co.

Montrose, Colorado, founded in 2017

stormkingdistilling.com

Inspired by a passion for whiskey, the owners have released wheat whiskey, bourbon and rye. The first single malt, a vatting of the 8 first batches, appeared in 2024.

Stoutridge

Marlboro, New York, founded in 2017

stoutridge.com

A distillery with direct fired stills and their own floor maltings. The range consists of vodka, gin, brandy and whiskey. Southern Ulster Single Malt was matured for 2 years in pinot noir barrels and finished in ex-Laphroaig casks This was followed by Quartarium Root and The Fragrant Coast.

Sugar House

Salt Lake City, Utah, founded in 2014

sugarhousedistillery.net

The first release from the distillery in 2014 was a vodka, followed by a single malt whisky. More releases of the single malt have followed including limited cask strength versions and finishes.

Sweetgrass

Portland, Maine, founded in 2007

sweetgrasswinery.com

Focusing from the start on wine and the distillation of gin, brandy, rum and liqueur, the distillery went on to producing malt whiskey. The latest batch of their Sunk Haze malt whiskey had been matured for eight years.

Talking Cedar

Rochester, Washington, founded in 2020

talkingcedar.com

The first tribal-owned distillery in the USA and the first distillery allowed in "Indian" country since 1834. A law against production

The master distiller at Tenmile Distillery is Shane Fraser who previously worked for Glenfarclas and Wolfburn in Scotland

of spirits on "Indian" lands introduced by Andrew Jackson in 1834 wasn´t repealed until 2018. Owned and run by the Chehalis tribe, the brewery/distillery produce a range of spirits including bourbon, rye and single malt whiskey. Released in 2024 were the 12 year old Singularity malt whiskey distilled at Westland as well as Blenders which is a blended malt with casks coming from both Westland and Talking Cedar. Leading the whisky programme at the distillery is Matt Hoffman who left Westland in 2023.

Tenmile

Wassaic, New York, founded in 2020

tenmiledistillery.com

Equipped with stills from Forsyths in Scotland, the distillery is focusing on gin, vodka and, most of all, single malt whiskey. The first single malt, fermented for seven days and named Little Rest, was released in April 2023 and has been followed by more expressions including maturations in oloroso sherry and port casks. The master distiller is Shane Fraser with a track record of working with Glenfarclas and Wolfburn distilleries in Scotland.

Timber Creek

Crestview, Florida, founded in 2014

timbercreekdistillery.com

Fermentation and distillation is on the grain and they use a traditional worm tub to cool the spirits. Releases include a rye, a wheated bourbon, a four grain whiskey and Florida Single Malt.

Town Branch

Lexington, Kentucky, founded in 1999

lexingtonbrewingco.com

In 1980 Dr Pearse Lyons founded Alltech Inc, a biotechnology company specializing in animal nutrition and feed supplements. Alltech purchased Lexington Brewing Company in 1999 and in 2008, two traditional copper pot stills were installed. The single malt range is currently represented by the 7 year old Town Branch Malt, the Single Barrel Reserve and an 11 year old cask strength version. An Irish style whiskey under the name Pearse is also available, aged 5, 7 and 12 years. The company also owns a distillery in Pikeville, Kentucky and one in Dublin in Ireland.

Triple Eight

Nantucket, Massachusetts, founded in 2000

ciscobrewers.com

Apart from whiskey, Triple Eight also produces vodka, rum and gin. The first bottles of a single malt were released on 8th August 2008 as an 8 year old. More releases of Notch have followed and currently there are three expressions aged 8, 12 and 15 years.

Two James Spirits

Detroit, Michigan, founded in 2013

twojames.com

Equipped with a 500 gallon pot still with a rectification column attached, the distillery has released vodka, gin, bourbon (even a peated version) and rye while a single malt is still maturing in the warehouse. Aged in ex-sherry casks the whiskey has been made from peated Scottish barley.

Up North

Post Falls, Idaho, founded in 2015

upnorthdistillery.com

Randy and Hilary Mann had their eyes set on malt whiskey when they started production but the first releases were honey spirits and apple brandy. The first release of North Idaho Single Malt Whiskey, aged for a minimum of 2 years, has been followed by more batches.

Van Brunt Stillhouse

Brooklyn, New York, founded in 2012

vanbruntstillhouse.com

The distillery made their first release of Van Brunts American Whiskey in 2012. This has been followed by bourbon, rye, corn and (in 2023) rice whiskey. The Van Brunt Single Malt is bottled irregularly, produced from a mash bill of several different brewer´s malts, fermented on the grain and matured in a variety of casks.

Vapor Distillery (formerly known as Roundhouse Spirits)

Boulder, Colorado, founded in 2007

boulderspirits.com

Since 2014 the owners focus on American malt whiskey but also make bourbon with an unusually high proportion of malted barley in the mash bill. Currently the distillery has four single malt whiskies in the range – Boulder American Single Malt Whiskey, a peated version of the same, one bottled in bond and one port finish. There is also a limited 7 year old bottled at 50%.

Venus Spirits

Santa Cruz, California, founded in 2014

venusspirits.com

Production is focused on whiskey, but gin and spirits from blue agave have also been released. The first single malt was Wayward Whiskey, matured in port and sherry casks and a limited peated version was released in early 2025.

Vikre

Duluth, Minnesota, founded in 2012

vikredistillery.com

Together with whisky - gin, vodka and aquavit are produced. Whiskies include top seller, now on its 12th batch, Sugarbush Whiskey and (temporarily out of stock) Iron Range American Single Malt.

Warfield

Ketchum, Idaho, founded in 2015

drinkwarfield.com

Warfield Organic American Whiskey (made from malted barley) was launched in 2019 and gin, vodka, brandy and beer is also produced. Small batch versions occur regularly with the 8th (Deke) launched in December 2024.

Woodstone Creek

Cincinnati, Ohio, founded in 1999

woodstonecreek.com

Opened as a farm winery in 1999, a distillery was added to the business in 2003. The first bourbon, was released in 2008 followed by a 10 year old single malt. Whiskey production is very small and just a handfull of releases have appeared since.

Wood´s High Mountain

Salida, Colorado, founded in 2011

woodsdistillery.com

The first expression, Tenderfoot Whiskey, is a triple malt and so is the release that followed, Sawatch, a 4-5 year old made from malted barley, malted rye and malted wheat. There is also the 5 year old Dawn Patrol made from 45% cherry-wood smoked barley and, released in January 2024, the 5 year old Distiller´s Reserve Tenderfoot.

Wright & Brown Distilling Co.

Oakland, California, founded in 2015

wbdistilling.com

The distillery is focused on barrel aged spirits. The first release, a rye whiskey, appeared in 2016 and was followed by a bourbon in 2017. Early 2020 it was time for the first single malt, a bottled in bond expression aged for 4,5 years with batch 4 (6 years old) launched in November 2023.

Canada

Shelter Point Distillery

Vancouver Island, British Columbia, founded in 2009

shelterpoint.ca

Founded by dairy farmer Patrick Evans who in 2005 switched to growing crops and four years later added a distillery. Distillation started in 2011 and the barley used is grown on the farm. Apart from whisky, gin and vodka is also produced. In 2016 a 5 year old single malt was released and today (although aged for seven years) the Classic is still the core expression. Other releases in a substantial range include Ripple Rock (matured in ex-bourbon and virgin oak), the triple distilled Montfort made from unmalted barley, Cask Strength and a 12 year old. There is also Smoke Point where the fumes from smoked driftwood and local peat is piped into the wood of the maturing casks. A recent release, and part of the Evans Family Reserve series, is a tequila finish and in 2024 their first widely available rye, Black Tail, appeared. In 2022 the majority of the distillery was sold to Nelson Investment.

Macaloney´s Island Distillery

Victoria, British Columbia, founded in 2016

macaloneydistillers.com

Founded by the Scotsman Graeme Macaloney the distillery is equipped with a one ton semilauter mash tun, 7 stainless steel washbacks, a 5,500 litre wash still and a 3,600 litre spirit still. Some of the barley is malted on site and there is also a craft beer brewery. Glenloy, the inaugural single malt and signature release, appeared in 2020 (later to be renamed An Loy) and is predominantly bourbon-matured. The rest of the core range is made up by An Alba (lightly peated and sherry matured), Cath-Nah-Aven (matured in a combination of ex-bourbon, oloroso and PX sherry casks), Siol Dugall (lightly peated) and Kildara and Killheigh (bot triple distilled single pot still). Regularly a vast number of single casks are released in three different series; Peated, Single Malt and Triple Distilled.

Glenora Distillery

Glenville, Nova Scotia, founded in 1990

glenoradistillery.com, glenbreton.com

Situated in Nova Scotia, Glenora was the first malt whisky distillery in Canada. The first launch of in-house produce came in 2000, an 8 year old named Glen Breton Rare and a 10 year old is now the core expression. Many other expressions have appeared over the years – 19, 21, 25 year olds and, not least, the 30 year old Triginta – the oldest North American single malt ever released. There have also been peated versions under the name Gleann Dubh as well as Glen Breton Ice, aged in an ice wine barrel and first launched in 2006.

Still Waters Distillery

Concord, Ontario, founded in 2009

stillwatersdistillery.com

Established by Barry Stein and Barry Bernstein, the distillery was recently taken over by Buck Hill Distilled Spirits. The distillery is equipped with a 3,000 litre mash tun, two 3,000 litre washbacks and a Christian Carl 450 litre pot still. The still also has rectification columns. The focus is on whisky but they also produce vodka, brandy and gin. Their first single malt, named Stalk & Barrel Single Malt, was released in 2013 and it was followed in 2014 by the first rye whisky. The range now consists of Rye and Single Malt, both bottled at 46% and at cask strength.

Other distilleries in Canada

Anohka Distillery

Parkland County, Alberta, founded in 2021

anokha.ca

Founded by former lawyer Gurpreet Ranu who also designed the stills that were manufactured in Portugal. The distillery is equipped with a hammer mill and a mash filter and the stills are direct fired. There is also a dunnage warehouse and all their their wheat and barley is grown locally. The first distillation of both peated and unpeated spirit was in January 2023 and the first release is anticiparted in early 2026.

Arbutus Distillery

Nanaimo, British Columbia, founded in 2014

arbutusdistillery.com

The distillery produces a wide variety of spirits including rye and single malt whisky. The first single malt appeared in 2018 and has been followed by more releases.

Bridgeland Distillery

Calgary, Alberta, founded in 2018

bridgelanddistillery.com

Equipped with an unusual copper pot still where the lyne arm is extended with a large copper spiral leading to a condenser. The Glenbow single malt was first released in 2022 followed by single pot still Innisfail in 2023 and Taber Corn Berbon 101 in 2024 and Artisan Collection Wheat Whisky in 2025.

Central City Brewers & Distillers

Surrey, British Columbia, founded in 2013

centralcitybrewing.com

One of Canada´s largest craft breweries added a distillery in 2013. The whisky is sold under the Lohin McKinnon Single Malt brand including special bottlings such as peated, tequila finish and one aged with cocoa from a local chocolatier. In November 2024 they received creditor protection and at the time of writing (April 2025) it remains to be seen what will happen.

Côte des Saintes

Mirabel, Quebec, founded in 2016

cotedessaints.com

The distillery grows their own barley and for the whisky a 3,000 litre still from Vendome is used. Head distiller is Matt Strickland who headed up research and development for Corsair distillery in Tennessee for many years. Their range of single malt whiskies is divided into three ranges; Premium, Prestige and Cask Strength.

Diony Distillery

Red Deer, Alberta, founded in 2018

dionydistillery.ca

The current range is based on a mash bill of at least 67% malted rye and a very long fermentation time of 10-14 days but there is also whisky made from malted barley maturing in the warehouse.

Dubh Glas Distillery, The

Oliver, British Columbia, founded in 2015

thedubhglasdistillery.com

The whisky is double distilled in an Arnold Holstein still and gin is also produced. The first release of a single malt was the peated Against All Odds in 2019. A large number of whiskies are released every year where the latest include the peated Dirty Little Secret, the rum-matured Shiver Me Timbers and Solitary Coast.

Eau Claire Distillery

Turner Valley, Alberta, founded in 2014

eauclairedistillery.ca

The distillery´s first limited single malt whisky appeared in 2017 with Anniversary Edition as well as Moscatel Cask and Tequila Cask in the Cask Series being the latest.

Ironworks Distillery

Lunenburg, Nova Scotia, founded in 2010

ironworksdistillery.com

While focusing on rum, brandy and vodka there is also the Heart Iron single malt which was first released in 2020. followed in 2023 by Blacksmith made from chocolate malt.

Last Straw Distillery

Vaughan, Ontario, founded in 2016

madebyhand.laststrawdistillery.com

A wide range of spirits are produced including whisky made from various grains (rye, corn, rice etc.). The only single malt so far, a 6 year old cabernet franc finish, appeared in September 2023.

Liberty Distillery, The

Vancouver, British Columbia, founded in 2010

thelibertydistillery.com

The distillery produces gin, vodka and a wide range of whiskies made from organic grain. Sold under the brand name Trust Whiskey, there are single malts matured in madeira, port, burgundy, bordeaux and sherry casks. There is also the limited 7 year old and sligthly peated Anniversary Cask Strength Whiskey.

Maison Sivo

Hinchinbrooke, Quebec, founded in 2014

maisonsivo.ca

Inspired by production of fruit brandies in Hungary where he grew up, Janos Sivo produces different kinds of spirit including whisky. Le Single Malt finished in Sauternes casks and Le Rye were both released in 2018. There is also the limited Le Sélection Single Malt.

Moon Distillery

Victoria, British Columbia, founded in 2012

moondistillery.ca

The distillery produces beer and a variety of spirits including malt whisky. Two of the latest single malts, Antifogmatic Bliss and 3 Sheets to the Moon, were accompanied by a series of three whiskies infused with cacao nibs, coffee beans and dark cherries.

North of 7 Distillery

Ottawa, Ontario, founded in 2013

northof7distillery.ca

First releases were gin and other spirits. These were followed by whiskies made from various mash bills and in 2022 the 5 year old (later releases 8 years old) North of 7 single malt appeared.

Anohka - an exciting, new Canadian distillery equipped with mash filter and direct fired stills

Odd Society Spirits

Vancouver, British Columbia, founded in 2013

oddsocietyspirits.com

The first two whiskies appeared in 2018; the Commodore single malt and the Prospector rye. They have later been followed by collaboration projects, working together with local breweries.

Okanagan Spirits

Vernon and Kelowna, British Columbia, founded in 2004

okanaganspirits.com

The first Okanagan distillery was started in 1970 but closed in 1995. In 2004 Okanagan Spirits was established and a distillery was opened in Vernon (and later, one in Kelowna). A variety of spirits including gin, vodka and whisky are produced. In 2013 the Laird of Fintry single malt was released where a number of different expressions have been releasecd since. Recent, limited single malts include the 5 year old Captain Short´s Triple Wood, the 10 year old Tatshenshini Glacial, and Primero finished in port pipes.

Rig Hand Distillery

Nisku, Alberta, founded in 2014

righanddistillery.com

The distillery produces a veriety of spirits with the first whisky appearing in 2017. Bar M was a blended whisky made from wheat, barley and rye. This was followed by the 5 year old Diamond S single malt, the Rocking R rye and the Lazy B corn whisky.

Sheringham Distillery

Langford, British Columbia, founded in 2015

sheringhamdistillery.com

While focusing on gin, akvavit and vodka the odd bottlings of Red Fife and Woodhaven whiskies have also appeared. In 2023 the distillery moved to a new location.

Spring Mill Distillery

Guelph, Ontario, founded in 2019

springmilldistillery.com, johnsleemandansons.com

Already in 1836 the Sleeman family built a distillery in St. David´s, Ontario. Almost 200 years later, John Sleeman opened up a whisky distillery in Guelph. The distillery is equipped with column stills for neutral grain spirits, corn- and rye whisky, traditional copper pot stills from Forsyths for malt whisky and wooden wash backs made in Scotland. There is also a small cooperage on site. The big seller is the straight whisky made predominantly from corn but they have also released a 4 year old sherry finished single malt.

Stillhead Distillery

Duncan, British Columbia, founded in 2017

stillhead.ca

All kinds of whisky including rye, wheat and "bourbon" style are produced, including malt whisky. Releases in the past few years include a 5 year old with a second maturation in Hungarian oak, the port cask finish Potent Port-ables and one matured in madeira casks.

Yukon Spirits

Whitehorse, Yukon, founded in 2009

twobrewerswhisky.com

All of the whisky produced is made from malted grains but not only barley but also wheat and rye. The first bottles of the 7 year old Two Brewer´s Yukon Single Malt Whisky were released in 2016 and the current portfolio is based on four styles; Classic, Peated, Special Finishes and Innovative, all released in batches of which there has been a total of around fifty.

Sullivans Cove has recently completed a substantial expansion including a new visitor centre

Australia & New Zealand

Australia

Lark Distillery

Cambridge, Tasmania, founded 1992

Pontville, Tasmania, founded in 2015

larkdistillery.com

In 1992, Bill Lark was the first person for 153 years to take out a distillation licence in Tasmania. The success of the distillery forced Bill Lark to bring in investors in the company to generate future growth and since 2018, Australian Whisky Holdings (AWH) holds a majority of the shares. In 2020, AWH changed name to Lark Distilling Co and in autumn 2021 they bought the Shene Estate, 30 minutes north of Hobart. Behind the Shene Estate distillery was Damian Mackey who started distilling whisky already in 2007. In 2016, with the aid of investor John Ibrahim and Anne and David Kernke, the opportunity came for him to move the production to the Shene Estate at Pontville. When Lark Distilling bought Shene, an already existing distillery with a 350,000 litre capacity and stock of maturing whisky was included in the deal. This gave the two distilleries (the original in Cambridge and the one at Shene Estate) a combined capacity of almost 600,000 litres. The Pontville distillery (Shene) was opened in 2022 in connection with Lark´s 30th anniversary and there are plans to increase the production to one million litres per year. The signature products in the Lark whisky range are the Classic Cask, Classic Cask Cask Strength, Chinotto Citrus Cask and Tasmanian Peated. Recent limited releases include The Knotted Tree and Golden Lark for the 2025 Lunar New Year and the Mizunara Oak in the Rare Cask Series. A new series, The Wilderness Collection, was recently introduced with Earth (focusing on peat) as the first edition to be followed by Sky and Sea.

Sullivans Cove Distillery

Cambridge, Tasmania, founded 1994

sullivanscove.com

Founded by Robert Hosken in 1994, Patrick Maguire joined the company five years later as head distiller and co-owner. In 2016, Maguire and the other owners sold the distillery to a company led by Adam Sable. In 2024 the distillery re-opened after a $14m revamp which included a completely new visitor experience as well as more equipment, not least two more copper pot stills, which tripled the capacity. The core range from the distillery comprises of American Oak, French Oak (where the barrels have contained tawny) and Double Cask. There is also the Old & Rare range with whiskies that are 16 years or older. The oldest bottling released so far was a 24 year old released in late 2024 and in 2025 an 18 year old from an ex-boubon cask and a 17 year old matured in an ex-tawny barrel appeared.

Bakery Hill Distillery

Kensington, Victoria, founded 1998

bakeryhill.com

The first spirit at Bakery Hill Distillery, founded by David Baker, was produced in 2000 and the first single malt was launched in 2003. In 2016, David was joined by his son Andrew and father and son started planning for a move to larger premises and adding a second still. The plan came to fruition in late 2023 when the distillery opened up in a new location in Kensington. Five different core expressions are available – Classic and Peated (both matured in ex-bourbon casks) and Double Wood (ex-bourbon and a finish in French Oak). Classic and Peated are also available at cask strength. One of the latest limited releases (in 2024) was Blunderbuss #3 with a second maturation of two years in stout barrels. In November 2024 they also released their first blended whisky.

Starward Distillery

Melbourne, Victoria, founded 2008

starward.com.au

The distillery was moved in 2016 to a bigger site in Port Melbourne and the year before Diageo invested in the distillery. The original stills (an 1,800 litre wash still and a 600 litre spirit still) were complemented in 2020 with a new 7,000 litre wash still while at the same time the old wash still became the new spirit still. The first Starward single malt was released in 2013 and the current core range consists of Nova and 100 Proof (both matured in Australian red wine barrels) and Solera (matured in casks that had held apera, the Australian version of sherry). There are also two blended whiskies made from malted barley and wheat - Two-Fold matured in red wine barrels and Panettone finished in tawny port. Recent limited expressions include Left-field, Botrytis Cask and Bourbon Cask #2.

Hellyers Road Distillery

Burnie, Tasmania, founded 1999

hellyersroaddistillery.com.au

Hellyer´s Road Distillery is one of the larger single malt whisky distilleries in Australia with a capacity of doing 120,000 litres of pure alcohol per year. The distillery is equipped with a 6.5 ton mash tun, a 60,000 litre wash still and a 20,000 litre spirit still. The pots on both stills are made of stainless steel while heads, necks and lyne arms are made of copper. The first whisky was released in 2006 and what can be considered as core range at the moment is made up of Double Cask and 7 year old Peated Single Malt. The distillery is in a position to release some of the oldest Australian whiskies available. A few of the more recent limited bottlings include a 19 year old peated, a 20 year old oloroso finish and a 22 year old matured in American oak casks.

Great Southern Distilling Company

Albany, Western Australia, founded 2004

distillery.com.au

The distillery is located at Princess Royal Harbour in Albany. In 2015, the owners opened a second distillery in Margaret River which is focused on gin production and in 2018 a third distillery, Tiger Snake in Porongurup, started production. The combined production is 400,000 litres of pure alcohol per year and the company also have their own maltings. The first expression of the whisky, called Limeburners, was released in 2008 and the core range now consists of American Oak, Port Cask, Sherry Cask and Peated – all bottled at 43% and aged 5 to 8 years. Every year a number of limited releases occur and one of the latest, in February 2025, was Year of the Snake finished in tawny port casks.

Archie Rose Distilling Company

Banksmeadow (Sydney), New South Wales, founded in 2014

archierose.com.au

What started as a fairly ordinary distillery, both in terms of size and production technique, was completely changed in November 2020 when their new distillery in Banksmeadow, Sydney was opened. This is now one of the largest distilleries in Australia with a capacity of 3,2 million litres of pure alcohol. What stands out is how the whisky (and other spirits) are produced. The mashing is done with a mash filter but the really unique thing is how they handle their different malts in the process. The whisky from Archie Rose was from the start based on a six-malt mash bill. In the new distillery, each malt variety is handled separately all the way from milling, through brewing, fermentation, distillation and maturation. Only after that is the whisky blended together. This way each malt variety can be handled with regards to its own specific attributes. Apart from producing rye whisky and peated and unpeated single malt, the distillery also makes gin, rum and vodka. The first whisky was released in 2019 and today there are two core expressions Single Malt and Rye Malt. Limited releases occur regularly with the Sydney Opera House Contemporary Single Malt in November 2024, matured in fortified wine casks, being one of the latest.

Overeem Distillery (former Sawford Distillery)

Kingston, Tasmania, founded in 2017

overeemwhisky.com

The history of the distillery goes back to 2007 when Casey Overeem founded the Old Hobart Distillery. Eventually he made a name for himself with his Overeem single malt and was also joined by his daugther Jane. In 2014, Old Hobart distillery was acquired by Lark Distillery and later by Australian Whisky Holdings. In 2020, the Overeem trademark and part of the whisky inventory was sold back to Jane (who was married Sawford) and her husband Mark. The equipment was not included and henceforth Overeem whisky is produced at the new Sawford (later renamed Overeem) distillery which is equipped with two stills from Knapp Lewer (1,800 and 800 litres respectively). The core range of Overeem single malts (aged for at least 5 years) consists of Port Cask, Sherry Cask and Bourbon Cask bottled at both 43 and 60%. In March 2023, the 12 year old Bourbon Cask single malt was launched. Recent limited releases include Man of Promise Reserve 2024 matured in muscat casks and, in February 2025, Slightly Peated Sherry Cask Marriage.

Launceston Distillery

Western Junction (near Launceston), Tasmania, founded in 2013

launcestondistillery.com.au

The equipment consists of a 1,100 litre stainless steel mash tun, stainless steel washbacks, a 1,600 litre wash still and a 700 litre spirit still. The first release, matured in Apera casks, appeared in July 2018 and since then a signature range has developed; Apera, Tawny, Bourbon, Bourbon cask strength and Peated. Apart from that, whisky matured in different types of casks, bottled on a batch basis, are also launched more or less monthly including a Carribean Rum cask in late 2024.

Chief´s Son Distillery

Somerville, Victoria, founded in 2017

chiefsson.com.au

The distillery is equipped with a 4,000 litre copper pot still and focuses on malt whisky. They currently have a core range under the name 900 made up of Pure Malt, Sweet Peat, American Oak, Standard Port Cask and Standard Single Cask. Other bottlings include Forge, The Tanist and Peated Malt. The Distiller´s Select series is made up of bottlings only available at the cellar door where the latest (in November 2024) had been matured in muscat casks.

Callington Mill Distillery

Oatlands, Tasmania, founded in 2019

callingtonmilldistillery.com.au

In 2018, John Ibrahim opened a 100,000 litre capacity distillery in Hobart. Three years later a larger distillery (500,000 litres) was opened in Oatlands. All the equipment (including two copper pot stills and eight washbacks) was made in Tasmania. In 2022, the Leap of Faith series of eight bottlings distilled at Shene and Old Kempton distilleries was released. In February 2023 the distiller´s first core range from their own production was launched consisting of El Sol, Invicta and Fusion. These were later followed by the peated Quagmire, Enigma, Madeira Nouveau Beginnings and the peated Supreme Courthouse in February 2025.

Other distilleries in Australia

5 Nines Distilling

Uraidla, South Australia, founded in 2017

5ninesdistilling.com.au

The whisky is made primarily with local barley and the first releases appeared in August 2020. Later versions have included one that was finished in a cask that had been seasoned with cola and one that had matured in a cask that had held altar (sacrificial) wine.

7K Distillery

Brighton, Tasmania, founded in 2017

7kdistillery.com.au

A wide range of gins were intially released followed by their first single malt in 2020. Two recent versions, in 2024, were a rum cask and a port cask.

23rd Street Distillery

Renmark, South Australia, founded in 2016

23rdstreetdistillery.com.au

With three stills, 7,500 litres each, this distillery focused on a variety of gin, vodka and rum to start with. In 2019 the first single malt whisky was released. The latest bottling was Year of the Snake in January 2025.

36 Short Distillery

Virginia, South Australia, founded 2014

36short.com.au

A versatile distillery producing gin, vodka, rakia and also single malt whisky using a 1200 litre copper pot still. On of the more recent, limited releases was Daicos 35 in March 2024.

78 Degrees (a k a Adelaide Hills Distillery)

Hay Valley, South Australia, founded in 2016

78degrees.com.au

With his 400,000 litre distillery, Sacha La Forgia has been leading the way when it comes to producing whisky from Australian native grains. His trials have been numerous and the first bottling in 2019 couldn´t even be called whisky since wattleseed (which was part of the mash bill) isn´t a cereal grain. The whisky is now sold under the name 78 Degrees with a Muscat finish as one of the latest releases.

Adams Distillery

Perth, Tasmania, founded in 2016

adamsdistillery.com.au

After less than two years of production, all the equipment was sold to make way for a huge new distillery which started production in 2019. In February 2021, the distillery burned to the ground but soon after the ressurection began and a new distillery was operational in summer 2023. March 2023 saw the release of Signature Series 2 bottled at either 42% or 59%. Limited releases in 2024 included two that had partly matured in prosecco and sloe gin casks respectively.

Aisling Distillery, The

Griffith, New South Wales, founded in 2015

theaislingdistillery.com.au

With a focus on malt whisky - gin, vodka and rum is also produced. The first two single malts were released in 2020 and currently there is the Heritage Collection represented by Tawny and Apera as well as the limited Preimhe Shiraz Baraille. and Cnoc Neamh.

Amber Lane Distillery

Wyong, New South wales, founded 2017

amberlanedistillery.com

Founded by Rod Berry and Phil Townsend and equipped with a 3,600 litre copper pot still, the distillery focuses entirely on whisky. The first core expression, Destiny, has been followed by Equinox and Liquid Amber and, in autumn 2024, the Alchemical Series; Earth, Water, Fire, Air and Quintessence.

Backwoods Distilling

Yackandandah, Victoria, founded in 2017

backwoodsdistilling.com.au

Equipped with a 1200 litre copper pot still with an attached column, the first distillation was in 2018 with an inaugural release in August 2020. Recent releases include single malts matured in muscat casks, stout casks and casks made from red gum.

Barossa Distilling Company

Nuriootpa, South Australia, founded in 2016

barossadistilling.com

Located in the historical Old Penfolds Distillery, the distillery released their inaugural malt whisky, the 6 year old Gallus Barossa finished for 12 months in a muscat cask, in September 2023.

Battery Point Distillery

Battery Point (Hobart), Tasmania, founded 2018

batterypointdistillery.com

With Jack Lark, son of whisky icon Bill Lark as the head distiller for the first four years, the distillery launched the first whisky in April 2021. Focus in on single malts matured and/or finished in a variety of casks; sherry, tawny, bourbon and IPA.

Bellarine Distillery

Drysdale, Victoria, founded in 2017

bellarinedistillery.com.au

The distillery released their first whisky in spring 2021. Since then the owners have embarked on a Flagship Series called Oak and Spirit with Oak as the first and Spirit due for release in 2025. A limited release in 2024 was Kestrel matured in Apera casks.

Black Gate Distillery

Mendooran, New South Wales, founded in 2012

blackgatedistillery.com

Apart from malt whisky, the distillery produces vodka and rum. The first single malt was in 2015 when a sherrymatured expression was released. More bottlings have followed, including several peated releases as well as an on-going collaboration series (Country to Coast) with other distilleries.

Boatrocker Brewers & Distillers

Braeside, Victoria, founded in 2012

boatrocker.com.au

Starting as a brewery a distillery was then added. Apart from gin, vodka and rye, single malt whisky is also produced. The first release was Seven Year Itch in 2021 followed by two manuka smoked whiskies matured in apera and red wine casks respectively.

Bogan Road Distillery

Quambay Brook, Tasmania, founded 2018

boganroaddistillery.com

Starting out as bottlers in 2016, Karin Ketelaar and Shane Spencer decided to build a distillery in 2018 to produce their own spirit. Gin and various liqueurs have already been launched while single malt whisky is still maturing in the warehouse.

Bunker

Spring Grove, New South Wales, founded 2020

bunkerdistillery.com.au

Equipped with a 1,250 litre pot still for whisky and rum and a 300 litre still for gin, vodka and other spirits, a 5 year old, peated single malt (apparently sourced since the distillery started in 2020) was launched in 2023.

Canberra Distillery, The

Canberra, ACT, founded in 2016

thecanberradistillery.com.au

The main part of the production is gin, vodka and various liqueurs.

Callington Distillery in Tasmania has an impressive capacity of 500,000 litres

The first single malt whisky, Old George Reserve, distilled in 2018 and matured in a PX sherry cask was first released in late 2021.

Cape Byron Distillery

McLeods Shoot, New South Wales, founded 2016

capebyrondistillery.com

A B Corp certified distillery situated on a macadamia farm. The original intention was to do only gin but in 2019 they also started producing malt whisky. A core expression was launched in 2022 and releases in 2024 include Serendipity, Tawny Cask, Stone Beer Cask and Mac. Liqueur Cask. For the latter, casks that had held macadamia liqueur were used for the maturation.

Castle Glen Distillery

The Summit, Queensland, founded in 2009

castleglenaustralia.com.au

Established as a vineyard in 1990, Castle Glen moved on to open up also a brewery and a distillery. Apart from wine and beer, a wide range of spirits are produced. The first whisky was released as a 2 year old in 2012 and the oldest version to date is a 12 year old.

Coburns (Station Line Distillery)

Burrawang, New South Wales, founded in 2017

coburns.com.au

Mark Coburn started production in spring 2017 and his business is very much focused on selling barrels of maturing whisky to customers. Coburns is one of very few Australian distilleries with its own peat bog for smoking the barley.

Coopers

Recency Park, South Australia, founded 2024

coopers.com.au

Coopers, Australia´s largest independent brewer, recently opened a whisky distillery on their premises. Equipped with copper pot stills from Scotland they will be using malt from their own maltings for the whisky.

Corowa Distilling Co.

Corowa, New South Wales, founded in 2010

corowawhisky.com.au

The distillery is focused entirely on single malt whisky using barley from their own estate. Corowa started distilling in 2016 and the current core range consists of Barrel House XB Peated, Bosque Verde, Corowa Characters, Mad Dog Morgan, Private Notes and The Ben Buckler. There is also the Lunar Series with Year of the Snake (matured in rum casks) as the latest.

Cradle Mountain Whisky

Cradle Mountain, Tasmania, founded in 2019

cradlemountainwhisky.com

The story behind Cradle Mountain Whisky goes back to 1989, thirty years before the current distillery started production. In that year Brian Poke distilled the first Cradle Mountain single malt at his Darwin Distillery. Production, although sometimes intermittent, continued under different names until 2015 when Cradle Mountain Whisky (including stock) was bought by the Lahra family. In 2019 they opened up a new distillery under the name Cradle Mountain. The owners now produce single malts such as A Walk in the Woods and The Forest Trail with Barrel 26 being the latest.

Craft Works Distillery

Capertee, New South Wales, founded 2018

craftworksdistillery.com.au

The first releases from the owner, Crafty Field, were collaborations with other distillers. The first whisky from his own production was I Am..., released in early 2021. Later releases include Capertee and 42.

Cut Hill

Hindmarsh Valley, South Australia, founded 2019

cuthilldistillery.com.au

Situated on the Fleurieu Peninsula the distillery produces single malt whisky under the brand name Keystone Release. There are two ranges named Stonecutter and Small Batch. One of the more recent, in November 2024, was Stonecutter #7 - Fire and Stone which had been matured in an ex-muscat cask.

Darby-Norris Distillery

Scottsdale, Tasmania, founded in 2018

darbynorrisdistillery.com.au

The distillery recently moved from Kelso to larger premises in Scottsdale. Gin, vodka and rum have been released but the first single malt hasn´t been released yet.

Demoiselle

Panuara, New South Wales, founded 2012

demoiselle.com.au

Famous for their absinthe and spirits made from agave, a 6 year old malt whisky has also been released.

Derwent Distillery

Dromedary, Tasmania, founded in 2019

derwentdistillery.com.au

Opened in spring 2022, whiskies distilled at other distilleries but matured an bottled at Derwent were released from the start. The first expressions from their own production, Botrytis Cask and Tawny Cask, appeared in February 2025.

Deviant

Somerset, Tasmania, founded 2016

deviantdistillery.com

The first two single malts appeared in 2023 under the name Somerset - Black Label and Blue Label. Both are more than 3 years old but the owners have also been experimenting with an enhanced maturation technique.

Dusty Barrel Distillery

Macclesfield, Victoria, founded 2020

dustybarreldistillery.com.au

The still is directly fired using gas and the neck is a gatlin type which means the vapours rise through a number of smaller pipes before they reach the condenser. The first whisky, made from five grains, was launched in November 2023 and was followed by a whisky made from rice.

Edge of the World Distillery

Burnine, Tasmania, founded 2019

edgeoftheworlddistillery.com.au

The focus is on malt whisky but they are also producing gin and other spirits, First malt release was in September 2023, recently followed by a Pinot cask and an Apera cask - both 5 years old.

Fannys Bay Distillery

Lulworth, Tasmania, founded in 2014

fannysbaydistillery.com.au

The distillery is equipped with a 400 litre copper pot still and they use a long (7-8 days) fermentation. The first whisky was released in

May 2017 and it is now available in four main versions - bourbon, sherry, pinot and port. Most of the releases are single barrels and recently they have started to bottle lightly peated versions as well.

Fleurieu Distillery

Goolwa, South Australia, founded in 2016

fleurieudistillery.com.au

A beer brewery was turned into a distillery in 2016 but whisky had been distilled already since 2014. The first single malt appeared in 2016 and has been followed by several more expressions. Some of the latest are Don Quixote matured in an apera cask and Tapestry from both bourbon and apera.

Furneaux Distillery

Flinders Island, Tasmania, founded in 2018

furneauxdistillery.com.au

Initially the fermented wash was brought in from Launceston distillery but recently the distillery moved to Furneaux and a brewhouse was installed. The first single malts appeared in 2020 and in 2022 a new range was launched; unpeated Sawyers Bay Double Oak and two peated - Flinders Island and Smoky Wedding. The latter has been made from a 50/50 combination of Flinders Island malt and Scottish malt.

Grove, The

Wilyabrup, Western Australia, founded 1995

thegrovedistillery.com.au

Starting as a wine producer a distillery using a German pot still was later added. All kinds of spirits are produced including malt whisky where currently small batch rum cask and muscat cask are the best sellers.

Headlands Distilling Co.

North Wollongong, New South Wales, founded 2018

headlands.com.au

A range of gin and vodka were the initial releases but in 2020, the first two single malts were launched, finished in apera and muscat casks respectively. In December 2024 a limited 5 year old malt finished in 8 Shades Stout casks from Resin Brewing was released.

Hillwood Whisky (Tamar Valley Distillery)

Hillwood, Tasmania, founded in 2018

hillwoodwhisky.com.au

The spirit is distilled in a 600 litre copper pot still. The first releases appeared in summer 2020 and today there is a wide range of single cask malts (some of them peated) matured or finished in a variety of different casks.

Hobart Whisky (formerly known as Devil´s Distillery)

Moonah, Tasmania, founded in 2015

hobartwhisky.com.au

The first core expression from the distillery was the bourbon matured Signature in 2020 which was followed by Sherry Cask and Tawny Port Cask. The limited Winter Feast 2024 had been matured in a combination of bourbon maple, tawny and ex-Islay casks.

Hunnington Distillery

Kettering, Tasmania, founded 2016

hunningtondistillery.com.au

Focusing on gin and vodka, the owners also produce small volumes of triple distilled single malt whisky. The first release appeared in August 2020 and has been followed by more bottlings.

Imbue

Melbourne, Victoria, founded 2019

imbuedistillery.com

A versatile distillery producing a variety of spirits including Angel´s Share single malt. The two most recent are the 3 year old Bourbon and Port.

Iron House Brewery & Distillery

White Sands Resort, Tasmania, founded in 2007

ironhouse.com.au

Established as a brewery but started distilling whisky in 2010. The first Tasman Whisky (as the brand is called) was released in 2019 and the core range currently consists of Port-, Sherry- and Bourbon Cask – all aged for more than 4 years. A recent bottling in 2024 was the 8 year old Distiller´s Release matured in ex-port barrels.

Joadja Distillery

Joadja, New South Wales, founded in 2014

joadjadistillery.com.au

The main part of the barley for the whisky is from their own fields. The first whisky was launched in 2017 with a multitude of bottlings following. Celebrating its 10th anniversary in 2024 a 4 year old single malt fully matured in ex-Moscatel casks was released.

Jones & Smith Distillery

Spring Hill, New South Wales, founded 2017

jonesandsmithdistillery.com.au

A craft distillery with Epoch gin as their main product. On the malt whisky side there are two main ranges - Classic Collection and the Signature Series. In November 2024 Distiller´s Release matured in French oak sherry casks and bottled at 54,5% was launched.

Kilderkin Distillery

Ballarat, Victoria, founded in 2016

kilderkindistillery.com.au

Equipped with a pair of copper pot stills, a range of different gins has been their focus. The first Goldfields single malt matured for 5 years appeared in 2023 and was followed in 2024 by a 6 year old.

Killara Distillery

Richmond, Tasmania, founded in 2016

killaradistillery.com

Founded by Kristy Booth, the succesful Apothecary gin has been on the market for quite a while and in 2018 it was time for the first single malt release – matured for two years in an ex-tawny port cask. One of the more recent releases was a 6 year old matured in ex-tawny and finished in an ex-Laphroaig cask in October 2024.

Kinglake Distillery

Kinglake, Victoria, founded in 2018

kinglakedistillery.com.au

The distillery is focused on malt whisky and the first release was in 2021. The current core range consists of O´Grady´s Stand, Full Noise and Double Wood. Limited releases in 2024 included a small batch version, finished in red gum wood.

Kitty Hawk

Brisbane, Queensland, founded 2017

kittyhawkdistillery.com.au

A Queensland brain surgeon, Dr Martin Wood, is one of the co-founders of this distillery making gin and single malt whisky. Releases of the latter include Kitty hawk Byron Double finished in a rum cask, American Flyer (rye cask finish), The ´120´ (apera finish and Stratus (oloroso sherry).

Lawrenny Distilling

Ouse, Tasmania, founded in 2017

lawrenny.com

The first two single malts, Ascension and Descension, were launched in 2020. The current core range consists of Heritage (apera and sherry matured), Homestead (bourbon, port and sherry) and, most recently, the peated River Mist. Meanwhile there is an ongoing range of limited releases named Cellar Collection.

Lisandras Distillery

Bayswater, Western Australia, founded 2019

lisandrasdistillery.com.au

A family owned distillery which was recently expanded. First whisky was launched in 2021 and this was followed by American Oak, Hungarian Oak and Double Cask.

Loch Distillery

Loch, Victoria, founded in 2014

lochbrewery.com.au

A combined brewery and distillery using the wash from their brewery for the whisky production. The first single malt was launched in 2018 and by late 2024, more than 40 different releases had been made.

Lower Marsh Distillery

Apsley, Tasmania, founded 2019

lowermarshdistillery.com

The owners produce malt whisky from barley grown on their own farm including malting it themselves. The spirit is matured in a variety of casks and the first bottlings appeared in 2021.

McHenry Distillery

Port Arthur, Tasmania, founded in 2011

mchenrydistillery.com.au

Originally equipped with a 500 litre copper pot still, a 3,400 litre still was installed in late 2022. The first whisky was released in 2016 and in 2024 they released their first 12 year old. There is also a peated version in the range.

The McLaren Vale Distillery

Blewitt Springs, South Australia, founded in 2014

themclarenvaledistillery.com.au

In 2020 the first two malt whiskies were released and in 2021 the distillery was expanded with more stills. The current core product is Australian Wine Cask Single Malt and several limited editions, matured or finished in wine casks from local wine producers, appear regularly.

McRobert Distillery

Armadale, Western Australia, founded in 2019

mcrobertdistillery.com.au

The owner produces gin and whisky. Apart from rye, corn and bourbon style whisky there are two single malts in the range, bottled at 40% and 61% respectively; Single Malt and Heavily Peated.

MCW (Mount Compass)

Mount Compass, South Australia, founded 2019

mcwdistillery.com.au

In 2012 the owners took over a wine property on the Fleurieu Peninsula and in 2019 a distillery was added. Vodka, gin, grappa but also malt whisky is produced.

Manly Spirits Co. Distillery

Brookvale, Sydney, New South Wales, founded in 2017

manlyspirits.com.au

The first single malt appeared in 2021 and there are currently three ranges of single malts under the brand name Coastal Stone; Signature Series, Element Series and Italian Luxe Series (maturation in different red wine casks).

Morris Whisky

Rutherglen, Victoria, founded 2016

morriswhisky.com

Traditionally making fortified wines since 1859 the Morris family added a distillery in 2016. Their signature release appeared in 2021 and has been followed by other expressions, most of which have been finished in the company´s own wine barrels.

Mountain Distilling

New Gisborne, Victoria, founded 2017

mountaindistilling.com

Focusing mainly on gin, vodka and (not least) agave spirits the distillery has so far also released the peated Red Gum Single Malt.

Mt Uncle Distillery

Walkamin, North Queensland, founded in 2001

mtuncle.com

The owners started out by producing gin, rum and vodka. Their first single malt was released in 2014 and the only current malt whisky is Watkins Whisky.

Nant Distillery

Bothwell, Tasmania, founded in 2007

larkdistillery.com

The distillery was founded by Keith Batt but was later taken over by Australian Whisky Holdings which has since been renamed Lark Distilling Co. The first bottlings were released in 2010.

Newcastle Distilling

Wickham, New South Wales, founded 2020

newcastledistillingco.com.au

A brewery/distillery with plenty of spirits on their repertoire. Victor Hingston single malt appeared in 2022 and recently a lightly peated version aged in port barrels was launched.

Nonesuch Distillery

Dodges Ferry, Tasmania, founded in 2018

nonesuchdistillery.com.au

Established as a gin distillery it soon expanded into making single malt whisky as well. Currently in the range are Pinot Cask, Double Oak and Paradigm. Recently a 5 year old made from corn, rye and barley was launched.

Noosa Heads Distillery

Noosaville, Queensland, founded in 2018

noosaheadsdistillery.com

Equipped with a 2,000 litre copper pot reflux still, the distillery launched its first products in 2019 – gin, vodka and a white malt (new make spirit). The first single malt whisky, Laguna, was released in spring 2023.

Old Kempton Distillery

Kempton, Tasmania, founded in 2012

oldkemptondistillery.com.au

Established as Redlands Estate Distillery, the distillery re-located in 2016 to Dysart House in Kempton and later changed the name to

Old Kempton Distillery. The first whisky appeared in 2015 and the core expression is Old Stables but limited bottlings include Classic Pinot, Classic Tawny and the 10th Anniversary Release.

Otter Craft Distilling

Lilyfield, New South Wales, founded 2017

ocdistilling.com

This small distillery has launched a wide range of vodkas and in summer 2019 the first single malt whisky was released. More than 30 bottlings have followed, always bottled as a single barrel.

Riverbourne Distillery

Jingera, New South Wales, founded in 2016

riverbournedistillery.com

Located close to Canberra, the distillery produces whisky, rum and vodka. The first two single malts, released in 2018, were The Riverbourne Identity and Supremacy followed by Ultimatum, Enigma, Initiative, Objective, Betrayal and Shiraz Brandy.

St Agnes Distillery

Renmark, South Australia, founded 1925 (whisky since 2016)

stagnesdistillery.com.au

Starting as wine makers in the late 1800s, the Angove family later became Australia´s leading brandy producer. In 2016 the fifth generation ventured into small scale whisky production as well and in late 2022 the first releases of Camborne single malt appeared. They were all single casks and finished in brandy, sherry, tawny and shiraz casks repectively.

Sandy Gray Distillery

Spreyton, Tasmania, founded 2016

sandygraywhisky.com.au

Gin and single malt whisky are produced and a larger still was installed in 2022. The first whisky was launched in 2019 and the owners are planning for larger volumes to be released from mid 2025. The latest had been matured in second fill tawny barrels.

Settlers Artisan Spirits

McLaren Vale, South Australia, founded in 2015

settlersspirits.com.au

Initially concentrating on gin, a new pot still in 2018 tripled the whisky production. The only single malt release so far is the port matured Settlers Single Malt.

Souwester Spirits

Margaret River, Western Australia, founded in 2016

souwesterspirits.com

The owner´s spirits (gin and malt whisky) are matured in ex-wine casks. A single malt, matured in an ice chardonnay barrique, was first released in 2020 and was followed in autumn 2024 by a lightly peated matured in the same type of casks.

Spring Bay Distillery

Spring Beach and Cambridge, Tasmania, founded in 2015

springbaydistillery.com.au

The first release was a gin followed in 2017 by a single malt. In 2019 they built a second distillery in Cambridge. The owners are working on a solera system and more whiskies, matured in port, sherry and bourbon casks, have appeared since. One of the latest had been finished in madeira casks and bottled at 50%.

Stillmaker and Sons Distillery

Montville, Queensland, founded 2019

stillmakerdistillery.com.au

A family-owned distillery entirely focused on single malt whisky. A private cask was bottled in early 2023 and the first official and general release is expected in 2025.

Sunny Hill Distillery

Arthurton, South Australia, founded in 2018

sunnyhilldistillery.com.au

A family farm since 1872, the distillery produces gin, vodka and liqueurs. The first single malt made from their own barley was released in 2021 and one of the latest (in August 2024) was Dual Quercus matured in a combination of American and French oak.

Tara Distillery

Nowra Hill, New South Wales, founded 2019

taradistillery.com

The first spirit was a gin in autumn 2020. Mashed, fermented and distilled in a 2,400 litre pot still on site there is also an Irish-style single pot still as well as single malt whisky, both of them still maturing although the Exile poitín has been released.

Taylor & Smith Distilling Co.

Moonah, Tasmania, founded in 2017

taylorandsmith.com.au

Using a self-built, direct-fired 400 litre pot still, the owners produce small volumes of gin and malt whisky. The first single malt was released in October 2020 and several more expressions have followed matured in bourbon, sherry, port or rum casks.

Timboon Railway Shed Distillery

Timboon, Victoria, founded in 2007

timboondistillery.com.au

The first whisky release (Port Expression) was made in 2010 and is still the signature whisky. Other bottlings include Christie´s Cut, Governor´s Reserve where the latest had been matured in tawny casks, Smoky Tom and, released in February 2025, the limited The Golden Trifecta matured in three different types of casks.

Tin Shed Distilling Co.

Nairne, South Australia, founded in 2013

tinsheddistillingco.com.au

The owners opened Southern Coast Distillers, in 2004. Eventually it was closed and a new distillery started in 2013. In 2024 they moved to Nairne. The Iniquity malt was launched in 2015 with the 5 year old Den´s Dram in 2024 as one of the latest. Other ranges include the Anomaly Series, the Gold Series and the Silver Series.

Tiny Bear Distillery

Knoxfield, Victoria, founded in 2017

tinybear.com.au

Currently the main product is various expressions of gin. The first single malt appeared in 2021 and recent expressions include Barrel 13 and Barrel 18 - both matured in wine casks.

Tria Prima Distillery

Mount Barker, South Australia, founded 2017

triaprima.com.au

Equipped with a 2,200 litre pot still the distillery is focused on malt whisky. The first single malts, the 3 year old Enchantress and Bruxa, were released in 2021. Today the production is made up of three series - Traditional, Rebis and Transfiguration. Batch 2 of Enchantress appeared in autumn 2024.

Turner Stillhouse

Grindelwald, Tasmania, founded in 2018

turnerstillhouse.com

Founded by ex-Californian Justin Turner, the distillery has so far been focusing on gin. A designated whisky still was installed in summer 2019 with the aim to produce both American style whisky as well as single malt. First releases of these are expected in 2025.

Waubs Harbour Distillery

Bicheno, Tasmania, founded in 2018

waubsharbourwhisky.com

The distillery was founded by Tim Polmear, his wife Bec and Tim´s brother Rob whi is the head distiller. The first whiskies - Waubs Original, Port Storm and Founder´s Reserve - appeared in April 2023 and in 2024 a limited rum cask was released.

Western Tiers

Westbury, Tasmania, founded 2021

westerntiersdistillery.com.au

Originally supplying distilleries with equipment, Mark Kolodziej and Tim Freeman opened their own distillery in 2021. With both gin and vodka in the range the focus is on malt whisky. Three expressions are available; Highland Lakes (ex-bourbon), Western Lakes (ex-port) and Thousand Lakes (ex-sherry).

White Label Distillery

Huntingfield, Tasmania, founded in 2018

whitelabeldistillery.com.au

This is an unusual distillery in the sense that it is working as a contract brewing and distilling company, producing for other clients. Their customers can either obtain wash for their own distillation or new make spirit distilled to their own specification. The equipment consists of no less than 16 stainless steel washbacks (4,000 litres each) and two pairs of copper pot stills.

Wild River Mountain Distillery

Wondecla, Queensland, founded in 2017

wildrivermountaindistillery.com.au

One of the highest elevated distilleries in Australia, they released their first single malt, Elevation, in 2019. The 13th batch, matured in an oloroso cask and bottled at 54,3%, was launched in August 2024.

Winding Road Distilling

Tintenbar, New South Wales, founded 2017

windingroaddistilling.com.au

Apart from single malt whisky, both gin and rum is produced. The first whisky was distilled in spring 2019 in a 1,250 litre copper pot still and the first release of the Hinterland Single Malt appeared in spring 2022 with a fourth release in March 2024.

Yack Creek Distillery

Yackandandah, Victoria, founded in 2015

yackcreekdistillery.com.au

Equipped with two stills with columns attached, the distillery produces malt whisky, rum, gin and vodka. The first whisky was released in 2019 and has been followed by more batches. The latest (027) in 2024 had been finished in casks that had held the unusual combination of red wine, smoky whisky, rum and beer!

New Zealand

Thomson Whisky Distillery

Auckland, North Island, founded in 2014

thomsonwhisky.com

The company started out as an independent bottler but in 2014, the owners opened up a small distillery with two direct fired stills using gas. First release was in 2018 and the current core range is made up by Rye & Barley, Manuka Smoke, Two Tone and South Island Peat. Recent limited expressions include Full Noise, a cask strength manuka smoked whisky and the unsmoked Allier matured in second fill French oak wine casks.

Pokeno Whisky Company

Pokeno, North Island, founded in 2018

pokenowhisky.com

The distillery was founded by Matt and Celine Johns, both with a long experience from the whisky industry in the UK and France. It is equipped with two copper pot stills (4,000 and 3,800 litres respectively) and the current capacity of 100,000 litres of pure alcohol will increase to 250,000 litres in 2025. There is also a cooperage on site. In August 2022 the first three single malts were released; Origin, Discovery and Revelation making up the current core range. There is also the Exploration series with Totara Cask, Winter Malt and Triple Distilled. Finally in the Single Cask series the two latest releases were Vino de Naranja (with an 18 month finish in orange wine casks) and Sunshine Limited Edition finished in local beer casks.

Cardrona Distillery

Cardrona (near Wanaka), South Island, founded in 2015

cardronadistillery.com

The distillery is equipped with 1.4 ton mash tun, six metal washbacks, one 2,000 litre wash still and a 1,300 litre spirit still. The first 3 year old whisky was released in December 2018 followed by Just Hatched. Next came three expressions under the name Growing Wings and in spring 2023 it was time for Full Flight – two 7 year olds, matured in bourbon and PX sherry respectively and bottled at cask strength. All these represented the earliest stocks from the distillery and were followed in 2024/2025 by Sherry Cask, American Barrel and Chardonnay Barrel as well as three single cask releases; Hiahia, Briar and Discaria. In September 2023 the distillery was acquired by Thai-based International Beverage (also owners of Inver House Distillers with five distilleries in Scotland) for an undisclosed sum. The founder, Desiree Reid, will remain as managing director.

Other distilleries in New Zealand

1919 Distilling

Auckland, North Island, founded in 2017

1919distilling.com

The owners started with a substantial range of gin and in summer 2020 the first single malt was released. Goleta, matured in ex-bourbon and finished in sherry casks appeared in June 2024. More releases can be expected in 2025.

Auld Farm Distillery

Scotts Gap, South Island, founded in 2017

aulddistillery.co.nz

For three generations, the Auld family have been growing grain on their farm and in 2017 Rob and Toni also added distilling. The barley comes from their own land and is malted on site. New make and an oat whisky (autumn 2024) have so far been released.

Herrick Creek Distillery

Christchurch, South Island, founded in 2020

herrickcreek.co.nz

This micro distillery has already launched gin and three types of whisky are produced - single malt from barley, corn and bourbon style. Dusky Whisky (a single malt corn whisky) has been released and whisky made from barley have been announced for 2025.

Kiwi Spirit Company

Golden Bay, South Island, founded in 2002

kiwispiritdistillery.co.nz

For two decades the distillery has produced a wide variety of different spirits including spirits made from Blue Agave as well as the unique Waitui Single Malt Manuka Honey where the whisky has matured in casks that had previously held manuka honey.

Lammermoor Distillery

Ranfurly, South Island, founded in 2018

lammermoordistillery.com

A "paddock-to-bottle" distillery with every step from organically growing and malting the barley through to distilling and maturation. The manuka smoked First Edition single malt appeared in 2020 and was followed by The Anzac Edition, The Jock Scott and the Special Reserve Double Cask in February 2025.

Reefton Distilling Co.

Reefton, South Island, founded in 2018

reeftondistillingco.com

Starting off by distilling gin, vodka and liqueur, the owners moved to new premises in 2021, added a second still and started producing Moonlight Creek Whisky which became available in 2025.

Scapegrace Distillery

Lake Dunstan, Otago, South Island, founded in 2024

scapegracedistillery.com

Founded in 2014 the company built a succesful business, not least based on their gin but also vodka and single malt whisky. All the spirits were contract distilled at another distillery. In summer 2024 they opened up New Zealand´s largest distillery in central Otago equipped with a 5,000 litre wash still and a 3,600 litre spirit still. There are three single malts from their first production; Ephemeral matured in American oak as well as the smoky Anthem and Vanguard, both from virgin French oak.

Spirits Workshop Distillery, The

Christchurch, South Island, founded in 2012

thespiritsworkshop.co.nz

For quite some time the distillery has been making spirits for others in their two copper pot stills including malt whisky for New Zealand Whisky. Recently, however, they have themselves released a single malt under the name Divergence. The latest releases include Virgin French Oak, OtagoPinot Barrel and Port Wood Single Malt.

Waiheke Whisky

Waiheke Island, North Island, founded in 2010

waihekewhisky.com

The distillery was founded by Mark Izzard and Richard Evatt on the Waiheke Island. They started by designing a unique, geodesic spirit still made up by a number of flat copper panels that were fitted together. In 2023 the distillery moved into larger premises with more washbacks and a new set of stills. New Zealand peat is used for a lot of the production and the first expressions include Moss, Seris 1, Bog Monster, Dyad I and II. and The Sweetwater. In October 2024 Failight was released which is a blend of their own whisky and a number of world whiskies created by Alan Winchester

A beautiful view from the Cardrona still room

Asia

China

Daiking

Zhangzhou, Fujian, founded in 2014

daikingtw.com

Without any international attention, this malt whisky distillery of a substantial size (a capacity of 8,4 million litres of pure alcohol) was opened already in 2014 and in 2019 their first whisky was launched in the domestic market. It is one of few Chinese malt whiskies that have so far reached markets in the rest of the world as well. The distillery is equipped with no less than five mash tuns (three semi-lauter and two converted starch cookers for brewing). There are 48 stainless steel wash backs with a fermentation time from 60 to 96 hours.A total of ten 10,000 litre wash stills and eight spirit stills, 6,000 to 10,000 litres, are housed in three still houses.

Laizhou

Qionglai, Sichuan, founded in 2021

laizhoudistillery.com

Laizhou distillery is owned by Shanghai Baccus, the biggest company in China in the ready-to-drink (RTD) segment and a subsidiary of Bairun. The distillery is equipped with eight copper pot stills made by McMillan in Scotland and equipped with condensers made of copper as well as stainless steel. In addition there are also 7 column stills. The distillery has the capacity to make 5 million litres of malt and 20 million litres of grain yearly. There is also a cooperage on site with nine coopers as well as a custom-made STR-system where wine casks are shaved, toasted and re-charred. The inaugural single malt appeared in 2024 together with a blend (70% malt and 30% grain).

Goalong

Liuyang, Hunan, founded in 2021

goalong.com.cn

The owners, Hunan Goalong Liquor (Miluo) Co., was established as a company already in 2012 to produce a variety of spirits. The distillery is situated in South Central China in a subtropical climate. In 2015 equipment for experimental whisky distillation was installed and in 2021 a completely new whisky distillery was commissioned with one large mash tun, 8 washbacks, 5 copper pot stills and one column still. The capacity (malt and grain combined) is 5 million litres and the owners have already released a range of single malts. An expansion of the distillery, including more warehousing and a visitor centre, is also underway.

Chuan

Emeishan, Sichuan, founded in 2021

pernod-ricard.com

It was only a matter of time before the large whisky producers from overseas would build their own whisky distilleries in China. Pernod-Ricard became first when they commissioned their Chuan Distillery in 2021. With an investment of $150m the distillery has been equipped with ten stainless steel washbacks with a minimum fermentation time of 78 hours and one pair of pot stills made by Forsyths. The distillery is spectacularly designed and also includes a visitor centre. In December 2023 Chuan Pure Malt Whisky, containing also Scotch whisky, was launched.

Mengtai

Ordos, Inner Mongolia, founded in 2023

In 2021 the equipment for an entire whisky distillery was shipped from Forsyths in Scotland to Ordos in Inner Mongolia. It is the first whisky distillery in the region and behind the project is Mengtai Group, one of Inner Mongolia´s largest private companies and mainly active in coal production and generation of electricity. Included in the equipment is a two ton mash tun and ten washbacks. One of two production lines, making "bourbon", was commissioned in May 2023 and production of malt whisky commenced in August.

Nine Rivers

Da Chi, Fujian, founded in 2024

nineriversdistillery.cn

A total of 160 investors from 28 countries are behind this project.

The impressive Laizhou Distillery

After a few years of discussions and planning land for the sizeable distillery was purchased in 2020 and in June 2025 the distillery had its first distillation trials. All the equipment is built in China apart from the stills which come from Forsyth. Initially three stills will be operating with space for another seven. The ultimate capacity will be 10 million bottles per year. The distillery has its own floor malting and a cooperage is currently being built. There will also be a visitor centre.

Yun Tuo

Eryuan, Yunnan, founded in 2023

Located at an altitude of 2,100 metres above sea level, this is Diageo´s first malt whisky distillery in China. The development has been supervised by master blender Jim Beveridge and master distiller Andrew Millsopp and the the distillery is carbon neutral. Trial production began in 2023 and full-scale production started in March 2024. The distillery, which will eventually be opened to visitors is equipped with a 7 ton full lauter mash tun, eight stainless steel washbacks and two pairs of stills.

Guqi Distillery

Bozhou, Anhui, founded in 2024

A joint cooperation between the famous producer of cognac, Camus, and producer of baijiu Gujinggong. The focus is on two styles of products; single malt whisky and whiskies infused with traditional Chinese herbs.

Chun´an Distillery

Chun´an, Zhejiang, founded in 2025

Family owned Angus Dundee Distillers, founded in 1988, is one of the larger Scottish whisky companies. They are acting as bottlers, blenders and producers and for almost 25 years they have been the owners of Glencadam and Tomintoul. Reecently they embarked on building a malt distillery in China. Located on the Qiandao lake near Fuwen village, the distillery will be commissioned in early 2026. Main parts of the equipment come from Forsyth in Rothes including an 8 ton semi lauter mash tun and two pairs of stills and the capacity will be 3,4 million litres of alcohol. There will also be substantial visitor facilities.

Dongwei

Dong-Ting Lake, Hunan, founded in 2020

thedongwei.com

A craft distillery owned by Weidong Wei who began distilling already in 2014 in a small pilot still. The distillery is equipped with two traditional Scottish-style copper pot stills, designed and built by himself. The wash still is 3,000 litres and spirit still 2,000 litres and the distillery has a capacity of producing 93,000 litres. Chinese barley (two-, four- and six-row) is used and the first 6 year old single malt was released in 2022.

India

Amrut Distilleries Ltd.

Bangalore, Karnataka, founded in 1948

amrutdistilleries.com

The family-owned distillery, based in Kumbalgodu outside Bangalore in southern India, started to distil malt whisky in the mid-eighties. The equivalent of 60 million bottles of spirits (including rum, gin and vodka) is manufactured a year, of which 1,5 million bottles is whisky. Most of the whisky goes to blended brands but Amrut single malt was introduced in 2004 and can now be found in more than 50 countries. The distillery was expanded with four more stills in 2018 and with a total of two mash tuns and 12 washbacks it now has the capacity of producing one million litres of pure alcohol. The fermentation time for the single malt is 140 hours and the barley is sourced from the north of India, malted in Jaipur and Delhi and finally distilled in Bangalore before the whisky is bottled without chill-filtering or colouring.

The Amrut core range consists of Indian (unpeated) and Peated Indian, both bottled at 46% as well as at cask strength as well as

In 2023 Diageo began production at their first whisky distillery in China - Yun Tuo

Fusion which is based on 25% peated malt from Scotland and 75% unpeated Indian malt. Special releases over the years, often released in new batches, include Two Continents, where maturing casks have been brought from India to Scotland for their final period of maturation, Intermediate Sherry Matured where the new spirit has matured in ex-bourbon or virgin oak, then re-racked to sherry butts and with a third maturation in ex-bourbon casks, Kadhambam which is a peated Amrut matured in ex oloroso butts, ex Bangalore Blue Brandy casks and ex rum casks, Portonova with a maturation in bourbon casks and port pipes, Amalgam comprising of Amrut as well as single malts from Scotland and Asia (with a peated version introduced in late 2018), Spectrum where the fourth edition had been matured in casks made of four varieties of oak, Double Cask, a 5 year old combination of ex-bourbon and port pipes and the 100% malted Amrut Rye Single Malt. A big surprise in 2013 was the release of the 8 year old Amrut Greedy Angels. That was an astonishing achievement in a country where the hot climate causes major evaporation. A few years later a 12 year old version was launched and in 2024 a 15 year old 75th anniversary edition was released – the oldest Indian single malt to date.

In 2020 the first triple distilled Indian whisky was released – Amrut Triparva – and in 2021 the sherry-finished Bagheera was launched. Late that year the first Master Distiller´s Reserve, a peated version matured in both bourbon and PX sherry casks appeared. A special range called Single Malts of India was launched in 2021 with the peated Neidhal being the first bottling. Distilled at another distillery it had been further matured and bottled by Amrut. A second installment, Kurinji, appeared in 2023 followed by the 10 year old Marudham in spring 2024.

John Distilleries Jdl

Goa, Konkan and Bangalore, Karnataka, founded in 1992

pauljohnwhisky.com

Paul P John, who today is the chairman of the company, started in 1992 by making a variety of spirits including Indian whisky made from molasses. Their biggest seller today is Original Choice, a blend of extra neutral alcohol distilled from molasses and malt whisky from their own facilities. The brand, which was introduced in 1995, is currently the world´s best selling whiskies. John Distilleries owns three distilleries and produces its brands from 18 locations with its head office in Bangalore and a huge distillery and visitor centre in Goa. The basis for their blended whiskies is distilled in column stills with a capacity of 500 million litres of extra neutral alcohol per year. In 2007 they set up their single malt distillery which was recently expanded with a larger mash tun and another two pot stills (a total of eight). The malt capacity is now 3 million litres. Malhar Indian Craft Gin was recently added to the portfolio and a completely new brand named Roulette (blended whisky, brandy, vodka and gin) has been launched. The large American spirit producer Sazerac owns 60% of the company while the rest is controlled by Paul P John.

The company released their first single malt in 2012 and this was followed by several single casks. Since 2015 the core range consists of three expressions aged 6 years or more; Brilliance - unpeated and bourbon-matured, Edited - bourbon-matured and lightly peated and Bold - heavily peated. In 2019 an entry level bottling named Nirvana, aged for 3 years and bottled at 40%, was also launched. In 2014, two cask strength bottlings were released in the Select Cask range and since then more expressions have been released; Oloroso, Pedro Ximenez, Madeira and Port. In 2025 three expressions for travel retail in India appeared.

Rampur

Rampur, Uttar Pradesh, founded in 1943

rampursinglemalt.com

Radico Khaitan, one of India´s oldest and largest manufacturers of India Made Foreign Liquor (IMFL), operates eight distilleries across India including four in Rampur (Uttar Pradesh), one in Sitapur, and three in Aurangabad (Maharashtra). Together, these facilities boast an annual distillation capacity of 321 million liters. They also have a distillery producing whisky from malted

Amrut was the initiator of Indian single malt which today has become popular all over the world

barley. An expansion in autumn 2019 increased the capacity of that distillery to 3 million litres per year and further expansion is underway which will take the capacity up to 5 million litres.

The first whisky brand from Radico (in 1998) was 8PM, which sells around 115 million bottles yearly. The first single malt release, the ex-bourbon matured Select, appeared in 2016 and since then Double Cask matured in bourbon and sherry casks and PX sherry have been released in the core range. Asava, in 2020, was finished in Indian cabernet sauvignon casks. This was followed in 2022 by Trigun and the limited Jugalbandi series. In spring 2023 Sangam, a blended malt made from whiskies around the world was released followed in 2024 by Barrel Blush.

Piccadily

Indri, Haryana, founded in 1967, whisky since 1994

piccadily.com

Piccadily Agro Industries was founded in 1952 while Piccadily Distillery was registered in 1967 and in 1994 they resumed distilling. The distillery has so far been equipped with two mash tuns (4.5 and 6.5 tons respectively), eight washbacks (60,000 litres each), three 25,000 litre wash stills and three 15,000 litre spirit stills - all pot stills stills and made from copper. A recent expansion has brought the capacity from 4 million litres of alcohol to 5.1 million litres and there are plans to also build a new distillery in Mahasamund in Chhattisgarh. Grain spirit is also produced and on a much larger scale. This makes Piccadily the largest independent malt producing distillery in India. In 2020, in a joint venture with Peak Spirits, they launched their first single malt whisky named Kamet. This was followed in 2022 with Indri which had been matured in a combination of ex-bourbon, ex-wine and PX sherry casks and in 2023, Indri Dru, a cask strength version was launched. Indri Triple Cask was released for the travel retail market in 2024 and in June 2025 Indri Agneya, a lightly peated version, appeared. The master blender behind the whisky is Surrinder Kumar who was the Amrut master blender for many years.

Other distilleries in India

Imperial Distillers & Vintners

Kundaim Industrial Estate, Ponda, Goa, founded in 2009

thecheersgroup.com

The company, which is part of the Cheers Group founded by Mohan Krishna, is the producer of a variety of different spirits including the Three Monkeys Single Malt. Equipped with copper pot stills, the distillery has a capacity of 1 million litres of alcohol.

Khoday

Bangalore, Karnataka, founded in 1906

khodayindia.com

Khoday is a company working in many areas, including brewing and distillation. The IMFL whisky Peter Scot was launched by the company already in 1968 and in spring 2019, the Peter Scot Black Single Malt was launched.

McDowell´s Distillery

Ponda, Goa, founded in 1988 (malt whisky)

diageoindia.com

Established in the late 1800s, the company (with seven distilleries around the country) produces the best selling whisky in the world, McDowell´s No. 1, with 377 million bottles sold in 2023. Owned by Diageo since 2014, the distillery also produces a very small amount of single malt whisky. In spring 2024 the brand was re-invented and the first release was Distiller´s Batch Indian Single Malt where the maturation involves four types of casks; ex-bourbon, virgin oak, cabernet sauvignon and shiraz.

John Distilleries recently increased their malt whisky capacity to 3 million litres

Mohan Meakin

Solan, Himachal Pradesh, founded in 1855

mohanmeakin.com

Founded as a brewery in 1820, possibly by Edward Dyer and incorporated as a company in 1855. It was taken over by H G Meakin in 1887 and finally, Narendra Nath Mohan acquired the business in 1949. Today, the company is making beer, whisky and rum. Their most famous brands are Old Monk rum and Solan No. 1 whisky. Their first general launch of a single malt whisky under the name Solan Gold Single Malt appeared in 2019.

South Seas Distilleries and Breweries

Mumbai, founded in 1984

southseasdistilleries.com

The family´s interest in distillation goes back to the early part of the 20th century but the distillery we see today was equipped in 1990 by Stewart McBain Ltd in Scotland and has later been expanded to produce larger volumes. In 2023 they released for the first time their Crazy Cock single malt which can be found in two versions - /Bourbon/Sherry and Peated.

Una Distillery

Una, Himachal Pradesh, founded in 2024

Scottish whisky producers have lately shown an interest in establishing distilleries in India and Una Distillery was founded by Ian Macleod Distillers (owners of Glengoyne, Tamdhu and Rosebank in Scotland). The distillery is equipped with a mash tun and nine washbacks made in India as well as two copper pot stills made by Forsyths in Rothes. The total capacity is one million litres of pure alcohol. The first distillation was in March 2024 and the distillery is using locally grown 2-row barley to get a diverse flavour profile and a higher yield compared to 6-row barley.

Israel

The Milk & Honey Distillery

Tel-Aviv, founded in 2013

mh-distillery.com

Israel's first whisky distillery, equipped with a stainless steel mash tun, six stainless steel washbacks and two copper stills. The capacity is 800,000 litres of pure alcohol. The first distillation was in March 2015 and the first, limited 3 year old single malt, made before the final equipment was installed, was released in May 2017. A Founder's Edition appeared in autumn 2019 and in January 2020 their first commonly available and current core expression, Classic, was launched. A series named Elements is based on maturation in ex-bourbon and STR casks with an addition of other cask types for each expression. Currently there are Sherry, Peated, Red Wine and Pomegranate wine casks expressions. Another limited range is Apex where the head distiller, Tomer Goren, is experimenting with malts having been fully matured or finished in unusual casks or in one of the different terroir-based warehouses located all around Israel. The 3rd. release of the Apex Terroir, aged at the Dead Sea (the lowest place on earth) was released in 2024. Another three different climate zone-matured expressions appeared in February 2025 - aged at the sea of Galilee, Jerusalem mountains and at the Desert in Arad.

A collaboration with Julius distillery in Israel was released also under the Apex series with a whisky finished in Grappa-style casks. A third range named Art&Craft focuses on different cask types and while the first edition in 2022 focused on ex-beer casks, the second batch in 2024 was all about dessert wine casks. In September 2023, the first Israeli whisky made entirely from Israeli barley was launched under the name Local Barley. This was followed in November by the Spirit of Hope single-cask series to fund donations for the victims of October 7th in the south of Israel.

Una Distillery in Himachal Pradesh was founded in 2024 by Ian Macleod Distillers

Other distilleries in Israel

Golani Distillery

Katzrin, founded in 2014

golanispirit.com

Founded by David Zibell, the distillery is equipped with two artisanal copper stills and some of the whisky is matured in wine casks from the nearby Golan Heights Winery. In spring 2020, a new, one ton mash tun as well as two more washbacks were installed and in autumn 2021 another mash tun, two more washbacks and two new 1,000 litre stills were added. The distillery is focusing on single malt from barley and on grain whisky (51% malted barley and 49% wheat). The first 3 year old whisky appeared in late 2017. A large number of different expressions, mainly single casks, have since been launched. There is also a range of single cask single malts named Unicask where the whiskies have matured mainly in casks that have previously held wine or brandy.

N.G.K. Distillery

Gan Hashomron, founded in 2021

ngk-distillery.com

Founded by Tomer Goren, Milk & Honey's Head Distiller and Amos Nir, in a collaboration with Milk & Honey distillery, it started distillation in May 2022. Equipped with one mash tun, three stainless steel washbacks and two stills, the distillery is producing a lightly peated whisky. An expansion of the distillery is currently underway. A founders collection presale was launched in 2024, offering a bundle of young single malts as well as a preorder of the Founders Edition, planned to be released in January 2026.

Pelter

Ein Zivan, founded in 2013

en.pelter.co.il

A boutique winery which expanded their production with a distillery equipped with an alembic still and producing whisky, brandy and arak in 2013. The first release of a single malt was a 3 year old and the latest had reached the age of 10 years.

Shevet Brewing & Distilling

Pardess Hanna, founded in 2017

shevet.co.il

Abrewery with a distillery attached equipped with two traditional copper pot stills. The wash from the brewery is distilled into whisky. The malt whisky is named Ruach and a special version (Stronger Together) was launched in autumn 2023 to raise funds for the survivors of the attack on the 7th of October.

Yerushalmi Distillery

Jerusalem, founded in 2017

yerushalmidistillery.com

This is David Zibell´s (owner of Golani) second distillery and equipped with a 3,000 litre wash still and a 2,000 litre spirit still it has a capacity of 150,000 litres per year. The idea is to concentrate the peated production to this distillery. The first distillation was in 2019 and they have released the peated single malt (35ppm) Mount Moriah and also four peated single casks in a range named Solum; Sessile Oak (new French charred oak), Pirate Oak (rum cask), Birra Oak (craft beer cask) and Dessert Oak (white dessert wine cask). Several more expression have followed since.

Golani - a craft distillery in the Golan Heights in Israel

Japan

Yamazaki

Mishima, Osaka, founded in 1923

suntory.com/factory/yamazaki/

The story of Japanese whisky started here, in earnest, when Shinjiro Torii built the first malt whisky distillery in Japan. Torii was a pragmatic man, so he decided to build his distillery close to center of commerce at the time, Osaka. The construction of Yamazaki distillery began in late 1923 and was completed the following year. The first spirit ran off the stills on November 11, 1924. The distillery started out with two pot stills but has been reconfigured and expanded many times over the years, first in 1957, and most recently in 2013, when four pot stills were added bringing the count to 16. There is lots of variety in terms of heating method, shape, size, lyne-arm orientation and condenser type, but that's typical of Yamazaki at every stage of production. Since 1988, eight of the washbacks are wooden whereas the other nine are stainless steel. With different peating levels for the barley, different yeast strains and a plethora of cask types, the variety of whisky types created at Yamazaki distillery is quite staggering. The most recent release to come out of the distillery was Yamazaki Story of the Distillery 2025 Edition.

Yoichi

Yoichi, Hokkaido, founded in 1934

nikka.com/eng/distilleries/yoichi/

Masataka Taketsuru established Yoichi distillery after leaving Kotobukiya (now Suntory) in 1934. He settled on the town of Yoichi, in the cold north of Japan, because the locale and climate conditions reminded him of Scotland, where he had studied whisky making. The first spirit ran off the stills in 1936, with the first product launched in 1940. Initially equipped with a single still that doubled as spirit and wash still, the distillery now houses 6 stills. Coal-heated and featuring straight heads and downward lyne arms, these produce a robust spirit. Although the 'house style' is peaty and heavy, people tend to forget that – like the other big distilleries in Japan – Yoichi is set up to create a wide range of distillates. Between various peating levels, yeast strains, fermentation times, distillation methods and maturation types, it is said that Yoichi is capable of producing 3,000 different types of malt whisky. The most recent release to come out of the distillery is the 2025 edition of The Nikka Yoichi 10 year old.

Fuji Gotemba

Gotemba, Shizuoka, founded in 1973

fujiwhisky.com

Fuji Gotemba distillery sits at the foot of Mt. Fuji, less than 12 km from the peak. The distillery was founded by Kirin Brewery, Seagram & Sons and Chivas Brothers as a comprehensive whisky distillery where all production processes – from malt and grain whisky distilling to blending and bottling – take place on site. Unlike most Japanese distilleries, which followed Scottish whisky-making practice, Fuji Gotemba distillery adopted production techniques and methodologies from Canada and the U.S. as well. After Seagram started selling off its beverage assets worldwide, Kirin became the sole owner of the distillery.

The distillery is well known for its uniquely different styles of grain whisky, made using column stills, a kettle and a doubler in a modular way. There are also ongoing projects to further diversify the flavor profile of their malt whisky. In 2021, two different sets of new pot stills and four wooden washbacks came into use. In 2023, the two large-size pot stills, which had been in use since the foundation of the distillery, were replaced with brand new ones. The latest major development on site as far as malt whisky production is concerned involves the use of locally-grown barley.

Hakushu

Hokuto, Yamanashi, founded in 1973

suntory.com/factory/hakushu/

Hakushu was built 50 years after the first Suntory malt whisky distillery and is nestled in a forest area at the foot of Mt Kaikomagatake in the Southern Alps. It is often referred to as 'the

The old practise of coal firing the stills is still in use at Yoichi Distillery

forest distillery': more than 80% of the site owned by Suntory is undeveloped. The original distillery was equipped with 6 pairs of stills. In 1977, capacity was doubled and another 6 pairs of stills added in a building next to 'Hakushu 1'. With its 4 mashtuns, 44 washbacks and 24 stills, Hakushu (1+2) was the largest whisky distillery in the world at the time. In 1981, Suntory built a new distillery, 'Hakushu 3' or 'Hakushu East' on the site, and decided to phase out production at #1 and #2 in favor of #3. Distilleries 1 and 2 had big stills, but all of the same shape and size, whereas #3 had a variety of stills with different shapes, sizes, lyne-arm orientations, heating methods and condenser types. What they were after was diversity and quality rather than quantity.

The distillery as it is operative now is Hakushu 3, albeit with the addition of two pairs of pot stills in 2014, bringing the total to 8 pairs, just like at Yamazaki distillery. It's also worth noting that there is a small grain whisky facility at Hakushu since 2010. The most recent release to come out of the distillery was Hakushu Story of the Distillery 2025.

Miyagikyo

Sendai, Miyagi, founded in 1969

nikka.com/eng/distilleries/miyagikyo/

Miyagikyo is Nikka's second distillery and legend has it that it took Masataka Taketsuru three years to find the perfect site for it. He settled on the valley that brings the Hirosegawa and Nikkagawa rivers together because of the quality of the water, the suitable humidity and the crisp air. Construction started in 1968 and was completed the following year. Originally known as 'Sendai', the distillery was renamed 'Miyagikyo' when Asahi took control of Nikka in 2001. At present, Miyagikyo is equipped with 22 steel washbacks and 8 huge pot stills of the 'boil ball' type with upward lyne arms, encouraging reflux which – given the slow distillation method (steam-heated) – results in a lighter, cleaner spirit. The site also houses two enormous Coffey stills imported by Taketsuru from Scotland. Moved from Nishinomiya in 1999, these are used to produce grain whisky (Coffey Grain) but, occasionally, are used to distill malted barley (Coffey Malt). Since 2017, they're also churning out Coffey Gin and Coffey Vodka. Production at Miyagikyo is in 3 shifts, 7 days a week. Every day 5 batches of malted barley are processed, with one batch using a massive 10 tons of malted barley. There used to be two mashtuns – one smaller and one bigger – in function of the difference in size between pot stills 1 to 4 and 5 to 8, respectively, but the small mashtun was removed in 2023 and an ingenious system was worked out that allows the use of just the big mashtun.

Chichibu #1

Chichibu, Saitama, founded in 2007

facebook.com/ChichibuDistillery/

Chichibu distillery was established in 2007 and started producing the year after. The set up is small and compact: a 2,400 litre mashtun (manually stirred with a wooden paddle), 8 mizunara washbacks of 3,000 litre each and a pair of 2,000 litre pot stills. Chichibu I is dedicated to non-peated production for 9 months a year, and to heavily-peated production for 1 month, the remaining 2 months being used for maintenance. There is also an area for floor malting on site. Between Chichibu I and Chichibu II distillery, there are 7 warehouses: six dunnage and one racked. Ichiro also has a fully operational cooperage a few minutes down the road from Chichibu I distillery. Since 2010, the Chichibu team has been making regular trips to Hokkaido to buy mizunara wood and the in-house coopers have been perfecting their mizunara-barrel-making skills since 2016. A very small number of casks are made out of local Chichibu mizunara. The latest 'big' single malt release is the Chichibu 10 year old, which hit the shelves in the latter half of 2025.

Chichibu #2

Chichibu, Saitama, founded in 2019

facebook.com/ChichibuDistillery/

Around 2014, Ichiro Akuto started thinking about setting up a second distillery. Unlike other whisky producers in Japan with multiple distilleries, he didn't go for a distinctly different location and environment. Ichiro stayed in his hometown and built his new distillery just a two-minute drive away from the 'old' one.

Coopering of mizunara casks at Chichibu Distillery

Construction began in April 2018 and the first spirit came off the stills in July 2019. There are many features of the new distillery that are the same as at Chichibu I, but the new distillery is five times bigger than the first one. At Chichibu II, 2 tons of malted barley are processed per batch. The water is the same as at Chichibu I. At Chichibu II, non-peated, lightly-peated, medium-peated and heavily-peated malted barley is used. Mashing takes place in a semi-lauter tun. The fermentation process takes place in washbacks made of French oak. The stills are the same shape as at Chichibu I and even the lyne-arm angle is the same (12° downward), but they are much bigger (10,000 litres and 6,500 litres respectively) and both stills are direct-fired. The first official, generally available bottling to come out of the new distillery – simply called Ichiro's Malt Chichibu Distillery II - was released in May 2025.

Other distilleries in Japan

Akkeshi

Akkeshi, Hokkaido, founded in 2015

akkeshi-distillery.com/en/

Inspired by Islay and with equipment and methods imported from Scotland, the goal of Akkeshi distillery is to create a whisky that is uniquely shaped by the environment. The production relies heavily on peated malt (50ppm), although non-peated malt is used as well. The distillery has two warehouses on site as well as two near the sea, to explore differences in maturation. Since August 2021, the distillery has also been maturing some of its spirit in central Hokkaido. The 18th release in the distillery's 24 Solar Terms series ('Touji') was released in February 2025. Interestingly, this was a single blended whisky with both malt and grain distilled at Akkeshi. The grain whisky is a 'single pot still grain whisky', made from all-Hokkaido ingredients (malted barley, wheat, rice and buckwheat).

Asaka

Koriyama, Fukushima, founded in 2015

sasanokawa.co.jp/asaka-distillery-en/

Sasanokawa Shuzo was founded in 1765. Whisky 'making' started in 1946 but exactly how is lost in the mists of time. Sake production forms the backbone of the company and that allowed them to ride out some of the tougher periods for whisky in Japan. To mark the 250th anniversary of the company in 2015, a proper malt whisky distillery was set up in a disused warehouse on site. By the end of the year, two small pot stills had been installed. The first single malt expression (Asaka The First) was released in 2019 and Asaka The First Peated was released the year after. Only 10% of the production is peated. The latest general release was the Yamazakura Single Malt Asaka 2025 Edition, released in May 2025.

Eigashima

Akashi, Hyogo, founded in 1919 (whisky since 1984)

ei-sake.jp/en/

On paper, this is the oldest whisky producer in Japan, having acquired a whisky production license in 1919, four years before Yamazaki. It took them four decades to get their act together, and another four decades to release their first single malt in 2007. The old spirit and wash still were retired in 2019 and replaced with new ones. In April 2023, a wooden washback was added to the distillery to extend the fermentation time and encourage the lactic acid fermentation. All production is matured on site in old single-story rickety warehouses in a bewildering variety of cask types.

Fugaku

Fujiyoshida, Yamanashi, founded in 2021

sasakawa-whisky.jp/en/

Located in the Fuji-Hakone-Izu National Park, at the foot of Japan's iconic peak. Production started in late 2023 and it is equipped with 6 Douglas fir washbacks and a pair of pot stills made by Miyake Industries (the wash still being direct-fired). The distillery has also been distilling a small amount of Golden Promise barley. No products have been released yet.

Fuji Hokuroku

Fujikawaguchi, Yamanashi, founded in 2020

Fuji Hokuroku Disitllery is a sideproject of Ide Jozoten, a well-

Fugaku Distillery has a direct fired wash still

known sake producer. The current president of the company, Yogoemon Ide, decided to expand into the field of whisky production and a tiny distillery was set up next to the historical sake brewery. The first milling took place in 2020 and the equipment includes two repurposed enamel-coated steel sake tanks and a single stainless steel still with copper plates in the neck. The distillery makes both malt and grain whisky during the warmer half of the year (when sake production is on hiatus). The distillery has recently filled some casks made from Mt. Fuji mizunara and chestnut.

Gakkogawa

Yuza, Yamagata, founded in 2021

gakkogawa.com/en/

Founded by the well-known sake maker Tatenokawa Shuzo the construction of the distillery was completed in July 2023 and production started in October. It is equipped with 5 stainless steel washbacks and a pair of pot stills (2,400 l and 1,200 l respectively). Most of the production is non-peated and filled into ex-bourbon wood, but the distillery also uses ex-bourbon barrels fitted with heads made from local mizunara. Bottles of newmake were released in March 2024..

Hanyu

Hanyu, Saitama, founded in 2021

hanyu-distillery.jp

The original Hanyu Distillery was mothballed in 2000 and demolished in 2004. Its whiskies have since become the stuff of legend, changing hands for many thousands of dollars a bottle. In 2002, Toa Shuzo became a subsidiary of Hinode Holdings Co., Ltd and recently it was decided the time was right to revive whisky-making. A brand new distillery equipped with a one ton mash tun, 5 stainless steel washbacks and a pair of steam-heated lantern-shaped pot stills based on the blueprints of the original Hanyu stills started production in February 2021. The first release from the new distillery ('Genesis') came out in 2024. The distillery officially opened to the public in May 2025 and regular tours are offered.

Hida Takayama

Takane, Gifu, founded in 2022

whisky-hida.com

Established by a local sake company the distillery is located in a closed elementary school in Takane city. Production started in May 2023. Four wooden washbacks are used – two of these made from oak and the other two from larch. The potstills are Zemon stills (of the type pioneered by Saburomaru distillery). The wash still has a capacity of 2,600 litres and the spirit still 2,200 litres. Most of the production is non-peated and is filled into ex-bourbon wood. The first product release is scheduled for the end of 2026.

Hikari

Konosu, Saitama, founded in 2020

Hikari Distillery is the brainchild of Eric Chhoa and is, for the time being, the closest whisky distillery from Tokyo. They are doing their best to stay out of the spotlight for the first few years and focus on creating quality malt whisky. The Flemish-style design of the buildings is quite striking. Inside the distillery, all equipment is on skids allowing for easy reconfiguration in the future, should the need arise. The equipment consists of a one ton mash tun, six stainless steel washbacks with a 4 day fermentation time and one pair of stills. From the start the distillery has been making whisky using non-peated malted barley imported from the UK. Occasionally, medium- and heavily-peated malt is used. There are two warehouses on site: a small dunnage-type warehouse and a larger racked-warehouse which was completed in the spring of 2022. In April 2024, the distillery purchased a plot of land next to the distillery to start growing two-row barley.

Hinokami

Makurazaki, Kagoshima, founded in 2022

satsuma.co.jp

The distillery is part of Satsuma Shuzo's existing complex dedicated to the production of barrel-aged barley shochu. The modern building houses 5 stainless steel washbacks and a pair of pot stills. The stills are lantern-shaped and fitted with ascending,

Fuji Hokuroku Distillery is a new venture from the well-known sake producer Ide Jozoten

narrow lynearms. Production started in February 2023. The wood policy is about 80% ex-bourbon wood and 20% ex-sherry wood. There is also a continuous still on site for the production of grain whisky as well as a cooperage.

Hishida

Osaki-cho, Kagoshima, founded in 2022

tensei-shuzo.com

The shochu producer Tensei Shuzo set up the distillery within the infrastructure of their existing shochu distillery, and are making use of a lot of the shochu equipment already in place to make malt in the summer and grain whisky in the winter. Production started in November 2022. For the malt whisky production, a stainless steel still fitted with copper 'honeycomb' packs in the neck is used for the first distillation and a copper hybrid still for the second distillation. The first product was released in March 2025, Hishida Distillery Newborn Prelude 1, aged for less than 3 years.

Iiyama Mountain Farm

Iiyama, Nagano, founded in 2016

kiyokawa-sake.co.jp/home

This distillery is built around a "farm to bottle" concept, which is no mean feat given the harsh winters in the area. Whisky production started in 2019. There are 4 washbacks made from Italian oak and 6 stainless steel ones as well as stills from Frilli in Italy. There is also equipment on site to make grain whisky. The distillery earned ISO 22000 certification in 2025, a recognition that is rare among Japanese distilleries and nearly unprecedented within the craft whisky field.

Ikawa

Shizuoka, Shizuoka, founded in 2020

juzan.co.jp/contents/ikawadistillery/

At the moment, Ikawa is the highest whisky distillery in Japan. Located in a UNESCO Eco Park in the Southern Alps at an altitude of 1,200m, this is also one of the most remote distilleries in Japan. It's a four-hour drive from the centre of Shizuoka City. The distillery is owned by Juzan Co., Ltd. and the equipment includes four stainless steel washbacks and one pair of stills with slightly descending lyne arms. Barley (peated as well as un-peated) is imported from Scotland. For the maturation, bourbon and sherry wood is used, but the company also has ambitious plans to make its own barrels using wood types other than oak, harvested from the forests surrounding the distillery. They are also experimenting with local wild yeast for the fermentation. The owners plan to showcase their non-peated whisky with a series of 'Flora' releases and their peated whisky with a series of 'Fauna' ones. The first two specimens of each appeared in late 2024 and dearly 2025.

Kaikyo

Akashi, Hyogo, founded in 2017

akashisakebrewery.com/the-kaikyo-distillery

Kaikyo Distillery is located on the site of the Akashi Sake Brewery, established by the Yonezawa family, which has been brewing since 1856 and distilling (albeit not whisky) since 1918. To mark their first century of distilling, a new stillhouse was built to house Forsyths stills and the building was named The Kaikyo Distillery. Together with Torabhaig Distillery (on the Isle of Skye), The Borders Distillery and Mossburn Distillers & Blenders, Kaikyo Distillery is part of a family-owned Swedish investment company. There is a close reciprocal relationship between the distilleries in Scotland and the team at Kaikyo in Japan. The aim is to produce a light, fruity spirit that will age well.

Kamui Whisky K.K.

Rishiri, Hokkaido, founded in 2020

kamuiwhisky.com

Kamui Whisky was established by husband-and-wife entrepreneurs Casey Wahl and Miku Hirano. The location they

Hishida Distillery in Kagoshima is one of many new distilleries originating from the shochu side of the business

chose couldn't be more remote: Rishiri Island off the northwestern tip of Hokkaido. It is equipped with two stills from Vendome in Louisville, Kentucky. Both are heated using steam jackets and cooled with miniature worm tubs. Production started in the fall of 2022 and the production is still very limited by necessity.

Kanosuke

Hioki, Kagoshima, founded in 2017

kanosuke-en.com

Kanosuke distillery is owned by Komasa Jozo, one of the leading shochu makers in Kagoshima prefecture. In 2015, Yoshitsugu Komasa, who represents the fourth generation of the family, picked some vacant land next to three warehouses where the company's shochu is matured and had the necessary equipment installed in the summer of 2017: a 6,000 litre mash tun, 5 stainless steel washbacks and 3 pot stills (6,000, 3,000 and 1,600 litres respectively) all with wormtub condensers. In 2022, five additional stainless steel washbacks were installed. In 2021, Diageo made an investment in the distillery through accelerator Distil Ventures. In 2022, five additional stainless steel washbacks were installed to ramp up production. Kanosuke is the first craft whisky distillery in Japan to have a core range consisting of a single malt (Kanosuke), a single grain (Hioki Pot Still) and a blended whisky (Kanosuke Double Distillery), with all components made in-house.

Karuizawa

Karuizawa, Nagano, founded in 2021

karuizawa-whisky.co.jp

Not to be confused with the legendary distillery of the same name that is long gone, this new distillery is the brainchild of Shigeru Totsuka, the 16th generation master distiller of Totsuka Sake Brewery. Totsuka acquired land in the town of Karuizawa and production started in December 2022. Master distiller is Yoshiyuki Nakazato who used to work at the original Karuizawa distillery. The pot stills are similar to the original stills, though slightly larger and sherry wood will play a key role in the maturation. No single malt will be released for the first decade.

Kita-Karuizawa

Agatsuma-gun, Gunma, founded in 2022

link-kitakaru.co.jp

Established by Tatsuhiko Sakamoto, the owner-bartender of Bar LAG in the Ginza district of Tokyo, this is one of the smallest distilleries in Japan. Whisky production started in July 2023. The first and second distillation takes place in one and the same pot still, which is a unique contraption with a body of stainless steel, but an alembic-type head and a lynearm made of copper.

Kobe

Kobe, Hyogo, founded in 2021

kobe-distillery.com

In 2021, trading company GrowStars decided to add a whisky-making facility to the existing alembic at "Michinoeki Kobe Fruit Flower Park Ozo" in Kobe. The alembic had been used for brandy-making in the past. The idea was to revive that but also add whisky production. A mash tun, two washbacks and a pair of pot stills were installed and whisky production began in the autumn of 2022. Most of the malted barley used is non-peated. Newborn 2024, containing spirit aged for 15 months, was released in 2024.

Komaki

Satsuma-gun, Kagoshima, founded in 2023

komakiwhisky.com/en/

A new project initiated by Komaki Jozo, a shochu producer that traces its history back to 1909. For the maturation of its spirit, the distillery uses a lot of Yakushima cedar, which should result in a unique and clearly identifiable taste profile when the whisky is ready.

Kanosuke Distillery was aided in the beginning by Diageo´s accelerator Distil Ventures

Komoro

Komoro, Nagano, founded in 2020

karuizawadistillers.com/en/

Komoro distillery is the brainchild of Koji Shimaoka, who worked in investment banking for over 20 years before moving into the hotel business in Karuizawa. Looking to bring back distilling to the Greater Karuizawa area, Shimaoka found the perfect site, in the city of Komoro. In 2020, he brought Ian Chang, formerly of Kavalan, on board as co-founding partner. There is a one ton mash tun, 5 stainless steel washbacks and 5 made from Oregon pine. Atypically, the spirit still is larger than the wash still (7,800 and 5,000 litres respectively). This setup enables the low wines of the two first distillations to be combined for one second distillation. The yearly capacity of the distillery is 500,000 litres of alcohol and the first spirit ran off the stills in June 2023. The spirit will be non-peated for the most part, but to honor Dr Jim Swan (Ian Chang's mentor), December will be set aside to make a mildly-peated whisky. The big news from the owners is that they are currently constructing a second distillery in Furano, in Hokkaido, scheduled for completion in 2028.

Kuju

Taketa City, Oita, founded in 2021

kujudistillery.jp

The distillery is located at an altitude of 600m in the majestic Kuju Plateau. For Shoji Utoda it is the realization of a dream he has harboured since the early 2000s. The distillery is equipped with a 0.5 ton mash tun, five washbacks made of Douglas fir and two stills from Forsyth. Both peated (40-50ppm) and unpeated malt is used and most of the production is filled into ex-bourbon wood. The first official single malt whisky release, 'Kuju The First', appeared in April 2025.

Kurayoshi

Kurayoshi, Tottori, founded in 2017

matsuiwhisky.com/en/distillery/

Kurayoshi first emerged on the Japanese whisky scene in 2015 as a brand rather than a distillery, with age-statement releases of 'Japanese pure malt whisky' at a time when age-statement Japanese whisky had become rare. The fact that Japanese whisky-makers don't swap stock made it easy for savvy consumers to figure out that the liquid in the bottles was imported in bulk from abroad. In 2017 they set up an actual distillery. They started with three small alembic-type stills. In 2018, they added two larger stills and slowly started to let people into their distillery.

Kyoto Miyako

Kyotamba-cho, Kyoto, founded in 2020

kyotoshuzo.com/en/distillery/

The distillery, owned by Kyoto Shuzo Co., is located in the Tamba highlands. All production takes place under one roof and the equipment includes four enamel-coated open tanks used as washbacks with a 60 hour fermentation and two pot stills with slightly descending lynearms. There is also a small alembic type still, used for the production of gin. The whisky products currently sold by the company appear to contain liquid sourced from abroad.

Maoi

Naganuma, Hokkaido, founded in 2008 (as a winery)

maoidistillery.com

Starting as a winery, a distillery (for both whisky and brandy) was added in 2021. Whisky production started in September 2022. The set-up includes a hand-stirred mash tun, two stainless steel washbacks and a hybrid still made by Forsyths with two columns

The owners of Komoro Distillery also have plans for a second distillery in Furano in Hokkaido

used for grain whisky and brandy. The company uses both local barley and local peat.

Mars Komagatake

Miyada village, Nagano, founded in 1985

hombo.co.jp/visiting/shinshu/

Mars Komagatake was built at the peak of whisky consumption in Japan, but 7 years into what would turn out to be a 25-year long decline, the doors were closed. The distillery was mothballed in 1992 and it wasn't until 2011 that the decision was made to fire up the stills again. In 2014, the old pot stills were replaced with brand new ones and in 2018, three Douglas fir washbacks were installed. As part of a massive 1.2 billion yen investment, 2019-2020 saw the construction of a new warehouse, new stainless steel washbacks and mashtun as well as a new visitor centre. Most of the barley is imported (both peated and un-peated) but in 2021 the first batch of locally grown barley was distilled. The most recent general release was the Komagatake 2025 Edition.

Mars Tsunuki

Minami-Satsuma, Kagoshima, founded in 2016

hombo.co.jp/visiting/tsunuki/

Towards the end of 2015, Hombo Shuzo started setting up a second distillery in their homebase of Tsunuki in Kagoshima with the first distillation in October 2016. The distillery is the playground of Tatsuro Kusano who learned the ropes at Mars Shinshu. Some things are the same as there but there are marked differences too not least in the approach to making whisky including the use of specialty malts, various yeast types etc. The most recent general release was the Tsunuki 2025 Edition.

Nagahama

Nagahama, Shiga, founded in 2016

romanbeer.com/whisky/

Nagahama, one of the smallest distilleries in Japan, was set up in a record time of 7 months as an extension of Nagahama Roman Brewery. The distillery started production in November 2016. Mashing and fermentation takes place in the equipment used for beer making. For the rest of the process, a small 'still room' with three 1,000 litre Hoga alembic-type stills was created. The most recent release, The Sixth Batch, appeared in July 2025.

Niigata Kameda

Niigata, Niigata, founded in 2019

kameda-distillery.com

Niigata Kameda is located in Kameda Industrial Park, close to JR Niigata Station. This station is serviced by the bullet train so, from Tokyo, it's the shortest trip to a whisky distillery. The distillery is a side project of Ohtani, the biggest maker of inkan (personal seals) in Japan. The first distillation took place in February 2021. Most of the malted barley (both peated and non-peated) is imported from Scotland, but some local Niigata barley is used as well. A small, automated malting machine was installed in 2022 and the plan going forward is to do the malting of local barley in-house. The first official single malt release (and also the first in their so-called Zodiac Sign series) was Ohtani Whisky – Pisces which was launched in March 2025.

Niseko

Hokkaido, founded in 2019

niseko-distillery.com

The distillery is the brainchild of Jiro Nagumo, CEO of the sake producer Hakkaisan Brewery. The equipment includes a Buhler mill from Switzerland, a one ton full-lauter mash tun from Slovenia, three Douglas fir washbacks made in Japan and a pair of pot stills from Forsyths in Scotland - one 5,500 litre wash still and a 3,600 litre spirit still. There is also a 600 litre hybrid Holstein still for the production of gin. The first whisky distillation took place in March 2021.

Nozawa Onsen

Shimotakai District, Nagano, founded in 2020

nozawaonsendistillery.jp/en/

The distillery is situated in Nozawa Onsen – a well-known tourist destination in Nagano prefecture – and whisky production began in January 2023. The head-distiller, Sam Yoneda, uses a mash cooker with direct steam injection and a crash-cooling jacket. It is used in conjunction with a mash filter. There are also stainless steel washbacks, a pair of lantern shaped pot stills and a gin still. It is currently the only Japanese craft whisky distillery using a mash filter, giving huge flexibility to develop unique flavour profiles.

Nukada

Naka, Ibaraki, founded in 2016

kodawari.cc

Nukada distillery was set up by Kiuchi Shuzo in a corner of their new Hitachino Nest brewhouse. In terms of output, it is the smallest whisky distillery in Japan. The 1,000 litre hybrid still is used to make whisky as well gin. The production volume varies from year to year and is limited by the fact that the staff also distill beers and make some of the Kiuchi liqueurs.

Okayama

Okayama, Okayama, founded in 2011

whiskyokayama.com/english/

Miyashita Shuzo was founded as a sake brewery in 1915. In 1994, they became one of the pioneers of Japanese craft beer. In 2003, the company started distilling some of their hoppy beer in a stainless steel shochu still. Then, in 2011 they got a license to produce also malt whisky – at first in the shochu still and since 2015 in a copper hybrid still. Production is extremely limited and bottlings are rarely seen. One of the latest one was Single Cask Okayama 2023 Wine Cask Strength (matured in an ex-amarone cask) in September 2023.

Ontake

Kagoshima, founded in 2019

nishi-shuzo.co.jp/ontake

The distillery was established by liquor producer Nishi Shuzo and is part of a golf course they own. The distillery is equipped with one mashtun, five stainless steel washbacks with a 5 day fermentation and two pot stills. For the time being, only non-peated malted barley is used. Most of the production is aged in oloroso butts but the distillery also uses pinot noir casks from their own winery in New Zealand. The most recent release is Ontake 2025.

Oriental Kanazawa

Kanazawa, Ishikawa, founded in 2016

orientalbrewing.com

Oriental Brewing, a craft brewer based in Kanazawa city, installed a hybrid still with 6 plates, three wooden washbacks and three repurposed enamel-coated steel sake tanks in summer 2022 and started distilling soon after. The aim is to launch the first whisky in 2025..

Osuzuyama

Koyu-gun, Miyazaki, founded in 1998 (whisky since 2019)

osuzuyama.co.jp/en/

Originally established as a shochu distillery. All ingredients are sourced locally and the equipment includes 15 fermenters made of Obi-Sugi, a type of cedar tree traditionally used for ship building. The barley is malted in-house using a propriety method called "box malting". A combination of stainless-steel shochu stills and a copper pot still is used. Several of the Osuzu Malt releases are aged in casks made of wood types other than oak (chestnut, cedar, sakura).

Rokkosan

Kobe, Hyogo, founded in 2020

rokkosan-distillery.com

The distillery was established by Axas Co., Ltd on top of Mt Rokko, at an altitude of 800m. The operation is tiny with only 40 batches per year but still offers tours to visitors. Malted barley (predominatly heavily peated) is milled off-site and brought to the distillery as grist. One mashtun and two stainless steel fermenters are used in conjunction with one Holstein still.

Saburomaru

Tonami, Toyama, founded in 1990

wakatsuru.co.jp/saburomaru/en/

Wakatsuru Shuzo started making whisky following the end of the Pacific War, but the company has been making sake since 1862. They focused on simpler whiskies but in 2016 they revitalized their distillery to produce malt whisky. A new mill and mashtun were installed in 2018. In 2019, the distillery started using a new pair of pot stills, the world's first cast copper pot stills also known as Zemon stills and in 2020, a single Douglas fir washback was added to the set-up followed by a second one in 2022. These are used for 24 hours after the first 4 days' fermentation in enamel tanks. In 2024 the production was doubled. The most recent release was the VI The Lovers. It was released (like its predecessors in this tarot series) in a standard version (at 48%) as well as a more limited cask-strength edition.

Sakurao Distillery

Hatsukaichi, Hiroshima, founded in 2018

sakuraodistillery.com/en/sakurao/

Sakurao may be a new distillery, but the liquor company behind it is not. Chugoku Jozo was established in 1918 and incorporated in 1938. Their liquor portfolio comprises shochu, sake, mirin and various liqueurs. Chugoku Jozo started 'producing' whisky in 1938 and until the liquor-tax change of 1989, their field was 'budget' whisky. In 2003, they launched the Togouchi brand which was made up of whisky imported from abroad. To mark the 100th anniversary of the company, a proper whisky distillery was set up at the company's main site. Initially, one Holstein hybrid still was used to make whisky, but in 2019 a new slightly bigger still of the same type was added. Both peated (20ppm) and unpeated spirit is produced. Casks are matured on site as well as in disused tunnels. Sakurao is a rare instance of a Japanese craft distillery with two permanently available single malts on the market: Single Malt Sakurao and Single Malt Togouchi.

Setouchi

Kure, Horoshima, founded in 2020

setouchidistillery.com/en

Setouchi Distillery is the most recent project of Miyake Honten, a company that traces its history back to 1856 when it started producing mirin, shochu and later sake. In the late 1920s, its products became the official military-use sake aboard naval ships. The new whisky operation (starting 2021) is relatively small but in August 2022, a pot still was added to the exisiting hybrid still. A The New Born Aged 2 Years was released at the end of 2024.

Shindo

Asakura City, Fukuoka, founded in 2021

shindo-lab.jp/distillery/

The distillery was built by Shinozaki Co., Ltd, the famous maker of shochu. Since the start many types of malted barley have been used but one month a year is reserved for heavily-peated (50ppm) production. Mashing takes place in a one ton semi-lauter tun and the distillery is also equipped with 5 stainless steel washbacks with water jackets and one pair of copper pot stills. The first official single malt release, Shindo Experimental 01, appeared in June 2025.

Shizuoka

Shizuoka, Shizuoka, founded in 2015

shizuoka-distillery.jp

The distillery is owned by Gaia Flow founder Taiko Nakamura and started producing in February 2017. Initially there were 5 washbacks at the distillery: four made from Oregon pine and one made from Shizuoka cedar. In February 2018, three more cedar washbacks were installed. The stillhouse has 3 pot stills: one from the old Karuizawa distillery and a new pair made by Forsyths in Scotland with the wash still being directly fired. The flagship single malt is Shizuoka United S, containing malt whisky distilled in both types of spirit stills.

Tamba

Tamba-Sasayama, Hyogo, founded in 2018

kizakura.co.jp/tamba/

Tamba distillery in Kyoto is owned by Kizakura Co., a liquor producer founded in 1925 and their distillery is based in an inland basin surrounded by mountains on all sides and blessed with a subtropical climate. Since 2004, shochu has been produced but the owners felt the humid location was also ideal for making whisky. At first whisky was produced using a stainless steel still but in 2021, two copper pots made by Forsyths were installed. Milling and mashing takes place off-site and both peated and un-peated barley is used. Fermentation takes place in one of two enamel-coated tanks of the type used in sake production. The distillery uses a variety of yeasts (distillers, sake, brewers, etc.) and maturation takes place in a dunnage warehouse on-site A few single malt expressions have been released to date, but they are very hard to find as they are mostly restricted to the on-trade.

Yamaga

Yamaga, Kumamoto, founded in 2021

yamagadistillery.co.jp/?eng

Being the first distillery in Kumamoto, Yamaga is equipped with a one ton mash tun, five stainless steel washbacks and a pair of pot stills. Both non-peated and heavily peated malt is produced. For the maturation, a warehouse on site with mobile racks and a capacity of 3,300 barrels is used. Yamaga Distillery is one of the few Japanese distilleries open to the public. The distillery is gearing up to release its first official single malt whisky.

Yasato

Ishioka, Ibaraki, founded in 2019

hinomaruwhisky.com/distillery

The owners (who founded Nukada distillery already in 2016) designed this distillery based on making a new type of whisky, using various kind of grains and different types of yeast. There's a four-roller mill, a 5,000 litre cereal cooker for step mashing and rice/buckwheat/corn cooking and a 6,000 litre lauter tun, four 12,000 litre stainless fermenters and four 6,000 litre wooden fermenters. There is also a 12,000 litre wash still and an 8,000 litre spirit still. The first distillation was in March 2020. Kiuchi Shuzo occasionally releases whisky distilled at Yasato and/or Nukuda distillery under the brand Hinomaru Whisky.

Yuza

Yuza, Yamagata, founded in 2018

yuza-disty.jp

Kinryu, the owners of the distillery, was founded in 1950 and was a joint venture funded by nine local sake producers, initially to make neutral spirit. Over time, they started making and selling shochu made in a continuous still. Overall consumption of shochu (as well as sake) has been on the decline for decades. To mitigate that, the company decided to start producing whisky and set up a brand new distillery in Yuza city. The first distillation took place in November 2018 and he most recent release, Yuza Aged 6 Years, was launched in June 2025.

Lebanon

Athyr (Riachi Winery & Distillery)

Khenchara, founded in 1839 (whisky since 2013)

athyrwhisky.com

Riachi winery opened in 1839 and while eventually also making arak, grappa and brandy the first whisky wasn´t produced until 2013. Local barley is used and the newmake matures in Lebanese oak sometimes with a finish in cedar wood. The first release of Athyr single malt was in 2019 and recently a 10 year old appeared.

Pakistan

Murree Brewery Ltd.

Rawalpindi, founded in 1860

www.murreebrewery.com

Started as a beer brewery, the assortment was later expanded to include whisky, gin, rum, vodka and brandy. The core range of single malt holds two expressions – Murree´s Classic 8 years old and Murree´s Millenium Reserve 12 years old. There is also a Murree´s Islay Reserve, Vintage Gold.

South Korea

Three Societies Distillery

Namyangju-si, Gyeonggi Province, founded in 2020

threesocieties.co.kr

With three distilleries having been built in the late 1980s and later closed, this is the first malt whisky distillery in modern times in South Korea. Two of the founders are Bryan Do, a Korean-American former game show host and Andrew Shand who started his career at Glenlivet in 1980. Located 30 kilometres north of Seoul, the distillery is equipped with a 5,000 litre wash still and a 3,000 litre spirit still – both from Forsyths and the capacity is one million litres of alcohol. There is also a 700 litre still for making gin, rye, bourbon and experimental spirits. Some of the barley is grown on the estate and the owners make use of Korean yeast and oak as well. The distillery´s flagship whisky, Ki One, appeared first in February 2023 and more expressions have followed.

Taiwan

Kavalan Distillery

Yuanshan, Yilan County, founded in 2005

www.kavalanwhisky.com/en

On the 11th of March 2006 at 3.30pm, the first spirit was produced at Kavalan distillery. This was celebrated in a major way a decade later when guests and journalists from all over the world were invited for the 10th anniversary. But it was not just to celebrate 10 years of whisky production but also to witness an expansion of the distillery which made Kavalan one of the ten largest malt whisky distilleries in the world! This rapid development may even have surprised the founder, entrepreneur and business man Tien-Tsai Lee, and his son, the current Chairman of the company Yu-Ting Lee. Early on, it was decided that expertise from Scotland was needed to get on the right track from the beginning.

With a background in both sake and shochu production, Yuza recently added also whisky to their range

Dr. Jim Swan was consulted and he developed a strategy including production as well as the future maturation. Jim Swan passed away in early 2017.

The distillery lies in the north-eastern part of the country, in Yilan County, one hour´s drive from Taipei. Following the expansion in 2016, the distillery is equipped with 5 mash tuns, 40 stainless steel washbacks with a 60-72 hour fermentation time and 10 pairs of lantern-shaped copper stills with descending lye pipes. The capacity of the wash stills is 12,000 litres and of the spirit stills 7,000 litres. Kavalan only uses a very narrow cut from the spirit run, leaving more foreshots and feints to accommodate a complex and rich flavour profile.

On site, there are two five-story warehouses and one seven-story warehouse, with a combined capacity of 300,000 barrels. The climate in this part of Taiwan is hot and humid and on the top floors of the warehouses the temperature can reach 42°C. Hence the angel´s share is higher than in for example Scotland - between five and seven percent. The distillery has its own cooperage where the preparation of the STR (shave-toast-rechar) casks plays an important part for the final character of some of their whiskies.

Since the first bottling of Kavalan was released in 2008, the range has been constantly expanded. In spring 2020, the core range was complemented by two bottlings being priced competitively to act as an entry level to the rest of the range. One of them was launched already in 2018 and is now called Distillery Select No. 1 while the other one is Distillery Select No. 2. Apart from them, the core range consists of Classic and an "upgraded" version of that called King Car Conductor. There is also the port finished Concertmaster which has been supplemented by Concertmaster Sherry and Vinho Barrique. Finally there are Ex-Bourbon, Oloroso Sherry, Wine and Port, all bottled at 46%, and Podium.

The range that first opened the world´s eyes to Kavalan was Solist first introduced in 2009. Matured in different types of casks these are all bottled at single cask strength and released in batches. The first two were ex-Bourbon and Oloroso Sherry and have been followed by Fino, Vinho Barrique, Brandy, Amontillado, Manzanilla, PX, Moscatel and Port. In February 2025 a Solist Palo Cortado completed the "sherry part" of the range. Another three bottlings are exclusively sold at the distillery visitor centre; Distillery Reserve Peated Whisky, Rum Cask and Madeira Cask. The distillery produces whisky from peated barley (10ppm) as well and in July 2025 a new series of two named Kavalan Peatist was launched. At the moment they are available exclusively in Taiwan. In 2023/2024 two travel retail exclusives appeared; Master´s Select Reserve No.1 (ex-Bourbon and lightly peated STR casks) and No. 2 (the same type of STR casks as well as port barriques). In September 2024, Kavalan Lán was launched with a maturation in ex-Bourbon, STR Wine and port casks and in March 2025 the distillery reached a milestone when they released their first bottling carrying an age statement on the label - a 15 year old.

Whisky is, of course, the main product for Kavalan but production of gin is also carried out. The first release in a series of triple distilled gins appeared in 2019. In 2020, the owners launched a "ready-to-drink" range called The Kavalan Bar Cocktail and since 2018 they are producing beer at a plant in Taoyuan. In 2019, Kavalan opened their first designated 'Cask Strength Whisky Bar' in the busy Zhongshan District of Taipei. Recreating the inside of the distillery´s warehouse, it was the only bar in the world to carry the full range of Kavalan whisky. This was later followed by a second bar at the distillery in Yilan where The Kavalan Garden Bar dominates the second floor of the Spirits Castle. There is also a Warehouse Tasting Room at the distillery where guests can taste whisky straight from the barrel.

Other distilleries in Taiwan

Funny Distillery

New Taipei City (Shulin District), founded in 2024

funnydistillery.com

Co-founded by the former distillery manager and master blender of Laizhou Distillery in Sichuan, China - Jeng-Ing Chen. The distillery is equipped with a hammer mill, a small mash tun, four washbacks and a modified Lomond-style still. Unusually the

The sherry "family" of Kavalan´s Solist range was completed in 2025 with the launch of Palo Cortado

fermentation is "on the grain" and both grain and malt whisky as well as rum is produced.

Holy Distillery

New Taipei City, founded in 2016

holydistillery.com.tw

The founder Alex Chang started out with rice whisky and later produced both a bourbon style whisky as well as the Salvation single malt and recently added rum to the range.

Nantou Distillery

Nantou City, Nantou County, founded in 1977 (whisky since 2008)

omarwhisky.com.tw

Nantou distillery is a part of the state-owned manufacturer and distributor of cigarettes and alcohol in Taiwan – Taiwan Tobacco and Liquor Corporation (TTL). Between 1947 and 1968 it exercised a monopoly over all alcohol and tobacco products sold in Taiwan. It retained the monopolies until Taiwan's entry into the WTO in 2002.

There are seven distilleries and two breweries within the TTL group, but Nantou is the only with malt whisky production. The distillery is equipped with a 2,5 ton full lauter mash tun and eight washbacks made of stainless steel with a fermentation time of 60-72 hours. There are two wash stills and two spirit stills. Nantou distillery also produces a variety of fruit wines and the casks that have stored lychee wine and plum wine are then used to finish some of their whiskies. In 2013 two cask strength single malts under the name Omar were launched. Three years later Sherry Cask and Bourbon Cask appeared and the two now make up the distillery´s core range together with Peated. Another range is called Liqueur Finish and they have all been finished in different wine or liqueur casks. Finally there is the Cask Strength series.

Thailand

Red Bull (Prakaan) Distillery

Mueang Kamphaeng Phet district, founded in 1988

prakaanmaltwhisky.com

A large distillery producing a multitude of spirits and since at least ten years, also single malt whisky. It is owned by one of Asia´s top drinks producers, ThaiBev, controlled by the Thai billionaire Charoen Sirivadhanabhakdi and his family. The main seller when it comes to whisky is the Blend 285 which is made up from whiskies distilled in Thailand and Scotland. In December 2024 the first malt whiskies were released in the Tribura Collection; Select Cask, Peated Malt and Double Cask.

Vietnam

Về Để Đi Distillery

Hanoi, founded in 2020 (whisky since 2023)

ve-de-di.com

Founded by Michael Rosen and Nguyen Hung Quan this is the first Vietnamese distillery producing malt whisky. Initial products were gin and creme de cacao and the first barrels of whisky were laid down in October 2023. Both whisky made from malted barley and corn whisky are produced. It is important to the owners to use local ingredients, partly to see what terroir can do for the spirits but also to support farming families from the Hmong people in the Northwest. The first release, Distiller´s Choice, appeared in August 2025.

Về Để Đi Distillery is the first whisky producer in Vietnam

Africa

South Africa

James Sedgwick Distillery

Wellington, Western Cape, founded in 1886 (whisky since 1990)

threeshipswhisky.co.za, bainswhisky.com

Distell Group Ltd. was formed in 2000 by a merger between Stellenbosch Farmers' Winery and Distillers Corporation, although the James Sedgwick Distillery was already established in 1886. The company produces a huge range of wines and spirits and James Sedgwick Distillery has been the home to South African whisky since 1990. The distillery has undergone a major expansion in the last years and is now equipped with one still with two columns for production of grain whisky, two pot stills for malt whisky and one still with five columns designated for neutral spirit. In 2022, a majority of Distell´s share holders accepted a take-over bid from Dutch brewer Heineken. In the whisky portfolio it is the Three Ships brand that makes up for most of the sales. The range consists of three blends; Select, the 5 year old Premium Select and the 3 year old Bourbon Cask. Furthermore there is the 10 year old single malt first released in 2003. A range called the Master´s Collection was introduced in 2015 with the idea to annually launch something limited in volume and a South African first. One of the latest was a 6 year old Chenin Blanc finish. In 2023 the pinnacle of Three Ships whisky was reached when a 21 year old was released! Apart from the Three Ships range, the distillery also produces South Africa´s first single grain, Bain´s Cape Mountain Whisky.

Other distilleries in South Africa

Boplaas Winery & Distillery

Calitzdorp, Western Cape, founded in 1880 (whisky since 2012)

boplaas.co.za

Now managed by the 6th generation of the Nel family the company has been distilling brandy since 1880. When whisky came into the picture it was mainly made from various grains but in autumn 2024 the first single malt made from Scottish peated malt, an 8 year old finished in tawny casks, appeared.

Helden Distillery

Parys, Free State, founded in 2018

helden.co.za

Apart from a Helden Single Malt there is African Bonfire Whisky in the range made from red sorthum and barley and matured in French oak and African indigenous camel thorn wood. One of the latest releases was the limited Enigma.

Incendo Distillery

Hartbeespoort, North West, founded in 2017

incendo.co.za

The distillery produces a wide range of spirits including whisky. Limited expressions of 3 year old single malt from barley as well as from other mashbills have been released under the name Lexicon.

Pringle Rock

Pringle Bay, Western Cape, founded in 2024

pringlerockdistillery.com

A distillery founded by Leigh Elves and he even made the stills himself. It is situated in a repurposed horse stable south of Cape Town and quickly earned a reputation for their Rockjumper Gin. Soon enough they added whisky production but the first release of that is still within 4 to 5 years from now.

James Sedgwick Distillery has defined the high quality of South African whisky

South America

Argentina

La Alazana Distillery

Golondrinas, Patagonia, founded in 2011

laalazanawhisky.com

Located in the Patagonian Andes, this is the first malt whisky distillery in Argentina. The distillery is owned and run by Nestor Serenelli and his wife Lila. The owners are firm believers in the "terroir" concept where local barley, water and climate will be expressed in the flavour of the whisky. A new twist on "terroir" came in 2022 when two casks of maturing whisky were brought to Marambio military base in the Antarctic to mature for another couple of years in extreme climate. The experiment was later repeated when two new casks were brought to another base with the intention of maturing them in an ice cave for eight to ten years. The distillery is equipped with a lauter mash tun, four stainless steel 1,100 litre washbacks with a fermentation time of 100 hours and two stills. The owners are also growing and malting their own barley. Besides the Classic and Organic malt, they do a lightly peated malt named Haidd Merlys. The owner´s first, limited 10 year old whisky was bottled in 2021. In autumn 2023 an unexpected collaboration between Penderyn distillery in Wales and La Alazana resulted in a Welsh/Argentinian whisky!

Other distilleries in Argentina

Emilio Mignone y Cia

Luján, Buenos Aires province, founded in 2015

emyc.com.ar

Owned by brothers Carlos and Santiago Mignone, this became the second whisky distillery in Argentina. The first distillation was in November 2015 and the distillery is equipped with a 300 litre open mash tun, a 600 litre washback with a 72-96 hour fermentation and two stills, directly fired by natural gas. The distillery was expanded in 2022 to an annual capacity of 6,000 bottles. The distillery has released a number of different editions; the EM&C Pampa Single Malt Classic matured in ex-bourbon barrels, released in 2019, the EM&C Pampa Single Malt Peated matured in PX sherry barrels, launched in 2020, the EM&C Pampa Single Malt Classic matured in ex-sherry barrels, released in 2022 and, the latest in 2024, a Peated edition that had been matured in ex-bourbon casks.

Madoc Distillery

Dina Huapi, Rio Negro, founded in 2015

madocwhisky.com

The owner is one of the founders of the first Patagonian distillery, La Alazana. In 2015, he left the company and brought with him some of the equipment, as well as part of the maturing stock to build a new distillery in Dina Huapi. The first distillation was in 2016 and a single malt bottled at 40% was soon released followed by more where Las Malvinas was one of the latest expressions.

Brazil

Union Distillery

Bento Gonçalves, founded in 1948 (whisky since 1972)

maltwhisky.com.br

The company started to produce wine, before focusing on malt whisky production from 1972. In the 1980's, it invested in its production facilities including a co-operation with Morrison Bowmore Distillers. Most of the production is sold as bulk whisky, but the company has recently re-started to release their own products since 2019. Their Single Malt core range includes 'Pure Malt' (Wine Cask Finish; Virgin Oak Finish; the peated Turfado and the heavily peated Extra Turfado) as well as 'Autograph' limited releases and 'Vintage' releases, including the Vintage 2005, possibly the oldest single malt released in Latin America.

Lamas Destilaria

Matozinhos, founded in 2019

lamasdestilaria.com.br

Started by the Lamas brothers this is now managed by the second and third generation Lamas family members. The craft distillery produces a wide range of spirits, including single malt whisky. Lamas' single malt whisky core range includes: Plenus, Verus, Rarus, and the smokier Nimbus and Nimbus Robustus. They also produce a blended whisky named Canem and sometimes use Brazilian native woods for the maturation resulting in special releases such as the recent Putumuju (*Centrolobium robustum*).

Chile

Last Hope Distillery

Puerto Natales, founded in 2017

lasthopedistillery.com

Founded by an Australian couple this is the southernmost whisky distillery in the world. While gin was their first release they always had whisky in their plan which is still maturing in their warehouse.

Tepaluma

La Junta, founded in 2017

tepaluma.com

Located in the Patagonian part of Chile, the owners started producing gin while malt whisky is still maturing in the warehouse. They are also looking to build a new distillery.

Uruguay

Larnaudie

Punta Colorada, founded in 2017

Being a passionate home brewer for ten years, Enrique Larnaudie eventually turned into distilling. The first Larnaudie single malt was released as a 3 year old in 2021 and now there is also a 5 year old in the range.

Nestor and Lila Serenelli - founders of La Alazana Distillery

The Year
that was

Including the subsections:
Single malt hot spots | The big players
The big brands | New distilleries

As 2024 dawned, the entire alcohol business felt uneasy of what would lay ahead as it entered the new year. The happy days of 2021 when the industry made a tremendous rebound after the first pandemic year (2020) seemed long time gone. The rate of improvement had continued in 2022, albeit at a slower pace. And then came the harsh downturn in 2023 that made the producers re-think strategies and bolster for rougher times ahead.

The main reasons for the 2023 set-back – inflation causing both lower household disposable income and increasing costs for the producers, and an insecure geopolitical climate – still prevailed in 2024 and an additional factor entered into the equation: the fear of tariffs.

With yet another four years of having Donald Trump in the White House, flashbacks of his first term in office came back. Those were the years of a trade war affecting not only spirits and wine but also steel and aircraft. It was a retaliatory process between the EU and USA with 25% tariffs, not least on Scotch, but also other spirits and wines heading for America and bourbon being imported to Europe. When Joe Biden took office in 2021 he, at least temporarily, removed these obstacles.

In June 2025 a deal was struck between USA and the UK (this time outside of the EU) where most exports to USA would be imposed by a 10% tariff. At the time of writing there are ongoing negotiations aiming to see if Scotch could be exempt from duty altogether. One month later an agreement between USA and the EU resulted in a general 15% duty on products imported to the USA which of course gave Irish whiskey a disadvantage compared to Scotch. Unlike the trade war during the first Trump term, there are no retaliatory taxes from the EU against USA. However there is a European list of potential targets, including bourbon, but this has been suspended at least until the beginning of 2026. Meanwhile a coalition of 57 alcohol industry organisations has warned president Trump that the agreed 15% tariffs on all goods from the EU could threaten 25,000 American jobs

If we look at total spirits volumes, sales were down in 2020 by 9% and then up by 3% in 2021 (with values climbing even more). That was followed by three consecutive years with falling numbers (in 2022 minus 1%, in 2023 minus 3% and in 2024 down by 2%). The fact that volumes fell three years in a row is of course alarming but the main reasons for these figures are that the declining sales of Asian national spirits (baijiu, shochu and soju) affected the whole sector. In 2024 three categories lost ground by 1-2% (brandy, rum and vodka) while whiskies remained unchanged and gin (+3%) and agave-based spirits (+1%) grew.

But there is more to it than financial factors and political instability causing this significant downturn in sales. One thing that has been on the agenda for quite a few years is that Generation Z (typically regarded to be 16-25 years) seems to be less interested in alcohol than their elders. The reason is generally thought to be an increased interest in, and concern over, health issues. However, recent studies show that this may be a somewhat simplified analysis. Even the millennials (the generation preceding Gen Z) consumed less but as they grew older, they seemed to fall into the same habits as older generations. Perhaps it's just a matter of delaying their alcohol debut.

A lot of possible reasons for a later debut have been presented recently. In 1991 over 64% of US high school seniors had been drunk at least once. By 2024, it was just 33%. When smartphones became ubiquitous the risk of being photographed and "shamed" on social media when being drunk became an issue and especially so at an age where you are starting either an academical or professio-

nal career. As these youngsters grow older and establish a social position where this type of images can be handled more causally or even ignored, they could become more comfortable with social drinking. One conclusion presented by Sophie Arundel on The Drinks Business is simply that the alcohol industry can expect a rebound in alcohol consumption from that generation as it matures.

However, it is probably not as simple as "wait and see" and then they'll buy. The new generation demands a new approach by the producers. Environmental and sustainability issues have become more important when choosing a brand and their interest and future loyalty also depends more on the authenticity of the brand. False claims not withstanding closer scrutiny will not go that far.

If we look at Scotch whisky export in the last five years, 2020 (the year of the covid outbreak) was a complete disaster, the two following years (and especially 2022) saw Scotch whisky in a major rebound while 2023 and – to a lesser degree – 2024 landed in an adjustment downwards from the inflated figures from the previous two years. But this also meant that the market adapted to a geopolitically much more insecure world as well as an inflation which eroded the disposable income for many households. If we try to look at the bright side (and why shouldn't we?) the rate has slowed down markedly as the downturn from 2023 continued in 2024.

Total value, which was down by 9.5% in 2023, was "just" down by 3.6% in 2024. And total volume was actually up by 3.9% which should indicate an adjustment from consumers towards more affordable whiskies. An interesting observation is that blended Scotch (both values and volumes) gained in 2024 while single malt Scotch took a significant blow – both volumes and values went down by close to 20%. This is a tell-tale sign of consumers having less to spend and at the same time contradictory to the current mantra that many consumers "drink less but better" – what in the whisky producer's world is known as premiumisation (read more about on pages 30-35).

While the figures for the last two years may indicate the coming of bad times for Scotch, one should keep in mind that all the six values in the table below, bar volumes of single malts, are actually higher than in 2019 – the last year before the pandemic.

SINGLE MALT SCOTCH - EXPORT 2024

Value:	-17.2% to £1.68bn
Volume:	-18.2% to 127.4m bottles

BLENDED SCOTCH* - EXPORT 2024

Value:	+3.7% to £3.63bn
Volume:	+5.8% to 1.2bn bottles

TOTAL SCOTCH - EXPORT 2024

Value:	-3.6% to £5.4bn
Volume:	+3.9% to 1.4bn bottles

* incl. bottled and bulk blend, bottled and bulk blended malt and excl. grain

The European Union

The EU continues to be the largest market for Scotch whisky in terms of volumes in spite of a decline of 1% compared to last year. It represents 35% of the global exports. In terms of values it has been number two since 2022 after Asia and Oceania. Sales in the EU fell by 5% in 2024. Like for most regions it was single malt that took the biggest blow – down 18% in values.

The European Union — Top 3

France	volumes	+2%	values	-12%
Spain	volumes	+2%	values	+6%
Germany	volumes	-6%	values	-14%

The French love their whiskies and for a great many years France was the number one export market for Scotch in volumes. It is only recently that India has managed to challenge that market and in 2024 they were again in the top spot with France coming in second. Volumes for France inched up 2% in 2024 while values dropped 12%. It was bulk exports that saved the year for France while bottled single malt declined by 28%. The French love affair with whisky is also reflected in an increasingly growing domestic production. There are now 175 distilleries producing but since production volumes generally are small, French whisky represent just 0.8% of the total domestic sales.

In second place we find Spain – a market with a historically strong connection with Scotch. Exports to the country have slowed down over the past two decades but in recent years the country has made a comeback. Volumes increased by 2% in 2024 but the surprising fact is that values also increased (+6%) contrary to most other markets. It was bottled blend that did the job while single malts went down by 30%. If we compare 2024 to the last figures from precovid (2019) sales have gone up by 9%. One has to travel to Asia to find such positive figures.

Germany lost its position from last year to Spain and ended up as number three with a loss in volumes by 6% and in values by 14%. Whereas Spain has increased since 2019, Germany is in a worse situation having slipped by 8%.

Asia and Oceania

While coming second in terms of volumes, Asia and Oceania has since 2022 been the most important region for Scotch whisky exports if we look at values. The figures for 2024 represented a mixed bag. Volumes were up by 6% (while the EU and North America were on the red side). If we look at values though, Asia and Oceania lost 12% – more than any other region except for Sub-Saharan Africa. When a region gains in volumes but looses in value, the explanation is usually less sales of single malts and this is exactly what happened. Both values and volumes were down more than 20%. Bottled blend increased in volume (but not value) while it was bulk export that saved the year.

Asia and Oceania — Top 3

India	volumes	+15%	values	+14%
Japan	volumes	+23%	values	+7%
China	volumes	-2%	values	-32%

In 2024 India took back its position from France as the world's number one Scotch export market. Both volumes and values were up by double digits driven by bottled and bulk blended whisky. Malts on the other hand were down by almost 20% in terms of values. While Irish whiskey experienced a volume increase in India of 58% last year, Scotch is still dominating the market when it comes to foreign whisky. No less than 86% of the value growth of imported whisky in 2024 came from Scotch. With the Chinese economy slowing down, the large producers of Scotch now see India as the main market to drive long-term growth. This is of course fuelled by the recent trade agreement between India and the UK where the, over the years much debated, 150% tariff on import of Scotch was halved to 75% with the aim to reach 40% within ten years. The forecast from IWSR is that Scotch whisky volumes in India

There are high hopes for the Indian market for Scotch as the tariffs have recently been lowered to 75% from the previous 150%

will grow at a CAGR of 7% between 2024 and 2029.

At the same time the interest in Indian made malt whisky is growing with several new distilleries, some of them owned by Scottish producers, coming on stream. In March 2025 the Indian Malt Whisky Association was launched which will work as a trade body establishing unified standards for Indian single malt whiskies. On one hand the growing volumes of Indian malt whisky could pose a threat to Scotch but on the positive side it could also grow the overall interest in malt whisky as a category.

In second place (in terms of volumes) we find Japan which is one of the largest importers of bulk Scotch (blends, blended malts and grain whisky that hasn't been bottled) in the world. Due to a softer legislation in Japan, this whisky is then blended with domestic spirit and often sold as Japanese whisky. If we look at values, Japan is in fourth place. Singapore, a well-known hub for re-export to other markets, is number one followed by Taiwan and India. In 2024, Japan was one of few countries in the region where values of imported Scotch was up and that by a healthy 7%, mainly caused by an increase of bottled and bulk blend. Single malts were down but to a much lesser degree (-5%) than India and China. A huge number of malt distilleries have been built in Japan over the past decade but their capacity is generally much smaller than those opened up in China and India and so represents a lesser threat to Scotch.

The third biggest Asian market in 2024 for Scotch in terms of volumes was China, with a decrease of just 2% during 2024. When we look at values the picture is completely different: These were down by a staggering 32% driven mainly by lower sales of single and blended malts. This means that China slipped form third to fifth place in values. It's not just Scotch that is suffering – the local spirit baijiu and, not least, cognac were also victims. On the winning side, possibly thanks to the emerging cocktail culture, were gin and vodka. The main reasons for the decline in China is the weaker financial climate (in part due to the very slow return to "normality" after the pandemic) but also the real estate crisis. In the future there is also the risk of tariffs being raised (which has already happened to cognac). For the future China will remain one of the most important markets for Scotch but it remains to be seen how quickly it will recover.

Finally we have to mention Taiwan. With just 25 million people this market has for a long time been extremely valuable for Scotch exports. To a certain extent (but much less so than in Singapore) part of the imports are re-shipped to other countries. The positive figures for 2023 (volumes +8% and values +1%) where however turned into a 12% decrease in 2024. That still rendered the country a second place in values.

North America

The disastrous 2023 for Scotch whisky exports to North America (volumes -14% and values -10%) changed for slightly better in 2024. Volumes were down by just 1% and values by 3%. The figures were saved by bottled blend and bulk whisky while single malts suffered severely; volumes slipped by 19% and values by 11%. The main issue here is of course what will happen in 2025. Last year was a year without Trump and tariffs and the summary of 2025 when the time comes can look very different.

North America — Top 3

USA	volumes	+4%	values	-1%
Mexico	volumes	-21%	values	-21%
Canada	volumes	+10%	values	-5%

Historically, USA has been the most important market for Scotch whisky exports. It all started with Prohibition (1920-1933) when American producers could not legally make whisky and their Scottish competitors quickly took advantage of the situation. The post WWII years further cemented the importance of the US market. For many years it has been number one in the world in terms of value and in 2024 it beat the number two, France, by a staggering 130%. While sales were down by 1% in 2024 the rate of decrease was still better than the year before (-7%). On the volume side the US market ranks as number three (beaten by India and France) but managed to increase by 4% in 2024. Like for many other markets in 2024 it was single malt that took the biggest blow. USA represents 81% of the values imported to the North America region. One alarming thing about the US market is that values of Scotch in 2024 are down by 9% compared to 2019. Most countries are still on the plus side compared to the last year before the covid pandemic.

Whether this is a trend that will continue remains to be seen. Of course, much of it depends on the tariff war between USA and the rest of the world. In April 2025 a 10% tariff was imposed on the UK by the American government which hit, among other products, Scotch whisky. While this is considerably lower than the 25% during the first Trump administration, it will of course hurt the export. At the same time a 10% overall tariff was imposed on the EU, thus including also Irish whiskey. Trade negotiations between USA and the EU were still ongoing at the time of writing and things could become worse for Ireland with tariff levels increasing to 20-30%. While the American market is important for Scotch producers, it is even more so for Irish distillers.

Mexico, in second place, saw values and volumes decrease during 2024 by 21% respectively. These figures follow a 2023 which was actually even worse and the market is now only in place 18 in terms of value on the world list of importers. Mexico is traditionally a blended Scotch market with malts representing just 3-4% of the total

Canada, finally, surpassed Mexico last year in terms of value (but not volumes) due to a smaller decrease in sales (-5%). Value of bottled blends were up by 11% while single malts fell by 14%.

Latin America and Carribean

In November 2023, Diageo issued a warning that the financial result for 2023/2024 could be severely impacted by slower sales in Latin America and the Carribean. This message led to the share price dropping 35%. The final figures for the region in 2023 were volumes down by a staggering 50% and values slipping with 45%. The fears for a repetition the following year, 2024, were of course strong but happily the region recovered: an increase of volumes by 19% and values by 22% was a slight consolation to producers that otherwise had to face a turbulent world market. And when most other markets saw a decline in single malt sales, this region was on the plus side in that category.

Historically Latin America and the Caribbean have been an important yet volatile region for Scotch. The re-occurring economic downturns have seen consumers looking for less expensive alternatives like locally produced spirits such as cachaca in Brazil, aguardiente in Colombia and pisco in Bolivia and Peru. It is a region hugely dominated by blends and single malt only make up 5% of the total value.

Latin America and Carribean — Top 3

Brazil	volumes	+23%	values	+36%
Panama	volumes	+44%	values	+10%
Chile	volumes	+15%	values	+11%

The biggest market is Brazil with 24% of the region's value. The country is now the world's seventh largest importer of Scotch when it comes to volumes and number 13 if we look at values. This an improvement compared to 2023 but the country still has a long way to go to re-establish its 2022 position. Bottled single malt sales make up just 3% of the totals in terms of value. In August 2024 Scotch obtained Geographical Indication (GI) status in Brazil just like tequila, cognac and champagne already enjoyed.

In second place we find Panama which has replaced Chile since last year. In terms of values though, the Dominican Republic is number two with an impressive surge of 70%. The trading conditions for Panama are special. The country has several economic zones with the Colon Free Trade Zone on the Atlantic side being the largest free-trade zone in the Western Hemisphere. This means that a substantial share of the Scotch imports are being distributed to other parts of Latin America and the Caribbean.

Chile made a moderate comeback in 2024 but as single malt constitute a mere 3% share of the totals, Colombia where single malts make up 6%, is actually ahead of them in terms of value.

Western Europe exc EU

There are only seven markets in the region and of the four regions that showed an increase in value during 2024, this was the one with the largest improvement – plus 29%. Volumes were up 11%.

Western Europe exc EU — Top 3

Turkey	volumes	+14%	values	+24%
Switzerland	volumes	-6%	values	-1%
Norway	volumes	+-0%	values	+13%

Of the Top 10 export markets in the world, Turkey is the one that increased the most during 2024 in terms of values (+37%). In the past decade, the country has made an incredible journey from being the 19th largest market for Scotch exports in 2014 to occupying place 9 just ten years later. The increase in the last few years could easily be interpreted as a big chunk of the export to Turkey being re-shipped to Russia due to sanctions on that country. That analysis however is probably too simple. The whisky scene in Turkey has changed dramatically over the past 10 years with more young consumers preferring whisky as opposed to wine. Currently whisky is the third most preferred

Scotch in Latin America is still very much about blended whisky and not least Black & White

alcoholic drink after beer and raki. Turkish spirits commentators notice that with 40% of the people aged under 25, the future for Scotch remains bright in the country. The increase in 2024 hit all categories – single malts and blends alike.

Regarding the other two countries, Switzerland decreased in both volumes and values whereas Norway showed a healthy increase – not least when it comes to single malts which gained 29% in terms of value.

Sub-Saharan Africa

The region didn't impress much in 2022 when all other regions were booming. Things didn't improve during 2023 when volumes decreased by 24% and values by 21%. In 2024 volumes were up by 4% but value continued down by 13%. The value of the region is the second smallest beating only Eastern Europe

Sub-Saharan Africa — Top 3

South Africa	volumes	+23%	values	-5%
Kenya	volumes	+43%	values	+59%
Nigeria	volumes	-8%	values	+6%

South Africa is, as always, the dominant market in the region but it's impact has clearly diminished. The last year before covid (2019) the country was among the top ten export markets. In 2024 it went from place 16 in terms of volumes to 14 but for values, slided from 22 to 26. It now represents 39% of the region's value (51% in 2022) and 54% of the volume (same as last year).

The two runner-ups have switched places since last year with Kenya now occupying second place. Already last year figures were on the positive side but this was emphasized even more in 2024. Unlike most other markets this year, the gains come from all categories including single malt. In third place we find Nigeria which has slowed down considerably compared to last year. Values were up by 6% driven mainly by single malts.

Middle East and Northern Africa

While it may be the second smallest region in terms of volumes it is substantially larger in value than both Sub-Saharan Africa and Western Europe ex EU. In 2024 volumes were up by 2% (following a decrease the year before by 22%) while values were up 4% (- 18% in 2023). Most of the recovery came from bottled blends..

Middle East and Northern Africa — Top 3

UAE*	volumes	+22%	values	+11%
Israel	volumes	+6%	values	+19%
Iraq	volumes	-42%	values	-35%

* United Arab Emirates

A major part of the imports to the UAE are destined for duty free sales and with the travel market being restored following the pandemic, sales of single malts (27% of the export to the country) continued to increase in 2024 by 15% in terms of values. The Israeli market suffered a backlash in 2023 with both volumes and values declining by double digits. The rebound in 2024 was impressive though; volumes up by 6% and, not least, values by 19%. Surprisingly it was blended Scotch that was responsible for the rise. Iraq, finally, is in third place with 7% of the regions total imports and figures were down dramatically in 2024.

Eastern Europe

This is the smallest of all regions and consists of Russia and some of the surrounding countries including parts of the Balkans. States traditionally included in Eastern Europe but being members of the European Community are not included here. The region did well in 2024 with volumes up by 21% and values by 20%. The surge was evenly spread between malts and blends.

Eastern Europe — Top 3

Russia	volumes	+23%	values	+25%
Ukraine	volumes	+35%	values	+44%
Georgia	volumes	+27%	values	+38%

Russia is still the main market in the region despite declining exports in 2023. In 2024 both volumes and values were up by a quarter. Since the Russian invasion of Ukraine in February 2022, the region has been difficult for the Scotch whisky producers to do business in, as it has for companies in other industry sectors. Trade sanctions against Russia were imposed in early 2022 but they didn't include a complete ban on exporting whisky. Bottles priced below €300 were exempt. On the other hand, there are producers who have stopped all exports feeling the pressure from their consumers to take a moral stance in the war.

Georgia and Ukraine have switched places since last year in terms of volumes and the latter is now in the second spot with an impressive surge which includes both malts and blends. In terms of values though, Georgia is well ahead of Ukraine.

Single malt hot spots

I often get asked the question which countries have a preference for single malt Scotch so let's have a look. In these figures, I have focused on the Top 45 markets and selected the 10 nations with the largest single malt share.

Single malt share of Scotch whisky imports 2024

	Country	Volume	Value
1.	Taiwan	50%	64%
2.	China	35%	65%
3.	Canada	33%	54%
4.	Sweden	27%	59%
5.	South Korea	26%	33%
6.	Singapore	25%	39%
7.	Denmark	18%	59%
8.	Nigeria	17%	57%
9.	Netherlands	15%	52%
10.	USA	15%	37%

If we instead take into account the number of people living in the respective countries, i. e. volume of single malt Scotch per capita, the ranking looks like this (and again we're talking about the Top 45 markets);

Largest single malt Scotch import per capita in 2024

1. Singapore
2. Latvia
3. Taiwan
4. Netherlands
5. United Arab Emirates
6. France
7. Sweden
8. Belgium
9. Uruguay
10. Australia

It is important to remember that both Singapore and Latvia (and to a certain degree Taiwan) serve as hubs for re-export to other markets and that a significant part of the volumes to the UAE are for travel retail.

The big players

Diageo

When the results for 2024/2025 (ending 30th June) were published, the figures showed a tiny decline of net sales by 0.1% to $20.25bn. Organic growth however was 1.7%. Annual operating profit tumbled by 27.8% to $4.3bn and while this seems alarming there are reasons for this large decline. Exceptional impairment and restructuring costs were a a heavy burden. If we instead look at operating profit before exceptional items, the decline diminishes to 4% and the sum is $5.7bn. The market seems to have captured the reasons behind the profit loss and the company's shares went up 6.7% when the report was published.

While volumes for Scotch (-2%), vodka (-4%) and rum (-3%) were all down, tequila improved by 15% and beer by 6%. It is also in these two categories we find the star brands. Don Julio tequila volume increased by an astonishing 41% and Guinness by 14%. Johnnie Walker on the other hand fell by 11% mainly because of weak sales in the US market.

Overall, reported sales in the American market grew by 0.8% and in Europe by 0.4% whiles sales declined in Asia Pacific by 4.8%. This was caused by a continued weak economy in China and couldn't be offset by an increase in India with 7%.

In terms of leadership it has been a couple of turbulent years for Diageo. In June 2023 the CEO at the time, Ivan Menezes, unexpectedly passed away. He was set to retire three weeks later and his successor Debra Crew had already been appointed. Her tenure, however, lasted just two years and in June 2025 she was succeeded as interim CEO by the former CFO Nik Jhangiani. He had been a driving force behind the company's Accelerate programme which was launched in May 2025 and was described as: "Across Diageo, we are embedding a more performance-driven culture, focused on speed, agility, continuous improvement, and leadership accountability." The plan includes a cost savings plan of $500m.

Jhangiani´s comments on the future were that sales growth for next year would be similar to this year's and that organic operating profit growth would be in a mid-single-digit percentage.

The last year has been filled with rumours on whether or not Diageo would dispose of any of their more than 200 brands and if so – which ones? Two possible sales suggested by some commentators were those of Guinness and the company's 34% stake in Moët Hennessy – the wine and spirits arm of LVMH. In January 2025 however, a Diageo spokesperson declared that they had no intention to sell either.

There have been several decisions taken in recent times in order to bring down costs in the company. One was not to continue backing Distill Ventures accelerator programme in the future although it remained uncertain what that would mean for the companies already involved in the scheme. Another action in March 2025 was to at least pause production at their Bulleit distillery in Lebanon, Kentucky – the third largest of its kind in North America.

Pernod Ricard

The vast majority of spirits producers told the same story when revealing their latest financial reports using terminology including tariffs, inflation and geopolitical instability and Pernod Ricard was no exception. What perhaps stood out a little bit is a comment from the CEO and chairman Alexandre Ricard when he, albeit expressing optimism over the future, stated that "volatility is here to stay."

In dry figures, the company's results for the year ending 30th June 2025 showed that sales were down by 3% to €10.9 billion while reported profits from recurring operations fell by 1% organically to €2.9 billion. In common with most of the big producers the blame was directed at declining markets, especially in the US and China. The analysts, however, had anticipated worse figures and, similar to Diageo, the share price went up when the results were revealed in the end of August. A cost-saving programme was introduced already in spring 2025 with a goal to generate savings of €1 billion over the next four years.

The company says it was hit badly in three of its four

Nik Jhangiani became interim CEO for Diageo in June 2025

Midleton Distillery, where Pernod Ricard´s Jameson whiskey is distilled, stopped producing temporarily during 2025

so called "must-win" territories - America (-6%), China (-21%) and travel retail. Regarding China a spokesperson said "we expect some improving trends in China towards stabilization." The one market that stood out in a positive way was India which now accounts for 13% of Pernod Ricard's business. Sales grew by 6% and Jameson became the biggest-selling brand of imported bottled spirits. In the calendar year 2024, Jameson increased volumes globally by 6%. Other whisky brands in the company that also grew include Ballantine's (+13%) and Chivas Regal (+4%) while 100 Pipers, Passport and Glenlivet were all in the red.

But Pernod Ricard is also about other spirits, not least cognac where Martell is their major brand. China has been an important market for a very long time but the relation has sometimes been strenuous. Chinese officials have accused European producers of dumping prices on brandy/cognac destined for China and in an attempt to help the Chinese brandy industry, duties were recently imposed on imported brands. Some companies were, however, exempted after negotiations in July 2025 and Pernod Ricard together with Rémy Cointreau and Hennessy belong to them. These are the same companies that Chinese officials used as examples to spark the anti-dumping investigation in early 2024.

Suntory Global Spirits

The origins of the company go back to 1899 when Shinjiro Torii opened an import store in Osaka. In 1923 he broke ground on the Yamazaki distillery which was the starting point of the Japanese whisky wonder. To this day the Torii family is still the principal owner of Suntory Holdings which entails a very diverse company with interests in spirits, soft drinks, beer, wine, RTD and products within health and wellness.

In 2014 the company bought Beam and an entire new company was founded – Beam Suntory. In April 2024 it was renamed Suntory Global Spirits and this is now the company responsible for its parent company's (Suntory Holdings) spirits operations

Financial figures for Suntory Global Spirits are not revealed in detail by Suntory Holdings but the parent company showed an increase in revenue in 2024 by 4.3% to 3,210 billion yen while the operational income increased by 3.8% to 327 billion yen. These are both impressive figures at a time when most companies involved in the alcohol business experience decline.

Even though the name Beam recently disappeared from the company name, it is Jim Beam that is the flagship brand. It remains the world's most popular bourbon and is number 8 on the top list of all whiskies. With an increase of 3% it sold 128 million bottles in 2024. Maker's Mark on the other hand decreased by 10%. The Japanese whisky side of the company is made up of brands such as Yamazaki, Hakushu, Kakubin and Torys to mention but a few.

Beam Suntory is also the owner of a portfolio of Scotch single malts where Laphroaig takes the lead followed by Islay neighbour Bowmore. The other three are Auchentoshan, Ardmore and Glen Garioch. Substantial investments have been made over the last couple of years in all five distilleries, aiming primarily at improving the quality rather than increasing the capacity. This approach to production by the Japanese owners is a sign of *monozukuri* at its finest. This Japanese word can best be translated to "the art of crafting things" and within the group there is a designated company (Suntory Monozukuri Expert Europe) with the task to fine tune production – either by honouring traditional methods or through innovation – in order to achieve the ultimate quality and flavours.

Brown Forman

The company is on the Top 10 list of the world's largest spirits producers and in the latest financial year (ending 30 April 2025) net sales fell by 5% to $4.0bn while operating profits were down by 22% to $1.1bn. This was quite a contrast to the previous year when profits were up by 25%. On the other hand, those figures were inflated due to the sale of the Sonoma-Cutrer wine business and also the sale of Finlandia vodka to Coca-Cola in November 2023.

One measure in order to mitigate the challenging times has been a 12% lay-off of the workforce (650 people) and the selling of their Louisville cooperage. Barrel making and repair will be outsourced instead.

In terms of markets, the US remained a tough one and there were challenges in developed markets such as the UK, Germany and Canada too. In Latin America things looked brighter, not least in Brazil where Jack Daniel's was doing well.

The company´s mega brand, Jack Daniel's, did fairly well with just a 1% decrease in sales and Woodford Reserve even managed to increase by 6%. If whiskey wasn't the problem then the tequila portfolio certainly was. Both El Jimador and Herradura saw declining sales by 13%. Chal-

Famous Grouse was recently sold by Edrington to William Grant & Sons

lenging macroeconomic conditions in Mexico was one main reason. What the company calls "Rest of Portfolio's" dropped by 33% but had to do with the aforementioned sale of Sonoma-Cutrer and Finlandia. Diplomático rum on the other hand, which was acquired from Spain's Destillers United Group in 2022, showed double-digit growth.

In 2016 Brown Forman took an interest in Scotch malt whisky when they bought BenRiach, GlenDronach (about to be expanded) and Glenglassaugh (with a brand new product range). A year before, the company also entered the Irish whiskey scene taking over Slane distillery in collaboration with the Conyngham family.

Edrington

In previous year's edition of this book we stated that both Diageo and Pernod Ricard had begun to feel the effects of slower sales for the global spirits & wine industry. Edrington however came out with flying colours. One year later even they experienced a downturn in sales and profits. In the financial year which ended 31 March 2025 core revenues (sales) were down 12% from last year to £1,069m, while profits before tax decreased by 30% to £258m.

Scott McCroskie, the CEO of Edrington, noticed a weaker demand for prestige products; "We saw performance hold up better at the lower price points, whilst sales of our top-end products slowed more sharply."

For a company such as Edrington this became serious. Their focus for more than a decade has been on ultra-premium Scotch with The Macallan as the flagship brand. It is the third best selling single malt in the world in terms of volumes but number one in terms of values. In recent years the interest in China for these expensive editions has been particularly strong but last year it was the core expressions that performed well instead. Highland Park and Glenrothes on the other hand showed a significant decline in sales.

One brand in the Edrington portfolio is consistently performing well and also so this year; Brugal rum shows resilience, not least in its home market, the Dominican Republic. For many years Edrington was not represented in the American whiskey category. In 2018, however, they bought a 35% share in Wyoming Whisky which was increased to 80% in 2023. Two strong brands are not part of the portfolio anymore. In autumn 2024 it was announced that Famous Grouse and Naked Malt would be sold to William Grant & Sons and a few months later the deal was approved the UK Competition and Markets Authority. Famous Grouse is one of the Top 10 blends in the world and number one in the UK. It seems obvious that there was no longer a place for a blend in a company focusing on prestige brands. The decline in sales for Edrington in 2024/2025 was more or less consistent across all markets with just a couple of exceptions – South Korea and Japan.

Edrington's principal shareholder is The Robertson Trust which has donated in excess of £350 million to charitable causes since 1961. Since 2020, the Japanese company Suntory owns 10% of Edrington as well as 25% of Macallan (a share they have held since 1989).

The big brands

Blended Scotch

The category that dragged down the total export figures for Scotch in 2023 was blended Scotch with a dramatic downturn in volumes of 21%. Single malts performed marginally better and even managed to increase in values. One year later roles were reversed. While single malts decreased by double digits, blended Scotch made a comeback with volumes rising 6%.

Before we dig in to the Top 10 – the list comes with a caveat; for 2024 there are no official figures for two of the brands – Famous Grouse and Grant's. We have therefore made cautious estimations based on figures from previous years and on the performance of other brands in the same price bracket. Hopefully we are not too far from the truth.

The number one, as always, is Johnnie Walker. The brand declined (-2%) for the second year in a row to reach 259 million bottles but this is still 17% more than in 2019, the last year before the pandemic and the third best year in history for the brand. Johnnie Walker is also the fourth best selling whisky in the world with three Indian brands occupying the first three spots.

Number two on the list is Chivas Brothers' Ballantine's which made a tremendous comeback in 2024 with an increase by 13% to reach 112 million bottles. These are also the best sales volumes the brand has ever experienced. Just like Johnnie Walker the range continues to increase, sometimes through unorthodox innovations. The latest, in 2025, was Ballantine's Sweet Blend. Since it's been bottled at 30% abv it doesn't qualify as a whisky but is labelled "spirit drink". The aim is to attract new consumer groups to the brand.

Since 2022 Chivas Regal has been number three on the list and with a 4% increase to 58 million bottles they defended the position in 2024. One success last year was the introduction of the Extra Smoky edition. In fourth place we find Grant's where we estimate the sales volumes to be 48 million bottles.

Place five in last year's book was held by one of Bacardi/Dewars two blends, namely William Lawson's. This year it is again a brand from the same owner but this time Dewar's. It retained the same volumes as in 2023 – 40 million bottles. In 2024 the owners launched a global campaign titled "Here's to the Story" emphasizing social interaction between people as well as experiences. Place number six is occupied by William Lawson's which has grown by 170% since the new millenium. The year 2024 was a disappointment though with sales going down by 9% to 38 million bottles

Famous Grouse comes in at seventh place with an estimated sales volume of 36 million bottles. It is still the number one whisky in the UK with an impressive market share of 25%. Apart from the UK, the brand is also hugely popular in the Nordic countries and in Eastern Europe. In 2025 the brand was sold by Edrington to William Grant & Sons.

Black & White in 8th position can look back at an impressive 14 years of continued growth. It is just in the last two years that sales have declined. In 2024 volumes were down by 6% to 35 million bottles. The brand is popular not least in Latin America and India

Number 9 is Label 5 owned by the French company La Martiniquaise who also owns Glen Moray distillery in Scotland. Sales were 29 million bottles – just as the year before. In 10th place, we find J&B which saw sales dropping by 4% in 2024 to 28 million bottles. Finally, we feel we need to mention a brand that was just about to join the Top 10 – White Horse. This iconic blend was registered as a brand in 1891 and in 2024 it managed to grow more than any other blend; plus 17% and a total of 25 million bottles.

Single Malt Scotch

As mentioned before, 2024 was not the year of Scotch single malt. Over the years we have come accustomed to the category continuously growing, but last year both volumes and values were down by almost 20% each. The category's share of total value for Scotch export was also down from 36% to 31% while the share of volumes is around 9%. If we divide total values of exported Scotch single malts by the equivalent of bottles exported, we get £13.23 per bottle which is an increase compared to the previous year.

Let's look at last year's sales development for the Top 10 Scotch single malts where all Top 10 are the same as the previous year and in the same order.

There is no official communication on Glenfiddich sales volumes for 2024 but since they were well in the lead in 2023 and with the closest contender, Glenlivet, declining in both 2023 and 2024 we feel confident to say that Glenfiddich was the best selling single malt in 2024. Sales in 2023 were 19.6 million bottles. In second spot Glenlivet continued to loose volumes for the second year in a row. Sales were down by 7% to 16 million bottles.

For the rest of the malts on the Top 10 list, there were no sales figures for 2024 available at the time of printing so what follows here is the position and figures from 2023; Macallan (12.1 million bottles), Glenmorangie (8.9 million), The Singleton (8.6 million), Balvenie (5.3 million), Talisker (4.4 million), Laphroaig (4.1 million), Aberlour (3.8 million) and Dalmore (3.3 million).

Finally, let's take a look at the top whiskies in North America, India and Ireland.

In North America, Jack Daniel's is the undisputed leader. It is also the sixth most popular whisk(e)y in the world with 169 million bottles sold in 2024 which was a volume decrease of 1%. In second place is the most sold bourbon in the world, Jim Beam, which is also the 8th most sold of whiskies in the world. A total of 128 million bottles were sold in 2024. It is followed by the Canadian whisky Crown Royal (96 million bottles) and two bourbons – Evan Williams (42 million and up by an impressive 13%) and Maker's Mark (32 million, down by 10%).

In India, we find six of the ten most sold whiskies in the world even though they cannot be sold in the EU as whisky since they are made from molasses rather than grain. The top 5 are McDowell's No. 1 (386 million bottles), Royal Stag (372 million bottles), Imperial Blue (275 million), Officer's Choice (256 million) and Blender's Pride (121 million). For a few of the usual big sellers (Original Choice and Bagpiper) there were no official sales figures this year.

Finally we have Ireland where Jameson has dominated and in many ways defined the category for a very long time. In 2024 the brand occupied place 7 on the Top whiskies of the world, selling 130 million bottles (up by 6%). Number two is most certainly (although no official figures have been disclosed) Tullamore Dew which sold 19 million bottles in 2023 while Bushmills comes in third with 13 million bottles sold in 2024.

New distilleries - Scotland

This part of the book deals with the embryonic distillery projects – those that haven't started producing yet. In those cases where neither funds nor planning permission has been obtained, the stories are more about visions rather than concrete actions that have taken place.

It is amazing and encouraging to see that in spite of the current downturn for Scotch, and most other spirits for that matter, there are still entrepreneurs planning for new distilleries. Admittedly, the ideas for a majority of these were hatched years ago when the prospects were brighter, but nevertheless – the optimism is still there. And to my knowledge none of the 60 plus distilleries that were opened since 2005 have been forced to close.

In the last couple of years focus has often been on new distilleries in Campbeltown and on Islay and we will come back to that later but for this year let's start on Isle of Skye. In 2022 Séamus Ó Baoighill and Seumas Gorman opened their 57° Skye craft gin distillery in Broadford in the southern part of the island. They are now looking to replace it with a new distillery which will also involve whisky production. A planning application was submitted in March 2025 and is still being dealt with. The equipment will consist of two stills and seven washbacks.

Heading north on the mainland we reach the Black Isle, the peninsula north of Inverness. This area carries a lot of weight in terms of whisky history. It was the location of the legendary Ferintosh distillery. Founded in the 1600s by the Forbes, it accounted for two thirds of all legal whisky in Scotland in the 1760s. It closed in 1785 but now there might be a new Ferintosh distillery emerging in the area. Morris Dalgetty, a local sheep farmer, has, together with Organic Architects, applied for permission to build a distillery on the Mulchaich farm north of Inverness.

While still in the area, Black Isle Brewery, established organic craft beer brewers since 1998, have had planning permission granted to build a state-of-the-art new brewery and distillery to the east of Inverness. The development will also feature a taproom, a shop and outdoor space for events and festivals. The distillery will be equipped with one pair of stills and it could be producing some time in 2026.

Heading further north we reach Castletown near Dunnet where Martin and Claire Murray were granted planning permission in 2022 to convert the historic Castletown Mill into a whisky distillery. Their company, Dunnet Bay Distillers, is already producing gin and vodka and the £4m project would finance a whisky distillery with four washbacks and one pair of stills. The two stills, manufactured by Speyside Copper Works, arrived in April 2025 and hopefully production can commence during 2025. The future whisky will be sold under the name Stannergill.

Let's head southwest to Giarloch in Wester Ross where Gordon and Vanessa Quinn have been operating their Badachro distillery since 2017 with gin and vodka production. Recently they submitted an application to the local council to expand the distillery into whisky production. They have already launched sourced whisky from an unnamed Highland distillery under the name Bad na h-Achlaise.

Heading further south we reach Inveraray. Here, at Inveraray Castle, the Stock Spirits drinks company submitted a planning application in April 2025 to build a £25 million distillery. Stock Spirits is one of the largest alcohol producers in Europe and acquired the Clan Campbell blended Scotch brand from Pernod Ricard in 2023. The distillery, with a two million litre capacity, will also house a visitor centre.

On the west coast of the Cowal Peninsula, the village Polphail was built in the 1970s to house workers on a planned oil rig construction plant nearby. However, the oil rig yard was never realized and the houses that had already been built turned into a ghost town and were finally demolished in 2016. In 2017, Sandy Bulloch, the previous owner of Loch Lomond Distillery, bought the site with the aim of building a distillery named Portavadie. The planning application was approved by Argyll & Bute Council in 2018 but then nothing materialized. Later the entire project (with a second approval in October 2022) was taken over by the Indian company Piccadily Agro Industries (known for their single malts Kamet and Indri) who have invested £15m in the site. It is at the moment uncertain if the project will go through but an amendment to the building application was submitted in June 2025.

From here, the step to Campbeltown seems natural. With around 25 distilleries operating in the early 1900s, only two (Springbank and Glen Scotia) survived and a third one, Glengyle, was re-opened in 2004. There are currently plans to double that number with three new distilleries.

Behind one of them, Dál Riata in the very heart of Campbeltown, we find Iain Croucher and Ronnie Grant. A planning application was approved in September 2023. With a capacity of 850,000 litres of alcohol, it will be equipped with a two ton semi-lauter mash tun, ten washbacks, a 10,000 litre wash still and a 7,200 litre spirit still. In April 2025, however, there were no signs of any construction work going on.

Another distillery in the Campbeltown area, and the one that seems to be closest to opening, was announced in June 2023. Brave New Spirits, an independent bottler established in 2020, received planning permission in August 2023 for a distillery by the name of Witchburn, to be located between Campbeltown airport and Machrihanish village at MACC Business Park. Powered by renewable energy sources, the distillery will have an impressive capacity of 2 million litres and will be equipped with 16 washbacks and two pairs of stills.

The planning application for the third distillery in the

The stunning location of Witchburn Distillery just north of Campbeltown

vicinity of Campbeltown was approved by the council in April 2024. The Dhurrie Farm north of the town will be converted from a dairy farm to a regenerative arable farm and a distillery named Machrihanish will be set up. The owners of Isle of Raasay Distillery, R&B Distillers, are behind the project. The 360 degree view from the distillery (and not least the planned visitor centre bar) will be spectacular. Machrihanish will be equipped with a mash filter, six stainless steel washbacks with cooling jackets, two 6,250 litre wash stills and two 4,000 litre spirit stills. There are also plans for small maltings on site. The barley used will be grown in the surrounding fields.

Over on Islay, Elixir Distillers, spearheaded by well-known whisky dealer and collector Sukhinder Singh and his brother Rajbir, finally got the green light in April 2021 to their planning application for Portintruan Distillery. The distillery, managed by the experienced Georgie Crawford, will be situated just outside Port Ellen on the road leading to Laphroaig, Lagavulin and Ardbeg. The contractors started with the foundations in July 2022. In April 2025 the majority of the internal vessels and large equipment were in place and the distillery is planned to be commissioned in late 2025. Equipped with 14 washbacks (eight wooden and six stainless steel) and two pairs of stills with directly fired wash stills, the distillery will have capacity to produce 1 million litres of pure alcohol. On-site floor maltings will produce between 60 and 80% of the barley needs. Fourteen houses for families working at the distillery are included in the project, as well as a visitor centre and an education facility. There are also plans for a micro distillery with two pot stills and a column still for experimentation and, possibly, producing other spirits, not least rum. This part of the distillery will have a hammer mill and a mash filter.

In 2014, Jean Donnay, at that time owner of Glann ar Mor distillery in France, secured a planning permission for Gartbreck distillery just south of Bowmore. Shortly after Hunter Laing became involved but later the two parties fell apart and Hunter Laing moved forward to build their Ardnahoe distillery on the northern part of Islay instead. Years later the Gartbreck site was bought by Chivas Brothers, already operating twelve malt distilleries on the Scottish mainland, and in October 2024 they announced that they would build their first Islay distillery. Since then their have been no further information from the company and no planning application has been submitted to the council.

Out on Barra in the Western Isles, a gin distillery has been running since 2017 and later vodka and rum have also been added to the range. It is the owners', Michael and Katie Morrison, intention to also include whisky production in a new distillery at Eoligarry. In December 2022 they received planning permission from the Comhairle nan Eilean Siar planning department and since summer 2024 they have raised £2.3m to finance the expansion. .

Back on the mainland and heading south we find Campbell Meyer & Co who own a 150,000 square ft bonded warehouse in East Kilbride, just south of Glasgow. In spring 2016, the company announced plans to add a distillery named Burnbrae. Little news has been shared since, but apart from filling, blending and bottling they may have added distilling as well.

Could it be that we will see Coleburn distilling again after 40 years in the shadows?

North of Glasgow, in Dumbarton, we find Loch Lomond Brewery which was established by Euan and Fiona MacEachern in 2011. They went on to distilling gin and vodka and with a new 1,250 litre wash still and a 950 litre spirit still it seems that they just recently embarked on producing malt whisky. No doubt they will be added to the active distilleries chapter in next year's edition of the Malt Whisky Yearbook.

Let's head east to Aberdeenshire – a region which rarely is covered in a "new distillery" context. This year however, there are two projects in planning. The first is the Bon Accord distillery which will be situated on Greyhope Road by the waterfront. Historically there was a Bon Accord distillery but this was situated in the centre of the town. It was established in 1855 and closed in 1913. One of the reasons for this name being reused in these modern times is that the distillery will be built on the site of the Bon Accord Drinks Company (producers of juice) which closed in 2000. It will be equipped with two stills and eight washbacks and a planning application was approved in January 2025.

To reach the other proposed distillery we need to leave Aberdeen and drive 30 minutes northwest to the village Kemnay. Jonathan Dunne has the intention of restoring the 19th century stables on the nearby Fetternear Estate and turn them into the Inverurie Distillery, equipped with two stills. A planning application was submitted to the council in February 2025 but at the time of writing no decision had been taken.

In the Speyside area, a long-closed distillery could be about to come alive. Dallas Dhu, founded in 1898 and closed in the infamous year of 1983 together with another ten distilleries, could be working again soon. Last summer, the long-time custodian of the distillery, Historic Environment Scotland (HES), announced that the business will reopen as a working distillery, with Aceo (owners of the independent bottler Murray McDavid) responsible for management of operations. All the equipment is still there and it remains to be seen if and when the distillery starts producing again.

While still on closed distilleries being resurrected, there is a fair chance that Coleburn (founded in 1897 and closed in 1985) might be distilling again in a few years. It is situated just north of Rothes and since 2004 the buildings have been owned by Dale and Mark Winchester. Their plan was to rebuild it into an entertainment centre which so far hasn´t materialised. Since 2014 the buildings have been used by Aceo (same company involved with Dallas Dhu above) to mature whisky. Recently it was revealed that there are plans underway to restore Coleburn into distilling. The owners have chosen Keith Cruickshank to supervise the transformation. Keith has spent the last 27 years as the manager of Benromach distillery near Forres.

Going further north, in Easter Fearn on the Dornoch Firth, just a few miles west of Balblair, the Brooke family (proprietors of the estate since 1893) are looking at building a whisky distillery. The family submitted a planning application to the Highland Council in May 2022 which was approved in October for a distillery equipped with one mash tun, ten washbacks and two pairs of stills and with a capacity of one million litres.

Heading south again, in 2021, Speyside Distillers announced that their lease of their current distillery site south of Kingussie would expire and that they were looking for a new site to build on. Rumours about the possible location floated around but in November 2023 a planning application for a distillery near Strathmashie (around 15 km west of the current site) was approved by the local council. It will be situated even closer to the Spey river than the current distillery. The planned equipment will be six wash backs with space for another six and there will be two pairs of stills.

Meanwhile, the new owners of the current Speyside distillery site since 2021 – Glasgow Whisky – are now rebuilding the distillery which, when on stream in 2026, will be named Glen Tromie Distillery. The capacity will be increased to 1.4 million litres and in July 2025 Graham Geddes, ex-manager of Jura distillery, joined the company.

South of Stirling, near Bannockburn, planning was approved in June 2025 for Auchenbowie distillery. It will be built in the dilapidated walled garden of Auchenbowie House which dates back to the 17th century. Construction is expected to begin in 2026.

Down in The Borders, near Kelso, approval was granted in April 2024 to alter buildings at Grahamslaw Farm to turn them into a distillery. The team behind it is led by Sarah Lang and included is also the legendary, former master blender at Chivas Brothers – Colin Scott. The manager for the upcoming distillery, which will be equipped with one pair of stills, is Sarah Fraser with her past in The Borders Distillery in Hawick and with Chivas Brothers.

Setting up another distillery in The Borders has been in R&B Distillers' plans for a long time by now. Eventually, they went ahead and founded a distillery on Raasay instead and now plan to build yet another on the Kintyre peninsula instead (the previously mentioned Macrihanish distillery). The company hasn't given up on The Borders though. Current aspirations include a micro grain distillery in Coldstream south west of Berwick-upon-Tweed and right on the border to England but this is probably 3-4 years into the future.

In 2017 Linlithgow Distillery west of Edinburgh was founded as a gin and vodka distiller. In 2024 the American investment group Billion Global Chase acquired a 75% stake with the intention of adding also a malt whisky distillery. The project is still in an early stage with a possible start within two years.

The only distillery in East Lothian southeast of Edinburgh has for many years been the classic Glenkinchie. Now it looks like they may get company in the near future. Eydent Distillers plan to build a distillery near Ormiston. One of the people involved is Jack Mayo who has been working with Glasgow and Holyrood distilleries previously. Apart from whisky the plans are to make also gin and other spirits. A planning application, awaiting decision, was filed in December 2024.

Finally a distillery is being built near Dunfermline in West Fife, 20 minutes north of Edinburgh. Privately run by a family, the owners have been working away quietly since planning permission was granted in 2022. One pair of stills were installed in summer 2025 and most probably the distillery will be added to the active distilleries chapter in the next edition of the Yearbook. Involved in the Knockhill distillery project is also John McDougall with 64 years in the industry.

Independent
bottlers

Independent bottlers play an important role in the whisky business. With their innovative bottlings, they increase diversity. A new and brilliant book on the topic is David Stirk´s *Independent Scotch – The History of Independent Bottlers* (ISBN 978-1-399-94553-0). The following are a selection of the major companies. Tasting notes have been prepared by Ian Wisnewski.

Gordon & MacPhail

gordonandmacphail.com

Established in 1895 the company is owned by the Urquhart family. Apart from being an independent bottler, there is also a legendary store in Elgin which moved from South Street to St Giles Shopping Centre in High Street while the old shop will be turned into a whisky experience venue. Early 2025 the shopping centre surprisingly closed and Gordon & MacPhail moved the shop next to Johnstons of Elgin. In 1993 they bought Benromach distillery and in 2022 they commissioned their second distillery, The Cairn close to Grantown-on-Spey. In July 2023 the owners surprised many when they announced that they would stop purchasing stock for independent bottlings from 2024. One reason for the decision is that more and more producers want to release their own bottlings, resulting in less available new make to buy. Going forward, the company will focus more on their own brands but also reassured their customers that they have maturing casks in stock that will last for several decades of independent bottlings.

Gordon & MacPhail´s part in establishing the interest in single malt Scotch before the vast majority of producers realised the potential, can not be overrated. Currently there are five distinctive ranges; Connoisseurs Choice consists of single malts. Over the years there have been bottlings from over 100 Scottish distilleries. Discovery is grouped under three flavour profiles – smoky, sherry and bourbon. Distillery Labels is a relic from a time when Gordon & MacPhail released more or less official bottlings for several producers. Private Collection features old single malts including bottlings from closed distilleries. Generations comprises the oldest and rarest whiskies in stock, including Glenlivet 80 years old in 2021. George Urquhart, second generation of the family, was instrumental to the success and popularity of single malts and to honour him there is a range named The Legacy of Mr. George. In October 2025 the company released the world´s oldest single malt to date. It was an 85 year old Glenlivet, matured in an American oak cask and bottled at 43,7%.

Glenlivet 1954, 43,7%

Nose: Sticky toffee pudding, overtones of apple crumble, orange marmalade and tiramisu.

Palate: Silky mouthfeel, sweet top notes and dry base notes together with crisp green apples, caramel sauce and underlying dry oak.

Glenburgie 1963, 54,4%

Nose: Chocolate truffles, marzipan, roasted nuts and barbecue notes extend to prunes in syrup and raisins.

Palate: Soft, silky mouthfeel, fruit cake with dried fruit intensifying, then tiramisu and espresso underlined by dry oak.

Berry Bros. & Rudd

bbrspirits.com

The world´s oldest wine and spirit merchant, founded in 1698! The famous address 3 St James´s Street, where the company has been since the start, was in 2017 returned to its appearance of 35 years ago and is now a space for consultations and a new flagship store opened just around the corner in 63 Pall Mall. In April 2024 a dedicated spirits shop was opened at 1 St James´s Street, connected to the Pall Mall shop which now focuses on wine. In summer 2025 the company also announced that they have plans to open a retail store in Washington, DC and in September that year Rob Symington (of Symington Family Estates, producers for five generations of Graham´s Port) joined the company as the UK managing director.

Berry Brothers had been offering their customers private bottlings of malt whisky for years, but it was not until 2002 that they launched Berry´s Own Selection of single malts. A series called The Classic Range, including Sherry and Peated, was released in 2018 with Speyside Traditional 16 year old as the latest addition. In 2021 the spirits range was revamped by way of the first bespoke spirits bottles in the company´s history including series such as Small Batch, Exceptional Casks and Perspective. In 2023 the The Collective series where they offer whiskies from distilleries around the world was launched and it was followed in June 2024 by the Odyssey Collection. In 2023 Berry Bros acquired a minority stake in England´s largest whisky producer, Cotswolds Distillery.

Glen Spey 2009 Glen & Valleys, 58%

Nose: Juicy apple crumble, further enrichened by Victoria Sponge and edge of oak.

Palate: Creamy mouthfeel, dark chocolate and light oak unfold, then extend with lemon meringue, juicy baked apples with raisins, and hint of maltyness.

Single Orkney 2006 Coast & Shores, 56,3%

Nose: Sea breeze, mineral water notes and oak with underlying lemon.

Palate: Velvety mouthfeel, tangy sea spray garnished by vanilla and a hint of coconut, then moves to brioche and creamy maltyness.

Signatory

signatoryusa.com

Founded in 1988 by Andrew and Brian Symington, Signatory Vintage Scotch Whisky soon became one of the most influential independent bottlers, not least for their ability to surprise consumers with extremely rare bottlings and often from closed distilleries. The most widely distributed range is Cask Strength Collection. Other ranges include The Un-chill Filtered Collection, the 100 Proof Edition, the Small Batch Edition and Symington´s Choice. Andrew Symington bought Edradour Distillery from Pernod Ricard in 2002 and the entire operations, including Signatory, are now concentrated to the distillery in Perthshire.

Ian Macleod Distillers

ianmacleod.com

The company was founded in 1933 and is one of the largest independent family-owned companies within the spirits industry. Gin, rum, vodka and liqueurs, apart from whisky, are found within the range and they also own Glengoyne, Tamdhu and Rosebank distilleries. And it doesn´t stop there; in 2024 they started producing at their Una distillery in Himachal Pradesh in northern India and in 2026 their new distillery on Islay, Laggan Bay, will open. Their biggest seller is the blended whisky King Robert II while their single malt range includes The Chieftain´s where a Cigar Malt is a recurrent bottling. Macleod´s Regional Malts are single malts chosen to represent the 5 whisky regions in Scotland. There are two As We Get It single malt expressions – Highland and Islay. The Six Isles blended malt contains whisky from the majority of whisky-producing islands while one of the top sellers is the blended Scotch Isle of Skye available at 8, 12, 18, 21, 25 and 30 years old. Finally, Smokehead, a heavily, peated single malt from Islay introduced in 2006, has become a huge success. The range was revamped in 2018 and several new expressions have been released including Smokehead Tequila Cask Terminado.

Isle of Skye 30 year old, 40%

Nose: Sticky toffee pudding, nutmeg and poached dried fruit, then hints of tea leaves, followed by butterscotch.

Palate: Luxurious, velvety mouthfeel yields fruitcake and butterscotch, then dry oak with further espresso and tiramisu highlights.

Isle of Skye 25 year old, 40%

Nose: Rich apricots and dates, ginger and nutmeg, toffee and tiramisu, then soft oak.

Palate: Silky mouthfeel, gingerbread, orange marmalade, a balance of sweetness-dryness, then vanilla creme anglaise with apricot indulgence.

Blackadder International

blackadder.com

Behind Blackadder is Robin Tucek together with his two children Michael and Hannah. Apart from Blackadder Raw Cask (bottled straight from the cask without any filtration at all), there are also a number of other ranges – Smoking Islay, Peat Reek, Peat Reek Embers, Statement, Chimera, Puff Adder and special bottlings of Amrut single malt. In recent years, three brands have become increasingly popular; Black Snake which is a vatting of casks finished in a single sherry butt, Red Snake which are single cask malts, always from first fill ex-bourbon and Sherry Snake from first fill sherry casks. All bottlings from Blackadder are uncoloured and un chill-filtered.

Murray McDavid

murray-mcdavid.com

The company was founded in 1996 by Mark Reynier, Simon Coughlin and Gordon Wright. In 2013 Murray McDavid was taken over by Aceo Ltd. and a year later they signed a lease for the warehouses at the closed Coleburn distillery for storing their own whiskies as well as stock belonging to clients. The bottlings are divided into eight different ranges; Mission Gold (exceptionally rare whiskies bottled at cask strength), Benchmark (mature single malts bottled at 46%), Mystery Malt (single malts where the distillery is not revealed), Select Grain (single grains), The Vatting (vatted malts), Crafted Blend (blended Scotch from their own blending) and Cask Craft (showcasing different wood finishes). The eighth range, Ultra, was recently introduced with extremely rare and old expressions. Aceo has also announced that they, in a joint venture with Historic Environmental Scotland, have plans to re-start production at Dallas Dhu distillery.

Duncan Taylor

duncantaylor.com

Founded in Glasgow in 1938 as a cask broker and trading company. In 2002, the company was acquired by Euan Shand and operations were moved to Huntly where they also run a whisky shop. Recently they opened The Bank Café & Restaurant and a whisky bar, The Club Room, also in Huntly. Duncan Taylor´s flagship brand is the blended Scotch Black Bull, a brand with a history going back to 1864. Black Bull was rebranded in 2009 by Duncan

Taylor and the range consists of several expressions – 12, 18 and 30 year old, Kyloe Original, Kyloe Peated Finish and Kyloe Sherry Finish. There is also the Nick Faldo Collection with old bottlings up to 55 years. The Black Bull brand is complimented by Smokin' which is a blend of peated Speyside, Islay and grain whisky from the Lowlands.

The portfolio also includes The Rarest (single cask, cask strength whiskies of great age from demolished distilleries), Dimensions (a collection of single malts and single grains aged up to 39 years), The Tantalus (a selection of whiskies all aged in their 40s), Battlehill (a range of single malts and single grains) and Rare Auld Grain (a selection of rare grain whiskies bottled at cask strength). The perhaps most popular range in recent years is The Octave. These are single malt whiskies matured for a further period in small, 60-70 litre ex-sherry octave casks. In 2019 The Octave Premium with substantially older whiskies, was introduced. Finally, the blended malt category is represented by Big Smoke, a young peated whisky available at 46% and 60%.

Black Bull 18 year old, 50%

Nose: Turkish Delight, floral hints, dried fruits, sherry overtones.
Palate: Long and intense with dark chocolate, herbal aromas and baked apple pie.

Black Bull 21 year old, 50%

Nose: Pine needles, vanilla, oatmeal crackers, fennel, chocolate, citrus and nougat.
Palate: Delicious notes of dried fruits, chocolate cake, dry smoke, cherry trifle, tiramisu, clove and cinnamon.

Scotch Malt Whisky Society

smws.com

The Scotch Malt Whisky Society was founded in 1983 and was owned by Glenmorangie Co from 2003 until 2015 when it was taken over by a group of private investors and later, Artisanal Spirits Company became the owner. Since 2021 it is listed on the London Stock Exchange. The society has more than 41,000 members worldwide and apart from UK, there is a network of international branches and partner bars in 26 countries around the world. The idea from the very beginning was to buy casks of single malts from the producers and bottle them at cask strength without colouring or chill filtration. The Society has played a significant role for the interest in single cask Scotch that has exploded in recent decades. The labels do not reveal the name of the distillery. Instead there is a number but also a short description which will give you a clue to which distillery it is. Around 500 casks are bottled every year. The SMWS operates four venues with bars and member rooms in Edinburgh (Queen Street and Leith), London (Greville Street) and Glasgow (Bath Street) and also works with partner bars around the world. In recent years, the range has been expanded to also include single grain, whiskies from other countries as well as rum, gin, cognac and other spirits.

Compass Box Whisky Co

compassboxwhisky.com

Compass Box celebrated its 25th anniversary in October 2025 and has been one of the most influential players on the Scotch whisky scene since it luanched in 2000. Not least thanks to the founder John Glaser who, with a background in the wines business, reinvented the Scotch category not least by being meticulous in the selection of oak for the casks. In 2024 Glaser left the company but still remains a shareholder. His role as Whiskymaking Director was taken over by James Saxon who, after seven years in the company, was succeeded by Angela D´Orazio in September 2025. She played a significant role in establishing Swedish whisky on the market when she was the master blender for Mackmyra. In 2019 she was inducted into the Whisky Magazine Whisky Hall of Fame. In 2015 Bacardi acquired a minority share of Compass Box which they offloaded in 2022 when Cælum Capital Limited took over a majority stake of the company. Compass Box has also been advocating more transparency in the industry where the customer is given as much information as possible about the contents of the bottle.

The company divides its ranges into core and limited. The Peat Monster (a combination of peated Islay whiskies and Highland malts), the blended malt Orchard House, the blended Scotch Nectarosity and the blended malt Crimson Casks are included in the core range. Limited whiskies are regularly replaced and at times only to resurface a couple of years later in new variations. Three of the latest expressions are the eighth edition of Flaming Heart, Secrets of Smoke and Brûlée Royale – a tribute to Versailles, home of the first ever crème brûlée. Finally there are two core blended Scotch, Artist´s Blend and Glasgow Blend.

Brûlée Royale, 49%

Nose: Creme brûlée and chocolate truffles with undertones of oak and linseed, then lemon meringue and pain au chocolat.
Palate: Silky mouthfeel, abundant creme Anglaise, sweet top notes and dry base notes, evolving with pear drops and caramelised demerara sugar.

Secrets of Smoke, 52%

Nose: Smoke wafting from embers, garnished with caramel and nutmeg, then subtle orange marmalade joins in.
Palate: Silky, velvety mouthfeel, creaminess balanced by luscious lemon meringue and lemon zest, with smoke wafting above, mid-way sweetness opens up and is more distinct than the subtle dryness.

North Star Spirits

northstarspirits.com

Founded in 2016 by Iain Croucher who used to work for AD Rattray before deciding to go it alone. The main North Star range consists of single cask malts and blended malts. In 2023 a new range named Periodical was introduced; 50 cl bottlings, presented at 50% abv and priced at £50. Tarot is a range of blended Scotch whisky where the grain part comes from North British distillery. Finally there is the new Obscurities & Curiosities where Croucher bottles odd and exceptional whiskies that he has found. Together with Ronnie Grant and other partners Iain Croucher has embarked on building a new distillery in Campbeltown named Dál Riata and a planning application was approved in September 2023.

Meadowside Blending

meadowsideblending.com

Donald Hart, a Keeper of the Quaich and co-founder of the well-known bottler Hart Brothers, runs this Glasgow company together with his son, Andrew. There are six sides to the business – blends sold under the name The Royal Thistle, single malts labelled The

Maltman, single cask single grains under the label The Grainman, Vintage Cask Reserve featuring ultra rare bottlings, Vital Spark focusing on single malts with "a maritime twist" and, introduced in 2020, The Granary with blended grain whiskies.

Master of Malt

masterofmalt.com

Master of Malt is an independent online retailer of much more than just "malt". Founder-owned and fiercely independent, Master of Malt has been bottling the world's most interesting whiskies since 1985 as perhaps the world's first mail-order independent bottler – sending out a monthly catalogue and receiving actual physical cheques and hand written order forms back a few days later. This year as a part of their 40th Anniversary they've given their labels some long overdue love, and made them available beyond the Master of Malt website for the first time.

Glendullan 14 year old year old, 59,6%

Nose: Apricots and pear drops with baked apples, cinnamon and caramel.

Palate: Lightly chewy mouthfeel, sweetness fills the palate then becomes the top note with dry oak and apple crumble beneath, caramel sauce then some maltyness.

Atom Brands

Atom Brands, part of the Atom Group which includes online retailer Master of Malt, Master of Malt Trade and the UK distributor Maverick Drinks, is the producer of an ever-increasing number of innovative new products (Dalry Milk, Burnt Ends) as well as independently bottled whiskies, rums, gins and other spirits from around the world. Included in their portfolio is Drinks by the Dram, the creators of the booze-filled Advent calendars, tasting sets and 30ml dram samples, as well as Bathtub Gin, Rumbullion!, That Boutique-y Drinks Company, Darkness, Wormtub, Project 173 and Atom Labs, the innovation "hits factory" behind Jaffa Cake Gin, &Whisky and Black Cannon.

Black Cannon 10 year old, 40,4%

Nose: Rich blend of chargrilled and fruity notes including creme de cassis, accompanied by liquorice and black leaf tea.

Palate: Indulgent mouthfeel with elegant sweetness that is more prominent than dry oakyness, and provides a canvas for liquorice and prunes, with light malty creaminess and lemon zest freshness emerging.

That Boutique-y Whisky Company

thatboutiqueywhiskycompany.com

That Boutique-y Whisky Company is an independent bottler founded in 2012, bottling unusual gems from distilleries around the world. For more than a decade, TBWC has been exclusively about single cask, small batch, limited edition and unrepeatable 50cl bottlings, but that changed in September 2023 when they launched their Core Range in 70cl bottles. In 2025 three new World Whiskies (a 10 year old Bourbon, a 21 year old Irish whiskey, and an 8 year old English Rye) joined the five original "core" offerings: Islay, Speyside, Highland, an ancient Blended Grain and a sherry cask-polished Canadian Corn Whisky.

Speyside 12 year old, 45,8%

Nose: Floral, fruity overture with apple crumble and pears, toffee, caramel and rich honey with a hint of chocolate, digestive biscuits and apples at the end.

Palate: Rich, creamy mouthfeel with fresh fruity top notes, becomes juicy with apricots and orange marmalade, hints of espresso and dark chocolate.

Darkness

darknesswhisky.com

Darkness first came to the market in 2016 and offers a range of intensely sherried whiskies. The first core expression, an 8 year old, was released in 2019. Each whisky undergoes an additional six months of maturation in sherry cask octaves. Whether it's the flagship whisky or one of the limited edition 50cl releases finished in Oloroso, PX, Palo Cortado, or Moscatel casks – Darkness provides a distinctive experience for sherried whisky enthusiasts.

Dailuaine 8 year old amontillado, 61,2%

Nose: Rich and rounded, raisins, dark chocolate, walnuts, toffee, prunes.

Palate: Luscious mouthfeel, indulgent flavours expand across the palate: espresso and dark chocolate merge into tiramisu, sweetness remains subtle with more dis tinct dryness, then a wave of chocolate truffles and walnuts.

The Whisky Agency

whisky-agency.de

The man behind this company is Carsten Ehrlich, to many whisky aficionados known as one of the founders of the annual Whisky Fair in Limburg, Germany. His experience from sourcing casks for limited Whisky Fair bottlings led him to start as an independent bottler under the name The Whisky Agency, a business that celebrated its 15th anniversary in 2023. There are several ranges including The Whisky Agency, The Perfect Dram and Specials with some unusual bottlings.

A Dewar Rattray Ltd

adrattray.com

Founded by Andrew Dewar Rattray in 1868. In 2004 the company was revived by Tim Morrison, previously of Morrison Bowmore Distillers and fourth generation descendent of Andrew Dewar, with a view to bottling single cask malts from different regions in Scotland. He was joined by his son Andrew and in 2011, the company opened A Dewar Rattray´s Whisky Experience & Shop in Kirkoswald, South Ayrshire. Apart from having a large choice of whiskies for sale, there is a sample room, as well as a cask room.

One of the company´s best-sellers is a single malt named Stronachie which is actually sourced from Benrinnes. There are currently two expressions, a 10 year old and a 10 year old sherry finish. In 2011 a peated, blended malt, Cask Islay, became the first in a new series called Casks of Scotland. There are now three expressions available – Cask Islay Classic, Cask Orkney and Cask Speyside – in different versions. The AD Rattray´s Cask Collection is a range of single cask whiskies bottled at cask strength and without colouring or chill-filtration while Vintage Cask Collection contains rare and old single malts. In 2020 a new range of single cask whiskies, The Warehouse Collection, was introduced. Bottled at either cask strength or 46% these are a mixture of full or part casks, 'bin ends' and remnants from casks that have be re-racked. Finally there is the House Malts range, exlusively available in the shop (and on line).

Cask Islay Classic, 46%

Nose: Coffee and walnut cake, hints of roasted coffee beans and background wafting smoke.

Palate: Soft mouthfeel, tiramisu with espresso notes then muscovado sugar, while chocolate mousse and dark chocolate emerge.

Stronachie 10 year old, 43%

Nose: Fresh lemon juice, camomile tea, honey, hints of lime and orange.

Palate: Lightly velvety, luscious mouthfeel, then camomile tea, juicy lemon and lime, waves of vanilla and butterscotch.

Douglas Laing & Co

douglaslaing.com

Established in 1948 by Douglas Laing, this firm was run for many years by his two sons, Fred and Stewart. In 2013, the brothers decided to go their separate ways. Douglas Laing & Co is now run by Fred Laing and his daughter Cara. Douglas Laing has the following brands in their portfolio; Provenance (single casks bottled at 46%), Premier Barrel (single malts in ceramic decanters) and Old Particular, a range of single malts and grains. The latter has also been expanded with two brand extensions; XOP and XOP "The Black Series". Finally there is a range named Double Barrel where just two single malts have been blended together.

A decade ago the company started a range that has become highly succesful. The first installment in the series that eventually was given the name Remarkable Regional Malts, was Scallywag – a blended malt influenced by sherried whiskies from Speyside. More versions have followed with Noir in 2025 as one of the latest. Regional Malts has been expanded over the years and now also includes Timorous Beastie from the Highlands with a no age statement and a 10 year old. Recent limited expressions include an 18 year old sherry edition, the 13 year old Meet the Beast and a 25 year old. Rock Island is a blended malt combining whiskies from Islay, Arran, Orkney and Jura and can be found without age statement, as a 10 year old, a Cask Strength and a Sherry Edition. Recent limited releases include a 16 year old. The Epicurean represents the Lowlands with a no age statement as well as the recent, limited Glasgow Edition #2. The Gauldrons is made from Campbeltown malts with is represented by a no age statement and sherry cask edition #2. The final regional whisky is Big Peat, a vatting of Islay malts. This was launched several years ago but was later included in the range. The core range is made up of a no age statement bottling and a 12 year old. Recent limited versions include a red wine cask finish, a 10 year old Mizunara Edition and one for Feis Ile 2025.

In 2019 the company bought Strathearn distillery west of Perth. In April 2024 they released the first expression that contained whisky made by both the previous owner and by Douglas Laing and this was recently followed by batch 2.

Strathearn Batch 2, 50,2%

Nose: Elegant, creamy mouthfeel, fruit trifle top notes with antique oak below, then oak takes over.

Palate: Elegant mouthfeel, simultaneously delivers fresh top notes and distinctly dry base notes, then crisp, juicy green apples with a hint of honey.

Rock Island 16 year old, 46,8%

Nose: Distinct oak frames sultanas, lemon curd, cider, then chocolate comes to the fore.

Palate: Full-bodied velvety, silky mouthfeel, opens with creamy vanilla and lemon zest followed by dry cider, sultanas then subtle oak emerges.

Hunter Laing & Co

hunterlaing.com

This company was formed after the demerger between Fred and Stewart Laing in 2013 (see Douglas Laing). It is run by Stewart Laing and his two sons, Scott and Andrew. The Hunter Laing portfolio consists of the following ranges and brands; The Old Malt Cask (rare and old malts, bottled at 50%), The Old and Rare Selection (an exclusive range of old malts offered at cask strength), The Sovereign (a range of old and rare grain whiskies), Hepburn´s Choice (younger malts bottled at 46%) and The First Editions. The latter was created by Andrew Laing before Hunter Laing was formed and is now a substantial part of the portfolio. Two subranges, the Author´s Series and Distiller´s Art paying tribute to famous British authors and artists, have later been added. In 2019, Scarabus, a single malt from an undisclosed Islay distillery, was released and now appears as a no age statement, a 10 year old and a Batch Strength. There is also the Journey series (Islay, Highland, Campbeltown and Hebridean) with blended malts from four different regions in Scotland. Finally there is a flagship blended Scotch named House of Peers

In 2018, Ardnahoe distillery was opened on the north-east coast of Islay near Bunnabhain. The distillery, with a capacity of making 1 million litres per year, was opened to the public in spring 2019. In May 2024 a limited, 5 year old inaugural release appeared and it was followed by the core expression Infinite Loch in September. In 2025 the range was expanded with Bholsa, matured predominantly in oloroso casks.

Balblair 34 year old Old & Rare, 43,3%
Nose: Fresh green apples and richer apple crumble with vanilla custard, then walnuts.
Palate: Luscious mouthfeel with lightly creamy vanilla, dark chocolate and cappuccino, extending with walnuts, light oak and richness.

Ardnahoe Bholsa, 50%
Nose: Vivid creosote, with embers lightly wrapped in butterscotch and Brazil nuts, then phenolics recede and brine becomes central with hint of chocolate.
Palate: Soft mouthfeel, flavours gradually open up with barbecue notes on a bed of sweetness with some fresh lemon zest and grapefruit freshness, then black olives.

Malts of Scotland

malts-of-scotland.com

A German bottler founded by Thomas Ewers in 2009. The backbone of the assortment is the Basic Line with three blended malts; Classic (18yo), Sherry (15yo) and Peat (10yo).Apart from other ranges of Scotch single malts, Ewers also has three ranges called Malts of Ireland, Malts of India and Whiskeys of America. Apart from a large number of single casks, there are two special series, Amazing Casks and Angel´s Choice, both dedicated to very special and superior casks.

Wemyss Malts

wemyssmalts.com

Founded in 2005, Wemyss Malts is an independent, family-owned company run by brother and sister duo William and Isabella Wemyss, whose centuries-old family heritage is rooted in Fife, on Scotland's East Coast. In 2014 they also opened their own distillery, Kingsbarns, a few miles south of St Andrews. The company is mainly known for its range of blended malts of which there are three core expressions – The Hive, Spice King and Peat Chimney. These are available at 46% un chill-filtered and also in limited edition batch strength. Recent limited releases include Bohemian Blossom, Nectar Grove and, released in 2024, the 25 year old blended malt A Quarter Passed. Another side of the business involves single cask single malts either bottled at 46% or occasionally at cask strength. All whiskies are un chill-filtered and without colouring. Finally, there are two versions of the blend Lord Elcho (NAS and 15 year old). In 2014, Wemyss launched the sherried Velvet Fig which resurfaced as a limited 25 year old in 2020. In early 2026 it is time for yet another appearance when a 12 year old will be launched.

The core range from the owner´s own Kingsbarns distillery consists of the 5 year old Balcomie, Doocot which has been matured in a combination of bourbon and STR red wine barriques and, released in 2024, Coaltown. They were complemented in 2025 with a 10 year old.

Kingsbarns 10 year old, 46%
Nose: Fresh, alluring floral notes, roses, then orange marmalade with some underlying chocolate and nutmeg.
Palate: Luscious indulgent mouthfeel, opens up impressively with balanced sweetness, creaminess, cider, digestive biscuits, and lemon meringue richness with lemon zest freshness.

Velvet Fig 12 year old, 46%
Nose: Mellow blend of spice and linseed, then fruit rises to the fore: figs, prunes, and apricot freshness.
Palate: Embracing, silky mouthfeel, richness wrapped in sweetness and underlined by oak dryness, becomes luscious with figs, prunes and hint of peaches.

Elixir Distillers

elixirdistillers.com

The company is owned by Sukhinder and Rajbir Singh, known by most for establishing The Whisky Exchange shops in London as well as being the largest on-line retailer of Scotch whisky in the world. In the beginning of October every year, they used to be hosting the iconic The Whisky Show in London, one of the best whisky festivals in the world and they have also been involved in the Old & Rare Show in Glasgow and London. A couple of years ago they sold The Whisky Exchange to Pernod Ricard. In 2002 they started as independent bottlers of malt whiskies operating under the brand name The Single Malts of Scotland. In 2009 a new range of Islay single malts under the name Port Askaig was introduced. The current core range consists of an 8 year old, Cask Strength a 15 year old and a 17 year old. Limited releases have included a 25 and a 45 year old. Elements of Islay, a series of malts, was introduced one year before Port Askaig. The three, main expressions are all blended malts; Cask Edit, Bourbon Cask and Sherry Cask and as a limited release, Campfire appeared in 2025. The first part of a fascinating series was introduced in early 2023 followed by the second act in 2025; The Macbeth Collection is inspired by the characters in William Shakespeare´s famous play and a total of 42 bottlings will be released.

Elixir Distillers is at the moment building Portintruan distillery on Islay on the outskirts of Port Ellen with a planned opening in late 2025 or early 2026. In 2022 they also bought Tormore Distillery in Speyside.

Port Askaig Cask Strength Small Batch, 59,1%
Nose: Distinct barbecue, charred notes, then vanilla emerges accompanied by earthy, forest, medicinal notes.
Palate: Velvety mouthfeel, immediate richness and separate sweetness envelope a core of barbecue and chargrilled notes, with dry base notes and waft of rising smoke.

Linkwood 11 year old SMOS, 48%
Nose: Creamy fruit trifle with hints of mango and creme caramel, then distinct lemon zest freshness with hint of elegant perfume.
Palate: Mellow mouthfeel, immediate sweetness continues to reach out across the palate with light creaminess, brioche, Victoria sponge, then digestive biscuits and hints of strawberry sweetness.

Single Cask Nation

singlecasknation.com

Initially Single Cask Nation was formed a a member´s club but later the owners decided to also start selling through retailers in USA, Europe and Canada. Although the focus is on Scotch, Single Cask Nation has over the years released more and more bottlings from distilleries in other parts of the world. In January 2024 the company was bought by The Artisinal Spirits Company.

The Ultimate Whisky Company

ultimatewhisky.com

Founded in 1994 by Han van Wees and his son Maurice. All whiskies are un chill-filtered, without colouring and bottled at either 46% or cask strength. The van Wees family also operate one of the finest spirits shops in Europe – Van Wees Whisky World in Amersfoort – with i.a. more than 1,000 different whiskies.

Svenska Eldvatten

eldvatten.se

Founded in 2011, in their range apart from whisky they have aged tequila and rum and they have also launched their own rum, gin and aquavit. They are also importers to Sweden of whisky from Murray McDavid, AD Rattray, North Star Spirits, Claxton´s, Single Cask Nation, Watt Whisky and Little Brown Dog.

The Vintage Malt Whisky Company

vintagemaltwhisky.com

Founded in 1992 the company supplies whisky to more than 35 countries. In 2022 they opened up a rum distillery in Port Ellen on Islay. The most famous brands in the whisky range are two single Islay malts called Finlaggan and The Ileach. The latter comes in two versions, bottled at 40% and 58%. The Finlaggan range consists of Old Reserve, Eilean Mor, Port Finish, Sherry Finish, Cask Strength and Red Wine Cask Matured. Other expressions include a range of single cask single malts under the name The Cooper´s Choice with a new sub-range, The Cooper´s Choice - The Golden Cut. There are also the Islay Storm single malt and the blended malt Smoke Stack.

Wm Cadenhead & Co

cadenhead.scot

A classic bottler established in 1842. The owners, J&A Mitchell, also own Springbank and Glengyle distilleries in Campbeltown. Their core range, Authentic Collection, is made up of single cask cask strength whiskies, exclusively sold in their own shops and on-line. Other collections are The Chairman´s Stock selected from the late chairman Hedley G Wright´s private collection, the Enigma series with unusual expressions and the Original Collection. They also have their own ranges of gin and rum.

Adelphi Distillery

adelphidistillery.com

Founded in 1993 by Jamie Walker and named after a distillery which stopped making malt whisky in 1907, the company offers a range of single malts bottled at cask strength. There are also two recurrent brands, Fascadale and Liddesdale, where the single malt differs from batch to batch. In 2015, the first two bottlings of a new brand named Fusion saw the light of day. The first release was The Glover – a vatting of single malt from the closed Japanese distillery Hanyu and two Scottish single malts. This has been followed by collaborations with Amrut in India, Starward in Australia, Zuidam in The Netherlands and Chichibu in Japan. The latest Fusion bottling, in 2025, was Cargill - a 5 year old in a collaboration with Cardrona distillery in New Zealand. Since 2014, Adelphi is also making whisky in their own Ardnamurchan distillery in Western Scotland. The first single malt from the distillery was released in October 2020. Recent bottlings include the second edition of The Midgie matured in bourbon, port and sherry casks and the AD/Sauternes Peated in autumn 2025.

Ardnamurchan The Midgie 2025, 48%

Nose: Finely tuned ripe orchard fruit and roses in full bloom, leading to lemon zest and digestive biscuits.

Palate: Silky mouthfeel, sweetness and luscious freshness glide across the palate balanced by maltyness and underlying dry oak, culminating in baked apples and cinnamon.

Cargill Fusion, 57,9%

Nose: Vanilla custard, cinnamon and mango, with underlying black tea leaves, then floral jasmine notes emerge.

Palate: Velvety mouthfeel with luscious juiciness, tiramisu, espresso and underlying oak dryness, with top notes of peaches and apricots, garnished by nutmeg.

Deerstalker Whisky Co

deerstalkerwhisky.com

Dating back to 1880, the Deerstalker brand was bought by Aberko Ltd in 1994. Currently there is one core single malt in the range, a 12 year old, and two blended malts - Peated Edition and Highland Edition. Limited Deerstalker single malts are released from time to time.

Morrison Distillers

morrisondistillers.com, carnmorwhisky.co.uk

Owned by a family with decades of experience in the Scotch whisky industry, the company´s most famous range is Carn Mor single malt whiskies. Other ranges include Mac-Talla with Islay single malts and Old Perth blended malts. In 2017 the owners also opened a distillery of their own in Fife, Aberargie Distillery., and the inaugural release is expected in early 2026.

Dramfool

dramfool.com

Bruce Farquhar sources his whisky from private individuals as well as from brokers. In 2021 a new range was added - the Jim McEwan Signature Collection where the different styles from Bruichladdich were represented. He was also the first to independently bottle Wolfburn.

Angel´s Nectar

angelsnectar.co.uk

Highfern Ltd fills and sells whisky under the name Angel´s Nectar. Current expressions include the blended malt Original, the single malt Oloroso Sherry Cask Edition, the single malt PX Sherry Cask Edition and an 8 year old single malt. There is also the 13 year old Cairngorms 4th Edition Single malt.

The Single Cask Ltd

thesinglecask.co.uk

Ben Curtis was a whisky distributor in south-east Asia before he started as an independent bottler in Singapore in 2010. Since then he has moved back to the UK. The business has grown over the years and the brand is now sold in the UK, Europe and Asia. The company also acts as a broker selling casks with both newmake and maturing whisky.

Selected Malts

selectedmalts.se

A Swedish bottler and blender specialising in single malts from Scotland but also from Sweden. In 2019 they released their own blended malt, Zippin, and later they became distributors for GlenAllachie, James Eadie and Milk & Honey in Sweden.

The Alistair Walker Whisky Co.

alistairwalkerwhisky.com

When Alistair Walker´s family sold BenRiach, GlenDronach and Glenglassaugh in 2016, he decided to start up as an independent bottler. The brand is called Infrequent Flyers and to date more than 160 bottlings have been released.

Watt Whisky

wattwhisky.com

When Mark Watt left Cadenheads he decided to start a company of his own together with his wife Kate who has a background working for both Springbank and Glenfarclas. Their philosphy is to mainly bottle single malt Scotch (but also grains and rums) at cask strength and without colouring or chill filtration. In autumn 2020 Mark, together with his friend David Stirk, launched a range of its own named Electric Coo.

The Whisky Baron

thewhiskybaron.co.uk

Jake Sharpe began the business trading casks as an investment but eventually started to sell bottled single cask malt to private customers. The current range is divided into Rennaisance, Founder´s Collection and the Signature series.

Lady of the Glen

ladyoftheglen.com

Hannah Whisky Merchants was founded by Gregor Hannah in 2012 and is mainly known for their brand Lady of the Glen with bottlings of single malt and single grain Scotch. Around 40 casks are bottled per year and the latest releases include a 26 year old Ben Nevis, a 31 year old Strathclyde single grain and an 11 year old Glen Elgin finished in an amontillado sherry cask.

The Islay Boys

islayboys.com

Mackay Smith and Donald MacKenzie bought the Islay Ales Brewery in 2018. Soon after they started as whisky bottlers and at the moment their range consists of Bårelegs Islay single malt and Flatnöse blended malt and blended Scotch. Lately they are working together with Ian Macleod to start production at the new Laggan Bay Distillery on Islay.

Asta Morris

asta-morris.be

Founded by former Malt Maniac Bert Bruyneel in 2009, the company started with whisky but has later also branched out into rum, cognac and calvados. The single malts released range from young and affordable expressions to old and are bottlings. A special project for Bert is his NOG gin which has been matured in some of his used whisky casks and is bottled in batches.

James Eadie

jameseadie.co.uk

Founded by Rupert Patrick who is the great-great-grandson of James Eadie, a Scottish blender in the 1800s. With a long background in the Scotch whisky industry Rupert set up as a independent bottler specialising in small batch and single cask Scotch. He also managed to recreate Eadie´s blend from the early days when he launched Trade Mark X. Apart from whisky, the company also published an astonishing book in 2022 – The Distilleries of Great Britain and Ireland. It is a 630 page compilation of long since forgotten articles (and amazing photos) about 124 distilleries written in the 1920s. This was followed up in 2023 by yet another tome, The Distillation of Whisky, with articles about whisky production in the late 1920s.

Claxton´s Spirits

claxtonsspirits.com

A company with a bonded warehouse on the Dalswinton Estate just north of Dumfries. This facility allows them to have an impressive scheme of re-racking, finishing, blending and bottling - rather unusual for an independent bottler. Focus is on single malt or single grain Scotch bottled at cask strength. The range is divided into three series; Warehouse No. 1, Warehouse No. 8 and Exploration. There are also the 10 year old single malt Glen Carrick, the 12 year old The Red Comyn, the 30 year old single grain Grain Barn and the blended malt Smoking Furnace.

Brave New Spirits

bravenewspirits.com

A fairly new independent bottler and blender with their own warehouse in Glasgow. Currently there are three ranges; Whisky of Voodo (small batch releases), Cask Masters (iconic whiskies often aged 30 plus years) and WhiskyHeroes (with spectacular labels). Other singular releases include single malts such as Old Smitty´s, The Highland Shepherd, McKintyre´s and Celtic Revival. There are also two blends – Lighthouse Whisky and Royal Cabinet. Currently the company is building the Witchburn distillery near Machrihanish airport north of Campbeltown.

Saltire Rare Malt

saltireraremalt.com

The founders have quietly been purchasing casks from a wide variety of distilleries over the last three decades and The Whisky Couple, Hans & Becky Offringa, were appointed curators of the extensive stock. SRM is located in Falkland, Fife, and operates its own warehouses and bottling line. In 2024 their first 6 single cask bottlings were launched and to date more than 20 expressions have been launched.

Goldfinch Whisky

goldfinchwhisky.com

A fairly new independent bottler in Glasgow founded by whisky veteran Andrew Macdonald-Bennett. They have a number of ranges; the Goldfinch Series focusing on single malts finished in a variety of different sherry casks, Paloma where palo cortado casks play the leading role in the maturation, the Wine series where Blair Athol has been finished in five different wine casks and the peated Kilnsman´s Dram.

The Heart Cut

theheartcut.com

Founded in 2023, by Georgie and Fabrizio the company showed a true interest in global whisky with their first 16 bottlings coming from 8 different countries. You can also subscribe to their Slow Whisky Club where you every two or three months will receive a whisky, beer and other things that will enhance your experience.

Spirits Shop Selection (Dong Fang Ming)

spirits.com.tw

A retailer and independent bottler established in 2014. They are one of few bottlers focusing on selecting casks that cater specifically to the Asian palate.

Whisky shops

AUSTRALIA

Nicks Wine Merchants
10-12 Jackson Court, East Doncaster, VIC, 3109
Phone: +61 (0)3 9848 1153
www.nicks.com.au
A supplier of all sorts of spirits and wines and with an extraordinary range of whisky with more than 500 Australian whiskies in the range!

The Odd Whisky Coy
25 Anzac Ridge Road, Bridgewater, SA, 5155
Phone: +61 (0)417 852 296
www.theoddwhiskycoy.com.au
On-line whisky specialist with an impressive range.

World of Whisky
Shop 11A, Cosmopolitan Centre
2-22 Knox Street, Double Bay NSW 2028
Phone: +61 (0)2 9363 4212
www.worldofwhisky.com.au
A whisky specialist with a wide range, most of them single malts.

The Whisky Company
PO Box 2559, Seaford, VIC, 3198
Phone: +61 (0)434 438 617
www.thewhiskycompany.com.au
One of the largest on-line retailers of single malt whisky in Australia with around 800 products currently in stock.

The Oak Barrel
152 Elizabeh St, Sydney, NSW, 2000
Phone: +61 (0)2 9264 3022
www.oakbarrel.com.au
Good range of Scotch but the range of Australian whiskies impresses the most.

AUSTRIA

Potstill
Währinger Straße 65, 1090 Wien
Phone: +43 (0)664 118 85 41
www.potstill.org
Austria's premier whisky shop since 1992 with over 1100 different single malts, including some real rarities.

Whisky Wien
Hahngasse 17, 1190 Wien
Phone: +43 (0)677 622 476 40
www.whiskywien.at
The former Cadenhead whisky shop but now with a new life.

Pinkernells Whisky Market
Alter Markt 1, 5020 Salzburg
Phone: +43 (0)662 84 53 05
www.pinkernells-shop.at
More than 500 whiskies are on offer and they are also importers of Maltbarn, The Whisky Chamber and Jack Wiebers.

Hirschenbrunner Spirits
Neustiftgasse 64, 1070 Wien
Phone: +43 699 1132 37 30
www.hirschenbrunner.com
A very well equipped store with more than 1,500 whiskies including many old and rare bottlings.

BELGIUM

Whiskycorner
Kraaistraat 18, 3530 Houthalen
Phone: +32 (0)475 416528
www.whiskycorner.be
A very large selection of single malts, more than 2000 different. Also other whiskies, calvados and grappas.

Crombé
Doenaertstraat 20, 8510 Marke
Phone: +32 (0)56 21 19 87
www.crombewines.com
A large assortment of Scotch is supplemented with whiskies from Japan, the USA and Ireland to mention a few.

We Are Whisky
Avenue Rodolphe Gossia 33
1350 Orp-Jauche
Phone: +32 (0)471 134556
www.wearewhisky.com
On-line retailer with a range of more than 800 different whiskies. They also arrange regular tastings every month.

Dram 242
Rijgerstraat 60, 9310 Moorsel
Phone: +32 (0)477 26 09 93
www.dram242.be
A wide range of whiskies. Apart from the core official bottlings, they have focused on rare, old expressions.

CANADA

Kensington Wine Market
1257 Kensington Road NW
Calgary, Alberta T2N 3P8
Phone: +1 403 283 8000
www.kensingtonwinemarket.com
The shop has a very large range of whiskies (more than 1500) as well as other spirits and wines. More than 80 tastings in the shop every year.

World of Whisky
Unit 240, 333 5 Avenue SW
Calgary, Alberta T2P 3B6
Phone: +1 587 956 8511
www.coopwinespiritsbeer.com/stores/world-of-whisky/
Specialising in whisky from all corners of the world. Currently there are over 1100 different whiskies in the range including some extremely rare ones from Scotland.

DENMARK

Whisky.dk
Vejstruprødvej 15
6093 Sjølund
Phone: +45 5210 6093
www.whisky.dk
Henrik Olsen and Ulrik Bertelsen are well-known in Denmark for their whisky shows but they also run one of the largest whisky shops in Northern Europe with an emphasis on whisky but also including an impressive stock of rums.

Juul´s Vin & Spiritus
Værnedamsvej 15
1819 Frederiksberg
Phone: +45 33 31 13 29

Lyngby Hovedgade 43
2800 Kongens Lyngby
Phone: +45 33 18 37 93
www.juuls.dk
A very large range of wines, fortified wines and spirits with more than 1100 different whiskies (800 single malts).

Whisky Watcher
Kongensgade 69 F
5000 Odense C
Phone: +45 66 13 95 05
www.whiskywatcher.com
Whisky specialist with a very good range, and also a nice assortment of champagne, cognac and rum.

Kalø Whisky og Vin
Ebeltoftvej 54, Feldballe, 8410 Rønde
Phone: +45 (0)71 90 82 40
www.whiskyogvin.dk
A shop with a carefully selected range of malt whiskies as well as other spirits, wine and beer. Regular tastings.

ENGLAND

The Whisky Exchange
2 Bedford Street, Covent Garden
London WC2E 9HH
Phone: +44 (0)20 7100 0088
90-92 Great Portland Street, Fitzrovia
London W1W 7NT
Phone: +44 (0)20 7100 9888
88 Borough High Street, London Bridge
London SE1 1LL
Phone: +44 (0)20 7631 3888
www.thewhiskyexchange.com

An excellent whisky retailer founded by Sukhinder and Rajbir Singh who recently sold it to Pernod Ricard. Started off as a mail order business, run from a showroom in Hanwell, but later opened up at Vinopolis in downtown London. Moved to a new and bigger location in Covent Garden a few years ago and have since then opened two more shops. The assortment is huge with well over 1000 single malts to choose from. Some rarities which can hardly be found anywhere else are offered thanks to Singh's great interest for antique whisky. There are also other types of whisky and cognac, calvados, rum etc.

The Whisky Shop
(See also Scotland, The Whisky Shop)
11 Coppergate Walk
York YO1 9NT
Phone: +44 (0)1904 640300
www.whiskyshop.com

7 Turl Street
Oxford OX1 3DQ
Phone: +44 (0)1865 202279

3 Swan Lane
Norwich NR2 1HZ
Phone: +44 (0)1603 618284

169 Piccadilly
London W1J 9EH
Phone: +44 (0)207 499 6649

3 Exchange St
Manchester M2 7EE
Phone: +44 (0)161 832 6110

25 Chapel Street
Guildford GU1 3UL
Phone: +44 (0)1483 450900

Unit 9 Great Western Arcade
Birmingham B2 5HU
Phone: +44 (0)121 233 4416

64 East Street
Brighton BN1 1HQ
Phone: +44 (0)1273 327 962

3 Cheapside
Nottingham NG1 2HU
Phone: +44 (0)115 958 7080

9-10 High Street
Bath BA1 5AQ
Phone: +44 (0)1225 423 535

Unit 1/9 Red Mall,
Intu Metro Centre
Gateshead NE11 9YP
Phone: +44 (0)191 460 3777

Unit 210 Trentham Gardens
Stoke on Trent ST4 8AX
Phone: +44 (0)1782 644 483

36 Royal Arcade
Cardiff CF10 1AE
Phone: +44 (0)29 2213 0033

12-14 County Arcade, Victoria Quarter
Leeds LS1 6BN
Phone: +44 (0)113 430 0158

1 Cathedral Close, Exeter EX1 1EZ
Phone: +44 (0)1392 968 088
The largest specialist retailer of whiskies in the UK with 23 outlets. A large product range with over 1500 Scotch single malt whiskies as well as other spirits, accessories and books. They also run The W Club, the leading whisky club in the UK where the excellent Whiskeria magazine is one of the member´s benefits. Shipping all over the world.

Berry Bros. & Rudd Spirits Shop
1 St James´s St, London SW1A 1EF
Phone: +44 (0)20 7022 8973
www.bbrspirits.com
A legendary company dating back to 1698! One of the world's most reputable wine shops but with an extensive and exclusive selection of malt whiskies, some of them bottled by Berry Bros. themselves. The company is also known as as well respected independent bottler of whiskies and rums.

The Wright Wine & Whisky Company
The Old Smithy, Raikes Road, Skipton,
North Yorkshire BD23 1NP
Phone: +44 (0)1756 700886
www.wineandwhisky.co.uk
An eclectic selection of near to 1000 different whiskies. 'Tasting Cupboard' of nearly 100 opened bottles for sampling with regular hosted tasting evenings. Great 'Collector to Collector' selection of old whiskies plus a fantastic choice of 1200+ wines, premium spirits and liqueurs.

Master of Malt
Unit 1, Ton Business Park, 2-8 Morley Rd.
Tonbridge, Kent, TN9 1RA
Phone: +44 (0)1892 888376
www.masterofmalt.com
Online retailer and independent bottler with a very impressive range of more than 2,500 whiskies, including over 2,000 Scotch whiskies and over 1,500 single malts. In addition to whisky there is an enormous selection of gins, rums, cognacs, armagnacs, tequilas and more. The website contains a wealth of information and news about the distilleries and innovative personalised gift ideas. Drinks by the Dram 30ml samples of more than 3,300 different whiskies are available also they also offer the Dram Club monthly whisky subscription service, as well as a Blend Your Own option, personalised whisky and has a gift finder to help with special occassions.

Whiskys.co.uk
The Square, Stamford Bridge
York YO4 11AG
Phone: +44 (0)1759 371356
www.whiskys.co.uk
Good assortment with more than 600 different whiskies. Also a nice range of armagnac, rum, calvados etc.

The Wee Dram
5 Portland Square, Bakewell
Derbyshire DE45 1HA
Phone: +44 (0)1629 812235
www.weedram.co.uk
Large range of Scotch single malts with whiskies from other parts of the world and a good range of whisky books. Run 'The Wee Drammers Whisky Club' with seminars and tastings. In October they arrange the yearly Wee Dram Fest whisky festival.

Hard To Find Whisky
1 Spencer Street, Birmingham B18 6DD
Phone: +44 (0)121 448 84 84
www.htfw.com
As the name says, this family owned shop specialises in rare, collectable and new releases of single malt whisky. The range is astounding - more than 3,000 different bottlings including more than 500 different Macallan. World wide shipping.

Nickolls & Perks
37 Lower High Street, Stourbridge
West Midlands DY8 1TA
Phone: +44 (0)1384 394518
www.nickollsandperks.co.uk
Mostly known as wine merchants but also has a huge range of whiskies with 1,900 different kinds including 1,300 single malts. They also organize Midlands Whisky Festival, www.whiskyfest.co.uk

Gauntleys of Nottingham
4 High Street, Nottingham NG1 2ET
Phone: +44 (0)115 9110555
www.gauntleys.com
A fine wine merchant established in 1880. The range of wines are among the best in the UK. All kinds of spirits, not least whisky, are taking up more and more space and several rare malts can be found.

Hedonism Wines
3-7 Davies St., London W1K 3LD
Phone: +44 (020) 729 078 70
www.hedonism.co.uk
Located in the heart of London, this is a temple for wine lovers but also with over 1,200 different whisky bottlings from Scotland and the rest of the world.

The Lincoln Whisky Shop
87 Bailgate, Lincoln LN1 3AR
Phone: +44 (0)1522 537834
www.lincolnwhiskyshop.co.uk
Mainly specialising in whisky with more than 300 different whiskies but also 500 spirits and liqueurs. Mailorder worldwide.

Milroys of Soho
3 Greek Street, London W1D 4NX
Phone: +44 (0)207 734 2277
www.milroys.co.uk
A classic whisky shop in Soho with a very good range with over 700 malts and a wide selection of whiskies from around the world. Also a whisky bar within the shop and bottles Scotch under their own label.

Cadenhead´s Whisky Shop
26 Chiltern Street, London W1U 7QF
Phone: +44 (0)20 7935 6999
www.cadenhead.shop
One in a chain of shops owned by independent bottlers Cadenhead. Sells Cadenhead's product range and c. 200 other whiskies. Regular tastings.

Drinkfinder
30 Fore Street, Constantine, Falmouth
Cornwall TR11 5AB
Phone: +44 (0)1326 340226
www.drinkfinder.co.uk
A full-range wine and spirits dealer with a great selection of whiskies from the whole world (of which more than 1,000 are Scotch).Worldwide shipping.

House of Malt
48 Warwick Road, Carlisle CA1 1DN
Phone: +44 (0)1228 658 422
www.houseofmalt.co.uk
A wide selection of whiskies from Scotland and the world as well as other spirits and craft ales. Regular tasting evenings and events.

The Vintage House
42 Old Compton Street
London W1D 4LR
Phone: +44 (0)20 7437 2592
www.vintagehouse.london
A huge range of 1400 kinds of malt whisky, many of them rare. Supplementing this is also a selection of fine wines.

Whisky On-line
Units 1-3 Concorde House, Charnley Road, Blackpool, Lancashire FY1 4PE
Phone: +44 (0)1253 620376
www.whisky-online.com
A good selection of whisky and also cognac, rum, port etc. Specializes in rare whiskies and hold regular auctions.

Mitchell´s Wines Merchants
354 Meadowhead, Sheffield S8 7UJ
Phone: +44 (0)114 274 5587
www.mitchellswine.co.uk
A vast amount of beers, wines and cigars is complemented by 500 single malt Scotch as well as a good range of world whiskies. Also includes a private bar for tastings.

The Spirits Room
Newlyns Farm, North Warnborough, Hook Hampshire RG29 1HA
Phone: +44 (0)1256 263 887
www.thespiritsroom.co.uk
Established in 2024 and with a very nice selection, this shop has focused on customer experiences. With almost 200 open bottles to try before you buy they also have plenty of tastings including whisky/food pairings.

FRANCE

La Maison du Whisky
20 rue d´Anjou
75008 Paris
Phone: +33 (0)1 42 65 03 16

6 carrefour d l´Odéon
75006 Paris
Phone: +33 (0)1 46 34 70 20

11 rue Tiquetonne
75002 Paris
Phone: +33 (0)1 53 40 81 77

(1 shop outside France)
The Pier at Robertson Quay
80 Mohamed Sultan Road, #01-10
Singapore 239013
Phone: +65 6733 0059
www.whisky.fr
France's largest whisky specialist with an exquisite range of brands and also many own-bottled single malts. La Maison du Whisky acts as a EU distributor for many whisky producers around the world. Also run the Golden Promise whisky bar in Paris.

The Whisky Shop
7 Place de la Madeleine, 75008 Paris
Phone: +33 (0)1 45 22 29 77
www.whiskyshop.fr
The largest chain of whisky shops in the UK also has a store in Paris.

GERMANY

SCOMA
Am Bullhamm 17, 26441 Jever
Phone: +49 (0)4461 912237
www.scoma.de
Very large range of c 750 Scottish malts and many from other countries. Holds regular seminars and tastings. The excellent, monthly whisky newsletter SCOMA News is also produced.

The Whisky Store
Am Grundwassersee 4, 82402 Seeshaupt
Phone: +49 (0)8801 30 20 000
www.whisky.de
A very large range of whisky of which ca 1200 are Scotch. The website is a goldmine of information, in particular the videos with Horst and Ben Luening.

Whisky Market Cologne
Luxemburger Strasse 257, 50939 Köln
Phone: +49 (0)221-2831834
www.whisky-market.com
Good range of malt whiskies (c 350 different kinds) including Cadenhead's bottlings. Other products include wine, cognac and rum etc. Arranges recurring tastings and also has an on-line shop.

Tara Spirits
Rindermarkt 16, 80331 München
Phone: +49 (0)89 26 51 18
store.tara-spirits.de
An excellent supplier of whiskies as well as gin and rum. Also holds regular tastings.

Home of Malts
Hosegstieg 11, 22880 Wedel
Phone: +49 (0)4103 965 9695
www.homeofmalts.com
Large assortment with over 800 different single malts as well as whiskies from many other countries. Also a nice selection of cognac, rum etc. On-line ordering.

Reifferscheid
Mainzer Strasse 186, 53179 Bonn
Phone: +49 (0)228 9 53 80 70
www.whisky-bonn.de
A well-stocked shop with a large range of whiskies, wine, spirit, cigars and a delicatessen. They also have a wide range of whiskies bottled especially for the shop.

Whisky-Doris
Germanenstrasse 38, 14612 Falkensee
Phone: +49 (0)3322-219784
www.whisky-doris.de
Large range of over 300 whiskies and also sells own special bottlings. Orders via email. Shipping also outside Germany.

Weinquelle
Lübeckerstrasse 145, 22087 Hamburg
Phone: +49 (0)40 300 672 950
Jacobsrade 65, 22962 Siek (showroom)
Phone: +49 (0)4107 908 900
www.weinquelle.com
An impressive selection of both wines and spirits with over 1000 different whiskies of which 850 are malt whiskies.

The Whisky-Corner
Reichertsfeld 2, 92278 Illschwang
Phone: +49 (0)9666-951213
www.whisky-corner.de
A small shop but large on mail order. A very large assortment of over 2000 whiskies.

World Wide Spirits
Am Söterberg 12, 66620 Nonnweiler
Phone: +49 (0)6873 800 990
www.worldwidespirits.de
A nice range of more than 1,000 whiskies with some rarities from the twenties. Also large selection of other spirits.

WhiskyKoch
Weinbergstrasse 2, 64285 Darmstadt
Phone: +49 (0)6151 96 96 886
www.whiskykoch.de
A combination of a whisky shop and restaurant. The shop has a nice selection of single malts as well as other Scottish products and the restaurant has specialised in whisky dinners and tastings.

Scotia Spirit
Friesenstrasse 16a, 50670 Cologne
Phone: +49 (0)221 78944370

Arnoldstrasse 2, 404 79 Düsseldorf
Phone: +49 (0)211 915992248
www.scotia-spirit.de
Two well-equipped shops where the one in Cologne also has a whisky bar with regular tastings.

Kierzek
Weitlingstrasse 17, 10317 Berlin
Phone: +49 (0)30 525 11 08
www.kierzek-berlin.de
Over 600 different whiskies in stock. In the product range 50 kinds of rum and 450 wines from all over the world are found among other products.

Smoke & Whisky
Wittelsbacherstrasse 14, 82319 Starnberg
Phone: +49 (0)8151-368223
www.smokeandwhisky.shop
A specialist on whisky and cigars (they even have a huge walk-in humidor). More than 700 different whiskies and rums.

Whisky For Life
Fahrgasse 6, 60311 Frankfurt am Main
Phone: +49 (0)173-6602413
www.whiskyforlife.de
Good range of malt whiskies and other spirits.

The Whisky Brothers
Glockengasse 8, 93047 Regensburg
Phone: +49 (0)941 99 22 44 15
www.the-whisky-brothers.de
A family run shop with more than 1000 whiskies and also a range of rum, gin etc.

HUNGARY

Whisky Shop Budapest
Veres Pálné utca 7., 1053 Budapest
Phone: +36 1 267-1588

Hadak útja 1., 1119 Budapest
Phone: +36 20 325 29 75
www.whiskynet.hu
www.whiskyshop.hu

Largest selection of whisky in Hungary. More than 900 different whiskies from all over the world as well as a large selection of other fine spirits. Most of them can be tasted in the GoodSpirit Whisky & Cocktail Bar which operates in the same venue.

IRELAND

Celtic Whiskey Shop
27-28 Dawson Street, Dublin 2
Phone: +353 (0)1 675 9744
www.celticwhiskeyshop.com
More than 900 kinds of Irish whiskeys but also a good selection of Scotch, wines and other spirits. World wide shipping.

ITALY

Whisky Shop
by Milano Whisky Festival
Via Ludovico Cavaleri 6, Milano
Phone: +39 (0)2 70017478
www.whiskyshop.it
The team behind the excellent Milano Whisky Festival also have an online whiskyshop with almost 700 different whiskies including several special festival bottlings.

Whisky Antique S.R.L.
Via Giardini Sud, 41043 Formigine (MO)
Phone: +39 (0)59 574278
www.whiskyantique.com
Whisky enthusiast and collector Massimo Righi owns this shop specialising in rare and collectable spirits – not only whisky but also cognac, rum, armagnac etc.

THE NETHERLANDS

Whiskyslijterij De Koning
Hinthamereinde 41
5211 PM 's Hertogenbosch
Phone: +31 (0)73-6143547
www.whiskykoning.nl
An enormous assortment with more than 1400 kinds of whisky including c 800 single malts. Arranges recurring tastings.

Van Wees - Whiskyworld.nl
Leusderweg 260, 3817 KH Amersfoort
Phone: +31 (0)33-461 53 19
www.whiskyworld.nl
A very large range of 1000 whiskies including over 500 single malts. Also have their own range of bottlings (The Ultimate Whisky Company). On-line ordering.

Wijnhandel van Zuylen
Loosduinse Hoofdplein 201
2553 CP Loosduinen (Den Haag)
Phone: +31 (0)70-397 1400
www.whiskyvanzuylen.nl
Excellent range of whiskies (circa 1100) and wines. Email orders with shipping to some ten European countries.

Ton Overmars Slijterij
Ton Overmars, Hoofddorpplein 11
1059 CV Amsterdam
Phone: +31 (0)20-615 71 42
www.tonovermars.nl
A very large assortment of wines, spirits and beer which includes more than 400 single malts. Arranges recurring tastings.

Wijn & Whisky Schuur
Blankendalwei 4, 8629 EH Scharnegoutem
Phone: +31 (0)515-520706
www.wijnwhiskyschuur.nl
Large assortment with 1000 different whiskies and a good range of other spirits as well. Arranges recurring tastings.

Wine and Whisky Specialist van der Boog - Passion for Whisky
Prinses Irenelaan 359-361
2285 GA Rijswijk
Phone: +31 70 - 394 00 85
www.passionforwhisky.com
A very good range of almost 700 malt whiskies (as well as a wide range of other spirits). World wide shipping.

NEW ZEALAND

Whisky Galore
834 Colombo Street, Christchurch 8013
Phone: +64 (0) 800 944 759
www.whiskygalore.co.nz
The best whisky shop in New Zealand with 750 different whiskies, approximately 400 which are single malts. There is also online mail-order with shipping all over the world except USA and Canada. Owned by Michael Fraser Milne who became a Master of the Quaich in 2019.

POLAND

George Ballantine´s
Krucza str 47 A, Warsaw
Phone: +48 22 625 48 32

Pulawska str 22, Warsaw
Phone: +48 22 542 86 22

Marynarska str 15, Warsaw
Phone: +48 22 395 51 60

Zygmuntą Vogla str 62, Warsaw
Phone: +48 22 395 51 64
www.sklep-ballantines.pl
A huge range of single malts and apart from whisky there is a full range of spirits and wines from all over the world. Recurrent tastings and organiser of Whisky Live Warsaw.

Dom Whisky
Wejherowska 67, Reda
Phone: +48 691 760 000, shop
Phone: +48 691 930 000, mailorder
www.sklep-domwhisky.pl
On-line retailer with a shop in Reda and another two in Wroclaw and Warsaw. A very large range of whiskies and other spirits. Organiser of a whisky festival in Jastrzębia Góra.

SCOTLAND

Gordon & MacPhail
The Courtyard, Johnstons of Elgin, Newmill, Elgin IV30 4AF
Phone: +44 (0)1343 545110
www.gordonandmacphail.com
This legendary shop opened already in 1895 in Elgin. The owners are perhaps the most well-known among independent bottlers. The shop stocks around 1000 single malt whiskies and more than 600 wines. Tastings are arranged in the shop and there are shipping services within the UK and overseas. The shop attracts visitors from all over the world and the company also owns two whisky distilleries - Benromach and The Cairn.

Royal Mile Whiskies
379 High Street, The Royal Mile
Edinburgh EH1 1PW
Phone: +44 (0)131 2253383
www.royalmilewhiskies.com
Royal Mile Whiskies is one of the most well-known whisky retailers in the UK. It was established in Edinburgh in 1991. The whisky range is outstanding with many difficult to find elsewhere. They have a comprehensive site regarding information on regions, distilleries, production, tasting etc. Royal Mile Whiskies also arranges 'Whisky Fringe' in Edinburgh, a two-day whisky festival which takes place annually in mid August. On-line ordering with worldwide shipping.

The Whisky Shop
(See also England, The Whisky Shop)
Unit L2-02 Buchanan Galleries
220 Buchanan Street
Glasgow G1 2GF
Phone: +44 (0)141 331 0022

Unit 16 Princes Square
Buchanan Street
Glasgow G1 3JN
Phone: +44 (0)141 320 0246

17 Bridge Street
Inverness IV1 1HD
Phone: +44 (0)1463 710525

93 High Street
Fort William PH33 6DG
Phone: +44 (0)1397 706164

52 George Street
Oban PA34 5SD
Phone: +44 (0)1631 570896

Unit 23 Waverley Mall
Waverley Bridge, Edinburgh EH1 1BQ
Phone: +44 (0)131 558 7563

28 Victoria Street
Edinburgh EH1 2JW
Phone: +44 (0)131 225 4666

Unit 18, Multrees Walk
Edinburgh EH1 3DQ
Phone: +44 (0)7721 973 463
www.whiskyshop.com
The first shop opened in 1992 in Edinburgh and this is now the United Kingdom's largest specialist retailer of whiskies with 23 outlets (plus one in Paris). A large product range with over 700 kinds, including 400 malt whiskies and 140 miniature bottles, as well as accessories and books. The own range 'Glenkeir Treasures' is a special assortment of selected malt whiskies. The also run The W Club where the excellent Whiskeria magazine is one of the member´s benefits.

The Scotch Malt Whisky Society
(venues)
28 Queen Street, Edinburgh EH2 1JX
Phone: +44 (0)131 625 7484

87 Giles Street, Edinburgh EH6 6BZ
Phone: +44 (0)131 554 3451

38 Bath Street, Glasgow G2 1HG
Phone: +44 (0)141 739 8810

19 Greville Street, London EC1N 8SQ
Phone: +44 (0)20 7831 4447
www.smws.com
A legendary society with more than 40 000 members worldwide, specialised in own bottlings of single cask Scotch whisky, releasing between 150 and 200 bottlings every year. The Society also bottles whisky from other parts of the world as well as gin, rum, armagnac and other spirits. Operates four venues in the UK and cooperates with partner bars around the world.

Whiskies of Scotland
36 Gordon Street
Huntly AB54 8EQ
Phone: +44 (0) 1466 795 105
www.thespiritsembassy.com
Owned by independent bottler Duncan Taylor. In the assortment is of course the whole Duncan Taylor range but also a selection of their own single malt bottlings called Whiskies of Scotland. A total of 700 different expressions. Also an on-line shop with shipping worldwide.

WhiskyBrother Dufftown
1 Fife Street, Dufftown
Moray AB55 4AL
Phone: +44 (0)1340 821097
www.whiskybrother.co.uk
The well-known whisky specialist in Dufftown was recently taken over by South African whisky profile Marc Pendlebury who also runs a hotel, bar and restaurant in the town.

Cadenhead's Whisky Shop
30-32 Union Street
Campbeltown PA28 6JA
Phone: +44 (0)1586 551710
www.cadenhead.scot
Part of the chain of shops owned by independent bottlers Cadenhead. Sells Cadenhead's products and other whiskies with an exscellent range of Springbank.

Cadenhead´s Whisky Shop
172 Canongate, Royal Mile
Edinburgh EH8 8DF
Phone: +44 (0)131 556 5864
www.cadenhead.scot
The oldest shop in the chain owned by Cadenhead. Sells Cadenhead's product range and a good selection of other whiskies and spirits. Recurrent tastings.

The Good Spirits Co. (3 shops)
23 Bath Street, Glasgow G2 1HW
Phone: +44 (0)141 258 8427

21 Clarence Drive
Hyndland, Glasgow G12 9QN
Phone: +44 (0)141 334 4312

(mainly wine and beer)
105 West Nile Street, Glasgow G1 2SD
Phone: +44 (0)141 332 4481
www.thegoodspiritsco.com
A specialist spirits store selling whisky, bourbon, rum, vodka, tequila, gin, cognac and armagnac, liqueurs and other spirits. They also stock quality champagne, fortified wines and cigars. There are more than 400 single malts in the range as well as whiskies from the rest of the world.

A.D. Rattray´s Whisky Experience & Whisky Shop
32 Main Road, Kirkoswald
Ayrshire KA19 8HY
Phone: +44 (0) 1655 760308
www.adrattray.com
Recently revamped, this is a combination of whisky shop, sample room and educational center owned by the independent bottler A D Rattray. A wide range of whiskies and tasting menus with different themes are also available.

Loch Fyne Whiskies
Main Street, Inveraray, Argyll PA32 8UD
Phone: +44 (0)149 930 2219

36 Cockburn St
Edinburgh EH1 1PB
Phone: +44 (0)131 226 2134
www.lochfynewhiskies.com
A legendary shop and with a second shop in Edinburgh since 2018. The range of malt whiskies is large and they have their own house blend, the prize-awarded Loch Fyne, as well as their 'The Loch Fyne Whisky Liqueur'.

The Carnegie Whisky Cellars
The Carnegie Courthouse, Castle Street
Dornoch IV25 3SD
Phone: +44 (0)1862 811791
www.carnegiewhiskycellars.co.uk
Opened in 2016, this shop has already become a destination for whisky enthusiasts. The interior of the shop is ravishing and the extensive range includes all the latest releases as well as rare and collectable bottles. International shipping.

Abbey Whisky
Dunfermline KY11 3BZ
Phone: +44 (0)1383 733 020
www.abbeywhisky.com
Family run online whisky shop specialising in exclusive, rare and old whiskies from Scotland and the world. Apart from a wide range of official and independent bottlings, Abbey Whisky also selects their own casks and bottle them under the name 'The Rare Casks' and 'The Secret Casks'.

The Scotch Whisky Experience
354 Castlehill, Royal Mile
Edinburgh EH1 2NE
Phone: +44 (0)131 220 0441
www.scotchwhiskyexperience.co.uk
The Scotch Whisky Experience is a must for whisky devotees visiting Edinburgh with an interactive visitor centre dedicated to the history of Scotch whisky. This five-star visitor attraction has an excellent whisky shop with more than 300 different whiskies in stock. Following an extensive refurbishment, a brand new and interactive shop has been opened.

Tyndrum Whisky
Tyndrum, Perthshire FK20 8RY
Phone: +44 (0)1301 702 084
www.tyndrumwhisky.com
The new name for Whisky Galore at The Green Welly Stop. It was established at a road junction between Glencoe and The Trossachs nearly 60 years ago. Well equipped with a nice range of Scottish single malts, grains and blends but also world whiskies and other spirits.

The Whisky Castle
6 Main Street, Tomintoul AB37 9EX
Phone: +44 (0)1807 580 213
www.whiskycastle.com
A legendary shop that specialises in single malts (more than 600) and single casks in particular. Also a range of whiskies bottled exclusively for The Whisky Castle.

Whiski Shop
4-7 North Bank Street
Edinburgh EH1 2LP
Phone: +44 (0)131 225 7224

119 High Street
Edinburgh EH1 1 SG
Phone: +44 (0)131 566 3095
www.whiskishop.com
www.whiskirooms.co.uk
Located near Edinburgh Castle, these two venues are a combination of a shop, tasting room, bar and restaurant. Also regular whisky tastings.

Robbie's Drams
3 Sandgate, Ayr, South Ayrshire KA7 1BG
Phone: +44 (0)1292 262 135
www.robbieswhiskymerchants.com
An extensive range of whiskies available both in store and from their on-line shop. Specialists in single cask bottlings, closed distillery bottlings, rare malts, limited edition whisky and a nice range of their own bottlings. Worldwide shipping.

The Whisky Barrel
Unit 3, Cupar, KY15 5JY
Phone: +44 (0)1334 650 353
www.thewhiskybarrel.com
Online specialist whisky shop based in Edinburgh. They stock over 3,000 single malt and blended whiskies including Scotch, Japanese, Irish, Indian, Swedish and their own casks.

Drinkmonger
100 Athol Road, Pitlochry PH16 5BL
Phone: +44 (0)1796 470133

11 Bruntsfield Place
Edinburgh EH10 4HN
Phone: +44 (0)131 229 2205
www.drinkmonger.com
Owned by Royal Mile Whiskies, the idea is to have a 50:50 split between wine and specialist spirits with the addition of a cigar assortment. The whisky range is a good cross-section with some rarities and a focus on local distilleries.

Luvian's
93 Bonnygate, Cupar, Fife KY15 4LG
Phone: +44 (0)1334 654 820

66 Market Street, St Andrews
Fife KY16 9NU
Phone: +44 (0)1334 477 752
www.luvians.com
A legendary wine and whisky retailer owned by the three Luvian brothers with a very nice selection of more than 1,200 whiskies (600 single malts).

The Johnnie Walker Experience
145 Princes Street, Edinburgh EH2 4BL
Phone: +44 (0)131 376 9494
www.johnniewalker.com

Opened in 2021 this extraordinary five storey venue in the middle of Edinburgh is dedicated to the world´s most sold whisky - Johnnie Walker. Tours and spectacular experiences can be booked and there are is a restaurant and a roof top bar. The shop on ground floor sells a variety of Johnnie Walker bottlings as well as a wide range of single malts from Diageo.

The Stillroom
Gleneagles Hotel
Auchterarder, Perthshire PH3 1NF
Phone: +44 (0) 1764 694 188
www.gleneagles.com
Located in the famous hotel, the shop has a well selected range of both rare and collectible whiskies.

Robertsons of Pitlochry
44-46 Atholl Road, Pitlochry PH16 5BX
Phone: +44 (0) 1796 472011
www.robertsonsofpitlochry.co.uk
With new owner since 2013, the shop has grown to become one of Scotland´s best. An extensive range of both whisky and gin is complemented by single malts bottled under their own label. There´s also an excellent tasting room (The Bothy).

Robert Graham Ltd (3 shops)
194 Rose Street
Edinburgh EH2 4AZ
Phone: +44 (0)131 226 1874

111 West George Street
Glasgow G2 1QX
Phone: +44 (0)141 248 7283

9 Sussex Street, Cambridge CB1 1PA
Phone: +44 (0)1223 354 459
www.robertgraham1874.com
Established in 1874 this company specialises in Scotch whisky and cigars. A nice assortment of malt whiskies is complemented by an impressive range of cigars. They also bottle whiskies under their own label.

Whisky & Wine
15 North Bridge, Edinburgh EH1 1SB
Phone: +44 (0)131 557 5105
Premium retailer specialising in whisky, cigars, fine wines, and hand cut crystal. Almost 1,000 varieties of global whisky and over 500 varieties of single malt Scotch, including rare and unique bottles. One of the only appointed cigar specialists in Edinburgh. Impressivec range of wines, gins, rums, cognacs, tequila and mescal. Regular tastings available.

Whisky Trail
223-225 High Street, Edinburgh EH1 1PE
Phone: +44 (0)131 225 7614
Long-running, family-owned drinks emporium focusing on old and rare whiskies, unique independent bottlings, and old and new world wines. Tastings available.

The Speyside Whisky Shop
110A High Street
Aberlour AB38 9NX
Phone: +44 (0) 1340 871260
www.thespeysidewhisky.com
Opened in 2018, the shop is situated in the very heart of Speyside, in Aberlour. The owners specialise in highly collectable single malts from a variety of distilleries. Also a wide selection of craft gins.

Inverurie Whisky Shop
1 Burnside, Burn Lane,
Inverurie AB51 3RY
Phone: +44 (0)1467 622412
www.inveruriewhiskyshop.com
An excellent wine and spirits shop with a very large range of whiskies including their own bottlings. Arranges regular tastings as well as whisky tours. There is also a regular whisky chat on-line called "The Blether" where people from the industry are invited to share their views.

Highland Whisky Shop
23 Castle Street, Inverness IV2 3EP,
Phone: +44 (0)1463 592 055
www.highlandwhiskyshop.co.uk
A fairly new whisky shop right by the castle in Inverness. Close to 400 different whiskies as well as other spirits and there is also a bar where you can create your own tasting.

Whisky Please
24 Heather Avenue, Glasgow G61 3JE
Phone: +44 (0)781 806 1010
www.whiskyplease.co.uk
Online retailer of whiskies and other spirits. A very nice presentation of each distillery with a picture and text.

The Islay Whisky Shop
Shore Street, Bowmore, Islay PA43 7LB
Phone: +44 (0)1496 810 684
www.islaywhiskyshop.com
A must for any visitor to Islay, this shop has an impressive range of Islay whiskies, some of them very rare and limited.

Aberdeen Whisky Shop
472 Union Street, Aberdeen AB10 1TS
Phone: +44 (0)1224 647 433
www.aberdeenwhiskyshop.co.uk
A nice selection of whiskies but also other spirits. Free tastings in the shop every Saturday.

Malts and Spirits
32 St John Street, Perth PH1 5SP
Phone: +44 (0)1738 871 403
www.maltsandspirits.com
A family-owned shop with around 400 single malts in the assortment. Also conducts regular tastings.

SOUTH AFRICA

WhiskyBrother (3 shops)
Shop 16 D Middle Mall,
Hyde Park Corner Shopping Centre,
Johannesburg
Phone: +27 (0)63 294 7285

Nicolway Mall (top level)
William Nicol Drive, Bryanston,
Johannesburg
Phone: +27 (0)81 081 8832

Bedford Centre (Inside mall, ground level)
Van Der Linde Road, Bedfordview,
Johannesburg
Phone: +27 (0)10 054 6007
www.whiskybrother.com
Three shops specialising in all things whisky - apart from 400 different bottlings they also sell glasses, books etc. as well as whiskies bottled exclusively for the shop. Regular tastings and online shop. Also run a whisky bar in Johannesburg with more than 1,000 different whiskies to try. The owner, Marc Pendlebury, is also the organiser of The Only Whisky Show in Johannesburg and Cape Town.

SWITZERLAND

P. Ullrich AG
Schneidergasse 27
4051 Basel
Phone: +41 (0)61 338 90 91
Another two shops in Basel:
Laufenstrasse 16 and Unt. Rebgasse 18, one in Talacker 30 in Zürich and one in Kramgasse 45 in Bern.
www.ullrich.ch
A very large range of wines, spirits, beers, accessories and books. Over 800 kinds of whisky with almost 600 single malt. Online ordering. Recently, they also founded a whisky club with regular tastings and offers. (www.whiskysinn.ch).

Eddie's Whiskies
Bahnhofstrasse/Dorfgasse 27
8810 Horgen
Phone: +41 (0)43 244 63 00
www.eddies.ch
A whisky specialist with more than 750 different whiskies in stock with emphasis on single malts (more than 500 different). Also arranges tastings.

World of Whisky
By Waldhaus, Via Dimlej, 7500 St. Moritz
Phone: +41 (0)81 852 33 77
www.worldofwhisky.ch
An extraordinary shop with more than 1500 single malts. They also have a bar in the Hotel Waldhaus am See (the largest in the world according to Guinness Book of World Records) with 2500 different whiskies.

USA

Binny´s Beverage Depot
5100 W. Dempster (Head Office)
Skokie, IL 60077
Phone:
Internet orders, 888-942-9463 (toll free)
www.binnys.com
A chain of close to 50 stores in the Chicago area, covering everything within wine and spirits. Some of the stores also have a gourmet grocery, cheese shop and, for cigar lovers, a walk-in humidor. Also lots of regular events in the stores. The range is impressive with more than 1850 whisk(e)y including 650 single malt Scotch, 700 bourbons, 300 rye and more. Among other products there are 900 kinds of tequila and mezcal, 450 vodkas, 480 rums and 275 gins.

Statistics

The information on the following pages is based on figures from Scotch Whisky Association (SWA), Drinks International and directly from the producers.

The Top 30 Whiskies of the World

Sales figures for 2024 (units in million 9-litre cases)

McDowell´s No. 1 (Diageo/United Spirits), Indian whisky — 32,2
Royal Stag (Pernod Ricard), Indian whisky — 31,0
Imperial Blue (Pernod Ricard), Indian whisky — 22,9
Johnnie Walker (Diageo), Scotch whisky — 21,6
Officer´s Choice (Allied Blenders & Distillers), Indian whisky — 21,3
Jack Daniel´s (Brown-Forman), Tennessee whiskey — 14,1
Jameson (Pernod Ricard), Irish whiskey — 10,8
Jim Beam (Suntory Global Spirits), Bourbon – 10,7
Blenders Pride (Pernod Ricard), Indian whisky — 10,1
Ballantine´s (Pernod Ricard), Scotch whisky — 9,3
Royal Challenge (Diageo/United Spirits), Indian whisky — 9,1
Crown Royal (Diageo), Canadian whisky — 8,0
8 PM (Radico Khaitan), Indian whisky — 7,2
Royal Green (ADS Spirits), Indian whisky – 4,8
Chivas Regal (Pernod Ricard), Scotch whisky — 4,8
Iconiq White (Allied Blenders & Distillers), Indian whisky — 4,5
Kakubin (Suntory), Japanese whisky — 4,0
Black Nikka Clear (Asahi Breweries), Japanese whisky — 4,0
Sterling Reserve (Allied Blenders & Distillers), Indian whisky – 3,9
Director´s Special (Diageo/United Spirits), Indian whisky — 3,6
Evan Williams (Heaven Hill), Bourbon — 3,5
Signature /Diageo/United Spirits), Indian whisky – 3,3
Dewar´s (Bacardi), Scotch whisky — 3,3
William Lawson´s (Bacardi), Scotch whisky — 3,2
Black & White (Diageo), Scotch whisky — 3,0
Maker´s Mark (Suntory Global Spirits), Bourbon – 2,7
Torys (Suntory Global Spirits), Japanese whisky – 2,4
Label 5 (La Martiniquaise), Scotch whisky — 2,4
J&B (Diageo), Scotch whisky — 2,4
8 PM Premium Black (Radico Khaitan), Indian whisky – 2,4

* For some brands that are usually on this list, the producers have chosen not to disclose sales figures for 2024. These include Original Choice, Bagpiper, Hayward´s Fine, Old Tavern, Grant´s and Famous Grouse.

Source: Drinks International, The Millionaires Club 2025

Global Exports of Scotch by Region 2024

Volume (litres of pure alcohol)

Region	000s of litres	Change in %
Asia & Oceania	117 242	+5,9
Eastern Europe exc EU	8 926	+21,2
European Union	136 628	-1,3
Latin America & Carribean	39 741	+19,4
Middle East & North Africa	13 095	+2,1
North America	47 921	-0,7
Sub-Saharan Africa	14 315	+3,6
Western Europe exc EU	14 786	+11,4
Total	**392 655**	**+3,9**

Value (£ Sterling)

Region	000s of £	Change in %
Asia & Oceania	1 571 066	-12,4
Eastern Europe exc EU	50 796	+19,9
European Union	1 482 523	-5,4
Latin America & Carribean	499 544	+22,4
Middle East & North Africa	276 568	+3,9
North America	1 161 845	-3,0
Sub-Saharan Africa	140 561	-13,0
Western Europe exc EU	214 802	+28,9
Total	**5 397 816**	**-3,6**

Source: Scotch Whisky Association

Export of Scotch Whisky 2024

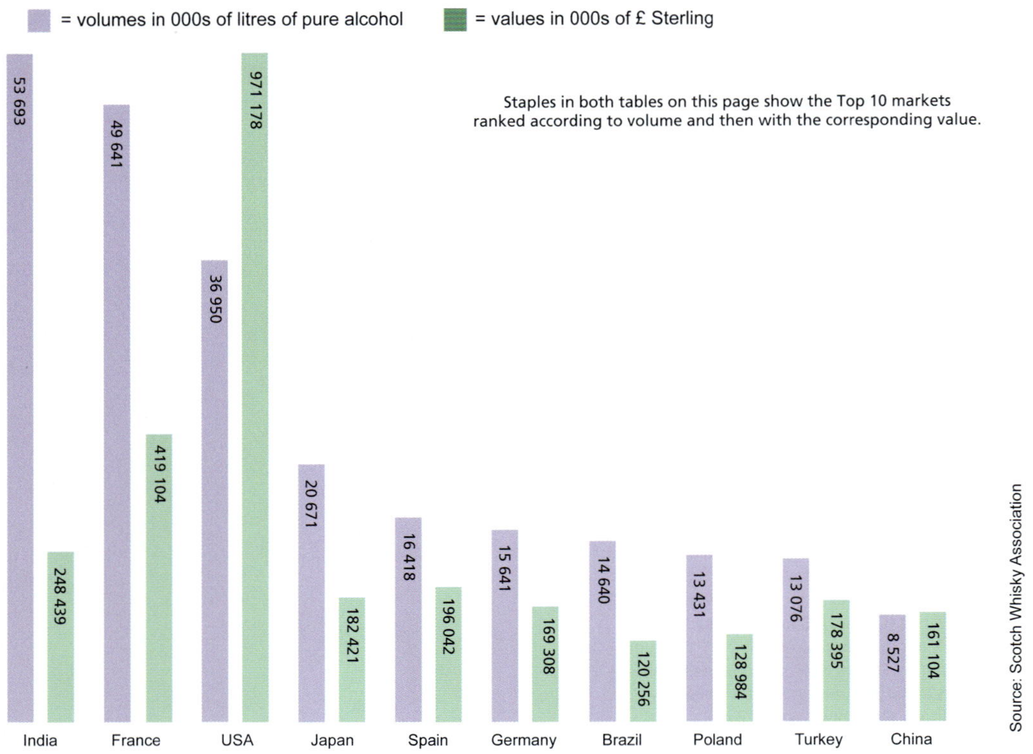

Export of Single Malt Scotch 2024

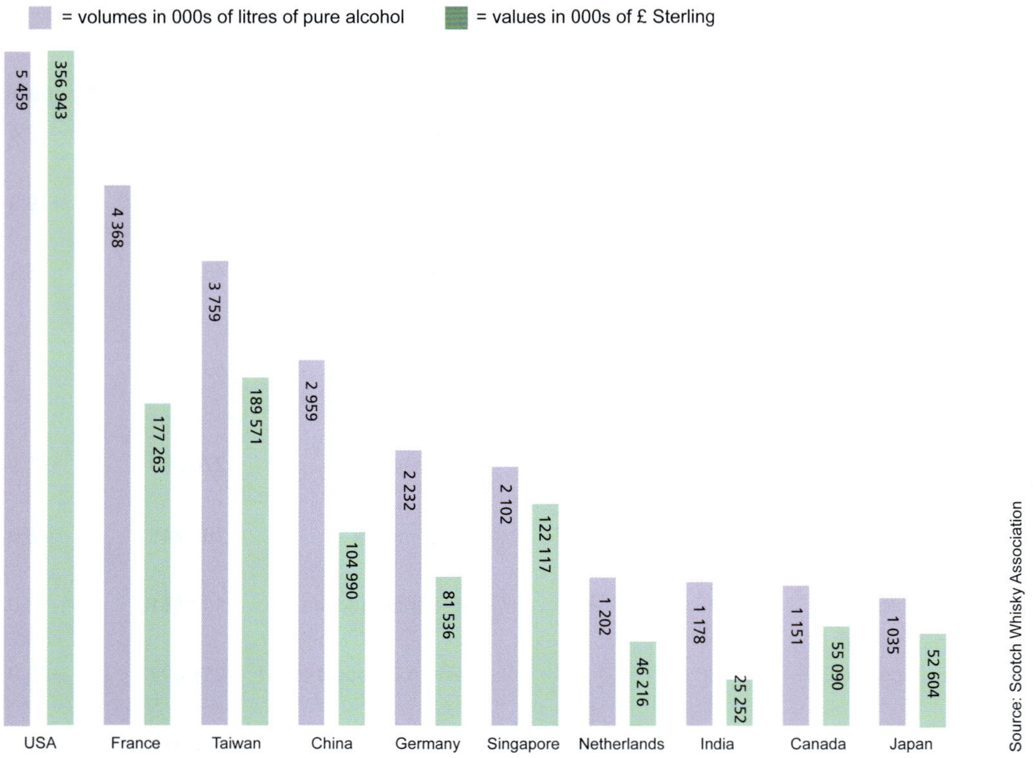

Distillery Capacity

Litres of pure alcohol - Scottish, active distilleries only

Glenfiddich	21 000 000
Glenlivet	21 000 000
Macallan	15 000 000
Roseisle	12 500 000
Ailsa Bay	12 000 000
Glen Ord	11 900 000
Teaninich	10 200 000
Dalmunach	10 000 000
Dalmore	9 000 000
Glen Moray	8 400 000
Glenmorangie	7 100 000
Balvenie	7 000 000
Caol Ila	6 800 000
Glen Grant	6 200 000
Aultmore	6 000 000
Dufftown	6 000 000
Glen Keith	6 000 000
Mannochmore	6 000 000
Auchroisk	5 900 000
Miltonduff	5 800 000
Glenrothes	5 600 000
Linkwood	5 600 000
Dailuaine	5 200 000
Glendullan	5 000 000
Loch Lomond	5 000 000
Tomatin	5 000 000
Ardmore	4 900 000
Clynelish	4 800 000
Tormore	4 800 000
Speyburn	4 600 000
Kininvie	4 500 000
Longmorn	4 500 000
Tamnavulin	4 500 000
Craigellachie	4 300 000
Royal Brackla	4 300 000
Glenburgie	4 250 000
Allt-a-Bhainne	4 200 000
Braeval	4 200 000
Glentauchers	4 200 000
Macduff	4 100 000
Glenallachie	4 000 000
Inchdairnie	4 000 000
Tamdhu	4 000 000
Aberlour	3 800 000
Bunnahabhain	3 800 000
Mortlach	3 800 000
Glenlossie	3 700 000
Benrinnes	3 500 000
Glenfarclas	3 500 000
Talisker	3 500 000
Aberfeldy	3 400 000
Cardhu	3 400 000
Laphroaig	3 300 000
Tomintoul	3 300 000
Inchgower	3 200 000
Lagavulin	3 200 000
Deanston	3 000 000
Tullibardine	3 000 000
Balmenach	2 900 000
Benriach	2 800 000
Blair Athol	2 800 000
Glen Elgin	2 700 000
Strathmill	2 600 000
Auchentoshan	2 500 000
Glenkinchie	2 500 000
Highland Park	2 500 000
Jura	2 500 000
Strathisla	2 450 000
Ardbeg	2 400 000
Cragganmore	2 200 000
Dalwhinnie	2 200 000
Fettercairn	2 200 000
Bowmore	2 150 000
Ben Nevis	2 000 000
Bladnoch	2 000 000
Bruichladdich	2 000 000
Glendronach	2 000 000
Knockdhu	2 000 000
Balblair	1 800 000
Port Ellen	1 700 000
Pulteney	1 700 000
The Borders	1 600 000
Glen Spey	1 500 000
Knockando	1 400 000
Glen Garioch	1 350 000
Glencadam	1 300 000
Scapa	1 300 000
Tobermory	1 250 000
Falkirk	1 200 000
Glengoyne	1 200 000
Lochranza	1 200 000
Glenglassaugh	1 100 000
Ardnahoe	1 000 000
Ardross	1 000 000
Balmaud	1 000 000
Brora	1 000 000
The Cairn	1 000 000
Laggan Bay	1 000 000
Rosebank	1 000 000
Oban	925 000
Ardgowan	900 000
Speyside	850 000
Glen Scotia	800 000
Aberargie	750 000
Glengyle	750 000
Lagg	750 000
Bonnington	720 000
Benromach	700 000
Burn O´Bennie	680 000
Kilchoman	650 000
The Clydeside	620 000
Kingsbarns	600 000
Annandale	500 000
Ardnamurchan	500 000
Glenturret	500 000
Royal Lochnagar	500 000
Springbank	500 000
Torabhaig	500 000
Harris	400 000
Port of Leith	400 000
Glasgow	365 000
Edradour	340 000
Jackton	300 000
Holyrood	250 000
Lerwick	250 000
Lindores Abbey	225 000
Isle of Raasay	220 000
Arbikie	200 000
Dunphail	200 000
Lochlea	200 000
8 Doors	150 000
Benbecula	150 000
Wolfburn	135 000
Glen Wyvis	120 000
Ballindalloch	100 000
Cabrach	100 000
Eden Mill	100 000
Ncn´ean	100 000
Daftmill	65 000
Kythe	60 000
Strathearn	60 000
North Uist	50 000
Orkney	30 000
Crafty	25 000
Abhainn Dearg	20 000
Uile-bheist	20 000
North Point	18 000
Toulvaddie	17 000
Dornoch	12 000
Moffat	12 000
Stirling	12 000
Deerness	10 000
Ben Cumhaill	7 000
Tiree	5 000
Blackness Bay	2 000

Summary of Malt Distillery Capacity by Owner

Owner (number of distilleries)	Litres of alcohol	% of Industry
Diageo (30)	126 225 000	28,5
Pernod Ricard (12)	71 700 000	16,2
William Grant (4)	44 500 000	10,1
Edrington Group (3)	23 100 000	5,2
Bacardi (John Dewar & Sons) (5)	22 100 000	5,0
Emperador Inc (Whyte & Mackay) (4)	18 200 000	4,1
Suntory Spirits (5)	14 200 000	3,3
Pacific Spirits (Inver House) (5)	13 000 000	2,9
Moët Hennessy (Glenmorangie) (2)	9 500 000	2,2
La Martiniquaise (Glen Moray) (1)	8 400 000	1,9
CVH Spirits (Burn Stewart) (3)	8 050 000	1,8
Ian Macleod Distillers (4)	7 200 000	1,6
Campari (Glen Grant) (1)	6 200 000	1,4
Benriach Distillery Co (3)	5 900 000	1,3
Loch Lomond Group (2)	5 800 000	1,3
Tomatin Distillery Co (1)	5 000 000	1,1
Elixir Distillers (Tormore) (1)	4 800 000	1,1
Angus Dundee (2)	4 600 000	1,0
InchDairnie Distillery Ltd. (Inchdairnie) (1)	4 000 000	0,9
The Glenallachie Distillers (1)	4 000 000	0,9
J & G Grant (Glenfarclas) (1)	3 500 000	0,8
Picard (Tullibardine) (1)	3 000 000	0,7
Nikka (Ben Nevis Distillery) (1)	2 000 000	0,4
Rémy Cointreau (Bruichladdich) (1)	2 000 000	0,4
David Prior (Bladnoch) (1)	2 000 000	0,4
Others (61)	24 200 000	5,5
Total (156)	**442 175 000**	

Shetland
ORKNEY ISLANDS
Wick
NORTH HIGHLANDS
Isle of Lewis
Isle of Harris
North Uist
Benbecula
SKYE
Kyle of Lockalsh
Inverness
SPEYSIDE
Loch Ness
CENTRAL HIGHLANDS
Aberdeen
Fort William
EAST HIGHLANDS
WEST HIGHLANDS
Pitlochry
Loch Tay
Oban
MULL
Dundee
Perth
St. Andrews
Loch Lomond
Stirling
JURA
Glasgow
Edinburgh
ISLAY
ARRAN
Campbeltown
Ayr
THE LOWLANDS
Dumfries
Stranraer

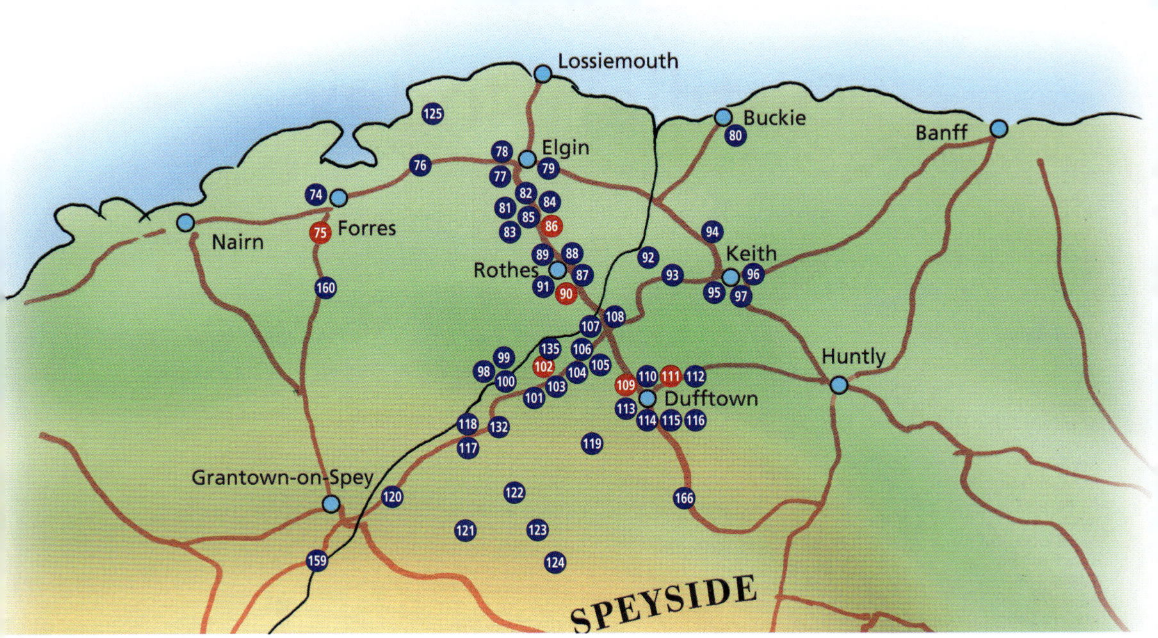

Distilleries in red letters are Speyside — **Active** — **Closed, mothballed, dismantled or demolished**

c = closed

164 8 Doors
148 Aberargie
39 Aberfeldy
106 Aberlour
127 Abhainn Dearg
126 Ailsa Bay
119 Allt-a-Bhainne
128 Annandale
134 Arbikie
62 Ardbeg
173 Ardgowan
25 Ardmore
147 Ardnahoe
131 Ardnamurchan
151 Ardross
58 Lochranza
49 Auchentoshan
92 Auchroisk
94 Aultmore
7 Balblair
132 Ballindalloch
165 Balmaud
120 Balmenach
113 Balvenie
19 Banff (c)
174 Benbecula
179 Ben Cumhaill
30 Ben Nevis
82 Benriach
104 Benrinnes
74 Benromach
9 Ben Wyvis (c)
180 Blackness Bay
57 Bladnoch
37 Blair Athol
153 Bonnington
138 Borders
66 Bowmore
124 Braeval
143 Brewdog
5 Brora
67 Bruichladdich
70 Bunnahabhain
155 Burnobennie
166 Cabrach
159 The Cairn
69 Caol Ila
90 Caperdonich (c)
99 Cardhu
142 Clydeside
6 Clynelish
86 Coleburn (c)
109 Convalmore (c)
178 Crafty
118 Cragganmore
108 Craigellachie
42 Daftmill
103 Dailuaine
75 Dallas Dhu (c)
11 Dalmore

135 Dalmunach
29 Dalwhinnie
45 Deanston
168 Deerness
144 Dornoch
110 Dufftown
160 Dunphail
136 Eden Mill
38 Edradour
154 Falkirk
32 Fettercairn
141 Glasgow
13 Glen Albyn (d)
105 Glenallachie
76 Glenburgie
34 Glencadam
23 Glendronach
116 Glendullan
85 Glen Elgin
35 Glenesk (c)
101 Glenfarclas
112 Glenfiddich
52 Glen Flagler (c)
24 Glen Garioch
18 Glenglassaugh
50 Glengoyne
87 Glen Grant
60 Glengyle
96 Glen Keith
55 Glenkinchie
122 Glenlivet
31 Glenlochy (c)
83 Glenlossie
14 Glen Mhor (c)
8 Glenmorangie
78 Glen Moray
12 Glen Ord
89 Glenrothes
61 Glen Scotia
91 Glenspey
93 Glentauchers
41 Glenturret
22 Glenugie (c)
28 Glenury Royal (c)
149 Glen Wyvis
140 Harris
2 Highland Park
152 Holyrood
102 Imperial (c)
133 Inchdairnie
80 Inchgower
47 Inverleven (c)
146 Isle of Raasay
171 Isle of Tiree
157 Jackton
71 Jura
68 Kilchoman
51 Kinclaith (c)
43 Kingsbarns
114 Kininvie

100 Knockando
21 Knockdhu
175 Kythe
56 Ladyburn (c)
63 Lagavulin
150 Lagg
176 Laggan Bay
64 Laphroaig
167 Lerwick
137 Lindores Abbey
79 Linkwood
48 Littlemill (c)
156 Lochlea
46 Loch Lomond
36 Lochside (c)
84 Longmorn
107 Macallan
20 Macduff
81 Mannochmore
15 Millburn (c)
77 Miltonduff
161 Moffat
115 Mortlach
145 Nc´nean
33 North Port (c)
170 North Point
177 North Uist
40 Oban
172 Orkney
111 Pittyvaich (c)
65 Port Ellen
163 Port of Leith
4 Pulteney
53 Rosebank
125 Roseisle
16 Royal Brackla
27 Royal Lochnagar
54 St Magdalene (c)
3 Scapa
88 Speyburn
26 Speyside
59 Springbank
169 Stirling
130 Strathearn
97 Strathisla
95 Strathmill
73 Talisker
98 Tamdhu
123 Tamnavulin
10 Teaninich
72 Tobermory
17 Tomatin
121 Tomintoul
139 Torabhaig
117 Tormore
158 Toulvaddie
44 Tullibardine
162 Uile-bheist
129 Wolfburn

2 Highland Park
3 Scapa
4 Pulteney
5 Brora
6 Clynelish
7 Balblair
8 Glenmorangie
9 Ben Wyvis (c)
10 Teaninich
11 Dalmore
12 Glen Ord
13 Glen Albyn (c)
14 Glen Mhor (c)
15 Millburn (c)
16 Royal Brackla
17 Tomatin
18 Glenglassaugh
19 Banff (c)
20 Macduff
21 Knockdhu
22 Glenugie (c)
23 Glendronach
24 Glen Garioch
25 Ardmore
26 Speyside
27 Royal Lochnagar
28 Glenury Royal (c)
29 Dalwhinnie
30 Ben Nevis
31 Glenlochy (c)
32 Fettercairn
33 North Port (c)
34 Glencadam
35 Glenesk (c)
36 Lochside (c)
37 Blair Athol
38 Edradour
39 Aberfeldy
40 Oban
41 Glenturret
42 Daftmill
43 Kingsbarns
44 Tullibardine
45 Deanston
46 Loch Lomond
47 Inverleven (c)
48 Littlemill (c)
49 Auchentoshan
50 Glengoyne
51 Kinclaith (c)
52 Glen Flagler (c)
53 Rosebank
54 St Magdalene (c)
55 Glenkinchie
56 Ladyburn (c)
57 Bladnoch
58 Lochranza
59 Springbank
60 Glengyle
61 Glen Scotia

62 Ardbeg
63 Lagavulin
64 Laphroaig
65 Port Ellen
66 Bowmore
67 Bruichladdich
68 Kilchoman
69 Caol Ila
70 Bunnahabhain
71 Jura
72 Tobermory
73 Talisker
74 Benromach
75 Dallas Dhu (c)
76 Glenburgie
77 Miltonduff
78 Glen Moray
79 Linkwood
80 Inchgower
81 Mannochmore
82 Benriach
83 Glenlossie
84 Longmorn
85 Glen Elgin
86 Coleburn (c)
87 Glen Grant
88 Speyburn
89 Glenrothes
90 Caperdonich (c)
91 Glenspey
92 Auchroisk
93 Glentauchers
94 Aultmore
95 Strathmill
96 Glen Keith
97 Strathisla
98 Tamdhu
99 Cardhu
100 Knockando
101 Glenfarclas
102 Imperial (c)
103 Dailuaine
104 Benrinnes
105 Glenallachie
106 Aberlour
107 Macallan
108 Craigellachie
109 Convalmore (c)
110 Dufftown
111 Pittyvaich (c)
112 Glenfiddich
113 Balvenie
114 Kininvie
115 Mortlach
116 Glendullan
117 Tormore
118 Cragganmore
119 Allt-a-Bhainne
120 Balmenach
121 Tomintoul

122 Glenlivet
123 Tamnavulin
124 Braeval
125 Roseisle
126 Ailsa Bay
127 Abhainn Dearg
128 Annandale
129 Wolfburn
130 Strathearn
131 Ardnamurchan
132 Ballindalloch
133 Inchdairnie
134 Arbikie
135 Dalmunach
136 Eden Mill
137 Lindores Abbey
138 Borders
139 Torabhaig
140 Harris
141 Glasgow
142 Clydeside
143 Brewdog
144 Dornoch
145 Nc´nean
146 Isle of Raasay
147 Ardnahoe
148 Aberargie
149 Glen Wyvis
150 Lagg
151 Ardross
152 Holyrood
153 Bonnington
154 Falkirk
155 Burnobennie
156 Lochlea
157 Jackton
158 Toulvaddie
159 The Cairn
160 Dunphail
161 Moffat
162 Uile-bheist
163 Port Of Leith
164 8 Doors
165 Balmaud
166 Cabrach
167 Lerwick
168 Deerness
169 Stirling
170 North Point
171 Isle of Tiree
172 Orkney
173 Ardgowan
174 Benbecula
175 Kythe
176 Laggan Bay
177 North Uist
178 Crafty
179 Ben Cumhaill
180 Blackness Bay

Distillery Index

Distillery Index

Distillery Index